02/2012

The Contours of American History

The Contours of
American History

William Appleman Williams

VERSO

London • New York

First published in 1961
Published with a new introduction by Verso 2011
New foreword © Greg Grandin 2011
The new foreword by Greg Grandin appeared in a slightly
different form in the *Nation* (July 1, 2009) and is repub-
lished here with the kind permission of that publication.

1 3 5 7 9 10 8 6 4 2

Verso
UK: 6 Meard Street, London W1F 0EG
US: 20 Jay Street, Suite 1010, Brooklyn, NY 11201
www.versobooks.com

Verso is the imprint of New Left Books

ISBN-13: 978-1-84467-774-0

British Library Cataloguing in Publication Data
A catalogue record for this book is available from the British Library

Library of Congress Cataloging-in-Publication Data
A catalog record for this book is available from the Library of Congress

Typeset in Minion by Hewer Text UK Ltd, Edinburgh
Printed in the US by Maple Vail

In memory of my father, and for my mother; parents who gave me by example the wisdom and the life inherent in both meanings of Napoleon's neglected axiom:

You commit yourself, and then—you see.

One may easily see history as only a succession of chances or conjunctures—but, if so, there is nothing to study, there are no correlations to be made between events, and in fact there is only a rope of sand, a series of non sequiturs which one can do nothing but narrate. . . .

But it is the optical illusion or the occupational disease of the research student to imagine that only the details matter, and that the details are all of equal value—that the statesman has no cohesive purpose but is merely a bundle of contradictions—and that everything is under the rule of chance, under the play of absurdly little chances—history reducing itself at the finish to an irony of circumstance.

Herbert Butterfield, 1959

I have always thought that a basic division among human beings is between those preoccupied with the question "How" and those preoccupied with the question "Why." This is a great "How" age. But "Why" remains unanswered, and will doubtless in due course again claim attention.

Malcolm Muggeridge, 1958

Contents

Foreword to the 2011 Edition: Reading *The Contours of American History* at Fifty

The schizophrenic discipline of the Historian is a harrowing way to stay sane.

William Appleman Williams,
The Roots of the Modern American Empire

"Why William Appleman Williams, for God's sake?" asked Arthur Schlesinger, Jr. in 1999 when he learned that Williams' *The Contours of American History* had been voted one of the 100 best nonfiction books of the twentieth century by the Modern Library. Schlesinger had spent the better part of half a century fighting the influence of Williams, describing him in 1954 as "pro-communist" to the president of the American Historical Association. In 1959 the *New York Times* picked Schlesinger's *The Coming of the New Deal* and Williams' *The Tragedy of American Diplomacy* as best books of the year, calling the first, in a nod to a liberalism still vital, a "spirited study" and the second a "free-swinging attack" on U.S. foreign policy, hinting at the raucous dissent to come. But forty years later, Schlesinger considered the fight won. The victory of the United States in the cold war had disproved Williams' jeremiads against an American empire careening toward disaster, while the concomitant collapse of the left had confirmed Schlesinger's position as curator of America's historical sensibility—liberal, democratic, pragmatic. Schlesinger was one of the Modern Library's jurors, and his own *The Age of Jackson* made the cut. Still, he couldn't keep Williams, dead for nearly a decade, out of the pantheon. For God's sake.

Williams was not the first historian to identify the United States as an empire, yet he was unique in linking domestic disquiet to a long history of expansion, which in his grandest formulation—*The Contours of American History*, reissued here on the fiftieth anniversary of its publication—he traced back to beyond England's Glorious Revolution, making him one of America's most consequential dissident intellectuals. His early criticisms of containment—Washington's post–World War II efforts to isolate the Soviet Union and limit the spread of communism—nearly got him blacklisted (the manuscript of *Contours* was subpoenaed by House Committee on UnAmerican Activities, perhaps the only work of interpretative history to have been so cited). They also got him labeled a moral relativist when in fact he was an ethical absolutist: what is good for the United States is a non-negotiable good for them. "And if all that the rumors of catastrophe mean," he said on America's bicentennial, "is that the barbarians will land at Plymouth Rock, I can only say that I will give over in peace. They would move us off dead center."

By this, Williams meant breaking the cycle in which outward movement through territorial conquest, market expansion or war becomes the default solution to all social ills, and he spent most of his career trying to identify the problem that expansion deferred. At his most polemical and Freudian, tendencies that escalated in tandem with the Vietnam War, he argued that "Americans denied and sublimated their violence by projecting it upon those they defined as inferior." And he was acutely attuned to how "moralizing about the failures of other countries" could be an excellent career move. Williams is considered the founder of New Left diplomatic history. Yet he should be more aptly remembered as a theorist of liberalism; his most important contribution—what makes his work so enduringly generative but at the same time often misunderstood—was to identify the arena of foreign relations as where normative ideas concerning how best to organize society got worked out. In particular, Williams argued that over the long course of U.S. history, liberalism's prime contradictions—the tension between community and private property, individualism and society, virtue and self-interest—was harmonized through constant expansion, first territorially then economically. Empire, he once wrote, "was the only way to honor avarice and morality. The only way to be good *and* wealthy."

William Appleman Williams was born in 1921 in the wheat and oat town of Atlantic, Iowa, founded after the Civil War and named, according to the historian, by a flip of a coin because it sat halfway between the two coasts. He credited his interest in politics and history to an underappreciated prairie cosmopolitanism (his mother and grandmothers were "liberated women"), one as open to the world's ideas as the local farmers were, via the Rock Island Railroad, to the continent's two great ocean markets. Educated at Missouri's Kemper Military Academy, he graduated from Annapolis and then served in the Pacific in World War II. At war's end, the Navy sent him to Corpus Christi, Texas, to train as a pilot. But in retaliation for his work with the NAACP—which, with the help of local communists, was taking on General Motors, King Ranch and the local Catholic Church—he was ordered back to the Pacific to take part in Operation Crossroads, an experiment that entailed the nuclear destruction of Bikini Atoll to test the effects of radiation on military personnel and equipment. A wartime back injury prevented his participation, sparing him the illnesses that afflicted many Crossroads alumni but leaving him in a shoulder-to-thigh cast for months. With little to do except read, he deepened his interest in history and philosophy. Shortly after he left Texas, an African-American activist was murdered. Williams often cited this and other instances of "routine violence" that demands for equality were met with, as well as his close-call escape from Crossroads, as contributing to his radicalization. "Yes, sir, that will make a socialist out of you," he once said to an interviewer, referring to the killing, "unless you are dead."

He began graduate school at Madison in 1947, the same year Wisconsin voters sent Joseph McCarthy to the Senate. McCarthyism, though, largely passed over Madison; the university's greater challenge was resisting liberal orthodoxy, along with the emerging scholarly support of containment. Williams remembered later in his life that the campus was alive with a postwar class of "alert veterans" outspoken on issues like the Korean War, an engagement "largely forgotten in all the talk about the silent generation of the 1950s and the activism of the 1960s." Also vital to campus life was "thoughtful dialogue with first-rate conservatives"—not today's mean-spirited ids to liberal superegos but scholars who honestly grappled with American history. Soon after graduating, following a stint at the University of Oregon, Williams took a position in Madison's Department of History, where he would have a considerable influence on the emerging New Left. He drew around him young bohemians and intellectuals—among them scholars who would go on to dominate diplomatic history, such as Lloyd Gardner, Walter LaFeber, and Thomas McCormick, but also pioneers in social history including Herbert Gutman and Joan Scott—compelled by watching him work out "an alternative radical critique to sterile Stalinism," as Gutman, Williams' teaching assistant, explained the attraction.

Above all, the University of Wisconsin-Madison was a stew of ideas, with émigrés from Europe and refugees from New York drawing on European social and cultural theory to reinvigorate older Progressive Era historiography. The German sociologist Hans Gerth introduced Williams to continental philosophy and Frankfurt School Marxism, which sent him "soaring," according to Paul Buhle and Edward Rice-Maximin in their excellent intellectual biography *William Appleman Williams: The Tragedy of Empire*. The Americanists brought him "back down to earth." At some point, Williams felt compelled to decide between thinkers who saw the world as a dynamic whole, such as Hegel, Marx and Spinoza, and those who viewed it as made up of "atomistic elements" only mechanically related. "I chose Spinoza," he said. He also chose Marx, "exhilarated" by his "capacity to see in one piece of evidence a set of relationships that reveal an economic truth, a truth about an idea, a social verity, and a political truth." He focused on diplomacy because "if there is a Spinozian whole for an historian, then it has to involve foreign policy and the periodization of history."

This self-description makes Williams sound more like a Hegelian than a Spinozian or a Marxist. Indeed, despite his searing indictment of empire, he was openly obsessed with the idea of America as the embodiment of a world spirit. "America," he wrote toward the end of his life, "is the kind of culture that wakes you in the night, the kind of nightmare that may [yet] possibly lead us closer to the truth." Williams was a serious, empirical scholar whose prose could be as dense as any academic's, but he often broke out of form to riff in a style as sprawling as his subject matter. "If we start with reform and go on to modernize, prosperity, improve, uplift," he said of the action words of American expansion, "then we come out with purify, put right, purgation, overtake, and never look back. Finally, we find stewards as policemen, which leads us backward and forwards to benevolence, surveillance, reform, paternalism, and systematic discipline in the name of progress." Intoxicated by the "dialectical tension" of "coming apart at the seams at midnight" and "stitching it back together in a sentence or two at 3 a.m.," Williams, a jazz drummer, often expressed himself with bop rhythm and beat imagery. "Assume the worst," he warned in his last great work, chanting its title with a frequency worthy of *Howl*'s Moloch: "empire as a way of life will lead to nuclear death."

The Contours of American History is an extension and deepening of ideas first worked out in what is now a better known book, *The Tragedy of American Diplomacy*, published in 1959, which Williams presented as an updating of Frederick Jackson Turner's "Frontier Thesis." Since the end of the nineteenth century, Turner's argument that the westward advance of the United States determined the unique character of American society had "rolled through the universities and into popular literature as a tidal wave." But most historians had misconstrued its importance, debating whether or not the frontier had closed when Turner said it did, in the 1890s, or if a continent of "free land" actually led to political or social democracy. The very term "frontier," Williams argued, emphasized the "static" over the "dynamic," distracting scholars from viewing the thesis as a "classic illustration of the transformation of an idea into an ideology," the influence of which extended into the twentieth century. The real task, Williams said, was to understand how Turner served as a guide to policy-makers, including presidents Theodore Roosevelt and Woodrow Wilson, who saw the American border not as a line to stop at but as one to cross.

Tragedy traced the nascence of America's modern, nonterritorial empire to the industrial crisis of the 1890s, which brought violence and strife and threatened much worse. There emerged in reaction a "convergence of economic practice with intellectual analysis and emotional involvement" that created a "very powerful and dangerous propensity to define the essentials of American welfare in terms of activities outside the United States." With profits falling, cities swelling, workers marching and agrarians protesting, the United States, far from being "thrown back upon itself," as Turner described the result of reaching the Pacific, cast further afield. Militarists might have been dreaming of national regeneration, farmers and industrialists of international markets, labor leaders of social peace and a slice of the pie, intellectuals of an outlet for individualism in a world of corporate concentration, and missionaries of deliverance, but all came to share a vision in which domestic progress and prosperity were dependent on unfettered expansion.

The result was the Spanish-American War, when the United States got Cuba and Puerto Rico, along with what Williams thought the real prize: the Philippines, a foothold in the Pacific needed to pre-empt Europe's and Japan's drive to divvy up China. The acquisition of overseas territory—as opposed to the fruits of mainland Manifest Destiny—provoked a great national debate between imperialists and anti-imperialists. This debate was ultimately reconciled by a third camp, which advocated an "Open Door" of market expansion; this would allow the United States to use its ascendant economic strength to best competitors while remaining free from the burdens of direct colonialism.

The Open Door promised perpetual peace. "In a truly perceptive and even noble sense," Williams wrote, its designers "understood that war represented the failure of policy." Yet the policy delivered constant conflict. The grail was the Chinese market. But rivals like Japan, czarist Russia and Germany kept getting in the way, embroiling the United States in its own Great Game of geopolitics and war. Rather than discrediting the Open Door, opposition heightened the magnetism of an idea presented as a moral—that open markets benefit all—uniting realists and idealists and pulling anti-imperialists into intervention. Neither revolutions in Mexico, China and Russia nor insurgencies against Marine occupations in the Philippines and the Caribbean were dealt with as effects of economic restructuring or U.S. militarism. Rather, missionary certainty blended with the ideal of self-determination into an all-encompassing "imperial anticolonialism," allowing Americans to believe that self-interest and the world's well-being were mutually reliant.

Thus hard-wired into the *Weltanschauung*—which Williams identified as a "conception of the world and how it works, and a strategy for acting upon that outlook on a routine basis as well as in times of crisis"—that drives the United States forward were the terms of its own denial, a point unintentionally affirmed by Adolf Berle, a brain-truster of FDR's presidency. Berle favorably reviewed *Tragedy* in the *New York Times*, thinking it a corrective to the excesses of the early cold war. Yet he quibbled with Williams' use of the word "imperialism"; the United States in the nineteenth century, he said, "did expand, but into empty land. It is one thing to conquer a subject people; another to occupy vacant real estate."

Tragedy appeared in stores a month after the Cuban Revolution, with deteriorating relations between Washington and Havana providing daily illustrations of many of its arguments. "A more saddening example," Williams remarked in a revised edition, "of reading world history since 1917 in terms of the Bolshevik Revolution would be very difficult to find." The ongoing influence of Frederick Jackson Turner was practically certified by Kennedy, who responded to Cuba and other Third World problems by declaring that "America's frontiers today are on every continent." Kennedy's 1961 Alliance for Progress (which Berle was instrumental in organizing) read like a screenplay based on *Tragedy*, with the United States in the dual role of preacher and constable, promoting both modernization and counterinsurgency to tragic ends in one country after another. And history continued to be kind to *Tragedy*'s arguments. "After all," said Williams in 1973, in response to his critics, "Korea, Cuba, Vietnam, Cambodia, and Chile did happen." So did, in his lifetime, Iran, Guatemala, Indonesia, Brazil, Laos, Argentina, Angola, Mozambique, El Salvador, Nicaragua and Afghanistan. Yet through it all he would continue to discern the same pattern of denial. "The essence of American foreign relations is so obvious as to have been often ignored or evaded," Williams wrote in 1972; the "American Empire just grew like Topsy."

William's use of the word "tragedy" to describe U.S. diplomacy is often taken as an indication, despite all his talk of systems, structures, and markets, of a moralism and voluntarism—an idealist hope that if only the Great Men of the liberal pantheon— FDR and JFK, among others—had honestly faced the dilemmas of capitalism they could have steered a different course. It is true that Williams, like all good Marxist existentialists of the 1950s and 1960s, wrestled with the limits of free will within history. He had read his Sartre. But well before he came on the scene, tragedy had become a favored genre of scholars operating within the "vital center" of American intellectual life, and the title of Williams' book was a subtle skewering of these sophisticates.

In fact, it might be the case that George Kennan—the person most associated with the U.S's early cold war containment policy—is responsible for the title of the book most associated with the New Left critique of that policy. I don't know if William Appleman Williams was in the audience when Kennan addressed the 1955 meeting of the American Historical Association, but if he was he would have heard the diplomat lament the way foreign policy often fell hostage to domestic partisan politics. It was a "pity" Kennan said, and a "tragedy." Kennan was not alone in striking a tragic note, for nearly all the men who morally and intellectually supported containment, among them Reinhold Niebuhr, Arthur Schlesinger, and Kennan himself, all did so by, at least partly, invoking the unperfectable dark heart of human-ity, a beating core of destructive irrationality. "History is not a redeemer, promising to solve all human problems in time," Arthur Schlesinger cautioned in 1949, in a *Partisan Review* essay nominally about the Civil War but really a brief for containment; it is rather a "tragedy in which we are all involved, whose keynote is anxiety and frustration." Other "tough-minded" liberal intel-lectuals summoned the force of instinct and passion in mass soci-ety as something of a *deus ex machina* to stress history's tragic dimensions. The notion that evil did not "proceed from a cruel system"—that is, a system that could be engineered to produce ever more virtue, as the Henry Wallaces of the world would have it—but from man's "dark and tangled aspects," as Schlesinger interpreted Niebuhr, helped transform liberalism from a politics of hope into one of fear.

The policy implications were clear: the New Deal was the outer limit of reform, beyond which lay the nether lands of totalitarianism, and the Soviets needed to be confronted with the same resolve with which the Union defeated the Confederacy and Franklin Delano Roosevelt beat the Nazis. The world needed to be policed; containment—not just of the Soviet Union but of the egalitarian, popular-front thrust of the New Deal as well—was justified by this ethic, and served as its concrete manifestation. In his infamous 1950 "Report on Latin America," for example, Kennan repeatedly cited "the tragic nature of human civilization in all those countries to the south of us" to recommend support for heavy-handed authoritarian governments. "The human existence is everywhere tragic," Kennan later wrote in his memoirs about his trip to the region, "that of Latin America is only tragic in its own manner."

Williams viewed this dramaturgical turn as a manifestation of America's "New Babbittry," a middlebrow provincialism that, despite gestures toward liberal internationalism, garrisoned American thought from the rest of the world—as well as from its own past. In the mid-1950s, Williams was recruited to write for *The Nation* by editor Carey McWilliams, himself recently brought from the West to revive the magazine, politically and financially besieged for taking an anti-anti-communist stance during the editorship of Freda Kirchwey. Both men favored a show-me skepticism in their dealings with East Coast intellectuals. But Williams, trained in European criticism and well read in Freud, was particularly unimpressed by the moral theatrics of their work and unconvinced by their justifying pretensions. "There is a great book to be written some day," he quipped, that could explain how historians like Schlesinger who blamed the cold war on Stalin's paranoia "came by the power to render such flat-out psychiatric judgments without professional training." At *The Nation*, McWilliams used the historian to lend "depth" to front-of-the-book reporting, giving him free rein to develop a prescient critique of still-unnamed neoconservatism. In a 1956 review/essay, Williams identified Hofstadter's celebrated *The Age of Reform*—with its heavy use of psychology to explain violent episodes in American history, including the Spanish-American War—as signaling a turning point in American thought. Absolved from having to examine the relationship between ideology and interests, liberals had rendered history into "myth." "Perhaps the major American casualty of the cold war," he wrote in another essay, "has been the idea of history."

And if not *tragic* then *ironic*. Both *Tragedy* and *Contours* could be read against Reinhold Niebuhr's 1952 *The Irony of American History*. Niebuhr was an anti-imperialist in his youth, yet *Irony of American History* served as something of a blank postdated check, underwriting intervention and liquidating its deficits. His interpretation of history as a series of "ironies" folded the violence involved in the rise of the United States—which Niebuhr and Williams described in strikingly similar terms—into a transcendent understanding of evil that was then, conveniently enough, projected onto the Soviet Union. In 1946, for instance, Niebuhr had called the bombing of Hiroshima and Nagasaki "morally indefensible." Six years later, *Irony*'s first page warned that there is an "element of tragedy" in the struggle of "freedom against tyranny." Though "our civilization" is "confident of its virtue it must yet hold atomic bombs ready for use so as to prevent a possible world conflagration."

Williams thought this a theology of evasion. It was easy to lampoon what he described as the "high noon" fantasies of Henry Luce's American Century. Yet hand-wringers like Niebuhr—whom Williams once called the "most sought-after soul sitter for American liberalism"—played their part in justifying expansion. Williams had no illusions about the Soviet Union, and he criticized its repression of intellectuals. Russians, he said, paid a "terrible price in terror and hardship." But he too could appreciate what he called history's "harsh irony": by bringing a preponderance of power to bear against the U.S.S.R., which emerged from World War II with an exhausted military, wasted farms and factories, ruined cities and a "sad, weary, and lethargic population," the United States eventually conjured up the enemy it feared; armed with the threat of containment, Stalin drove "the Soviet people to the brink of collapse" until he turned his country into a nuclear power.

Containment-intellectuals drew heavily from Freud, Marx, and even Christ, wrote Williams, but they did so in a way that suppressed their "utopianism." "Freud's objective was to know the irrational in order to discipline and control it," he said in *Contours,* not adjust to or flee from it. The same is true regarding Marx's notion of alienation and Christ's idea of sin. All three "insisted that the only important frontier was man in society—not man on a frontier. To them, the frontier was harmful because it was precisely what Turner called it: an escape from the chance to become fully human" (that it is difficult to say where Turner in his famous essay says anything along these lines speaks to Williams' interpretive imagination). But by denying that humanity could achieve "great and noble goals," Niebuhr and other cold war liberals point in only one direction: outward. Like the pragmatists that came before them, they offered a "philosophy without a Utopia," which was "like a sky without the stars. It is very inspiring until it gets dark"—that is, until it is time to go to war and a supposedly independent and critical-minded realism melts like snow in May (think, Williams says, of John Dewey and World War I). Today, Niebuhr's celebrated "modesty" is often held up as an alternative to neoconservative hubris. Williams though identifies in it the same merry-go-round foreign policy ethic that emerged after 1898. He called it "containment-liberation": an idealism that gets us in, and a realism that keeps us there while promising to get us out.

But if Schlesinger, Niebuhr and the rest of the "New Babbitts" wanted history as dinner theater, Williams could do that too. In 1955 Williams produced a *Nation* "fable," casting the cold warrior as a composite of four historical types: Puritan, Planter, Hamiltonian, and Homesteader:

> The Puritan elected himself America's first elite. He originally intended to establish a righteous Eden. His handmaiden was to have been Calvin's Virgin of unexploited wealth. But the Devil, cleverly camouflaged as the noble savage, already claimed the Virgin. Thus the Puritan had first to contain and defeat the red man … But the pietistic intensity of his awareness of the Devil withered the Puritan's sense of purpose. Morality ceased to be the means of communicating with God and the guide to the good life … Only the Devil, warned the Puritan, spoke of the general welfare. Thus the Puritan gave way to the Planter, who comforted and wooed the Virgin … Not until the Puritan pointed to the evil of the slave did the Planter and the Virgin take up the language of noblesse oblige. It was then too late. The hell of a fellow who occasionally feeds the neighborhood does not become m'Lord through rhetoric …

And on it goes, with Williams introducing the Hamiltonian empire builder, who vanquished the Planter, and the Homesteader, a potential repository of a non-imperial America but compromised by his ties to the Hamiltonian and the Planter. At this point Williams was an assistant professor at the University of Oregon, a land-grant university tucked into a remote corner of the continental United States. Yet here he was, precociously seizing on the then-influential "myth and symbol" school of American studies to sweepingly reinterpret all of U.S. history. He perversely cast FDR not as a Hamiltonian but as a Planter who renovated noblesse oblige for the industrial age and reconciled the Homesteader (Henry Wallace!) to the "machine." Williams made the story's endpoint 1955, hoping that Soviet nuclear power would rescue history from the "Puritan memory hole" and free Eisenhower from crusaders who mistook "catechism for wisdom."

This "fable" actually helps decode Williams' subsequent writings, in particular his recurrent concern, elaborated in full in *Contours*, with the externalization of morality: "good" came to be understood as expansion ("Calvin's Virgin"), whereas anything that stood in its way—from American Indians to the Confederacy, from the Soviet Union to the Third World—was "evil." "Americans became very prone to define their rivals as unnatural men," he wrote, "almost, if not wholly, beyond redemption."

Throughout his career, Williams repeatedly called on citizens to use, in his phrase, "history as a way of learning" to "get closer to the truth." "It is only by abandoning the clichés that we can even define the tragedy. When we have done that," he wrote, "we will no longer be acquiescing in the deadly inertia of the past." Williams' attempts to explain exactly what this meant were often abstruse. But at least one model for what he had in mind was offered by postwar British social historians.

After receiving his doctorate from the University of Wisconsin-Madison, in 1950, Williams spent some time studying Labour economics at the University of Leeds, where exposure to British history confirmed his criticisms of U.S. scholarship. Unlike in the U.S., where the reaction against the Progressive historians led to the academic kitsch Williams would pit himself against, in Great

Britain the move away from economism by scholars such as R. H. Tawney, Hugh Trevor-Roper and Christopher Hill resulted in a serious engagement with ideas, both religious and secular, and their relationship to class, political action, and large-scale change. It was here, exposed to the self-aware scholarship of an empire in decline, that Williams began to work out his account of an empire in ascendance, and in denial.

Published in 1961, *The Contours of American History* went well beyond anything Williams did in *Tragedy*. Where *Tragedy* in many ways can be read as an updating of Charles Beard, *Contours* offered a wholly original interpretation, reaching deep into thirteenth-century British history to identify the motor contradictions of what eventually would become known as liberalism. In doing so, the book in effect presented the story of the United States as *the* story of capitalism. Williams largely ignored the heated debate between Tawney, Trevor-Roper, and Hill—over, for instance, whether it was a rising or falling gentry that sparked the English Civil War—and instead focused obsessively on what he believed to be the heart of the matter: "the whole question of private property in its relation-ship to the state and to religious values"; or, "how to reconcile the Biblical injunction to promote the general welfare and common good of God's corporate world and its creatures" with the "growing propensity to define God's estate as the civil society in which the individual Christian resided."

Others in the 1950s, such as John Rawls and Louis Hartz, considered the problem of "property" in liberal thought, particu-larly as it related to the difficulty of achieving social democracy within a capitalist framework. Yet Williams was perhaps the first to link these questions explicitly to imperialism—or, more precisely, to realize the way expansion in a liberal society warps any consid-eration of the dilemma. For Williams, the development of mercan-tilism from a fitful set of notions and practices concerning trade, expansion, money, private property, poverty, wealth, hierarchy, and domestic welfare in the thirteenth century into a mature *Weltanschauung* in the eighteenth produced two fundamental tenets, notable less for their content than the frankness with which intellectuals across class and theological lines held them to be true: first, expansion was necessary to overcome what Williams described as the "political economy of English backwardness," that

XXVI   THE CONTOURS OF AMERICAN HISTORY

is, to integrate agriculture and manufacturing and to maintain peace and order in a society roiled by change; second, there existed no natural harmony between private interests and the common-weal. Both needed to be nurtured and balanced by strong public action.

The nuances were many, but the common ground firm: radical Levellers and Anabaptists might have had a more "thoroughgoing" program to subvert the rights of property, but upper-class mercantilists like Lord Shaftsbury and Sir James Steuart, while believing that "self-interest was the main engine of human action," also knew that limits had to be placed on individual rights, that "men had to act consciously and rationally to keep the system functioning," and that "welfare was the product of policy, not of Providence." As to the vaunted individualizing thrust of the Protestant Ethic, Williams reminded readers that at no time did "Luther construct a hierarchy of labor which implied that godliness came with worldly success," and that while later Protestants might have downplayed a "stress on corporate values in favor of individuals and worldly goods . . . Calvin himself never did so."

It is liberalism then that is the great "heresy." By this, Williams didn't mean liberals rejected Christian mercantilism's concern for the general good of God's earthly estate. Rather, they inverted the terms, insisting that the "general welfare" is *derived* from the "supremacy of individual liberty." This apostasy was driven by the deepening complexity of civil society, the rise of new and shifting coalitions organized along ever more intricate and competitive interests, which clouded the social awareness Williams esteems in Shaftsbury and Steuart. The very success of the system "prompted men to overlook the fact that it was a man-made system, and to assume instead that it was a natural order which would operate indefinitely with little or no attention."

It would be half correct to understand Williams as something of a Red Tory himself, and Williams wouldn't have disagreed. He could be placed alongside contemporaries, such as Christopher Lasch and even E. P. Thompson, whose criticisms of liberalism often seemed to be facing backwards, to the forge, farm, and family, to a time of true community and unalienated individuality. Williams was in the upswing of a New Left generation that understood the problem to be not so much capitalism as corporate liberalism and the bureaucratic welfare state, and Williams lamented a society that forced individuals to give themselves over to large-scale organizations, be they the federal government, the giant corporation, or impersonal labor unions. His criticism of the New Deal was insistent, and left him with more than a few admirers among conservatives.

But Williams' brief in defense of Shaftsbury and Steuart seems like a straightforward (and decidedly not libertarian or precapitalist) advocacy of state planning and corporate paternalism. This, I think, points less to a gap between concept and ethics than to what makes his analysis singularly perceptive, prophetic even, yet at the same time difficult to integrate into subsequent scholarship.

Reading *Contours* now, more than thirty years after the insurgence of the New Right—which not only shows no signs of abatement but today embraces an American Exceptionalism defined nearly exclusively as individual supremacy—one appreciates just how remarkably attuned Williams was to the power of Lockean liberalism in driving the U.S. forward, and outward. Few social critics in the early 1960s, perhaps with the exception of Louis Hartz, thought the problem was too much individualism; many rather focused on what they identified as a dissolution of individuality, which was blamed, depending on perspective, on the welfare state or commodity production. Much of this work was influenced by theories of social alienation affiliated with the Frankfurt School, especially the joining of psychoanalysis and Marxism to argue that monopoly capitalism had stripped away the traction from everyday life needed to generate dialectical political struggle and ego formation. Where earlier moments of capitalism generated the self that stood at the center of the liberal ideal, its modern, totalizing incarnation produced subjects that were unmoored, unformed, subsumed into, at best, the modern bureaucracy and mass culture, or, at worst, the totalitarian party. Much of this influence was covert. It worked its way into the sociology of scholars like David Riesman, whose *The Lonely Crowd*, published a decade before *Contours*, talked of the rise of rootless "other-directed people" who are "at home everywhere and nowhere." By the early 1980s, Christopher Lasch, who translated Frankfurt School arguments into a U.S. vernacular, was describing the dominant type in modern life as the "minimal self," trapped in a lifelong pursuit of shadows, sublimated to technology, pastoral therapy, sex, and advertising. Neoconservatives would build on the kind of insights offered by Riesman and Lasch to develop an effective politics that attacked the social softness of the welfare state. Many scholars on the left developed a different, though not too different, argument, focusing on the fragmentary, protean nature of subjectivity that was never whole to begin with—a focus which, in retrospect, seemed completely unprepared to anticipate the Right's ability to renew itself through a reconstituted Lockean individualism.

Like Riesman and Lasch, Williams read Adorno, Horkheimer, Fromm, Marcuse, and Freud. Yet what sets him apart from these thinkers was an insistence that the effects of social and psychic alienation were relocated into the realm of expansion, and that the defining characteristic of "the age of corporate capitalism" was not so much the suppression of the individual that rises in earlier periods but its reproduction, in distorted, increasingly aggressive and unaware form, on the frontier.

Williams' interpretation of John Locke's thought in *Contours* as "experimental, neo-hedonistic individualism" is in many ways typical for his time. But if others had already identified "America's philosopher" as capitalism's primal mystifier, it took Williams to point out that that mystification could only be maintained through constant expansion. He identifies in Locke's philosophy three keys to understanding what a few years earlier in *Tragedy* he named as "imperial anticolonialism." The first, described above, is an inversion of Christian mercantilism's terms. The "collective good" in the Lockean formulation was no longer understood to be maintained through an acceptance and regulation of individualism but was now dependent on unleashing that individualism. Second, Locke's followers, if not Locke himself, subtly transposed this presumed harmony of interests between the collective and the individual on to the question of empire. As did the mercantilists, Locke "theoretically and practically" knew his philosophy to be utterly dependent on expansion. Profits from the empire made it possible both to "define freedom for citizens of the Metropolis as the crucial issue" and to avoid "fundamental questions concerning the nature and allocation of responsibility in society." Later advocates of laissez faire would extend this evasion of responsibility to the question of empire itself, absolving themselves from having to assume liability for the consequences of a foreign policy that in effect financed their ethics. Third, Locke's celebrated individualism was little more than Hobbesian authoritarianism dressed in "liberal rhetoric," for it was founded on a circular logic that enforced conformity. Locke granted men the inherent right to "control their labor and property" and to challenge any state that did not protect this right; it follows then that those who challenged the state from a perspective that did not affirm individual supremacy were "unnatural men and hence beyond the pale." As Captain Yossarian put it in Joseph Heller's war novel—which, also published in 1961, could be read as *Contours'* literary companion—"Whoo, that's some catch, that catch-22." "It's the best there is," came the reply.

Beginning with Shaftsbury and ending with Dean Acheson and Martin Luther King, Jr., along the way synthesizing and reframing existing scholarship on every important phase and event of U.S. history and indexing literature, architecture, and art to an epoch's particular mode of production, Williams uses Locke's initial slight of hand—capitalism's original Catch-22—to unlock the black box of American Exceptionalism and reveal its nested, mutually reinforcing assumptions. These include:

—a definition of the commonweal as dependent on unfettered individual rights, and the persistence of that definition even as other industrial societies have accepted the legitimacy of social democracy;

—the enduring, deepening, and increasingly aggressive propensity, absent a positive vision of a social community, to understand the collective good exclusively in negative terms, as the removal of obstacles to the pursuit of individual interests;

—the increasing dependence, also related to the lack of a positive ideal of the commonweal, on expansion to absorb the conflicts, stratifications, inequalities and concentrations of wealth that come from an unleashed pursuit of individualism;

—thus the increasing externalization of morality, in which expansion is identified as "good" and impediments to expansion "evil;"

—a projection of the Lockean fallacy that a harmony of interests exists

between individual self-interest and the collective good into the realm
of foreign relations, which allows both a denial of the consequences of
empire and an ability to pass off the U.S. particular as universal;
—the rhetorical celebration of the individual yet the actual enforcement of conformity;
—and the rhetorical celebration of minimal government yet the actual
construction of a fortified state pursuing militarism abroad and mass
incarceration at home to remove disruptions to a harmony of interests
presupposed as natural.

While Locke infused the Declaration of Independence's spirit,
it was the mature mercantilists, Shaftsbury and Steuart foremost among them, who bequeathed their historical vision and
social awareness to America's architects of law, particularly to
James Madison, empire's great "theorist" who was "nothing if not
comprehensive." Williams quoted a phrase of Madison's every
chance he could: "Extend the sphere" and "you make it less probable that a majority of the whole will have a common motive to
invade the rights of other citizens." Demands for a leveling of
wealth could be defused by opening up "surplus social space."
Thomas Jefferson once proposed redistributing property each
generation as a way of retaining republican virtue in a small
place, but he abandoned the idea to become, in Williams' words,
the "epic poet" of the "urge to escape, to run away and spend
one's life doing what one wanted—or in starting over again and
again." And so the history *Contours* describes as taking centuries
to unfold in Great Britain passes in but six decades in the United
States, as the brief but politically potent "age of mercantilism"—
expansionist but consciously organized, running from the 1760s
to the 1820s—falls to the "animal vigor" of the "age of Jacksonian
laissez faire."

In the United States, with its open frontier and easy enemy,
the elemental tension within liberalism didn't so much dialecti-
cally progress as unspool. It's worth pulling out the following two
passages not just to illustrate the point but to highlight the quirki-
ness of Williams' prose and, for someone who had to fend off
charges of economic determinism his whole career, the respect he
pays to ideas and aspirations:

To say [that the Puritans] sought a chimera is to give up the intellectual and moral struggle: they asked the right questions and struggled
for the right answers. Nonetheless, like the little girl with a curl in the
middle of her forehead, these early Puritans had a kink in their ideology; when they went wrong, they went very, very wrong. Devoted to
the ideal of a corporate community guided by a strong moral sense,
they developed a great talent for misinterpreting any opposition.
From the outset, for example, they were prone to view the Indians as
agents of the Devil waiting to test their convictions. . . . But that definition externalized Evil, thus making it an object to be overpowered
rather than an internal, human weakness to be contained until transformed. . . . This propensity to place Evil outside their system not only
distorted the Puritans' own doctrine, it inclined them toward a solution which involved the extension of their system over others. Here
was a subtle convergence of religious and secular ideas, for mercantilism also emphasized the necessity as well as desirability of expansion
in economic and political affairs. It externalized secular evil by arguing that domestic poverty could in the last analysis be overcome only
by taking away wealth from others. Far from wanting no more to be
left alone, New Englanders developed a solution to their religious and
secular difficulties which prompted vigorous action against an external cause.

This desire to be "left alone," he noted in an earlier essay, could only
be realized by total war (which, after his experiences in World War
II, was another theme that preoccupied Williams); the "American
dream" for the country to become "a world unto itself," he observed
with a mordancy that later in life would at times slip into mania,
is not as "isolationist a policy as we have liked to think." "Gunfire
removed the hardy," Williams wrote in 1980, and displacement and
disease extirpated the rest: "the coughs, the sneezes, and the laying
on of hands were like the bombs over Hiroshima and Nagasaki."
    As to the high, conscious vision of Founding Fathers like
Madison, the resort to the frontier as a safety valve led to social-
barbarization and the emergence of a deep anti-intellectual individualism. Here, the register really is tragic, since, for Williams,
the dispossession of historical awareness is a social catastrophe we
all have to bear:

Expansion west has been formulated as an answer to the crucial problem of controlling private property in order to achieve the general welfare. But it was in fact an evasion—and no very subtle or sophisticated one—of that central issue. For given a continent easily conquered and ruthlessly exploited it was not too difficult to accumulate the lowest necessary amount of public wealth while at the same time allowing private individuals and groups to acquire unlimited riches. For the same reasons, the expansionist thesis of the mercantilists also encouraged a nonintellectual approach to human affairs. Problems could be solved by growth. For men who valued intellectual achievement so highly, and knew it as vital in providing men with a sense of purpose and meaning, this was perhaps the greatest irony of their own labor and influence.

That Williams understood liberalism largely in sacred terms, as an attempt to "sanctify the processes of this earth," is what allowed him to escape the economism of Charles Beard, who described but couldn't explain the transition from a quasi-isolationist diplomacy based on realist national interests to the moralistic internationalism that reigned after 1898. One of Williams' great insights was to insist that these divides were false, that both sides of the apparent division—realism and moralism, and isolationism and internationalism—were expressions of liberalism's obfuscation of the contradiction between self-interest and the collective good. During the Age of Corporate Capitalism, Woodrow Wilson emerges as the epoch's organic intellectual, a "Christian capitalist" who applied nineteenth-century notions of individualism to the corporation and then worked to build an interstate order aligned to that application.

Faced with a stifling concentration of monopoly wealth and political influence that threatened to derail the whole system, Wilson appealed to Lockean natural law not to challenge amalgamated power but to institutionalize it. The role of government was defined in strictly negative terms, limited to removing obstacles (monopolies) that interrupted the efficient harmony of interests presumed to exist between the common good and self-interest pursuing beings, with corporations now included among those beings. Actual individuals, left to chase their natural right to self-interest in the increasingly ineffectual electoral arena, lost their power to "initiate, or even control, affairs that affected" them "immediately and fundamentally." In turn, Wilson's postwar foreign policy was an "almost literal" application of corporate liberalism to the world at large: "The League of Nations became the state, and its function was to maintain order and enforce the rules of the game at the international level," with the idea that the global removal of impediments to the capitalist "harmony of interests" would produce universal peace and prosperity. If a colony or country challenged the ideal of property rights—such as Japan, Mexico, Russia, and China—or sought to realize the promise of self-determination to "achieve their goals in their own fashion," the challenge was understood as a perverse, unnatural disruption of the presumed harmony and dealt with as such. Some of these countries could of course exercise their franchise in the new Parliament of Man, yet a handful of powerful empires continued to exercise mandatory powers. Like individuals in a polity ruled by corporations, "every nation could vote," Williams writes, "but nothing could be done." Thus the domestic becomes the foreign, America the world, and the transfer of a "simple (if not crude) concept of natural law" into the realm of foreign policy "as neat a circle as ever drawn freehand." Catch-22 indeed.

From this point forward, Williams presents successive U.S. presidents as paralyzed by the narrow range of choices facing them, leading them, during moments of crisis, to reinforce rather than transcend the old order. "Fleeing forward," as he later described the ongoing evasion. The arching narrative of Contours at times endows abstractions with human agency: "The Weltanschauung of Laissez Faire Engenders a Civil War," is one of its subtitles. Yet individuals are never ground down in history's gears. In an insightful reading of Edgar Allan Poe as a profound appraiser of the mystifications and terrors of laissez faire, Williams describes the writer as a "brilliant creative force" who "struggled with the central problem of art and existence: how to subordinate the parts of the whole in order to achieve overall meaning and significance while at the same time retaining the integrity of the individual elements." It's a struggle Williams shared, for despite all his talk about understanding history as a "system" he rendered particular people with an intimacy beyond the reach of most historians, of whatever political persuasion.

General Douglas MacArthur "had an instinct for the viscera," and his lunge for power stemmed as much from the dynamics of the military-industrial complex as from the frustrations of his Scottish aristocratic family's three-generation bid to break into American politics. "One has to touch one's cap," Williams said, to any "man sitting on that combination of personal and social dynamite, and somehow keeping it under control." He's especially appreciative of politicians who grasp the dilemma: Abraham Lincoln's strength was to "abstract himself from himself," and while his sanctification of private property made him the "philosopher of the marketplace," the older, more humble Lincoln "sensed the weaknesses of that philosophy and tried to lead its triumphant advocates toward a more humane and responsible conception of man and society." But his efforts failed, and following the Civil War, "the *soul* of *laissez faire went marching on* into a world of vastly different substance and proportions." Then there's his portrait in a latter essay of "Ol' Lyndon" Johnson, "first and always" a "*southern* white who grew up wandering hither and yon across that no man's land that divides the lowers from the maybe middles," his Confederate "consciousness of being first among the damned" making him aware of the New Deal's betrayal of African-Americans in ways Northern patricians like John F. Kennedy never could understand. One has the feeling Williams knew these people, or men very much like them, during his service in the Pacific and his time in Corpus Christi.

Williams died in 1990. He lived long enough to sense the importance of the election of Ronald Reagan but short of the time needed to grasp its full significance, or just how farsighted he was in identifying individual supremacy as the enduring feature of American Exceptionalism. He might have been surprised, however, or at least impressed, with the seemingly unstoppable success the New Right has had in organizing a mass movement, and advancing an ideal of a common good, around a reconstituted Lockean individualism. Even before the rise of Reagan, he held out hope that the left could seize on states' rights to break up the U.S., overthrow corporate rule, and end the empire; in an underappreciated essay, *America Confronts a Revolutionary*

World, he called for a reappraisal of the decentralizing thrust of the Articles of Confederation, reminding "radicals" that "states' rights can be invoked and honored to create a socialist community as well as to defend slavery." That of course didn't happen, and states' rights remain a central plank of the U.S. New Right as a vehicle for individual supremacy.

Williams, however, would recognize in the New Right a perfect circle of cause and effect, with dynamics similar to what he identified as taking place during the Jacksonian "Age of Laissez Nous Faire": a violent assault on the Third World in the 1980s, launched simultaneously with an undermining of the United States' industrial base, kicked off a cycle of speculative capitalism that continues to this day. This in turn eroded the middle-class virtue and patriarchal authority established by the New Deal, resulting in social and psychic dissolution that the New Right stemmed by resurrecting the ideal of a bounded, disciplined, property-holding and natural-rights-bearing male self—an ideal that could only be maintained by constant mobilization against its perverse and unnatural opposite: welfare queens, criminals, feminists, Latin American communists, gays, Muslims, and migrants. Put another way, concrete violence hastened abstract violence, which was healed by more concrete violence, creating a perpetual feedback loop.

It's Williams, in other words, who explains the sundering of Arthur Schlesinger's "vital center," the unprecedented polarization of U.S. politics and its downward spiral, and how Barack Obama's fundamentally mild policy efforts at halting that spiral can credibly be cast as an assault on "American Exceptionalism," as an effort to turn the United States into if not Zimbabwe then a run-of-the-mill European social democracy. Williams would see in Obama, despite the backlash against him, a familiar capitulation to received wisdom, an expected rotation back to "realism" and "pragmatism" after the excesses of "idealism"—an inability to break the cycle or challenge the fundamental premises that underwrite domestic economics and foreign policy. Under the banner of perpetual war, and in the shade of concentrated corporate wealth and power greater than anything Williams could have imagined, the soul of *laissez faire again marches into a world of* vastly different substance and proportions.

To end, then, with Schlesinger's opening query, why William Appleman Williams? Because as history has shown, things can always get worse.*

Greg Grandin

---

*   After *Contours*, Williams wrote a number of book-length essays, including *The Great Evasion: An Essay on the Contemporary Relevance of Karl Marx and on the Wisdom of Admitting the Heretic into the Dialogue about America's Future*; *America Confronts a Revolutionary World*; *Empire as a Way of Life*; and one more fully researched monograph, *The Roots of the Modern American Empire: A Study of the Growth and Shaping of Social Consciousness in a Marketplace Society*, published in 1969, which is worth a reappraisal in itself. *Roots*, almost impenetrably dense and, unlike *Tragedy* and *Contours*, thick with footnotes, reconsiders the expansionist vision Williams had previously attributed to urban financiers and industrialists in the 1890s, tracing it earlier back to the Agrarian populists in the 1860s. Since the majority of the labor force at the time were farmers, it was a much more pessimistic argument than he had made before regarding the widespread, mass psychological support for empire, one that in many ways echoed what he had previously criticized in Hofstadter. At the end of the book, Williams tries to escape the corner he has backed himself into by quoting Max Horkheimer: "Again and again, ideas have cast off their swaddling clothes and struck out against the social systems that bore them." Recently, there has been a reconsideration by U.S. historians of agrarian Populists as modern expansionists, confirming without crediting arguments Williams made 40 years ago. See the William Appleman Williams Papers, held by Oregon State University, for a complete bibliography; available at osulibrary.oregonstate.edu.

Preface to the 1966 Edition: Concerning Such Matters as Authors, Reviewers, Readers, and Even the Book Itself

Raymond Chandler and William Faulkner shared some of the same insights into the nature of being an historian and a writer, and they warned against reading the reviews of one's own books. Both men understood that a writer's creativity, integrity, and performance are perpetually threatened by the urge to defend or assert himself, and to be praised by his peers and superiors. And they realized that the more an author fulfilled these natural and healthy needs by satisfying his reviewers, the more he would write to and for his reviewers. The writer would thus warp his own insights and perceptions, and turn away from his true audience.

The writer and the reviewer are engaged in separate dialogues with the same protagonist—the reader. The writer's responsibility is to offer himself directly and honestly, and at the highest level of performance he can reach, to the reading public. The reviewer's obligation is to do the same *in order to inform and guide the reader's dialogue with the writer*. When the author and the reviewer substitute each other for the reading public, they deny their separate purposes and responsibilities.

I was impressed with the validity of this insight offered by Chandler and Faulkner long before I began to write books. I found the vast majority of formal and public exchanges between authors and reviewers to be dull, childish, petty, or irrelevant. A good many managed to display all those qualities. There were a few exciting personal duels, but neither the bluster nor the blood contributed to any fundamental enrichment of the reader's dialogue with the author. The tiny number of such confrontations that did help the reader involved an investment of time and energy by the author that he could have used far more creatively in a way that I will describe later.

The warning from Chandler and Faulkner was further verified when I disregarded it. I doubt if any man has either the confidence or the discipline to ignore the reviews of his first book. Certainly I did not. But in reading them I gained a fuller understanding of what Chandler and Faulkner were talking about. Some reviewers mistake the public or professional for the personal arena. There is a legitimate purpose, and potentially great value, in a serious confrontation between professionals. Ted Williams could and did teach other men how to raise their batting averages. The tough, candid, private exchanges between Maxwell Perkins and Tom Wolfe, and between F. Scott Fitzgerald and Ernest Hemingway, were fruitful. And I have read personal correspondence between historians that engaged and enlarged the minds of both men and improved their subsequent work.

But such direct personal relationships have nothing to do with reviewing, and the attempt to promote that kind of a dialogue in a review has provided many examples of trying to do a good thing in the wrong way and in the wrong place. The reviewer has the extremely difficult task of helping the reader to initiate and sustain his own creative relationship with the author. There are very few serious writers from whom we cannot learn something, even if it is sometimes negative, and the reviewer fails unless he helps engage the reader in that educational process.

Any book, however excellent, can be ostensibly destroyed by using one of two simple techniques. The reviewer can list the author's secondary or incidental judgments which are eccentric or otherwise at odds with received truth, combine these with a compilation of the slips and errors that inevitably occur during the process of publication, and present the sum total as substantive failures which demolish the author's work. The other procedure involves finding a fulcrum outside the author's conceptual system and applying the lever of routine intelligence. This offers the reader the illusion of professional destruction.

Such wrecking exercises may meet certain psychological needs of the men who undertake them, and may even provide temporary distractions for others, but they should not be confused with helping the reader understand, evaluate, and benefit from what the author has created. Hence they are particularly indefensible when performed by professionals before an audience of professionals.

Other reviewers use a book as either an excuse or an opportunity to begin their own dialogue with the reader about issues and subjects that are largely—if not totally—divorced from the author's work. The reviewer has the right, and should be encouraged, to initiate and sustain his own independent relationship with the reading public. But he only confuses, and hence misleads, the public when he does so in the guise of reviewing.

Such reviewers are so involved with their own labors that they are particularly unable to establish any significant rapport or empathy with the author and his work. Yet such *simpático* is essential to creative reviewing. This does not mean that the reviewer must praise or even accept all that the author says. (There is a great misconception, somehow, that to identify, in order to understand, is of necessity to agree or approve or acquiesce. But neither a secular logic nor a moral imperative unites the two acts. One can understand and still disagree.) Yet the reviewer has to understand the author in the fundamental sense of *simpático* if he is to speak creatively and helpfully about the author's work to the reading public. Opposition or praise that are based on no more than personal projection, preference, or pique do not help third parties reach their *own* conclusions.

The experience of reading the reviews of my first book, *American-Russian Relations, 1781–1947*, and considering them seriously, also suggested to me that authors are probably capable of writing some of the most critical and useful reviews of their own work. This may not be true of those who produce nothing beyond the one book that is proverbially said to be in every man, but it is most likely the case with a good many writers who are engaged in a sustained creative effort. Writing is an act of learning and maturation as well as a display of insight and ego, and I know many writers who have discussed their past work with an exciting combination of candor, affection, ruthlessness, and imagination.

Those who doubt this proposition might profitably read the correspondence of Malcolm Lowry, and particularly his essay replying to the negative commentary prepared for a publishing house that was considering his manuscript.*

All this by way of saying why I decline to provide a running commentary on the reviews that were printed in response and reply, in hope and disappointment, and in fear and anger when *Contours* was first published in 1961. The gentle insistence of an unusual editor, Ivan Dee, who is also a rare human being, persuaded me to read all those documents. And the experience verified the remark once made by Merrill Jensen, a colleague whose mind and heart have informed and warmed my life, that the temptation to review the reviewers is almost irresistible.

But Chandler and Faulkner are correct, and I am not concerned with writing to and for the reviewers. I have been, and I remain, concerned to carry on a dialogue with the reading public about the way we Americans have lived our individual and collective lives, about the consequences of thinking and acting as we have, and about how we can use that knowledge to extend and deepen our humanity in the present and the future.

I think that a few of the reviewers made stimulating and helpful contributions to that dialogue, even though they disagreed in varying degrees, and ways, with what I offered the reader. The trench warfare initiated by other critics, whose posture and thought was almost wholly negative, contributed little either to the dialogue between myself and the reader or to their own conversation with the reader. The mistakes they discovered did not destroy my substantive argument. Most of their criticisms of my analyses and interpretations were based upon sloppy reading of my actual presentation, upon insufficient factual evidence to carry the weight of their rebuttal, or upon the lack of sufficient *simpático* to grasp fully the nature of the alternate explanations I offered.

Nothing I can write will transform them into close and attentive readers. Transcribing all my research notes into supplementary

---

* M. Lowry to J. Cape, January 2, 1946: *Selected Letters of Malcolm Lowry*, edited by Harvey Breit and Margerie Bonner Lowry (New York: Lippincott, 1965), 57–88.

text and commentary for them would fill at least another volume as large as this. The willingness to be *simpático* is a challenge that each man must meet for himself. If he is psychologically strong enough to do so, then the only issue is whether he musters the courage to face a new idea that might change his mind and thereby his life.

My reply to the reviewers, finally, is simply to invite the reader (old and new) to give this book his close and sustained attention; and to engage me in dialogue about what we Americans have been and done, what the consequences have been, and what we can learn from that experience that will help us go beyond our present limitations and use our creative powers more effectively and more morally.

The book would be somewhat different if I had just written it, or if I had taken six months to revise it extensively. The factual slips and oversights would be corrected. It would be longer in order to provide more detailed expositions of some points that are probably cryptically presented, and to offer further examples in support of some interpretations and judgments. And the events since 1960 would be integrated into the analysis. But none of these are primary, substantive matters. I have not changed my mind about the validity of my broad conceptual framework or periodization of our history, or about the relevance and usefulness of my interpretation of central events, ideas, and institutions. I think that the book, carefully read and seriously considered, extends our knowledge of ourselves.

There is some point, however, in responding directly to one question that was put to me by the great majority of the several hundred readers who wrote personal letters after they had finished the book, and by a similar number with whom I have talked directly. Some of these men and women enjoyed wealth and power; others endured low incomes and the pain of living in a world largely shaped and controlled by others. Most of them, of course, were members of that vast area we call the middle class. Yet all of them were troubled by the questions they felt the book had raised but had not answered: What should we do now, and where do we go from here?

When I wrote this book I argued that History was a way of

learning, a way of mustering knowledge, courage, and will to break free of the past. I see no reason to change that view. I see only a more pressing need to break free—a greater urgency, that is, to honor those of our traditional ideals, values, and practices that remain creative; and a more insistent necessity to create new visions, virtues, and procedures to replace those that have reached their potential and survive only as conventions and rationalizations that impede the building of an American community.

We already have a Great Society. Indeed, this is a good part of our trouble. We are role-players in a huge and powerful system that is increasingly capable of creating the actors it needs out of the human beings it is supposed to serve. But acting the part written by the system destroys both our essential humanness and our essential Americanness.

The nature and the pervasive strength of contemporary industrial society lie at the heart of the problem. Critics such as Walter Lippmann recognize this power, and its consequences, and hence see that it is necessary to go beyond the Great Society to the Good Society. But it is not enough to aim only as high as a Good Society. For the Good Society is also predicated upon the existing system, and for that reason it can offer nothing more than greater material ease, a more relaxed acceptance of our limited scope and significance in the system, and hence a further hedonizing, privatizing, and narrowing of our existence. The Good Society can give us greater fulfillment, but only in a more limited role. It is a beguiling but tranquilizing objective.

Our true goal should be an American community. Now community is a process as well as an achievement, and the process is more important. Community as process is the ever-deepening understanding of our nature and potential as human beings, and the sustained creation of ways of living together that are appropriate to that nature and potential.

The fundamental conflicts within and between human beings in society arise out of contending propensities that are common to all men and women. These can be described and discussed in several ways, but in thinking about community it seems useful to do so by defining two sets of paired opposites. One of these polarities involves the tension between power and love—between the exercise of one's will over another, and the confluence of oneself with another. Power is a mine-his relationship. Love is an I-Thou relationship. The other polarity involves the tension between acquiescence (or passivity) and participation (or involvement). Clearly enough, there is an interrelationship between the two sets of opposites. True love is predicated upon full mutual involvement, and pure power for one requires acquiescence by another.

These polarities of power and love, and passivity and involvement, operate within a broader context. All living organisms need and seek an integrated relationship with their environment. Hence an ecology between human beings can be established—at least for a time—on the basis of power and passivity, as well as through involved, participating, and reciprocal love. Those are the basic patterns, and hence the two irreducible forms of *functioning* government are benevolent despotism and democracy. There are of course gradations between these primary modes, and pathological extensions of each, but such patterns are derivative and not independent.

Thus there are two kinds of community. One is the community established through the practice of benevolent despotism. It is predicated upon power for the few and acquiescence by the many; and it is sustained by an understanding on the part of the few that they can hold their power only by resolving the tension between power and love, by taking care of the many. Such action creates a reciprocal bond between the many and the few. Stratification, limitations, and exclusions are made tolerable, and even creative in some respects, by the spirit and practice of *noblesse oblige*.

The few pay for their power (and wealth) with an adulterated love. They accept the responsibility for meeting the fundamental economic and political requirements of living together as an organized society. And they also grant the many a rudimentary respect: within specified areas, and within certain limits, the few leave the many alone to their own devices. For their passivity about power, therefore, the many are rewarded with an opportunity, restricted though it is, to create a limited community of their own based on participation and love. The resulting culture of the many under benevolent despotism has often been vital and warm, if also crude and circumscribed.

Many benevolent despotisms have existed in the west as well as in the East, and a good number of them have generated important material, intellectual, and cultural improvements. The problem with benevolent despotisms has never been whether or not the could or did function. They can and they have. The difficulties are practical and moral: can the form sustain itself as one kind of community, and does it offer the resolution of the tensions between power and love, and between passivity and participation, that is *most* appropriate to our nature as human beings? So far, at any rate, the answer to both these questions is no. They break down because they fail to satisfy the demands for love and participation.

This judgment should not keep us from recognizing that a sizable part of American history (from the establishment of the colonies through the election of Andrew Jackson) can in many fundamental respects be considered part of the general history of benevolent despotisms. Nor should it blind us to the great achievements of that period. But we do have to confront the truth that, despite the framework of representative government, power of the real, operational, and consequential kind was divided—at the local and the national level—on a highly skewed basis between the many and the few. To cite but the most obvious examples, the masters ruled the slaves, the metropolis ruled the territories, and even the Jeffersonians were dominated by an aristocratic hierarchy.

Yet the few were largely responsible and benevolent as well as powerful, intelligent, and competent; and they did create what can fairly be called an American community of the aristocratic variety. They also generated economic and cultural development. Indeed, American mercantilism may be the highest achievement in the entire history of benevolent despotisms: its creators and rulers actually resolved the paradox inherent in the very combination of benevolence and despotism by accepting peacefully the transition to a closer approximation of democracy.

But these aristocrats did not create a community based on love and participation. Neither did their successors, whose approach was largely keyed to competing for power and wealth. That is why today we still confront the challenge of creating a community as a democracy. The ideas and the ideals that compose the related conception of the Great and Good Societies are really no more than an attempt to adapt the mercantilism of the Founding Fathers to contemporary circumstances. They are thus simply variations of benevolent despotism. If realized, therefore, they would offer us no more than an affluent version of power and acquiescence.

The second kind of community, both as process and achievement, is neither aristocratic nor stratified, skewed nor paradoxical. It is democratic and equitable, straightforward and loving. This kind of community involves, in its nature per se and as the essence of the method of realizing it, a different hierarchy of values. Love comes before power and participation before passivity. Equity and equality come before efficiency and ease.

Man is made for great adventures and great achievements; he is not made for mammoth, centralized organizations. He creates best in conjunction with, not under direction by. And he most nearly approaches love in evolving relationships with other human beings, rather than in organized and structured associations with other role-players. It is easy to say, of course, that these are verities impossible to realize. The answer is that never before have we been able to realize them.

But we now confront these possibilities as real choices. We *can* provide ourselves with the material basis for a truly human life and also produce enough to help other human beings achieve the same position. We *can* do so, moreover, while simultaneously decentralizing our economic and political institutions, so as to enable us to live at the scale, and in the kinds of relationships with ourselves and each other, appropriate to our nature.

We can no longer take refuge, or seek escape, in the question of whether or not we can become truly human.

We can.

The question now is whether or not we *will*.

W.A.W.
Madison, Wisconsin, 1966

Preface: History as a Way of Learning

To study history is always to seek in some degree to get beyond the limitations and preoccupations of the present; it demands for success an effort of self-transcendence.

Arthur O. Lovejoy, 1939

Relieved and exhilarated by their triumph over the Axis Powers in 1945, Americans seemed to have assumed that their traditional dream of becoming a world unto themselves was about to be realized. Far from having become disillusioned (or isolationist), they appeared casually confident that their earlier visions of Manifest Destiny were materializing as the reality of the present. Though vaguely uneasy about the full extent of its powers, most Americans looked upon the atom bomb as a self-starting magic lamp; even without being rubbed it would produce their long-sought City on the Hill in the form of a *de facto* American Century embracing the globe.

It was generally taken for granted that such benevolent Americanization of the world would bring peace and plenty without the moral embarrassments and administrative distractions of old-fashioned empires. And so, having created the most irrational weapon known to man, Americans proceeded with startling rationality to abandon the mass army as their principal strategic weapon. Armed only with their bomb, they then generously offered to help everyone become more like themselves. "We are willing to help people who believe the way we do," explained Secretary of State Dean Acheson, "to continue to live the way they want to live."

Had Americans applied their intelligence, humanitarianism, and power to the paradox of plenty without purpose within their own society and to the needs and aspirations of their fellow humans throughout the world, it is possible that their self-centered dream would have been transformed into a vision of brotherhood among men. Instead, they calmly asserted that they had disarmed, a confusion of the truth so complete as to befuddle even their opponents. On the one hand, American leaders explained that The Bomb kept the barbarian at bay while he was collapsing under the economic and political pressures exerted by the United States. On the other hand, they righteously condemned his failure to disarm while they kept a monopoly of nuclear weapons. Their promises of self-restraint served only to add a touch of arrogance to the double standard of their morality, a morality as dangerous and destructive as their weapon.

Some years later, after the Russians accepted the American logic of disarmament-by-nuclear-fusion and produced their own hydrogen bomb, the United States was forced to confront its own dilemmas with more candor and concern. But even earlier, throughout an era which might be called The Years of Babbitt's Confidence, Americans had become increasingly perplexed, anxious, and frustrated. Not even McCarthyism, a particularly virulent epidemic of the anti-intellectualism of the frontier, could cope with the harsh realities of a world in revolution. In attempting to exorcise their fears, overcome their spiritual and intellectual malaise, and resolve their dilemmas, Americans in surprising numbers next turned more formally and directly to history for an explanation of their predicament and a program (if not a panacea) for the future.

As a result, and despite the natural charms and cultivated coquetry of psychology, sociology, and economics, Clio became involved in another of her many affairs with a society in search of reassurance and security. American foreign service officers retired to write memoranda for today's diplomacy in the form of history books while historians took leave of absence to become acting foreign service officers. Many businessmen underwrote the reconstruction of selected portions of their past, while some historians made a thriving business of carefully culled segments of the heritage of America.

And convinced of the validity of the underlying assumptions of such activities, numerous communities legislated history into the curriculums of their schools.

Many observers interpreted this enthusiasm as a sign that America was solidly afoot on the road to salvation. Without denying the virtues and values of history, there is nevertheless considerable reason to doubt whether the evidence is that persuasive. Even the most casual review of this particular renaissance reveals the persistence of two phrases, "history shows" and "history proves," used to establish *ex post facto* the validity of a policy or attitude already entertained by the writer. Instead of being treated as the study of the past and present in which thinking, reasoning, and reflection might lead to insights and perception, history appeared more often to be viewed as a grab bag from which to snatch footnotes for an a priori opinion.

But History is one of the most misleading—and hence dangerous—approaches to knowledge if viewed, or practiced, as a process of reaching back into the past for answers sufficient unto the present and the future. For although historical consciousness can be a powerful tool with which to improve our lives and our world, it is little more than a demonic sorcerer's apprentice unless the history of which we become conscious is something more than a brief in defense of some particular proposal. The purpose of history is not to explain our situation so that we settle down as what C. Wright Mills has called Cheerful Robots in This Best Possible of All Worlds. Neither is its function to propel us into orbit around some distant Utopia. Indeed not. History's great tradition is to help us understand ourselves and our world so that each of us, individually and in conjunction with our fellow men, can formulate relevant and reasoned alternatives and become meaningful actors in making history.

Considered in this light, History is a way of learning. As such, it begins by leaving the present; by going back into the heretofore, by beginning again. Only by grasping what we were is it possible to see how we changed, to understand the process and the nature of the modifications, and to gain some perspective on what we are. The historical experience is not one of staying in the present and looking back. Rather it is one of going back into the past and returning to the present with a wider and more intense consciousness of the restrictions of our former outlook. We return with a broader awareness of the alternatives open to us and armed with a sharper perceptiveness with which to make our choices. In this manner it is possible to loosen the clutch of the dead hand of the past and transform it into a living tool for the present and the future.

As with any such enterprise, this essay in review and interpretation is apt to be misjudged in two ways. In the first place, it is not intended to be, and does not offer, a detailed reconstruction of the American past. That work, which might be compared to the product of the research lab in the natural sciences, is a continuous process sustained by all historians. This essay draws extensively upon such investigations by other scholars. In addition, independent research in the primary sources has been pursued in many areas of the American experience. Basically, however, the essay is the result of standing back and thinking about the available knowledge of America's past in an effort to grasp the nature and significance of the relationships—the causes and the consequences—of what is known. It is thus an effort to provide three things: (1) a fundamental description of the structure and circumstances—the reality—of American society at various periods; (2) a characterization of the definition and explanation of the world entertained by Americans at different stages in their development; and (3) various explanations of the way such views of the world arose out of the immediate and remembered reality and in turn changed that reality.

By its very nature, an essay of this type invites misunderstanding of a second kind. Any effort to comprehend and survey the history of a nation by defining and elucidating a few central outlooks and attitudes is risky because of the great difficulty involved in picking the crucial themes. Some concepts are so huge and spongy that they absorb everything; when squeezed they squirt a never-ending stream of homogenized tables of contents. Others are so narrow and hard that they leave nothing but a peep-hole into the garden of evidence; the focus is superb but the field is often irrelevant.

The tool used in the present study is the concept of *Weltanschauung*, or definition of the world combined with an explanation of how it works. Every sane adult has such an inclusive conception of the world which cuts across and subsumes personal motives, group interests, and class ideologies. This point needs to be emphasized, for in recent years many historians have relied extensively on the

psychology of the irrational in developing their analyses and interpretations. As a result, they seem to have confused consciousness
of purpose with conspiracy. Now neither contingency nor madness
is absent from history, but the vast majority of significant figures
on the stage of history act consciously and purposefully (if usually
routinely) within their conceptions of the world. Hence to assert,
or assume, that the choice of interpretations lies between irrationality, chance, and conspiracy is to distort the nature of history
almost beyond recognition. History written from that point of view
becomes little more than a bag of tricks dumped upon the living.

This essay reviews and attempts to make sense out of American
history by reference to three conceptions of the world which are
traditionally associated with economic thought and action. The
approach is open to two criticisms: it can be charged that this
means that all thought is economic, and it can be claimed that it
implies that ideas have no life of their own. There are two answers
to these caveats.

First, some ideas which originate as instruments of specific interests ultimately break their narrow bounds and emerge as broad,
inclusive conceptions of the world. Herbert Spencer made this
point in convincing fashion. "I do not think," he answered a critic,
"that *laissez-faire* is to be regarded simply as a politico-economical
principle only, but as a much wider principle—the principle of
letting all citizens take the benefits and evils of their own acts: not
only such as are consequent on their industrial conduct, but such
as are consequent upon their conduct in general."

Secondly, it should be obvious that ideas persist for a long time
after their immediate relevance is gone, and therefore may act as
independent variables in later circumstances. For this reason, and
because of the practical problem of organizing any written history,
it is always an arbitrary choice as to which—reality or existing
ideas—will be discussed first. This essay opens with an outline
of an existing idea and proceeds to discuss the way it was altered
fundamentally by circumstances.

Following this introduction, which deals with the rise and decline
of British mercantilism during the two centuries prior to the revolution of 1776, American history is presented as being defined in three
periods, each of which is characterized and powered by a basic view
of the world. They are: The Age of Mercantilism, 1740–1828; the

Age of Laissez Nous Faire, 1819–1896; and the Age of Corporation Capitalism, 1882–1960s. Within each of these epochs the interrelationships of ideas and reality are seen to develop according to a dynamic which is described as having several stages.

At this point the historian confronts his most specific problem of synthesis and presentation. Unless he breaks the process of change into phases he cannot write about it save in a constant going to and fro that exaggerates the diffuseness and tenuousness of reality. He can err by making reality too complex—too "thisey and thatey"—as well as by forcing it into an oversimplified schematic system. Yet by organizing his report or reconstruction in the form of stages he risks creating a jerky and artificial impression of what is in reality a continuous and interrelated process.

The present essay attempts to strike a balance between these dangers by defining enough stages to provide a sense and feel of the changes while at the same time describing the predominant outlook and practice of the age in question. Thus each of the three broad divisions opens with a section on the Triumph of the Rising Order, in which an effort is made to characterize the essential reality, assumptions, theory, and policies of the then accepted conception of the world. Since all views of the world arise during and out of an order that they replace, and cannot triumph save as the old order dies, these dominant ideas are confronted almost immediately with a reality different from the one used as data in their own construction. This confrontation, discussed as A New Reality for Existing Ideas, eventuates in a *modus vivendi* through a third stage, The Adaptation of the Accepted Order. So adjusted and established, the accepted outlook next literally transforms reality and in doing so gives birth to new assumptions and ideas. As this challenge moves toward its own ultimate triumph, however, the existing outlook ripens and fulfills itself in practical and intellectual affairs.

Lest there be any misunderstanding, each of the three main epochs—of Mercantilism, of Laissez Nous Faire, and of Corporation Capitalism—is described, analyzed, and discussed under the following headings.

    I.   The Triumph of the Rising Order
   II.   A New Reality for Existing Ideas
  III.   The Adaptation of the Accepted Order

IV. The Transformation of Reality and the Inception of New Ideas
V. The Fulfillment of the Passing Order

Though it is possible and indeed accurate, therefore, to speak of an overriding outlook, an equal emphasis is placed on conflict and change, upon the efforts of men to recognize and direct or inhibit such changes, and upon the development of new explanations of reality which come ultimately to replace the formerly accepted order.

The method of history is neither to bypass and dismiss nor to pick and choose according to preconceived notions; rather is it a study of the past so that we can come back into our own time of troubles having shared with the men of the past their dilemmas, having learned from their experiences, having been buoyed up by their courage and creativeness and sobered by their shortsightedness and failures. We shall then be better equipped to redefine our own dilemmas and problems as opportunities and possibilities and to proceed with positive rather than negative programs and policies. This enrichment and improvement through research and reflection is the essence of being human, and it is the heart of the historical method.

Let us abstract ourselves from today's predilections and tomorrow morning's headlines, therefore, and begin again by entering the mind of Anthony Ashley Cooper, First Earl of Shaftesbury, as he grappled with the problem of ordering the British Empire after the Cromwellian Revolution. The time is the middle of the 17th century and the Age of Mercantilism is rising on the far-flung foundations of the Age of Discovery and Exploration. In his conscious and purposeful efforts to manage trade and the affairs of the colonies, Shaftesbury is struggling to deepen and consolidate a maturing conception of the world and to formulate programs and policies that will be appropriate and effective. He is of course concerned with his own power and fortune. But to stop there is to rest on the lowest rung of the ladder of understanding. Our concern is with his conception of the sources of that power, its relationship to the reality of his time, the purposes for which it can and should be used, and the best means for its employment.

The Contours of American History

Introduction: British Mercantilism as the Political Economy of English Backwardness

God alters no law of Nature.

ˋ   John Preston, Puritan theologian, c. 1620

The rebellions of the belly are the worst. The first remedy or prevention, is to remove by all means possible that material cause of sedition, which is want and poverty in the estate. To which purpose serveth the opening and well balancing of trade; the cherishing of manufactures; the banishing of idleness.... The increase of any estate must be upon the foreigner, for whatsoever is somewhere gotten is somewhere lost.

Sir Francis Bacon,
Of Seditions and Troubles, 1628

Commerce, as an affair of state, was widely different from the mercantile part ... [and hence] trade, as a point of policy and government, consisted of many articles.... Many of these things did not lie within the prospect of the merchant, much less within his power, care or consideration; and, therefore (the distinction being made between the magistrate's and the merchant's duty), he proposed that, instead of a Committee of the Privy Council, a select Council might be established to take care of the welfare of our colonies, and the trade and navigation of the kingdom. [This] Council should consist of such gentlemen as would be more concerned in the generality of the trade of the nation, and the right management of it, than in the profit of any particular trade, which might possibly have too much sway with private merchants.

The First Earl of Shaftesbury to King Charles II, 1670

All the imaginable ways of increasing Money in any Country are these
two: Either to dig it in Mines of our Own, or to get it from our Neighbours.
. . . Nor, indeed, things rightly considered, do Gold and Silver drawn out
of the Mine equally Enrich with what is got by Trade. . . . Riches do not
consist in having more Gold and Silver, but in having more in propor-
tion than the rest of the World, or than our Neighbours, whereby we are
enabled to procure to ourselves a greater Plenty of the Conveniences of
Life than comes within the reach of Neighbouring Kingdoms and States.

John Locke, 1691

The time may come when the . . . colonies may become populous and
with the increase of arts and sciences strong and politike, forgetting their
relation to the mother country, will then confederate and consider noth-
ing further than the means to support their ambition of standing on
their legs.

Nehemiah Grew,
English Mercantilist, 1707

NEW MEN AND OLD PROBLEMS

Anthony Ashley Cooper, more usually known as Lord Ashley or
the first Earl of Shaftesbury, was a man of the world in an age
when the world had become immense. Short in stature, he was
smart in substance and sophisticated in style. Samuel Pepys, that
fabulous guide to the upper reaches of mid-seventeenth-century
English society, had him right: Shaftesbury was "a man of great
business, and yet of pleasure and drolling too." Fleeing from
England after his plot to overthrow Charles II was discovered,
Shaftesbury's disguise aroused the suspicions of a maidservant.
His reaction was typically suave: he told his aide to "go and make
love to her" so that having been compromised she would hesitate
to turn informer.

No doubt other men of his time employed similar diver-
sions in moments of crisis, and the episode does not account for
Shaftesbury's importance in British and American history. But it
does provide a sense of the man's temperament and style, and it
does dramatize his central role in the ferment going on in England
after the collapse of Oliver Cromwell's commonwealth and the
restoration of the Stuart monarchy. Other such glimpses reinforce

this estimate. He could host a formal dinner so memorable that one as blasé as Prince Cosmo de Medici asked for and kept the menu for over thirty years, sending Shaftesbury a yearly bottle of wine to mark the anniversary. Yet he was also a hero to Englishmen for his successful fight for the Act of Habeas Corpus and his vigorous resistance to the abuses of Charles II. When acquitted of charges of treason, his release from the Tower of London was greeted with "halloawing and hooting" in the court, and observers of the time reported that "the rabble lighted bonfires, the bells rung," and there was "such public rejoicing in the city that never such an insolent defiance of authority before was seen."

Since the English Revolution had left a wound as yet unhealed on the political and social nerve-endings of those in authority, the description is probably exaggerated. For all that, it is true. Shaftesbury not only conceived and executed the idea of an organized political following in the city, but he gathered about him from the countryside a nucleus of leadership that in a few years carried through the Glorious Revolution of 1688 and then took power as the Whig Party. The Crown, indeed, was caught between Shaftesbury's powerful threat to its prerogative and the incompetence of most of its own advocates. Called in to reorganize domestic affairs and to guide the consolidation and further expansion of an empire which had been neglected during the Revolution, Shaftesbury became Chancellor of His Majesty's Exchequer in 1661, and President of the Council of Trade and Foreign Plantations in 1672, before ultimately being driven into exile and death in Holland in 1683. During the same span of years he played a key role in founding the colony of South Carolina and through it all was an active member of the Royal Society, participating in its scientific experiments and investing his wealth in their practical development.

Yet Shaftesbury's significance is only half explained by a summary catalogue of his more striking achievements. For throughout those years he had at his side as friend, physician, and confidential advisor none other than John Locke, more often known in the United States as "America's philosopher." American history comes into much sharper focus once it is realized that Locke derived many of his ideas from his experience as an intimate member of Shaftesbury's mercantilist entourage. Those ideas formed an important element in the system of thought that exerted so much influence upon the Founding Fathers. For many men, indeed, Locke became *the* philosopher of the Anglo-Saxon *Weltanschauung* that emerged from the English Revolution. On the one hand, his statement of an experimental, neo-hedonistic individualism based on the value of labor and the rights of property pointed the way toward Adam Smith's manifesto for laissez-faire capitalism. At the same time, however, Locke's broad defense of the existing state as a trustee for society and his harsh judgment on those who did not behave as natural men served to justify the status quo and invest its defenders with an enthusiasm which often transformed them into righteous crusaders against social innovations and new ideas.

Considerably more taciturn and withdrawn than Shaftesbury, who wived several women and in other ways lived at the center of society, Locke was temperamentally inclined toward the introspection which served as one of his principal tools in exploring and analyzing the nature of man and society. Though by no means a recluse, and certainly not indifferent about his attractiveness to women, this propensity to think things over stopped him on the near side of several opportunities for permanent liaison—sexual or political. So too, no doubt, did the example of Shaftesbury's difficulties and disappointments with a son, his confinement in the Tower, and his ultimate exile. Perhaps even more persuasive was the ambivalence of Locke's own early life. Born of stout Puritan ancestors with strong Royalist sympathies, a combination by no means unusual despite the stereotype which links Calvinism with vigorous dissent, Locke obtained an education at Oxford which challenged his traditional outlook and at the same time opened up several careers. Inclined strongly toward the ministry, he nevertheless exhibited abilities and interests in science, medicine, and secular philosophy.

When they met in Oxford in 1666, therefore, Shaftesbury and Locke confronted each other with common interests and complementary personalities. Shaftesbury's resulting offer of patronage pulled Locke away from religion to political philosophy, and also enabled and encouraged him to develop his medical and scientific interests. Privy to high-level economic, political, and scientific discussions, and called upon to cooperate in developing Shaftesbury's plans in those areas, Locke grappled with the fundamental questions of man and society and with the practical problems confronting the leaders of England.

Shaftesbury and other English leaders were confronted with the necessity and the opportunity to refine and extend the policies and programs which, however modified, had survived the turmoil of the English Revolution. Their basic predicament was something of a paradox. In a political sense, the revolution had never been completed. Not uncommonly, the coalition against the Crown had included conflicting interests and approaches to the ideal society. But unlike many revolutions, the dominant group within the movement lacked a firm consensus on any positive program. As a consequence, Cromwell's regime disintegrated.

Behind the dilemma of what to do after replacing one king with another lay fundamental economic and social troubles which would have made it difficult for any group of leaders to have erected a framework of government and undertaken a long-range program. Though it had a large navy, a few established colonies, the beginnings of an industrial economy, and visions of more of all three, England was still a predominantly agricultural nation. Compared with other nations of that time, it was a relatively backward, underdeveloped, poor society. Challenged at its own coastline, and abroad, by stronger, ambitious nations, it was plagued at home by disorganization, unrest, and poverty. The familiar phrase "Merrie Old England" is not very accurate: life was anything but merry for the great majority. Though there had been many positive economic changes since the coronation of Elizabeth I in 1558, England's progress toward a diversified and more balanced economy and social structure had not proceeded far enough to overcome its inertia and sustain such improvement through its own momentum—let alone generate recovery from the civil war.

Neither had any new sense of community and ethic of mutual responsibility emerged to replace the ideal (and the actuality) of the integration so characteristic of feudalism and manorialism. Religious groups quarreled among themselves and with secular interests which in turn clashed with each other. Despite a general, though reluctant, agreement that something had to be done, it was extremely difficult for Shaftesbury and others to organize a new coalition to restore the monarchy. His ultimate objective, that of building a political party oriented toward the general welfare, posed an even greater challenge. From the economic imbalance to the ideological free-for-all, England was a troubled land.

In these fundamental and pervasive respects, therefore, Shaftesbury and Locke, along with their contemporaries, were confronted by the same kind of problems that their predecessors had faced a century before. Their feeling of backwardness, weakness, and isolation only reinforced a natural inclination to approach the difficulties of the post-revolutionary 1660s with a very similar outlook and to employ many of the same specific solutions. These assumptions, ideas, and policies are usually grouped together under the heading *mercantilism.*

As with all such broad and inclusive terms, mercantilism can be criticized on two grounds. Sometimes it is employed indiscriminately to lump together all the ideas, programs, and actions that developed between 1550 and 1783. Used in this way, the concept of mercantilism is misleading because it suggests the existence of a rigid system and raises the false issue of explaining a sudden change in the late eighteenth century. Other scholars have chosen one specific aspect of the epoch between Elizabeth I and George III and drastically restricted their definition of mercantilism by concentrating on that particular feature. This usage is just as unsatisfactory, for it implies that there was no general outlook characteristic of those years.

But since there was such a *Weltanschauung,* and since the term mercantilism is firmly associated with that period, it seems useful to retain the name and give it specific substance and meaning. For considerable understanding of American history develops from thinking of mercantilism as the general definition and explanation of the world developed and acted upon by Englishmen between 1550 and 1763 and reviewing its development through the interplay of circumstances, interests, and ideas. It is in this setting that the broad significance of Shaftesbury and Locke becomes apparent. Shaftesbury was carrying the past into the age of the Restoration and trying to adjust it to modified circumstances. Locke was preparing to synthesize that adaptation and project it into the next century. Yet both men were initially guided by the assumptions that had shaped earlier efforts to solve the same problems.

THE ROOTS OF THE ENGLISH POLITICAL ECONOMY

Two ancient themes lay at the center of the outlook which Shaftesbury struggled to sustain and develop more extensively as English

Mercantilism. One was the Biblical injunction to promote the general welfare and common good of God's corporate world and its creatures. The second was the growing propensity to define God's estate as the civil society in which the individual Christian resided. In this fundamental sense, therefore, the rise of mercantilism is the story of a struggle to retain and adapt an original Christian morality during the dynamic secularization of a religious outlook as an agrarian society was transformed into a life of commerce and industry.

During its origins and early evolution, an epoch which extended from the time of Edward I down to the outbreak of the English Revolution in 1640, mercantilism retained a strong religious character. Religion was *the* way of thinking, of making basic sense of the world, and economic development occurred within that framework. The gradual shift from a self-contained agriculture to the production of wool (and later, cloth) and to the opening up of mining, trade, and manufacturing was undertaken and managed by men who entertained a deep sense of God's will. Few were fanatics, but most were believers.

This religious ethic, moreover, was based on a corporate conception of society which stressed the relationships and responsibilities between man and man. Not only does this raise serious doubts concerning the cliché that the Protestant Ethic, and particularly Puritanism, accounts for economic progress, but it emphasizes the point that the various elements of mercantilism first appeared in an incomplete and unorganized manner. Thus Edward I, who ruled between 1272 and 1307, expelled some foreign economic enterprises, focused the English wool trade in Antwerp, and made several unintegrated moves to control domestic commerce.

But the long war with France (1333–1360), combined with domestic unrest at home, prompted—and enabled—Edward III to go even further. Not only were his efforts significant in his own time, but they established precedents in the body of common law that the American colonists were often to cite more than four centuries later; the American definition of treason, for example, derives from Edward III's reign. Edward also initiated various policies concerning the political economy that had a similar influence on later Englishmen. He attempted to fix wages and prices and to balance the relationship between them so that the laborer would not suffer unduly from wartime inflation; in return he demanded that every man work when jobs were available. As this *quid pro quo* indicates, mercantilism was grounded in the idea of a mutual, corporate responsibility. God's way was based on such reciprocal respect and obligation, and Jerusalem provided the example to be followed.

During his reign between 1377 and 1399, Richard II endeavored to coordinate and extend the somewhat random policies of his predecessors. Further economic progress demanded an organized effort; the competition of foreign powers had to be countered more effectively, and the increasing social and economic conflict within England, symbolized by the Peasant's Rebellion of 1381, had to be controlled and moderated before it should rip society apart. Hence Richard favored English shippers and traders by the Navigation Act of 1381, and tried to acquire enough gold and silver to keep England out of debt and at the same time buy needed items from foreign countries. His drive to establish what the Crown called a "well and rightly governed kingdom" was an effort to accumulate at a *national* level the social and economic capital for England's present security and future progress. Quite naturally, and for that matter, logically, Richard disciplined those who opposed or disrupted the program and rewarded those who supported it. His courts openly decreed that those who "serve the general weal stand in special favor with the law."

Critics of the King's policy fought back by seeking privileges within the system and by initiating theoretical and popular arguments for free trade. It is essential to realize, however, that this campaign was not concerned with free trade as it is understood today. Free traders of the early period wanted to break down the domestic system of corporate organization, centralized direction, and reciprocal responsibility in order to win special advantages for themselves. Far from agitating for open world trade, they were enthusiastic advocates of an expanding but strictly English empire.

The same imperial vigor characterized the outlook and actions of Henry VII between 1465 and 1509. He commissioned the voyages of John Cabot and other explorers and adventurers, negotiated commercial treaties with Denmark and other countries, and in numerous ways encouraged Englishmen to shove, elbow, and wiggle their way into the scramble for empire. As this increasing emphasis on trade and empire indicates, commerce was the dynamic element in England's economic evolution. Although territorial expansion within the home islands and into overseas areas was undertaken at a later time for the same reasons, commerce was the activity that provided the added increment of capital which underwrote further development at home.

Hence the basic issue was simple: Should the merchants be allowed to run unchecked with no effort being made to control and balance the economic changes and the social consequences which followed in the wake of their activities? From almost every point of view, the answer supplied by England's existing traditions was negative. The king's specific and general political objectives reinforced that outlook; he could risk neither unlimited power in the hands of the merchants per se nor the probability of their excesses provoking rebellion in the lower classes (and in the old agrarian aristocracy). From the economic angle, untrammeled freedom for the merchants did not produce general economic improvement. Food production, for example, was sadly neglected in the rush to wool-raising and mining. Finally, even the merchants came to realize that they had to have a more unified and balanced society in order to attract other segments of society to support the Crown in undertakings that would help them to expand their overseas operations. It should be apparent, therefore, that mercantilism was anything but the narrow ideology of the commercial interest, for while it stressed the need for trade and was supported by the merchants, it defined the problem as one of directing such activities so as to produce the common good.

By the beginning of the sixteenth century, however, any English effort to reap the rewards of the Age of Discovery and Exploration was hindered by several difficulties. Spain, Portugal, and France were more firmly established throughout the new imperial world. Their control of the gold and silver stolen or mined in America complicated the troubles brought on by the English Crown's distressing habit of financing its needs by debasing the currency. The Dutch, for their part, were approaching a position of dominance in the realms of fishing, shipping, and trade. Confronted by this reality, the English soon articulated a cardinal tenet of mercantilist thought: The best—if not the only—way to get wealth and welfare was to take them away from somebody.

Even this was not an immediately productive approach, for England had to develop the goods and services to run an empire and to take advantage of the markets conquered or created by colonization. Seemingly suspended in limbo between the old world of Christian feudalism and manorialism and the new age of commerce, England's domestic affairs and institutions were confused and inefficient. And any effort to grapple with these difficulties was complicated by Henry VIII's break with Roman Catholicism.

RELIGION AND THE RISE OF MERCANTILISM

Prior to his break with Rome, Henry VIII seemed to be succeeding with the staggering task of carrying through an English Reformation within the universal Catholic Church. But the fundamental issue was much broader. Whether viewed from within or without the framework of the Papacy—that is, considered by Luther and Calvin or by the Jesuits—the central religious, intellectual, and practical problem was how to cope with the *general* breakdown of the old church and its explanation of man and the world. Henry's rupture with Rome dramatically confronted him and his subjects with the need to decide what to put at the center of their individual and collective lives in place of the universal church. Salvation having been taken out of the hands of the Papacy, the issue became that of where it was to be dropped—in the lap of the state or in the hands of the individual? But this was only half the difficulty; for if the state were to be charged with such responsibility, then was the responsibility to be discharged according to social (that is, inclusive and corporate) values or by the principles of personal, arbitrary monarchy?

Henry's answer, toward which he had been moving throughout his reign, was that the state in the form of God's monarchy assumed the role and the functions of the old universal church. What Henry had done in his own blunt way was to sanctify the processes of this world. Small wonder that his earlier polemics against Luther were withdrawn from the royal stationer and replaced by a new discourse on the divine right of kings. God was not wholly excluded from this modified outlook, but now He was seen to be operating at one stage further removed. A special religious institution no longer existed; it had been first blended and ultimately integrated with a secular organization. And whatever laws might be passed, the only effective means by which the church and the state could again be separated was by denying God's *direct* will in secular affairs. This assault was finally organized and carried, even though Henry was neither the conscious instigator nor the victim.

He nevertheless opened the main gate to the conflict by dealing out the confiscated church properties to his supporters. As in earlier years on the European continent, this act raised the whole question of private property in its relationship to the state and to religious values. Originally church leaders had considered property no more than a necessary evil. St. Thomas Aquinas modified this tradition in two respects: first, he asserted it was a positive asset, both natural and good; then he promptly declared that the state had to regulate property for the common good. This doctrine was accepted and generally honored, if also evaded, for many centuries.

But confiscation revived, as among the Anabaptists and the Levellers, the earlier stress on common property. In England, this outlook ultimately won literary treatment and presentation in Sir Thomas More's *Utopia*. Others considered this a dangerously retrogressive theory and set out to sanctify private property per se. Those who undertook that effort differed among themselves, and the result was a long period of confused and contradictory competition. Both Luther and Calvin exemplified the ambivalence. In his notorious castigation of the peasants for revolting against their masters, for example, Luther also attacked the rulers for their failure to honor the corporate values and responsibilities of their religion. At no time, furthermore, did Luther construct a hierarchy of labor which implied that godliness came with worldly success.

Calvin was even firmer in his emphasis that *any* calling offered a satisfactory place in which to exercise one's discipline in the Lord's way. Even more significantly, he insisted that a man with two callings was bound by the true principles of Christ to choose the one which contributed most to the common good. And for many years those who took Calvin's name struggled to honor the injunction. Later Protestants de-emphasized this stress on corporate values in favor of individualism and worldly goods, but Calvin himself never did so.

When it reached a climax in England a century after Henry's death, this confusion and conflict over private property took three principal forms. Oliver Cromwell's revolutionary army divided sharply over the issue. Some upper-class conservatives charged the Anabaptists and Levellers with subverting the rights of property.

The Levellers replied that property was being protected at the cost of political rights, social welfare, and human beings themselves. But while opposing the thoroughgoing nature of the Levellers' program, other upper-class leaders accepted limits on the rights of private property and tried to maintain the tradition of corporate Christian welfare upon which mercantilism was based. Yet the Levellers defended their radical position by reference to the same ideal. In a persuasive way, therefore, both the upper-class mercantilists and the lower-class radicals derived their outlook from the same basic interpretation of Christianity. In 19th-century England, such conservatives were appropriately called Tory-Radicals.

By realizing this it is possible to gain a vital insight into that contemporary liberalism which defends the rights of private property and asserts the supremacy of individual liberty while at the same time advocating the general welfare. For although such liberals show superficial similarities to the mercantilists, they are considerably removed from that conservative tradition of the common good. Such liberals usually label Karl Marx a heretic and consider socialism a heresy, but the reverse is much closer to the truth. The liberal tradition stems from the triumph of laissez-faire individualism over corporate Christianity. Marx and other socialists reasserted the validity of the original idea in response to the liberal heresy. That is, indeed, one of the basic explanations of socialism's persistent relevance and appeal in the 20th century.

It should therefore be clear how it was that Henry VIII touched off an unending controversy by taking over church lands in England. While he strengthened men who accepted his ideal of a powerful divine monarch, he also assisted those who wanted a more democratic and socially responsible state, and helped still others who emphasized individualism and private riches. At the same time, Henry made a great—if unintended—investment in the economic diversification and progress of the nation. Dramatized by one of the great country leaders who turned his abbey into a crude factory, the result was not only new industrial enterprise, but a blurring of the old distinction between agrarian and urban activity and wealth. Men who came to maturity after those changes had altered the structure of English society (and Shaftesbury was one such man) reached different conclusions as to what should replace the church at the center of men's lives, and they took their ideas, as well as their interests, into politics.

For the time, a combination of events favored Henry's conviction that a divine monarchy should provide meaning and direction for English society. As he bluntly stated in his defiant reply to the Pope in 1533, "It is manifestly declared and expressed that this realm of England is an empire." Reflecting the same attitude, the classic religious images of the flock and the family were transferred from the church to the state. And in its more practical aspects, Henry's solution was anchored in the traditions of English rule from the time of Edward I and Richard II.

England's economic conditions at the time of Henry's break with Rome were confused and contradictory. Domestic diversification and growth had begun in a moderate way as the wool trade shifted to the cloth business and became more complex, and as the metal and other industries were organized. The nation nevertheless remained a backward and poor country whose international exploits were as yet insufficient to accelerate its improvement. It is conceivable that a nation could accomplish economic development with a bare minimum of centralized control and coercion. But at least three things would be required: a long period of peace defined as more than just the absence of open war; extensive outside assistance; and a highly enthusiastic and pervasive agreement among the vast majority of the society upon the objectives sought and the means to be employed, a consensus that would in effect serve as a substitute for centralized power and authority.

Such happy circumstances did not prevail for England during the sixteenth and seventeenth centuries, and the result was a steady growth in mercantilist thought and action. Nothing illustrates this as clearly as the Tudor response to the economic and social crisis that developed near the end of Henry VIII's reign. Between 1500 and 1522 a great burst of activity in the wool trade with Antwerp brought a corresponding advance in English economic life. But by 1550 the nation was again on the edge of stagnation and violence. English traders persisted in trying to force the price despite obvious warnings that they had almost saturated the market. The dilemma was very real: the boom was about to collapse, yet England had to export wool or "fall dangerously sick." Hence the crisis served to strengthen even further two of the fundamental ideas of mercantilism: that exports were the key to prosperity and social stability, and the corollary that nothing was more dangerous than a surplus of goods.

Abandoning the *ad hoc* approach, England's leaders undertook a general, coordinated program to reorganize and rationalize the entire woolen industry by establishing specifications and standards of production and marketing, and by limiting its size (and hence destructive competition) through the principle and institution of apprenticeship. This system of industrial training, for which John Locke later manifested vigorous enthusiasm, also served to provide some control over unemployment. Going beyond these proposals, the parliament then laid an entirely new emphasis upon the importance of maritime activities (shipping and fishing) and stressed the need to go abroad in search of new markets and precious metals.

This legislation consolidated the outlook and practices of earlier monarchs. Englishmen were henceforward to argue about who should control the central government but not to dispute the validity of the national state or its active role in society. This crucial struggle matured during the reigns of Elizabeth I, Charles I, and James I (1558–1641). Hence it is useful to consider those years as a unit save for some emphasis on Elizabeth's role in the era. Her personality, temperament, and style were magnificently appropriate to the tradition and the circumstances. She symbolized the final stages of the past and transformed them into the beginnings of a new epoch.

THE MATURATION OF THE ENGLISH WELTANSCHAUUNG

Elizabeth's reign marked the apex of early mercantilism as a broad conception of the world still fundamentally oriented around a religious ideal of corporate morality and responsibility. Her successors, Charles I and James I, were also capable and strong rulers who knew what they were about, even though the English Revolution is usually associated with their names as a mark of failure. James I was particularly concerned with the welfare of the lower classes; his paternalism was morally sincere and prompted many of his actions. Taken together, those three rulers effected the consolidation of the mercantilist outlook.

Four ideas formed the core of this *Weltanschauung*. First, the state was the institution for achieving wealth and welfare. Second, and as implied by the first, good fortune did not happen by itself: it was the result of men making good policies. As should be apparent, the mercantilist did not believe in the famous hidden hand of Adam Smith. Third, the state had an obligation to serve society by accepting and discharging the responsibility for the *general* welfare. This does not mean that mercantilism was a rudimentary form of socialism. Though it sometimes joined in mixed enterprises, it usually delegated opportunities to men as individuals or in corporate associations. Fourth, the world was defined as known and finite, a principle agreed upon by science and theology. Hence the chief way for a nation to promote or achieve its own wealth and happiness was to take them away from some other country.

Two phrases of the time capture the spirit of this maturing mercantilism. One, "this manor of England," appears repeatedly in the literature of the age and delineates perfectly the sense of national self-consciousness and integration. The other, an ancient Roman axiom from Marcus P. Cato, was used almost as often to dramatize the drive for export markets: *opportet patrem familias vendacem esse, non emacem*—"it behooves the husbandman to be a seller and not a buyer." Surrounded by turmoil and danger (there was one year of peace between 1600 and 1667) and beset by internal tensions and discord, English leadership devoted its energies and abilities to an effort to translate that image and that rule of thumb into reality.

This urge to unity, balance, and self-sufficiency had been gathering strength for many years. *The Tree of Commonwealth*, an essay published about 1509, argued that a man should not indulge himself to "pull from this tree at his liberty of every of these fruits;" rather should he practice restraint for the common good. And as others before him, Richard Hooker emphasized in 1597 that such a balanced order was neither fortuitous nor the result of divine intervention, but was rather the "work of policy." The principle was written into an Order of the Privy Council in 1622: "This being the rule. . . . Whosoever had a part of the gain in profitable times . . . must now in the decay of Trade . . . bear a part of the public losses, as may best conduct to the good of the public and the maintenance of the general trade."

Beginning with Elizabeth and continuing for a century and a half, the mercantilists sought to accomplish five tasks: erect the framework of a political and economic system; modify, centralize, and consolidate the older but still useful units of society; encourage and direct the development of a new political economy; balance that evolution; and expand the resulting system abroad. Early and continuing attention was given to economic and administrative affairs. Thus the Parliament of 1563 passed legislation encouraging food production, a relief measure for the poor, an act designed to improve the navy as a means of securing more wealth, tariff regulations, and an elaborate Statute of Artificers calculated to put the nation to work in a rational and balanced manner, and called for a concerted effort to diversify and expand overseas trade and colonization. Similarly, a national system of weights and measures, monetary standards, taxation, and codified law were established. Administrative reforms and innovations, though in no sense entirely rational or equitable, created an organizational hierarchy capable of acting in a far more routine and effective manner. To accomplish all this, the functions and the authority of the old towns and guilds were destroyed or transferred to the central government. These and similar actions created the form and substance of a national system of political economy.

Agriculture was a key problem because it lagged behind the new enterprises in commerce and industry. It is simply wrong to think of mercantilism as an outlook that ignored the farm. Along with other leading mercantilists, Sir Josiah Child, Josiah Tucker, and Shaftesbury stressed the need for a balanced economy. They accepted as a matter of course the axiom enunciated by George Coade. "Between the Landed and Trading Interest in this Kingdom," Coade explained, "there ever has been and ever will be an inseparable Affinity. They naturally furnish each other with all the Conveniences of Life, and no real Preference can be given either to the one or the other."

Even if initially approached as nothing more than the ideology of the trading interest, this side of mercantilism is not surprising. Mercantilists represented a personal merging of landed and commercial operations, and they realized that agriculture was vital to self-sufficiency in war and peace, and to solving the problem of winning export markets. Agricultural improvement, explained Malachy Postlethwayt, would "render the price of the necessaries of life no more than one half, or even one third what it is at the present. This will inevitably reduce the general price of labor . . .

and will not this render all our fabrics and manufactures cheaper
. . . ? Hereby we cannot fail . . . to augment the value of our exports
beyond that of our imports; this will gradually increase the balance
of our trade." A great deal of official attention was devoted to
increasing food production. Land reclamation, conservation, and
technological improvements were encouraged and supported by
the government, and territorial expansion complemented such
domestic efforts.

Commerce and industry enjoyed similar favors. Elizabeth
ordered foreign merchants, for example, to spend their profits
before leaving the country. And despite the fear that England was
overpopulated, skilled foreigners were encouraged to immigrate
and accelerate the nation's development. This was a classic example of economic decisions furthering religious and intellectual
toleration, for most of such artisans were strong Protestants. As for
tariffs, they were seen as the fountain of prosperity and power. "So
it is now," explained the Protectionist Act of 1562, "that, by reason
of the abundance of foreign wares brought into this realm from the
parts of beyond the seas, the said artificers are not only less occupied, and thereby utterly impoverished . . . [but] divers cities and
towns within this realm greatly endangered, and other countries
notably enriched." Beginning with a specific proscription against
certain goods for a stated time, the program was rapidly generalized. Protectionist advocates asserted that the tariff would provide
revenue and employment, protect and foster young and important industries, strengthen the military power of the nation, and
thus produce a system that through its exportable surplus would
create new capital for further improvement at home. By the end
of the period, the Book of Rates under James I opened with a wry
tongue-in-cheek justification of the policy: "If it be agreeable to
the rule of nature to prefer our own people before strangers. . . ." A
more rhetorical remark could hardly have been made.

Several reasons account for the practice of delegating opportunities and responsibilities to private individuals and corporations.
Political motives were important, but they should not be overemphasized. In both its forms, general and joint-stock, the corporation enabled larger amounts of capital to be organized and put to
work in a more rational and fruitful manner. Considered in one way,
mercantilism was a set of policies designed to accumulate capital

at the national level and the corporation a means to this end. Even the practice of granting monopolies, which came to be grievously abused and thereby to provoke serious resistance, was a natural and obvious way to initiate projects in a rapid and vigorous manner.

Mercantilism's emphasis on corporate responsibility is drama- tized by the Statute of Artificers (1563) and various Poor Laws enacted throughout the age. The legislation concerning artificers was an elaborate effort to create and sustain some balance and order in the process of economic development and in its attendant social consequences. Wage rates (and their relationship to prices), migra- tion within the country, terms and conditions of employment, and the principle of a seven-year apprenticeship were all written into an integrated system enforced by the strengthened national govern- ment. Poor Laws complemented this involved legislation by prohib- iting begging, placing pauper children in apprenticeship, establish- ing a system of collecting and distributing alms among the aged and infirm, and putting the poor to work in special enterprises.

Though in some respects harsh and confining in their impact on the individual (it may be remarked that slow starvation, aliena- tion, and vagabondage also have their peculiar disadvantages), these laws were predicated upon the idea that poverty, instead of being a personal sin, was a function of the economic system, and that the general welfare was the responsibility of the government. Prior to 1640, at any rate, such a conception of welfare was shared by Catholics, Protestants, and others who stressed a more secular- ized idea of a natural law binding on all men.

Following Calvin's ideas very closely, pre-Revolutionary Puritan leaders such as William Perkins defined a calling as "a certain kind of life, ordained and imposed on man by God, for the common good." William Gouge, Richard Sibbes, and John Cotton were other Puritan divines who stressed the same conception of a mutu- ally responsible corporate community. All agreed that a specific calling was subordinate to the general welfare; even men who had several callings were to choose among them "not for it selfe, but for the good of the whole bodie."

This outlook provided the intellectual framework within which particular issues like unemployment acquired meaning. One famous report described the country as populated by far too many men who "cheat, rob, roar, hang, beg, carp, pine and perish," and many leaders wrestled with the problem of those "which do not live idly at home, and are burdenous, chargeable and unprofitable to this realm." Unemployment and its camp follower, social unrest, threatened England—the lower classes as well as the Crown and the privileged orders. The anxiety reinforced the feeling that England was overpopulated; "the people, blessed by God, do swarm in the land, as young bees in a hive." Sir Francis Bacon spoke for a large majority when he concluded that the "material cause of sedition [was] want and poverty in the state," and that such "rebellions of the belly [were] the worst." Lower-class spokesmen revealed the anguish of the suffering more personally: "Alas, Man! What should we do? The world is hard."

Bacon was only one of many writers who concluded that expansion offered the best solution of both the specific difficulties and the general problem. Though more often remembered as a preacher who wrote somewhat erotic poetry when not in the pulpit, John Donne supported expansion because it would "sweepe your streets, and wash your doores, from idle persons, and the children of idle persons, and imploy them." William Cecil, one of Elizabeth's closest advisers, argued bluntly that "by lack of vent [for surpluses] tumults will follow." And Sir Humphrey Gilbert, an early leader in the expansionist movement, explained that his operations would "prove a general benefit unto our country" by finding or establishing enterprises "to the great relief and good employment of no small number of the natural subjects of this realm."

This expansionist push of the early seventeenth century produced a vigorous drive for exports and colonies. Designed to achieve markets, resources, and bases for the security and extension thereof, the campaign developed around an integrated set of ideas. Though considered necessary in the strictly military sense for defense, the navy rapidly came to be seen primarily as an instrument of economic improvement. The basic objective was a strong merchant marine and a large, regularized trading empire. Both objectives can be seen in the legislation of 1563, which declared that "it is necessary for the restoring of the navy to have one day more in the week ordained to be a fish day and that day to be Wednesday." Sometimes referred to as "political Lent," the Wednesday fish law reveals as much about the influence of economics on religion as does almost any single episode in English history.

This concept of an overseas economic empire as the means to improvement at home synthesized the mercantilist's concern for agriculture with his support for commerce. It gave meaning to the territorial wars against Wales and Ireland and brought about a change in English thinking about precious metals. Breaking with the bullionists, who emphasized the acquisition of money to balance their international accounts, the mercantilists viewed money as a means of developing the domestic economy itself. All such specific ideas and policies were synthesized in the doctrine of a favorable balance of trade. John Hales offered a somewhat embellished translation of Cato that was borrowed by many other writers between 1550 and 1660: "For he weare no good husband that will bie more in the market than he selleth there againe." Otherwise, Hales warned, "We should empoverish ourselves and enrich the strangers." William Lane was even blunter, arguing that foreign sales must be greater, for by "so much shall our common-wealthe be yerely gainers of them, and they not of us, and we to lyve off them and they not off us."

Colonization was a fundamental part of the view that wealth had to be taken away from others and integrated into a self-sufficient empire. As William Penn once remarked, England did not found the colonies in order to be praised by later historians as the disinterested mother of independent parliaments. "Nothing is more untrue," concludes Oxford Professor A. L. Rowse, Britain's distinguished historian of Elizabethan expansion, "than the Victorian saying that that empire came into being in a fit of absence of mind: nothing much is apt to come into being in that way. It was the result rather of a conscious, deliberate and tenacious campaign . . . on the part of the elect spirits of the nation."

Early charters were distinctly feudal in nature, defining the colonies as "a fief held of the Crown of England." And just as the other elements of mercantilist thinking were pulled together in the early seventeenth century, so too were the first efforts made to tighten up the colonial relationship between the mother country and the overseas possessions. Virginia's charter was put under the Crown, Massachusetts was subjected to the first in a long series of regulations and pressures conceived to pull it back from the near edge of *de facto* independence, and Maryland's charter stated explicitly that all its exports were to be marketed in or through England. And Charles I moved in 1634 to bring all the colonies under a central commission empowered to legislate on matters "concerning either the state public of the said colonies, or utility of private persons and their lands, goods, debts, and successions."

As with the affairs of trade, this movement to consolidate the colonies was greatly accelerated and intensified by the serious depression of 1622. Itself the dramatic culmination of a 70-year period of fluctuation between good and bad conditions, the depression heightened all the fears and hopes of the era. Writing against that background, Thomas Mun provided one of the most striking and influential statements of the mercantilist outlook. Arguing that domestic, or internal, trade did little more than balance itself out without producing any increase in real wealth, and that precious metals did not buy improvement, Mun, on the eve of the English Revolution, worked out a magnificent synthesis of the mercantilist *Weltanschauung*. "The main thing," he explained, "is to possess goods; if you have them you will get money. He that hath ware hath money by the year." Lacking mines at home or in the colonies, he argued, "the ordinary means therefore to increase our wealth and treasure is by foreign trade, wherein we must ever observe the rule to sell more to strangers yearly than we consume of their value." "Behold then," he concluded in a powerful and famous phrase, "the true form and worth of foreign trade, which is the great revenue of the King . . . the school of our arts, the supply of our wants, the employment of our poor, the improvement of our lands, . . . the terror of our enemies."

Accepted by the great majority of Englishmen, this credo of mercantilism nevertheless failed to provide an automatic solution to the nation's problems. Economic development takes time, even under the best conditions, and the depression of 1622 only reinforced a natural impatience. The feeling was strengthened by the growing feeling that the Crown was not providing equitable and efficient leadership. Such dissatisfaction and latent unrest appeared in the great attacks on monopoly and in the campaign for freer domestic trade. But it is vital to realize that these objectives were sought within the mercantilist framework and not as part of a new system of economic and political philosophy.

Though such criticism had been voiced at least fifty years earlier, a major assault on monopolies erupted in the last years of Elizabeth's reign. Elizabeth's troubles can be sensed by realizing that such favors had been extended far beyond the area of new, major, or key industries. A monopoly on the import and resale of steel in an under-developed country, for example, could be defended by rational economic argument. But the same exclusive policy made little sense when applied to the making of flasks, powder-boxes, and paper, or to the printing of the Psalms of David or the law of the realm.

Edwin Sandys, an eminent Protestant merchant who protested monopolies on religious and secular grounds, was a typical leader in the campaign. "All free subjects are born inheritable as to their lands," he reasoned, "so also to the free exercise of their industry in those trades whereto they apply themselves and whereby they are to live." Another anti-monopolist applied the idea of balance in nature to the specific situation at hand. A more equal distribution of wealth and opportunity was not only more equitable, but "too much fullness doth puff up some by presumption, and too much emptiness leaves the rest in perpetual discontent, the mother of desire of innovations and troubles."

Other speakers sustained the same themes in later debates. Monopolies were criticized as being based "upon misinformation and untrue pretences of public good," and as "tending to the general hurt of others." In one of his more striking analogies, Sir John Colepeper compared monopolies to a plague. "Like the frogs of Egypt," he thundered, they "have gotten possession of our dwellings and we have scarcely a room free from them; they sip in our cup; they dip in our dish; [and] they sit by our fire." The secular nature of the whole attack emerged in a pamphlet of 1645, where another writer summed up the specific charges against monopolies with the accusation that the practice "trencheth upon the native Rights of the freeborn subject . . . tending to the diminution of Trade." These men were not attacking mercantilism per se, only its abuses. They wished further access to the system for themselves and other Englishmen, but they entertained no thought of abandoning all controls or of embarking upon what later came to be known as free trade.

On the other hand, the gradual secularization of the religious concept of a corporate society weakened the sanction for the ideal of a common good. The idea was not immediately destroyed, but men came to assault the King's Christian responsibility in the name of their individual natural right to private property as well as under the banner of their corporate Christian duty. At least for a time, however, the resulting ideology provided all elements of the revolutionary movement with a common language and hence a sense of sharing the same objectives as well as the same enemy. Some groups retained the original sense of corporate religious responsibility that was so strong in the thought of Calvin and Luther. Others, particularly in the lower classes, developed faiths of their own in Anabaptism, millenarianism, and even mysticism. But again, many were infused with a secular outlook which, as then formulated, placed far less emphasis on mutual obligation and general welfare. Lacking a firm consensus on one ideal of the common good or on a program for its realization, the ideology of the English Revolution left its triumphant advocates with the fundamental problem of providing any intellectual and moral cement for the new regime.

These considerations suggest that the English Revolution was, like most revolutions, the product of an alliance between elements of the upper class and a larger segment of the middle and lower classes. The line that divides a society on the eve of revolution does not run horizontally, separating classes into two neatly defined and wholly antagonistic groups. Neither does it run vertically, splitting it into armed camps according to functional differences such as agriculture and industry. The fault line of revolution is a diagonal, cutting down across the society through functional *and* class lines. This was particularly true of England in 1640, for economic development after 1550 had thoroughly confused the distinction between pure agrarian and pure commercial-industrial operations. The predominant pattern was one of landed interests involved in trade—and vice versa.

Evaluated as part of the long-term drive for general economic improvement, this characteristic involvement in land and trade casts considerable light on the argument among English historians as to whether the revolution was caused by a "rising gentry" or a "falling gentry." Since the gentry were not aligned as a group on either side, the debate is cast in misleading terms. The question is asked in such a way that it is impossible to give a satisfying answer. It seems more revealing to ask whether it was a struggle between the "risen gentry" and the "rising gentry." For in fact it is not surprising to find some gentry who were commercial, industrial, and financial leaders supporting the Crown, even though the majority of these groups favored the Revolution. They had gained access to such activities and profits through royal favor. Other predominantly agrarian gentry sided with the parliamentary forces for economic or ideological reasons. Members of the lower classes divided in much the same way. Some supported the Crown in keeping with the tradition, and practice, of a quasi-feudal but socially responsible government. Others viewed the Revolution as a means to a similar but more modern state, and a final group, joining with the "middling sort," saw it as a way to improve their individual position and fortune in keeping with their natural rights as Englishmen.

SHAFTESBURY AND THE CRISIS OF ENGLISH MERCANTILISM

Though denounced by many of his contemporaries and harshly criticized by many historians, Shaftesbury was probably the central figure in England's effort to retain mercantilism's original sense of corporate responsibility during the revolutionary crisis. A true farmer who knew his seeds and soil, he was also an imaginative and successful merchant, industrialist, and colonizer. Having matured in the revolution of 1640, he played a key role in the revolution which restored Charles II to the throne; and his ideas, political organization, and friends were crucial factors in the Glorious Revolution of 1688 which consolidated parliamentary power against the monarchy.

Born higher in the traditions of "this manor of England" than in the hierarchy of government, Shaftesbury was educated by "a strong Puritan" tutor, who turned him less toward dissent and revolution than toward the precepts of *noblesse oblige*. Bacon's writings were probably the strongest secular influence in his early training. This background predisposed Shaftesbury to the ideal of stewardship and the role of trustee, and the tendency was strengthened by the death of his mother when he was seven years old. Two years later he was fatherless—"fatherless but a baronet and the owner of a large estate." As Shaftesbury recalled, "a time of business which overtook me early . . . forced [me] to learn the world faster than my book."

Not too surprisingly, Shaftesbury was not one of the early revolutionary leaders. But neither did he rush to join the King. It was not until the spring of 1643, that he finally took the field with the forces of the Crown. His family associations and his connections in London seem

sufficient to explain the hesitant decision. He proved a reluctant reactionary, however, and within the year went over to Oliver Cromwell.
Though certainly a vigorous—even ruthless—field commander,
Shaftesbury had little enthusiasm for Cromwell's religious zeal or his
Puritanized version of the personalized, centralized state. Breaking
with the great leader, he went into opposition once again and began
to devote his energies and abilities to the basic problems unresolved
by the Revolution.

The great virtue of revolutions is that they create the circumstances in which a society's problems *can* be solved. They are not to
be criticized or damned for failing to produce a model community
on the morning after the final battle. It is enough that they open the
way for men to reexamine their values and difficulties in a spirit
of rededication and creativity. For it is the essence of being human
to assert that mere existence is insufficient unto life. Shaftesbury's
recognition of this truth and his decision to commit his considerable influence and powers to the central issue of reconstructing
England as a better society is the measure of his greatness.

The dilemma created by the failure of the revolution to establish any institutional framework for society had priority. And since
Shaftesbury insisted that "poverty and necessity [were] no faults"
of the individual but rather the consequences of a poor system, it
was with this problem that he was concerned. With considerable
anxiety, he took a leading role in the restoration of the Stuart kings
in the person of Charles II. "We do now sit down just where we did
begin," he admitted, and put in his oar to keep history from drifting
around in a vicious circle. His principle of action was simple: "It
belongs to us to have some care into whose hands we commit the
management of the commonwealth." Appointed Chancellor of His
Majesty's Exchequer and Under-Secretary of the Treasury in 1661,
he set himself "steadily and actively to the business of governing
England." An astute foreign representative in England concluded
within two years that Shaftesbury was "almost the only man that [I
see] to look after business, and with the ease and mastery that [I]
wonder at him."

Shaftesbury, however, was by no means the only important
leader of the national effort to lift England onto the high road of
welfare and happiness. Sir George Downing, although as "mean,
hateful, and treacherous" a man as walked the age, nevertheless

provided vigorous and brilliant leadership in the intellectual and bureaucratic work of formulating and administering specific policies. Benjamin Worsley played an important role as one of Shaftesbury's close associates. And Sir Josiah Child and Sir William Petty were molders of public opinion in addition to their services as confidential advisors; their ideas influenced many people of the time and were to influence later historians and economists as well.

Shaftesbury nevertheless deserves special emphasis. His range of interests and activities spanned the human spectrum and marked him as a unique figure even in an age of virtuosos. Involved in banking, commerce, agriculture, and industry, he also supported science and philosophy as a patron and member of the Royal Society. His talent for innovation and organization made him an excellent administrator. Perhaps most important of all, he brought to each of those activities a considerable degree of political sophistication.

In his outlook and actions, therefore, Shaftesbury exemplified the whole man who took the long view. His domestic and foreign policies were the complementary halves of classic mercantilism. In domestic affairs, he moved quickly to put the operations of the Treasury on a fair and regular basis, repaying government loans strictly according to chronological sequence without favoritism. Next he restored and strengthened the policy of inspecting manufactured goods for quality and tried to regulate prices within reasonable limits. Finally, he made great efforts to revise the tax structure on more equitable and realistic grounds and to establish a routine and effective system of collection.

Shaftesbury fully accepted the key assumption of mercantilism that foreign policy was the key to domestic welfare. Beginning with his role in framing the Navigation Law of 1651, which reenacted the Elizabethan system based on a *national* monopoly of imperial commerce and development, he quickly became a key figure in empire affairs. By itself, however, the Act of 1651 proved insufficient unto England's difficulties. The revolution and its associated disorders had disrupted domestic progress, sidelined England while the Dutch and the French were expanding apace, and encouraged (and enabled) the American colonies to strike out on their own.

In response, jealousy and frustration reinforced the logic of mercantilist ideas, and together these considerations overpowered Cromwell's religious interest in a Protestant alliance with the Dutch.

Shaftesbury vigorously supported the first war against the Dutch (1652–1654) as a move to recover lost ground and enforce the reenactment of the navigation acts. Though rewarding in some respects, and hence serving to verify the axiom that the way to wealth was through taking it away from somebody else, the war did not provide a fundamental solution to England's economic problems.

Despite the diversification and improvement which had taken place since 1550—and it was by no means inconsiderable—Charles II stepped ashore in a country still, or at any rate once again, plagued by economic difficulties. "For is it not the general complaint and out-cry of the City," commented the Reverend David Barton of St. Margarets as late as 1669, "that there is a universal decay of Trade?" Pessimists wailed that trade was "almost totally lost," and even the more hopeful bemoaned "the necessity of parting every year with vast sums of money to make the balance of trade even, because we import much more than we export." Barton no doubt spoke for the majority when he gave his explanation of "the true cause of the distemper: Either a Foreign Nation ingrossing Trade abroad, or the Magistrates neglect of Trade at home must bear the blame."

THE IDEOLOGY AND POLITICS OF THE CORPORATE WELFARE

Shaftesbury and his colleagues faced strong opposition from specific interest groups as they labored to reestablish and improve the mercantilist system. They steadily opposed such efforts to subvert the common good in the name of private property. "Private advantages," warned Samuel Fortrey, "are often impediments of public profit." Shaftesbury agreed: "Where the merchant trades for a great deal of Profit, the nation loses." Openly attacked in 1662 by a group of London merchants who complained that the new navigation system was "destructive of his Majesty's trading subjects," Shaftesbury refused to surrender his ground. He and other mercantilists also saw the challenge to their program inherent in the power of the largest joint-stock companies and trading corporations. Their response to that danger was twofold. First, they tried to keep the big companies from squeezing too much out of the economy and from creating a private empire of their own over which neither the Crown nor the Parliament had effective authority. Second, they worked to centralize control of the empire and its policies in a committee responsible to Parliament as well as to the Crown and composed, in Worsley's phrase, of men more "concerned in the generality of the Trade of the nation and in the good of the management of it than in the profit of this or that particular Trade."

Shaftesbury and his colleagues fully agreed with Petty that "there is but a certain proportion of trade in the world," and with Child that "foreign trade produces riches, riches power, power preserves our trade and religion." Their emphasis on markets for English products was therefore a central part of Restoration mercantilism. Sir George Peckham stressed the fear of unrest contingent upon unemployment, explicitly defining export markets as a way of avoiding riots among those who "live here idly to the annoy of the whole state." And the pamphlets, as well as the formal policy memorandums, were filled with the search for "a far better vent," and proposed policies which would "cause a mighty vent" for English goods, ships, capital, services, and loans.

The navigation acts of the next century were designed to achieve that goal, but basic to the system were the laws of 1660–1661 which specified three restrictions: (1) all trade was to be carried in English (*including colonial*) ships; (2) foreign merchants were excluded from the trade of the colonies; and (3) certain goods in the colonies could be exported only to England or to other English colonies. Two years after this, the Staple Act made England the depot for all trade from the colonies to Europe (and later, vice versa). Domestic policies supplemented these principal laws. The old centralized, paternalistic monopolies were scrapped, and the greater part of the empire was opened in fact, if not in law, to all Englishmen. Free trade, at least in its *original* meaning of fewer restrictions *within* the system, became very much a reality for Englishmen within the empire. Manufacturers were given encouragement in the form of bounties (or subsidies) and protection in the form of tariffs. And the colonies, in their turn, were guaranteed military security and a virtual monopoly of the English market.

Bluntly warning the King in 1669 that "the decay of land rents and trade" remained unchecked, Shaftesbury launched a campaign to consolidate the affairs of commerce with those of the colonies and produce an integrated and balanced system. He recommended assistance for manufacturing and "all encouragement to the promoting of our fishery and advancing our plantations, the increase of our shipping and multiplying our seamen." Upon successfully forcing its creation in 1670, Shaftesbury in 1672 assumed the presidency of the Council of Trade and Plantations. Shortly thereafter he brought Locke in as secretary to the organization. Collaborating easily with Worsley and Locke, Shaftesbury made recommendations which often led to "pronouncements ... contrary to the private interests of the merchants" for the simple reason that he was openly and militantly concerned with "the welfare of our said Colonies and Plantations and of the Trade and Navigation of these our kingdoms."

"In the beginning America was the world," Locke was to remark in a revealing passage of his *Second Treatise on Government* (first drafted no later than 1681), and it had been the problem of the American part of the empire that lay at the center of the whole mercantilist system at the time that Shaftesbury set about his official labors in 1660–1661. Founded by men who thought of themselves as creating a schism in the state, Massachusetts and its satellites had manifested considerable independence by 1630. Severely restricted by an economic geography which limited its agricultural operations, the area very soon began to develop an economy—and an outlook—which was more competitive with that of the mother country than it was complementary to it. The term "New England" was far more than a romantic, nostalgic name; it quickly became an accurate descriptive term.

The English Revolution accelerated such developments throughout the colonies by cutting off the emigration of people and money and forcing the colonists to strike out on their own. And what began as a necessity became in the minds of some a positive virtue. By the time of the Restoration, the Earl of Sandwich and others were quite outspoken in their fear that New England would put together a system of its own and become "mighty rich and powerful and not at all careful of [its] dependence upon Old England." Shaftesbury shared such anxieties and recognized the difficulties in dealing with the situation.

Perhaps nothing illustrates the maturity of Shaftesbury's mercantilism as clearly as his preference for a policy of patient firmness pending the broad, complementary integration of the political economy of two regions. Certainly the evolution and persistence of just such a pro-British attitude on the part of many American colonists north of Philadelphia tends to verify his analysis. Shaftesbury's attitude also helps to explain why mercantilism, as contrasted with

the imperialism that developed after 1740, operated in a more
relaxed manner. As a philosophy of the general welfare over the
long haul, mercantilism was less driven to exploit every immediate
situation to the last degree.

Though often ridiculed or contemptuously dismissed, the
constitution which Shaftesbury, assisted by Locke, prepared for
the colony of South Carolina reveals another facet of this concern
with corporate responsibility and the common good. While the
criticism that the charter of South Carolina was a neo-feudal
document is largely true, it nevertheless misses the point—indeed,
several points. For one thing, Locke's association with the project
suggests that he was not the unrestrained individualist Americans
often picture him to be. The document also suggests the weakness
of the generally prevalent idea that the United States by-passed
any connection with feudalism. Over and above the fact that such
a thesis ignores a great part of the early history of the country,
it would appear that the interpretation is based on a confusion
about the differences between feudalism and manorialism and
the relation of the two. Manorialism was a system of organizing
production—almost exclusively agrarian production. It was an
economic system with no necessary connection with feudalism;
and in some cases existed independently and without leading to
feudalism.

Feudalism, on the other hand, was a *political* system and philosophy involving an interlocking network of freedoms, duties, and
obligations between individuals inhabiting specified areas of land.
Anchored to the idea of balanced relationships, it was composed
of a whole series of *imperium in imperio*. The weakest individual
was usually bound to several superiors standing between himself
and a final authority, but the highest lord had reciprocal obligations to the lowest man in the order. And not only could a given
vassal also be a lord; by the ninth century the whole concept of
vassalage had lost much of its implication of unfreedom.

This suggests, and rightly so, that a fief—the territorial area held
by a vassal who was also a lord—had many things in common with
the later city, township, county, and state. It was an area ruled by local
leaders under specific conditions and within explicit and implicit
limits specified by a superior power. But the lord accepted reciprocal duties and responsibilities. As a political system designed to

solve the problem of ruling large areas under the assumption that a small state was the only feasible unit of direct government, this cardinal principle of feudalism was the very backbone of England's colonization in North America.

It is essential to realize that the republicanism of the 16th and 17th centuries was a political theory clearly derived from feudalism. A more extended representation began with demands from within the system; the other part of the transformation involved no more than shifting the unit of government from the individual (who took the vows of fealty to an overlord) to the state or other subdivision, which took a similar oath to the nation. American leaders were not only conscious of this heritage of their own constitution, but they understood that the theory that small states were both necessary and more desirable conflicted with the explicit emphasis on expansion in mercantilism. Their resolution of this contradiction opened the way for the republican empire which they ultimately established.

During the intervening years, Shaftesbury defined the relationship between the colonies and the mother country within a framework of reciprocal obligations. Given such a system, he assumed that each party would enjoy its own realm of freedom and yet contribute to the common good. Both factors are revealed in Shaftesbury's subtle plan whereby the colonies, and in particular South Carolina, would develop their trade in a manner that would subvert the Spanish Empire. "Planting and Trade is both our design and your interest," he explained to colonial critics whose short-range view distorted the purpose of various restrictions on exploitation; "and if you will therein follow our directions we shall lay a way open to you to get all the Spanish riches in that country with their consent, and without any hazard to yourselves." And despite his inability to realize the broad plan in his own time, Shaftesbury's vision was ultimately verified by the commerce of Charleston and Baltimore.

Both at home and in the colonies, Shaftesbury was basically concerned with the problem of working out some resolution of the tension between the Crown and Parliament, and between the individual and the state. Growing ever more aware that Shaftesbury's leadership posed a major threat to the arbitrary power of the Crown, Charles II finally dismissed him from office in 1673, shortly after he had helped carry through, for the Asian trade and other commercial objectives, a third war against the Dutch. "[I am] only laying down my gown," Shaftesbury openly warned the King, "and putting on my sword."

True to his rhetoric, Shaftesbury quickly launched an assault on the King's personal and dynastic ties to Roman Catholicism. He argued (with considerable foresight) that a king of one faith could not successfully rule a population having a fundamentally different commitment. And having opposed Cromwell's crusading righteousness, he also turned his back on the post-revolutionary distortion of Calvin's original concept of calling. Led by such preachers as Richard Baxter, many Protestants, including some Puritans, replaced with another analysis the Elizabethan and early Stuart view that poverty was caused by the economic system. They now began to assert that poverty was a function of sin, especially lust and laziness; their new thesis defined individual, worldly success as a sign of religious virtue. Though himself something of a Deist, Shaftesbury nevertheless remained true to the old concept of a corporate welfare that was rooted in Calvin's injunction to labor faithfully in one's calling in behalf of the common good. Shaftesbury's combination of Deism and a deeply religious sense of responsibility for the corporate welfare was a forerunner of the attitude of colonial Episcopalians such as James Madison; they were to separate church and state while retaining the essence of the theology.

Despite the neo-orthodoxy of his own views, Shaftesbury supported toleration within the non-Catholic community with two arguments. The first derived from the post-Revolution assumption that England had become underpopulated, and its logic was strictly mercantilist. More people would produce more goods and at lower wage rates; this in turn would increase England's ability to win markets away from the Dutch and the French. Thus slavery was encouraged in the colonies, home-folk were urged to produce large families, emigration of skilled labor was discouraged and restricted, and in 1622 the Poor Laws were revamped to integrate the paupers into national economic production through government work projects.

For the same reason, many mercantilists suggested that immigrants be encouraged by promises of religious toleration as well as by guarantees of employment. Sir William Petty, for example, argued that "indulgence must be granted in matters of opinion." Shaftesbury offered a far more thorough proposal. Advising the King that the nation's welfare "depends not so much on anything, on this side of heaven, as on the multitude of your subjects," he recommended that immigrant nonconformists be welcomed and tolerated. Turning the logic about, he then proposed to populate the colonies by allowing dissidents at home to emigrate and "enjoy the liberty of their mistaken consciences."

Shaftesbury also made a powerful theological argument for toleration. Men were always striving to know more of the Truth, he asserted, but "it is a far different thing to believe, or be fully persuaded of the truth of the doctrine of our Church, and to swear never to endeavor to alter" it. Willing to "burn for the witness of it, if Providence should call him to it," Shaftesbury nevertheless considered other men equally devoted. In this commitment he found the strength to fight militantly against all attempts to limit Protestant dissent, and to stand for the right of "every other sort of nonconformists [to] have the liberty to assemble, for the exercise of their own manner of worship."

Shaftesbury was also active in reforming the law. Though less famous than his important efforts in behalf of the Habeas Corpus Act (1679), his labors to save and reform the Chancery Courts were possibly more significant. The Courts were corrupt and inefficient at the time of the Restoration, and Shaftesbury's vigorous supervision restored their reputation, enhanced their performance of justice, and undoubtedly saved them for their later evolution into the Court of Equity. In many ways, for that matter, he conceived of the law as one of the basic substitutes for the old religious sanction in behalf of a corporate sense of the common good. After being dismissed by the Crown, he threw down his challenge in those very terms. "The King is king by law," he flatly asserted, "and by the same law that the poor man enjoys in his cottage." During the same year, 1675, he carried the attack to the very principle of divine right. "In a word," he cried, "if this doctrine be true, our Magna Charta is of no use; our laws are but rules among ourselves during the King's pleasure."

Shaftesbury had been moving toward this climax ever since he had broken with Cromwell over the same issue of personalized government. He had done so, moreover, on the broadest possible grounds—an effort to provide a secular substitute for the traditional religious ideal and practice of the corporate welfare. Taking one of his cues from James Harrington, the leading philosopher of history during the epoch of the Revolution, Shaftesbury then added two ideas of his own. Arguing from an extensive study of earlier societies, Harrington had concluded that revolutions were caused by a shift in the nature and distribution of economic power. Thus any revolutionary government had to stabilize the altered economic relationships by creating appropriate political institutions. This could best be done by dividing the powers and responsibilities of government and weighting each of them in favor of a different economic and social bloc within the society.

Seeing deeper into the heart of the matter, Shaftesbury realized that such a system would not work without an institutionalized organization capable of actually running the government and at the same time standing beyond the power of the King. He was equally concerned to find an organization that would give the individual a sense of purpose, commitment, responsibility, and involvement in the affairs of the nation. Groping and fumbling his way, he concluded that the political party was the answer.

By modern academic standards, Shaftesbury's theory of the political party was not very sophisticated, but it cut through to the essentials. He argued that the party had to be concerned with, and organized on the basis of, ideas and policies which offered its members a set of significant objectives. Such clearly delineated standards and purposes provided the best guarantee that government would neither stagnate, degenerate into tyranny, nor become a meaningless scramble for place and pelf. He was correct, for the dangers he foresaw are precisely the causes of the alienation of men from other men and from their own humanity.

Convinced that the restored monarchy was devolving toward just such a tyranny, Shaftesbury organized the Whig Party. Drawing on his deep knowledge of the whole of England (even his enemies admitted that it was unmatched), he built an alliance between citizens of all classes in London and the leaders of the English countryside. It was a powerful coalition; so strong, indeed, that had Shaftesbury been in better health it might have brought about the Glorious Revolution some five to ten years sooner.

Organized as the Green Ribbon Club (and in some respects carrying on the traditions of Harrington's Rota Club), Shaftesbury and his lieutenants, meeting at the King's Head Tavern, brought modern politics into existence. They were the first to provide voters with free transportation to the polls, and their pamphlets and public rallies would be the envy of many contemporary politicians. All this was to one specific purpose: the supremacy of elected parliaments. Without that victory, Shaftesbury warned, "our laws, liberties, lives, and estates should become in a short time at the will of the prince."

Shaftesbury also pushed many specific reforms; perhaps the most important was his demand for regular parliaments at short intervals. He also fought bribery and the practice of rigging elections through the rotten borough. He likewise demanded a uniform election system and secret voting. By 1681 he was ready to have Parliament sit in defiance of dissolution by the King. Thoroughly frightened (and properly so), the Crown struck back by raising the specter of another civil war and issuing warrants for the arrest of Shaftesbury. It thus frightened and divided his followers and forced him to adopt the life of a hunted animal. Beaten down and desperately ill, Shaftesbury fled across the Channel in November, 1682. Two months later he died of exhaustion and a sense of failure.

He was in fact triumphant. Shaftesbury's individual acts, his ideas, and his party saved for England a crucial sense of corporate welfare. To Americans he bequeathed two legacies: a concept of responsibility and self-discipline for the common good, and his influence on John Locke. Shaftesbury was one of the most liberal men of his time, and he fortunately transmitted some of his attitude and ideas to the young Locke. In the beginning Locke was a vigorous, even dedicated Royalist; unquestionably Shaftesbury modified those views. Unhappily, the influence was limited. For whatever reason, Locke failed to grasp or act on Shaftesbury's central insight that corporate responsibility is the key to a meaningful as well as wealthy life; he offered instead the polarities of conformity and unrestrained individualism.

JOHN LOCKE AND THE DECLINE OF CORPORATE RESPONSIBILITY

Developing his own thoughts on government as Shaftesbury's career came to a dramatic end, John Locke significantly modified his patron's tradition in two significant respects, both revisions being concerned with the central dilemma of resolving the tension between the individual and the state. He did so, moreover, in so eminently simple and persuasive a manner that he convinced a great many people that the problem no longer existed. The result and the reward were momentous: Locke's philosophy eclipsed the more rigorous and substantial outlook evolved by Shaftesbury, and in the process became the central theme of a later American Weltanschauung. But in fact, Locke begged the whole issue.

Both theoretically and practically, Locke's individualism was dependent upon expansion and empire. And only by setting aside the entire question of the relationship between the mother country and the colonies could he define freedom for citizens of the Metropolis as the crucial issue. As a result, the tension between the individual and the state centered upon the access to and division of the rewards of empire. Fundamental questions concerning the nature and allocation of responsibility in society were discounted by Locke because he assumed the existence of a stable and profitable empire. Pointed toward a hedonism of that character, his followers soon became utilitarians and ultimately embraced pragmatism.

At the same time, Locke undercut the very individualism he proclaimed so loudly. He defined the relationship between the state and the individual in such a way that the individual was in reality charged with justifying his resistance to the state instead of the state being held strictly accountable to the individual according to a corporate value system. This was nothing new, for Hobbes and others had advanced similar arguments before the Revolution, but Locke sustained the tradition while clothing it in liberal rhetoric.

Going even further in this direction, Locke defined the natural man as one who did not cause trouble by asserting and acting upon different standards. This axiom extensively reinforced the authoritarian bias of his philosophy. For by this reasoning it became unnatural to exercise one's individuality in a manner or for a purpose which conflicted with the accepted norms. While it is true that these limits may be broad, and may even be extended under the circumstances of an expanding or secure empire, it is also true that they become progressively narrower under less permissive conditions. And at that point, unfortunately, conformity becomes, within Locke's philosophy, the only acceptable form that responsibility can assume.

Born of stout Puritan ancestors and educated within that outlook, Locke came to maturity as a talented if orthodox conservative. He feared disorder hardly less than Hobbes, and in 1656 his disgust

erupted in a description of the nation as this "great Bedlam England."
By 1660 he was "a wholehearted monarchist," "a man of the Right,
an extreme authoritarian." But always a sophisticated trimmer,
and constantly fretting about his reputation, Locke adjusted to
the circumstances of the Restoration without risking his career in
support of Shaftesbury's intellectual and political commitments. As
Locke himself remarked: "People are not so easily got out of their
old forms as some are apt to suggest."

Once Shaftesbury's restraining hand was gone, Locke's mercantilism became much narrower in outlook and oriented ever more
closely to the property interests of the upper class. His policy paper
in 1697 on the problem of unemployment and pauperism was
harsh and severe: an appalling document, judged by any standards. His monetary proposals had the effect of extracting sizable
sums from the citizenry for the benefit of the Crown and a few
special groups. And his foreign policy reveals even more the extent
to which his individualism and democracy relied on the principle
of imperial expansion.

Locke's totally relative definition of wealth was based on an
ever-expanding empire. "Riches," he explained repeatedly, "do
not consist in having more gold and silver, but in having more
in proportion than the rest of the world, or than our neighbors."
Hence "our growing rich or poor depends ... only on which is
greater or less, our importations or exportations of consumable
commodities." Locke completed the argument by explaining that
agriculture would decay if trade failed to sustain an indefinite
expansion. By Locke's argument, the only way to achieve welfare
was to take enough away from others to raise the national average.

Given this analysis of wealth and welfare and how to attain
them, Locke understandably emphasized property rights, a labor
theory of value, the sanctity of natural (i.e. normal) behavior, and
the power of the state itself. An individual's right to wealth implied
that he controlled his labor and his property without qualifica-
tion. Men were justified, said Locke, in criticizing the existing
state of affairs in the name of this individualism, but when they
did so from any other point of view they became unnatural men
and hence beyond the pale. Thus all men owed their loyalty to the
state which protected these rights and standards and extended the
national empire. When, in dire and unique circumstances, such

individualism was threatened, men could revoke their loyalty—
but only after a majority had reached that conclusion.

Locke no doubt agreed with Harrington's thesis that an extension of voting rights need not subvert the position of propertyholders: weighted representation, a division of government powers,
and imperial expansion would prevent such an outcome. Most
Englishmen read Harrington and Locke as philosophers of a once
dangerous revolution which had become a reassuring status quo.
American colonists, on the other hand, ultimately found in those
writers the logic and justification for a conservative revolution.

This is not as contradictory as it might appear. Considered in
England, or in any other country that was the metropolis of a going
empire in which a revolution had been stopped and stabilized
short of the truly radical objectives proposed by a sizable group
of its supporters, Locke's system could offer no justification for
continued—or new—revolution. For by definition he advanced no
objective beyond hedonistic pleasure and avoidance of pain; and
the citizens of the mother country enjoyed such rewards. Only the
colonial subjects of the empire could find a sanction for revolution
in Locke. Even for them, however, the appeal was invalid as long
as their position improved, or at least held its own. Locke authorized revolution only in negative terms and under the most extreme
circumstances; indeed, over half the American Declaration of
Independence is taken up in satisfying those criteria.

"God gave the world to men in common . . .," Locke admitted,
"[but] He gave it to the use of the industrious and rational (and
labor was to be his title to it), not to the fancy or covetousness of
the quarrelsome and contentious." From this premise he argued
that while "the end of civil society is present enjoyment of what this
world affords," it was equally true that "the first and fundamental
law . . . is the preservation of the society, and (as far as will consist
with the public good) of every person in it." Otherwise there would
be "no peace, no security, no enjoyment, enmity with all men and
safe possession of nothing, and those stinging swarms of misery
which attend anarchy and rebellion." Locke could hardly have been
stronger in his emphasis: ". . . the end of civil society being to avoid
and remedy those inconveniences of the state of nature . . . by setting
up a known authority which every one of the society ought to obey."

Locke thus asserted that *any* society had to be considered just until a *majority* of men exercised their senses and their reason to reach a different conclusion. A man who differed prematurely, he pointed out, "becomes degenerate, and declares himself to quit the principles of human nature, and to be a noxious creature." Under those circumstances "the execution of the law of nature is in that state put into every man's hand, whereby everyone has a right to punish the transgressors of that law to such a degree as may hinder its violation." For Locke, therefore, individualism was a right and a liberty reserved to those who accepted a status quo defined by a certain set of natural truths agreed upon by a majority. Within such a framework, and it is a far narrower set of limits than it appears at first glance, the natural laws of property and labor were deemed sufficient to guide men's pursuit of happiness.

As can be seen, Locke's individualism contained all the elements of the kind of laissez faire advocated a century later with such persuasiveness by Adam Smith in his famous essay *The Wealth of Nations*. Both men are often thought of as advocates of weak or minimal government, but this impression is less than half true. Given a national system capable of obtaining riches, Locke and Smith advocated a modification of government authority and regulations *within one part of the system*. Even in that sense, however, both men made it quite clear that the state had very definite duties toward property and the maintenance of order. Neither of them proposed that the government should abandon its responsibility for sustaining and extending such an imperial system. The basic question was not whether there should be an *internal* relaxation, for upon that point they were agreed; the issue was whether the system was large and strong enough and sufficiently developed to permit such liberality without provoking another general crisis.

THE DILEMMAS OF SUCCESSFUL MERCANTILISM

Just such an early campaign for domestic laissez faire coincided with the favorable reception given to Locke's ideas in the 1690s. A combination of events had produced a striking improvement in England's economy during the thirty years after the Restoration. The efforts of men like Shaftesbury and Downing had been complemented by more general factors. Internal peace freed men and money for the rehabilitation of old enterprises and the expansion of new undertakings in manufacturing and the reexport trade. The wars against the Dutch brought concrete gains (if only psychological ones) and buttressed the enforcement of the mercantile system, which in itself was systematized and rationalized. Finally, the English colonies had developed far enough beyond the initial stage of survival to play a positive and contributing part in the empire.

As a result, Englishmen began to agitate more vigorously for freer trade. Monopolies and severely confined trade again came under attack. But the demands did *not* include the cry for international free trade as this came to be defined in later years. "It is necessary," explained Nehemiah Grew, "so far as it may promote the Interest, not of any Company but of England, that every English merchant should be free, so it is that all English plantations should be bound, bound I mean to trade with England alone."

Supporting this drive for freer trade *within* the system, an English court ruled in 1705 that "all people are at liberty to live in this place, and their skill and industry are the means they have to get their bread; . . . consequently it is unreasonable to restrain them from exercising their trades within this place." Six years later, in an even more important decision, Lord Chief Justice Parker sustained that argument: "no free man . . . should be robbed of his own property or his liberties or his free customary rights . . . [and these] have always been taken to extend to freedom of trade." As the judge no doubt knew, he was exaggerating; America is not the only society in which the courts follow the economy and the elections.

Even some mercantilists, such as Sir Francis Brewster, were beginning to favor modifications of the old regulations though they were not ready to abandon their basic ideas. "Trade indeed will find its own Channels," Brewster admitted, "but it may be to the ruin of the Nation if not Regulated." These difficulties and dilemmas were produced by the very success of the system. *This was as true for colonial as for domestic affairs.* As the empire prospered, so did the Americans. Given extremely favorable access to the English market, a full share in the shipping business, increasing manufactures and services from England, as well as the protection afforded by the Royal Navy (and the King's Army), the colonies enjoyed their own accelerated improvement. It is misleading to think of them as nothing but a conglomeration of log cabins, possum caps, and handgrown corn cakes. They had produced cities, fortunes, and leaders of their own, and the stratification of an established society was visible to all.

This progress prompted steadily increasing concern in England. American industry was feared as particularly ominous, and called forth a series of laws designed to strangle the rival posthaste. The Woolen Act of 1699 was prefaced by the explanation that such products of America were "exported from thence to Foreigne Markets heretofore supplied from England which will inevitably sink the value of Lands and tend to the ruine of the Trade and Woolen Manufactures of this realm." A year later the Board of Trade ruled explicitly that all manufactured items in America "ought to be imported from this kingdom." Perhaps the greatest testimony to the progress of the American colonial economy came in 1751 and 1764, when England sought to stop the colonials from printing their own money. Sometimes interpreted as a sign of weakness, the need of more money was in fact an indication that the colonies were bursting the imperial bonds. They were on the verge of creating their own system within the British Empire.

Americans thus benefited in their own fashion from the same wars that gave the English economy an extra boost. For just as they had gained at the expense of the Dutch in 1654 and 1663, so the English won "substantial and permanent gains . . . at the expense of France, the greatest industrial nation of eighteenth-century Europe." As often is the case during wars, and particularly in nations which escape physical damage (as did England between 1660 and 1763), the increased demand opened the way for new ideas. Quickly adapted and applied to industrial undertakings, these innovations created new jobs and a greater domestic market. Opportunities for employment multiplied and the competition among capitalists for a share of the labor force increased.

As far back as the 1630s, Thomas Mun had sensed what the consequences of such a pressure on the labor market would be for traditional mercantilist thought. "The riches of a nation," ran an argument typical of the era, "arise out of the labor of its people exported to foreign markets." The logical, and practical, outcome of that thesis was a policy favoring slavery and bare subsistence wages. But low wages also put a ceiling on the effective demand generated among the workers. And a persistent emphasis on exports tended to produce a rise in domestic prices (because of delays and short-ages) that in turn decreased domestic demand even further and thereby created conditions favorable to unrest and radical agitation. Such theoretical possibilities were becoming practical realities by the 1740s.

It was becoming apparent that, despite its general success, the system was producing a domestic imbalance. On the one hand, the drive and sense of purpose manifested by earlier mercantilist leaders was giving way to the spirit of irresponsibility and the ethics of the scramble. On the other, greater incentives had to be offered in order to sustain demand and avoid "large-scale emigration or social disturbances." Whether they "contributed systematic treatises or ephemeral pamphlets," concludes Professor A. W. Coats, "many contemporary authors were, consciously or unconsciously, groping their way towards the concept of an optimum wage level—one which would reconcile the interest of the agricultural producers, the exporters of manufactures, and the wage earners themselves."

In these respects, therefore, the mercantilists were no longer united on a few basic policies which they were confident led to opulence and power. Their growing concern over the optimum kind and degree of regulation necessary to sustain the improvement of the country was extended and intensified by several other factors. Instead of being characterized by competing ideas about the objectives of national and individual life, and the means appropriate for reaching those goals, English politics came to be typified more and more by shifting coalitions organized (and disrupted) on the basis of personal and group interest. The very success of mercantilism prompted men to overlook the fact that it was a man-made system, and to assume instead that it was a natural order which would operate indefinitely with little or no attention.

The result was a progressive intensification of bureaucratic infighting, corruption, and legislation for interest rather than for corporate welfare. Along with the rising advocates of laissez faire, a growing number of mercantilists became less interested in policy than in exploiting existing opportunities. As a result, problems of empire were slighted or handled in a negative and unimaginative way. Such an approach made it almost certain that any later effort to compensate for the neglect would take on the character of an all-encompassing campaign to reassert the power of the Metropolis over the colonies.

THE DECLINE OF MERCANTILISM AND THE AMERICAN REVOLUTION

This decay of the standards and performance of mercantilism served to strengthen and invigorate the continuing battle for laissez faire. Its advocates concluded that mercantilism had served its purpose and should be abandoned. But they also insisted that the empire was the foundation of this ability to have more freedom at home; hence they were not opposed to a tightening up of the empire itself. The colonies were to become less free in order that the mother country might enjoy more liberty.

This shift from the mercantilist conception of empire toward an imperialistic outlook became increasingly apparent after 1715. English investments were protected by strict controls over colonial currency established in 1751 and through a law of 1731 which made colonial property legally forfeit for debts. Articles such as copper, furs, and special forest products were added to the list of goods reserved for England. And the principle itself became law in 1742 with an official proclamation emphasizing the duties of the colonies toward the mother country.

This imperialism of the laissez-faire outlook was reinforced by the problem of governing and controlling events in the vast areas taken from France directly, such as Nova Scotia and Canada, and was accentuated by the difficulties of limiting and directing the westward movement of the colonists once the French began their retreat. Many Englishmen argued that these issues could not be handled in the way that the mercantilists had dealt with commerce and the original colonies. Territorial administration and relations with the Indians called for the exercise of extensive authority from London. And the colonies themselves had reached the point where they had begun to think of themselves as having the ability, the need, and the right to conduct many of their own affairs.

All those perplexing issues merged in two debates which came to a climax in England after the final victory over France in 1763. One was a vigorous argument between mercantilists and advocates of laissez faire over the best way for England to retain its supremacy among the world empires and at the same time keep from being overtaken by the poor countries. The second was a struggle between George III and his opponents over the question of leadership in

England. Interwoven in an extremely complex way, these two conflicts promoted an attempted tightening up of the British empire. And that in turn ultimately provoked and encouraged the colonists to initiate the creation of an American empire.

Touched off by David Hume's assertion that England would find it impossible to maintain the world supremacy it enjoyed at the moment, the intellectual and theoretical argument soon settled down to a debate between Adam Smith and Sir James Steuart. Taking place during the 1750s and the 1760s, this discussion determined the climate of opinion for many years before the publication of the big books which summarized the conflicting views. Smith's *Wealth of Nations* appeared in 1776, nine years after Steuart's *Inquiry into the Principles of Political Oeconomy*; but the publication dates are very misleading if taken as signifying the beginning of the disagreement. The books were the final statements in an argument lasting nearly twenty years.

The basic significance of the differences between Smith and Steuart is clear: they reopened the central issue posed by Shaftesbury and similar early mercantilists and offered different conclusions and recommendations. Though mercantilism originated as the articulate statement of the needs and desires of the commercial interest, three other aspects of its mature *Weltanschauung* are nevertheless of paramount importance. First, trade *was* the dynamic element in the nation's early development. Second, the mercantilists correctly asserted that society was an interrelated system composed of conflicting, competing, and cooperating interests; and for that reason men had consciously to manage their affairs to accommodate and balance the various parts and to advance the general welfare. Finally, the mercantilists generalized their ideas beyond their own interests to include the entire nation. This was partly because of their conception of society as an integrated (even organic) unit and partly because of their personal awareness that all the parts were interrelated.

At the crucial juncture of the Restoration, Shaftesbury realized that mercantilism could develop in one of two ways. It could sustain the image and the ideal of society and the general welfare, or it could slide back into a narrower and ultimately extreme emphasis on group and personal interest. Shaftesbury held fast to the broader ideal. His protégé Locke turned toward a hedonistic individualism. A century later, when Shaftesbury's theoretical alternatives had materialized as the two roads open to England, Smith argued for individualism while Steuart upheld the broader vision of purposeful action for the general welfare.

As with Shaftesbury and Locke, Steuart and Smith shared one crucial assumption: whatever the local or domestic means of achieving welfare, it could not be accomplished without an empire. The key difference lay in the view shared by Shaftesbury and Steuart that conscious, positive policies were necessary to sustain the reality of corporate, mutual responsibility within society and to improve the general welfare. The four protagonists also agreed, however, that self-interest was the main engine of human action. This did not mean that they were pocketbook determinists; they were quite aware that ideas played an important part in defining self-interest. Steuart was willing to grant, moreover, that it was often "the combination of every private interest which forms the public good."

Beyond that point, however, Steuart's views diverged dramatically from those of Smith. He was convinced from observation and analysis that the exchange economy of the capitalist system suffered from an inherent tendency to get out of balance. As it did so, it produced unemployment, political unrest, and the probability of social revolution. Denying that the competition between contradictory self-interests provided an automatic corrective for this inevitable instability, he insisted that men had to act consciously and rationally to keep the system functioning satisfactorily.

Steuart's acceptance of the responsibility "to provide food, other necessities and employment, not only for those who actually exist, but also for those who are to be brought into existence" dramatized his reassertion—contrary to Locke and Smith—of the moral imperative that had been so strong in early mercantilism and that Shaftesbury had labored so hard to reinvigorate and sustain. Steuart's thought signified the high point of British mercantilism in theoretical sophistication and in its concern for the national well-being over the long run. Entertaining no thought of total regulation and quite willing to give individuals a broad area for independent action, Steuart nevertheless insisted that welfare was the product of policy, not of Providence nor of the automatic workings of Newton's Great Clock nor even of the mysterious powers of Adam Smith's "hidden hand."

Though it came out in curious ways, Adam Smith had considerable respect for the power of Steuart's argument. In his public remarks, Smith almost never admitted the existence, let alone the intelligence, of Steuart. Yet his correspondence makes clear that Steuart was *the* antagonist. In particular, he implicitly acknowledged the strength of Steuart's argument about the inherent instability of capitalism. He also refused to attack state action as such, an important point often overlooked by the more careless or enthusiastic advocates of laissez-faire free enterprise. At several points, indeed, he emphasizes that the state is responsible for key actions. In others, his remarks suggest that he was attacking the corruption of the ideal of mercantilism as much as the outlook per se.

This is certainly true in the crucial sense that Smith predicated his entire system on the existence of an empire. Along with many Scotsmen, Smith was at once a nationalist and a British imperialist. In 1766 he even prepared a special study of Roman colonies for Lord Shelburne, an undertaking designed to further the efficiency and productivity of the empire. Smith's basic argument was that "Britain was already a rich country and hence there really was no need for the government to safeguard advantages which we were not in danger of losing." He nevertheless stressed the constant need to extend the market; accepting the assumptions of the mercantilists, he hinged his entire argument on the existence of an expanding "vent for surpluses."

By Smith's own emphasis, the key to *The Wealth of Nations* is the axiom that "the surpluses must be sent abroad." Thus, as he explained, it was the existence of the empire which made it possible to rely rather upon the division of labor than upon mercantilist policy to sustain and increase the wealth of the rich country. "A rich nation," he concluded, "must always in every competition of commerce and manufactures, have an equal, or superior advantage over a poor one." This is the context within which Smith was ultimately willing to acquiesce in the political independence of the American colonies; a large part of the empire remained undisturbed, and, he was confident, England would retain its vital economic supremacy over America.

In the simplest sense, that is to say, the "hidden hand" upon which Smith relied to sustain laissez faire was nothing more nor less than an empire which gave the Metropolis an a priori advantage in development over other countries. Under those circumstances, the balance of trade was "very advantageous" to England. Men could proceed to indulge themselves "in the way that they judge most advantageous to themselves." As with John Locke, Smith based his individualism on empire and the absence of factions in the body politic; faction, according to Smith, "obstructs all public business" and disturbs the easy workings of a natural order. Ironically, therefore, Smith was in this at one with the French physiocrats who wanted a strong government to protect a predominantly agrarian society, and with Englishmen such as Viscount Bolingbroke who argued the necessity of a strong Patriot King to clamp down on factions that were threatening to tear society asunder.

Clearly enough, George III took his cue from Bolingbroke rather than from Smith; but in his insistence on an end to faction and on the retention of the empire he was acting on the cardinal axioms of Smith's own argument. As a firm believer in divine right, George III was also anxious to reassert the prerogative of the Crown and assert his own personality. Emphasizing the virtues of laissez faire, many of the King's critics (both then and later) found it an easy matter to present him in an unfavorable light. But the breakdown of mercantilism did involve corruption and the loss of purpose and responsibility. Hence, while it is easy to argue that George III's cure for such unrestrained individualism was worse than the disease, the issue is not that simple—the disease was very real and very dangerous.

Even the Americans were ultimately to discover that the assumption that empire solves all problems proves less satisfying in its long-run results than in its momentary profits and pleasures. As the last of the great mercantilists, Steuart understood very early what Americans of a later century were to learn only after they had used a weapon of mass destruction that threatened the individual and corporate welfare of unborn generations. For the living do bear, in Steuart's moving phrase, a responsibility for the welfare "of those who are to be brought into existence."

James Madison, the commanding mind of the American gentry and the sage of the Founding Fathers, ultimately adopted and then adapted the mercantilism of Steuart as the morality and the policy by which to transform the feeble colonial confederation into a mighty republican empire. Before the final break with London, moreover, it was only with great reluctance that Madison's predecessors abandoned their desire and effort to reestablish the outlook and the policies of Shaftesbury and Steuart in the councils of the British Government. And even the determined rebel minority who conceived, sustained, and finally realized the idea of independence shared the same basic image of America as a mercantilist empire. Through its defeat in Britain, mercantilism was reborn in America.

The Age of Mercantilism

1740–1828

Private Vices, by the dextrous Management of a skillful Politician, may be turned into Public Benefits.

Bernard Mandeville, 1714

Mercantilism thus meant primarily that, under the pressure of new intellectual enlightenment in various spheres, people were, for the first time, directing their deliberate attention to aims which they had long cherished unreflectingly.

August Heckscher, 1935

CHAPTER ONE

The Triumph of the Rising Order

Shall we whine and cry for relief, when we have already tried it in vain?
George Washington, 1774

We do not want to be independent, we want no revolution.
Joseph Hewes, 1775

We have it in our power to begin the world over again.
Thomas Paine, 1776

We must rebel some time or other, and we had better rebel now than at any time to come; if we put off for ten or twenty years, and let them go on as they have begun, they will get a strong party among us, and plague us a great deal more than they can now.
Joseph Hawley to Samuel Adams, 1776

Though it might have seemed far-fetched in the 1670s, Shaftesbury's strategy to subvert Spain's American empire by capturing its trade (and bullion) had proved its validity within two generations. His similar expectation that the commercial colonies would develop closer economic and social ties to England was also being verified. South Carolina and its southern neighbors were redirecting the Indian and Spanish trade down the Ashley and Cooper rivers toward the wharves of Charleston; Pennsylvanians and New Englanders were carrying Spanish pieces of eight to London in payment for manufactures; and British ships of the home marine were making regular trading voyages along the coast of South America.

Working within the framework of attitudes and policies established during the Restoration, the American colonies and England had constructed a complementary empire. Far more relaxed in tone and routine than it appeared to many later observers—and certainly not a tightly ruled imperialism—this mercantilism had produced a surprisingly close approximation to the idea, and even the ideal, of a commonwealth. Though he committed himself to independence sooner than most colonists, Samuel Adams began with nothing more than a determination to reform the affairs of Massachusetts. And even when he broadened his attack to include England's colonial policy, his initial objective was no more than to reestablish the old mercantilist system with the kind of liberal rule that Massachusetts had enjoyed under Governor Thomas Pownall.

Pownall's outlook, like that of Benjamin Franklin, his friend and fellow speculator in Ohio lands, was that of the nabob. Such rising upper-class colonials assumed they would ultimately inherit the empire; in the meantime they sought to further their economic and social welfare by making alliances with various groups in English society and in the British government. Though they did not verbalize it as explicitly or as formally, and lacked the power to act on it overtly, the great majority of colonists shared the basic assumptions of the nabob and aspired to emulate him. Like their leaders, most of them were hesitant or indifferent toward independence until the morning of the break with England. And many of them never bothered to fight after the war began. As for Franklin and his fellow nabobs, it was only with great reluctance that they joined Adams and his revolutionary allies in Virginia in making a bid for an independent empire.

THE SOUTH AND THE RISE OF AN AMERICAN GENTRY

Further developed than any of its neighbors, Virginia was the symbol and the leader of the colonies south of Pennsylvania. Negro slavery was the mainspring of that society. Slaves handled the great crops of tobacco, rice, and indigo that provided the security for the wealthy indebtedness of the region, and their masters contributed leadership in social, political, and economic affairs. As a practice and as an institution, Negro slavery in the American colonies developed within the logic and politics of English mercantilism. Slavery was the gravest weakness of that system: the frayed and raveled end of the strand of mercantile economic theory which stressed the importance of a large, cheap, and controlled labor force that could produce a staple surplus for export. And in this instance, theory was eminently practical as well as persuasive. African chiefs proved only too ready to supply such human exports. They had been doing it for centuries. Scrambling for empire along every great circle route on the globe, English traders entered the dirty business in an organized fashion when Charles II chartered the Royal African Company in 1672. After that monopoly was broken in 1697 (as laissez faire put its foot in the English door), the industry became even more extensive and degraded as other Englishmen joined colonists from Salem and Rhode Island to parlay the normally narrow margin of profit into a lucrative and lamentable commerce.

Most 17th-century Englishmen were harsh and offhand about slavery. The vigorous nationalism and anti-foreignism of mercantilism reinforced the existing discrimination against the Negro because of his different color, religion, and culture. Yet at no time did the planters of Virginia or other southern colonies manage to convince themselves that slavery was beyond morality. For that matter, southerners were periodically assailed by questions about its economic advantages. Many thought that the cost of slaves (the "Profits arising thereon [are] so very great") explained the persistently unfavorable balance of trade, and hence indebtedness, of the region. Others questioned whether slavery was efficient, adding that the southern economy needed more men with diversified skills, industry, and initiative.

Such economic doubts were reinforced by the sense of social and corporate responsibility which was strong in the secular philosophy consciously modeled on that of the English gentry, and in the religious doctrines of the established Anglican church. George Washington and other planters of the late colonial era anticipated the demise of slavery long before the inspiring rhetoric of the Declaration of Independence reminded the colonists of their responsibilities as free Englishmen. As a leader who saw the need to diversify the economy of his region, Washington combined both an economic and a moral argument in his candid critique of slavery.

Yet many influences converged to sustain the dreadful institution. Though not as straightforward as Patrick Henry, many planters shared his preference for having someone else do the hard work;

he spoke bluntly about "the general inconvenience of living without them." Others had frenzied imaginations which transformed legitimate (and intelligent) concern about the difficulties incident to emancipation into scenes of orgiastic violence, biological decay, and wholesale poverty. Yet—during the colonial era, at any rate—it was the economic arguments that seem to have been the most powerful.

Washington's program for developing a diversified agriculture and local industry made a great deal of sense, but the majority of the planters could not translate it into reality. Their debts to London middle-men, which Thomas Jefferson later spoke of as being inherited for generations, increased as the value of their tobacco declined. These economic scissors snipped away their freedom of maneuver. As even Washington admitted (and he was an exceptionally efficient and wealthy planter), "goods [were] for the most exceedingly dear bought." Probably most planters tried to raise more of their own food, and some experimented with a few acres planted for the West Indies market, but the majority continued to abuse their land with the same old commodity crops.

As tobacco declined in value on the European market, the planters sought a solution within the traditional framework of mercantilism. They proposed to limit production and improve quality. With virgin land lying open to the west, however, not many of them could command the discipline to restrict their output. But they did combine their efforts to raise more of the staple with the idea of quality controls and inspections, and with the traditional mercantilist system of centralized depots. Together with the steady exhaustion of the soil, this campaign to expand production reinforced the existing drive to the west for more land. When they did not simply elbow them out and onward, the planters and speculators leapfrogged over the yeomen and frontiersmen, and thus southerners of different classes came into common conflict with British regulations limiting expansion beyond the mountains.

Such an emphasis on expanding production steadily strengthened the conclusion drawn from earlier experience that gang labor provided the only way to make a profit on staple crops. Though it was possible to raise tobacco, and later cotton, on smaller units of cultivation, this profitableness of gang labor became one of the chief arguments—or excuses—for maintaining the slave system. It should not be imagined, however, that the planters were unique in defending slavery. Southern yeomen aspired to own their own slaves (many realized the ambition), and white workers in such cities as Charleston organized against free Negro labor (as in the shipbuilding yards) at an early date.

In later years, after coming under militant attack from the critics of slavery, southerners often replied by emphasizing the achievements of their culture. Though not justifying Negro slavery in America and often exaggerated, the argument had a certain validity. For the best of the south was exceptionally good; it was mature, responsible, respectful of learning, civilized, and urbane. Moral without being priggish, the planter aristocracy probably comprehended the verity of original sin at least as well as most of the New England theocracy. And though their reforms may have been weakened by an overly developed propensity to compromise, such men did avoid the arrogance of self-righteous crusading. Long before the tradition of the Cavalier was somewhat belatedly imported after 1660, southerners had begun to advance their own version of the life of the English gentry, and it evolved rapidly through the 18th century.

Like many other southern mansions, that of William Byrd at Westover, Virginia, was less elegant but nevertheless comparable to those of many English estates. Commanding a fine vista of the James River, its bold and imposing structure featured a mahogany stairway and housed a magnificent library of 4,000 volumes. And in the ports, such as Annapolis to the north, great homes like the Hammon-Harwood house designed by William Buckland typified a similar pattern of living. Though this southern architecture might be described rather as a solidly appropriate style rendered in good taste than as great art, it was justly admired.

St. Michael's church in Charleston was likewise an impressive symbol of the gentry's culture. Presumably because as a group they were far less prone than some other colonials to discuss every issue in a theological vocabulary, because they separated church and state by law, and because Thomas Jefferson came to be considered the symbol of the entire society, it has often been assumed that the southern aristocrats were Deists in all but name or men for whom sitting in church was one of the chores of their class. But James Madison and many others among the southern gentry were deeply, although not ostentatiously, religious in the Anglican tradition of the corporate church. While vigorously opposed to bishops running the state, and increasingly tolerant of dissent, they retained a strong sense of inclusive Christian social morality. Washington's Farewell Address, for example, emphasized that such an ethic was essential to sustaining the ideal and the practice of the general welfare.

Samuel Matthews of Virginia was typical of the many planters whose names do not get into every history book, but who nevertheless exhibited a strong sense of social responsibility. He managed his own affairs with care and success, took an active part in local government, and tried to anticipate and prepare for the development of the region. Although they may have sent their sons to England for an education, men such as Byrd and William Fitzhugh also worked to establish colonial colleges and lower schools. In all these respects, they labored to improve life in the present as well as to develop a tradition and found a family dynasty with its own coat-of-arms. And as for the tradition, they proved so successful that some back-country southerners ultimately rebelled against those who ignored or abused it.

This southern aristocracy developed several contrasting though complementary styles of life. At one extreme, some of its merchants and professional men represented an almost exclusively urban and commercial influence. Joseph Hewes and James Iredel of North Carolina typified that pattern. Further south, the Charleston merchants and factors like Henry Laurens revealed an even greater similarity to their British counterparts. Indeed, many of them came to feel that they had so much in common with their trans-Atlantic prototypes that they were extremely disinclined to break the connection. Christopher Gadsden in Charleston was a notable exception, becoming a vigorous advocate of independence.

On the other hand, many planters were practically pure agrarians. Similar in their outlook to some of the patroons along the Hudson in upper New York, these men stayed close to the land in thought as well as in routine. This mode of life and its associated view of the world ultimately prompted them to take up and adapt the basically feudal philosophy of the French physiocrats. Though placing great emphasis on individual freedom and local self-government, they dominated the economic, political, and social life of their counties and regions in an aristocratic style that was often benevolent and almost always effective. In later years, the leaders of this group in the south were Virginians like John Taylor of Caroline and John Randolph of Roanoke; in the north, New York's George Clinton was the outstanding figure.

Despite the difficulties in doing so, a significant number of planters were by 1740 developing still another pattern of life which resembled that of the English gentry. Whether in Maryland, Virginia, or other southern colonies, this group maintained city houses, were governed as to their clothes and coaches, silver and lace, manners and anecdotes by the latest London fashions, and similarly extended their other interests and tastes. Charleston was perhaps the exemplar of this more cosmopolitan existence; yet as the center of government and society as well as of trade fairs, and boasting the College of William and Mary founded in 1693, Williamsburg was also a focus of the urban-commercial-agrarian life; and Annapolis, in those days a far more important port than Baltimore or Norfolk, developed along similar lines.

Like its English predecessor, this colonial gentry also diversified its economic activities. Virginia began offering bounties on cotton (and on linen cloth) in 1730, and within a few years some entrepreneurs were beginning to experiment with wheat and other crops as a supplement to their staples of tobacco, rice, and indigo. Local manufacturing emerged alongside this extended agriculture. Robert Carter invested in a Baltimore ironworks, Colonel Scarburgh produced shoes and malt, and George Washington loomed woolens as an integral part of his plantation enterprises as well as drawing up plans for the future of Virginia's iron industry. Such men as Thomas Johnson of Maryland and Robert Beverley of Virginia thought along the same lines and brought forward specific ideas, as with Johnson a plan for a Potomac Canal and Beverley a program for a Virginia mercantilism. Washington rapidly assumed the leadership of this group. It was by no means all talk; by 1775 Maryland and Virginia had 82 blast furnaces producing iron.

Men such as Washington made it evident that the image of the gentry and the ideal of a diversified and balanced society that was associated with it was steadily gaining strength and being translated into reality during the 18th century. In another way, the founding of Georgia in 1732 revealed the persistence of the mercantilism that Shaftesbury had done so much to consolidate almost three generations earlier. Beginning with the idea of a planned economy, Georgia's leaders emphasized the importance of corporate development. Undertaken for "the more direct and better convenience of the inhabitants," the colony's road-and-ferry legislation specified that the citizens recognize their responsibility to work on such projects. And commodity-inspection laws were instituted on the ground that it was "in the interest of the colony that all lumber exported be honestly and faithfully made." After slavery was legalized in 1750, the Georgia aristocracy moved even more rapidly toward their own version of the attitudes and policies which had been maturing in the older colonies.

Virginia and South Carolina had similar work laws underwriting labor on roads, canals, and public buildings. South Carolina's legislation of 1749 for "regulating the price and assize of bread" was an avowed manifestation of the corporate responsibility to control "covetous and evil-disposed persons" who acted only "for their own gain and lucre" and thus "deceived and depressed . . . especially the poorer sort of people." Virginia's law "to prevent the exportation of bad and trash tobacco" emerged from the mercantilist's basic conception of political economy; such conduct contributed directly "to the great decay of trade" and thereby weakened the entire colony. And Georgia's laws on price-fixing and its limitation on the rate of interest were likewise designed "to encourage trade."

Intellectual and policy responses to this increasing colonial maturity took two principal forms. Those who wholeheartedly accepted the framework of the British Empire maintained the outlook of the nabob who ruled at home through a combination of his local wealth and his connections in the Metropolis. Men of that view exhibited no particular impatience for the independence that they assumed would come in the future. Largely because of opponents in the colonies who stood ready to challenge his supremacy once independence arrived, the nabob was against a break with the mother country under all but the most extreme circumstances. As a classic figure of this group, Laurens of South Carolina once asserted that he "felt much more pain" over independence when it finally arrived than over the death of a son. This attitude reflected the normal political evolution of the upper class in a colonial system and occurred in India and other British possessions as well as in America. Most southern planters, as well as the majority of colonial leaders in

Pennsylvania and New York, held and acted upon this conception of the world.

On the other hand, some southern mercantilists like Gadsden and Washington infused the attitude and role of the nabob with a vigorous self-consciousness that moved rapidly toward independence. Ultimately they were joined by planters like George Mason of Virginia and Willie Jones of North Carolina who entertained a more narrowly agrarian view of the world. The age, intelligence, and expanded interests of these native mercantilists all help to explain the difference in their outlook. It was not only that many of them were young, but also that they came to maturity when their society and their class had established a tradition and a style of their own. Richard Henry Lee, for example, was typical of a younger generation impatient for leadership in a vigorous society.

With the decline of the tobacco market, such men intensified and extended their interest in western lands and invested in nonagricultural enterprises. And for similar reasons, they also manifested an increasing desire to enter the general world market with their surpluses. Acutely aware of the possibilities of an undeveloped continent, they recognized the problems to be surmounted and faced up to them persistently and astutely. Both Johnson and Washington concluded that the diversified economic development of the Potomac waterway to the west would help to weaken the institution of slavery as well as to sustain the position and the power of the coastal gentry as the colonies expanded inland. As that argument implies, they had a vision of an American empire from an early date.

NEW YORK AND PENNSYLVANIA: FINISHING SCHOOLS FOR THE AMERICAN NABOB

In contrast, no similar group of leaders in the middle colonies developed and committed itself to this emerging American mercantilism until just before the Declaration of Independence in 1776. Even then they were exceedingly reluctant revolutionaries. Many key figures in Pennsylvania and New York fought hard for a compromise with England. To many of them, reconciliation must have seemed a Jacob's ladder to safety from a rising sea of relentless competitors and lashing critics. Thus it is not surprising that the expansionists among them thought primarily in terms of mixed English and colonial companies, nor that a significant number of these nabobs ultimately left America to become important leaders in England and other parts of the empire. From their inception, these middle colonies were the home and hearth of the loyal nabob.

Established by the Dutch as a fur-trading depot in the 1620s, New York remained a comparatively small colony for many years. Extensive commitments in men, money, and interest were not forthcoming; both the government and the Dutch West India Company were initially more interested in an empire in Asia, Africa, and Brazil. Moving belatedly to salvage some of its investment by capturing more English and French trade in America, the Dutch government in 1638 made New York a free port in all but name. The strategy worked brilliantly but not immediately and not for the Dutch. Always a center of the fur trade, New York began to expand and diversify its commerce. Tenant farmers could accurately complain that many fields "lie fallow and waste," but agricultural surpluses and shipping services provided enough capital to launch the city's booming economic growth. In a short time the port attracted, and produced, an increasing population of sailors, merchants, and laborers. They were a wild ethnic mixture with a speculative outlook on life and a sometimes vulgar and unfocused cosmopolitanism that further weakened the colony's loyalty to the Dutch.

Had the French acted vigorously, pushing down the river valleys from Canada, the history of the world might have become a different story. But however poor an English king he became as James II, the Duke of York performed magnificently in seizing New York in 1664. Providing a sorry preview of what was in store for his subjects at home, the Duke then mismanaged the job of ruling his conquest. He was no match either for the entrenched landed aristocracy, the rising merchant interest, or the restive and aggressive lower class. Giving up in frustration and failure, he sold off great chunks of the original grant and went home to fail again.

Having defeated their second "mother country," the New York patroons proceeded to consolidate their local control. As they did so, they created an integrated gentry typical of the age of mercantilism. Thus, as they made economic investments in commerce and shipping, they married into the rising elite of merchants and lawyers in New York. Sitting astride one of the most extensive and rapidly expanding trade centers in the colonies, this New York gentry became highly prone to take its well-being for granted. It was not that they were lazy or lacked initiative; it was simply that their fortunes seemed to billow as naturally as the sails of their ships in a fresh trade wind. Handling everything from luxury furs to beeswax, dried venison, and porkers on the run, their exports of agricultural commodities and semi-finished raw materials provided the basis of a commerce with Europe and the West Indies that dramatized the general development of the colonies. And by the 1740s some of them had begun to invest in banking and manufacturing while others turned their attention to speculative opportunities in the west.

Since they at least acknowledged the same tradition of the corporate Anglican religion that guided many southerners, it might be assumed that the New York gentry evolved a similar conception of social responsibility. This was not the case. Under the impact of disorganized and shifting outside authority, extensive and mixed immigration, and almost unchallenged local power, the New Yorkers created a caricature of the gentry. Politics became a treacherous and generally pointless scramble within the aristocracy. James De Lancey commanded one faction dedicated to keeping the upstart lawyers and merchants in their place. He was opposed by William Livingston who attempted to rally support among the smaller merchants and even the laboring class. The primary result of his strategy was to create a growing sense of solidarity and organization among his ultimate opponents; led by such popular figures as Isaac Sears and Alexander McDougall. As for the upstate yeomen and tenant farmers, they were generally ignored by both factions and only slowly began to organize their own philosophical and practical opposition.

Though De Lancey played an important part in founding King's College, and a few others indicated some awareness of the responsibilities of the gentry, most New York aristocrats continued to devote most of their energies to trade and the gay life. De Lancey's son was something of an extreme, but nevertheless typical, example. Principally concerned with "cock-fighting, horseracing, and women," he once led such a carousing invasion of Philadelphia as to frighten the fathers of that city—as well as its mothers (and no doubt even some of its daughters). There was a more favorable side to such revelry, however, because, in conjunction with the great (albeit unnerving) tradition of the sailor on shore leave, it helped New York to establish a pattern of entertainment that was broader in every sense of the word than any to be found in the other colonial cities.

As might be expected in such a commercial center, New York also supported the evolution of the daily newspaper and the tradition of a free (if slandering and scandalous) press. Beyond that, the city was culturally backward. Cadwallader Coldein's *History of the Five Nations,* a review of the Indians and the wars incident to taking their land, was the only book produced in the colony that was worthy of serious attention. And while such painters as Lawrence Kilburn and John Wollaston provided many portraits for the elite, their subjects were seemingly averse even to the kind of tension that helps create a great graphic image. Yet, in a way that was revealing, the focus in most of their likenesses was the wide expanse of shimmering light ricocheting off the satin waistcoats that covered the full bellies; in this sense, at any rate, the artist did transmit a hint of the deeper reality, for many members of the New York gentry opposed independence even after the fighting began.

Though many of them reacted similarly, the Pennsylvania leaders included men of a vastly different style with a far broader image of the good life. For despite the fact that Benjamin Franklin's amatory abilities and adventures might indicate the opposite, William Penn founded Pennsylvania as what he always referred to as "The Holy Experiment." Under more appropriate circumstances, Penn might have been one of the great benevolent despots. Governing in that style, and guided by his Quaker faith in the goodness of men and his sophisticated mercantilism, he made the very best of the geographical and human resources at his disposal.

Established between 1680 and 1682, Pennsylvania rapidly overtook older colonies and by 1740 was challenging them for political and economic leadership. England's post-Restoration economic boom helped the colony get off to a quick start, and within two years Philadelphia boasted more than 350 dwellings. Political and religious controversies in England and on the Continent helped to maintain a steady flow of immigrants, and the early settlers encouraged others to share the bonanza. Penn exploited these favorable circumstances through judicious mercantile policies and astute propaganda. As a pioneering master of what later public-relations experts were to call the "soft sell," his advertising campaigns in Europe combined a promise of wealth and grandeur with a candid and psychologically clever warning that the lazy and untalented might better stay where they were. Western Europeans responded eagerly. Encouraged by leaders of their own such as Francis Daniel Pastorius, Germans (and some Dutch) arrived with an outlook sympathetic to the established Quaker religion. Unusually content with their own company and capable of building thriving communities by their own skill in carpentry, farming, weaving, wood-working, pottery, and shoe-making, these men and women were willing to accept the political and social leadership of the Quaker aristocracy on the eastern coast. This involved no great sacrifice, for they had their own society and culture, and those who became particularly successful managed to move quietly into the inner councils of government.

These experiences were so generally satisfying, and accounts of them so persuasive, that in Europe some Germans worried lest their sons abandon promising futures at home for the opportunities in America. Perhaps nothing is as revealing of the evolution of life in the colonies as a sharp letter of complaint written by a German family to a son in England. Trying to shame him into abandoning a plan to emigrate to Philadelphia, a brother disparaged the ambition. "From appearances," he wrote snidely, "you wish perhaps to become an English nabob." Apparently attracted by just that prospect, the errant brother sailed for Pennsylvania.

Other immigrants from Scotland and Ireland were less adaptable; they were more driven by religion, more harried by memories of earlier troubles, and less sophisticated in their image of success in America. Finding the seacoast and its immediate hinterland settled, they tramped on through to the frontier, some of them spilling down across the Appalachians into the southern uplands on the way. Hardworking as they were, many had reserves of energy which they turned toward politics and expansion. Far more aggressive than the Germans (from whom, ironically, they got their deadly long rifles), these predominantly Presbyterian settlers mixed religion and economic grievances into a back-country brew that finally fermented into overt opposition to Quaker rule.

Anything but radicals, they wanted little more than a greater share in the existing government. More representation was their general cry, and their specific complaints converged on taxes and Indians. Opposing some excises (such as those on the liquor they made), they concentrated on getting more help against the Indians who checked their freebooting advance into the Ohio valley. And as they began to produce surpluses from the rich land, they added the argument that farm-to-market roads and canals would serve to speed up the war against the red men.

Many of the shopkeepers and workers in Philadelphia, as well as the seaboard gentry, resisted such demands for economic and political reasons. Busily engaged in enjoying and developing existing opportunities, or organizing to win a greater share of them, they had little inclination to weaken their own position. But one group of Quaker leaders opposed aggressive western expansion (and the resulting violence against the Indians) for reasons of religious principle. One can quarrel with their assumptions but not with their logic or motivation. Their hospitals, secondary and higher schools, and philanthropic projects revealed a commitment to the spirit of *noblesse oblige* unsurpassed in America. When finally confronted with the ultimate choice of abandoning their central premise of non-violence or giving up political power, they chose the latter. Easy as it is to call such men impractical, and as conveniently persuasive as the label may be after the Indians are no longer a problem, a little reflection suggests that those Quakers bequeathed America one of its great moments of philosophic insight and moral courage. For the Indians were, after all, human beings, and they did have a society which the colonists and their sons destroyed.

Had the expansionists and such of their leaders as Benjamin Franklin and Robert Morris tried the Quaker program of gradual, equitable, and peaceful dealings with the Indians, they and the latterday critics of the Quakers would seem more persuasive. A recent assertion that Americans enjoyed free security as well as free land throughout most of their history, and that these factors explain the nation's development is hardly half the story. What is missing is the pattern of total war developed and put into operation against the Indians and then transferred to later opponents. Initiated by the colonists in a mood of self-righteous arrogance out of gluttony for land they often never even cleared, let alone cultivated, such total war extracted a terrible physical and moral price for security. It also planted in the American mind an assumption of omnipotence that was to prove costly. The Quakers stood out against this policy and ethic at a time and in a way that does credit to their intelligence, their values, and their courage.

Poor Richard's aphorisms were faint echoes of that morality. For this very reason, no doubt, they appealed to many men who were rising to the top in Pennsylvania's bubbling pot of opportunity and success. But as in other colonies, the issue in political economy was not should there be any controls, but rather what kind. Pennsylvania regulated various phases of the market system, established government loan offices and land banks, and also encouraged local wage and price-controls affecting butchers, innkeepers, bakers, and other concentrated or monopoly trades. A law of 1725 revealed the spirit that was so prevalent in the southern colonies; it was passed to prevent the export of inferior flour which would threaten "the credit of our trade and the benefits thence arising."

Combining (and controlling) the colony's natural resources and its ambitious, skilled labor force, Pennsylvania's seaboard gentry developed a highly diversified economy based on surplus food production (including processed flour), livestock breeding, rough manufacturing, and all phases of domestic and international trade. Guided by a generally mercantilist outlook, Philadelphia's leaders gained rapidly on their rivals in Boston and New York. This intracolonial competition played an important role in ultimately determining attitudes toward British policy after 1763. As the old leader falling behind, Boston proved to be the most militant and aggressive opponent of the Crown's decision to tighten up the empire. In the meantime, Pennsylvania's rapid progress provided context and springboard for Benjamin Franklin's fabulous career.

Though in some respects he appeared to be an advocate of laissez faire, Franklin was actually a nabob who wanted free trade in the same sense that the English gentry demanded greater access to the opportunities of the empire. A man who came so close to living by the what-is-is-right credo, that on major issues he broke the rule but once, Franklin accepted the empire and set out to sustain, expand, and exploit its opportunities. He succeeded. His twenty-five years as a printer, culminating in his becoming publisher of *The Pennsylvania Gazette* and *Poor Richard's Almanac*, established his fortune. Along the way he had time to learn four languages, found the Philadelphia Library, the American Philosophical Society, and an academy, and organize the Junto, a private intellectual club in which many rising leaders developed their economic and political ideas. He retired from active business at an age when most men were just reaching for the top and turned to sophisticated scientific tinkering, empire politics, and majestic schemes of land speculation.

Franklin's famous experiments with electricity, as well as his more prosaic modifications of existing ideas and gadgets, were a tribute to his learning and to his speculative, almost childlike curiosity. There is nothing inherently wrong with such an attitude, but it should not be confused with that of science. To a scientist the design of the experiment is the essence of the discipline, and by this criterion Franklin was only a lucky, albeit clever, amateur.

This once-in-an-epoch combination of the dedicated amateur's *expertise* with the casual flair and style of the dilettante is what proved so irresistible. The frontiersman needing a better fireplace made Franklin into the same kind of hero as did the member of a European salon who was searching for proof that the scientist was a good fellow like himself. But praiseworthy though it is, an interest in the results of science is vastly different from an understanding of the method and a willingness to accept its discipline. Because of his role in blurring this vital distinction, it may very well be that America's later propensity to think that playing with nature, or technological facility, is the same thing as the scientific spirit goes back to Franklin.

In any event, it is difficult to think of Franklin as a scientist if only because he invested so much time and intelligence in land speculation. Along with his British allies, one of his regular associates in those enterprises was Thomas Wharton, whose name, appropriately enough, now graces a school of business at the University of Pennsylvania which originated as Franklin Academy. As the leader of such ventures, Franklin carried on an intricate and delicate—albeit militant—struggle for control of the Ohio frontier and hence the continent.

The essence of Franklin's outlook was the British mercantilism he borrowed from Sir William Petty. As a man who thought England's radical John Wilkes an "outlaw," and who maintained for many years that George III was "the best king any nation was ever blessed with," Franklin was in no sense a revolutionary. Working within the existing framework and in close association with English leaders, he hoped to outflank domestic rivals like the Virginians led by George Washington and place Pennsylvania in the direct line of succession as the center of a mammoth British Empire. In his view, sustained expansion would keep the people busy farming and in that way turn them from domestic manufacturing while creating a limitless market for British manufactures. It would also "continuously draw off" the unemployed in eastern cities and thus decrease the chances of urban unrest.

Franklin abandoned this truly magnificent strategy very late and with great reluctance. Only his broad mercantilist vision and his opportunism kept him from becoming a Loyalist along with so many other men in Pennsylvania, New York, and New England who had also developed their careers and ideas within the assumptions of the nabob. And as Franklin later admitted, the strength of those precepts made it difficult, even for a man with his perception of the main chance, to adapt his political economy to the circumstances of independence. This insight offers an important clue to the reason why the leaders of the revolution were younger men, or at any rate men with a clearer conception of a self-defined corporate society.

NEW ENGLAND AND THE IDEOLOGY OF CALVIN'S CORPORATE SOCIETY

Though they had insisted on their separateness and self-contained independence from the summer they stepped ashore on the wrong piece of real estate and managed to survive only with the help of the Indians, many New Englanders were just as slow as Franklin to accept the idea of a final break with England. For men who claimed to be the Children of God, most of them were strangely slow afoot when it came to striking out on their own. They seemed to prefer the garden of empire that the British Board of Trade had created and that the Royal Navy walled off from misguided interlopers.

Just such a vision of a City on the Hill had guided the founders of New England during their earlier efforts to purify the corporate society of England's late Tudors and early Stuarts. Only after failing in the effort did they decide that America was "the place where the Lord will create a new Heaven and a new Earth." Those early leaders understood and honored Calvin's thought with its strong emphasis on the integration of economic and other affairs in a corporate whole. Like the Virginians who were more religious than is sometimes realized, the New England Puritans were more concerned with problems of political economy than their theological polemics might indicate. For that matter, many of them came to America for immediate and personal economic reasons as well as to attain long-range ideological objectives.

Though carried to the near edge of fanaticism by their theology, such men nevertheless were Englishmen who had matured during the pre-Revolutionary consolidation of mercantilism. While still in England, they argued with considerable justice that their triumph would not upset the political economy of mercantilism but would only organize and administer it with greater rigor and success. As with Calvin, they distinguished aristocracy, monarchy, and democracy as the three forms of government and concluded in agreement with him that a mixture of aristocracy and democracy offered the best compromise.

John Winthrop's sense of the general welfare was strong and included the realization that the relationship between prices and wages had to be taken into account when working out a general system of economic regulation. John Cotton had a similar concern for the common good and the economic policies calculated to promote it, and Cotton Mather advanced a theory of taxation based on the principle of a progressive rate and the assumption that the receipts would be used for public benefits. Another New Englander sounded like Shaftesbury and other English mercantilists of the 17th century: "Whilst men are all for their private profit, the public good is neglected and languisheth." As his contribution to this discussion, Increase Mather emphasized the fact that social welfare is not the automatic product of profits. "Sometimes," he noted, "one man by seeking to advance himself has brought great misery on whole nations." And the persistence of this outlook was revealed a century later. "*Trade* or *Commerce*," concluded an essay on the good republic, "is an Engine of State, to draw men into business, for the advancing and enobling of the Rich, for the support of the Poor, for the strengthening and fortifying of the State."

Considered in this context, the characterization of Calvinism and Puritanism as philosophies based on making fine distinctions takes on a deeper significance. For as can be seen, there were two crucial decisions constantly demanding to be made. First, it had to be determined whether critics were attacking the idea and ideal of such a corporate community or merely proposing different means for building and sustaining it. Second, it was vital to decide when "enobling the Rich" began to subvert "the support of the Poor." Or, to illustrate the problem in a way which calls attention to the Puritan's less than puritanical outlook on life, consider the issue of liquor. Winthrop and Mather agreed that the "wine is from God, but the Drunkard is from the Devil." The difficulty was in deciding how to hinder the Devil without denying God.

Rather than to view New Englanders as either all ideology or all practicality, it seems more accurate to describe them as men living in terrible and unremitting tension between, on the one hand, the confidence that their ideal was correct and, on the other, the anxiety generated by a fear of destroying the ideal by enforcing it too rigorously or having it undone by outsiders. John Cotton came to face this dilemma as a result of his understanding and friendship with Anne Hutchinson. Winthrop had the same problems in his relationship with Roger Williams. Both men finally came down on the side of enforcing loyalty to the ideal. But they did so with a rending reluctance which, given their outlook and experience as committed men who had led the colony through extreme difficulties, is more a tribute to their consciousness of the dilemma than it is proof of their blind fanaticism.

The point is not that Williams and Anne Hutchinson were wrong. The issue is to get beyond the stereotype of the Puritan. However one chooses between the contestants, it should be apparent that the Puritans were a great deal more than bluenoses dedicated to spoiling everyone's good time. What they wanted was a good time with an equal emphasis on the good rather than a complete stress on the time. To say that they sought a chimera is to give up the intellectual and moral struggle: they asked the right questions and struggled for the right answers.

Nevertheless, like the little girl with a curl in the middle of her forehead, these early Puritans had a kink in their ideology; when they went wrong, they went very, very wrong. Devoted to the ideal of a corporate community guided by a strong moral sense, they developed a great talent for misinterpreting any opposition. From the outset, for example, they were prone to view the Indians as agents of the Devil waiting to test their convictions—even though their theology implied very strongly that the red men were members of the

Invisible Church. But that definition externalized Evil, thus making it an object to be overpowered rather than an internal, human weakness to be contained until transformed (or, in the case of the Indians, to deal with them as co-equal Children of God).

This propensity to place Evil outside their system not only distorted the Puritans' own doctrine, it inclined them toward a solution which involved the extension of their system over others. Here was a subtle convergence of religious and secular ideas, for mercantilism also emphasized the necessity as well as the desirability of expansion in economic and political affairs. It externalized secular evil by arguing that domestic poverty could in the last analysis be overcome only by taking wealth away from others. Far from wanting no more than to be left alone, New Englanders developed a solution to their religious and secular difficulties which prompted vigorous action against an external cause.

Even so, and in the same way that they were at first ambivalent toward Williams and Anne Hutchinson, they were initially cautious in opposing the demand brought forward in the 1620s and 1630s for broader participation in political affairs. Raised by wealthy men as well as by the middle and lower classes, this attack on restricted government might easily have succeeded. But when the rulers hesitated, only a small number of the critics stepped forward and declared themselves free men. Convinced that such caution indicated a lack of conviction, the oligarchy swung shut the gate and slammed home the bolt. Not even the halfway covenant of 1662, by which the children of the converted were admitted to partial church membership, reopened it. For by that time the leaders had consolidated their position and altered the meaning of the old ideal.

Embarking upon a campaign of righteous persuasion which often became outright intimidation, and upon a bloody trail of persecution, the church fathers punished the courageous, exiled the bold, and terrified the timid. As early as the 1650s, an old man was doubled over in irons for 16 hours and then lashed 100 times with a tarred rope. Far from "enobling the Rich, and support[ing] the Poor," this horrible travesty on the ideal of a corporate community culminated some 20 years later in the witchcraft trials. It is of course true, and fortunate, that not many people were killed, but that is only half the ledger. None were saved. Unless, perhaps, it was Winthrop himself; there is a story about him which suggests that on his deathbed he saw his mistake. Asked to sign a warrant for the banishment of another heretic, he refused: "No, I have done too much of that work already."

During those same years, Winthrop and his successors consolidated their political position at home and within the empire. Winthrop's attitude is wonderfully revealed by an episode in which he had to borrow the royal ensign from a visiting ship so that the captain of the vessel could report in London that he had seen it flying over the colony. "Our allegiance binds us not to the laws of England," explained Winthrop, "any longer than while we live in England." While he agreed with those Englishmen who thought it desirable to exercise more authority over New England, Shaftesbury refused to panic over the colony's freedom. His assumption that the colonists would come to accept the basic principles of the empire was generally correct. As in other colonial regions, New Englanders fought more or less effectively for local authority while accepting the restrictions of the Navigation Acts and the compensating rewards of trade and naval protection.

In the century that followed Winthrop's militant resistance, Massachusetts and its neighbors evolved a dynamic and stratified society led by the merchant aristocracy. Poor farm land, boundary restrictions in their charters, and the opposition of the French, Indians, and New Yorkers (and each other) combined to make New Englanders into miners of the sea. There was some agricultural farming, as well as tree harvesting, and some city men owned or speculated in land; but the boulders of New England produced more poets, pamphleteers, and politicians than landed gentry. Fishing, shipbuilding, processing operations in flour, lumber, and alcohol, and colonial and international trading created the private fortunes, the training grounds of decision makers, and the economic weather for the entire region.

Slave trading was an integral part of the system. Some old-time merchants even called it "the first wheel of commerce." Though an exaggeration, the profits on "black ivory" purchased many a prayer book and Bible and spilled into collection plates from Providence to Boston. "We have seen," cried one critic of the miserable business, "molasses and alcohol, rum and slaves, gold and iron, in a perpetual and unholy round of commerce." As that comment suggests, New Englanders developed a complex economy; it was simple only in essentials. Codfish were graded and exported to the appropriate market, top fillets went for flour and tobacco down the coast, and the rest to the Mediterranean for salt and wine or to the Indies. Whale-chasing was successful in its own right and ultimately created a young candlemaking industry in Rhode Island. Naval stores and ships were supplied on order for England as well as for traders in Boston. At the center of the whole system were the merchants who handled everything from marine insurance to retail sales across the counter, and the rising body of colonial lawyers who knew the ropes of such an economy in both senses of the term.

Considerable insight into New England can be gained by comparing it, instead of contrasting it, with the Southern colonies. The obvious differences can be overemphasized to the point of serious misunderstanding, for there were many similarities. Both were pocket-deep in the business of slavery. Both upper classes were opposed by the lower orders within their regions. And both groups of leaders valued artistic achievement. Thomas Hancock's great house on Beacon Street in Boston, for example, was the merchant's version of Mount Vernon. New England's John Singleton Copley, furthermore, was *the* colonial painter. Gifted among colonial artists with exceptional visual perceptiveness, Copley had a unique ability to create the illusion that is more real than reality. His portrait of Samuel Adams, for example, calls up an image of Calvin that reveals the essential Adams far better than does any written study of the man.

These two societies held yet other elements in common. Though both groups found it ever more difficult to maintain the rate of growth within England's mercantilist empire that they had grown accustomed to, neither of them reacted by embracing independence en masse. Finally, and perhaps most important of all, each had an outlook rooted in a religious conception of the good society as a balanced, corporate system originally shared by their Puritan and Anglican ancestors in England. Perhaps it is not as surprising as it sometimes appears, therefore, that Massachusetts and Virginia ultimately struck the alliance which defeated Great Britain. Or, in another way, that one of the great philosophic and literary documents of American history is the correspondence between John Adams and Thomas Jefferson.

As also in Virginia, moreover, the New Englanders who took the lead in the revolutionary movement were men committed

THE TRIUMPH OF THE RISING ORDER 99

to that ideal of corporate responsibility and welfare. Jonathan Edwards, Samuel Adams, and John Adams played particularly important roles in sustaining the morality of a corporate society and the political economy of a balanced mercantilist state. All were products of the educational system founded by the early theocracy and its secular leaders. Learning was not only a part of religion in the basic sense (how else could the Bible be emphasized?), but it was considered vital for the training of preachers and for the general prosperity of the society. Fines for the neglect of education were levied in Massachusetts as early as 1642, and within five years teachers were given special consideration. Whether Harvard was founded for secular or religious objectives is not really the issue; both were part of the corporate entity in 1636.

But this early devotion to the corporate ideal was weakened as Massachusetts and the other colonies in New England extended their boundaries and their prosperity. Religion was not abandoned, but the wealthy "river gods" of the Connecticut Valley and the merchants of Salem, Boston, and Providence gradually redefined the meaning of the crucial term, the elect. From signifying membership in Calvin's corporate religious community it came to mean the upper class of that society. Furthermore, since the leaders dominated the political system, they began to equate the elect with the elected. By this casuistry they gave themselves a happy aura of liberalism in an age when laissez faire was beginning to challenge the corporate emphasis in mercantilism.

Jonathan Edwards assaulted their outlook with tremendous vigor and passion. Professor Perry Miller's description of the campaign is appropriately bare and explicit: Edwards "demonstrated to New Englanders of 1734 that they had ceased to believe what they professed, and that as a result the society was sick. He did not merely call them hypocrites, he proved that they were." In defining religious commitment as an affair of the heart, in considering that only God is worthy of worship, in placing high value on the intellect and on education, in valuing and respecting self-government, and in asserting that there were positive, pragmatic consequences of being sober, honest, responsible, and willing to work—in all these respects Edwards was a man who left his life as a monument to the positive side of Puritanism. Perhaps even more important, having ultimately recognized that the principal danger of his outlook lay in turning politics into a crusade, he did all that he could to moderate that unhappy tradition.

Intellectually, or theologically, Edwards reasserted and insisted that Calvinism was a religion for none but the strong at heart; it confronted men with a harsh world and offered them no quarter. Either they lived together as the children of God or they lived together as animals. "Frauds and trickishness in trade," Edwards thundered, supplemented the casual callousness "in taking any advantage that men can by any means obtain, to get the utmost possible of their neighbor for what they have to dispose of, and their neighbor needs." Worst of all, men "take advantage of their neighbor's poverty to extort unreasonably from him those things that he is under a necessity of procuring." Edwards explained this decay by man's natural tendency to confuse his interests with those of the Lord, a propensity encouraged and even justified by the false theology of such English preachers as John Taylor and Daniel Whitby. Edwards was not alone among New England theologians in recognizing that these ideas emerged with the parallel economic progress of the mother country and the colonies. Jonathan Mayhew of Boston saw the connection and candidly tailored the corporate cloth of Calvinism to fit the individualism of John Locke and Adam Smith. Not so Edwards. Accepting the challenge to Christianity that was implicit in this evolving laissez-faire business ethic, he attacked its theological (and hence intellectual) premises.

Men like Taylor and their American admirers had done a very simple and effective thing; they raised once again the obvious question about Calvinism. If man is truly predestined, how then can he be asked to be good? For the doctrine to be tenable, they concluded, it had to grant that men were open to persuasion by God's agents and therefore had a will and volition of their own. As they admitted, theirs was a religion in which the disarming plea of insufficiency was enough to excuse any but the most blatant failure to honor the way of the Lord.

Edwards replied with a torrent of moral scorn directed by the hell-fire logic of a deep and brilliant believer. Neither cause and effect nor the experience of free will can be made intelligible and coherent, he insisted, without an inclusive conception of the universe. Suffering has no significance and no dignity outside such a world, and tolerance based on indifference, or the lack of any positive position, is nothing but an evasion of the whole point about toleration. For like suffering, toleration is meaningful only when the person involved truly cares about the issue; otherwise it becomes an insufferable arrogance. Hence the essential corporate character of Christian society: what belongs together belongs together, whether or not it is benevolent or pleasant. And to assert against this the claim that man is adequate is to commit the most grievous sin of all. No man is an end in and of himself.

Yet the other side of this religious conflict and revival that came to be known as the Great Awakening also had significant consequences for America's developing self-consciousness. For one thing, Edwards's targets were powerful figures in New England society, and their vigorous faith in their own self-interest ultimately prompted many of them to favor a war for independence. Having reached that conclusion, they made important contributions to its success. In a quite different way, religious leaders like George Whitefield of England influenced a large number of colonists. Whitefield had none of Edwards's moral integrity or intellectual rigor. His sermons (a more apt term might be performances) combined the free-will argument that man could save himself with the idea that salvation meant a return to Calvin's original ideas and ideals. Such a have-your-cake-and-eat-it-too doctrine had a broad appeal. Scotch-Irish Presbyterians and Congregationalists could join with men of the Dutch Reformed Church in responding to this approach; it seems, for example, to have inspired Patrick Henry in Virginia as well as Sam Adams in Massachusetts.

"I was in my field at work," recalled one New Englander who was roused by this theology. "I dropped my tool that I had in my hand and ran home to my wife, telling her to make ready quickly to go and hear Mr. Whitefield preach at Middletown, then run to my pasture for my horse with all my might, fearing that I should be too late." Having worked up such a lather on himself as well as on his animal, the man was caked with a thin film of mud when he rode into the cloud of dust raised by the arrival of other men and women who had reacted in the same fashion.

Whitefield consciously spoke to "the rabble" as well as to "the great and the rich." In rhetoric and impact, if not in motivation, this was an equalitarian Christianity, and some men like John Wise went on to secularize it even more explicitly as a democratic political philosophy.

In that very limited sense, therefore, the Great Awakening was a colonial version of the Levellers' far more rigorous, and radical, religious enthusiasm. But only an insignificant number of Levellers developed in America, and to speak of colonial radicals in referring to such men as Isaac Sterns or Sam Adams is to distort the term beyond any serious or useful meaning.

COLONIAL MATURITY: THE ACHIEVEMENT OF BRITISH MERCANTALISM

But in a less rigorous way, as a movement based on the individual's discovery (or rediscovery) of self within a group, the Great Awakening did reinforce and extend the rising self-consciousness that the colonists were exhibiting in economic and political affairs. By the 1740s, when the English government gave way before the persistent entreaties and pressures of the South Sea Company and officially supported the penetration of Spain's empire in the New World, the American colonies were mature societies infused with an increasing confidence. When the war against Spain erupted into a general European conflict aimed at France, for example, Massachusetts planned, financed, and won a campaign against Louisburg. Costing more than £50,000, this assault captured the fort which commanded the trade routes and fishing grounds of the North Atlantic and controlled access to the St. Lawrence and the interior of the continent. When forced to give it up in 1748, Massachusetts gorged itself at the table of frustrated ambitions.

Similar clashes occurred during the next decade as Virginia, Pennsylvania, and New York disagreed with London's policies on the Indians and westward expansion. And with the outbreak of the French and Indian War in 1756, the conflict took on some of the characteristics of a struggle between two English-speaking empires. Following the mercantilist axiom that trading with the enemy was permissible if the opponent gave up more than he got, the colonials in Boston and Pennsylvania continued (and expanded) their commerce with the French West Indies. England was furious. Firing writs of assistance as one might use grapeshot, it moved in to enforce its restrictions. Hiring James Otis, a lawyer crony of Sam Adams, to defend them, the merchants accepted the challenge. As all good lawyers are wont to do, and doing it with "a torrent of impetuous eloquence," Otis transformed an earthy economic conflict into a noble constitutional issue.

British officials had warned of a rising militant self-consciousness fifteen years earlier. "Whether grown wanton by prosperity or whatever . . .," reported Lt. Gov. George Clark of New York in 1741, the colonists were by their acts reinforcing "a jealousy which for some years has obtained in England, that the plantations are not without thoughts of throwing off their Dependence on the Crown of England." As if to prove the point, William Bradford of Philadelphia started the *American Magazine* the same year, and by 1757 it was referring to the colonies "as a nation." Governor Lewis Morris of New Jersey agreed with Clark that some colonists were "grasping at the whole authority of Government."

Statistics help to explain this concern. Colonial population had mushroomed from 250,000 in 1700 to about 1,400,000 in 1750. And having produced an irrelevant one-seventieth of the world's pig and bar iron in 1700, the colonies were racing toward the one-seventh share they would turn out in 1775. By that time, their production was more than that of England and Wales combined. In a more general sense, the colonies had evolved an economic system. However compartmentalized it might be by the particularism of each colony, the resources, skills, and attitudes of the colonists had created a common and interdependent economy. They made shoes as well as iron, furniture as well as ships, and guns as well as rum. Their own lumber, livestock, and food could sustain a family or a settlement. And their trade with Europe, Africa, and the West Indies brought them other goods as well as capital. The colonies were so far along toward integration that one of the most common complaints concerned the lack of a compulsory system of weights and measures.

Such maturity was also revealed in the growing awareness of differences between classes and groups. This was not surprising: the colonies had been founded as sharply divided societies (consider the planter and the indentured servant), and a man with 1,000 acres or a ship to mortgage could always get wealthy faster than the man who had to stop and clear the trees from his family plot or save a stake while building ships for someone else.

A Plymouth tavern-keeper named Thomas Morton observed and protested such stratification less than a generation after the first settlements were established. William Davyes and John Pate led an unsuccessful rising in Maryland in 1676. Almost simultaneously,

John Culpeper headed a similar movement in South Carolina and was saved from severe punishment only when Shaftesbury intervened in his behalf. New York artisans and small merchants organized protest movements further north. And in Massachusetts the struggle over the land bank revealed similar internal divisions as well as a conflict between the bank and the English government, a consideration which encouraged the supporters of the bank to feel that domestic welfare might depend on winning independence.

Far from being radical uprisings, these rebellions revealed a persistent concern to restore and strengthen the ideal and the practice of a corporate society in which responsibilities and benefits are shared. Led by Nathaniel Bacon in Virginia during 1676, the first major colonial uprising defined its objectives in exactly those terms. While the rebels complained with particular bitterness about the lack of support against the Indians, their list of grievances is anything but a call for laissez faire and most certainly not a program of Levellers. Rather did they damn the governor for "specious pretences of public works," for failing to initiate measures for "fortification, towns, or trade" or for "liberal arts, or sciences," for abusing the system of justice, and for violating the Crown's rights by making a *personal* monopoly of the beaver trade. Such fidelity to the accepted code of a corporate mercantilist state gave them every right to assert that "we cannot in our hearts find one single spot of rebellion or treason."

Just a century later, the Regulator movements of the North and South Carolina backcountry manifested a similar outlook. Pointing out that men stole their horses and then sold them to the Dutch and the French, they demanded protection for their property and punishment for those who violated the regulations of the empire. They also petitioned for an equitable share in the government from which they requested such public benefits as schools, better poor laws, price-control and quality-inspection laws, and bounties for agriculture. Their attack on church leaders is particularly revealing, for they requested a vigorous reassertion of the corporate ideals and a wholesale distribution of Bibles. A program more typical of Anglican mercantilism would be difficult to imagine, and it is not surprising that such men supported the mother country when the revolution finally began.

That phrase, "the revolution," is in many respects a misnomer for there was no single decision to go to war. There were 13 different governments in America. Founded as separate colonies, developing different though complementary interests, and having waged their respective battles against Royal governors and the mother country, these governments were reluctant to give up any of their self-determination. Massachusetts typified their attitude when in 1754 it refused to support Franklin's proposed union on the grounds that "it would be subversive of the most valuable rights and Liberties of the several Colonies included in it." On the other hand, the colonists did have a vision of sharing a common future.

"What scenes of happiness we are ready to figure to ourselves!" cried a not atypical colonist in 1759. "You cannot well imagine," wrote another a year later, "what a Land of health, plenty and contentment this is among all ranks, vastly improved within the last ten years." And as early as 1755 an American geographer named Lewis Evans commented that Massachusetts was headed toward an empire of its own. But so was Virginia. Worried and upset "at the largeness" of his debts, delayed and frustrated in his plans for western development and land speculation as early as 1761, and anxious to diversify the economy of the entire region, George Washington had begun to think as a leader of an American system. When he complained about poor or damaged imports from England, his London agents told him to send them back. Finally he exploded: it was impossible. How "can a person, who imports bare requisites only, submit to be a year out of any particular article of clothing, or necessary for family use. . . . It is not to be done. We are obliged to acquiesce."

IDEOLOGY AND INDEBTEDNESS:
THE LEVER AND FULCRUM OF INDEPENDENCE

As Washington and his peers like George Mason along the Potomac Valley grew ever more restive, the British government embarked upon a program to confine them further. Loyal Englishmen had been suggesting the virtue of that approach as early as 1747. "The colonies at this Time are arrived to a State of considerable Maturity," judged William Douglas in Boston: "perhaps it would be for the Interest of the Nations of Great Britain, and for the Ease of the Ministry or Managers at the Court of Great Britain, to reduce them to some general uniformity."

This concern with uniformity is the basic explanation of English policy after the final defeat of the French in North America in 1763. George III and his supporters (though not the mere hangers-on at Court) wanted a uniformity that had its roots in the doctrine of the divine right of kings. He sought it as a Patriot King for its own sake, and as a way to get money from the colonies in order to win his political battle in England. Others saw such control as the prerequisite for laissez faire in England: if policy was to be abandoned for interest at home, then policy had to triumph throughout the empire. Men could not pursue their enlightened self-interest unless there was a stable foundation on which to make their rational calculations, one which would withstand the violence of their competition and the shock of their mistakes. For quite different reasons, therefore, the king and many of his enemies agreed that the colonies had to be brought into line.

Having first placed restrictions on the settlement of the west in 1761, England announced on October 7, 1763, its decision to extend and enforce such limitations. Other edicts and laws followed in rapid succession during the next two years. Typical of the new approach was London's revocation of a controlled price system for the Indian trade as "doubtful in its principle"—a clear indication of the rising laissez-faire outlook in England. The colonists were more directly antagonized by a revenue law usually known as the Sugar Act (1764), which threatened to wipe out the margin of profit in the West Indies trade. It was followed by new restrictions on colonial money (1764), and demands that the colonists help finance the maintenance of British troops in North America (1765).

Then Parliament passed its first direct tax in the form of the Stamp Act, another revenue measure which raised the cost of legal documents, newspapers and Franklin's *Almanac*, and even playing cards. This not only threatened to raise the cost of business, but it soured a man's anticipation of a friendly game of cards—he had to ante up an extra time for the King. Finally, just when the colonists thought they had won a general victory in their bitter fight over the Stamp Act, England passed the Townshend Acts (1767). Consisting of taxes on colonial imports such as glass, lead, paint, paper, and tea (which was the national drink much as coffee is today), the legislation also erected special commissions and courts to enforce the collection of the money and punish offenders.

The colonists, whose self-consciousness and confidence had been intensified by the victory over the French, were affronted by the inclusive nature of these regulations and taxes. The new legislation also jarred their identification with the empire, and intensified the economic difficulties they were experiencing in a postwar depression. Massachusetts struck back on June 6, 1765, with a call for a meeting of the colonies to determine the strategy and organize the forces of a counterattack. Though not at that time the unchallenged leader of colonial resistance that he became in a few years, Samuel Adams was nevertheless the moving spirit of this first step toward independence and empire. Together with Virginians like Richard Henry Lee, Mason, and Washington, Adams and his New England allies made the Revolution.

Although he has been explained and interpreted as everything from a Leveller (and hence a radical of his time) to a neurotic haunted by a father image, Adams is best understood as a true Calvinist and thoroughgoing mercantilist. From an early age, he received religious training as a strict Congregationalist from his mother who had "severe religious principles." His father was a deacon of Boston's Old South Church. Emerging from this background, he developed views on the relationship between religion and politics that were subtle and complex. On the one hand, he staunchly advocated and defended the "free exercise of the rights of conscience," and vigorously opposed any participation by the organized church in secular affairs. Yet he was against allowing Catholics to hold public office because of what he considered their divided loyalties; either their commitment to Rome was meaningless, in which case they were hypocrites, or they would follow the Pope in a conflict of values with the electorate. At the same time, he defended a modicum of state support to organized Protestantism on the ground that the church played a vital role in maintaining a firm corporate ethical system and in providing insurance against anarchy.

As with Calvin, Adams was a militant spokesman for the supremacy of civilian authority over military leaders and institutions. And when ethical crises arose he was always willing "to step forth in the good old cause of morality and religion." As he acknowledged in later years, his central purpose was to make Boston "the *Christian Sparta*" of the world. "I am *in* fashion and *out* of fashion, as the whim goes," he commented in a revealing letter of 1768. "I will stand alone. I will oppose this tyranny at the threshold, though the fabric of liberty fall, and I perish in its ruins." Coordinated with the other aspects of his thought, his very candid remarks about "the *Christian Sparta*" and his willingness to pose the issue in terms of an either-or choice indicate that Adams became a revolutionary in the circumstances of his time precisely because he was a Calvinist dedicated to the ideal and the reality of a corporate Christian commonwealth. Calvin himself had followed that course, and his ideas and logic would propel a true follower along the same path. There seems little doubt that the words of Jonathan Edwards carried the spirit of true Calvinism into the well-prepared mind of Samuel Adams. Once there, it infiltrated the ideas of Shaftesbury, Locke, and Harrington to produce a man who signed many of his militant polemics as "A RELIGIOUS POLITICIAN."

Though he accepted Locke's statement of natural rights and based his political theory and practice on that principle, Adams also stressed explicitly the dangers of individualism. Hence he set himself firmly against men who defined liberty as "nothing else . . . but *their own liberty*." Adams was not a laissez-faire individualist who thought that the competition between enlightened self-interests would produce the general welfare. "Liberty no man can truly possess," he amplified, "whose mind is enthralled by irregular and inordinate passions; since it is no great privilege to be free from external violence if the dictates of the mind are controlled by a force within, which erects itself above reason." "Religion and public liberty of the people are intimately connected," he concluded: "their interests are interwoven; they cannot subsist separately."

Given the existence of a Christian corporate commonwealth, or the possibility of reforming such a society that had slipped away from the ideal, there is nothing in Adams's thought to justify a revolution. "The man who dares to rebel against the laws of a republic ought to suffer death," he asserted, because under those circumstances "sedition is founded on the depraved and inordinate passions of the mind; it is a weak, feverish, sickly thing." But if such a corporate Christian republic did not exist, or had decayed past the power of internal reform, then the same criteria enabled Adams to advocate revolution. Indeed, his principles forced him to do so. Thus any opponent of the true commonwealth became a public enemy. Adams ultimately cast Britain, and its agents and allies in the colonies, in that very role. Flatly declaring that "the Colonies were by their charters made different states by the mother country," Adams concluded that the new British policy was sedition against the original and true principles of the empire commonwealth.

Never sympathetic to "utopian schemes of levelling," Adams assumed a causal relationship between property and freedom. "These must stand and fall together." Thus Britain's move to tax the colonists was critically important: it "greatly obstructed" their trade and made the economic situation "very uneasy." As for Boston in particular, it "lived by its trade" and therefore had the "deepest concern" about the new policy. For Adams, the conclusion was obvious: acquiescence in such economic restrictions would make every colonist a "bond slave" by depriving him of the basis of his freedom. The Masters of Harvard agreed, asserting in 1765 that the new regulations "made it useless for the people to engage in commerce," and for that reason the laws could "be evaded by them as faithful subjects."

It seems doubtful that Adams sought *immediate* independence prior to 1770. His early polemics and letters stress the idea of forcing England to return to mercantilism. Take the natural and extensive profits of that system, he told them, and be satisfied. For that purpose (though perhaps from the outset for independence), Adams organized a propaganda network and a local political party supplemented by an extralegal police force known as the Sons of Liberty. Aided by such key allies as James Warren and John Adams, he used this machinery to maintain constant pressure (much of it in the form of physical intimidation by his street mobs) on Boston merchants. His purpose was to keep them in line on the economic embargo against British goods, and to make them do business without the stamps decreed in 1765. Counting on the pocketbook motive of the merchants, he assumed this would prompt the Boston traders to put similar pressure on the merchants in other colonial ports to keep them from taking all the profits. He also encouraged, prodded, and incited the Sons of Liberty and other similar groups throughout the colonies to exert their own power for the same purposes.

Lest the great importance of Adams be overemphasized, it should be made clear that each of the 13 colonies traveled its own road to independence. Adams could no more have singlehandedly bullied or bamboozled them into doing the same thing at the same time than he could have maneuvered his election as Pope. He had help, and lots of it, from several sources. Other lower- and middle-class leaders in the seaboard cities organized their own political clubs and street gangs, and deployed them as Adams used his own organization in Boston. Charles Thompson, for example, is often referred to as "the Sam Adams of Philadelphia." Isaac Sears and John Lamb were clever and militant leaders in New York, and in 1770 Alexander McDougall became a hero in jail for his role in opposing supplies to the British troops in the city. And further south, Patrick Henry and George Rogers Clark provided similar leadership for agrarian dissidents.

Upper-class leaders such as Joseph Galloway and John Dickinson of Philadelphia, Philip Schuyler and Robert Livingston of New York, and the majority of southern merchants were initially willing to support the kind of vigorous resistance to British policy advocated by Adams. But they never went beyond the idea of forcing England to restore the old order. "A little rioting," as one of them put it, "is a good thing." Beyond that point, however, such nabobs were openly afraid, as Governor Morris explained, that the colonies would fall "under the worst of all possible dominions . . . the dominion of a riotous mob." Franklin was even willing, in the earlier years, to accept a tightening up of the empire and "make as good a night of it as we can."

Persuaded, prodded, and intimidated by its more militant elements, this coalition forced England to back down. Turning to the classic mercantilist weapon of economic sanctions, it adopted and ultimately enforced by extralegal (and strong-arm) organizations the strategy of refusing to import British goods. Led by Washington, Mason, Lee, and Henry, Virginia effected the general consolidation of this movement in 1769. This non-importation cut deeply into England's trade, which dropped almost a £1,000,000 in one year. As expected, British merchants and manufacturers reacted vigorously, demanding a modification or change of policy. It is more difficult to determine the effects of the concurrent agitation by Wilkes and other radicals in England, but since they were using the American issue for their own purposes it probably encouraged British leaders to retreat. Even more important than these effects in England, however, was the experience and organization that non-importation provided for the Americans.

Combined with the scrambling for position between and within the English parties, these direct and indirect results of non-importation produced successive repeal of the Stamp Act (1766) and of all but one of the Townshend Acts (1770). And though England kept a tax on tea, the American coalition collapsed. New York and Rhode Island abandoned non-importation, and the other colonies hurried to reopen their own trade. Unfortunately for those who favored such compromise, neither Sam Adams nor the British Government would leave them alone. Adams launched a determined campaign to establish a corporate Christian and mercantilist American empire.

Like his allies in Virginia, Adams was thus a revolutionary without being a radical. And while other popular leaders in the colonies spoke for interest groups that wanted a greater share of upper-class well-being and political authority, only a tiny and insignificant group of individuals offered anything remotely resembling a radical program. Some of Adams's counterparts in other colonies stressed an extension of popular government more heavily than he did, for example, but none challenged the assumptions of the existing order. Had the revolution come a generation later, it is very probable that one wing of the popular movement would have developed such an attack on established institutions. But whether judged within the predominant mercantilist outlook, or against the standards of the laissez-faire philosophy that was gaining power in England, the colonials were far from radical. In either case, the crux of the matter was the Levellers' demand that private property be replaced by social property so that the Christian concept of commonwealth could be fully developed. The colonials had not reached that point by 1776.

Hence they emphasized freedom of action and empire. "It is the business of America to take care of herself; her situation depends upon her own virtue," Adams declared at the end of 1770. "Arts and manufactures, ordered by commerce, have raised Great Britain to its present pitch of grandeur. America will avail herself of imitating her." A year later, Philip Freneau and Hugh Henry Brackenridge caught the spirit of that outlook in their militant *Ode to the Rising Glory of America*. And Adams's mercantilist emphasis on manufacturing was typified in the expanding enterprises that were developing in every colony. The Boston Society for Encouraging Industry and Employing the Poor (a mercantilist title if ever there was one) established a spinning school in 1769. The New York Society for the Promotion of Arts, Agriculture, and Oeconomy began to grant premiums for domestic production and apprenticeship schools in 1765. And by 1775 The United Company of Philadelphia for Promoting American Manufactures had 400 female employees. Even more significant was the way in which Americans reacted to the Tea Act of 1773 as a specific threat to American manufacturing as well as a general danger to the system.

Many Americans feared that the principle behind the East India Company's monopoly on tea would gradually be extended to other goods and thus give England control of all colonial wealth. Adams recognized and seized his chance: in December, 1773, his Boston Sons of Liberty chucked the tea into Boston Harbor. England retaliated in kind, combining the Coercive Acts against Boston itself with the Quebec Act directed against all the colonies. The latter law not only took part of the west north of the Ohio river and gave it to Canada, but it closed off the rest of the transmountain area and granted Catholics in Canada full religious freedom. This combination gave Adams everything he needed: a city as a martyr, a basic religious and ideological issue, and a fundamental economic grievance. Calling explicitly for "AN AMERICAN COMMONWEALTH," he warned of English control over colonial Protestant churches, emphasized the danger of Catholic infiltration from Canada, and called flatly for continued westward expansion.

"An empire is rising in America," Adams exulted, calling for the annexation of Canada, Nova Scotia, and the fishing banks. "We can subsist independently of all the world." He was ready even then to "fight it out, and trust to God for success." Most other Americans were not. Without his allies in Virginia (and in the streets of Philadelphia and New York), Adams would have failed to defeat the nabobs and their compatriots—the loyal, the indifferent, the cautious, and the fearful among the general populace. Perhaps it is too much to say that the hinge of empire broke on the September day in 1774 when George Washington walked into the Continental Congress wearing his blue-and-buff uniform as commander of the Fairfax County Volunteers. Yet the symbolism of the act must have been almost as great to his contemporaries as it appears looking back at the scene with the knowledge that in less than two years he was to be commander-in-chief of an American army. Long before Jefferson had finished his last revision of the Declaration of Independence,

Washington was in the field against the enemy. One frustrated loyalist had foreseen the result as early as February, 1775: "Adams, with his crew, and the haughty Sultans of the south juggled the whole conclave of the Delegates."

As a planter who had opposed the British years before 1763, and who had worked out broad and specific plans for American development, Washington concluded it "highly necessary that something should be done." Deeply concerned that Britain's policy was "starving" colonial manufactures, as well as draining the coffers of the trader and the farmer, Washington saw the issue in absolute terms. "Our all is at stake," he declared to George Mason on April 6, 1769. Other southerners came to share that conclusion during the next five years. Jefferson's witty definition of a planter as "a species of property annexed to certain mercantile houses in London" was accepted by Oliver Wolcott, Thomas Mason, and others, and caught the spirit of the growing support for freedom, property, and empire.

Thus it was that on July 17, 1774, Mason and Washington prepared the Fairfax County Resolves, the southern manifesto of independence. Objecting to being treated as "a conquered country" after a century of enjoying the "reciprocal" and "mutual benefits" of mercantilism, they described the new imperialism as a program "calculated to reduce us from a state of freedom and happiness to slavery and misery." Calling for a "firm union" of the colonies, they demanded an end to *all* trade with Britain by November, 1775, if the new policies were not revoked. Significantly, they included slaves in this total nonintercourse that was to be enforced by extralegal associations empowered to embargo violators in the colonies. Finally, they urgently recommended "temperance, fortitude, frugality, and industry, and ... every encouragement in their power, particularly by subscriptions and premiums, to the improvement of arts and manufactures in America."

On the next day, Washington served as chairman of the county meeting called to consider the document. Exhibiting the same determination he later showed in battle, he rammed it through without discussion. And within a fortnight, the local militia which had been drilling under his command was officially recognized. Since it is true, despite one of the great myths of American history, that Washington was a firm advocate of political parties based on ideas and principles, it is perhaps useful to see him as the Shaftesbury of the American Revolution. In any event, he and Adams symbolized the two mainstreams of colonial society that engulfed England in defeat.

THE TRIUMPH OF AMERICAN MERCANTILISM

As they converged on Philadelphia in 1774, Adams and Washington caught the nabobs in a classic squeeze play. A New Jersey merchant analyzed his (and his group's) dilemma with great perceptiveness on the eve of the Congress. He insisted that the colonies could and should adjust their differences with the King in order to preserve the imperial system and hence their own wealth and welfare. "We ourselves," he pointed out, "have happily lived and enjoyed all the liberty that men could or can wish." The alternative was the "blood and destruction" that would be brought on by "the sedition, nay treason that is daily buzzed into our ears" by the advocates of independence. Yet the coming Congress, he concluded fearfully, might be swayed by the men who wanted "a new empire."

As a member of the Congress thoroughly aware of its composition, Galloway agreed with "Mr. Z" from New Jersey. Magnificently led by himself, one group of delegates sought a "remedy which would redress the grievances justly complained of" and thereby lay the basis for "a more solid and constitutional union between the two countries." Supported by men like John Hancock, Silas Deane, Robert Morris, and John Rutledge, Galloway's strategy suggests a striking analogy with the policy of "No Peace—No War" advocated by Leon Trotsky when the Bolsheviks were threatened by German conquest in 1917 and 1918.

Opposing him, concluded Galloway, were men whose plan "was to throw off all subordination and connection with Great Britain." Sam and John Adams were the public heroes of this group, but they were in fact partners with Gadsden, Washington, and Lee from the south, and men like Roger Sherman and George Clinton from the colonies around Massachusetts. Actually, both "Mr. Z" and Galloway oversimplified the composition of the Congress. There was a third bloc composed of men such as John Dickinson (Philadelphia), John Jay, James Duane, and Robert Livingston (all from New York) who wanted to negotiate a return to the system as it existed before 1763.

Galloway seized the initiative September 28, and presented his plan to coordinate the colonies and then establish a new union with Great Britain. A month of vigorous open debate and even more strenuous private negotiations (and intimidating rallies staged by Thompson) finally defeated it by one vote on October 23, 1774. In the tradition of all great revolutionaries, Adams, Washington, and Lee exploited their victory with ruthless *élan*. Declaring for "life, liberty, and property," they jammed through a militant attack on the Quebec Act, legislated into illegal law the principles (and some of the language) of the Fairfax Resolves, and established traditional mercantilist regulations on prices "so that no undue advantage" or suffering would result for any members of the new nation.

Massachusetts promptly set the pattern for other colonies with a formal legislative call for American manufactures. Arguing that the colonists were now a "family," the revolutionaries declared that the liberty, happiness, and welfare of families depended on "the less occasion they have for any articles belonging to others." Not only did those heirs of Calvin and the Puritans thus beat Thomas Jefferson to the idea of using "happiness" as a more felicitous synonym for "property" (one wonders if John Adams suggested the same substitution to Jefferson), but they did so in a context of images that went back to early Tudor mercantilism. Specifically, the recipe for happiness included a call to improve "the breed of sheep"; to charge "only reasonable prices"; to manufacture nails, steel, tin-plate, salt-peter, paper, guns, powder, glass, buttons, and dyes, and to refine salt.

As this document suggests, British mercantilism bore a subtle and complex relationship to the American Revolution. It did not cause the conflict in the narrow sense because it had given way to the imperialism of laissez faire. But British mercantilism had provided the protection and the essential assistance by which a scattered group of pitiful settlements matured into 13 strong, militant, and self-conscious states. It also equipped the leaders of that society with a set of attitudes, assumptions, and ideas about policy that can only be understood as an American mercantilism. Thus when English leaders dropped mercantilism, the Americans picked it up and ran toward independence.

American leaders were very conscious of the crucial role played by imperial expansion in the mercantilist conception of the world. When he was only 20 (in 1775), John Adams thought it "likely" that "the great seat of empire" would soon be in the colonies. Members of Parliament sensed the vigor of this thinking among the colonists, and often asked their informants about the growth of this drive toward "*an independent empire*." British ministers anticipated Frederick Jackson Turner in explaining America by its drive to expand. Americans, wrote Lord Dunmore to Lord Dartmouth on December 24, 1774, "for ever imagine that the Lands further off are still better than those upon which they are already settled." Could any skeptics have heard John Adams exactly eight months later, their doubts would have vanished. Strongly implying that any nabobs who still hankered after a reconciliation with England had better get off the fence and either sail for London or see their tailors for a set of blue-and-buffs, Adams called for the Second Continental Congress to get on with the business of writing "a constitution to form for a great empire."

On January 9, 1776, Thomas Paine followed with *Common Sense*, the great propaganda document of the era, a truly artistic work. Like the *Federalist Papers* of a decade later, it was also an accurate guide to the general way in which colonists thought about the world. It was only common sense, Paine asserted, that there was "something absurd, in supposing a Continent to be perpetually governed by an island." Since more than one-third of the tonnage of Britain's trade empire was carried in ships built by the colonists, it was obvious to him that farmers, planters, and other Americans would "always have a market while eating is the custom of Europe." Such magnificent sarcasm (perhaps produced by an extra decanter of brandy, since he never wrote without such medication for thinker's and writer's cramp) was followed by an outline for a mercantilist empire complete with a national debt, a national bank by which to measure and use it, and a navy.

Southerners quickly joined the chorus. "Empires have their zenith—and their descension to a dissolution," explained William Henry Drayton of South Carolina; "The Almighty ... has made choice of the present generation to erect the American Empire. ... [It] bids fair, by the blessings of God, to be the most glorious of any upon Record." Ever practical man that he was, Sam Adams had long before singled out Canada and the fishing banks for the early attention they received in the military campaigns (and in the Articles of Confederation which specifically mentioned Canada as an acceptable member). And even at that early date George Rogers Clark concentrated his attention on westward expansion.

"Prudence" might well dictate, as Jefferson explained in the Declaration of Independence (and as Locke made abundantly clear), that established governments should not be overthrown "for light and transient causes"; but then an independent empire was no light and transient cause. Following Locke like a schoolboy copying his lesson, Jefferson then recited the "long train of abuses and usurpations" which justified the act and saved the colonists from being classed as unnatural men. And as any good agrarian naturally would, particularly when he was a young revolutionary writing a manifesto, Jefferson equated property and happiness. The alliance between Massachusetts and Virginia could not have been symbolized more aptly or revealingly.

Distinguished and honorable advocate of reconciliation that he had been, Joseph Hewes had already acted on his appreciation of the facts: "Nothing is left now," he remarked on March 20, 1776, "but to fight it out." There was of course a great deal more left to do, and perhaps the most difficult task was to come to terms with the harsh fact that new empires were not welcomed by their elders in the 18th century.

CHAPTER TWO

A New Reality for Existing Ideas

There is an overweening fondness for representing this country as a scene of liberty, equality, fraternity, union, harmony, and benevolence. But let not your sons or mine deceive themselves. This country, like all others, has been a theatre of parties and feuds for near two hundred years.

John Adams, 1817

No time is to be lost in raising and maintaining a national spirit in America. Power to govern the confederacy, as to all general purposes, should be granted and exercised.

John Jay, 1783

Unless some speedy and adequate provision be made beyond that of the Confederation, the most dismal alternative stares me in the face.

James Madison, 1783

We are fundamentally wrong. The first Thing to be done is for Congress to have a Revenue.

John Adams, 1786

I hope our land office will rid us of our debts, and that our first attention then, will be, to the beginning a naval force of some sort.

Thomas Jefferson, 1785

Something must be done, or the fabric must fall; it certainly is tottering.

George Washington, 1786

THE DREAM AND THE REALITY OF INDEPENDENCE

Infused with enthusiasm and ambition, driven by what they considered the necessities of circumstance, or simply carried along by events, the colonists went to war for life, liberty, and property (*alias* happiness). While most were aware of the difficulties confronting them, many were nevertheless extremely optimistic and assertive. Though they often sneered at the upstart, the European powers immediately raised their guard. Aware of America's rapidly expanding commercial power (it listed almost 40 per cent of the empire ships in 1775), they disliked the prospect of such vigorous competition. Spain in particular feared the impact of revolution in the colonial world. And even France, the crucial ally, spoke candidly of its concern to limit "the plans of conquest of the Americans."

Franklin tried to reassure such skeptics, but he was not too successful. For one thing, he kept insisting rather bluntly "that no other power will judge it prudent to quarrel with us." Men considerably less brilliant than Vergennes could see the discrepancy between protestations of modesty and claims to omnipotence. They were likewise able to draw the obvious conclusion from the persistent use of the phrase, "this rising Empire." It was more than a coincidence that it was used by advertisers in Philadelphia newspapers, by southern planters, and by intellectual leaders in New England.

The war momentarily sapped some of this cockiness. As with the midshipman who awakes on graduation morning as the most courted man in the Navy only to become by sunset the lowest ranking officer in the fleet (which puts him a notch or two below a good many enlisted men), so the Americans discovered that with independence they became a relatively backward, underdeveloped, and weak nation. Having begun by demands on England to restore the mercantilism of the years prior to 1763, Americans won the argument by creating circumstances in which they would have to devise and build their own mercantilist system.

For that very reason, as well as because of their personal and group ambitions, they never stopped thinking and talking and acting in terms of empire. Joseph Galloway, one of the nabobs who retreated to England at the outbreak of the war, provided an amazingly accurate prophecy of this pattern of events. Entitled "Cool Thoughts on the Consequences of American Independence," and published in 1780, it is a remarkable document that justifies a long excerpt. "When she shall have a separate and distinct interest of her own to pursue, her views will be enlarged, her policy exerted to her own benefit. . . . She will readily perceive that manufactures are the great foundation of commerce, that commerce is the great means of acquiring wealth, and that wealth is necessary to her own safety. . . . It is impossible to conceive that she will not exert her capacity to promote manufacturing and commerce. . . . Laws will be made granting bounties to encourage it, and duties will be laid to discourage or prohibit foreign importations. By these measures her manufacturing will increase, her commerce will be extended . . . until she shall not only supply her own wants, but those of Great Britain herself, with all the manufactures made with her own materials."

Eager as they were to get on with that happy future, the states were immediately confronted by serious difficulties. England was too strong to be defeated by random efforts and without aid. Some men were disillusioned early. By the summer of 1777, for example, Silas Deane was thinking about "an accommodation of friendship and alliance" with England that would lead to a three-way integration of political economies with Russia. "It is easy to foresee that Great Britain, America, and Russia united will command not barely Europe, but the whole world united."

This was certainly the clearest, and perhaps the earliest, statement of an idea and objective that ultimately was accepted as policy by one group of Americans led by Alexander Hamilton and Rufus King: America would become the strongest member, and closest associate of the Metropolis, in a British imperial system that encompassed the globe. Thus did one group of nabobs modify and sustain their image of the good society. A smaller number of that persuasion were ready to go back into the empire long before the war was won and clung to the idea for a generation after the peace treaty. But most Americans honored their vision of an independent empire. Not only did the alliance with France sustain this dream, but without it the revolution would very probably have failed.

An equally troublesome problem had its origins in the varied and vigorous particularism of the states, in the conflict of economic and class interests, and in the personal rivalries of the leaders. In a moment of utter disgust, John Jay vented his dismay in a bit of classic description. "What with clever wives, or pretty girls, or pleasant walks, or too tired, or too busy, or you do it, very little is done, much postponed, and more neglected." As a result, an early and growing consensus began to develop around the idea that the original Articles of Confederation had either to be revised in fundamental respects or replaced by a new agreement and organization. It is conceivable, perhaps even possible, that the government of the Confederation could have discharged those and similar tasks. To have done so, however, it would have had to have persuaded or forced the states to surrender their powers over internal taxation and the tariff. They were not so persuaded, and the Congress never considered the use of force. Even had those minimum requirements been met, it seems very doubtful that such a government would have had either the power or the prestige to manage the commercial and continental empire that was so clearly in the minds of the revolutionary leaders.

Sometimes praised and defended as an institutional framework that protected the individual and the group against usurpations by the rulers, the Articles of Confederation would very probably have been workable only by indirectly extending and centralizing power. That might easily have led to more undemocratic government than the Constitution did. Though personal and social welfare were far more adequately provided for under the Articles than many historians have allowed, it is nevertheless doubtful that the Confederation was appropriate to a dynamic, expanding, and relatively underdeveloped country. Yet that is precisely what America became from the moment it declared for independence. At any rate, a good number of the states stopped attending Congress because so little of a positive nature was accomplished, and at least half the politically active adult population ultimately supported the movement to create a stronger, more centralized government.

In the meantime, however, the states bickered among themselves (and pouted) almost as vigorously as they fought England. This particularism drew its strength from many roots. Founded as separate units, their political and economic experience was gained as small societies which dealt with each other as independent entities. Their sense of identity was deep and intense. Modern ideas and emotions of States' rights are but a feeble reflection of the original phenomenon. In addition, political theory of that age was both an engine and a caboose of immediate experience. It tagged along from the age of feudalism and was then called upon to supply the intellectual power to rationalize and reinforce existing circumstances and objectives. Primarily and directly derived (though by no means exclusively) from the French philosopher Montesquieu, it asserted that democratic and republican governments were irrevocably limited to small societies.

Three broad groupings of states and would-be states formed the protagonists in a broader fight for influence and predominance in the new nation. To be understood, this alignment has to be described in two ways, functionally (or economically) and ideologically (or philosophically). Divided from the others by the border between Maryland and Pennsylvania, the economic life of the southern states was primarily organized as large-scale staple-crop agriculture. North of that line the states were principally occupied in manufacturing, banking, and commerce of all kinds. This fundamental pattern is merely modified, not invalidated, by the existence of surplus-producing agriculture in the north and merchants (and mechanics) in the south. The crossover of economics and ideology became increasingly important, but between 1776 and 1787 it was not a crucial factor. Far more important in those years was the rapid development of a surplus producing diversified agriculture west of the mountains. This happened very quickly and played a major role in the rise of a movement to establish a strong central government.

In the meantime, however, the revolutionary leaders seemed to abandon their mercantilism in favor of free trade. But most Americans considered free trade a tactic for attaining the strategic objective of having an empire of their own. Lacking an established government, a developed and integrated economy, and an effective army and navy, the new confederation had to have help. Free trade appeared the obvious way to get it at the least possible cost and risk. "Trade must be free to all," explained Sam Adams, "as to make it the interest of each to protect it, till [we] are able to protect it. This the United States must do by a navy."

Making it quite clear that "nothing less is at stake than the dominion of the sea, at least the superiority of naval power," John Adams, Arthur Lee, and even Franklin could unite on empire even though they disagreed on other issues. Like Sam, John Adams also thought of free trade as a useful weapon for "preserving the respect" of France, thus avoiding any chance of becoming the ward of an ally. Seeking "to produce a balance of power on the seas," Adams wanted a navy as quickly as it could be built. It was a tool for fashioning "the foundations of lasting prosperity." No doubt he was concerned for the fisheries, but then so were others outside New England. What Adams and other American mercantilists saw in free trade was a temporary means to obtain help, check competitors, and break into the pattern of world trade while they established America as an independent power respected and feared by Europe.

They may have dreamed, for a moment or two after a victory like Saratoga, that America would demolish all British and French restrictions. But only a minute minority really believed that free trade would be accepted by the rest of the world. A few pessimists argued that America was too weak to try anything else; they thought a navy was a "wild, visionary mad project." And some had been attracted by the world of Adam Smith. Yet even such ostensibly physiocrat free traders as Jefferson quickly realized that such a policy could easily prevent the United States from developing its own system.

Though not every law was perfectly framed nor wholly enforced, the legislation of the Congress and the states revealed the predominance of the mercantilist outlook. The general drive for more representation in government did *not* signify a desire to establish weaker governments; the objective was a more responsive, and more responsible, institution that would do the various things wanted by the farmer and the mechanic as well as by the landed and commercial gentry. These groups all sought broad governmental assistance. Some of the new state constitutions reflected the moderate successes of the lower and middle classes. State capitols were relocated further inland, election districts were increased and redrawn in a more equitable way, more frequent elections were required, and the legislature was often strengthened against the executive and judiciary.

Though it produced significant results (if only in the form of frustrated and intensified ambitions), this *political* campaign should not be misunderstood. No state became the plaything of the farmers and the mechanics. In several cases, for that matter, and particularly in the south, though also in Massachusetts and New York, the gentry tightened its effective control. Early failures in enforcing price controls are misleading, for even modern governments have encountered difficulties in that area. And paper-money inflation, which won the support of some groups, had been the avowed program of one group of English mercantilists since at least the 1690s. By the end of the war, the states were passing navigation acts and protective tariffs and granting bounties and subsidies to special sectors of the economy.

Several states authorized central banking institutions, as in New York, Maryland, Pennsylvania, and Massachusetts. A momentarily successful campaign to establish a national bank also began at an early date. Supported by Thomas Paine, George Washington, and James Madison, as well as by more narrowly commercial spokesmen such as Robert Morris, the Bank of North America was founded in 1781. And even the agrarians who successfully repealed its Pennsylvania charter wanted to reestablish the state loan office of colonial times. The real struggle was not so much whether as it was how and by whom.

Morris rather than Alexander Hamilton was the central figure in the creation of this first quasi-public bank. Morris wanted the bank to "exist for ages," since in his view the "salvation of our country" in some measure depended on it. He also understood the bank's role in attaching "many powerful individuals to the cause of our country by the strong principle of self-love and the immediate sense of private interest." Morris enjoyed his full share of both of those reserves of human action, but he also had a vision of the nation "twenty years hence, when time and habit have settled and completed the Federal Constitution of America." Morris failed in his effort, but Hamilton, though neither more astute nor more original, was more fortunate.

Private individuals and groups also undertook such traditional mercantilist objectives on their own and exerted pressure on the state governments to extend (as in poor laws) or increase such benefits. Men like Matthew Carey and Tench Coxe were beginning to work out and advocate general, if somewhat rudimentary, theories and programs to explain and accelerate the establishing of such systems. The *Weltanschauung* of mercantilism was so generally accepted that, as Madison later complained regarding Virginia, some states ultimately went overboard and passed laws so rigorous and extensive that they almost literally isolated themselves as political and economic units.

This enthusiasm for mercantilism combined with the realities of the war and the postwar era to produce a series of fundamental difficulties and several raw conflicts of interest. English mercantilism, the essentials of which the colonists had taken over, evolved principally from an initial statement of the interest (and hence policy) of the commercial groups. Lacking much land, trade was the capital accumulating element in the British system. While there was a conflict between the city merchant and the country squire, it was resolved by the interpenetration of the two groups and the realization that land simply could not create enough surplus wealth for general economic growth.

Then, when land was won by conquest and colonization, it was physically removed from England. Neither the rich nor the poor had to bother themselves with adjusting the basic assumptions of their political theory to the increased riches. They ruled the new land as an empire and argued how to divide the additional wealth and welfare without fretting over the question of adjusting representative government to the new circumstances. For many generations, therefore, they remained ignorant of—or cheerfully evaded—the contradiction between, on the one hand, the mercantilist principle of wealth and welfare through expansion and, on the other, the political axiom that a state had to be small to be republican (or democratic) and the moral definition of welfare that had come down from Christianity.

Americans were not so fortunate. For, while they could expand their trade without raising such issues, they also had a continental empire of land at their back door. This made it impossible to avoid several theoretical and practical issues. First, it was necessary to adapt a theory of economic growth and welfare that stressed commerce as the dynamic element to a situation in which land, and hence wealth, was available almost for the taking. Second, the conflicts between political, moral, and economic theories had somehow to be resolved so that republicanism could be sustained within a contiguous empire.

THE WEST AS AMERICA'S PANDORA'S BOX

From the very beginning, this rough-and-tumble struggle during the Confederation era toward a centralized mercantilist government developed around the issue of the western lands. This came to symbolize not only the concern of the upper class about the attitudes and actions of the lower orders, but also the struggle between commercial and landed interests, the dilemma of expansion versus self-government, and even the question of slavery. In its origins, the issue was whether American claims to western and southern lands and to commercial freedom on the Mississippi should be abandoned in return for aid from Spain.

Congress first gave priority to Canada and the fisheries. They were "essential to the welfare" of the Confederation. Formal claims to Florida were tacitly abandoned. Buoyed up by military gains, Congress then refused in October, 1780, to trade any claims to navigation through New Orleans into the Caribbean. Spain would not talk seriously on those terms. "Not a single nail would drive," John Jay reported from Madrid. With another turn in military affairs, Congress again reversed itself. On February 15, 1781, it advised Jay he could give up navigation rights below 31° north latitude in return for significant help. And in August it approved "such further cessions" as might be persuasive or necessary.

Now in many ways Jay was a pivotal figure during those years, and it is crucial to watch him closely from the outset. For while he was unquestionably a vain and ambitious conservative, he was also a vigorous and intelligent man who very soon became an American mercantilist deeply concerned to remove the difficulties in the way of the nation's development. On these latter grounds he balked at his last instructions from Congress. No doubt he was offended by the casual treatment he was given in Spain, but his policy had deeper origins than a scar on his ego. Taking the long-range view that America would hold the Mississippi boundary, he frankly told Congress that he was "less certain" than Congress itself apparently was of the wisdom in giving up the navigation of the river. "In my opinion," he bluntly said, "[it will] render a future war with Spain unavoidable."

As victory became apparent, Congress once again reversed itself and closed off negotiations with Spain. Two aspects of this episode are important. The final decision by Congress was in many ways one of the first key compromises between the commercial groups, who were not primarily concerned with the west (many of them were openly antagonistic), and the southern agrarians who did attach great importance to the region. Though defeated, the northerners remained in the Confederation. Jay's behavior makes it clear, moreover, that he was not—as has often been said—a pro-English Federalist. Armed with this insight, it is possible to make more sense out of the later fight over western policy and commercial issues.

In the meantime, however, the American objective in the peace negotiations was to expand as far as possible. American leaders quite consciously and purposefully worked out their arguments "by recurring to first principles" because by that strategy "our pretensions [are] placed upon a more extensive basis." Adams was firmly convinced that "nothing could restrain" his countrymen from going clear to the Gulf of Mexico. Nor did he wish otherwise. Other northerners such as Robert Livingston (who called boundaries "the first point of discussion") added their support. So did many southerners as, for instance, Edward Rutledge, for whom "the boundaries are everything," and Madison, who fretted about the "dangerous phraseology which may be used in designating our limits." Jay vigorously supported these demands, explaining that America was going to expand into "a great and formidable people."

But while united against England and France, the gentry and those commercial and financial groups involved in land speculation turned on each other for control of the west. This at once led to a bitter fight between two interest groups in which the attendant personal economic motives played a noticeable role. The usual political shenanigans were also very prominently displayed. But this was also a conflict between those who saw the west primarily as an area to be controlled by and for special interests in the east and those who assumed that the region would rather quickly become a self-governing part of the Confederation. The division here was not on a simple struggle of land against commerce. Many southerners agreed that the west should be brought along slowly.

In its first phase, however, the fight took the form of a duel between the Virginia expansionists and the rest of the states. A resolution was finally effected when Virginia ceded its claims in December, 1783, on condition that Congress would not turn them over to others (such as Franklin), but would instead use the new wealth for the benefit of the Confederation. As these conditions suggest, the decision resulted from several factors. Virginians reluctantly concluded that they could not control the empire they claimed. Squatters and marauders were already taking the land and creating the conditions for a major Indian war. Virginians also fretted about the problem of maintaining republicanism in a large state and were openly fearful that the Confederation was in danger of splitting up into three or more smaller units. At the end of 1783, for example, only five states had delegates in Congress. "Unless some speedy and adequate provision be made beyond that of the Confederation," Madison warned, "the most dismal alternative stares me in the face."

This cession by Virginia of its lands was in many respects the apex of the small-state theory of republicanism in America. The finest practical statements of that political and economic outlook were the related 1783–1784 proposals by Jefferson, its then leading exponent, for organizing and governing the territory. As finally passed, the Ordinance of 1784 divided the trans-Appalachian west into ten relatively large states, each entitled to immediate self-government. Statehood would come when the population matched the smallest of the original states, and they were to pledge eternal union with the existing Confederation. And in a provision that symbolized the climax of the early antislavery sentiment in America, a consensus led and primarily composed of southerners, Jefferson proposed to exclude slavery from the region after 1800. Though it was dropped from the final law just before passage, this slavery proscription was reintroduced into the later, and in other respects quite different, Northwest Ordinance of 1787; hence it seems just to link it with Jefferson's original proposals.

But while his market and social interests as a planter and his education as a physiocrat strongly inclined Jefferson toward small states and local self-government dominated by a benevolent aristocracy, he either sensed or rapidly became aware of the dilemmas of that outlook. Territorial expansion was one way to resolve such difficulties, for it offered economic relief to the planter and protection against the lower orders to the aristocrat. Jefferson advocated such expansion, and intrigued for it, from an early date. But as indicated in his *Notes on Virginia* (one of the early literary and analytical classics of the new nation), he also sensed the physiocratic nonsequitur in arguing for free trade and at the same time opposing a navy.

This side of the millennium, at any rate, free trade was possible through one of several ways. A nation could maintain a large navy and enjoy free trade within its nautical empire, or it could make an

alliance with a power of that sort, or through fortuitous circumstances and a naval force strong enough to control certain key areas
(such as the Caribbean) it might exploit extensive commercial
liberties as a neutral. But all these possible solutions pointed away
from physiocracy and toward mercantilism. For that matter, so did
the kind of power and organization required for territorial expansion. Jefferson never gave up his vision of an idyllic solution to the
problem, and in 1819–1821, did indeed ultimately retreat into the
isolation within the south that it implied, but in the circumstances
of independence he rapidly modified his practice along mercantilist lines. The resulting discrepancy between his rhetoric and his
actions made him a perplexing but not incomprehensible figure.

Within three years, Jefferson's noble statement of the small-state
philosophy was on the verge of defeat. That evolution culminated
when the forces of American mercantilism established themselves
on Constitution Hill in 1787. Jefferson's own retreat points up a
key aspect of this shift: the reaction against his view of 1783–1784
came from *within* the south and the mercantilist bloc as a unit,
as well as from the small group of northern traders who thought
primarily in terms of an accommodation with Great Britain.

This movement away from the Articles of Confederation
was influenced by several factors: Britain's refusal to reopen its
economic empire to America, Spain's continued assertion of title
to the Mississippi and its navigation, the rapid economic and
psychological development of the west, and the manifestations of
serious, if only as yet symptomatic, social unrest which suggested
that the aggregate statistics of economic recovery did not tell the
whole story about its viability or its geographic and class distribution. Because it crystallized attitudes which had been maturing
for years, because it led to a stalemate inside the Confederation,
and because this in turn provoked a concerted drive to change that
system, the central event would seem to be Jay's negotiations with
Spain over the Mississippi question.

Jefferson's Ordinance of 1784 had no sooner been passed than
three things happened simultaneously. Northern speculators and
conservatives opened a campaign to revise it. James Monroe left
Philadelphia to reconnoiter the west. And Jay opened talks with
Spain in which he was charged by Congress with obtaining the
right of navigation through New Orleans and recognition by Spain

that the Mississippi itself, not its eastern bank, was the boundary between the two nations.

The effort to revise the Ordinance of 1784 was in no sense a juggernaut powered by a monolithic motive and guided by a one-track organization. Among other considerations, it was at least passively supported by a good many southerners for their own reasons. Without question, however, the speculators from Pennsylvania and other states were militantly active in opening and pushing the battle. No doubt their pocketbook nerve had suffered one of its spastic seizures, and they wanted Congressional control of the west so that they could dip their quivering—in some cases desperately quaking— hands into that great reservoir of healing wealth. Yet it is impossible to explain the revisionist movement wholly in terms of speculators, men who were truly indifferent to any other aspect of the issue.

Speculation actually honed the edge of several existing policies. One group around men like Timothy Pickering were old commercial nabobs to whom the west meant almost nothing except danger. Their primary objective was a hierarchal society ruled by a conservative oligarchy that had intimate—if not formal— economic, political, and social ties with England. Others were closer to Rufus King and Alexander Hamilton, who had begun to modify this view into a more complex and subtle outlook. They feared and disliked popular government, but they nevertheless had accepted the results of the war as it established an independent American society. On the other hand, they visualized the future of the United States in terms of an Anglo-Saxon empire run from their side of the North Atlantic basin. For all these reasons they favored a strong central government maintaining close relations with England and preferred to strike some kind of compromise with members of the southern gentry. But King, in the early days at any rate, was ready to consider secession and what he termed a northern "sub-confederation" as a last resort.

King was not only the early leader of this group who proposed many of the specific ideas later advanced by Hamilton (such as an alliance with England to penetrate and control Spain's colonies), but he was the clearer thinker and more astute politician of the two. Ultimately accepting the triumph of a wholly American mercantilism, he then laid the foundation of a new party sustaining the conservative tradition and representing the economic interests that were effecting the transition to industrialism. For the time, however, King wanted to control the west as a check on social unrest and the cost of labor in the east. His problem was to accomplish this while retaining control of the area, avoiding war with England, and reaching some agreement with southern leaders.

Jay's inability to win quick concessions from Spain gave King his opening. But while it might appear, and to some southerners did appear, that Jay shared King's outlook, the foreign secretary was in fact an astute spokesman and co-leader with John Adams of still another group in the north. Jay's maturing from a nabob to an American mercantilist had been rapid and thorough. By the end of 1783 he had embraced once and for all the political economy and ideology of American mercantilism. From the beginning, Jay and many other early American leaders saw the law and some supreme judicial institution as the secular cement that would replace a state religion in such a corporate society. On the other hand, Jay's deep Anglicanism undoubtedly lay behind that general view.

As early as March, 1783, he told the British to stop bluffing and accept the new facts of empire politics: America was "like a globe, not to be overset." He even welcomed European opposition as a blessing because it strengthened "a *national* spirit." "Good will come out of evil," he concluded in a bit of typical mercantilist philosophy. Foreign antagonism would make "our yeomen . . . as desirous of increasing the powers of Congress as our merchants now are," and produce a situation in which "domestic manufacturers would then be more encouraged." Jay was likewise ready to go to war against the Barbary pirates: it "does not strike me as a great evil. . . . Besides, it may become a nursery for seamen, and lay the foundation for a respectable navy." He also encouraged "the turn to the China and India trade" that Robert Morris and a few others had started several years before.

These aspects of Jay's outlook make it possible to draw important distinctions among northern leaders. King, for example, thought the Barbary interference in trade was "magnified." On the other hand, and whatever the apparently vast extent of his private raids on the gross national income while he was in charge of the Treasury, Morris emerges as a vigorous American mercantilist. As with the land speculators of that group, the *Weltanschauung* does not in any sense excuse the flabbiness of private morals; they misused their positions to improve their own fortunes. But neither does their political economy explain their misconduct, and their outlook was far more American than the view of other merchants and financial leaders who thought about the United States primarily in terms of England. Unlike Hamilton or King, Morris wanted "to see a foundation laid for an American navy." Along with men like Samuel Shaw of New York and John O'Donnell of Baltimore, Morris vigorously supported trade with Asia, and reveled in the jealousy such activities provoked in England. He was enthusiastic over the prospects of "an independent empire" in America.

Morris and Livingston (and Jay, also, prior to 1784) exemplified those northerners who steadily broadened an initially more narrowly commercial outlook into a mercantilist *Weltanschauung*. Livingston, for example, began as a trader and speculator who saw and pursued his business operations within a general theory of economic maturation. In his view, development occurred in a succession of stages defined by particular kinds of activity. Arguing that the newly independent states were in the commercial stage, he was at first disinclined to throw his influence behind any broad program to encourage manufacturing. According to him, and despite the growing number of manufacturers who agitated for such a policy, the attempt was premature and artificial. It would undercut the rate of commercial profit and thereby retard the accumulation of capital at home (and from abroad). That would in turn decrease the general rate of economic growth and actually delay the establishment of manufacturing on a solid footing. Through the 1780s, however, Livingston's thinking evolved along classic mercantilist lines, and offered a striking illustration of how a restricted interest idea could and did break through its own limitations.

But Jay and John Adams were the giants among northern mercantilists. "We concur so perfectly in sentiment, respecting public affairs and what ought to be done," Jay wrote Adams on November 1, 1785, at the end of a long, searching exchange on American problems, "that I find no occasion to enlarge on those heads." It was just as well that Jay enjoyed the comfort of his rapport with Adams at that hour, for he was soon burst in upon by a harried and almost frantic Monroe just back from his trip to the west. He had seen the west, and its vigorous vitality and independence confirmed his old fears and added some new ones.

Easterners were to suffer this kind of traumatic experience for many generations, and Monroe's case illuminates all of them. Even before he left on his trip, he had questioned Jefferson on the wisdom of granting home rule to Kentucky and the other settled areas west of the mountains. He argued for handling the region more like a colony. This imperial attitude and mercantilist outlook was also revealed in his support for the agitation to strengthen the existing government under the Articles of Confederation. He was ready, by the end of 1784, to pass navigation acts designed to "take some share in the carrying trade," and tariffs "to encourage domestic industry in any line."

Indeed, the militancy and thoroughness of Monroe's mercantilism is difficult to exaggerate. His formal reports to the Congress in the spring and summer of 1785 assumed that "the oldest and wisest" states would continue that kind of political economy, and urged the United States to respond in kind. The object of trade, he pointed out, was "to obtain, if possible, the principal share of the carriage of the materials of either party." Hence America should retaliate vigorously: "strike more deeply into their commercial system. . . . Essentially would their gen[eral] commercial interests, and at the same time promote those of these States. . . . Press them in every vulnerable part, and . . . pursue it to the utmost extent that our interest admit of, until we obtain what we seek."

Wearing these spectacles, Monroe saw the west as a Pandora's box of troubles for the gentry of the east. It was wild, exciting, and irresponsible, yet it was necessary for the gentry's wealth and welfare. Thus arose in practical and immediate terms the double dilemma of American mercantilism: how to reconcile the political commitment to republicanism and representative government with the necessity of expansion and at the same time effect a compromise between the landed and the commercial mercantilists. Monroe's original answer was close to the one finally adopted, but in his panic over the west he almost fumbled away the chance to put it into operation.

Monroe's program had three main points. First, repeal Jefferson's small-state, self-government approach to the west and substitute a straightforward colonial policy for the short run, ultimately giving local government and statehood to the west as it calmed down and accepted eastern modes, manners, and leadership. Second, support

the west against Spain, England, and the Indians in order to fore-
stall secession and prevent foreign influence from penetrating the
area and perhaps even leading to annexation. Third, combine these
two policies with a system of mercantilist legislation and risk the
chance that the northerners who opposed such a program would
try to establish their own confederation with close ties to England.

Patrick Henry responded with some enthusiasm. Charles
Pinckney of South Carolina was also favorable, remarking very
simply that any other approach "would destroy the hopes of the
principal men in the Southern States in establishing the future
fortunes of their families." Not only were there speculators in the
south, but the southern gentry saw the west as a capital fund to
retire the national debt, and hence a good share of their particular
debt. Monroe subsumed all such interests in his broad mercantilist
conception: "Under the direction of Congress," he wrote Madison,
"the produce of that country will be in trade the source of great
natural wealth and strength to the United States." This realization
that the west was becoming an area of commercial agriculture
was perhaps the most important observation that Monroe made
during his excursion beyond the mountains.

Preoccupied with these general aspects of the western problem,
Monroe did not immediately attack Jay. His first opponent was
Jefferson, who had fathered the illusion that the west would stay in
the Confederation under a relaxed and narrowly agrarian system.
Had he remained in the country instead of accepting the job of
handling relations with France, Jefferson might have fought any
revision of the Ordinance of 1784 with all his considerable abilities. On balance, though, this conclusion seems doubtful. Jefferson
wanted the west as badly as any other American-empire man in or
out of Virginia, and even before he departed to take up his duties
in Paris he agreed on the neccessity of legislation to establish parts
of a mercantilist system.

In any event, Monroe and his alliance of mercantilists, which
included northern and southern speculators, revised Jefferson's law
and produced the Northwest Ordinance of 1787. Monroe described
it almost perfectly in a letter to Jefferson: it was based, he explained,
on "a colonial government similar to that wh[ich] prevailed in these
States previous to the revolution, with this remarkable and important difference that when such districts shall contain the number of

the least numerous of the thirteen original states for the time being they shall be admitted into the confederacy."

The distinction emphasized by Monroe is an important one. It separated southern mercantilists from those northerners who, like Gouverneur Morris, wanted to rule the west and other conquests "like a province" with no plan for final self-government. Perhaps this difference was part of the same outlook that led the early gentry to criticize slavery and anticipate its demise. What sometimes goes unnoticed in emphasizing that the west had been put back in a checkrein (as it most certainly had) is the significant compromise between northern and southern mercantilists on the issue of slavery. It was banned in the Northwest Territory. This agreement opened the way for the later compromise in the Constitutional Convention. It also indicated the way that American mercantilists would solve the dilemma of freedom and expansion; an expanding nation would provide enough wealth and welfare for a republicanism which included slavery.

Sprouting in this fashion, the idea that expansion was the key to prosperity and republicanism soon matured and came to govern American politics for at least a century. In the meantime, and concurrently with his efforts to revise the legislation concerning the west, Monroe lashed out at what he considered a fundamental attack on this axiom of expansion. Ever since returning from the west, Monroe had heard rumors that Jay's talks with Spain were going badly. Prior to the late spring of 1786, he discounted them. Then, in June, he opened a bitter assault on Jay as a northerner who was willing to destroy the south by abandoning the west. Though Monroe admitted that his analysis was "presumptive only," he nevertheless charged that there was "an intrigue on foot under the management of Jay." "I have a conviction in my own mind," he wrote Jefferson, "that Jay has managed this negotiation dishonestly." Monroe's assumption about the cause of the trouble was wrong, but it says a great deal about the gnawing fears that some leaders in the south entertained concerning the lawyers and merchants in the north.

Jay fought back in a style and with an *élan* that was rarely surpassed among the Founding Fathers. Bluntly denying that he was secretly and literally selling the west down the river, Jay confronted Monroe *and* the Pickering-King group with an almost irrefutable analysis and recommendation. Without hesitation he declared that a "treaty disagreeable to one half of the nation had better not be made" because it would lead to disunion and catastrophe. This made it clear that he was not simply a pro-English conservative, but an American mercantilist ready to compromise.

Jay then reminded Monroe that neither England nor France was willing to let America inside their respective empires. This meant, he pointed out with great patience, that commerce was not able to function effectively as a way of accumulating capital for the further development of the United States. Jay next explained that the west could not perform that function all by itself. It could contribute its share only when the settled regions had an opportunity to earn capital in a general commerce. The exchange of goods for goods was nothing more than a definition of the old colonial system, and a revolution had been fought to end that bondage.

Looking about for a workable answer, Jay concluded that the best solution in sight was in *temporarily* abandoning America's maximum claims on the Mississippi and in New Orleans in return for access to the Spanish empire in the Western Hemisphere *and in Asia*. Trade with Spain would not only meet the existing emergency but would give Americans an additional bargaining weapon in their negotiations with England and France. Provided a breathing space, the country could pull itself together, erect a mercantilist system, and then go on to take the Mississippi and New Orleans.

Finally, Jay hit hard at Monroe and others on the Indian question. Not only did this turn the charge of dishonesty back on his critics, but it raised the basic ethical issue in mercantilism's theory of producing domestic welfare through expansion over other peoples. "Our people," he boldly reminded the southerners, "have committed several unprovoked acts of violence against them." Aware that the Canadians were thoroughly disgusted with American behavior in foreign affairs—"Were old Matchioavell alive," one of them concluded in anger, "he might go to school to the Americans to learn Politics more crooked than his own"—Jay emphasized the imperialism of the Confederation itself. Randolph Downes had already blasted his fellow Congressmen with a searing description of a law passed in 1783: for "imperial aggressiveness and outright effrontery this document takes a front rank in the annals of American expansion." The criticism had little effect. Congress continued in the empire tradition. "You are a subdued people," it told the Indians a year later. "We shall now, therefore, declare to you the conditions, on which alone you can be received into the peace and protection of the United States." It would seem that the principles of unconditional surrender and total war appeared rather early in American history.

"Would it not be wiser," Jay asked Jefferson, "gradually to extend our settlements as want of room should make it necessary?" As that remark suggests, Jay was a perceptive and intelligent American mercantilist who was trying to develop a program that would produce a strong nation and system of political economy, and who was at the same time a man keenly aware of (and trying to solve) the moral dilemma inherent in his outlook. Jefferson evaded the issue, as he did throughout his life. Madison had a far better grasp of the situation and told Monroe rather sharply that Jay had "a train of reasoning which has governed him. . . . If he was mistaken, his integrity and probity, more than compensate for the error." Jay was wrong on one significant point: he underestimated the extent and the rapidity of the west's maturation as a surplus-producing agricultural society. He also made one judgment that can be debated endlessly. He assumed, quite in keeping with his upper-class conservatism, that the west was an underdeveloped society that *should* be brought along slowly until it came of age politically, economically, and socially.

But Monroe too assumed this. Therein lies the crucial importance of the fight between them: it jarred all American mercantilists into the stark realization that they had to compromise in order to build the kind of society that they wanted. And in this important respect, Jay's answer to Monroe served as a catalyst in the growing consensus for a stronger central government. Southerners such as Madison, William Grayson, Edward Rutledge, Henry Lee, Richard Henry Lee, and George Washington understood that Jay was correct in assuming that the United States could ultimately take what it wanted from Spain if it survived the immediate crisis. But they realized better than Jay the great risk involved in any *overt and formal* commitment to his policy. They knew that the west might easily revolt (and that some hotheads had already written their own marching songs) if his analysis should be accepted as policy and translated into a treaty. Hence they blocked him in the Congress although they shared his broad outlook.

This recognition of the need to control the existing west while the east gained strength and cohesion—a combination that would then generate further expansion—played an important role in the rapid growth of the movement for a more powerful central government. In the immediate sense, for example, the stalemate over a treaty with Spain undermined the effectiveness and the prestige of the Congress. But this consensus did not produce any immediate relaxation of the tension within the evolving mercantilist coalition. For its members were fully aware that going slow in the west depended upon their ability to accelerate the economic development of the eastern states. Unless they could accumulate capital individually and collectively, and simultaneously prevent or control eastern social unrest, they would be unable to meet either the needs or the demands of the west, let alone satisfy the minimum requirements for their ideal solution to the problem.

Thus they were faced with the necessity of dealing quickly and effectively with the corporate, inclusive crisis in commercial and manufacturing affairs that had matured almost coincidentally with the western issue. This crisis cannot be understood if it is defined as no more than—or primarily as—a postwar economic depression. This was one of its features, but the basic question was whether the established economy of the seaboard metropolis was threatened with severely limited growth or actual stagnation because it was proscribed or isolated by the British and French empires. Many mercantilists, including Washington, were aware by late 1785 and early 1786 that the postwar depression seemed to be over and that recovery of a kind had begun. What worried all of them—and frightened a good many—was the cause and the nature of that recovery. Whatever their social theories or political philosophies, they saw recovery as being based on the creation of an unbalanced, quasi-colonial economic relationship with Great Britain. Accurately enough, they realized that this threatened their very existence as a strong, self-governing society.

THE GENTRY AND "THE ABSOLUTE NECESSITY OF SOME GENERAL SYSTEM"

The phrase "independent empire" was purposely not used in the preceding sentence. Some American leaders retained the basic outlook of the nabob and were therefore strongly pro-British. They could join the truly American mercantilists in a drive for a strong domestic government and agree that it should be used against internal unrest if necessary, while none the less opposing any vigorous policy against England. But the great majority of American leaders did view the problem from the perspective of their own mercantilism. One of several men could plausibly be singled out as the most important figure in rallying this consensus to the action that led to the Constitutional Convention in 1787. Such a choice would ultimately have to be made between Jay, John Adams, and Madison. As in the coming of the revolution itself, the movement for a strong central government had 13 centers, and once again the north and the south provided the synthesizing leadership. This time the honors probably go to Madison and the Virginia gentry.

To emphasize the difficulty, and the somewhat artificial nature, of such judgments, it may be noted that no one analyzed and defined the crisis more neatly than Elbridge Gerry of Massachusetts. Reviewing the economic tactics of the war, when free trade and reciprocity treaties with the most-favored-nation clause were used in an effort to break into European empires, Gerry concluded that they had become positively dangerous. America was a backward country, he explained to Jefferson, and hence its treaties with the small, relatively unindustrialized powers of Europe meant little. And should such nations negotiate treaties with London or Paris, the American economy would be placed in a very unfavorable position. The policy had to be changed. "We otherwise must be their Tributary . . . this favoured Nation System appears to me a System of Cobwebs to catch Flies." And in that era, at any rate, Americans saw themselves as one of the flies.

John Adams also explained similar truths to Jefferson and, along with Madison, seems clearly to have given the future sage of Monticello an intensive course in mercantilism. For that matter, Adams was a vigorous instructor to the entire American seaboard. As Congress officially told him as early as 1783, his logic and industry "have had a very good effect." Convinced as early as 1780 that England would pose a threat even after independence had been won, and determined to build a "genuine system of American policy," Adams persistently campaigned for a navy and warned as early as 1781 that the pro-English merchants would have to be closely watched lest they lead America back into the Empire. Asserting America's "natural right to the carrying trade," he undertook to "brace up" the Confederation in order to "encourage manufactures, especially of wool and iron," to pass navigation laws, to build a navy, and in all respects to construct a new empire.

Though older and hence less active than during the years of the revolution, Sam Adams vigorously supported the same program. Jay's role was more significant. Not only was he a high officeholder in the Confederation, but perhaps no one, not even Adams or Madison, was as ready as he to go as far in constructing a mercantilist system at such an early date. Unless America did so, he explained to Congress in 1783, "we shall soon find ourselves in the situation in which all Europe wishes to see us, viz., as unimportant consumers of her manufactures and productions and as useful laborers to furnish her with raw materials." America was in "a delicate situation," he warned Washington early in 1786, and urged immediate action. As with so many others, Jay looked forward to the day when Americans could make their agreements with other countries "more and more correspondent to their [own] views and Wishes."

Many southerners were almost as vigorous. Arguing in 1785 for the need of a "deep and radical change" in the Confederation, Monroe advocated putting "the political economy of each State . . . entirely under the hands of the union. The means, necessary to obtain the carrying trade, to enc. domestic [manufacturing] by a tax on foreign industry, or any other means . . . will depend entirely on the union." And by January, 1786, Monroe emphasized his concern to come "upon *the ocean* as a *commercial people*." Against this background, Monroe's ultimate selection of John Quincy Adams as Secretary of State seems almost a routine projection of his mercantilism.

Washington was more directly occupied with specific projects in and around the Potomac River Valley designed to develop the commercial and industrial resources of that region and open up a central communications route to the Mississippi. Such a plan, he argued, would lead to the decline of slavery as the south developed a diversified economy, and would centralize the entire country around the home of the gentry. "The earnestness with which he espouses the undertaking is hardly to be described," Madison noted, "and surely he could not have chosen an occupation more worthy of succeeding . . . than the patronage of works . . . which will extend commerce, link [the seaboard's] interests with those of the Western

States and lessen the emigration of its citizens by enhancing the profitableness of situations which they now desert in search of better."

For all his localized activity in Virginia and Maryland, Washington was keenly aware of the general crisis. "Something must be done," he wrote Jay in 1786, "or the fabric must fall; it certainly is tottering." As he thought about the new government that was needed, he concluded that basic natural resources should be controlled and dispensed by the central government according to a plan of balanced development rather than by the principle of first come, first served, and the public welfare take the leftovers.

Hugh Williamson of North Carolina was another active mercantilist from the south. So was the member of the gentry from Maryland who concluded that it was vital to establish a system which would make it possible to "feel ourselves superior to the Commercial frown of britions." That accomplished, "imagination itself would scarcely be capable of keeping pace with our increasing wealth and importance." And from Yale, Ezra Stiles wrote Jefferson in the same vein. Aware of the social unrest that was simmering in some of the colonies, Stiles recommended a strong central government and expansion as the proper remedies.

Thomas Jefferson also moved further toward mercantilism. Free trade was "impossible," and true reciprocity presented "difficulties insurmountable." "We are not free," he admitted under the hammering of Jay's logic, "to decide this question on principles of theory only." Hence he accepted the arguments of Adams for a "navigation act against Great Britain." Such a program would very probably lead to wars, Jefferson concluded, and for that reason he reiterated his earlier acceptance of "the necessity of some naval force."

But Jefferson was simply not a leader at that crucial juncture. "I own myself at a loss what to do," he admitted to Jay on January 27, 1786. What in fact he did do was follow Madison, Monroe, Jay, and Adams. Having accepted their analysis and the broad outlines of their program, he first proposed a war on the Barbary pirates. He even advocated, and dickered to organize, an alliance with other interested powers. Then he turned to westward expansion across the Mississippi to the Pacific and the markets of Asia. Not too surprisingly, Jefferson began about this time to argue for smaller states in the west because they would be easier to control.

Throughout this period, Jefferson was still trying to break into the French mercantilist system and thus open a vent for American tobacco and other surpluses. Though successful in specific instances, he never did crack the system itself. He also stressed the importance of reopening the West Indies trade. He considered it "indispensably necessary" and saw in a mercantilist system the weapon that would force England to capitulate. Integrating territorial expansion and commercial expansion, he outlined a broad strategy which he followed for many years. "Our vicinity to their West Indies possessions, and to the fisheries, is a bridle which a small naval force, on our part, would hold in the mouths of the most powerful of these countries. I hope our land office will rid us of our debts," he concluded in a letter to Jay, "and that our first attention then, will be, to the beginning of a naval force of some sort."

Others were equally concerned about the commerce of the Indies. Like Jefferson, Robert Morris wanted westward expansion (it would attract Canadian capital and "secure the Indian trade") as well as the island business. John and Samuel Adams were especially concerned to reopen it, since they viewed it as an integral part of "the natural system of the commerce of the United States," as well as specifically important to Boston. Others stressed the argument that access to the Indies would establish a re-export system embracing "*all parts* of the world."

Several other developments strengthened and accelerated this mercantilist drive toward a powerful central government empowered to co-ordinate the landed and commercial-manufacturing interests in one system and at the same time expand it in all directions. One of these was the increasing activity in manufacturing and an associated agitation for government aid. John Adams had reported in 1780 that Europe was worried lest America "become the greatest manufacturing country, and thus ruin Europe." Though America had not even approached that strength by 1786, there was a great deal of interest and activity. And the corporation, as a modification of the old joint-stock company, had already appeared as a means of solving the problems of capital accumulation and organization.

New York's Central Committee of Mechanics was founded in 1785 and soon thereafter became the Manufacturing Society of New York. An Association of Tradesmen and Manufacturers in Boston was matched by the Pennsylvania Society for the Encouragement of

Manufactures and Useful Arts. And mechanics in both cities began to demand protection against English imports for such of their own wares as naval supplies and leather goods. Southern states provided the same kind of aid and comfort supplied in the north. North Carolina, for example, gave bounties for iron production as well as for staple crops. Connecticut and New Hampshire encouraged their nascent manufacturing in similar ways. Pennsylvania and Massachusetts went even further, offering straight cash loans and even granting land for some factories. Other companies projected major transportation systems, as with the Potomac Company and the Great Dismal Swamp undertaking. Similar charters were granted for ventures on the James River and in South Carolina, and for bridges like the one authorized over the Charles River in Massachusetts in 1785. Some of these projects, like Washington's Potomac operation, demanded interstate co-operation of a fairly extensive nature. The rest served to increase and dramatize the need for a national economy.

In a different way, Noah Webster also campaigned for a unified system. His first spelling book of 1783 was timed perfectly, and the introduction spoke pointedly of the intellectual tools needed by "this infant Empire." Another of his many volumes followed shortly, and he went on the road from Massachusetts south to peddle his rhetoric and his ideology along with his word-books. His prefaces as well as his speeches made it apparent that he was dedicated to one object: to "encourage genius in this country, [so that] the EMPIRE OF AMERICA will no longer be indebted to a foreign kingdom for books." Following the same approach in politics, Webster described the Confederation as "a burlesque on government" and vigorously supported the campaign for a stronger, truly national institution.

Two other events which reinforced that movement were manifestations of social discontent and anxiety; Jay and Adams, among others, viewed them as omens to be ignored only at the risk of losing independence. First in origins was the Society of the Cincinnati, organized in 1783 under the direction of General Henry Knox and other extremely conservative veterans of the war. Though in some respects founded on the rather ghoulish camaraderie of all soldiers who have survived combat, the leaders of the society also entertained somewhat vague but vigorous ideas about conservative *coups d'état,* and the type of visions that led to wild or grandiose speculative investments. A broad cross section of the country reacted negatively. Led by Sam Adams, who thought it "might in time, revive the old feudal system," Massachusetts flatly and officially denounced the Society as potentially "dangerous to the peace, liberty and safety of the United States in general."

Washington managed to effect basic changes in the organization, but the fears and opposition lingered on into 1786 and 1787. Thus, while the Society itself vigorously supported the idea of a stronger government and agitated for such changes, many men who wanted the same thing argued that one of the virtues of a new government would lie in its ability to control such factions. As had been the case with Shaftesbury at the time of the Restoration in England, many American mercantilists in the circumstances of 1786 began to be seriously worried that the strife between factions would combine with the particularism of the states to destroy the government and lead to a voluntary or forced return to some kind of colonial status.

At this juncture James Madison began to take the lead in promoting a more powerful government capable of dealing with the country's many problems and opportunities. "The necessity of harmony in the commercial regulations of the States," he explained to Jefferson on January 22, 1786, "has been rendered every day more apparent." Madison and other leaders of Virginia and Maryland first thought to approach the problem by extending Washington's economic collaboration to the political level and thus counteract the particularistic mercantilism of the states. Virginia adopted resolutions defining the dangers and calling for a regional meeting to discuss the crisis. Even before it convened, however, the Potomac gentry widened their appeal to include all the colonies. Worried that other states would procrastinate, or openly oppose the projected conference, and that nothing would come of the effort, Madison explained his deep concern to Jefferson.

Madison had been working toward such a summary statement of his political economy ever since 1784. Free trade, he had concluded, was a chimera: "all others must concur" before it could work, and neither England nor France would voluntarily dismantle their own successful systems. Hence the "only" thing to do was to create a government that could pass "retaliating regulations of trade." Thus convinced of "the absolute necessity of some such general system," his object was a government with the power "to counteract foreign plans," "encourage ships and seamen," "encourage manufactures," provide revenue, inspire (and enforce) "frugality" in peace, and enact "embargoes in war." If such needs could not be satisfied within the Confederation, then Madison was willing to change the form of government.

Far more concerned with the narrower view of the northern merchants "so exclusively occupied in British commerce" than about the feasibility of the sophisticated mercantilism he had borrowed and adapted from Sir James Steuart and other Englishmen, Madison summed up his analysis in a letter to Jefferson on March 18, 1786. "Another unhappy effect of a continuance of the present anarchy of our commerce will be a continuance of the unfavorable balance on it, which by draining us of our metals furnishes pretexts for the pernicious substitution of paper money, for indulgences to debtors, for postponements of taxes. In fact," he concluded in a sentence that foreshadowed his famous essay No. 10 in the *Federalist Papers*, "most of our political evils may be traced up to our commercial ones, as most of our moral may to our political."

As he awaited the meeting which had finally been arranged for at Annapolis, Madison began to grapple with the central dilemma posed by the contradiction between the expansionism of mercantilism (and of economic interest) and the political theory which asserted that republicanism could work only in a small state. He concluded that the existing low ratio between population and land would prevent lower-class rebellion or aristocratic tyranny for some years. But the conclusion left him with the problem of postponing such a crisis as long as possible. "No problem in political Oeconomy has appeared to me more puzzling," he admitted to Jefferson on June 19, 1786, "than that which relates to the most proper distribution of the inhabitants of a Country fully peopled. . . . What is to be done with this surplus?" His first answer drove him right back on the barbs of the old dilemma. For "a more equal partition of property" which would ease the problem could be achieved only by expansion or by some communal arrangement.

Here was the heart of the matter for all mercantilists: Were the Levellers correct in insisting that the only way to build a corporate Christian commonwealth was through severe restrictions on private property? If so, that meant extensive losses and restrictions for Madison and other upper-class leaders. Unwilling to accept this answer, Madison turned back toward expansion as the way to have welfare *and* the enjoyment of private property. Expansion would not only supply enough property for all, in the narrow economic sense, and a surplus of resources for national development, but these considerations would make it easier to honor the demands of the corporate ethical system. Or, at least, so ran the logic. But that left Madison once again confronted by the argument that republicanism in large states—or empires—quickly degenerated into lower-class movements for communal property, or upper-class oligarchy, or personal tyranny.

Madison had not squared this mercantilist circle by the time of the Annapolis Convention in September, 1786. Neither had any of the other delegates. Even worse, many states had not bothered to send representatives to the meeting. Evidence of the antagonism and suspicions between individual states and regional groupings, this unconcern also indicated the extent to which 13 brands of mercantilism were competing for the market. But men like Tench Coxe from Pennsylvania and Alexander Hamilton from New York gave Madison some hope. Coxe was almost ready with a broad mercantilist program that both Hamilton and Madison were to draw upon within five years. And though he saw dangers in Hamilton's personal drive and administrative verve, Madison also realized that they were the twin cylinders of a powerful engine for basic change in the government.

Convinced that a bold act was needed, for his own future as well as for that of the country, Hamilton proposed to usurp the authority of Congress and issue a manifesto for another meeting. In a way that revealed his persistent concern with the morality of government and the risk of tyranny, Madison caught the coattails of the New Yorker before he went the last step and suggested a *coup d'état*. Perhaps Hamilton himself would have hesitated, but as one of his friends later remarked, his views became "more & more enlarged and comprehensive as we approached the crisis of our destiny." Madison and the other delegates at Annapolis did agree, however, that some kind of decisive action was essential. "Every days delay," Madison fretted, increased the chance that nothing would be done in time to avoid a catastrophe. Hence the meeting adjourned after preparing a militant call for a general review of the Articles of Confederation at a new convention.

Though as individuals or as a group they certainly had a suffi-
ciency of personal ambition and economic interest, men who
composed the coalition for a strong central government were
also motivated by an upper-class awareness of a very real crisis
in the existing system and were determined to establish a better
one within the philosophical assumptions of the era. For them the
issue was not mercantilism versus laissez faire; it was the failure
of mercantilism as applied at the level of 13 particularistic states.
All of them were worried that the west, which they talked about as
their colonial area, was on the verge of internal revolt or external
conquest. They were determined to prevent the disintegration of
the revolutionary victory whatever their differences as to its ultimate form and direction.

Hence it is doubtful that Shays' Rebellion in Massachusetts was a
traumatic experience for the established leaders of the Constitution
Movement. That resort to violence was shocking and dramatic.
But it was also merely the most recent episode in a long pattern
of discontent and unrest among the middle and lower classes that
originated before the revolution, manifested itself in mutinies in
the Army during the war, and continued after peace had returned.
It reemphasized a fear that had been a long-term resident in their
social and class consciousness. The greatest effect of Shays' impact
was a weakening of the confidence of those who had ignored the
Annapolis meeting on the assumption that mercantilism at the
state level would resolve their problems and realize their ambitions
and desires. They clearly reacted by becoming actively interested
in a stronger national government.

But it is often forgotten that the rebellion *was crushed quickly
and completely. Shays did not rally the countryside.* This suggests
that it had an influence on the Constitution Movement beyond
the way that is sometimes thought. Having quashed it, men began
to think about how to prevent future outbreaks as well as how to
control them more routinely. Jefferson provides a good example of this reaction. At first he was disturbed and worried; very
little of his famous remark about watering the tree of liberty with
the blood of patriots can be found in his early letters about the
event. It was the work of "mobs" and was "absolutely unjustifiable."
Furthermore, it emphasized the danger of losing the west through
similar outbreaks.

But Jefferson was soon calmed by letters from other conservatives who took a more balanced view of the event. "Don't be allarmed," wrote John Adams, ". . . all will be well, and this Commotion will terminate in additional Strength to the Government." Jefferson saw the point. "Unsuccessful rebellions indeed generally establish the incroachments on the rights of the people which have produced them," he wrote Madison after reflecting on the letter from Adams. "An observation of this truth should render honest republican governors so mild in their punishment of rebellion, as not to discourage them too much."

Jefferson's next reaction was no less revealing: he worked out an explanation of the revolt in classic mercantilist terms and recommended appropriate mercantilist policies for preventing such outbreaks in the future. The cause, he concluded, was the lack of export markets. That not only had rendered the specific groups unable to pay their taxes or their debts, but the taxes and the debts resulted from the corporate economy's inability to raise capital, including government revenue, in the traditional way. Another consequence was the inability to finance vigorous wars against the Indians, and that further upset the men who fell in behind Shays. The remedy was "to open the Mediterranean" and to establish a national system strong enough to wring concessions from England and France.

Jefferson's analysis of Shays' Rebellion and his programmatic response symbolized the fundamental strength of the Constitution Movement. Neither its tactics nor its procedures were wholly democratic, but it was not a conspiracy in any meaningful sense of that term. It was a well-organized campaign by a coalition of America's upper-class leadership determined to establish the institutions appropriate to an American mercantilist empire. And just as Jefferson's retreat from the doctrines of agrarian free trade and compartmentalized self-government was powered by the appeal and logic of expansion, so would the new national government rely on the same engines in its search for prosperity, democracy, and the general welfare.

CHAPTER THREE

The Adaptation of the Existing Order

It may be said that the new Constitution is founded on different principles, and will have a different operation. I admit the difference to be material. It presents the aspect rather of a feudal system of republics, if such a phrase may be used, than of a Confederacy of independent States. And what has been the progress and event of the feudal Constitution? In all of them a continual struggle between the head and the inferior members, until a final victory has been gained in some instances by one, in others, by the other of them. . . . This form of Government, in order to effect its purposes must operate not within a small but an extensive sphere.

Extend the sphere, and you take in a greater variety of parties and interests; you make it less probable that a majority of the whole will have a common motive to invade the rights of other citizens; or if such a common motive exists, it will be more difficult for all who feel it to discover their own strength, and to act in unison with each other.

James Madison, 1787

If we remain one people, under an efficient government, the period is not far off when we may defy material injury from external annoyance; when we may take such an attitude as will cause the neutrality we may at any time resolve upon to be scrupulously respected; when belligerent nations, under the impossibility of making acquisitions upon us, will not lightly hazard the giving us provocation; when we may choose peace or war, as our interest, guided by justice, shall counsel.

George Washington, 1796

[Our success] furnishes a new proof of the falsehood of Montesquieu's doctrine, that a republic can be preserved only in a small territory. The reverse is the truth.

Thomas Jefferson, 1801

CONFLICTING PHILOSOPHIES AND POLICIES OF
THE CONSTITUTION MOVEMENT

As they opened their proceedings by electing George Washington president, and by going into secret session, the members of the Constitutional Convention presented an imposing cross section of the American upper class. While a few of the delegates confined their philosophies and programs within the perimeters of their interests, most of them revealed the breadth of vision and the sense of long-run essentials so characteristic of class-conscious leaders. Had they not been class-conscious in this fundamental sense, they might never have compromised their immediate-interest conflicts; indeed, it is very difficult to imagine such institutional architecture being achieved by men of any society who were not so guided by a consciousness of class. Thus it seems appropriate to view the Constitution as the result of a long, difficult, and at times bitter bargaining session which finally produced a consensus on a program advanced by the key figures of the American gentry who were guided by the precepts of mercantilism.

Leaders such as Madison and Washington were supported in their conception of the Constitution Movement, both in and out of the convention itself, by men from the north as well as other southerners. William R. Davie, Alexander Martin, and Hugh Williamson of North Carolina, and John Blair of Virginia, joined such men as Thomas Mifflin, Robert Morris, and Thomas Fitzsimons of Pennsylvania, and John Langdon of New Hampshire in advocating and accepting most features of such a program. The point at issue here is not the party to which these men ultimately adhered, nor the conflicts between their economic interests and the variations in their social philosophies, but rather the proper kind of political economy and government that they thought the new nation ought to have. And in this sense, even though they were not members of the convention, John Jay and John Adams symbolized the northerners who entertained the same basic views.

Two other groups participated in the making of the Constitution. One included such men as Timothy Pickering and Fisher Ames, and was represented in the convention by Rufus King. These men had a well-developed and sophisticated interest, philosophy, and program to which they were deeply committed and which they advanced with vigor. Shippers and merchants with auxiliary interests in land speculation and finance who had been exceedingly reluctant revolutionaries, or even loyal nabobs who had returned after the war, they continued to define their future in terms of England. Exceedingly conservative in social and political affairs, they presented the superficial appearance of American aristocrats; living well, with fine homes and appointments, they feared and despised popular government. Centered in New England and the middle colonies, but supported by allies in Charleston and elsewhere throughout the states, they wanted a strong central government to protect and facilitate their interests, but their political economy was defined by the narrow idea of profits at home through connections with England. From the eve of the convention through the War of 1812, their outlook prompted them periodically to threaten secession in order to rejoin the British Empire.

A second particularistic segment of American leaders was narrowly agrarian in outlook. Represented in the convention by such spokesmen as George Mason and Edmund Randolph of Virginia, and on many issues by Luther Martin and John Mercer of Maryland, all of whom refused to sign the Constitution itself, these Americans were guided by the ideas of men like John Taylor of Caroline, John Randolph of Roanoke, and Governor George Clinton of New York. Both in his personal influence and through his writing, John Taylor was the foremost philosopher of the group. While verbose and often turgid, his ponderous tracts on *An Examination of the Late Proceedings in Congress* (1793) and an *Inquiry into the Principles and Tendencies of Certain Public Measures* (1794) were more important (as well as less blasphemous) than the polemics written by J. Thompson Callender and others. And Taylor's grand attack on John Adams, *An Inquiry into the Principles and Policy of the Government of the United States* (1814), was the definitive statement of the agrarian-physiocratic doctrine in American history.

In the United States, as well as in France and England, physiocracy represented a concerted effort to sustain the life and the economy of feudal medievalism in an age of science, commerce, and industry. Under such circumstances it became the highly sophisticated outlook and program of an agrarian interest engaged in an emotional as well as practical assault on existing reality. It was, to borrow the phrase of a sympathetic French scholar, the idea and ideal of a "feudal utopia" transferred to the 18th century.

American physiocracy can be understood only by abandoning the common but mistaken view that feudalism and manorialism were the same thing. Feudalism was essentially a *political* system of organization which as early as the 11th century had lost most of its denotation of unfreedom. Based upon the hierarchic organization of mutual obligations and responsibilities, feudalism posited the overall corporate organization of individually defined units of society. As a social order, feudalism was highly stratified; on the other hand, it was possible, though not routine, to move upward in the system. But as far as economic organization was concerned, feudalism as a political and social system not only could exist without manorialism, it did just that in various parts of Western Europe. Thus, while America would seem for the most part to have skipped manorialism (it did exist in New York and parts of the south), it most certainly did not bypass feudalism.

Starting with the classic assumption of small states founded on agriculture, the physiocrats derived their philosophy from the Stoics, Aristotle, St. Thomas Aquinas, and Locke. Taylor, for example, understood quite well that Locke was a conservative political thinker who combined individualism with strong government at the top of the system. And on more than one occasion, John Randolph ended a soliloquy in praise of Locke and individualism with a climax of this sort: "I am an aristocrat. I love liberty, I hate equality." Such American physiocrats also appropriated Locke's theory of the mind in its narrowest meaning. Accepting the proposition that men learned from reality, they took it to mean that the reality they knew was all there was to learn, or, at best, that there was no possibility of developing a theory any more subtle than a conflicting-interest definition of reality. This meant that the only true ideas were agrarian ideas; hence their philosophy was the ideology of an interest group.

In external affairs, the physiocrats believed in commutative justice in which exchanges had to be equal, value for value. Internal justice, on the other hand, was distributive according to the standing of the various orders of society. To secure both kinds of justice, the government had to be strong and controlled by the highest order which would use its power to intervene as necessary in social and economic affairs. While their contributions were valued and respected, inferior ranks could participate only within well-defined limits. Yet the physiocrats also believed that land qualified a man as a full member of natural society; in circumstances providing surplus land, as in America, this made them democratic in the broad sense. But it did not change the basic axiom of restricted rights and liberties for the lower orders. And there is no doubt that the great majority of Virginia's landed aristocracy made it their business as well as their theory to keep a firm hand on the implements of state.

Thus, while the physiocrats argued for unrestricted competition, they declared that merchants, manufacturers, shippers, and bankers were ineligible to compete. The principle of distributive justice did not apply to those categories. Perhaps the most difficult dilemma confronted by the physiocrats was the problem of finding markets for their agricultural surpluses without at the same time encouraging shippers and manufacturers. Even if they relied on foreign merchants, as was their wont, and insisted upon natural money (precious metals or specie) in the transactions, they were still impaled on their definition of those in the carrying trade and its attendant occupations as immoral and parasitic "traffickers."

The best thing the physiocrats could do was to oppose such evil within their own society. Hence it is not very difficult to understand why such men as Randolph opposed wars for commerce, even when the trade involved the exportable surpluses of western agriculture. Since it would offer a wider market, they reluctantly tolerated domestic manufacturing if the enterprises were small and local, if native workers and raw materials were used, and if the labor was not employable in agriculture. But they much preferred territorial expansion in order to solve the problems of soil exhaustion and to maintain a low ratio between population and wealth. While strongly individualistic, even in some respects liberal and democratic, the physiocratic doctrine was for these and similar reasons the strictly limited outlook of an interest group.

Taylor, Randolph, and even Patrick Henry nevertheless capitalized on its emotional appeal and on its superficial correspondence with existing reality throughout much of the country. Defining America as "one great farm, and its inhabitants one great family," Taylor proceeded logically to define property as "the chief hinge upon

154 THE CONTOURS OF AMERICAN HISTORY

which social happiness depends." But to the physiocrats property was nothing but land. Since there was only one interest, there was no call for more than one political party—the agrarian. Following his own rules, Taylor later played a key role in changing Virginia's election laws to make sure that Jefferson would win in 1800. In this fashion, and to their own satisfaction at least, Taylor and other southern physiocrats could agree with Mason's dictum that "never was [there] a government over a very extensive country without destroying the liberties of the people" and yet at the same time justify an empire. For as long as the agrarians ruled, there would be no despotism. As for wars, Taylor defined only two legitimate excuses: defense and "to promote emigration to richer lands."

But since *corporation* was one of those words "which are innately despotick," Taylor understandably became obsessed with the financial manipulations involved in banking or government-funding operations. For the same kind of reasons, Taylor never fully trusted Madison's politics and ultimately went into open opposition. On the main domestic issue facing American physiocrats, that of whether to define Negroes as serfs (with the consequent prospect of freedom, as under feudalism) or as property per se, Taylor honored the origins of his thought. He accepted and looked forward to the end of slavery; at least, he did so until he concluded that the attack upon it was in reality an assault directed by the corporations and the "traffickers" upon an agrarian utopia which the south was creating.

Jefferson's position on slavery was almost identical with Taylor's, yet the master of Monticello was no unwavering disciple of physiocracy. But neither was he a firm mercantilist. This ambivalence in Jefferson suggests that his most famous protagonist, Alexander Hamilton, occupied a comparable spot at the other end of the spectrum of America's constitutional coalition. Jefferson's demon took the form of a lifelong hankering after the physiocrat's feudal utopia realized with the aid of science. As he wrote in 1785, his dream was "to practice neither commerce or navigation, but to stand, with respect to Europe, precisely on the footing of China." Even later in his career he described Taylor as the man with the answers: "But I fear," he concluded sadly, "it is the voice of one crying in the wilderness." Turning for guidance to Madison, whom he described as "the greatest man in the world," Jefferson cherished his dream and at the same time became rather more than half an American mercantilist.

His entire career can be understood as the attempt of a physiocrat to use mercantilist means to realize his feudal utopia.

Hamilton also borrowed and manipulated mercantilist policies to create a strong state. But he was more narrowly driven by his own ambition, and his vision of the good society was far less balanced, democratic, or independent. Hamilton's devil was the image of himself at the head of an American-British empire embracing most of the world. His foreign and domestic policies became increasingly weighted against the nascent manufacturing and predominant agrarian interests in favor of the pro-English mercantile faction. His grand object was a scheme involving his leadership of a joint aggression with the English against Spanish America. And when it came to a question of investing his own funds, Hamilton preferred land speculation to American manufactures. Professor John C. Miller, in many ways the most subtle and convincing biographer of Hamilton, has put it as kindly as possible. "Hamilton was never prepared to purchase American nationalism at the price of exacerbating Anglo-American relations." Yet, given the relationship between the two societies, that was the only bid that would win the prize.

Jefferson, on the other hand, understood the comparative imbalance between England and America, and was in the last resort willing to accept the costs and the implications of modifying it. Hence he moved toward support for American shipping and manufactures. Whatever its short-run impact on the pro-English carrying trade, and even on the small merchant and consumer, his embargo was designed to preserve and extend America's economic independence. And it actually did function to create a composite political economy. The real irony of the embargo is not so much that it antagonized a good many of Jefferson's own followers at the time, nor even that it led to the War of 1812, but rather that it stimulated the economic development of groups which ultimately destroyed Jefferson's physiocratic society.

Unlike Jefferson, who was abroad as American minister to France, Hamilton, during the Constitutional Convention, candidly presented his views on the good society. But while his mind and logic were "damned sharp," as Robert Morris later remarked, the majority of the delegates had different ideas of the abstract good as well as of the practical possibilities. His call for an almost omnipotent executive, and his advice that the states "ought to be extinguished, new modified, or reduced to a smaller scale" doomed his plan. Some men agreed with him, or at least with the essentials of his position, but they knew that such a government could not be peddled to the people. Others had more fundamental objections, chief among them a strong commitment to representative government.

The idea of balanced government was also deeply entrenched in the thinking of the delegates. Those who had not read Harrington had very probably seen the argument as advanced by Francis Hutcheson (*A System of Moral Philosophy*), or John Witherspoon in his *Lectures on Moral Philosophy*. Witherspoon's advice was classically direct: "Hence it appears that every good form of government, must be complex, so that the one principle [or monarchy, aristocracy, or democracy] may check the other." Hutcheson agreed that the elements of government "should be divided." John Adams also provided a clear analysis and statement of the same theory. Published in 1786 and widely read, his essay *A Defense of the Constitution of Government of the United States* was a hardheaded, even pessimistic analysis based on sex, hunger, and wealth.

Adams provides a further illustration to modify the common view that the Founding Fathers were men who relied on practical experience as against theory. For as Adams and others made perfectly clear, they defined experience to include the study of history and political science as well as the learning-by-doing involved in running a business. Intellectual achievement was the key to their success. "I must study politics and war," Adams explained in a letter to his wife, "that my sons may have the liberty to study mathematics and philosophy . . . navigation, commerce, and agriculture, in order to give their children a right to study painting, poetry, music . . . and porcelain." Reflecting on the ancients, as well as on Harrington, Bolingbroke, and Locke (all of whom he read several times), Adams concluded that "the controversy between the rich and the poor [was] . . . as old as the creation, and extensive as the globe." It was the engine of history and the cause of despotism, anarchy, and tyranny.

To resolve the mercantilist's dilemma, how to use private property to achieve the corporate welfare and yet prevent interest and faction from running roughshod over the common good, Adams stressed the importance of a firm and active sense of justice. He also argued that a representative government of divided and balanced departments offered the best "check and control" against monarchy, oligarchy, and anarchy. Yet while he emphasized the need for a central government with a powerful executive, he also took it for granted that the principle and practice of popular government was beyond challenge. Since he candidly avowed his belief in the existence and virtues of his own class, and was personally inclined to be abrupt, touchy, and even arrogant, a good many people accused Adams of being a monarchist. He was in fact one of the truest defenders of representative government the nation ever had.

THE CONSTITUTION AS A FEUDAL AND MERCANTILIST INSTRUMENT OF GOVERNMENT

Despite the consensus on the idea of a strong, balanced national government, the members of the Constitutional Convention faced the need to make several broad compromises. One involved the extent to which they could consolidate the government and still have it accepted by the public. Not only were Hamilton's extreme views abandoned, but Madison's desire for a national veto over state legislation was likewise given up. Even so, many critics thought the final degree of centralization was far too extreme. Another group of compromises concerned the conflicts between the various interests in society, and between the existing sovereign states, over their relative power inside the new government. Both the large states and their smaller neighbors feared discrimination at each other's hands, but these antagonisms were finally resolved by the formula of proportional power in the House of Representatives and equal standing in the Senate. In practice this worked to strengthen even further the division of authority within the three branches of the government, and even within the Legislature.

Still another compromise dealt with the definition and recognition of slaves. Here the importance of antislavery feeling among the southern gentry played a vital role. The southerners' ethical, as well as economic, opposition manifested itself in two important ways. On the one hand, they insisted that in making the census for political purposes a slave be counted as three-fifths of a man. Though the demand was a means of protecting their interest in the allocation of representation in the Congress, it also reflected the basic feeling of the gentry that the Negro was a human being who should ultimately be freed. Hence the seemingly callous arithmetic is misleading if interpreted in a narrow framework. Southerners also accepted the near certainty that the slave trade would be prohibited within a generation, and that, too, amounted to a tacit definition of the Negro as a human being. As in the land law of 1787, the south compromised in the writing of the Constitution. Though not an antislavery document in the active sense, therefore, it did open the way toward the end of slavery if the practice was viewed as an institution, as the gentry did, rather than as a personal sin of the master, as abolitionists did in later years.

The persuasive mercantilism of most of the delegates manifested itself in many ways. Export taxes, for example, were explicitly proscribed; the states were also forbidden to interfere in the national system of import duties. Direct taxes were authorized, as was the power to regulate commerce, coin money and determine its value, emit bills of credit, and conduct foreign relations. The government was also empowered to enact a "uniform Rule" on citizenship, a "uniform Law" on bankruptcy, "the Standard of Weights and Measures," and "to promote the Progress of Science and useful Arts" by patent and copyright laws. And finally, as an arbiter for the system, "one supreme Court" was explicitly authorized.

This direct reference to a judicial system and a Supreme Court underscores the extent to which Americans had come to consider the law the secular equivalent of religion as the cement of their mercantilism. Lawyers and merchants from the north had developed this view over a long period of experience, and it is not surprising to find men who had filed briefs against the Crown in hopes of settling disputes of basic interest being willing to give the law such a vital role in their own system. But the agrarians also accepted the principle and the practice of judicial review. In Virginia, for example, the case of *Caton v. Commonwealth* (1782) was decided on the basis of judicial supremacy and by the court declaring the unconstitutionality of a law.

While this conception of the law was essential to bind the various elements of mercantilism to a common standard, it lacked the positive and dynamic impetus in building the common welfare that organized religion had provided in an earlier age. Many of the Founding Fathers were individually men of strong religious faith, but they also believed in the separation of church and state. Hence they tried to provide an alternative in the ideal of secular corporate justice.

It was, as they knew, the kind of an internalized restraint that had to be developed if self-interest and private property were to function satisfactorily as means to the general welfare. Along with Adams, Jay, Jefferson, Monroe, and other mercantilists, Madison persistently emphasized the vital role of a strong sense of justice: the ideal had to be pursued with vigor if the Constitution were to produce the good society—"the national welfare"—that he sought.

This concern was an integral part of Madison's effort to establish a government which would combine "the requisite stability and energy in government, with the inviolable attention due to liberty and to the republican form." The result of his disciplined intellectual application to the problem was a series of letters and short essays in *The Federalist* that remain as one of the nation's most brilliant statements of a grand theory of sociology and historical change. They are also one of the magnificent examples of concise writing in the English language.

Starting with fundamentals, Madison defined the problem as one of controlling faction. Now to a mercantilist in Madison's day, a faction did *not* mean a political party. As the term was employed then, a faction was an interest group defined by functional criteria bent on preferential treatment or outright aggrandizement. Madison even used the word *interest* and specified "a landed interest, a manufacturing interest, a mercantile interest, a moneyed interest, [and] many lesser interests." Quite aware that such factions were conditioned by the psychological make-up of their members, particularly their leaders, and by the accident of birth which deposited a man in a particular place in a given political economy, Madison nevertheless concluded that "the most common and durable source of factions has been the various and unequal distribution of property. Those who hold and those who are without property have ever formed distinct interests in society."

Dismissing a solution based on imposing the same views on everyone, Madison presented a fourfold answer to the problem of preventing faction from ripping society asunder. It put first the ideal of justice, for which a constant personal and social struggle had to be waged. This meant practicing self-restraint as well as adhering to the principles of equity and common law. Next came the division of powers within the government. Such a system of checks and balances, staggered as they were in terms of tenure of office and methods of access, would do much to prevent any faction or interest from capturing complete control of the government. Then Madison worked out a broader balance between the states, the people, and the central government. Sometimes called "Dual Federalism," his plan was to divide the national system between the people and the states. In developing it, what Madison did was to draw on the old feudal principle of interlocking powers and responsibilities. He realized that this was an innovation. "It may be said," he wrote to Jefferson, "that the new Constitution is founded on different principles, and will have a different operation. I admit the difference to be material. It presents the aspect rather of a feudal system of republics, if such a phrase may be used, than of a Confederacy of independent states."

Not only may the concept *feudal* be used, it provides the most accurate insight into the true nature of the Constitution. It is a document based on feudal principles. Just as in the feudal age, the individual citizen was beholden to, but was also the responsibility of, the highest lord (or the national government). He had the same relationship with his state government (a lower lord), which in turn had (as a vassal to the top lord) reciprocal ties with the national government. As long as the citizen participated directly and actively at both levels, and as long as the states remained significant elements in the political economy of the system, the individual was protected and at the same time able to play a meaningful role in governing himself.

Madison ultimately realized that a crisis would occur when and if the citizen ceased to have significant leverage on the political economy. This happened in fact as the corporation replaced the individual in the narrow economic sense and subsumed the state as the element of social decision-making in the broader sense. While he did not foresee that particular form which the crisis was to take, Madison did recognize two other dangers. Conflict was inherent in a feudal system of organization. "And what," he asked rhetorically, "has been the progress and event of the feudal Constitution? In all of them a continual struggle between the head and the inferior members, until a final victory has been gained in some instances by one, in others, by the other of them." This brought Madison right back to the old problem of maintaining the balance between the various elements and to the dilemma defined by the expansionism inherent in mercantilism as opposed to the theory that republicanism could exist only in small states.

Madison resolved both difficulties by standing feudal theory on its head. He simply asserted that a large state would weaken the influence of faction, would provide inherent protection for private rights, and—*as he explicitly said of the west*—would provide "a mine of vast wealth to the United States [which is capable] under proper management, both to effect a gradual discharge of the domestic debt, and to furnish, for a certain period, liberal tributes to the federal treasury. . . . This form of Government, in order to effect its purposes, must operate not within a small but an extensive sphere." "Extend the sphere," he concluded, "and you take in a greater variety of parties and interests; you make it less probable that a majority of the whole will have a common motive to invade the rights of other citizens; or if such a common motive exists, it will be more difficult for all who feel it to discover their own strength, and to act in unison with each other."

Madison meant exactly what he said when he referred to the new government as "the Empire," and the opponents of the Constitution interpreted his language to mean a sustained policy of expansion. As one of those who led the fight against the new government, Patrick Henry decried this drive for empire. "Some way or other," he mocked them, "we must be a great and mighty empire." Insisting that republicanism was "only calculated for a territory but small in extent," Luther Martin of Maryland also attacked the Constitution on those grounds. He thought it the work of men who wanted "one great and extensive empire, calculated to aggrandize and elevate its rulers and chief officers far above the common herd of mankind, to enrich them with wealth, becircle them with honors and glory."

Though Edmund Randolph finally voted for ratification, George Mason, Richard Henry Lee, and those in the north such as George Clinton fought to the bitter end. Almost every opponent accepted Madison's description of the new arrangement as a feudal system and agreed with him that it would produce a running war between the central government and the states. They assumed that the states would lose—and the people also. The response of others was ambivalent. Though worried about individual rights, Elbridge Gerry thought the plan had "great merit, and, by proper amendment," could be accepted. While he wanted "an energetic government" to exercise "an absolute control over commerce," James Monroe recognized the danger inherent in Madison's feudal system. Sam Adams had similar "doubts"; recognizing the truth in Madison's description of the plan as a feudal system, he fretted about the dangers of "*imperia in imperio.*" Still, Adams admitted that it was "highly valuable" because of its power "to regulate commerce, to form treaties." Jefferson was generally pleased with the document, "especially in pecuniary and foreign concerns." He reported that he "read and contemplated its provisions with great satisfaction." Along with Adams and a good many others, however, Jefferson desired more explicit protection for the individual.

The kind of close attention given the document by Jefferson and Adam suggests that the ratification of the Constitution cannot be explained by reference to a political and propaganda coup. Madison admitted that the country was "certainly in the dark" until the document was signed and released, and that initiative clearly favored the advocates, as also did the sense of general crisis and the feeling that something had to be done. Yet the opponents of the Constitution were recognized leaders drawing upon the traditions and interests of small state government and appealing to a broad cross section of American society.

The willingness of the pro-Constitution coalition to compromise probably decided the issue in their favor. Their opponents won amendments designed to protect the individual and secure his basic rights of speech, property, and defense. Combined with the general sense of urgency, this understanding about the first ten amendments was very likely the determining factor, even though it seems highly probable that half the voting population favored the new system. Nevertheless, the favorable decision of men like Sam Adams helped—as did a few bargains struck within such key states as Virginia and New York. And it is important to remember that the vote on the Constitution can only be described as the lowest order of democracy: men given the chance to say nothing more than yes or no on such a basic decision are not participating very extensively in the management of their own affairs.

THE DOMESTIC WAR FOR INDEPENDENCE

Once the Constitution was ratified and the formality of electing Washington as the first President disposed of, American leaders began their struggle to create the government for which they had a charter. Their efforts were marked by militant, and at times impassioned, conflicts over the issues of independence, economic development, balance and justice, representative government, and expansion. As a key figure in those controversies, Alexander Hamilton was the most audacious, undemocratic, and immediately successful leader of a faction in American history. He generalized a highly sophisticated program devised by the pro-English commercial and financial interest into a prospectus for the nation and thereby created such antagonisms and discontents that the hard core of his interest group was ultimately driven from power forever.

Hamilton did not scheme to deliver America into the hands of the British. He merely struggled to consolidate the domestic power of his faction and then achieve and dominate an intimate *rapprochement* with the British Empire. Since commerce was a capital-accumulating sector of the economy, part of Hamilton's interest-defined program and policies contributed to the general development of the United States. It also gained him initial support from men who recognized that consequence of his specific proposals and whose immediate interests were favored by the legislation he sponsored. But Hamilton was not an American mercantilist concerned with building a balanced political economy. Despite his famous report on the subject, he never pushed manufacturing as an integral part of the economy and in fact opposed the efforts of others to accelerate its development.

Hence it is a fundamental mistake to assess Hamilton on the basis of either the immediate or the long-range consequences and benefits of the work of such mercantilists as Adams and Madison. After all, Madison and a majority of the gentry (and even some of the physiocratic followers of Taylor) supported the broad objective of Hamilton's program to fund the debts of the Confederation and assume the obligations of the states. The legislation would not have passed without their votes, and for that reason it is simply wrong to picture Hamilton as a solitary, embattled, and far-sighted hero who saved the new government. It is not even sensible, let alone equitable, to praise him as a unique leader for something that would have been done anyway.

Having sensed the nature of Hamilton's outlook and the limited character of his program, Madison took the initiative in the first Congress of 1789. Asserting that it was an issue of "the greatest magnitude" that "requires our first attention, and our united exertions," he called on April 8, 1789, for the construction of an independent, balanced political economy. Dismissing the theory of free trade, and bluntly warning that England's superior economic power had bound America in "commercial manacles, and very nearly defeated the object of our independence," he called for immediate action on a broad front. He recommended a mercantilist system to protect commerce, to sustain and extend the "rapid advances in manufacturing" through duties running up to 50 per cent, to provide a revenue for the government, and to secure the fisheries, because they were, "perhaps, the best nurseries for seamen of any employment whatever" (and he wanted "a school for seamen, to lay the foundation of a navy"). He even wanted a duty on beer that "would be such encouragement as to induce the manufacture to take deep root in every state in the Union." He sought, in short, "to teach those nations who have declined to enter into commercial treaties with us, that we have the power to extend or withhold advantages as their conduct shall deserve."

A good many southerners joined representatives from the north in supporting Madison's efforts to use "the fostering hand of government" to create the common good in an independent empire. Men from New Jersey and Pennsylvania agreed that the issue was "the prosperity and welfare of the United States," and "deemed it prudent to emancipate our country from the manacles in which she was held by foreign manufactures." President Washington pledged his assistance to a Delaware society for the promotion of manufactures. And having campaigned in support of the Constitution for just such purposes, Tench Coxe, a leading political economist of his day, was agitating for a program "to *foster and encourage*, but *not to force* manufactures" as a way of binding the north and south together and guaranteeing a prosperous independence.

Hamilton would have none of these programs. Mustering his followers in Congress, he blocked Madison by substituting a moderate revenue tariff bill that could be praised for its protective principles without danger to his own objectives. Then he proposed direct taxes on the middle and lower classes, a public debt, and a national bank. Despite their awareness that Hamilton's methods of centralizing the debts immediately favored the mercantile and banking factions,

Madison and other mercantilists, and even some of the narrow agrarians, were willing to contribute this extra subsidy to the north because they realized the necessity and the broader benefits of the actions.

Madison insisted, however, on challenging the equity and other implications of Hamilton's methods. In stressing the importance of justice to those "original sufferers," the first holders of the Confederation debt, and to the states (including Virginia) which had paid part of their arrears, Madison was no doubt thinking also about the possibilities of organizing some general opposition to Hamilton. But there is no reason to question Madison's sincerity: politics and justice are compartmentalized entities only in the mind of the cynic.

Madison raised another basic issue in arguing that the funding of the state debts and the creation of a national bank involved the power of the national government under the Constitution. *Regardless of the proposals, and whether one approved or disapproved them,* Madison insisted that the people had to decide in cases where there was a question about the constitutionality of the government's authority to act. Otherwise, he protested, the feudal balance between the citizen, the states, and the national government would be upset by a series of *ad hoc* interpretations that extended the power of one element in the system. One had to play by the rules or else the game became a crude scramble for power. Madison's objections to interpreted powers thus went far beyond a narrow concern for States' rights, and was a much more fundamental and sophisticated opposition than Taylor and other physiocrats offered.

Madison also opposed Hamilton's Bank of the United States because he was not convinced that it was necessary. Along with John Adams, he realized the useful role of basic financial institutions if the economy was to grow and prosper. But both men feared that such a bank, managed as it would be by private entrepreneurs, would exert a preponderant influence on the economy and thereby usurp part of the effective power of the people and the government. Since the large corporation did come to hold precisely such an indirect as well as direct sway in American government, Madison and Adams must be credited with a high degree of perception and foresight.

On the other hand, Hamilton's arguments that the Bank would serve a positive and creative economic function were much stronger than the criticisms made by physiocrats such as Taylor. They simply did not understand the role that credit and banks could play even in such an agrarian society, let alone their function in a balanced economy. Hamilton's role in establishing the Bank was in many ways the most positive and creative act of his career. Granted that Robert Morris had prepared the way, Hamilton sustained the idea and created the institution.

In the matter of manufactures, however, Hamilton has received far more repute than he deserves. He never revealed, either in the famous report on the subject or in his other actions, the kind of support for American manufacturing with which he is credited, or which might be expected of an American mercantilist. Indeed, the Congress *ordered* him on January 15, 1790, to prepare a report on manufactures. *Hamilton did not comply until December, 1791.* During the intervening two years, moreover, his other actions cast grave doubts on his interest in developing a balanced and independent mercantilist economy. First he encouraged the English to resist the renewed efforts of Madison and Jefferson (the latter had become Secretary of State) to modify British trade restrictions. Then he turned to direct taxes, instead of to import duties, to raise additional revenue.

Nor is his famous *Report on Manufactures* actually the mercantilist document that Hamilton's admirers have claimed that it is. Dismissing protective tariffs and outright prohibition of selected imports as offering no assistance, Hamilton emphasized the value of bounties paid by the American government to selected enterprises. But bounties could only be paid from domestic taxes such as the whiskey excise; and they involved an obvious kind of discrimination against selected taxpayers. Likewise, the distribution of the favors would depend upon political approval from Hamilton's group, and they did not provide any real protection against the shiploads of lower-priced English goods.

As a matter of equity as well as of economics, therefore, the bounty proposal was not very favorably received. Sensing the similarity between Hamilton's proposal and the old system of monopolistic grants that had caused so much trouble during Elizabeth I's reign, the great majority of American manufacturers reacted negatively. And their suspicions were intensified by the speculative, monopolistic character of Hamilton's own Society for Useful Manufactures incorporated in New Jersey. Along with fishermen and other Americans forced to compete with the British, such men began to look to Madison for leadership in building an American system.

They also reacted favorably to Jefferson's strong argument that the long-range solution of their difficulties was "to find markets." Here they turned to France, not only for economic reasons, but because they agreed with John Adams that it was the "natural ally" of the United States in a world dominated by the economic and naval power of Great Britain. The outbreak of the French Revolution gave added force to the argument. Most Americans at first responded favorably to that upheaval. Even so conservative a leader as John Marshall of Virginia was to recall that the great majority were pleased and enthusiastic. And Washington's early attitude, reinforced by recent difficulties with England, was also favorable to France.

On the other hand, Washington was a cautious man who took an extremely long-range view of the developing American empire. Fearing the possibility that war would destroy the nation, or perhaps rip it up into antagonistic subdivisions even if it were not conquered, he concluded that America had to stay out of the developing conflict between England and France. Whatever his assessment of the factors, he decided to give ground to the English on commercial issues in order to preserve peace, secure the Western frontier which the British and the Indians continued to violate, and gain time for the material and psychological maturation of the nation. On April 22, 1793, he declared that the country would "pursue a conduct friendly and impartial toward the belligerent powers."

Other societies, likewise just emerging as nations from an experience as colonies, were to follow a similarly neutral policy after World War II, and for the same basic reasons—they were weak and primarily concerned with establishing themselves as independent nations. And in a comparable fashion, many Americans of that earlier time initially exhibited considerable favoritism for the revolutionary side of the conflict. Both attitudes were particularly strong among those who also opposed Hamilton's openly anti-republican program which hurt them economically. Beginning to coalesce as formal organizations (usually known as Democratic-Republican Societies) which were encouraged and helped by Madison and his supporters, men combined praise for the French with criticism of Hamilton and his allies in America.

Americans of that persuasion received Citizen Genêt, the new French representative, with a favoritism that frightened many conservatives and even aroused Washington. The President soon reacted militantly against the Democratic-Republican Societies. Genêt temporarily eased the crisis by his outrageous disregard of American neutrality. Pro-Revolutionary though they were, the enthusiasts had no comparable fervor for war. But they did continue their attacks on Hamilton. These responses suggest two crucial points: first, Americans who approved the Revolution were more anti-British than pro-French; second, as their wild rhetoric and vigorous political action indicated, they were more excited and upset about events in America.

Sensing that such was the case, and weary of trying to work out a compromise with Hamilton within the cabinet, Jefferson resigned as Secretary of State on December 31, 1793. Washington's attempt to establish and maintain a mercantilist coalition immediately lost its momentum. Hamilton saw the opportunity and moved to seize it for his own. But just before he left office, Jefferson fired a broadside at the New Yorker. His Report on Commercial Privileges and Restrictions of December 16, 1793, was an important document in two respects: it documented Jefferson's move away from the *policy* of the physiocrats (though he was to retain his emotional and social commitment to their vision of an agrarian utopia), and it signified his willingness to accept the essentials of the mercantilist program. Admitting that he preferred the ideal of free trade (arguing that America would gain the most that way), Jefferson acknowledged that it was unworkable unless every other country also adopted it.

Hence a system of "heavier and heavier" shipping discriminations and protective duties had to be put into effect against those who refused fair treatment to the United States. Jefferson may have entertained a fond hope that such retaliation would open the door to his agrarian utopia, but he explicitly recognized that such a system would encourage general manufactures as well as those of the household variety. Not only did he accept this result, but he recommended that the *state* governments should "co-operate essentially, by opening the resources of encouragement which are under their control." He also noted that such a program might easily attract foreign manufacturers who would bring capital along with their knowledge. Jefferson very probably retained his attachment to home manufactures, but the crucial point is that he formally proposed to aid the other kind. John Taylor of Caroline, high priest of the physiocratic faith, recognized this important shift and soon began to criticize Jefferson very vigorously as one who had fallen away from the true church.

As a realist, and blossoming politician, Jefferson no doubt realized that organized manufacturing was beginning to benefit from the new economic interrelatedness of the country and from the conflict in Europe. By the time that Jefferson resigned, for example, both Boston and Philadelphia employed over 2,000 workers. Washington was particularly pleased by the rapid increase in small workshops throughout the nation. Enterprises of that kind produced the bulk of American manufactures for several decades, but the corporation form of organization was increasing in popularity for industrial and commercial operations. Within a decade more than 20 were operating, and North Carolina and Massachusetts had passed special laws facilitating their creation and expansion.

Armed with Jefferson's Report, Madison again took the offensive against Hamilton on January 3, 1794. Since free trade "required what did not exist—that it should be general," Madison proclaimed his mercantilism. "To allow trade to regulate itself is not therefore to be admitted as a maxim universally sound. Our own experience has taught us that, in certain cases, it is the same thing with allowing one nation to regulate it for another." Madison thus reached the same conclusion that Adam Smith had advanced in *The Wealth of Nations*. Both saw that an advanced industrial country had a decided advantage in its economic dealings with a relatively backward country.

Having presented the essence of his argument, Madison bluntly specified the source of the nation's difficulties. England was being "very arbitrary and tyrannical," and "extremely atrocious." As for Hamilton's commercial faction, Madison concluded that its ideas "might not be an American opinion." Madison was appealing not only to the manufacturers who were skeptical of Hamilton's professed interest in their activities, but also to the northern and southern merchants and producers who were becoming ever more insistent that something be done to reopen the West Indies trade. Britain had closed it in 1783, and had never relaxed its regulations on a general basis.

Hamilton answered through Representative William Smith of Maryland, who often gave the speeches that Hamilton prepared. Since England did not discriminate against America more than against anyone else, he argued, it therefore did not discriminate against America. (Congressman Smith was bluntly accused of "subterfuge and a spirit of quibbling" for mouthing such sophomoric sophistries.) As for American manufactures, Smith continued for Hamilton, they were "out of the question." Thus appeared Hamilton's appendix to his earlier Report on Manufactures; an addition that clarified the meaning of the earlier document beyond serious question.

Hamilton's supporters went on to make it perfectly clear that they agreed on "shunning everything that may wear the appearance of commercial warfare" with England. Appropriately enough, in view of the non-intellectual origins of that policy, Fisher Ames spoke in openly anti-intellectual accents. "We follow experience too little," he complained, "and the vision of theorists a great deal too much." Another opponent attempted to defeat Madison by ridicule. "The gentlemen for the resolutions were like some kinds of amphibious animals. If you attack them on the land they fly into the water; if you attack them by water they fly to land." It was a funny remark, but it was also one that cut through to the heart of the issue: American mercantilism versus pro-British commerce.

While he finally managed to block Madison's comprehensive program, Hamilton could not hold all his allies any longer. By a wide margin 58–38, the Congress authorized an embargo and unmistakably revealed its impatience with Hamilton as well as with the British. Feeling ran so high that secession was openly proposed and discussed. In private talks with John Taylor of Caroline, Rufus King even made a direct bid for pacific dismemberment of the country. The outer edges of the coalition that Washington had attempted to build seemed about to break off and establish two new nations. And as if that were not trouble enough, the west began to reassert its demands and to threaten independent action to get what it wanted. Maintaining the attitude he had revealed during the fight between Monroe and Jay, Washington continued his efforts to develop the west slowly and to come to some general settlement with the Indians.

WASHINGTON'S STRATEGY OF EMPIRE

Before blaming Washington for all the troubles that followed, it should be remembered that he had neither a strong nor a free hand. Jefferson, for example, had been dickering over the conquest of the Floridas (including New Orleans) ever since 1787. His diplomatic maneuvers included encouraging emigration and covert support for expansionist Kentuckians and other westerners. As for the Indians, Jefferson assumed that they would be thoroughly defeated if not literally destroyed. Westerners generally agreed, and began to back Jefferson for national leadership.

Washington's efforts to stabilize the west all but collapsed when the Indians defeated the American General Arthur St. Clair in November, 1791. Westerners were convinced that the British were intriguing to reconquer the entire Mississippi basin. Between the drive for New Orleans, the Indian problem, and the general sentiment for expansion, Jefferson wrote that the Kentuckians were "restrained from hostility by a pack thread." Washington stopped the Kentuckians and their sympathizers with a blunt warning to keep the peace or face a two-front war.

While the President's final strategy had superficial similarities to the proposals offered by Rufus King and other pro-English leaders, it was actually quite different. As one who described British acts as "hostile and cruel," Washington was not looking toward some increasingly close and permanent relationship with Britain. He wanted to avoid war, check British influence on the Indians, and ease the redcoats out of the western frontier posts. Concluding that a settlement along those lines would stabilize the situation and thereby create the circumstances for steady development, he sent John Jay to London. But Jay's mission was only half the program. It was also necessary to place the nation "in a complete state of military defense, and to provide *eventually*, such measures, as seem to be now pending in Congress, for execution, if negotiations in a reasonable time prove unsuccessful." As he knew, Washington was undertaking a delicate and risky maneuver.

Hamilton's intrigue wrecked whatever chance it had to succeed. He privately assured the English that they need not fear the growth of manufactures in America and told the British minister that "it was the settled policy of this government in every contingency, even in that of an open conflict with Great Britain, to avoid entangling itself with European connections." While this was not a promise to abandon force in dealing with England, it was a clear indication that Hamilton was opposed to an open break. Confident that America would fight alone if it ever came to it, the British relaxed and gave Jay nothing more than a few diplomatic crumbs.

Almost nobody in America was satisfied with the treaty. It provided no immediate, fundamental relief for American trade; for that matter, it seemed to threaten new limitations on the power to retaliate. The one big gain concerned the west, where the English agreed to give up the frontier forts. But many thought that should have been done ten years earlier. Southerners were particularly disgusted by the failure to gain satisfaction for the slaves that were taken or freed. And many merchants pointed out that the West Indies were still closed.

Jay defended his work on four grounds. It preserved the peace, secured the western forts and boundary, won access to the East India (or Asian) trade on an unrestricted basis, and thus broke "in upon the navigation act" in such a way that promised the "*further extension* of commerce" throughout the British system. Hamilton's argument was far different. He emphasized England's right to stand fast because it was struggling with "a question of national *safety*," whereas America was concerned only with "a question of commercial convenience and individual security." Not a few merchants joined a majority of farmers in concluding that Hamilton was placing the safety of England above the independence of America.

Washington's problem whether to accept the treaty was complicated by the armed protests against the whisky tax which had erupted in July, 1794, just as Jay arrived in London. The President erroneously interpreted both that action and the wild, vulgar, and extensive protests against the treaty as signs of incipient revolution. In at least two ways, however, that extreme conclusion provoked action which temporarily relaxed the tension. Not only did Washington's decision to use troops produce a sudden soberness among the whiskey distillers, but the absurd and at times hilarious mismanagement of the campaign by Hamilton, who had jumped at the chance to get back on horseback, did more than a little to make the New Yorker a less awesome figure.

Even so, Washington knew that his decision to press for ratification of the treaty was "very serious business indeed." He was again helped by his opponents. Those critics who went beyond the existing broad limits of permissible personal abuse generated a reaction in favor of the President. And despite the efforts of such opponents to block the treaty by refusing to appropriate the necessary funds, a maneuver which Madison himself deemed unwise, Washington continued to reassert his control over the situation. He gained further strength when he won concessions from Spain on the Florida boundary and commercial rights on the Mississippi and in New Orleans. And even as those benefits were being formalized (October, 1795), General Anthony Wayne routed the Ohio Indians and cleared the territory for settlement, commerce, and the fur trade.

Washington was suddenly, and in part fortuitously, in a position to retire gracefully. As farewell advice, he admonished his country-men to calm their fears and take advantage of the opportunity that was theirs to become the leading power of the world. Cautioning them not to allow geographic and economic differences to produce disunion, he suggested that it would be wise to maintain an explicit system of religious "national morality" as cement for the country as well as a guide to the common welfare. And he was particu-larly insistent that the citizenry take direct responsibility for any modifications in the constitutional framework. Irresponsible shifts in the balance of authority would "create, whatever the form of government, a real despotism." Changes should be effected "by an amendment in the way which the Constitution designates." "Let there be no change by usurpation," he urged, in a clear defense of what Madison termed a feudal system of republics.

As for men who questioned the viability of one government for "so large a sphere," Washington judged that "there will always be reason to distrust the patriotism" of such critics until they were proved correct. There was no present reason to reexamine it. "If we remain one people, under an efficient government, the period is not far off," he confidently predicted, "when we may defy material injury from external annoyance; when we may take such an attitude as will cause the neutrality we may at any time resolve upon to be scrupulously respected; when belligerent nations, under the impos-sibility of making acquisitions upon us, will not lightly hazard the giving us provocation; when we may choose peace or war, as our interest, guided by justice, shall counsel." Far from being a call for isolation, what Washington issued was a mercantilist manifesto for an unchallengeable empire. Whatever one thinks of the logic, or of the goal itself, Washington's Farewell Address remains one of the great documents of America's Age of Mercantilism.

THE STATESMANSHIP OF JOHN ADAMS

As one who entertained the same *Weltanschauung* as Washington, John Adams tried several times to create a mercantilist cabinet including southerners as well as northerners. Failing that, he listened carefully to those like businessman Albert Gallatin of Pennsylvania who were active members of the Madison group. Had Madison and Jefferson given him more overt assistance, as at least once they considered doing, a great deal of private and social pain might have been avoided. Instead, Adams became the first President faced with a Congress controlled by *two* opposition parties and confronted abroad by two major empires, each of which offered cause for war. Finding no men with quite the will or the sense of justice to help him, Adams courageously burned his political bridges ahead of him and acted alone to secure peace for the country. It was one of the greatest acts of American leadership, and set a standard of statesmanship that few have equaled.

As soon as he took office, Adams was confronted at home and abroad by major opponents. Hamilton left the cabinet and set about to run the country through his control of the Federalist Party. He came uncomfortably close to doing so. At the same time, Madison and those of his political lieutenants such as John Beckley of Virginia and Frederic A. C. Huhlenberg of Pennsylvania commanded enough national strength to create additional difficulties for Adams. An almost exact parallel existed in foreign affairs, where England and France alternated in raising the greatest havoc with American ships, sailors, and commerce. Adams never wavered from his objective of keeping America neutral while gaining strength enough to win practical recognition of the right to trade with both belligerents. But Hamilton wanted war against France and, if possible, a Gargantuan invasion of South America with the British. Madison and Jefferson favored France for economic as well as ideological reasons (exports to France gained steadily for a time after 1794) and were militantly anti-British. Neither of them, however, wanted to rush into war.

Riding the current of popular reluctance to go to war, Adams maneuvered between the two blocs. Choosing his men carefully (the politics was important, but the outlook of the men more so), he dispatched John Marshall, Charles Pinckney, and Elbridge Gerry to Paris to negotiate a new treaty of trade and friendship. When they failed, as the result of a French blunder and their own pride and nationalism, Adams realized he was in trouble. A general wave of anger against France gave Hamilton an opportunity to push for war. Adams admitted that it might ultimately be necessary, but disagreed vigorously with Hamilton. Aware that the British were again acting in the west as well as continuing their seizures of American commerce, Adams advocated a thoroughly mercantilist strategy designed to protect the United States against either European power.

"We ought," he recommended, "without loss of time, to lay the foundation for an increase of our Navy to a size sufficient to guard our coast, and protect our trade." Having no illusions about the British—they were determined "to engross the commerce of the world to themselves"—Adams fought Hamilton as best he could. He got no direct help from Madison and Jefferson. Finally, in February, 1798, Adams acted on his own and broke with Hamilton over assigning top priority to building up a navy. "I have always cried, Ships! Ships!" Adams accurately recalled in later years. "Hamilton's hobbyhorse was Troops! Troops!"

Humorous or not, the point was crucial. Hamilton launched a major campaign to consolidate his power at home and then ally it with England against France and to conquer parts of Spanish America. "Nothing but an open war can save us," he cried, in both fear and determination. By "us"—at least according to the British—Hamilton meant "the men of fortune, of weight and character [who favored] a close connection with Great Britain as the only wise system of American politicks." In a brilliant, albeit nearly fanatic, outburst of driving leadership, Hamilton jammed through major elements of his program. His supporters voted increases in the Army and a land tax to pay for them, and also approved new loans. They then moved against their opponents—real and fancied—with the Naturalization Act, the Alien Act, and the Sedition Act. While no doubt given a more ominous cast by the crisis, the first two were commonplace pieces of legislation familiar to all countries in 1789.

They remain so today. The sedition law, on the other hand, was a vicious catch-all bill obviously designed to put Hamilton's critics out of circulation.

Adams should have vetoed the bill: *his* ethical and philosophical principles demanded such action. On the other hand, Madison and Jefferson should have been giving Adams open and coordinated help against Hamilton: *their* ethical and philosophical principles demanded such action. All three men failed at a crucial moment in the development of a corporate, social responsibility to accompany the political economy of mercantilism. But private and group interest triumphed over public duty, and civil war seemed almost certain. Hamilton and some of his associates talked of marching into Virginia and dividing it into smaller states. Virginians openly considered secession.

Though it was not at all their explicit purpose, Madison and Jefferson finally acted at that moment of passion in a way that did strengthen Adams's hand. They wrote, and maneuvered into formal presentation by two states, a pair of manifestoes that defined the crisis in exceedingly blunt terms and probably checked the rush to violence. In view of his early and persistent attachment to the utopia defined by John Taylor of Caroline, it is not surprising that Jefferson's resolutions (adopted by Kentucky in 1798) were the most extreme. Arguing that the state had "*an equal right to judge for itself, as well of infractions* [of the Constitution] *as of the mode and measures of redress,*" Jefferson raised the clear implication of secession by claiming the right of a state to declare "void and of no force" such laws by the national government. More concerned to maintain the union by revitalizing his idea of a feudal balance and aware that Jefferson's argument was not very well received in other states, Madison's resolutions in Virginia were milder. Emphasizing the danger of warping the feudal balance "into an absolute or, at best, a mixed monarchy," he was trying to shock the nation into blocking Hamilton's drive for consolidated power.

By that time, Hamilton was discussing an alliance with Britain. Adams was outraged: "This man is stark mad, or I am." He had taken enough from what he later termed the "fools who were intriguing to plunge us into an alliance with England, and endless war with all the rest of the world . . . and, what was worse than all the rest, a civil war, which I knew would be the consequence of the measures the heads of that party wished to pursue." Reporting that France had indicated "a disposition to do us justice," he moved rapidly to sign a treaty and thereby water the sand under Hamilton's feet.

Magnificently courageous in conception and execution, the maneuver avoided war. It also cost Adams his public career. Hamilton saw to that. Defeated by Jefferson in the election of 1800, Adams retreated to Massachusetts where he groomed his son for future leadership. Jefferson himself had written in 1797 that he, too, was "happier at home." It was probably true. By temperament more a man of thought than of action, he disliked politics despite his early "spice of ambition" and the gift of guile that has helped many a political leader. He was most at ease when pursuing his intellectual interests and social pleasures as the master of Monticello. Yet he personified the dream that was already beginning to haunt Americans: a society of free and independent men made equal and prosperous by the bounty of nature. Holding that vision himself, Jefferson extended his ambition into a sense of duty and a sizable willingness to put his ideas into operation.

Without the work of Madison, Beckley, and others like them who built the political organization that elected him, it seems doubtful that Jefferson would have gone beyond the leadership of Virginia. Assisted by the failure of Hamilton's policies (and the New Yorker's vicious fight with Adams), Madison and a band of energetic and talented local leaders put together a coalition of mechanics, planters, merchants, yeomen, and manufacturers that ruled the country for 30 years. It was a classic merging of interests and ideas under the *Weltanschauung* of mercantilism. Organized in the city as well as through the back country and the tidewater, that first Republican party attracted Hamiltonians like Fitzsimons of Pennsylvania as early as the election of 1800. Within a decade it had won such northerners as John Quincy Adams, William Plumer, and William L. Gray (probably the wealthiest merchant in America). Jefferson's attempt in 1798 and 1799 to change the party's name to Whig was appropriate, for it represented the same convergence of landed and urban groups of both upper and lower classes that Shaftesbury had organized in the 1670s.

It seems doubtful that Jefferson ever became a mercantilist in the full philosophical sense. He always honored the image of an agrarian utopia in which property in land would guarantee liberty, prosperity, and happiness. Yet under the tutoring of Madison and the pressure of the changes that were taking place in America, Jefferson accepted and employed mercantilist programs and policies between 1791 and 1820. Perhaps he actually changed his views during those years. More probably he continued through that period to view mercantilism as a way to achieve a good society modeled on the feudal vision of the physiocrats. Ultimately realizing that the attempt was subversive of its avowed objective, he repudiated the political economy of mercantilism and tried to work out an appropriate and effective physiocratic program.

When he entered the White House, however, Jefferson was fully prepared to follow Madison's lead in such matters. "If the commercial regulations had been adopted which our legislature were at one time proposing," he wrote in 1797 after Madison's campaign of 1794 had been defeated by Hamilton, "we should at this moment have been standing on such an eminence of safety and respect as ages can never recover. But having wandered from that, our object should now be to get back, with as little loss as possible, and when peace shall be restored, endeavor so to form our commercial regulations that justice from other nations shall be their mechanical result." And even at that time he was thinking of an embargo and other measures to strengthen America's *"native capitalists."*

While Jefferson had strong emotional and intellectual ties with France (among them a grand attachment to an extremely attractive woman), the vigor of his skepticism about Britain was not merely the reverse side of that involvement. As early as 1791, for example, he had offered an astute analysis of the unbalanced relationship with England and the reasons it should be changed. Unless it were changed, he concluded, Britain's preponderant economic power in commerce, finance, and manufacturing would seriously restrict American development and perhaps even undercut political self-government. He wanted a national commerce as the "handmaiden of agriculture"; therefore, he added, it "will be cherished by me both from principle and duty." "The day is within my time, as well as yours," he reassured William Short in 1801, "when we may say by what laws other nations shall treat us on the sea. And we will say it." Not even Washington anticipated more.

Whatever the temporary restraints, Jefferson expected American expansion to "cover the whole northern, if not the southern continent." He could not "contemplate with satisfaction either blot or mixture on that surface." Thus, while he spoke of civilizing the Indians, he urged his countrymen to "press upon them" until they were out of the way. With most Americans of his time, he considered re-colonization as the best solution to the slave question; but he also thought it would be wise to "combine it with commercial operations, which might not only reimburse expenses, but procure profit also." As for critics who complained that he was not active enough as an expansionist, Jefferson had a ready answer: they "would be cruelly mortified could they see our files." And indeed they would.

Whether as participants on the frontier, or as leaders and supporters in the east, the great majority of Americans accepted some variant of the expansionist philosophy. Jedidiah Morse, Congregational minister and author of the justly famous *American Geography*, asserted that the United States had "risen into Empire" with the ratification of the Constitution. "It is well known that empire has been travelling from east to west," he reminded his readers. "Probably her last and broadest seat will be America . . . the largest empire that ever existed." Albert Gallatin, a leading Pennsylvania businessman who was one of Jefferson's close associates, was inclined to view expansion as essential. "If the cause of the happiness of this country was examined into, it would be found to arise as much from the great plenty of land in proportion to the inhabitants . . . as from the wisdom of their political institutions."

Jefferson neatly summarized America's maturing mercantilism. America's success, he wrote in 1801, "furnishes a new proof of the falsehood of Montesquieu's doctrine, that a republic can be preserved only in a small territory. The reverse is the truth." Believing this, Americans were soon to go to war against Great Britain for trade and land and shortly thereafter to assert their primary position in the whole of the Western Hemisphere.

CHAPTER FOUR

The Transformation of Reality and the Inception of New Ideas

The larger our association, the less it will be shaken by local passions. . . .
Thomas Jefferson, 1804

We are going to fight for the reestablishment of our national character . . . for the protection of our maritime citizens . . . to vindicate our right to a free trade, and open markets for the productions of our soil now perishing on our hands; . . . in fine, to see some indemnity for past injuries, some security against future aggressions, by the conquest of all the British dominions upon the continent of North America.
Andrew Jackson, 1812

Acquiescence in the practice and pretensions of the British Government . . . would recolonize our commerce by subjecting it to a foreign Authority. . . . Experience warns us of the fatal tendencies of a commerce unrestricted with Great Britain, and restricted by her pleasure and policy elsewhere. Whilst the limited Market would continue overcharged with our exports, the disproportionate imports from it, would drain from us the precious metals, endanger our monied Institutions; arrest our internal improvements, and would strangle in the cradle, the manufactures which promise so vigorous growth.
James Madison, 1812

What! Shall this great mammoth of the American forest leave his native element and plunge into the water in a mad contest with the shark?
John Randolph of Roanoke, 1806

I do not believe in the practicability of a long continued union. . . . I am therefore ready to say, "Come out from among them, and be ye separate."
Timothy Pickering, 1804

I know and see every day the extent of geographical feeling and the necessity of prudence, if we mean to preserve and invigorate the Union.

Albert Gallatin, 1816

THE FOUNDING FATHERS AND THE FRONTIER THESIS

Set alongside De Tocqueville's remark that Americans were "haunted by visions of what will be," Jefferson's persistent concern with his physiocratic dream raises the perplexing question of why no one provided a classic didactic statement or fictional presentation of the American Utopia. Americans were strong on propaganda and vague assertion, but weak on firm conceptions. That loyal nabob and royal Governor of Massachusetts, Thomas Pownall, had said about as much as anyone. He defined America merely as a "New System of Things and Men, which treats all as they actually are, esteeming nothing the true End and perfect Good of Policy, but that effect which produces, as equality of Rights, so equal Liberty, universal Peace, and unobstructed intercommunication of happiness in Human Society."

The same absence of particulars, of some idea of how people were to *live*, strikes the reader of the famous poem "The Rising Glory of America" by Freneau and Brackenridge. They spoke of empire "Stretch'd out from thence far to the burning line," and of "num'rous ships of trade," but not of the society itself. Hector St. John de Crèvecover said little more in *Letters from An American Farmer*. He saw empire as the circumstance that "tended to regenerate" the colonist: "new laws, a new mode of living, a new social system." Of the new system, however, he said nothing. He merely talked about the existing order revived by a surplus of property: "to become a free man, invested with lands, to which every municipal blessing is annexed!"

A stronger case might be made for saying that James Fenimore Cooper defined the American utopia in his series of novels. Yet in fact he outlined two American utopias. One was the eastern aristocracy, and that was hardly either unique or idealistic in 1800. The other was the frontier of Natty Bumppo. *But that was not a society.* It was a man and a few comrades establishing a rudimentary ecology.

Cooper's women were singularly lacking in substance and almost literally absent in fact. As for the men, D. H. Lawrence described a typical one rather aptly: "hard, isolate, stoic, and a killer." Bumppo killed only when necessary, and with a piety, to be sure, but piety toward nature and animals is not necessarily piety toward men; transferred to humans, the attitude often produces an appalling arrogance.

Only Jefferson's *Notes on Virginia* remains for serious consideration. Here, at any rate, was a society of human beings. But here also was the traditional stress on property, land, and freedom within a hierarchical order. "Those who labor in the earth are the chosen people of God, if ever he had a chosen people, whose breasts he has made his peculiar deposit for substantial and genuine virtue." But that definition of the good society as a stratified, corporate community based on private property in land was far less significant *as a utopia* than the vision which had been advanced by one wing of the English Revolution, that of a corporate Christian commonwealth based on social property. Along with a few others, Sam Adams sustained parts of this ideal, but even he cramped it into a conservative, property-bound form. And for Jefferson as for Adams, expansion was the only way that the benefits of the system could be extended. Indeed, expansion was the only thing that made sense of Jefferson's famous motto about letting each generation make its own decisions. Either the phrase documented his total naïveté, which is of course absurd, or it meant that there had to be room and resources for everyone to start over.

Like Cooper, therefore, Jefferson had to accept the frontier as the only possible definition of an American utopia. All else already existed. But the frontier in this meaning was a process of becoming, not of being, and hence substituted motion for structure as its end. Motion as a substitute for structure is possible only so long as there is unlimited room to move in. When confined without the discipline provided by an ideal, such social motion produces aimlessness or chaos—or perhaps the final ordering of some utopia. And when it actually came to be so confined, Jefferson's south had nothing to guide it but the image of a feudal utopia created for it by Jefferson himself and John Taylor. That trapped the south, for by definition the utopia of Taylor and Jefferson had to expand or stagnate. The first act of that southern expansion was of necessity a move to acquire the freedom of action to extend itself. Secession was that first act of expansion.

But the industrial and agrarian utopias of the north and west also relied on expansion for success. Free farmers were Jefferson's ideological camp followers; merchants and industrialists could choose between the expansion explicit in mercantilism or inherent in laissez faire. Men who had neither the education nor the wealth to live as aristocrats naturally placed a similar emphasis on the frontier. For that matter, the frontier in some ways took the place of formal education; a kind of nonintellectual learning by surviving and succeeding became part of the American attitude at an early date. That Jefferson, who valued the intellect so highly and did so much to establish the University of Virginia, should also have contributed to that side of the educational ledger is an often neglected facet of his physiocracy.

As should be apparent, this conception of the frontier defined it not as a boundary but as an area to enter and occupy. Reinforcing the old antagonism toward England, such aspects of the frontier as a utopia would seem to do a great deal to explain America's steadily growing conviction that it could not live with any other nation occupying any significant part of the North American continent. Viewed through Lewis Carroll's looking-glass, this attitude could be defined as isolationism. But like the very expansionism implicit in mercantilism's static view of the world, this definition of utopia as a frontier produced a policy that was anything but isolationist. It was militantly, even aggressively, expansionist.

Jefferson moved quickly to initiate a western advance. His confidential message to the Congress of January 18, 1803, requested money for an expedition "to provide an extension of territory which the rapid increase of our numbers will call for." Avoiding all euphemisms, this meant that he was preparing expansion not only south, but west *across* the Mississippi *before* he knew that France was willing to sell the Louisiana Territory. His argument was bold even though his procedure was a classic of guile: expansion was necessary for democracy and prosperity. The Indians, for example, would thus be removed, and control of the Mississippi would end the question of egress to world markets. "The interests of commerce," Jefferson concluded in reference to the Pacific trade, "place the principle object within the constitutional powers and care of Congress, and that it should incidentally advance the geographic knowledge of our own continent can not but be an additional gratification." Expansion, not science, was the engine of the Lewis and Clark Expedition.

Had Jefferson and other Americans been forced to choose between a war with France and no further expansion at that time, they might have worked out some clear conception of the kind of society they wanted to build. But the fortuitous ease with which they acquired the 828,000 square miles of the Louisiana Territory served to convince them that expansion was a safe and cheap cure-all for their needs and difficulties. The Senate vote of 24 to 7 was an index of the national sentiment on expansion in its ideological as well as its obvious economic aspects.

Although they may appear a bit surprising in view of his vigorously expansionist messages of 1801 and 1802, Jefferson's qualms about the constitutionality of the purchase may have been completely sincere. He was far too astute to miss the implications of the move for the feudal balance of republics that Madison kept worrying about. But as Madison had done in 1787, and obviously paraphrasing Madison's argument as his own, Jefferson resolved the dilemma in favor of expansion. His second inaugural address, March 4, 1804, was a hymn to Madison's theory. The taxes to pay for the expansion, Jefferson explained, made expansion possible; the expansion would lower taxes. "Who can limit the extent to which the federative principle may operate effectively?" he concluded. "The larger our association, the less it will be shaken by local passions."

Westerners enthusiastically embraced this expansionist theory of democracy and prosperity. A Kentuckian boasted, for example, that his countrymen were "full of enterprise and although not poor, are greedy after plunder as ever the old Romans were, Mexico glitters in our Eyes—the word is all we wait for." It was not so much the word that they awaited as it was the election of enough of their fellow expansionists to control Congress. That came in 1810 and 1811; meanwhile the region developed rapidly as a producer of agricultural surpluses for commercial markets. Continued settlement of the Appalachian and Upper Ohio regions, as well as of Kentucky and Tennessee, tripled the population of the west between 1800 and 1810. Moving along the Mohawk River route, the trail to Pittsburgh, and the Wilderness Road in the Shenandoah Valley, a good many of the increasing number of immigrants simply bypassed the east. These people made the west function as a safety valve for the eastern seaboard in the truest sense. The cities and other settled regions never had to contend with them as economic, political, or social problems.

Westerners were soon enjoying their own religious revivals under the leadership of men like James McGready, whose Cane Ridge Meeting of 1801 rivaled anything George Whitefield had produced in colonial New England. Methodist and Baptist churches grew rapidly, and in Kentucky finally merged with Barton W. Stone's followers to form the Christian Church. Although some western ministers were vigorously anti-education, the revivals not only led to the rise of a large number of religious schools (thus delaying secular state-supported education), but also provided an impetus for the organization in 1810 of the American Board of Commissioners for Foreign Missions. While the Board's activities in the Mediterranean and the Far East ultimately contributed to the character (and the problems) of American foreign policy, the immediate result of such religious enthusiasm was to strengthen the west's self-consciousness. As a partner on the frontier, God provided reassurance in the wilderness and strong sanction for action against opponents who blocked the way to more land and trade.

THE ACHIEVEMENTS AND DILEMMAS OF
JEFFERSONIAN MERCANTILISM

This rapid economic development in the west produced an export trade from Tennessee and Mississippi as early as 1801. Kentucky, Indiana, Michigan, and Ohio were shipping surpluses down the Mississippi by 1806. And Pittsburgh, which was rapidly becoming known as "the western workshop," had its first iron-rolling mill in operation by 1811. It was not Pittsburgh, however, that undercut Washington's plan for a Virginia iron and industrial complex that would subvert slavery.

That blueprint was torn up by the businessmen who built a textile industry in England and by the American inventors who produced the cotton gin that handled the rough processing of the crop. Although antislavery sentiment continued to grow in line with Jefferson's cry of anguish—"We are truly to be pitied"—southern planters, after the slave uprising known as the Gabriel Plot of 1801 in Virginia, tightened up their controls and turned their gangs of black labor into the fields with renewed confidence. By 1820 they had captured the British market. But they also sold increasing amounts to northern industrialists. By the time that Jefferson retired in 1809, there were over 80 cotton mills in the country. And one of them, the Boston (Waltham) Manufacturing Company, had organized all its operations into one integrated system.

Other manufacturers were producing nails and cards by semiautomatic machines, and Seth Thomas clocks had become an established commodity. Indeed, almost half of the immigrants who came between 1783 and 1812 established themselves in nonagrarian jobs. Usually known as the inventor of the cotton gin (which he probably was not), Eli Whitney actually made a far more important contribution to America's industrial development. Along with Simeon North, he worked out the idea—and the production line—for interchangeable parts in manufactured goods. Starting with guns, the application of the principle became in many respects the key to modern industrial society. Other Americans were beginning to make machines, a particularly important element in economic independence.

Between 1800 and 1816, banking operations expanded from 29 institutions to 246. Society was becoming stable enough for life insurance companies to begin entering the field alongside their maritime predecessors. And the corporation form of organization received a big boost from the New York law of 1811, which permitted general incorporation without special applications and restrictions. Most of the early corporations were in transportation, an indication that the merchant capitalist and the commercial trader played key roles in the early economy. American ships handled over 90 per cent of the nation's trade by 1805, and exports had zoomed to $108,000,000 by 1808. Three years later, John Jacob Astor's American Fur Company had established a base on the Pacific at the mouth of the Columbia River, close cooperation by Jefferson providing a striking indication of the evolving mercantilism of the Republican party leadership.

In the meantime, however, the central issues of politics and government were defined by the problems of building such an American mercantilist system. As a prime source of wealth and welfare, the great western reserve of land presented several of those

problems. Indian policy, for example, continued to provoke arguments between those who wanted to be more equitable and those
who stressed expansion. Despite the excited, even wild, enthusiasm for land, a surprising number of Americans were uneasy about
the policy of unrestrained conquest and tried to halt the aggressive
destruction of Indian society. Jefferson often borrowed their rhetoric
but his practice was rather different. His economic policy toward the
Indians provided a good summary of his attitude. He was "glad to see
the good and influential individuals among them in debt; because we
observe that when these debts get beyond what the individuals can
pay, they become willing to lop them off by a cession of lands."

Land policy was in essence a problem of resolving three
competing claims in a workable program. As a source of wealth,
the land could be used for the accumulation of private or social
riches. And, given a system of politics based on property, land was
crucially important in maintaining the political balance of a large
nation. Designed to establish settlers on the soil and also provide
national revenue, the evolving pattern culminated in the law of
1820. Concluding that the earlier credit system stimulated speculation, the Congress reestablished cash payments while lowering
the price to $1.25 per acre and permitted sales of 80 acres and
more. Speculators still accumulated fortunes, but the law worked
well enough to dramatize the central problem of creating a national
economic system. Westerners demanded government aid in transportation and commerce.

Both in theory and practice, the principle of government assistance had become widely accepted. South Carolina, for example,
passed a typical law in 1808 for "the establishment and encouragement" of manufactures. Pennsylvania helped finance various
enterprises, granted cash subsidies to others, and proclaimed "the
duty and interest of all governments to prevent fraud, and promote
the interests of just and useful commerce." A typical writer in
Massachusetts thought it "manifestly erroneous" that people "are the
judges of their interests, and consequently should be allowed to regulate them unobstructed." Such laissez faire was "subversive to the end
and aim of all governments." As the governor pointed out in 1809,
the state had accepted the responsibility of "making and executing
just and practicable laws of inspection on manufactured articles."
John Adams summarized the situation accurately in his comment

that "democrats and aristocrats all unite" on the basic axioms of mercantilism.

National debate centered on four issues: internal improvements, banking and monetary policy, commercial discriminations, and aid to manufacturers. Mechanics and merchants alike petitioned for continued trade discriminations, predicting "a total stagnation in our shipbuilding" and commerce if these were lowered or abandoned. Any relaxation would be "a fatal blow," explained still others, and would be "extremely injurious to the agricultural and the mechanical classes of our citizens." Jefferson responded by maintaining the discriminations that he had recommended in 1793 and by undertaking the naval war against the Mediterranean pirates that he had suggested even earlier. These policies did not completely solve the crisis confronting a weak and backward country caught in the middle of a world war; yet for a time, as the profits of neutral trade brought a flamboyant prosperity, two purely domestic issues gained priority.

Both of these, internal improvements and national finance, became the principal concern of Albert Gallatin. A vigorous defender of civil and religious liberties and a strong advocate of an educational system, Gallatin had favored internal improvements and central banking ever since his service in the Pennsylvania legislature during the 1790s. Other Jeffersonians such as Senator Thomas Worthington of Ohio and Superintendent of Patents William Thornton advocated similar plans and provided important support, but Gallatin was the central figure in both areas. His plan was simple: use the receipts from land sales to promote economic development, and then sustain, control, and balance it through assistance to manufactures and by a national financial system.

Gallatin's masterpiece was his majestic report of April 8, 1808, on a national transportation and communications network designed to strengthen the sense and reality of "community." His proposed ten-year plan made Hamilton appear a fumbling amateur. Having accepted Madison's stress on expansion, Gallatin sought to make the theory work. Concerned with "justice" and a "still more intimate community of interests," he tried to minimize the dangers of separatism "by opening speedy and easy communications" throughout the nation. He proposed four main avenues: coastwise from Maine to Georgia; across the mountains through New York, Pennsylvania, and Virginia into Kentucky and Tennessee; across the four major isthmian blocks (Cape Cod, Delaware, New Jersey, and the Dismal Swamp in Virginia and North Carolina); and into the Great Lakes region.

Two years later, in 1810, he reported on manufactures. Stressing their vital importance to balanced growth and independence, he recommended a program of cash subsidies and other government aid to accelerate their development. But, as he realized, the long-range solution would be provided by an expanding home market stable enough to encourage large investment, *and by the establishment of economic independence vis-à-vis England's superior industrial system.* As did Madison and others, Gallatin understood perfectly the unfavorable consequences of free trade to a relatively backward, underdeveloped economy. This very issue of England's power over the American economy finally subverted his program. As he put it, his ten-year plan became "inexpedient" during a war with the most advanced industrial power in the world.

In the meantime, Gallatin encountered difficulties at home. While he secured an initial grant from land sales in Ohio and with that money began construction of the National Road west to the Ohio River in 1806, he promptly ran into the kind of particularistic opportunism that produced a hodgepodge of pork-barrel legislation instead of a coherent program. Here, of course, was the other side of Madison's expansionist solution to the danger of faction. For it also weakened the sense of community and made it difficult to establish a check on private and group property interests that undercut the general welfare. But supported by such men as John Quincy Adams, who also favored integrated development in preference to a patchwork of local projects, Gallatin initiated and preserved the idea of a truly *national* system.

Jefferson accepted the principle of such internal improvements, emphasizing education as well as canals, but he raised the issue of constitutionality. So did Madison, who feared that such a plan would unbalance his "feudal system of republics." Both men put their case directly: if the Congress undertook a ten-year plan of the magnitude and with the consequences inherent in Gallatin's program without explicit public approval in the form of a constitutional amendment, then a process of interpreting the constitution would have started that could end only in monarchy or some other form of tyranny.

Both men had similar reservations about continuing the national bank. But understanding and accepting Gallatin's argument that it would balance and stabilize the monetary system, and agreeing that destroying it would cause "much individual and probably ... no inconsiderable public injury," Madison concluded that the bank should be maintained. Jefferson, on the other hand, never overcame two fundamental reservations, and his skepticism helped block a recharter in 1811. Like Madison, but with more insistence, he worried lest the bank in time become an institution that cut across all regional and political lines. Doing so, he reasoned, it would subvert the authority of the states and hence replace or override them as an institution in the political economy. It would do so, moreover, outside the constitutional framework. This would not only recast the entire balance of power that the constitution established, but the bank would effect the change as an institution which was not in any way directly responsible to the people. He feared the end result would be a kind of "vassalage" imposed on both the individual and the government.

Jefferson's analysis was extremely perceptive, and basically his criticism was valid. Any economic institution organized on a national basis but essentially controlled by a group of private citizens would make economic decisions that affected all aspects of society without its powers being defined in the Constitution or checked by public participation and direct responsibility. This was anything but an irrational or irrelevant argument by an agrarian who did not understand economics. It was an astute analysis of the relationship between economic power and its social and political consequences, and our modern industrial corporations, together with the Federal Reserve Board itself, have verified it.

In his own physiocratic way, Jefferson had raised once again the crucial issue for mercantilists: How does one use private property to accomplish social ends without giving way to the narrower view? But to raise the question was not enough, and Jefferson's position had a fundamental weakness. He answered his own intelligent analysis of danger with an anti-intellectual conclusion that there was no way to have the benefits of the bank while controlling its potential harm. Without any doubt, Jefferson's position strengthened the coalition of businessmen such as Henry Clay of Kentucky and Isaac McKim of Maryland and agrarians such as John Taylor of Virginia and his western followers who fought the bank for the greater glory of their interests and principles. Symbolizing such opposition, Vice-President Clinton of New York in 1811 cast the deciding vote against rechartering the bank.

Despite their victory, Taylor and his physiocrat compatriots were by that time caught in a difficult contradiction between their theory and the mercantilist reality of their world. Given the general attack by Britain and France on American shipping, Taylor and Randolph had two choices: they could go to war, or they could simply acquiesce in British domination of the seas and its comparable industrial power vis-à-vis the American economy. As the philosophers of a faction, their logic took them, by quite a different route, to an agreement with the pro-British merchant group: no war with England. Put simply, the opposition to the War of 1812 was a coalition of the groups that had never wholly accepted an American mercantilism.

Neither Jefferson nor Madison wanted a war with Great Britain. They were not fanatic Anglophiles. But both men did fear the long-run consequences of the economic imbalance between the two systems and sought by economic power to break out of the relationship by persuading England to acknowledge America's right to trade throughout the British Empire and with other nations. When they first came to power, Madison and Jefferson kept Rufus King in London, hoping that his long associations and sympathies would facilitate some kind of equitable settlement. England continued its economic warfare. So next they sent Monroe on a special mission, just as Washington had sent Jay, but backed him up with economic measures to indicate the seriousness of their policy.

Jefferson and Madison refused to consider the draft treaty that Monroe negotiated as anything more than a basis for further discussions. With considerable justification, Monroe insisted that he had secured everything that could be obtained without recourse to war. But Madison favored using the economic measures that, at the request of the British, had been postponed during the negotiations. Madison admitted that they would cut into the wartime prosperity but emphasized that manufactures would be "efficiently fostered. . . . No event can be more desirable." His feelings hurt and his confidence undercut, Monroe came home. Taylor and Randolph welcomed him as a potential ally in their campaign against the mercantilism of Madison and Jefferson. Arguing that nothing more than the parasitic carrying trade was at issue, Randolph turned his full fury on the administration. "What!" he demanded. "Shall this great mammoth of the American forest leave his native element and plunge into the water in a mad contest with the shark? . . . I, for one, will not mortgage my property and my liberty. . . . You will come out without your constitution."

A CLASSIC WAR FOR TRADE AND TERRITORY

Randolph's lance for physiocracy was broken by the British, who on June 22, 1807, attacked the *U.S.S. Chesapeake.* War seemed unavoidable. "If the English do not give us the satisfaction we demand," Jefferson snapped, "we will take Canada, which wants to enter the Union; and when, together with Canada, we shall have the Floridas, we shall no longer have any difficulties with our neighbors; and it is the only way of preventing them." (As an example of a society blaming its troubles on others, this would seem almost unsurpassed.) As one who had always understood that impressment "materially injure[d] our navigation, more indeed than any restrictions," Gallatin argued that the time had come for a showdown. Declaring himself willing to accept the label "political heretic," John Quincy Adams gave Jefferson "hearty wishes for [the] success" of his countermeasures. "Who shall dare," he thundered, "to set limits to the commerce and naval power of this country?" Jefferson and Madison retaliated with an embargo calculated to bring British leaders back to the negotiating table more inclined to compromise. This did play a major part in bringing on the English panic and depression of 1809–1810; the logic was correct, but American patience was not equal to the trial.

For the embargo and subsequent versions of the same kind of economic pressure also brought on troubles at home. Combined with Britain's continued disruption of American commerce and with the frontier drive against the Indians and for more land, domestic economic difficulty led to the War of 1812. Ohio legislators anticipated the argument of the War Hawks as early as 1808, asserting that England "has so materially affected the whole commerce of the United States, that it has almost put a stop to our circulating medium." And within a year Kentuckians were describing the British Orders in Council "prohibiting and interrupting all commerce to the continent [as] the only cause of the [westerners'] embarrassment."

"Let the agriculturist and manufacturer, therefore," exploded

Cramer's Magazine Almanac in 1810, "join hands and bid the jarring world defiance." This, though a bit oversimplified as any one-sentence summary has to be, is what happened during the following two years. Acting as in most of their mercantilist conflicts, Americans quite consciously and purposefully went to war for their export trade, for more land, and to check Britain's engrossing of the home market for manufactures. It was a war for economic independence and expansion undertaken after a long period of frustrating experiences and unrewarding negotiations concerning everything from the West Indies trade to the persistent decimation of the complements of American ships at sea. Quite naturally, it was a war of passion and anger.

Despite all that has been written about the War of 1812, Madison provided the best interpretation of the various elements that produced it; an extensive analysis of the evidence bears out this judgment. Calling the Congress into special session in November, 1811, Madison emphasized his "deep sense of the crisis" created by Britain's "war on our lawful commerce." Having requested war preparations, he then asked continued support for "the just and sound policy of securing to our manufacturers the success they have attained." Replying on January 8, 1812, to a South Carolina resolution of support for his policies, Madison explained that seemingly strange reference to manufacturing and in general outlined the nature of the war.

"Acquiescence in the practice and pretensions of the British Government," he declared, "is forbidden by every view that can be taken of the subject." Having mentioned impressment, he went on to stress the explicitly economic factors. "[Such acquiescence] would recolonize our commerce. . . . [And] experience warns us of the fatal tendencies of a commerce unrestricted with Great Britain, and restricted by her pleasure and policy elsewhere. Whilst the limited market would continue overcharged with our exports, the disproportionate imports from it, would drain from us the precious metals, endanger our monied Institutions; arrest our internal improvements, and would strangle in the cradle, the manufactures which promise so vigorous a growth. Nor would the evil be confined to our commerce, our agriculture, or our manufacturers. The Shipowners and Shipbuilders and mariners must be equally sufferers."

Although the main engine of the war drive was the western

agrarian demand for free access to world markets, some element of every group mentioned by Madison did in fact support the resort to force. A good many Pennsylvanians, for example, along with other northerners, rather liked the idea of a fight with "those modern Buccaneers, who have carried their calicoes for sale throughout the world at the point of the bayonet. . . . Who have wrapped the four corners of the earth in flames for a monopoly of manufactures." And the New Jersey legislature emphasized the connection between impressment and the disruption of "lawful commerce." Henry Clay's impassioned cries for expansion carried him to the forefront of the western agrarians who pushed for war. "A war will give us commerce and character," he announced on December 31, 1811, almost as though he were making a New Year's Resolution for the country. America had to have a "vent" for its surpluses. "Sir," he thundered at one of his critics, "if you wish to avoid foreign collision you had better abandon the ocean; surrender all your commerce; give up all your prosperity."

So many congressmen repeated this theme in all its imaginable variations that the *Annals of Congress* was at times a veritable gusher of mercantilist rhetoric about the necessity of export markets. A Kentuckian said it was war "or formally annul the Declaration of our Independence." A Tennessean blamed the depression of 1807–1810 on "no markets," and added that it was not over yet. North Carolinians had a preference for arguing that it was a question of "the profits of both planter and merchant." And Jonathan Roberts of Pennsylvania joined William H. Crawford of Georgia and John C. Calhoun from South Carolina in warning that war was the only alternative to "absolute recolonization." The hour of decision had come, cried Langdon Cheves: "This nation is inevitably destined to be a naval power."

Such militants as Clay talked openly about expansion into Spanish America and Canada. As for the propriety of such an offensive war, William Giles of Virginia asserted that the "wise framers" of the Constitution had it in mind: "those virtuous and patriotic men had too much wisdom to restrict Congress to defensive war." "Canada," remarked Clay, "is the avowed object." And by March, 1812, a group was meeting to plan the states that would be carved out of the northland. Other members emphasized Florida and even Cuba as desirable objects of conquest, and a few stressed the virtue of using the war as an excuse to finish off the Indians. Though it is true that the British were not in fact inciting the Indians, that point is not too significant in understanding the war spirit; a good many Americans *thought* that they still were and acted accordingly.

Several factors would appear to account for the delay in going to war. Randolph's militant opposition slowed the pace for a time. Arguing that "it was our own thirst for territory, our own want of moderation," that provoked the Indians, he also warned of the danger of a slave rebellion and attacked the subversion of republican principles that would accompany such a war for empire. Stressing the "danger arising from the black population," which was already excited by the ideas of the French Revolution and the rebellion in Santo Domingo, he mocked those who were "talking of taking Canada [while] some of us were shuddering for our own safety at home." Although Calhoun replied with open scorn for such a public confession of failure as a planter, Randolph's blunt discussion of the problem probably won some votes among his own generation of southerners. Directly accusing Madison of embracing the policies of English mercantilism as his own, Randolph urged Congress to consult "the good old planters" and then forget about war.

A good many northerners, including John Jacob Astor and other leading New Yorkers, indicated that they agreed with James A. Bayard of Delaware: "Postpone the war, and we will submit to the embargo till November." This group seemed seriously to think that economic pressure would bring victory if persisted in a bit longer. Others wanted a delay in order to employ the classic mercantilist device of trading with the enemy for a time in order to build up strength more rapidly. The question of how large an army and navy and how to raise and deploy them also divided men who at heart favored the war. Madison's request to increase the regular army met stiff resistance from those who feared it would undermine representative government. And the debate over whether to build a coastal force, a big fleet, a squadron that could control the West Indies colonies, or simply arm merchantmen and send them scurrying after anything flying a Union Jack so divided the Congress that no firm decision ever was reached.

Those two prolonged debates had a great deal to do with the lack of any well-organized and prepared force in being when war was finally declared. But so, too, did the general cockiness of almost all the pro-war congressmen. They had a timetable for victory that would have made a modern tank commander hustle. Only the survivors of Hamilton's pro-English faction seriously considered organized opposition to the conflict. Their Hartford Convention of 1814 considered separation but abandoned the idea, at least for the moment; they might have tried to carry it through had the war not ended within a few months. Instead, they turned their support in behind Rufus King's campaign to reassert northern power in domestic politics.

VICTORY DISGUISED AS STALEMATE

While America suffered extensive damage, did not conquer Canada, and failed to break open the British economic empire, it is nevertheless a mistake to conclude that the country lost the War of 1812. For one thing, it had fought the world's strongest industrial power to a draw and a negotiated peace. In the process it had gained cohesion, confidence, and strength. Understanding this, Britain signed a commercial treaty in 1815, and then a boundary convention in 1818. Accepting the balance of forces on the Great Lakes, it also extended the 49th parallel to the Rockies and left the Oregon territory moot for ten years. This decision provided a symbolic contrast with England's prolonged occupation of the old frontier posts after the Revolutionary War. Spain also recognized the significance of the war; if it entertained any doubts, Andrew Jackson's wild foray into Florida in 1818, a jolting reminder that his victory at New Orleans was no fluke, was no doubt convincing evidence that America had not been tamed by Britain. Spanish leaders abandoned Florida shortly and agreed by February 22, 1819, to a generous boundary settlement running clear to the Pacific.

America emerged from the war with a manufacturing industry to complement its strength in agriculture and shipping and with a firm consensus on the policies of mercantilism. Writing very candidly to Benjamin Austin of Boston in 1816, Jefferson indicated that though he might cling to his physiocratic dream, he realized that it now seemed beyond reach. "We must now place the manufacturer by the side of the agriculturist." "I contend for the interests of the whole people of this community," declared Calhoun, who was rapidly being acknowledged as the leader of a new generation of southerners. "I am not here to represent my own state. I renounce the idea." John

Quincy Adams spoke of agriculture, commerce, and manufactures as "linked in union together," and defined the duty of the Congress as being "to conciliate them in harmony together." Monroe concurred, stating flatly that since manufactures required "the systematic and fostering care of the government," it was "of great importance" to provide such assistance. A French diplomat caught the significance of what he called "this fusion of political principles," and recognized that American mercantilism had come of age.

Nothing revealed the persuasiveness of this sense of community more clearly than the tariff debates of 1816 and 1818. In keeping with their earlier views, Madison and Monroe responded to the petitions for continued protection by supporting tariff legislation that promised to strengthen a national political economy. Pennsylvanians and other northerners had pushed such bills for several years, and the superficially surprising feature of the tariff debates in 1816 and 1818 was the extent and vigor of southern support. In reality, of course, the southern gentry had provided the most striking leaders of American mercantilism ever since the eve of the Revolution, and their advocacy of an inclusive conception of political economy was neither new nor strange. Some southerners were no doubt interested in developing manufactures in their own region, particularly textiles and other small industry, but the main southern support came from men with a broad national outlook.

Along with other Americans, such southerners had come to realize by 1816 the danger inherent in Britain's both absolute and relative preponderance of industrial power. Certainly enough Englishmen were telling them about it. Lord Brougham's warning was typical: he thought it "well worthwhile to incur a loss upon the first exportation of [English manufactures], in order, by the glut, TO STIFLE IN THE CRADLE THOSE RISING MANUFACTURES IN THE UNITED STATES." Southerners like Calhoun and Thomas Newton, and even William Downes, realized that domestic manufactures were essential to national defense and the general economic welfare. They also viewed tariffs as a source of revenue to pay for the war and to finance internal improvements. Their support of the tariff was based on the vision of a strong, balanced economy that would insure the independence and the common prosperity of the nation.

As the war ended, Calhoun emerged as the most intelligent and

forceful candidate to become the new leader of American mercantilism. With a keenness rivaled by few of his peers, he quickly
recognized the dangers inherent in Madison's theory of preserving
democracy and prosperity by expansion. America was "a surface
prodigiously great in proportion to our numbers," he explained
in 1817: hence "the rival jealousies of the States," and the "selfish
instincts of our nature" might easily tear the country apart into
warring competitors.

Openly worried that disunion might be the price of disprov-
ing Montesquieu's theory that republicanism was limited to small
states, Calhoun revealed a "deep solicitude" for the need to take
"the most enlarged views." "Selfish interests" could be ignored in a
small state, perhaps, but an empire required a strong awareness of
"the common good." It was "necessary" for each group and region
"to concede something" to others. Such compromise was essential
to accumulate the capital "to diffuse universal opulence": many
needs were "on too great a scale for the resources of the States or
individuals." There were "higher and more powerful considerations" than private profit or regional gain; the very "strength and
political prosperity of the republic" was at stake.

Calhoun understood and admitted that "what is necessary for
the common good may apparently be opposed to the interest of
particular sections." But he insisted on the equity and the necessity
of compromise: "It must be submitted to as the condition of our
greatness." Probably no other American leader except John Quincy
Adams looked so squarely into the central dilemma of mercantilism,
the constant conflict between private property and the corporate
welfare. And like Adams, Calhoun realized that the common good
would give way to private interests and ambitions were the tension
not controlled by everyman's commitment to the larger goal. Such
dedication to the general welfare was not only for Americans "the
condition of our greatness," it was the measurement of greatness for
any mercantilist society. That it set so high a standard for its adherents was the triumph of the mercantilist *Weltanschauung*.

Madison was of course aware of the problem, but he approached
it more indirectly. Perhaps he concluded that it was impossible to
achieve and maintain so high a level of public responsibility without
placing severe restrictions on private property, or even that it was
impossible under any circumstances. In any event, he emphasized

more and more the importance of preventing his "feudal system of republics," which he referred to in later years as "Dual Federalism," from drifting into monarchy or anarchy. "In the great system of political economy, having for its general object the national welfare," he wrote in a brilliant summary of his position in 1819, "everything is related immediately or remotely to every other thing; and, consequently, a power over any one thing, if not limited by some obvious and precise affinity, may amount to power over every other." Hence a broad plan of internal improvements, which he strongly favored, could not safely be started without a constitutional amendment. Private property and balanced government were implicitly at issue, and the public should declare itself directly. Writing a decade later, in the winter of 1828–1829, Madison predicted a major crisis in about a century. By that time, he concluded, expansion would have come to an end, and the great majority of people would be without property that was productive; under those circumstances the danger of monarchy or class war would be very high.

In his capacity as President, Madison clearly followed the political economy of mercantilism. In that vein, he supported the postwar efforts to continue economic pressure against Britain in order to break into the empire trade. Not even the booming commerce with and through Cuba eased the Americans' determination to reestablish their predominance in the West Indies and extend it beyond them. Madison judged the restrictions "unjust"; perhaps even more important, he thought the restoration of this trade essential to his efforts "to restore harmony to the discordant parts of the United States." For the time, however, retaliatory legislation was unsuccessful. Trade was not reopened until 1830.

Other national efforts were more immediately rewarding. Opposition to the slave trade produced in 1819 a tougher law that offered rewards for information about violations and established the death penalty for American smugglers. And the early antislavery impulse joined hands with the mature spirit of commercial expansion to produce by 1822 the first American overseas colony. Founded by the American Colonization Society at Monrovia, Africa, this outpost received expatriated slaves and enterprising traders with little discrimination. But as a solution to the slavery problem it was far less effective than it was later to become as the entering wedge for the American penetration of Africa.

THE SPROUTING SEEDS OF LAISSEZ FAIRE

More immediate in its consequences, however, was the consensus among Madison, Gallatin, and Calhoun that prompted the
reestablishment of a central Bank of the United States. The need
was great. The war had powerfully extended and accelerated the
development of the country, and such economic growth generated
monetary problems that required some kind of general solution.
Local and regional banks could and did create credit, but they
did so in ways that rendered it unreliable and expensive. Many
of the banks were narrowly conceived as profit-making ventures,
and their directors had little or no sense of public responsibility.
Even the more stable ones, limited as they were in their geographic
and economic range of operations, simply could not facilitate the
balancing of credit within the nation and with other countries. The
result was a general inflation and loss of confidence.

Moving to meet the crisis, John Jacob Astor and a few of his
friends such as Stephen Girard of Pennsylvania proposed to create
their own private national bank in New York. Madison opposed
the move because the institution would have been "free from all
legal obligations to cooperate with public measures." Supported by
Clay, who candidly admitted that he had been wrong in opposing the recharter of the bank of 1811, Calhoun took the lead in
creating a new bank over which the government would have some
authority. Angered and disturbed by the laissez-faire banking
of the war period—it "divests you of your rights"—he explicitly
aimed to establish an institution that could "remove those disorders" from the economy. Madison approved the bill in 1816.

Even so, speculators and men of narrow business views
entrenched themselves in the private half of the board of directors and almost wrecked the bank before it was fully organized and established. Indeed, their policy of loose credit (for
higher profits) helped bring on the panic and depression of
1819. Postwar development had boomed with the renewed
movement into the west and the heavy demand for foodstuffs
in Europe. Twelve thousand wagons reached Pittsburgh in
1817, and in the previous year the region north of Mississippi
had shipped almost $10,000,000 worth of goods into New
Orleans. Land speculation was literally fantastic. Touched off

by the rapid decline of European markets and accelerated by the failure of big mercantile houses like Buchanan and Smith of Baltimore, the boom collapsed.

A Kentuckian reported from the west that "a deeper gloom hangs over us than was ever witnessed by the oldest man." Cotton prices were almost halved. People either left for the frontier or demanded government help. Relief laws were passed throughout the west, and the entire country turned on the new bank as it tightened its credit controls. Langdon Cheves knew what he was walking into when he took charge of the bank in 1819 in an effort to save and reform it before it collapsed. It was an act of public service for which he was ever afterward damned. For what he had to do was restrict new loans, call in old ones, and in other ways reorganize the entire operation. His policies did a great deal to save the economy from further difficulties, but they also created an enmity among local and regional banks—and their publics—which was never to be forgotten.

The bank became "THE MONSTER," and none of its later virtues or services ever changed that image. In this fundamental sense, therefore, the panic of 1819, which had been brought on by the mercantilists' fear of limiting private property too much (as well as by the pressure of special interests), had the ironic effect of touching off a vigorous drive to be done with mercantilism and replace it with the philosophy of laissez nous faire, "let us do as we please." Southerners, for example, began to turn away from Calhoun's mercantilism toward Taylor's physiocracy. And westerners such as Thomas Hart Benton of Missouri began to fill hours of congressional debate with declarations of their independence.

Though it signified the rise of manufactures to a position of parity, the division of the congressional Committee on Commerce and Manufactures in 1819 also symbolized a breaking apart of the integrated thought of mercantilism. Having been nurtured by mercantilism, manufacturing was about to become a faction and step forth as a spokesman for laissez faire. A similar meaning was implicit in the translation and publication in America of the works of Jean Baptiste Say, a French economist who carried the ideas of Adam Smith and the early physiocrats to their logical conclusion. Say argued that complete freedom of trade and unrestricted enterprise would produce welfare and happiness for everyone. Despite vigorous attacks on the new "let-us-alone policy," its spokesmen began to pick up support from other reformers whose proposals were at least implicitly antimercantilist.

Philanthropic movements had been a part of English mercantilism from an early date, and had continued in that tradition in America; but some of the new leaders began to stress private charity in place of the public benevolence of the earlier period. As a move to curtail social unrest its function remained similar, and many of its acts produced significant social gains. Yet in being handled by private citizens and dealing more with individuals per se, the new approach did indicate an important change in outlook. Similar implications were apparent in the campaigns for debtor relief, in the broad list of reforms (from temperance to conscientious objection to war) advocated by a group in Mount Pleasant, Ohio, and in the growing opposition to slavery throughout the north.

Such tendencies were particularly noticeable in the proceedings of the New York State Constitutional Convention of 1821. For though the substitution of tax payments for property ownership as the criterion for voting was not of itself antimercantilist, the general tone of the debate indicated a growing strength in individualism and laissez faire. It was as if the works of John Locke, briefly used in 1775 and 1776 as a convenient authority for the right of revolution and then shelved in favor of mercantilists like Sir James Steuart, were being taken down again as a guide for exploiting and enjoying the opportunities that mercantilism had created. For while some of Locke's ideas were quite influential during the revolutionary period, it was not until the 1830s that he established himself as the philosopher of individualism.

Similar implications of laissez faire appeared in New York's determination to proceed independently with the construction of the Erie Canal in 1817. Eager to take advantage of its geographically favorable position to consolidate its role in exploiting the development of the west, and impatient with Madison's fears about interpreting the Constitution into tyranny, the state undertook the project on its own. Mercantilist in being a government enterprise, the approach nevertheless indicated the rising spirit of let-us-alone. It was, indeed, a preview of one of the principal forms that laissez nous faire would take after the collapse of mercantilism at the national level. As such, and particularly because it was ultimately so successful, it unquestionably helped to destroy that order.

For the time, however, the *Weltanschauung* of mercantilism remained predominant. Revealing the general attitude, Tammany Hall issued a manifesto for renewed concern with the "national economy," and called for policies to keep the nation "one great family." Quite aware of the increasing interest in what he called the policy of "let us alone," Madison reiterated his old judgment. It requires, he commented adversely in 1819, "a similarity of circumstances, and an equal freedom of interchange among commercial nations, which have never existed." Monroe, Adams, Clay, and Calhoun agreed, and they sustained an American mercantilism for another decade. But their very successes assured their inability to maintain it any longer than that.

CHAPTER FIVE

The Fulfillment of the Passing Order

The [Missouri] question could be settled no otherwise than by a compromise.

John Quincy Adams, 1821

Whatever may be the abstract doctrine in favor of unrestricted commerce, [it] . . . has never occurred, and cannot be expected.

It is believed that the greater the expansion, within practicable limits, and it is not easy to say what are not so, the greater the advantage which the States individually will derive from it. . . . It must be obvious to all, that the further expansion is carried, provided it be not beyond the just limit, the greater will be the freedom of action to both [National and State] governments.

James Monroe, 1822

The views and policy of the North Americans seem vainly directed toward supplanting us in navigation in every quarter of the globe.

Lord Liverpool, 1824

Must we not say that the period which he [Washington] predicted as then not far off has arrived?

John Quincy Adams, 1826

It is most desirable that there should be both a home and a foreign market. But, with respect to their relative superiority, I cannot entertain a doubt. The home market is first in order, and paramount in importance.

Henry Clay, 1824

CRISIS AND COMPROMISE IN A RENEWED STRUGGLE FOR THE WEST

Significant in its own right as the worst economic crisis yet suffered by Americans, the panic and depression of 1819 also marked the beginning of a decade of fundamental transition in American society. On the one hand, the *Weltanschauung* of American mercantilism was translated into a series of philosophic and practical manifestations that documented its power and achievement. Even when defeated by Andrew Jackson in 1828, for example, John Quincy Adams was supported by 44 per cent of the voting public. Yet Jackson's victory measured the extent to which the various elements of the system created by American mercantilists had broken into segments that were defining the common good in terms of their own particularist interests.

The first collision of these conflicting developments produced the crisis of 1819–1821 over the admission of Missouri as a slave state. Representing the culmination of internal southern migration into the old northwest, Missouri matured as an agricultural and commercial political economy dominated by slaveholders and merchants who were supported by yeomen accepting slavery. Since Alabama had just been received into the Union as a slave state, Missouri leaders anticipated no opposition. Instead, they walked onto glowing coals of what was thought to be the dead ashes of the Hamiltonian faction. To some extent that expectation was valid, for men such as Rufus King had stopped defining American problems in terms of relations with England. They still leaned toward London, but primarily they were concerned to strengthen their place in the American political economy. The new group still composed a faction, but it was more broadly based in the maturing commercial-manufacturing sector of the economy and counted far more supporters outside New England than had its predecessor.

Thus a major crisis developed when, on February 13, 1819, James Tallmadge of New York introduced a resolution in Congress to prohibit the admission of Missouri as a slave state and to free all its existing slaves within a given period. Tallmadge was in many respects an innocent incendiary who apparently intended to start no more than a slow fire of humanitarian opposition to slavery that might illuminate his own career more brightly. Instead, it erupted into a blazing struggle between two sectors of the political economy.

King seized control of the issue with the idea of ending what he termed the southern monopoly of government. Candidly admitting that he was "very imperfectly acquainted" with the issue of slavery per se (upon which he had "not bestowed much consideration"), King's immediate objective was to reestablish the influence of the northern commercial-manufacturing interest in national affairs. He was not sympathetic to slavery, but that issue was not his primary concern. Nor did many of his associates and supporters give it a high priority. As men who were beginning to see the west as a practical reservoir of economic and political wealth, they were among the first eastern conservatives to redefine the west as a necessity and an opportunity instead of a liability. They were beginning to view the frontier as their utopia, just as had the gentry ever since the 1760s.

When it began, and even throughout its two-year life, the Missouri Crisis was more a fight among political leaders than a great national issue. It had some influence on the congressional elections of 1820, but obviously did not result in a mass attack on either slavery or the south. King turned to northern antislavery advocates for support *after* he launched his campaign. Even more important, it was the strength of the antislavery feeling among southern leaders that provided the key to the final compromise. They admitted that it was a "deplorable evil," and pointed to their active support of the colonization program as proof of their concern.

Concerned about the danger of upsetting the balance of the Constitution, and about the parallel adjustments between the various elements of the political economy, most southern leaders were not only contrite about slavery, but manifestly anxious to compromise. A good many of them agreed with a resolution from Kentucky which defined the danger as that of a congressional usurpation of power; a fear that Congress would emerge from the conflict with the power to subordinate any state "to perpetual vassalage, and reduce it to the condition of a province." And quite aware that the struggle was far more about control of the west than over the institution of slavery, most southerners were always ready to settle for dividing the continent along the latitude line 36° 30′ westward from the Mississippi. That was the final result. Losing the support of northerners who were antislavery but not pro-faction, King was defeated.

Men such as John Quincy Adams and Madison were nevertheless deeply disturbed by the implications of the crisis. "Should a state of parties arise founded on geographical boundaries, and other physical and permanent distinctions which happen to coincide with them," Madison fretted, "what is to control those great repulsive masses from awful shocks against each other?" Adams feared that nothing would. Jefferson agreed, but embarked upon a course of action that helped to destroy the very corporate ethic of mercantilism that might have averted civil war. Recommending that the University of Virginia define education as teaching its students to be self-conscious southerners, and advising his compatriots to send their sons to such reliable schools instead of to northern institutions, he encouraged a thoroughly conservative, even negative, kind of regionalism. Repudiating his earlier support for manufactures, he denounced protection and emphasized the virtues of physiocracy. In view of his remark that John Taylor of Caroline followed the true philosophy but was unfortunately crying in the wilderness, Jefferson's actions suggest that he decided to join Taylor and transform the wilderness into a southern paradise. Certainly that was the impression and the advice that he bequeathed to his successors.

Implicitly, therefore, Jefferson finally provided a definition of the good society. It was a version of the physiocratic feudal utopia uncontaminated by outside influences and maintaining itself through the magic of the frontier and free trade. Together with Taylor, Jefferson thus created the illusion that ultimately became the romantic fiction of the antebellum south—a land of magnolias, mammies, and maidens watched over by benign and benevolent barons. Had he instead freed his slaves (even sending them to Africa), and thus honored the vision of a feudal utopia (for serfs were *not* slaves), the image of him as an apostle of American democracy would then have more substance. But in the end he was unable to define freedom save in terms of personal property in the form of other human beings.

ADAMS, MONROE, MARSHALL, AND CLAY—PROTAGONISTS OF AN AMERICAN SYSTEM

For the time, however, the implications and the consequences of the positions taken by King and Jefferson were overshadowed by the last accomplishments of American mercantilism. Perhaps the most striking of these was the role of internal improvements in sustaining national development despite an extended period of economic sluggishness and rapidly increasing immigration. Roughly 14,000 people entered America from abroad during every year of the 1820s. Their spirit and skills no doubt put a floor under the confidence of Americans at a time (e.g., 1824) when corn sold for eight cents a bushel, wheat for twenty-five, and a barrel of flour brought $1.25. Such figures can be misleading if read to mean a prolonged, desperate depression. The country maintained and even extended the development of its resources throughout the decade. But measured against the rapid growth during the years of the embargo, and particularly the immediate postwar years, the figures indicated a slower rate of economic progress.

A good many mercantilists concluded that these conditions provided the best argument against laissez faire. "Whatever may be the abstract doctrine in favor of unrestricted commerce," President Monroe remarked in his annual message of December 3, 1822, the necessary conditions have "never occurred, and cannot be expected." Unlike an increasing number of southerners, Monroe also continued to favor tariff protection for manufactures. Anticipating the day that America would be "a manufacturing country on an extensive scale," and having given "full consideration" to the opposition arguments, he recommended "additional protection" in December, 1823. And despite the growing propensity of manufacturers to view the tariff as a policy for them to manipulate for the narrow advantage of their interest or faction, most supporters of the act of 1824 still viewed it as within the framework of mercantilism.

Henry Clay also intensified his labors in behalf of the program of internal improvements and tariffs that he began calling "an American System." "Commerce will regulate itself!" he sarcastically conceded to his critics. "Yes, and the extravagance of a spendthrift heir . . . will regulate itself ultimately." Clay argued that the constitutionality of internal improvements, as well as the delegation of explicit powers such as those over commerce, was settled by precedent, and his efforts in Congress were mainly directed toward holding enough southern votes to pass various pieces of legislation. He was aided by Hezekiah Niles and Matthew Carey, who advocated the American System incessantly in *Niles Weekly Register* and countless articles and pamphlets.

More sophisticated popular arguments were advanced by Frederick

List, who was accurately described by a contemporary as a "high-class publicist." Probably the most respectable theoretical argument for the American System came from Daniel Raymond, whose *Thoughts on Political Economy* (1820) was the most systematic endeavor to recapitulate the ideas of British mercantilists and apply them to the American scene. In reality, the efforts of List and Raymond were feeble echoes of the English giants such as Petty, Child, and Steuart, and none of them could overcome the suspicion that they were spokesmen for an industrial faction that was merely using the rhetoric of mercantilism for furthering the objectives of an interest group.

Intellectually as well as politically, therefore, Clay received his most effective help from Monroe and Adams. Both men realized that there was more to mercantilism than economics. Monroe persisted in his conviction that "one system" of interrelated and balanced parts would accomplish "great national purposes" and "promote the welfare of the whole." Despite its rambling and redundant length, Monroe's special message of 1822 on internal improvements is one of the most illuminating and rewarding documents of the era. Written to explain his veto of a particular bill, the essay was a noble plea for a constitutional amendment that would save the whole idea of an interconnected and mutually responsible system.

Monroe warned of three basic dangers confronting the nation. Continued expansion without a sense of corporate responsibility would produce "sectional interests, feelings, and prejudices" that might disrupt "the bond of union itself." But undertaken without a constitutional amendment, internal improvements would also upset the balance of the Constitution and produce tyranny and ultimate violence. Furthermore—and here Monroe was clearly speaking for the southerners who had reacted so vigorously against the implications of the Missouri Crisis, as well as for all men of property—such action without a constitutional amendment would establish ominous precedents for the outright seizure or other infringement of private property.

But Monroe's concern for the rights of private property should not be wholly attributed to the rising vehemence of southern concern for slavery. For one thing, his essay came four or five years before that outcry began its first crescendo. More importantly, the conflict between the rights of property and the common good was a dilemma implicit in mercantilist thought. Monroe put his finger on the conflict and asked for a public resolution. Without an amendment, there was no warrant to allow property "to be examined by men of science; . . . to authorize commissioners to lay off the roads and canals; . . . to take the land at a valuation if necessary, and to construct the works." Nor was there any sanction to go into business on such an extensive scale. Failing any such amendment, Monroe could only fall back on the magic of expansion to provide a way out of the impasse. America had a "system capable of expansion over a vast territory not only without weakening either [state or national] government, but enjoying the peculiar advantage of adding thereby new strength and vigor."

John Quincy Adams was more willing to devalue property rights in favor of the general welfare. His first annual message of December 6, 1825, was thus the great statement of the philosophy and the domestic program of American mercantilism. Two issues lay at the heart of the problem: "the dominion of man over himself" as well as over other people and nature, and the responsibility of the present generation for "the unborn millions of our posterity." Hence Americans "must still, as heretofore, take counsel from their duties, rather than their fears." Adams was unquestionably a Calvinist, and the rigors of that philosophy no doubt cramped his personal style, but he was also a man who belied the common assumption that a Calvinist lived in fear. He challenged America to become truly unique by mastering its fears. It was Jefferson and his followers who did not face up to the tension that freedom involved. They denied it was possible to be free *and* disciplined. Adams insisted that was the only meaningful definition of freedom.

"The great object of civil government," Adams declared in his first annual message, "is the improvement of the condition of those who are parties to the social compact." To that end he recommended "laws promoting the improvement of agriculture, commerce, and manufactures, the cultivation and encouragement of the mechanic[al] and of the elegant arts." His Secretary of the Treasury, Richard Rush, filed a supporting report which expanded on this "intimate connection" between manufactures "and the wealth, the power, and the happiness of the country," and proposed "timely and judicious measures" designed to "organize the whole labor" of the country in order "to lift up [its] condition." Speaking directly on his own, Adams concluded his message with a set of detailed proposals embracing roads and canals, a national university, scientific exploration and research, and literature. And as proof that men could put the common good above personal and party considerations, he proceeded to make presidential appointments (even in the cabinet) on the basis of quality rather than political allegiance.

Nor were the results of this movement for an American System limited to such rigorous and moving documents. Notwithstanding his reluctance to move very far without full constitutional sanction, and despite the growing opposition from southerners, Monroe did approve the General Survey Act of 1824, and that law introduced a period of extensive involvement. River and lighthouse appropriations were followed by a whole series of government interventions in the form of stock purchases in mixed enterprises. Government became an economic partner, for example, in the Chesapeake and Delaware Canal, the Louisville Canal (around the falls on the Ohio), the development of the Dismal Swamp route, and the Chesapeake and Ohio Canal.

In four years the Adams Administration spent almost as much on internal improvements as had been allocated in the previous twenty-four. Indeed, by 1826 the government was the largest single economic entrepreneur in the country. It handled more funds, employed more people, purchased more goods, and borrowed more operating and investment capital than any other enterprise. For generations that are reputed to have believed in weak and minimal government, the Founding Fathers and their first offspring created a rather large and active institution. A coincidence of ground-breaking ceremonies on July 4, 1828, was to symbolize both their accomplishments and the persistence of the pattern they established. Only a few miles away from where Adams turned dirt for the Potomac-Ohio Canal, other men were to begin the first railroad to the west. And the principle of government assistance to private companies was to know no greater application than in the pattern of land grants to railroads unless, perhaps, it was in the direct and indirect subsidies to corporation enterprise during World War I and World War II.

In their own time, Monroe and Adams also facilitated and approved the continued recovery and maturation of the national bank. Having saved it from its own worst enemies and rehabilitated its routine operations, Langdon Cheves resigned. He had taken as much abuse as he could stand and far more than most men would have endured. Nicholas Biddle of Philadelphia succeeded him. In Bray Hammond's recent words, "as naive as one to whom the world has been singularly kind may be," Biddle was somewhat like Adams in thinking that the effective and responsible performance of public duties was sufficient to its own perpetuation.

But Biddle was quite unlike Adams in being a man who reveled in the pleasures of life while discharging its duties. He could write a bit of witty, flirtatious doggerel to a casual female acquaintance that made Adams's labored efforts at poetry seem as brittle as baked raw clay. He could also be as unyielding as a granite crag to stockholders who complained that his profit reports were too skimpy. Biddle managed the bank to facilitate the development of the country without the wild ups-and-downs so often characteristic of an expanding economic system. He did a better job than the directors of the Bank of England. Under his leadership the bank not only established a national system of credit balancing which assisted the west as much as the east, and probably more, but sought with considerable success to save smaller banks from their own inexperience and greed. It was ultimately his undoing, for what the militant advocates of laissez nous faire came to demand was help without responsibilities. In their minds, at any rate, that was the working definition of democratic freedom.

Their first attempt to destroy the bank by bleeding it to death through local taxes was blocked by Chief Justice John Marshall, who wrote the principles of American mercantilism into the legal procedure and the law of the land. Even before Marshall laid down such guideposts, however, the lower courts had affirmed one of those principles in cases dealing with labor-union action. During the colonial and revolutionary periods, some local mechanics had organized by trades (in particular the shoemakers and tailors), and by 1799 they were bargaining collectively with employers and using such weapons as the strike and the social boycott to strengthen their position. A strike of this kind in Philadelphia raised the issue whether the mercantilist industrial code of Tudor England was to apply in America. At first upheld in all particulars, it was used to declare that even combinations to raise wages were illegal conspiracies against the common good.

That total proscription was modified by a New York court in 1809 by a decision legalizing organizations to improve wages. But further action which was "too arbitrary and coercive, and which went to deprive their fellow citizens of rights as precious as any they contend for" was defined as conspiracy. The distinction was reinforced by a Pittsburgh decision in 1815 which proscribed mechanics from acting "by direct means to impoverish or prejudice a third person, or to do acts prejudicial to the community." Later cases during the 1820s upheld that view. As in England, such an outlook was not only mercantilist in its explicit references to the corporate responsibility of labor organizations, and in its clear attack on the monopoly power of guilds, but its implicit meaning was very similar—labor would benefit with and from the general improvement of the political economy.

Marshall's Supreme Court decisions were important because he was concerned to strengthen such a national system and because he, too, ruled against monopolies in the economic sphere. As a member of the Virginia gentry with holdings in land, insurance companies, canals, banks, and even early railroad ventures, Marshall was a firm advocate of mercantilism. He favored a "paternal legislature" that would support internal improvements through mixed companies and in other ways encourage and regulate the economy. Thus he upheld the sanctity of contracts and included charters of incorporation within that definition.

On the other hand, he sensed the potential danger of corporations being given a certain kind of "immortality" and "individuality" by such rulings. He explicitly declared, in any event, that a corporation should "not share in the civil government of the country." Acts of incorporation did not confer an individuality that gave "political power or a political character." It would appear that Marshall was trying through such specific restrictions to prevent the development of what later Americans described as the "invisible government" of large corporate enterprises. He also invalidated monopoly charters, as in the case of *Gibbons* v. *Ogden* (1824) concerning a steamboat franchise in New York. These decisions bear a striking resemblance to the key documents of the struggles in England to open up the system created by mercantilism, and yet at the same time prevent any one element from destroying the balance of the political economy.

Marshall had already pointed out in the case concerning the

national bank (*McCullock* v. *Maryland*, 1819) that "a corporation is never used for its own sake, but for the purpose of effecting something else." Thus the bank was constitutional because the government was "intrusted with such ample powers, on the due execution of which the happiness and prosperity of the nation so vitally depends." He added somewhat later that the purpose of the Constitution was "to maintain an uniform and general system." "Throughout this vast republic, from the St. Croix to the Gulf of Mexico, from the Atlantic to the Pacific, revenue is to be collected and expended, armies are to be marched and supported." Marshall's support for expansion, which became explicit in his decision in the case of *American Insurance Company* v. *Canter* (1828), was implicit in his mercantilism and sharpened by his fear of what would happen if it stopped. He fretted that "the price of labor will cheapen, until it affords a bare subsistence to the laborer."

Marshall's thoroughly mercantilist decisions were delivered in a prose that was as vigorous as his philosophy. For that matter, most of the great art of the Age of Mercantilism appeared in the constant discussions and debates over the problems of the political economy. Some of the speeches during the Missouri Crisis, for example, were magnificent rhetorical achievements. Rufus King and William Pinckney were particularly powerful and stylish. John Sergeant of Pennsylvania won a unique accolade from Randolph of Roanoke, who at his best could crack syntax like a whip. *"Never speak again! Never speak again!"* cried Randolph, half-persuaded by the performance.

John Quincy Adams also provided a good many documents of enduring literary significance. So had Madison, whose letter to Jefferson of October 24, 1787, in which he reviewed the proceedings of the constitutional convention, outlined the "feudal system of republics," and summarized his theory of expansion, provided a typical display of his abilities and set a high standard of performance. Adams nevertheless produced several items that were superior. His diary, for example, can be resisted only by those whose feeling for life is so underdeveloped as to count as nonexistent. And his *Report Upon Weights and Measures* is in many respects the classic document of the Age of Mercantilism. It is philosophy, ethics, political economy, and policy integrated in a government report that he wrote while executing a particularly heavy load of duties as Secretary of State.

Pointing out that men began by measuring everything in terms of their own bodies, Adams argued that the formation of society demanded that they get beyond this egoistic universe of the self. One's identity must be sustained through a sense of proportion based upon an acceptance of standards designed to order "the multiplying relations between man and man now superadded to those between man and things." Such "standards should be *just*" and "uniform" because of their great "influence upon the happiness and upon the morals of nations." The issue is of "momentous importance" because it affects such apparently disconnected elements as the safety of seamen and the welfare of the individual housewife. "The home, the market, the shop" have to trust each other: a contradictory, double standard "enters every house, it cripples every hand," and thus effects the "well-being of every man, woman, and child, in the community." No other philosopher or political economist in the world ever personalized and humanized the elementary problem of weights and measures—or any other mundane but vital element of their system—in a comparable manner. The document was, and remains, a magnificent triumph of the *Weltanschauung* of mercantilism that transcends its time and place.

THE MONROE DOCTRINE AS THE MANIFESTO
OF THE AMERICAN EMPIRE

Adams also played a key role in formulating the Monroe Doctrine, a statement of the expansionism inherent in American mercantilism that was clearly the manifesto of the American empire. Though it is generally treated as the cornerstone of American diplomacy, most analyses of the doctrine emphasize its negative aspects. It is thus presented as a defensive statement of the territorial and administrative integrity of North and South America: no further colonization, no transfer or extension of existing claims, and in return America would not interfere in European affairs. This standard interpretation neglects three major facts: the men who formulated it were concerned as much with European commercial and economic expansion as with its schemes for colonization; they viewed it as a positive, expansionist statement of American supremacy in the hemisphere, and Monroe actually intervened in European politics with the very same speech in which he asserted that Europe should stay out of American affairs.

Aware that the political economy of the United States was established, and properly interpreting the results of the War of 1812 as being fundamentally favorable to its position in the hemisphere, American leaders reached an obvious conclusion. If they could exclude further European penetration as Spain's authority collapsed, then the United States would remain as the predominant power in the hemisphere. Monroe thus reasserted the expansionist thesis at the end of his message of December 2, 1823, which announced the doctrine. Having urged further support for manufactures and internal improvements, as well as warning Europe off Latin America while he encouraged the Greek revolution, he concluded with this well-nigh classic paraphrase of Madison's theory. "It is manifest that by enlarging the basis of our system, and increasing the number of States, the system itself has been greatly strengthened in both its [state and national] branches. Consolidation and disunion have thereby been rendered equally impracticable."

As one who was equally familiar with Madison's theory of expansion (he mentioned it specifically in his eulogy of Madison), Adams fully expected the United States to acquire Cuba, Texas, and other tidbits of territory in North America. But he was at least as concerned with establishing American commercial supremacy as he was with blocking further colonial experiments by European nations. This balanced expansionist sentiment behind the Monroe Doctrine was well revealed in the congressional discussions about Oregon which some thought was threatened by Russia as well as by England. Francis Baylies of Massachusetts might have been expected to concern himself with the "magnificent prospects" of the Pacific commerce, but he also quoted Napoleon to emphasize his support for territorial expansion: he "never uttered words of more wisdom than when he said, 'I want ships, commerce, and colonies.' " Robert Wright of Maryland called for expansion because "there is less danger of separatism in a confederacy of 20 or 30 States than in one of a smaller number."

Senator James Barbour agreed. "Our advance in political science has already cancelled the dogmas of theory. We have already ascertained . . . that republics are not necessarily limited to small territories. . . . Whether America is capable of indefinite extent, must be left to posterity to decide." And speaking for a growing consensus, John Floyd of Virginia accurately concluded that "all contemplate with joy" continued westward expansion. It would provide land for farmers, "procure and protect the fur trade," "engross the whale trade," and "control the South Sea trade. . . . All this rich commerce could be governed, if not engrossed, by capitalists at Oregon."

Adams shared such commercial interest in the Northwest, and it contributed to his thinking about the Monroe Doctrine. Even more in his mind, however, was the importance of trade with Latin America. By 1820, when Adams, in his instructions to American agents, described it as "deserving of particular attention," this trade had developed into a significant commerce that vigorous European intervention would curtail and perhaps even destroy. Baltimore specialized in flour and furniture, but Salem, New York, Philadelphia, and even New Orleans, shipped shoes, cotton textiles, fertilizer, pitch, and lumber into such cities as Rio de Janeiro. The carrying trade was also important. American shippers carried Asian goods to Chile, Argentine beef to Cuba, and European items to the entire region. British agents reported to Foreign Secretary George Canning that Americans controlled the Argentine flour market, that their tonnage in Uruguay was "greater than that of any other nation," and that Peru's commerce with Asia "has been entirely engrossed by the North Americans."

Aware of this strong position, Henry Clay predicted that in half a century Americans, "in relation to South America," would "occupy the same position as the people of New England do to the rest of the United States." The implications of Clay's remark unquestionably disturbed some southerners in 1820 as much as the validity of his prediction was to upset Latin Americans in the 20th century. His enthusiastic campaign to establish an American System embracing the hemisphere was important for several reasons. Promising "mercantile profits," an influx of Spanish gold, and markets for the farmers and other entrepreneurs of the Mississippi west, he also assured his countrymen that the expansion of America's ideological principles would provide military as well as economic security. Being like the United States, he argued, the new countries would not be prone to oppose its basic policies.

Adams was wary of Clay's rambunctious ideological assertiveness, but he was fully agreed on the importance of commercial activity. His instructions of May 27, 1823, to an American agent who was being sent to Colombia left no doubt about his basic strategy. The American political economy was now strong enough to take advantage of its great relative superiority over the emerging new nations. "As navigators and manufacturers, *we* are already so far advanced in a career upon which *they* are yet to enter," he explained, "that we may, for many years after the conclusion of the war, maintain with them a commercial intercourse, highly beneficial to both parties, as *carriers* to and for them of numerous articles of manufacture and foreign produce."

As he explicitly noted, Adams was aware that the United States had reached the point anticipated by Washington in his Farewell Address: the *Weltanschauung* and the political economy of mercantilism had built a nation strong enough to secure many of its objectives through economic power. And on becoming President he proceeded to act upon the fact, recommending in 1826 that the United States attend and take the lead in a proposed conference of the new Spanish-American republics. Explaining to the Congress what Washington had meant, Adams pointedly drew the obvious conclusion. "Must we not say," he asked rhetorically, "that the period which he predicted as then not far off has arrived?" The answer was obviously "Yes," and Adams proposed to adjust the nation's foreign policy to fit the new circumstances. Economic predominance would mean effective control without limiting America's freedom of action.

But Adams ran into stiff opposition. Southerners disliked his proposal on several counts. They understood the domestic implications of his remarks about a mature economy—it meant a weakening of their position. Many of them also coveted Cuba as new slave territory, and they were not interested in encouraging the general revolutionary fervor lest it triumph on the island in the form of a colored republic—or at home as slave revolts. Even more significant, however, was the criticism leveled at Adams by a good many northerners. They cornered him with his own earlier opposition to indiscriminate expansion. Far from representing merely a delaying action by the south, the debate over the Panama Conference was a fundamental argument about America's mercantilist foreign policy and its implications for future domestic affairs.

THE UNRESOLVED DILEMMA OF AMERICAN MERCANTILISM

Neither Adams nor other leaders could any longer evade the issue: Was expansion so absolutely essential to American democracy and prosperity that it had to be sustained despite the fact that it might well subvert the basic principles of self-government, and even the existence of the union? Adams might draw a distinction between territorial expansion and expanded trade connections but that did not enable him to wriggle free of the dilemma. For he wanted Texas and the Pacific coast, and he understood perfectly the political consequences of America's greater economic power in dealing with underdeveloped nations. Nor was he unaware of the implications of all the agitation to spread American ideas, principles, and institutions throughout the world.

As early as 1821, on the Fourth of July, in fact, he had delivered a devastating criticism of that kind of expansion. The true America, he warned, "goes not abroad in search of monsters to destroy. . . . She well knows that by once enlisting under other banners than her own, were they even the banners of foreign independence, she would involve herself, beyond the power of extrication, in all the wars of interest and intrigue, of individual avarice, envy, and ambition, which assume the colors and usurp the standard of freedom. . . . She might become the dictatress of the world; she would no longer be the ruler of her own spirit."

Having rendered this unequivocal judgment, Adams might well have squirmed five years later when Senator Levi Woodbury of New Hampshire rose in Congress to ask if the President still adhered to that standard. "Are we so moonstruck, or so little employed at home, as, in the eloquent language of our President on another occasion, . . . to wander around abroad in search of foreign monsters to destroy?" Representative Alexander Smyth of Virginia spoke for still others who opposed any effort "to propagate our system on the other side of the Atlantic." "If there be a mode of destroying civil liberty," he echoed Adams, "it is by leading this Government into unnecessary wars."

The hour of decision had arrived. In one area, moreover, the mercantilists responded with great moral courage and *élan*. All the key leaders opposed the rising tide of laissez-faire aggressiveness against the Indians. Whatever the inherent "difficulty" or related political problems connected with dealing with them equitably, warned Madison, "it is due to humanity" to make such efforts. "They have claims on the magnanimity, and, I may add," Monroe agreed, "on the justice of this nation, which we must all feel." At least Calhoun did, and vigorously asserted that "on every principle of humanity the continuance of similar advantages of education ought to be extended to them." For the doubters, he had extensive evidence gathered from experienced teachers. It was "almost uniformly favorable, both as to the capacity and docility of the youths. Their progress appears to be quite equal to that of white children of the same age; and they appear to be equally susceptible of acquiring habits of industry." Hence the nation should put an end to the "evil" of "the incessant pressure of our population, which forces" the Indians out of their homes despite treaties to the contrary.

Adams and Clay agreed, and made vigorous efforts to prevent Georgia from uprooting Indians who were accepting the ways of American civilization. But confronted with a choice between federal troops in the south or the defeat of the Indians, Adams acquiesced. Georgia drove them west. It was a wrenching choice, and perhaps a fateful one; seeing one state defy the national government with impunity, Mississippi followed the same course and also succeeded. Far more than either the Kentucky Resolutions of 1799, or the South Carolina proclamation nullifying the tariff of 1832, it was the actions of Georgia and Mississippi that laid out the route to secession.

Perhaps Adams sensed this implication, for he ultimately concluded that domestic reforms took priority over further expansion. In that respect, at any rate, Adams proved capable of breaking free of the expansionist dogma of mercantilism. That had not been the case with Monroe. He had admitted that "so seducing is the passion for extending our territory" that it might destroy the union. But he had held fast to the concept of mercantilist empire, denying that expansion subverted republicanism. "On the contrary," he proclaimed on May 4, 1822, "it is believed that the greater the expansion, within practicable limits, and it is not easy to say what are not so, the greater the advantage which the States individually will derive from it. . . . It must be obvious to all, that the further expansion is carried, provided it be not beyond the just limit, the greater will

be the freedom of action to both [national and state] governments."
There could be no misunderstanding Monroe's choice. "There is
no object," he asserted in his last annual message on December 7,
1824, "no object which, as a people, we can desire, which we do not
possess, or which is not within our reach." In Monroe's mind, at any
rate, expansion was one "of our institutions."

Clay came to doubt whether the beneficent results of expansion were so "obvious." He and Adams shared by 1828 a "great
concern" over the implications of the expansionist thesis. But in
fundamental respects it was Clay who made the most astute and
devastating analysis of the danger and proposed the most relevant remedy. Even as early as 1820 he sensed that "a new epoch
has arisen," and called America "deliberately to contemplate" the
changed situation. "The call for free trade," he concluded in 1832,
"is as unavailing, as the cry of a spoiled child in its nurse's arms,
for the moon, or the stars that glitter. . . . It has never existed, it
never will exist."

Clay understood that free trade defined in that manner was
little more than a euphemism for a massive commercial empire. It
was, "in effect," he concluded, "the British colonial system that we
are invited to adopt." Then he quoted a British leader to make the
point absolutely clear: " 'Other nations knew, as well as [ourselves],
what we meant by "free trade" was nothing more nor less than, by
means of the great advantages we enjoyed, to get a monopoly of all
their markets for our manufactures, and to prevent them, one and
all, from ever becoming manufacturing nations.' " It was therefore
a choice, concluded Clay, between making the home market "first
in order" or embarking on a search "for new worlds . . . for new
and unknown races of mortals to consume this immense [surplus]
of cotton fabrics."

Not only did Clay thus attack the very plan that Adams had
advanced in 1823 for structuring America's future relations with
Latin America, but he drew an amazingly accurate picture of the
policy American manufacturers would advocate and help establish
within less than 65 years. For by the 1890s, when they became deeply
worried by precisely such surpluses, manufacturers of textiles and
other goods turned to Asia and Latin America for markets, and
to their own government for aid and assistance in exploiting their
"great advantages" over the economy of underdeveloped countries.

Both in its early part and at the end of the 19th century, their American system differed considerably from the one Clay had in mind.

Yet American mercantilists had built an economic and political system strong and flexible enough to survive 60 years of sustained exploitation and misuse by the advocates of laissez nous faire who triumphed in 1828. They even provided many of the central ideas that later Americans turned to in an effort to restore some balance, meaning, and purpose to their society. The accomplishments of the three Adamses, Madison, Jefferson, Washington, Gallatin, Calhoun, and Monroe comprised a truly magnificent testimony to the relevance and the quality of the mercantilist *Weltanschauung*, and to the spirit and energy of the Americans who transformed it into institutions and an established political economy. In fundamental respects, and to an extensive degree, Americans have been, and still are, living off the intellectual and economic capital accumulated during the Age of Mercantilism.

This very durability of some of their ideas makes it easier to recognize and understand their failures. Perhaps the most apparent weakness of their outlook lies in their argument that representative government, economic prosperity, and personal happiness all depend on expansion. They formulated this idea so rigorously and advanced it so vigorously and persuasively that Americans have never been able to examine it critically in an equally disciplined spirit. Until past the middle of the 20th century, at any rate, it became an integral part of their emotional and even psychological make-up. The power and persistence of ideas in the face of changing reality was never more amply documented. Whether cast in the overt form of slogans about an expanding economy or in the more complex ideology and myth of the frontier, the thesis that wealth and welfare hinged upon expansion provided daily a reminder of the Age of Mercantilism.

But the frontier theory of history was in reality only the most striking symptom of the basic failure of American mercantilism. It had been formulated as an answer to the crucial problem of controlling private property in order to achieve the general welfare. But it was in fact an evasion—and no very subtle or sophisticated one—of that central issue. For, given a continent easily conquered and ruthlessly exploited, it was not too difficult to accumulate the lowest necessary amount of public wealth while at the same time allowing private individuals and groups to acquire unlimited riches. For the same reasons, the expansionist thesis of the mercantilists also encouraged a nonintellectual approach to human affairs. Problems could be solved by growth. For men who valued intellectual achievement so highly, and knew it as vital in providing men with a sense of purpose and meaning, this was perhaps the greatest irony of their own labor and influence.

As the mercantilists knew, the construction of a successful economic system and the acquisition of personal fortunes was not the greater part of their *Weltanschauung*. Beyond those goals they were concerned with the *public* welfare and the spirit of a true corporate commonwealth. Hence the mercantilists were caught in their own argument: if property was essential to the individual's sense of identity, then it was by the same logic the basis of any public identity; the sense of *ours* was as vital as the sense of *mine*. But granted that the circumstances of world war and revolution were extremely difficult and the temptations of a continent extremely great, it is nevertheless true that the mercantilists never overcame their bias in favor of private property.

That they came as close as they did—and with men like Madison, Calhoun, and John Quincy Adams it was very close—is enough to justify high praise. They defined the problem so clearly that no one can ever know them and enter the plea of ignorance. A harsh judgment after the fact is perhaps unnecessary, for their failure brought its own consequences in the triumph of laissez faire. For them that was punishment enough. Unwilling in the final showdown to make a fuller commitment to social property in the name of a corporate commonwealth, they had no effective defense against the men who demanded that private property and interest be given full scope and unrestrained liberty in the name of individualism.

The Age of Laissez Nous Faire

1819–1896

> *Our age is wholly of a different character, and its legislation takes another turn. Society is full of excitement; competition comes in place of monopoly; and intelligence and industry ask only for fair play and an open field.*
>
> Daniel Webster, 1824

The Triumph of the Rising Order

The policy of leaving individuals, partnerships, and States, as much as possible to secure their own interest, in their own way, is the only good evidence that the government is founded in reason and justice, and not in error or fraud.

John Taylor of Caroline, 1824

It is said to be the age of the 1st person singular.

Ralph Waldo Emerson, 1827

I care for nothing about clamors, sir, mark me! I do precisely what I think just and right.

Andrew Jackson, 1828

JOHN TAYLOR AND THE VICTORY OF LAISSEZ FAIRE

Dynamic, liberating, and creative, the soaring spirit and animal vigor of the Age of Laissez Nous Faire transformed America from an established newcomer in the society of nations into the world's leading industrial country in less than three generations. Yet its twin dogmas of expansion and competition exacted a high price for success. Civil war, grave social disorders, and the progressive disillusionment and alienation of a sizable segment of society were the scars and open wounds it bequeathed to its heirs. The open field for fair play became first a military battleground and finally the restricted arena dominated by the giant corporation.

For a time, however, the majority of Americans were probably blessed with more liberty than any men in the modern age have known. In a spectacle that was at once terrifying and ennobling, they came unbelievably close to shaping themselves and their world in their own image. This breaking away from the mercantilist conception of a corporate commonwealth was recognized and elaborated upon by artists as well as politicians, by crossroad wits as well as formal philosophers. Perhaps none of them, even the most accomplished or famous, captured the realities and the implications of the Age of Laissez Nous Faire more accurately and with greater insight than Erastus Salisbury Field, an amateur painter from Massachusetts who mastered the techniques of primitivism long before Grandma Moses charmed Americans of the 20th century. As his contribution to the centennial celebration of independence, Field prepared a massive work (13 by 9 feet) entitled *Historical Monument of the American Republic*. It was a startlingly accurate and eerie image of the United States in the Age of Laissez Nous Faire.

Field's conception of the foundation of American society was a rectangular, three-story groundwork done in a severely simple and imposing classical style which heightened the sense of organic strength and durability created by the mass itself. But from that base arose eight separate and wildly polyglot towers. Not only did they differ from each other in their styles and shapes, but the various levels of a given tower revealed variations of a vaguely basic design. Near the top, seven of the towers were once again connected, in a modified figure-8 pattern, by railroad tracks laid on sweeping steel bridges over which trains sped purposefully from tower to tower. The eighth column, lower than the rest and unconnected save through the common base but placed strategically center-front, was reserved for the Constitution and Abraham Lincoln. And on a majestic mall in the foreground appeared a sizable body of troops on parade.

Though certainly undistinguished as formal art, Field's painting creates a strange charm as well as a ram-like image. The weakest aspect of the painting as primitive image is the lack of any direct visible connection between Lincoln's tower and the other columns. This is a serious omission because it was the professional politician as much as the railroads which provided the connecting tissue (and nerves) for the various elements of society during the time of laissez faire. And Lincoln was most certainly a keen, sophisticated, and generally triumphant politician.

The politician as he is known and thought of in the 20th century is a creature of laissez faire. Onrushing divergent streams of economic development, undercurrents of frontier savagery, and the steady pressure exerted by a surplus of wealth-to-waste eroded and distorted the corporate philosophy of mercantilism. Leadership ceased to be defined by the problems and responsibilities of *general* development; the encompassing view, based upon a sense of inter-related wholeness and community and defined by a system of equity and balance, failed to withstand the forces it had done so much to create. Leadership became instead a task of representing a specific element of the system and attempting to secure its objectives through conflict and compromise with the other elements.

Given the change, the politician became a separate, professional functionary in society. This did not mean that the politician became irrelevant or inferior; his role merely changed. His function was indispensable, legitimate, and honorable. It could of course be exploited for narrow gain or distorted into special pleading. But at his mundane best the politician became a competent and honest spokesman and broker, and could become a statesman by disciplining himself to stand outside his own interest and see it as part (albeit the most important part) of the entire system. Yet it is illuminating to note that the Compromise of 1850 was initiated and sustained by Henry Clay, who had matured within the framework of American mercantilism. Compared with politicians of the new era such as Thurlow Weed and Amos Kendall, or even Martin Van Buren, the leaders of mercantilism were men of broader vision and greater perception of the long-range implications and consequences of their actions.

For these reasons, many of them, like Madison and John Quincy Adams, had worried about the practical results of applying the ideas of laissez faire as early as 1819. But neither Adams nor Clay were able to sustain the structure of mercantilism against the force of its centrifugal triumphs. By 1826 they were confronted by the splintering of the political economy along several lines of tension. North Atlantic society wanted internal improvements, a protective tariff, and a land policy that would control westward expansion in the way that John Jay had outlined in 1785. Most of its leaders had come to accept the west, and some of them already saw it as the key to their future well-being. But they wanted to guide its development and connect it to eastern progress in a subsidiary relationship. This attitude weakened their ties with the westerners, even though the latter shared the seaboard's desire for internal improvements and were willing to bargain and compromise on the details of the tariff.

Both north and south of the Ohio River, however, westerners emphasized the clash between established entrepreneurs and the rising on-the-make small capitalists. They valued the liberty to get rich more than the opportunity to build a commonwealth. Hence they defined democracy far more in terms of unrestricted rights than in terms of corporate responsibilities. But so, too, did an increasing number of mechanics and small tradesmen in the east. While many of the forces disintegrating mercantilism were functional (such as the manufacturers against the shippers) and sectional (as with the south versus the north), one of the most persuasive was an intensifying class antagonism between large, well-established, upper-class entrepreneurs and smaller, upward-moving operators. Some of the latter, such as Andrew Jackson of Tennessee and Martin Van Buren of New York, had by the 1820s become wealthy men; but in their careers and their attitudes they provided models for emulation and symbols of leadership for others who had similar aspirations. Such class consciousness was a particularly dynamic force because it united men across lines that were otherwise divisive.

Still another conflict emerged within the coastal upper class. Planter agrarians of the Taylor-Randolph variety could agree with their northern counterparts on the usefulness of high land-prices in the west, but not much else. They denied the need of internal improvements by the national government, charged inequity in the allocation of those that had been undertaken, and asserted they would ultimately destroy free government (and perhaps property rights) by subverting the central principle of that "*imperium in imperio*" which Randolph called the very heart of the Constitution. Randolph also defined the tariff as the weapon with which northerners were about to reduce the south to "a state of worse than colonial bondage." In his own way, therefore, Randolph made the same analysis of the state of the political economy that Adams had offered when preparing the Monroe Doctrine, but he applied it *inside* the country instead of externally in relation to the Spanish colonies. "If you draw the last shilling from our pockets," he roared during the tariff debates of 1824, "what are the checks of the constitution to us?

A fig for the constitution! When the scorpion's sting is probing us to the quick, shall we stop to chop logic?" None of his audience had to guess as to his answer.

While in agreement that the tariff could make southerners "the serfs of the system," Calhoun was nevertheless reluctant to abandon the ideals and the achievements of a national corporate outlook. But two events pushed him in that direction. His constituency in South Carolina increasingly accepted the Taylor-Randolph analysis and thereby confronted him with a political ultimatum. Senatorial tenure and the possibility of White House tenancy were at stake. At the same time, and without any direct pressure, Calhoun interpreted the proceedings of the Harrisburg Convention on the Tariff (1827) as a sign that the northern conception of protection was undergoing a basic change. He concluded that instead of being viewed as a dual-purpose tool for defense and for developing the general political economy, it was rapidly being defined as a lever for lifting extra profits out of the south's pocket. Calhoun's estimate of the trend was accurate, though he probably exaggerated the extent to which it had developed by 1827. Northern industrialists were formulating their policy as manufacturers per se far more than as one element of a balanced and corporate society.

Loyal to that mercantilist outlook, and aware that the tariff could provoke a serious crisis among its adherents, John Quincy Adams soon advocated a compromise. But the older generation of leaders lacked sufficient support to maintain such a balanced program. This breakdown of the *Weltanschauung* of mercantilism, in which the attitudes and policies of northern businessmen were as subversive as the resurgence of the physiocratic outlook in the seaboard south, was the negative half of the coming of laissez faire. On the positive side, the southern agrarians and many western and northern entrepreneurs shared an active commitment to a strikingly different explanation of how individual, group, and national development could be speeded up and extended. For a time, at any rate, the new outlook was a binder that proved stronger than the differences over specific issues and policies.

Derived from the assumption of a natural order so emphatically and persuasively asserted by John Locke and the French physiocrats, and then refined, codified, and presented in the magnificent rhetoric and convincing syllogisms of Adam Smith and Jean Baptiste Say, the philosophy of laissez faire promised wealth, welfare, and happiness through the freedom to do what one wanted. Men were thus told what they hankered to hear: by following their bellies, their egos, and their pocketbook nerve they could become moral agents, accumulate profits, contribute their share to the general welfare, and at the same time extend and strengthen the area of liberty and freedom. Just as with mercantilism, laissez faire clearly originated as the short-run rationalization and long-range utopia of various rising and special interests. But similarly integrating those elements into a hierarchy of values, the *Weltanschauung* of laissez faire was no more a narrow philosophy of the bank account than its predecessor had been.

But teased and tempted by a rich and voluptuous continent, it was all too easy for men to emphasize economic liberty, particularly since Calvin's successors—to say nothing of his heretical followers—had already revealed a strong propensity to read worldly success as a sign of election to God's favor. According to the Scriptures as well as to Adam Smith's *Wealth of Nations*, therefore, it was moral to pursue one's self-interest because the Hidden Hand would reconcile all conflicts into the general welfare. Competitive free enterprise thus become the master carpenter of a moral community.

This new outlook became prominent in the debates over American policy toward the Greek Revolution of 1822–1823. Daniel Webster's resolution to send an American agent to encourage the revolt met with little enthusiasm from President Monroe or Secretary Adams, but a good many congressmen responded to his argument for action in behalf of America's "diverse interests in the Mediterranean." Other northerners agreed that the move "contemplate[d] opening new commercial relations." Aid for Greece would help "form a powerful check upon the barbarous dependencies of the [non-Christian Turks] in those seas, and give facility to that commercial enterprise which now finds its way only to one port of European Asiatic Turkey." Thus was the heathen also defined as an economic despot. And a good many westerners, like David P. Cook of Illinois, added their support to a crusade for Christian liberty which also promised foreign markets. Arm in arm, religion and laissez faire had mustered for their first campaign for freedom.

But southerners like George Cary of Georgia and Joel Poinsette of South Carolina were skeptical of the alliance as well as opposed to any direct action. Poinsette in particular warned that the abstract discussion of other people's freedom "has a native tendency to unbase the mind; to throw it completely off balance; and its discussion is therefore to be approached and conducted with the utmost caution." They stressed the connection between a crusading religious and political attitude and the interests of commerce and manufacturing even more in later years, when northerners turned their attack on planters as evil tyrants. Poinsette's thesis about the desirability of proceeding with some care and humility when entering upon an examination of the freedom of others is not invalidated, however, by such a connection between the private interest and the general idea.

Yet in one of the most striking ironies of American history, it was John Taylor of Caroline, the southerner *qua* southerner, who became the philosopher-king of the new *Weltanschauung*. Though he looked back to a feudal world for his inspiration (and his utopia), his basic ideas and program offered convenient and powerful weapons for the advocates of laissez faire. "Abolish exclusive privilege . . .," he thundered in 1822, "and vindicate the inviolability of property, even against legislatures." "The policy of leaving individuals, partnerships, and States, as much as possible to secure their own interest, in their own way," he added in 1824, "is the only good evidence that the government is founded in reason and justice, and not in error or fraud."

Along with a high percentage of southerners, Taylor's views attracted Van Buren and many other northerners. William M. Gouge, for example, was a southern patronage appointee of President Jackson who was consulted on many economic issues. Like Taylor, he flatly asserted that "corporations are unfavorable to the progress of national wealth." Ogden Edwards, a delegate to the New York constitutional convention of 1821, was another supporter. His thesis was simple: "we have too much legislation." Edwards defined the governor, for example, as "a watchful sentinel to guard us from evil." And again following Taylor, men like Edwards and Van Buren combined their individualism with a system controlled by well-organized and powerful political machines and headed by strong leaders. As John Locke had discovered when trying to reconcile a strong king with the right of revolution, this was obviously a dilemma, even a contradiction, in the philosophy of laissez faire. But

Edwards provided a typical resolution. He advocated a situation in which "the people may lie down and rest in security." While an apt image in connection with governmental action in the affairs of the political economy, it did not apply to the individual's enterprises. Edwards bespoke the popular desire to be able to forget about politics in order to concentrate on business.

Taylor also had a powerful protégé in the west who was likewise fond of the kind of secular morality typified in Edwards's use of the term "evil" in connection with politics. "I can hardly figure to myself," concluded Senator Thomas Hart Benton of Missouri, "the ideal of a republican statesman more perfect and complete [than Taylor]." A vigorous businessman and probably the best constitutional lawyer in the nation, Benton was a classic figure of the Age of Laissez Nous Faire. He thoroughly understood that the government continued to have three important responsibilities under the new outlook: it had to maintain the basic framework of a system (such as that of money and the rule of law); it had to preserve the competitive situation by acting against monopolies and by helping new or weak entrants into the scramble; and it had to be the agent of expanding and protecting the market place, which was the key to the individual competition producing the general welfare.

Highly responsible and effective as a politician of his outlook, Benton pushed through some of the earliest successful attacks in behalf of laissez faire. He ended government operation of lead mines in Missouri in favor of private companies. And calmly explaining that the War of 1812 had been worth "all the blood and treasure" that the west had contributed because it removed British influence in the fur trade, Benton demanded that the governmental system of trading posts, designed and initiated by George Washington, be discarded in favor of wide-open competition among any and all Americans. Benton's close association with Astor's American Fur Company no doubt influenced his campaign, but it did not modify his commitment to free competition.

His constant efforts in behalf of the western farmer included support for the right of preemption, relief acts for those who had difficulty in meeting their land payments, and for lowering the price of land that was not purchased within a specified time after being put on the market. He also agitated militantly against the Indians, and vigorously pushed commercial and territorial expansion. And convinced that "the monarch and the republican can no longer breathe the same atmosphere," Benton was willing to use force when and if it became necessary to carry out such an enlargement of the market place of capitalism and freedom.

MARTIN VAN BUREN AND THE NEW POLITICS

Benton was symbolic of the vast majority of westerners who supported the Hero from the Hermitage for President. Beginning well before the election of 1824, Jackson's western followers organized such support by stressing his military achievements and his success in rising from a log cabin to a planter's mansion. He was winningly vague on everything except his hates, which were undistinguished by anything except their violence. But he was a hero of economic independence and, as one of his lieutenants remarked, "one cup of *generous whiskey* produces more military ardor, than can be allayed by a month of reflection and sober reason."

In one important respect, however, the far more aristocratic Calhoun did more to democratize presidential politics than either Jackson or Van Buren. For he was the one who destroyed the narrowly based and tightly controlled caucus system through which candidates were selected. Thus it is misleading to view Van Buren as the man who engineered Jackson's election. Directly and indirectly, others contributed as much if not more, though, as with Calhoun, that had not been the original intention. Van Buren's more viable and more considerable warrant for fame is his grasp of the new role of the politician in an age of laissez faire. Charging Monroe with "heretical" sins for having embraced mercantilism, and describing Adams's views on appointment by quality as "pernicious," Van Buren took the groundwork of his philosophy from Taylor and Jefferson and set out to organize a working consensus of the various interests accepting that outlook.

Van Buren's operations in New York and Washington reveal and clarify the regional and national coalition between rising businessmen, yeoman farmers, southern planters, and northern mechanics that is generally labeled "Jacksonian Democracy." It was an unstable alliance between a rising bourgeoisie on the make and a quasi-feudal landed aristocracy directed against the established harbingers of an industrial order. Jackson personified the ambition, the attitude, and the objectives of those groups and justly gave his name to the movement. But Van Buren was in many essential respects the man who managed to consolidate and sustain a combination that persistently threatened to, and ultimately did, disintegrate in violent antagonisms.

Van Buren's personal career provided a miniature of the triumph of laissez faire. Beginning as the son of a tavern keeper, he entered law at 14 and ultimately became a "very rich man" with all the upper-class graces; "as polished and captivating a person in the social circle as America has ever known," remarked a contemporary. As a confirmed worshiper at the shrine of Jefferson and Taylor, he was unencumbered with philosophical second thoughts. "It is only when the natural order of society is disturbed . . . that the wages of labor become inadequate." To avoid any misunderstanding, let it be emphasized that Van Buren's definition of labor was the same as Robert Rantoul's, which included bankers and similar businessmen in the approved category of those "who *do something for a living*." After all, Van Buren himself had intimate ties with the financial community.

Gifted with a fine sense of timing and tactical understanding, Van Buren also understood the strategic axioms of laissez-faire politics. Perhaps his most notable victory was the building of an effective alliance between New York business interests and the state's aspiring mechanics. In some ways, of course, that was not too difficult in view of labor's commitment to property rights and laissez faire. "The great object of the struggles of the Democracy," explained William Leggett, who was one of the most militant spokesmen of the ambitious mechanics and smaller businessmen, "has been to confine the action of the General Government within the limits marked out in the Constitution." Sure that the "prosperity of rational men depends on themselves," he wanted little more than "a system of legislation which leaves all to the free exercise of their talents and industry within the limits of the general law." Freedom of action and the "protection of property" were the key axioms of that outlook.

Van Buren integrated the mechanics and the aristocrats in a political machine (The Albany Regency) that was as autocratic and centralized as any the mercantilists ever organized. Mavericks were simply not tolerated. A contemporary who knew the rules and methods of The Regency at first hand left a very candid description of its procedures: "Except he would swear allegiance to the powers that be, it was useless for him to look for an appointment." Unlike the mercantilists, however, The Regency wanted to establish free competition. "Equal rights for all," demanded an articulate mechanic, "and special privileges for none." Identical standards of natural law were applied to political affairs. As William Marcy of The Regency's board of directors explained bluntly, all was fair in politics as well as in love and war: "To the victors go the spoils of the enemy."

Van Buren's tie with eastern mechanics became even more important as manufacturing and commerce continued to institutionalize themselves in the factory and wholesaling systems centered in urban society, for the union movement slowly gained strength as a response to the continued success of the employers. Boasting 16 member units, the General Trade Union of Boston had counterparts in New York, Baltimore, and Philadelphia. Carpenters, leather workers, sail- and pump-makers, bakers, and coopers joined hands with weavers, tailors, and ironworkers. Organizing as Workingmen's Parties, they sought lien laws, and monetary standards, to guarantee themselves some minimum amount of wages under all circumstances, longer credit arrangements (six months was not too unusual as existing practice) for consumer purchases, tax revisions, anti-monopoly laws, an end to imprisonment for debt, the ten-hour day, more equitable arrangements for militia duty, and freedom from competition with prison labor.

They also stressed education, viewing it as the lever by which they could become successful enterpreneurs: education for reflection's sake was not their objective. It would be unfair and inaccurate to describe their approach as anti-intellectual; their definition of education tended to be nonintellectual. They were concerned with more than rudimentary vocational training; allowing for the differences of time and the nature of the economy their approach might be compared to that of our modern schools of commerce and business. Concerned to train infantry for the battle against the "aristocracy of talent and place," labor spokesmen agitated for public schools that would inculcate "a just disposition, virtuous habits, and a rational self-governing character"; disciplined to this standard, their sons would be able to take care of themselves in open competition.

As a leader of the upper classes, Horace Mann of Massachusetts approached education as an effective means of social control as well as a philosophical ideal. Warning his peers that social unrest would become a serious danger unless the lower orders were given a share of the increasing wealth, he argued that education would solve the problem. While the rich would remain rich, the lower classes would respond to the training of their minds by improving their fortunes and turning away from the "wanton destruction of the property of others." Thus the order would be saved and improved.

"What surer guaranty can be capitalist find for the security of his investments," Mann asked rhetorically, "than is to be found in the sense of a community morally and intellectually enlightened?" Such economic leaders as Thaddeus Stevens and Abbot Lawrence saw the logic and accepted the responsibility, and from an early date helped to spread Mann's ideas. Putting his principles into action as the official leader of education in Massachusetts from 1827 to 1837, Mann lengthened the school year and pushed the construction of 50 new public (and free) high schools.

Other men such as Yale-graduate Josiah Holbrook extended adult education through the lyceum movement. This may have been more actively intellectual, since it offered lecturers like Ralph Waldo Emerson and, in the early years, emphasized natural science. On the other hand, its meetings tended to become ceremonial and social affairs which served as forums for the discussion of practical and immediate issues. Whatever the balance between the production of heat and the stimulation and discipline of thought, the movement had a wide following. Established on a national basis by 1831, it claimed some 3,000 units in 15 states within four years.

Even the more radical wing of the labor movement based its program on Mann's equation of education and property rights. Thomas Skidmore's plan, presented in his *Rights of Man to Property* (1829), proposed to sustain true laissez faire by outlawing the practice of inheritance. A similar spirit permeated Stephen Simpson's statement of an individualistic labor theory of value in the *Workingman's Manual* (1831). He indignantly explained that it was "a perversion" to accuse labor of "contending for an *equality of wealth* or a community of property." Hence the slogan of the Workingman's Party—"equal education ... equal property ... equal privileges"—should not be interpreted as a rallying cry for early socialism. It was an exhortation to establish the framework for thoroughgoing laissez faire.

LIBERTY AND BONDAGE IN THE SPIRIT OF JACKSONIAN DEMOCRACY

Jackson's inaugural reception was a magnificent manifestation of this same spirit. Swarming into the White House from all parts of the country, and ignoring the formality of invitations, his exuberant followers turned satin-covered chairs into footstools, tapestries into throw-away napkins, and windows into doors. Appropriately permissive (and justly concerned for his personal well-being), Jackson abandoned the market place of revelry in favor of more secure quarters at Gadsby's Tavern. Jackson also took the part of Peggy Eaton, a vivacious barmaid who had married a cabinet official after a long and satisfying courtship, in her difficulties in breaking the established patterns of Washington's social élite. But the inaugural reception documented the unfettered triumph of laissez nous faire in a classic manner.

Taking office with a general philosophy of leaving "individuals and States as much as possible to themselves," Jackson selected his key advisors by this criterion. As a group of successful bankers, railroad-builders, land speculators, and general promoters which also included the director of the nation's telegraph monopoly, the General's friends were persuasive spokesmen for, and examples of, the Age of Laissez Nous Faire. "Things will take their course in the moral as well as in the natural world," explained Amos Kendall of the Kitchen Cabinet, and cautioned the Congress to "be content to let currency and private business alone."

This triumphant philosophy became the editorial viewpoint of the party's key magazine, *The Democratic Review*. "The best government is that which governs least," announced the leading essay in the first issue. "Legislation has been the fruitful parent of nine-tenths of all the evil, moral and physical, by which mankind has been affected since the creation of the world." Even a "strong and active democratic *government*, in the common sense of the term, is an evil differing only in degree and mode of operation, and not in its nature, from a strong despotism." Jackson's supporters eagerly spread the gospel and applied the doctrine of good works. Lower-echelon political leaders such as James K. Polk proclaimed the great faith of "enterprising freemen" and closed ranks behind Van Buren's leadership to control the Congress.

Elsewhere a good many ordained ministers began to expound the doctrine of laissez faire as though it were a newly discovered book of the Bible. Francis Wayland's *Elements of Political Economy* proclaimed that "every man is allowed to gain all he can." The Reverend John McVickar revealed that the principles of public wealth were the same as those for accumulating private riches. And Gilbert Vale, turning his religious education to secular purposes, became an influential circuit-riding economist in support of the cause. Stressing the importance of having enough land to take care of the poor, he provided a succinct summary of the success of this secular missionary movement. "Let us alone," he reflected with some pride, "is, generally speaking, the language of the merchant, the manufacturer, and the farmer; or, at least, do no more than remove impediments."

Jackson himself took charge of removing the major impediments. His first acts were to halt government subsidies to small-arms manufacturers and veto a bill for internal improvements in Kentucky. Though clearly a political broadside aimed at Henry Clay's fortress, Jackson's veto of the Maysville Road project was also an ideological manifesto. Bluntly proclaiming the danger inherent in the whole principle, he admitted that piecemeal grants had some justification. But even those were "unsafe." Unless they were approved with great caution, they "would of necessity lead to the subversion of the federal system." And there was no warrant at all for continuing to operate the projects as a business venture. Sure of his strength, Jackson poured salt in the wound by challenging Clay to engineer a constitutional amendment outlawing such vetoes.

At the same time, Jackson fully understood the role of the government (and particularly of the President) in sustaining and extending the basic framework of a laissez-faire political economy. While willing to compromise on the specific issue of the tariff, he moved vigorously, openly threatening force, against South Carolina's inclination to carry laissez faire to the point of nullifying national laws. Such action, Jackson slashed back, "is to say that the United States are not a nation": it was "incompatible with the existence of the Union." Arguing in a similar vein, he used troops against strikers who, in his view, were interfering with the government by stopping work on the construction of the Chesapeake and Ohio Canal.

Jackson manifested a similar concern for the national system by signing trade treaties with Siam and Great Britain and by demanding that France pay its long overdue damages against American shipping. And concluding that Indians "can not live in contact with a civilized community and prosper," he defied Chief Justice Marshall's effort to retain some equity in the new order and drove them west where they would not interfere with the free progress and prosperity of democracy. Culminating in a particularly cruel forced march, the Indians were forced to give up their all too successful efforts to adapt to the white man's system.

This tension between the minimum demands of a national system and the freedom it was supposed to make possible came to an early climax in the crisis over the national banking system. One group within the Jacksonian coalition approved the bank (and said so in an able congressional report) because it stabilized the monetary base of economic activity while at the same time providing an expanding credit (or capital) system. However profound the truths of laissez faire, such heretics doubted that credit could regulate itself. And as men who knew whereof they spoke, they wryly observed that some people were always richer than the rest.

Jackson galloped on. Sure of the truth that had been revealed to him during the Panic of 1819 when he and Benton had been hurt by tight credit, he was convinced that precious metals would in fact provide a natural and self-enforcing money system. Supported and constantly encouraged by several special interest groups, he thundered on to destroy "THE MONSTER." Wall-Street bankers naturally approved such an attack on Philadelphia's power. And politicians like Van Buren and Kendall screened the class and functional differences between agrarians, businessmen, and mechanics behind an ideological dance of the seven sophistries.

In a performance that laid bare the crippled spirit of laissez nous faire, the Jacksonians denied their central axiom that men were masters of their own fate. Instead, they retreated before the *possibility* that a national bank *might* undermine the government and democracy. It was a sensible and legitimate fear, but the surrender said more about the men of laissez faire than all their lyrics in praise of the free individual. Jackson faced the British and the Indians with great courage, but he quailed before the vastly more significant challenge of restraining one's own freedom of action in favor of society's well-being. Instead of controlling and using the bank, as had the mercantilists, the Jacksonians abandoned the field to their fears.

A similar retreat became evident in other quarters; many of the most articulate of the laissez-faire philosophers and artists withdrew into their own community *on the edge* of Boston, there to carry Ralph Waldo Emerson's axiom, "TRUST TO YOURSELF" to its logical (and almost deadly) conclusion. Mixing the romanticism of Samuel Taylor Coleridge with a travesty of Calvinism to produce a potent ideology called transcendentalism, they began to talk to themselves instead of to others, an other, or to God. By thus transcending society itself, they abstracted man into a set of principles which they ultimately presented as moral absolutes.

This doctrine of innate ideas justified a self-reliance that defined restraint as being immoral. Thus fortified, the poet William Cullen Bryant could simultaneously campaign for a nationalistic assertion of American verse, thoroughgoing laissez faire and free trade, and the repeal of all laws limiting interest rates. Usury was thus defined as an essential ingredient of free expression. Emerson never went that far (and Bryant performed more intelligently as a newspaper editor), but his pseudo-mystical doctrine of individualism constantly teetered on the edge of substituting personal exhilaration and impulse for rationality and social morality. It liberated men, but it did so in the name of an oversoul whose influence in this world was rather less than even the Hidden Hand that guided the system of Adam Smith.

"I simply experiment," Emerson explained: "an endless seeker with no Past at my back." He did uphold the value of education, calling it "the mother of national prosperity," but only to discount politics. Any accommodation to the system was "a loss of so much integrity." While capable of being defended under several easily imaginable circumstances, the view was unrewarding even within its own framework unless matched by some vision of a new order. Emerson denied the need. The state had no justification once it had educated a man. At that point "he needs no library, for he has not done thinking; no church, for he is a prophet; no statute book, for he is a lawgiver; no money, for he is value."

Having thus stated a theory of the withering away of the state in the Age of Laissez Nous Faire, Emerson had to come to terms with its existence and services. He did so by making personal property the touchstone of his compromise. "Money . . . is, in its effects and laws," he declared, "as beautiful as roses. Property keeps the accounts of the world, and is always moral." Men of such tremendous artistry as Emerson could survive these contradictions by living off their reserves of imagination and powers of abstraction—and their property. Those who needed more communion with the realities of human society either changed their outlook, struggled to some resolution of the dichotomies, or simply crumpled under the strain.

As a competent poet who lacked the power to transcend such troublesome details, Jones Very disintegrated and spent the last 40 years of his life expounding and elucidating a doctrine of "will-less existence." In a terrible way, he managed to transcend life itself. Margaret Fuller, an exceptionally talented woman of the group, was more fortunate. She went to Europe and was reborn in a tempestuous affair. Losing her husband and child in a disaster at sea, she provided one of the most poignant commentaries on the entire transcendentalist movement. "Had I only come ten years earlier. . . . So much strength has been wasted by abstraction."

Nathaniel Hawthorne ultimately reached a similar conclusion. Perhaps grasping the implications of *The Scarlet Letter* (the adultery is an abstraction that never became human or comprehensible) he recognized that he always stood just outside his characters and the society that he created for them to live in. To preserve his own independence, he almost destroyed them. His women always verged on a passionate act but in the end contented themselves with a substitute, such as having ideas about washing dishes. Like Margaret Fuller in her early years, Hawthorne's emancipated women had emancipated themselves from life.

Even his societies lacked any institutional substance. Nevertheless, Hawthorne's achievement as an artist was great. And in his last works he became fully aware of his own weakness. Comprehending the breakdown of Calvin's original vision of a corporate Christian commonwealth, he came finally to understand that the residue needed to be transformed into a new conception of community. Perhaps this insight was all that a man of his experience could grasp; it was a crucial truth, but he remained content with the evasive, though pleasant, duality that it provided.

Far more involved in the society of men, and incomparably the greatest poet of laissez faire, even Walt Whitman finally recognized the one-sidedness of his outlook. In a way that dramatized Jackson's evasion of the real issue in the bank fight, Whitman was prone to follow the path of least resistance. Like the transcendentalists, he started with "a simple, separate person" only to end up with the demand that society reform itself in his image. Whitman's politics were typically laissez-faire. "Under the specious pretext of effecting 'the happiness of the whole community,' " he pontificated, "nearly all the wrongs and intrusions of government have been carried through." Social reform thus became a matter of personal regenera-tion: men should "not look to precedents and legislative bodies for aid." When concerned by a problem, therefore, Whitman walked away, as many of his heirs from Mark Twain to William Faulkner were to do, and became "a way farer down the open road."

In this respect, and as indicated by his wild enthusiasm for nation-alistic expansion prior to the Civil War, Whitman was a poet of the frontier process by which democracy and prosperity were linked to an aggressive foreign policy. But he was also the first poet of the city, which he knew intimately from the grinding sorrow of its slums to the wonderful joy of a walk or a ride through its exhilarating diver-sity of cement, iron, and wet grass. Vastly more aware of the reali-ties of life than a man like Emerson, he infused the language with a vernacular vigor and inventive freedom that surpassed any European achievement. And despite, or perhaps because of, his bisexuality, he made it possible to treat sex as a subject in American literature.

To the degree that they sculpted and painted nudes, or infused their portraits with the essence of femaleness, as Thomas Sully did in his study of actress Fanny Kemble, American artists should be credited with a similar advance. Sully was typical of the best of them, for his image of Kemble also revealed the not-herself-not-anyone character of a great stage personage as well as her awareness that she could work at a higher artistic level than her audiences could understand or tolerate. A few of Ralph Earl's disciplined and sparse sketches of Jackson were almost as good. And Thomas Cole carried the basic ambivalence of lais-sez faire into his work, painting literal landscapes for the entre-preneurs who patronized him, while for himself he composed great scenes of religious and ethical decay sapping the strength of empires. A similar concern for the wholeness and interrelat-edness of things typified the sculpture of Horatio Greenough. Asserting that "God's world has a distinct formula for every function" long before Frank Lloyd Wright designed his fame on the same axiom, Greenough insisted that true achievement could come only by "mastering the principles."

Yet the art triumphs of the Age of Laissez Nous Faire that were appropriate to it were those of such men as William Sidney Mount and George Caleb Bingham. Honoring Mount's injunction to "paint pictures that will take with the public—never paint for the few, but the many," Bingham's *Fur Traders Descending the Missouri* gave Americans, and any others who were interested, some truly magnificent images of the Age of Laissez Nous Faire. And no one surpassed Mount's comment, in his drawing *The Power of Music*, on the poignancy of race relations in the United States. Spiritually so intimate and yet practically and physically so distant, the white man and the Negro shared a momentary relationship through a song that seemed to fill all of them with an awareness of the deeper tragedy.

A similar sense of laissez faire was provided by such architects as Robert Dale Owen, who favored the Gothic style because it allowed a "free play of anachronism." Books like Asher Benjamin's *Practical House Carpenter* (14 editions between 1830 and 1857) enabled journeyman builders to combine Greek and Gothic exteriors with the wildest kind of interior eclecticism. Such buildings provided the three-dimensional footnotes for James Fenimore Cooper's astringent comment. "You are in a country in which every man swaggers and talks, knowledge or no knowledge; brains or no brains; taste or no taste. They are all *ex nato* connoisseurs."

CHAPTER TWO

A New Reality for Existing Ideas

[Government] was not intended to . . . create systems of agriculture, manufacturing, or trade. . . . Few men can doubt that. . . . A system founded on private interest, enterprise, and competition, without the aid of legislative grants or regulations by law, would rapidly prosper.

Martin Van Buren, 1837

We are for leaving trade free; and the right to combine is an indispensable attribute of its freedom.

William Leggett, 1837

[A corporation] is, indeed, a mere artificial being, invisible and intangible; yet it is a person, for certain purposes in contemplation of law, and has been recognized as such by the decisions of this court.

Chief Justice Roger B. Taney, 1839

The Union, next to our liberty, most dear. May we always remember that it can only be preserved by distributing equally the benefits and burdens of the Union.

John C. Calhoun, 1830

If the State cannot survive the anti-slavery agitation, then let the state perish.

William Lloyd Garrison, 1836

THE THEORY AND THE REALITY OF THE MARKET PLACE

As generally presented and accepted, the *Weltanschauung* of laissez faire was based on what was presumed to be a simple if not obvious truth. Individualized free competition in an open and fair society would produce specific happiness and the general welfare. But the assumption of free competition was actually predicated upon three other unspoken premises: that domestic society was sufficiently balanced and unfettered to insure that such conflict remained creative, that the market place continued to expand, and that other nations accepted and acted on the key axioms. All other things being equal, ran the argument, competition would generate progress.

Yet as Madison, Monroe, and other mercantilists often pointed out, these essential other things never were equal. Various individuals and groups were always insisting that they needed assistance, either to enter the game as an equal or to remain competitors. Often they did need it. Even under the most favorable circumstances, the very process of competition led to the destruction, failure, or bare survival of the less successful. While it promised a diversity of life, therefore, the dynamic of the system carried it toward a situation in which a few triumphant elements dominated the political and social economy. Hence the system always required a considerable amount of tinkering in order to keep it in working condition. Since these realities contradicted the central premise (and corroded the utopia) of the system, it was not unnatural that men were constantly on the lookout to find and eradicate the *one* evil—or to discover the *one* great equalizer—and thus establish the necessary conditions for uninhibited progress toward perfection.

Such troubled advocates of laissez faire faced still another difficulty. Usually thought of as a philosophy and a system of individualism, by which is meant the single human being, the competition and conflict of laissez faire actually occurred at many different levels. In addition to the individual, there were organized groups such as corporations, labor unions, and reformers; political subdivisions such as parties and the states; social and economic units which became self-conscious sections or regions; and, in the broadest sense, nations themselves in the world arena. These units also competed on several levels: economic, political, and intellectual-social. And given the argument that competition produced welfare, it should not be too surprising to realize that laissez faire served subtly (though persuasively) to condition men to accept armed conflict with righteous attitudes.

Hence Van Buren's sanguine restatement of the principles of laissez faire as he became President did not match the realities he soon encountered. Government, he reminded the faithful, "was not intended to . . . create systems of agriculture, manufacturing, or trade." "Few men can doubt," he concluded, "that their own interest as well as the general welfare of the country would be promoted by . . . A system founded on private interest, enterprise, and competition [which], without the aid of legislative grants or regulations by law, would rapidly prosper."

Honoring the identical faith, Chief Justice Roger B. Taney, who had served earlier as Jackson's attorney general, rendered a militant decision against monopolies in the Charles River Bridge case. Declaring that restrictive charters delayed progress, and that the country would be "thrown back . . . to the last century and be obliged to stand still" if they were not destroyed, he announced the new political economy and opened the market place to all competitors. But Taney's opinion also confirmed the corporation as a legitimate unit of competition. And that aspect of the court's decision amounted in the long run to a death sentence for individualized laissez faire, for the independent businessman proved incapable of holding his own against the corporation.

In the short run, however, it was Jackson's economic polity which brought on many of Van Buren's troubles. After destroying the national bank with his veto, Jackson transferred government funds to selected state banks. Already expanding their loans in competition with other local and regional banks, the favored institutions responded by further extending themselves. Accentuating his a priori commitment to hard money, the resulting economic orgy led Jackson to issue his specie circular of 1836, by which he lived up to his ancient preference for precious metal and at the same time sought to stabilize the wild boom. His return to the monetary principles of the Middle Ages would no doubt have pleased John Taylor of Caroline, but it had less happy effects on the political economy.

Unfortunately coinciding with a drop in exports and a poor crop season in 1835, the deflationary monetary circular counterbalanced the effect of distributing over five million from the treasury surplus to the states (because it removed the specie from the banks), and played a key role in the development of a major crisis. As Jackson had joyfully anticipated, the maneuver toppled many of the speculators whom he thought selfish, unprincipled, and evil. But it also bowled over a good number of upright mechanics, farmers, and small entrepreneurs. Labor leaders such as Leggett of New York had urged and praised the specie circular in the belief that it would give the mechanics an honest wage, undepreciated by inflation and the discounts on the notes of weak banks. But they soon found themselves confronted by increasing prices and growing numbers of unemployed in northern cities. Van Buren's cherished alliance between northern businessmen and mechanics, and southern planters, began to break apart under the pressure of class consciousness and regional economic conflicts.

Organized as the Equal Rights Party even before the shock of the Panic and depression, the more radical wing of New York politics provided an early example of the proliferation of political parties that was characteristic of the age of laissez faire. Often quick to criticize European countries for their multi-party systems, Americans seem prone to forget that between 1835 and 1896, they conducted their own politics in a very similar fashion. Economic and social conflict was the characteristic of the age, and it took political form as early as the 1820s, when a mechanics' organization held the balance of power in Philadelphia. Though with steadily decreasing significance, the phenomenon continued into the 20th century.

Standing for thoroughgoing reform in the tradition of laissez faire, the New York dissidents challenged the aristocratic governors of Van Buren's Regency machine and demanded more vigorous action against local and regional financial powers, a system of direct taxes, and election by direct popular vote. For a moment in February, 1837, when the depression struck hard, they turned to direct action. Urged on by posters that were blunt and threatening—"BREAD, MEAT, RENT, and FUEL! *Their prices must come down!*"—the response was militant. Crowds raided grocery stores and for a period of a few days led some conservatives to fear a general uprising. But the movement's respect (and ambition) for property checked them well short of a fundamental critique of the existing order.

Such conservatism also limited the effectiveness of leaders like Frances Wright, a striking and inspiring woman who combined femininity and social criticism in an explosive package. Mechanics and upper-class reformers responded to her appeals but did not take up her more basic reforms with equal enthusiasm. Indeed, they asked her to play down some of her more fundamental attacks on the system. And early proletarian leaders such as Mike Walsh of New York, who argued that the shift from Monroe and Adams to Jackson and Van Buren was "nothing but a change of masters," attracted an even smaller following. The shock of the panic passed and the labor movement remained an association of would-be entrepreneurs organized to secure reforms that would open the way for them to scramble to the top. Depressions only dramatized labor's commitment to laissez faire; lacking any firm conception of an alternative order, they responded to such crises by competing for the remaining jobs rather than by seizing the opportunity to change the system.

Buffeted by the gales of laissez faire, utopian experiments sank in the sea of continental property. They appeared irrelevant, if not stupid or dangerous, to men who assumed that welfare, and wealth, were a matter of time and labor. Albert Brisbane's image of an America organized in self-sufficent communities of 1,600 souls had little appeal to men whose immediate problem was to dispose of cotton and wheat surpluses. And while John Humphrey Noyes was undoubtedly correct in arguing that the jealousy provoked by property and sex caused a good share of men's troubles, the majority preferred the competition to preempt such rights over a disciplined struggle to sublimate their impulses in a cooperative commonwealth. As with Whitman, most Americans evaded the challenge of Noyes's communal community at Oneida, New York, by blaming their troubles on other property holders or in joining the free-for-all for more property.

RELIGIOUS HERESY AND THE ASSAULT ON SLAVERY

Having destroyed the bank, that primeval monster in the garden of laissez faire, the Jacksonian safari in search of the secular and institutional evil that would explain the malfunctioning of the system began to converge with a moral crusade developing out of John Locke's definition of the natural (and unnatural) man, the breakdown of Calvinism, and the philosophical ruminations of the transcendentalists. As the sustained vitality of the revival movement of 1799 and 1800 had suggested, religion in the age of laissez faire was in essence a series of variations on the Arminian heresy that had plagued Calvinism (and Jonathan Edwards) in the New England of the 1730s and 1740s. Encouraged by the secularization of God's will in the philosophy of Adam Smith and his followers, the religious advocates of free will soon reduced Calvin's social morality to a code of personal righteousness that paralleled and reinforced the individualism of Locke. The free man thereby became *ipso facto* the moral man. He was also the natural man.

A more portentous distortion of Calvin's corporate philosophy would be difficult to imagine, particularly in a society which had come to define freedom and liberty in terms of the right to vote and the right to become an independent entrepreneur. Here was the bedrock meaning of the transition to laissez faire. American history between 1828 and 1896 is largely the story of the multiple tensions among an attempt to apply the criteria of laissez faire, the realities of the situation, and a growing recognition that the implications of the effort were subversive of the very freedom it was supposed to create and guarantee. For if a man is free only if he holds property, then he is a mere product of material wealth. The new *Weltanschauung* liberated him only to set a horrible trap.

Nothing dramatizes the distortion of Edwards's theology more ironically than the role of his brilliant and devoted student, Samuel Hopkins, in transmitting the spirit of the Great Awakening to men who had abandoned the corporate ethic for the Arminianism and secular laissez faire of Stoddard and Whitefield. For himself, Hopkins did not make the equation between morality and laissez-faire individualism. His attacks on slavery stemmed from a corporate philosophy that held all Americans responsible for slavery and hence obligated to devise a mutual and institutional solution. His approach pointed toward some form of emancipation compensated by the national government which would lead into gradual integration of the Negro with the rest of the political and social economy.

This institutional approach to slavery did not disappear with Hopkins. Even some of the transcendentalists like William Ellery Channing, for example, initially (1835) made a similar analysis. And while quite different in being New York businessmen instead of Unitarian ministers, Arthur and Lewis Tappan in the beginning also favored that kind of solution. In the short space of six years, however, both the Tappans and Channing had embraced the kind of individual moralizing that typified the convergence of laissez faire, the secular morality of natural law, transcendentalism, and Arminian Protestantism. As a preacher who took the evangelical fervor of Hopkins and Edwards but abandoned their corporate ethic

in favor of individualized religion, Charles G. Finney was a key entrepreneur of that merger. Finney asserted that every man had a responsibility for helping to erect a framework within which every other
individual had a chance to save himself. Until late in life, moreover,
Finney also believed that he and his associates had the truth that
could save anyone.

Religion thus embraced the task of reforming the moral world
so that laissez faire could function in the political, social, and
economic spheres. Theology had been adapted to the decline of
mercantilism and the triumph of laissez faire. And having been
so accommodated, it began to function as a powerful engine driving the change on toward its logical conclusion, the purification
of the entire system. While ideological pioneers of the 1730s like
Stoddard were probably aware that they were changing the essence
of Calvin's doctrine to conform to their economic interests, it is
unlikely that many Americans of the 1820s and 1830s realized
that they were altering their religion. They were not hypocrites.
They were simply men of their era who had never been trained or
encouraged or led to examine—let alone question—the relationship between their interests and their ideas.

Just as Jackson had defined and asserted the essential supremacy of the national framework of the political economy against
the freedom of a single element like South Carolina, so religious
leaders like Finney and Theodore Dwight Weld asserted the moral
imperatives of the order. Only moral men could attain the general
welfare through the indulgence of their various self-interests. Since
only free men could be moral, the slaveholder was by definition
the most immoral. But free men had also slipped into evil ways.
Having thus declared open season on the whole of human error (or
as they termed it, sin), the moral reformers undertook a good many
crusading expeditions into the jungle of man's fallibility. Their base
camp was a privately recreated universe roughly comparable to the
environment of the Old Testament—once again it was the Chosen
People against all comers in a fight for righteousness.

Some reformers no doubt saw themselves as heroes in the romantic novels of Sir Walter Scott that enjoyed such tremendous popularity in the United States, but then many southern slaveholders did the
same. Each group brought more to Scott than it took away. It seems
more probable that they were men who either made the transition

from mercantilism already possessing a strong moral system, or emerged in the world of laissez faire and proceeded, either by conviction or revelation, to define it in terms of religious morality. John Quincy Adams offers a good illustration of the first category which further suggests that the older group was strongly inclined toward an institutional resolution of the slavery issue.

Younger men like Finney and Weld were advocates of laissez faire. But being men of religious conviction, they could hardly be expected to become entrepreneurs in the ordinary sense. They saw themselves as trustees whose basic interest and responsibility in a laissez-faire world was the business of reform. It appears more than coincidental, for example, that the Tappan brothers also established the first credit-rating system in the country. Their emphasis on the need for a set of fixed and well-defined rules by which to play the game does a great deal to explain the support they received from the middle class. Men of that group wanted guarantees that their enterprise would be rewarded. And the steady transformation of the abolitionist crusade into an antislavery campaign for free land suggests even more strongly that the underlying element in the situation was the *Weltanschauung* of laissez faire.

Seen through the prisms of religious forms and language, the secular principles of laissez faire appeared as a utopian revelation. Though fears of economic competition played an overt role to some extent, most of the violent and bigoted reaction against the increasing number of immigrants (7,912 in 1824, 76,242 in 1836, and 369,980 in 1850) was anti-Catholic in origin. It was grounded in the view of Catholicism as the worst of the old corporate and institutional religions headed by evil men who crushed liberty and violated freedom. The burning of a Massachusetts convent in 1834, the combined anti-Catholic and antislavery actions of men like Lyman Beecher, and the formation of the Native American Association in 1837 were thoroughly entwined aspects of the same outlook. A similar antagonism manifested itself in the anti-Masonic agitation of 1827–1831 in New York. Here again the relationship between the axioms of laissez faire and the definition of the enemy is apparent. Going rapidly into politics, the anti-Masons became the first third party to stage an open national nominating convention (1831).

Other reformers concentrated on the dangers of tobacco, alcohol, and meat-eating. While the crusades for temperance and a pure

American race remained serious forces in American politics for nearly a century, the antislavery campaign soon became the dominant theme of the general drive to establish a proper moral framework for laissez faire. The sermon was appropriately simple: abolish slavery and the free system would flourish beyond all dreams. Along with Weld and Finney, William Lloyd Garrison completed the transition to a wholly individualized definition of the problem. Slaveholders became *the* evil, and nothing mitigated their sin. The trouble was bad *men*, not an institution.

Garrison hurled the absolute challenge. "If the State cannot survive the anti-slavery agitation, then let the State perish." Even though they were uneasy over slavery, the great majority of Americans drew back from such extreme abolitionists whose reform threatened the very system it was supposed to save. Garrison and others were physically attacked by northerners in several states, and leaders from all parts of the country, whatever their views on slavery, grew increasingly concerned to limit the impact of the agitation. But absolutist language finally provoked the irrevocable act: in 1837 abolitionist editor Elijah Lovejoy was murdered by a mob in Alton, Illinois.

Men like Garrison were exhilarated. The tragedy gave them a martyr and forced the country to confront the issue more directly. It also brought the abolitionists new converts like the wealthy and talented Wendell Phillips, some of them becoming key leaders in later transforming abolitionism into a more general political movement. Weld further stirred the fire by publishing his exposé of the evil, *American Slavery As I See It,* in 1839. As an indictment of the slaveholder, his tract typified the extreme individualist nature of the abolitionist movement. And despite the fact that Weld was willing to accept the Negro as a man capable of equal achievement, he offered no plan for dealing with the results of emancipation.

Perhaps nothing so reveals the crucial role of laissez-faire philosophy in understanding the abolitionists: whether they agreed with Weld about the capabilities of the Negro, or held him to be an inferior person, as most did, they simply assumed that he would take his place as a competitive unit in the system. Preferring to ignore the moral implications of the freedom to starve, the abolitionists also escaped the need to think seriously about their own responsibilities as liberators—or about the possibility that an institutional approach to slavery might produce more effective and more moral results.

But the abolitionists were in the mainstream of what is generally called American radicalism. It was a radicalism that defined the individual's freedom from restraint as the crucial element of the good society. It rejected the idea of restrictions or discipline being accepted in order to establish and sustain the circumstances for individual and group creativity. That was dismissed as conservative or reactionary. Such a radicalism relied on expansion to underwrite its individualized freedom, and in keeping with that pattern the abolitionist movement soon embraced such a program.

In the meantime, the crisis generated by Lovejoy's murder marked the high point of the early abolitionist movement. In little more than a decade it had introduced and sustained the idea of direct action to resolve a national issue and had established an absolute definition of democracy that excluded many men, if not an entire section, on the grounds that it (or they) were evil. But it also strengthened the less extremist wing of the antislavery movement. Men who were appalled by Garrison's vulgarity, irresponsibility, and questionable sincerity turned to political action in support of a program to end slavery within a Constitutional framework. Organized in 1838–1839 around James G. Birney, an ex-Kentucky slaveholder, the Liberty Party won an immediate response in New York. Despite its more moderate tone and policy, it was interpreted by edgy southerners as a political force that might someday turn the power of the central government against them in favor of abolition. Northern purists, on the other hand, slandered it as an agent of the Devil.

THE EVOLUTION OF THE SOUTHERN PREDICAMENT

The impact of these early moral, ideological, and political attacks by the abolitionists was increased because they hit the south during a critical juncture in the area's development. The old seaboard south seemed to have entered the last stage of its decline as a center of commodity agriculture. Slave prices, for example, had fallen to $400 by 1828. This produced in Virginia, among other consequences, a new generation of leaders seriously interested in working out some program for ending slavery. Though largely upper-class conservatives, these men negotiated a tenuous alliance with western yeomen, a coalition that they hoped would give them the power to adjust Virginia's economy to the new industrial and agricultural order. They were opposed by established planters who feared a wholesale assault on property rights as well as upon their existing position, and who were appalled by the prospect of a sizable plurality of free Negroes. In many respects, therefore, the situation can be understood as the moment of truth for Washington's old idea that Virginia should diversify its economy and in that manner end slavery and maintain its position of national leadership.

The two groups clashed in the Virginia Constitutional Convention of 1830 in one of the crucial debates in American history. Erupting in the context of a depression in tobacco, cotton, and slave prices, the conflict seemed at first to veer in favor of those who proposed an institutional approach to emancipation. But entrenched in political and social power, and making effective use of the specter of abolitionism and a society dominated by free Negroes, as well as emphasizing the expense of compensated emancipation, the defenders of slavery finally won. The debate continued in the first sessions of the new legislature, however, both because of the continuing strength of the antislavery group and in response to the crisis provoked when a free Negro preacher named Nat Turner sparked a slave uprising in 1831. Pointing to the key role of the free Negro in all slave revolts, and to the free-wheeling operations of others like William Johnson of Natchez (a barber who became a model of laissez-faire entrepreneurship), the proslavery group overrode its critics.

Antislavery organizations all but vanished from the south within five years. Slavery's victory was consolidated by the revival of commodity prices, the increasing intensity and vitriol of Garrison's attacks, and the developing division of the west into northern and southern sections. A good many commentators have concluded that the combination of the Erie Canal and the cotton gin produced the Civil War, and in a highly generalized sense the observation has validity. But it overlooks the crucial role of foreign markets for cotton and for the food crops of northern farmers, and it neglects the simultaneous expansion of the home market. That revival and expansion of the market was the key to the rapidly divergent development within the west between 1825 and 1846.

Little more than a fort in 1833, Chicago exploded into a city within a decade. What had been wilderness became $15,000 lots along the Illinois-Michigan Canal. In such a young and booming country (one foreign visitor recalled that he saw neither "an old man nor a gray hair") a man in Illinois could almost handcraft his career by reading law in a crossroads general store. But even so, many young men of the region, along with some of their fathers and grandfathers, were moving on to the black earth of the Iowa Territory and risking the tortuous struggle through the Indian country across the plains and mountains to make a claim in Oregon's lush Willamette Valley.

Already beginning to get the appropriate agricultural tools and machinery from American manufacturers, the upper Mississippi Valley was a region committed to the principles and myths of laissez-faire individualism with an ardor that was uncritical and unrestrained. Promising freedom and prosperity, the frontier was reinforced as the symbol of all that was good and necessary. And it did bring wealth, political freedom, and social acceptance to many men and women, and more particularly to their children. But it also produced a paradoxical mystique. One half of it was as hard-souled as any in the world, with one eye roving for the next unclaimed watering-place or likely looking acreage and one hand on a gun. Though the other half was in contrast warm and humane and cooperative, its fundamental nature was one that encouraged the evasion of the less obvious but subtly vital problems of social and personal relations. Indians were to be killed and the land was to be taken. By creating a mirage of an infinity of second chances, the frontier almost institutionalized everyman's propensity to evade his fundamental problems and responsibilities.

Yet in providing wealth and personal satisfaction for many, the frontier also worked its magic on easterners who never ventured west of Baltimore or Charleston—or Concord. Extending Rufus King's earlier appreciation of the importance of controlling the west, easterners began in the 1830s to stress the means of doing so through politics (Van Buren), economics (the absentee landowners), and education (the abolitionists). Edward Everett, a Massachusetts leader who thought that expansion was "the *principle* of our institutions," argued that educational control would bring massive returns on the investment. "We can," he exhorted Boston capitalists, "from our surplus, contribute toward the establishment and endowment of those seminaries, where the mind of the west shall be trained and enlightened." A more candid definition of education as an instrument of social control would be difficult to find.

Tidewater planters harbored the same fears of the brawling southwest, but they had less of a problem: that part of the west adapted the political economy of the older south. Making his father's poverty-induced dream come true, Stephen F. Austin established a colony in Texas as the first step in capturing the Mexican and Pacific trade. It quickly attracted northern yeomen, eastern businessmen, southern planters, and freebooters from every region. But that venture was only the most dramatic example of the general process by which, without any plot or conspiracy but only the magnificent flowering of self-interest, the southwest saved the southeast.

By 1834 the new states along the gulf coast were producing more cotton than the Atlantic seaboard. Committed to a capitalistic commodity agriculture based on slave labor, the southwest began to import its slaves from South Carolina and Virginia. Old planters, and their sons, thus prospered with the new. By 1837, slaves in Virginia brought $1,100; from 17 cents a pound in 1820 and as low as 10 in 1827, the price of cotton jumped above 30 cents in the 1830s. Coupled with the antislavery agitation, this fantastic transformation of the old south into a new trans-Mississippi cotton economy and the concurrent extension of the old northwest frontier of Pittsburgh and Cincinnati into a trans-Mississippi west populated by merchants, manufacturers, and farmers produced vital political consequences.

As an area even more agricultural than the rest of the nation (90 per cent as against 70 per cent), the south became increasingly aware of its special circumstances. It had but a third of the white population and only a tiny fraction of the country's industrial production. Yet through its international cotton sales it earned much of the nation's needed capital. The paradox produced on the part of the south a steadily increasing self-consciousness compounded of pride in its achievements, nervousness over its difference, and sensitivity about the equity of national policies initiated by northern businessmen and western farmers. Concerned about its backwardness in matters of local internal improvements, educational investments, and political reforms, it initiated a movement to catch up in those respects. To a surprising degree, and one often overlooked by its critics, the south at first concentrated on its internal affairs despite the persistent vehemence of abolitionist criticism.

Reinforced by that attack from the outside, such self-consciousness sparked the beginning of a firm conception of the south as a separate and integrated region. Writers like William Gilmore Simms and Mark Littleton began to think as southerners despite their familiarity with the north. Simms, for example, became a great planter with 15 children, and his stories stressed the positive aspects of such a grand existence. So, too, the work of John P. Kennedy. One of Kennedy's novels, *Swallow Barn*, was an early version of the magnolias-and-maidens myth: its aristocratic whites and devoted blacks drifted about a feudal utopia so profitable that no one ever mentioned money.

More practical leaders began to talk about the need for a balanced southern economy. Ultimately leading to a revival of neo-mercan-tilist thinking, the first result of this outlook was a firm picture of the south as one competing unit within the national system of lais-sez faire. Rising in the Congress on December 27, 1837, Calhoun presented six resolutions designed to establish the rules for compe-tition at this sectional-national level. His restatement of the old Madisonian view that the Constitution had created a "feudal system of republics" was accepted. So was his protest against Garrison's propaganda. A majority could also agree that the national govern-ment should not be used by one element of the system to attack another. Even the safeguards for existing slavery were accepted in a modified form. But when it came to his proposal to denounce those who opposed expansion because it might extend slavery, Calhoun met defeat. That resolution was tabled.

In some respects, of course, Calhoun's effort to win a consen-sus on the expansion of the market place was blocked by outright abolitionists and others who feared the political influence of the slavery issue and by men who favored expansion but thought it unwise to raise the issue so bluntly. Jackson, for example, wanted Texas in the worst way but considered it dangerous to move too fast. The fundamental explanation of Calhoun's defeat, however, would seem to be found in an unorganized consensus of western agrarians and eastern businessmen who defined the market place in terms of individual free labor and the corporation.

THE EARLY STRUGGLE OVER DEFINING FREEDOM
UNDER LAISSEZ FAIRE

Each of these major national units—the planter, the free individ-ual entrepreneur, and the organized businessman—was beginning to define the national system in terms of the circumstances that favored his particular ability to compete. But laissez faire could also be defined as a system that gave all such elements equal freedom to compete throughout the nation. Calhoun asked for a consensus on that principle, even though he was well aware that the planter would never win in certain areas. But the rising leaders of institutionalized industrialism and the entrepreneurs of food-crop agriculture were already favoring a set of rules that gave them a basic advantage against their toughest competitor. Thus began a system-shaking argument about first principles.

At the same time, moreover, a second basic issue was formulated when the corporation was openly accepted as a legitimate unit of competition. Jacksonian Democracy revealed its fundamentally laissez-faire nature in promulgating this view. Chief Justice Taney, the old Federalist crony of Jackson himself, and William Leggett, the left-wing leader of reform in New York, agreed completely that groups were legitimate competitive elements within the framework of laissez faire. "We are for leaving trade free"; Leggett declared in 1837, "and the right to combine is an indispensable attribute of its freedom." Taney handed down an identical ruling in the same year. In a decision that specifically opened banking to all citizens, he sanctioned the corporate form of organization.

"There is perhaps no business which yields a profit so certain and liberal as the business of banking and exchange," he explained, (from his own experience); "and it is proper that it should be open as far as practicable to the most free competition and its advantages shared by all classes of people." Free banking acts in Michigan and New York extended the principle of general incorporation laws that states like North Carolina and Connecticut had adopted earlier. New York courts not only approved the form in 1838, but for purposes of competition in the market place explicitly equated such corporations with the individual. Taney added the final sanction. The corporation, he explained in an opinion of 1839, "is, indeed, a mere artificial being, invisible and intangible; yet it is a person, for certain purposes in contemplation of law, and has been recognized as such by the decisions of this Court."

Though not yet the predominant institution of business organization, partnerships remaining both more numerous and characteristic of the key segments of the economy, the corporation steadily gained favor. By 1860, for example, iron manufacturing was rapidly adopting the form, and other elements in the industrial economy of the north, such as railroads, were also moving in this direction. Further facilitated by the rationalization and acceptance of the factory system, the growth of manufacturing was revealed in many ways. Large capital investments, the integration of various phases of production, and mass output were ceasing to be unique or even unusual by the 1840s. Steadily expanding the market through and beyond their respective regions, the manufacturers gave a tremendous impetus to wholesaling, credit organizations, and newspaper advertising.

Perhaps the most striking aspect of northern industrial development, as well as the most crucial, was the establishment and extension of the railroad system. For in addition to being a business in its own right, railroading acted as an accelerator of other industries. Not only did it enlarge the market for manufactures, but it underwrote new construction work, facilitated and encouraged the filling up and mature settlement of the trans-Appalachian region, and provided the farmer with better connections with the cities and export centers. Recognizing these benefits, as well as responding to more direct entreaties, pressures, and enticements, both the states and the national government began subsidizing the railroads as early as the 1830s. Liberal grants of the right of eminent domain, cash gifts, and credit facilities were extended by Georgia and Virginia as well as by Indiana and Michigan. In a few states like Michigan, for that matter, the government built railroads and then disposed of them to private entrepreneurs. Congress did its part with rebates on iron duties (and later a general exception), land grants, and gifts of other raw materials.

This rising momentum of industrialism turned the economist Daniel Raymond completely away from mercantilism toward a theory of laissez faire based on the freedom of the manufacturing corporation. An even more striking illustration of the change was provided by Henry Carey, son of persistently mercantilist Matthew. Wealthy and socially acceptable at an early age—an appropriate symbol of the earlier successes of mercantilism—Carey presented his economic views in an essay on *The Harmony of Nature* (1836). Arguing a rather sophisticated version of Smith's laissez faire, he stressed three interrelated principles: happiness and the general welfare were most effectively produced by giving men of property the freedom of action that was theirs by natural law, and in particular by recognizing that even greater (and faster) rewards would be gained by encouraging and accepting the industrial corporation and other large business enterprise.

Carey's political economy provides an insight into the ideas and actions of Daniel Webster of Massachusetts, whose oratorical powers and abilities as a lawyer and general counsel for the upper class made him one of the key politicians of the northern business community. Webster did not follow Carey in the way that a young lawyer plagiarizes Blackstone—in that respect his mentors were the wealthy entrepreneurs who retained him—rather it is that Carey's views help to clarify the particular kind of nationalism which Webster advocated and represented after swinging over to support the tariff in 1828. It is often suggested that Webster changed his basic ideas as his constituents shifted from shipping to manufacturing. This interpretation explains him as a man of regional particularism and laissez faire who became a spokesman of government intervention, and coincidentally a unionist instead of a sectionalist.

Though such an analysis is correct in the sense that Webster shifted from free trade to protection, and dropped the rhetoric of regionalism for the metaphors of nationalism, it nevertheless produces a serious misunderstanding of the nature of his nationalism and that of the industrializing north. Webster denounced labor organizations and smeared those who questioned the wisdom of general incorporation laws as "un-American." Manufacturers and other industrial leaders wanted a national system, to be sure, just as they sought government aid in the form of tariffs or railroad subsidies. But they defined that system quite narrowly and explicitly because all they did was to extend their particular version of laissez nous faire to the entire society.

As such, therefore, neither they nor Webster advocated the inclusive, balanced kind of corporate nationalism that had been characteristic of the mercantilists, or that Daniel's resounding phrases implied. Primarily concerned with the freedom to industrialize the entire economy, such nationalists soon came to prefer overseas economic expansion to the acquisition of additional territory. Their opposition to the latter kind of expansion has led some commentators to conclude that they were anti-expansionists in general. But not only were they expansionists in the strict sense of foreign policy, but they were also expansionists in their relationship with other elements of American society. One of Webster's ostensibly nationalistic maneuvers, for example, was a grandiloquent gesture of defiance against the old regime during the Hungarian Revolution of 1848–1850; yet it in fact represented just such a policy of ideological and commercial expansion as he had advocated at the time of the Greek Revolution. And northerners of his outlook wanted to control the trans-Mississippi west under a similarly restrictive program.

Webster and his constituents wanted a national industrial system in which the government would provide direct and indirect subsidies to the favored element, and which would not limit that group's efforts to integrate the entire political economy on its own terms. Neither Webster nor large northern businessmen wanted the slavery issue to erupt in violence, but their concept of the Union offered a less than reassuring future to the south. It was Henry Clay, not Daniel Webster, who accepted industrialism and attempted to deal with it in a truly national manner. He tried very hard to adjust the ideology of laissez faire to the realities of America through a reinvigoration of his mercantilist American System, and then to institutionalize that resolution in a political party. But he was defeated by the coalition of competing units that formed Jacksonian Democracy, even though that alliance was soon to disintegrate in civil war.

CHAPTER THREE

The Adaptation of the Existing Order

The great object [of the American System] . . . is to secure the independence of our country, to augment its wealth, and to diffuse the comforts of civilization throughout the society. . . . That . . . can be best accomplished by introducing, encouraging, and protecting the arts among us. . . . By . . . blending and connecting together all its parts in creating an interest with each in the prosperity of the whole. . . . And, mixing the farmer, manufacturer, mechanic, artist, and those engaged in other vocations together.

Henry Clay, 1830

I ain't greedy for land. All I want is jist what jines mine.

Frontiersman, c. 1840

Members of this floor [of Congress] . . . know the advantages of having a "West" to go to, where they were forced from many of the embarrassing circumstances, from family influences, from associated wealth, and from those thousand things which, in the old settled country had the tendency of keeping down the efforts and enterprise of our young men.

Congressman Jacob Brinkerhoff of Ohio, 1845

Foreign powers do not seem to appreciate the true character of our Government. Our Union is a confederation of independent States, whose policy is peace with each other and all the world. To enlarge its limits is to extend the dominions of peace over additional territories and increasing millions.

President James K. Polk, 1845

You must abolish the system or accept its consequences.

Orestes Brownson, 1840

Never, never shall you extend your institution of slavery one inch beyond its present limits. . . . If you will drive on this bloody [Mexican] war of

conquest to annexation, we will establish a cordon of free states that shall surround you; and then we will light up the fires of liberty on every side, until they melt your present chains, and render all your people free.
Congressman Columbus Delano of Ohio, 1846

We do not intend to stand still and have our throats cut.
Jeremiah Clemens of Alabama, 1849

HENRY CLAY AND THE ATTEMPT TO REVIVE AND ADAPT MERCANTILISM

Since they denied the necessity, desirability, or morality of any sustained effort to coordinate and direct the affairs of society, the advocates of laissez faire were impaled on the horns of an obvious dilemma when the system failed to function satisfactorily. Their warrant authorized them to deal only with fundamental issues: that is, defining the market place, certifying the units of competition, and specifying the rules of the game. Though they were dedicated to liberty and freedom of action, and did indeed throw open many gates in the society, the proponents of laissez faire were at the same time narrowly confined by their philosophy. In that respect, at any rate, they were less free than the mercantilists, who could deal with a basic question like the need and usefulness of a national bank by concentrating on controlling its power, and who could approach slavery as an institutional problem of the political economy rather than as a personalized sin.

As revealed in their assertion that the open conflict of self-interests would produce the general welfare, and in the persistent use of moral terms of judgment—by Jackson and the mechanics, as well as by Emerson and the abolitionists—the men of laissez faire were constantly thrown back on first principles. As a result, every spot of trouble became a sore point at issue. In one sense, of course, the resulting tension was a powerful engine of development. It provoked the advocates of laissez faire to change reality to conform with their a priori ideas and ideals, thus generating a tremendous momentum to manhandle nature and provide a better life. But such a drive to reshape reality could easily become a crusade to override men who disagreed with the axioms of laissez faire. And that could lead to violence.

Fearing just such an eventuality, Henry Clay struggled between 1834 and 1851 to reestablish and institutionalize the key ideas and policies of his mercantilist American System. The effort was neither as irrelevant nor as feeble as his ultimate failure might indicate. For one thing, the serious depression which began shortly after Van Buren's inauguration in 1837 raised basic questions about the ability of laissez faire to deliver on its promises concerning personal happiness and the general welfare. And the President's repeated assertion of laissez-faire dogma did little to generate recovery or to satisfy the demands from various groups and sections for assistance or other special treatment.

Clay did not need much encouragement to view such critics as potential supporters for the American System. He believed in his approach and wanted to be President. And by 1839 there was a much larger industrial base upon which he could build than there had been in 1824 or 1828. Hence he was in a position to exploit the increasing political importance of cities as the population ratio in favor of the farm dropped from 15 to 1 in 1800 to 10.4 to 1 by 1830 (and was to sink to 5.5 to 1 by 1850). Industry was also beginning to provide a steadily increasing and more stable market for labor, commence, and agriculture that strengthened his arguments about the interrelationships of the economy and the primacy of the home market. This was an important factor, and helps to explain the persistent Whig strength despite the party's rather poor showing in national elections.

Clay's economic policies had an obvious appeal for many businessmen in the north, but his program also won a following among merchants and other commercial leaders in the south. And some of the large planters, whose operations were as much commercial as agrarian, responded favorably. Such men of both sections not only had opposed Jackson's destruction of the bank but were further united by the bond of social conservatism. North-south philosophic and economic ties of this nature persisted to the outbreak of the Civil War and were a force for compromise as well as a source of votes for Clay and the Whigs. Clay also attracted a good many northern mechanics and laborers who responded to his emphasis on protection for the home market. He also won strength in the west because of his concern for internal improvements. And his strenuous efforts to distribute the surplus revenue from land sales to the states helped to moderate the westerners who really wanted free land, and who looked at Webster and concluded that the Whigs were little more than spokesmen for big business firms such as the Appleton Company in textiles or the Boston and Sandwich Glass Company.

Despite such support, Clay was unable to organize a real party. He had no access to national patronage, and no programmatic coalition had been brought together in the Congress. Hence the Whigs, in winning the election of 1840, had to rely on personal followings, their ideological persuasiveness, and political techniques borrowed from Jackson and Van Buren. Picking up the central philosophical theme of the Adams Federalists—"What would become of the poor without the rich?"—such Whig intellectuals as Edward Everett and William Ellery Channing developed a somewhat sophisticated argument that there was an identity of interest between labor and capital.

Stressing the reciprocal relationship between classes, they advanced a diluted version of the old mercantilist, corporate *Weltanschauung* that they distorted to fit the world of laissez-faire capitalism. By combining with the business aristocracy to establish and maintain a floor under free enterprise, they explained, the mechanic and the yeoman (and their sons) would win either way they played their hand. Since such an agreement would underwrite a never-ending prosperity, they could either relax with a share of the rewards that would steadily increase in absolute, if not relative, terms, or they could rapidly accumulate enough capital to become independent entrepreneurs on a larger scale. Granted an acceptance of the capitalist system, the argument was persuasive. Indeed, it was still to be very much alive in the 1960s. And even Calhoun enjoyed a brief flirtation with some elements of northern labor by proposing a variation on the same theme: in his version, labor was to gain by joining responsible southern planters to defeat the grasping business community.

Strikingly effective in 1840, the deeper significance of this Whig social philosophy was that it laid the foundation for a more permanent alliance between eastern and western advocates of laissez faire. In a real sense, therefore, it was the ideology that prepared the way for the Republican Party. Its more immediate success was facilitated by Whig astuteness and disingenuousness in presenting their presidential candidate, William Henry Harrison, as a western frontier farmer who had emerged from a log cabin to become a military hero and a democratic friend of the common man. Combined with their selection for Vice-President of John Tyler of Virginia, a States' rights southerner who had turned against Jackson, this campaign strategy thoroughly frustrated and defeated the Democrats. "We have taught them to conquer us!" cried one Jacksonian in anguish and disgust.

Clay entered the new Congress with a driving determination to legislate his national program into law. Had Harrison lived, Clay might have succeeded; at least he might have won a trial for his American System. But Tyler's militant loyalty to the ideas of John Taylor of Caroline and his own narrow definition of southern interests blocked Clay's plan to integrate the tariff, a bill for distributing land-sale funds to the states, and a new national bank. Clay resigned in March, 1842, apologizing for his arrogant aggressiveness in the Congress and explaining it as a manifestation of his concern for the nation, and then turned to strengthening the party (and his own position) for the election of 1844.

Clay's subsequent defeat in 1844 is often ascribed to the impact of the slavery issue in New York, where the 15,812 votes won by Birney's Liberty Party are said to have cost Clay the state by 5,106. While plausible, dramatic, and arithmetically impeccable, the argument is not convincing. After all, Clay could also have won the election by capturing a mere 2,554 votes from Polk. Thus it seems more likely that Clay lost New York in the east, where a complexity of specific and general developments reflected the renewed vigor of laissez faire. For one thing, New York bankers and their associates were not anxious to compete with another national bank. And as the depression ended in a rising swell of prosperity that lasted until the Panic of 1857, Clay's program of balanced national development became less attractive to other groups as well. They wanted to be left free to exploit their advantages.

The attitudes of mechanics and laborers, who in the modern sense of the term were becoming more numerous with the steady growth of the factory system, typified that outlook. Encouraged by the ruling of the Massachusetts Supreme Court in *Commonwealth v. Hunt* (1842) that unions were of themselves "not unlawful," they reorganized and reopened the campaign for a ten-hour day. Within two years, for example, the New England Workingmen's Association mustered 200 delegates from local unions for a regional conference in Boston. Van Buren's strong tie with New York labor was strengthened by this revival, and by several associated events. Labor had thrown its support to the yeomen who worked the large upstate manors on long-term and unrewarding contracts from the aristocrats. And as that conflict erupted into violence, the Democrats benefited when Whig Governor William H. Seward used troops against the yeomen.

Seward was an exceedingly astute politician, furnishing a classic example of the professionalization of the role, and his principled advocacy of laissez-faire freedoms supported by mercantilist internal improvements had won the support of urban immigrants and farmers as well as of businessmen. Under different circumstances he might have pushed Clay into the White House, particularly as his political partner was the cynical but exceptionally efficient Thurlow Weed of New York. But Seward's power was seriously weakened by the revolt of the farmers, by the rising state debts incident to his lagging program of internal improvements, and by the tacit approval (or outright support) given by Whigs to the anti-foreign agitation in New York City. The Democrats gained immeasurably. And since Birney's vote showed no significant increase, Clay very probably lost on the nativist issue in the east.

In the broader sense, moreover, Clay could have won the election without New York. But his inability to carry Pennsylvania and his loss of Michigan, Indiana, Illinois, and Missouri tells more about the election than does the antislavery issue. The rising expansionist sentiment defeated Clay. Whig anti-foreignism, which lost Philadelphia as well as New York City, for example, was but the negative side of that nationalistic fervor. And though slavery had become entwined in the issue of expansion as a result of Calhoun's anti-British campaign to acquire Texas, it had come about in a complex way. Not all antislavery men were against expansion. Neither were all expansionists proslavery. A good many in both groups were still willing to accept a *quid pro quo* between northern and southern expansion. For that matter, a large plurality of westerners, and an important minority of northeasterners, probably wanted Texas as badly as did the southerners. And when it is realized that Birney's party

was already leaning toward expansion for northerners and westerners, and that the Democrats promised Oregon as well as Texas, Clay's
defeat is to be seen in a broader context.

LAISSEZ FAIRE AND THE FRONTIER THESIS

Thus the election of 1844 provides a key insight into the shifting
nature of laissez-faire politics. From concerning itself with destroying mercantilist restrictions in the market place, it was turning to the
expansion of the market place for the ostensible benefit of everyone.
More and more Americans saw this as the way to adapt the system
to the troublesome realities of their situation. Texas provided the
dramatic example, but the main consideration is that expansion had
become the lowest common denominator of America's laissez-faire
politics. Politicians were quick to grasp and exploit the meaning of
this. While many stressed the specific interests of their constituency
or region, others developed a more inclusive view of the whole process and its relation to American development.

The consensus was impressive, including as it did key politicians
from Massachusetts and New York as well as Ohio and Illinois, and
from Michigan as well as Mississippi. Many leaders like Seward and
Benton talked candidly about commerce and farms; others took the
high ground of emotion and theory. Convinced that they could "run
faster, sail smarter, dive deeper, and fly farther than any other people
on the face of the earth," many Americans concluded that expansion
was a natural and inevitable reward for their superiority. And whether
limited to personal interests or extended to regional and national levels,
the argument of economic necessity won wide acceptance. Anticipating
the day, which he thought less than a generation away, when America
would be the "*first nation* on the earth," Walt Whitman shared the
general belief that such expansion was morally just as well as necessary.
"It is for the interest of mankind that its power and territory should be
extended—the farther the better." Or as Jackson had said, and Polk was
to reiterate, American expansion "extended the area of freedom."

Similar keen and revealing arguments came from the south and
west. Openly afraid that staying at home would create a "great and
fearful pressure" on society, Thomas R. Dew of William and Mary
College defended expansion in 1836 lest "the great safety valve of
the west will be closed." By 1845, Congressman Jacob Brinkerhoff of

Ohio had adapted the thesis for the north. Urging vigorous action in Oregon and Texas, he described such areas as "a home for our prosperity." "Members on this floor . . . know," he added, "the advantages of having a 'West' to go to." And Secretary of the Treasury Robert J. Walker of Mississippi, who was no enemy of northern expansion, integrated many such arguments into his departmental report of the same year. As might be expected of a land speculator and banker with railroad investments, Walker firmly believed that prosperity would "be best promoted" by wide-open laissez faire. Attacking the fallacy of the home market, and thus emphasizing the necessity of further expansion, he also argued that Texas was "a safety valve" through which slavery would evaporate. As Madison before him, Walker seemed to think that the diffusion of slavery would weaken it and turn the Negro into a wage laborer.

Despite their many other differences, Tyler and Polk agreed on the expansionist axiom of laissez faire. Both also included the south as a competing unit of the system in full and good standing. Tyler turned to expansion as the way to rebuild his political health after Clay left the administration. In favoring this remedy he played a key role in emphasizing expansion as the solution to America's problems. Tyler was most successful in Asia, perhaps because the north and the west shared an interest in that area and its continental approaches. Missionaries, for example, were concerned to carry their "principles" and "doctrines" to the Indians of Oregon and the more seductive heathens of Hawaii and China. In Hawaii, their powers of persuasion led to churches, marriages, and land titles. Together with traders, whalers, and shippers—who carried their own versions of the true gospel—the missionaries soon created a situation very similar to the coincident colonization of Texas. "Could I have forgotten the circumstances of my visit," one tourist remarked of Hawaii in 1833, "I should have fancied myself in New England."

Pioneer farmers, planters, and speculators were more interested in the open acres of Texas, Canada, California, and Oregon. Businessmen also looked to such colonization as a source of profitable trade, investment, and speculative ventures. And although they were beginning to show interest in European commerce, the traders, shippers, naval leaders, and even exporters of American manufactured goods concentrated on the Pacific coast, Hawaii, and Asia. Supported by many westerners and southerners as a national effort, the expedition of

Commodore Charles Wilkes in 1839 was specifically charged to find harbors, "easy of access, and in every respect adapted to the reception of vessels of the United States engaged in the whale-fishing, and the general commerce" of the Pacific.

Building on the foundation laid by Robert Morris and John Jacob Astor, later northeastern merchants such as Thomas H. Perkins, Gideon Nye, and Asa Whitney were by 1838 petitioning the Congress from Canton as well as from Boston for vigorous diplomacy in their behalf. Supported by naval officers such as Commodore Laurence Kearney and missionaries such as Peter Parker (who saw the navy and commerce as the allies of Christianity, and who ultimately laid claim to Formosa in the name of this unorthodox trinity), their campaign soon produced official results. Tyler subtly extended the Monroe Doctrine to Hawaii, and, stressing the importance of markets for American manufactured goods as well as the carrying trade, secured a treaty with China that won Americans the privileges of extraterritoriality as well as trading rights in key ports.

Having thus acted in keeping with what he termed "the magnitude and importance of our national concerns, actual and prospective, in China," Tyler attempted to repeat the performance in Oregon, California, and Texas and thereby win the Presidency in his own right. Making a similar campaign appealing to all potentially interested groups, he held forth "a wider and more extensive spread to the principles of civil and religious liberty." Tyler's mention of religion was of course sincere, but it was also politically astute and historically revealing. Many Protestants favored expansion into Mexico as well as Oregon in order to carry the gospel south into Catholic countries; and more than a few American Catholics thought they could handle church affairs in Mexico better than the native hierarchy. But Tyler never had a chance. The leaders of the Democratic Party had no more intention of permitting him to steal their program of expansion for all sections than of allowing Van Buren to cripple it by blocking the annexation of Texas.

This mushrooming enthusiasm for expansion provided a dramatic contrast to the vigorous and perceptive criticism of laissez faire that had been developing since 1837. One such critic was Edgar Allan Poe, who came as close to being completely alienated from American society and yet utterly devoted to its potential as anyone in the nation's history. He would have been a key figure in the misnamed "lost generation" of the 1920s, or in later movements that criticized mature capitalism. A brilliant creative force, he struggled with the central problem of art and existence: how to subordinate the parts of the whole in order to achieve overall meaning and significance while at the same time retaining the integrity of the individual elements. His triumphs and insights, which fathered symbolism and other important movements, mark him as one of the truly great American artists.

As typical campaigns in his assault on the *Weltanschauung* of laissez faire, Poe stuck pins in the utilitarians and the wild nationalistic expansionists. But while all his serious work reveals another facet of his condemnation (the debasement of love, for example, or the utter isolation of the individual), his famous story of *The Pit and the Pendulum* is perhaps the most subtle yet devastating fictional attack on laissez faire ever written. Presented as a horror story, the key to the tale is the kind of horror that it really portrays. Captured and imprisoned by the rulers of a system that demands absolute ideological conformity, Poe's protagonist holds to his own values through extended interrogation, a trial, and a series of rigorous ideological lectures. The experience, relates the hero, "conveyed to my soul the idea of a *revolution*" as the only way to deal with such a society.

Overcome by "nausea," he awakens in a torture chamber convinced that he is "without hope"; his humanity is all but destroyed. The familiar sequence follows: despite his rational efforts, he avoids death in the pit only by "accidentally" discovering it; then he is strapped to a pad beneath a razor-sharp pendulum which is lowered toward him at an agonizingly slow rate while it widens its arc and thus picks up enough momentum to make an incision clear through his backbone. By that time, he recalls, "long suffering had nearly annihilated all my ordinary powers of mind. I was an imbecile—an idiot."

Escaping this destruction by rubbing his food on his fetters and thus putting the gluttony of a pack of rats to work for him, he realizes that the fiery movable walls of the chamber are squeezing him into the pit. Only the fortuitous arrival of a conquering general rescues him: he is saved by armed resistance, and by the forces of a foreign revolution at that. Just as a description and critique of laissez faire, the story would be a classic: from the first accidental survival in the market place, through the episode in which the "first time I thought" prompts the hero to use the greed of others to accomplish his private objectives, to the deadly constriction of the market place. If by chance he survives, the individual is then alienated and finally destroyed. Poe lived out the pattern of the story, dying alone in the streets of Baltimore.

While avoiding such a tragic death, Poe's most notable ideological compatriot came to the same philosophical conclusion: "You must abolish the system or accept its consequences." Originally an enthusiastic and effective intellectual leader of Jacksonian Democracy, Orestes A. Brownson of Massachusetts dramatically came forward in 1840 with an all-encompassing critique of the movement and its philosophy. "All over the world," he announced in one of those sentences that explode when the reader is halfway into the next one: "All over the world . . . the workingman is poor and depressed, while a large portion of the non-working men . . . are wealthy." Then he struck directly at the philosophers of individualism like Emerson. "Self-culture is a good thing, but it cannot abolish inequality nor restore men to their rights."

Brownson next mocked the irrelevance of the laissez-faire slogan that "every man become[s] an independent proprietor." "The middle class," he explained, "is always a firm champion of equality when it concerns humbling a class above it, but it is its inveterate foe when it concerns elevating a class below it." "No matter what party you support, no matter what men you elect, property is always the basis of your governmental action." Quite aware of the rising expansionist fever, and realizing that fundamental reforms had little or no chance until it was checked and reversed, Brownson tried to counter it by pointing out how the growing dominance of the large business enterprise had changed the role of the frontier.

Further expansion would not solve the contradictions of laissez faire. "The wilderness has receded, and already the new lands are beyond the reach of the mere laborer, and the employer has him at his mercy." Brownson's alternative was a cooperative and corporate religious commonwealth. Arguing that "God gives to every nation an aristocracy," and that "a Duke of Wellington is much more likely to vindicate the rights of labor than an Abbot Lawrence," Brownson became a Catholic in 1844, and sought thereafter to work out some programmatic approach for such a society. But by that time expansion had entrenched itself as the popular answer to America's problems. Everybody wanted expansion; the argument was about expansion where and for whom.

Hence Henry Clay's irresolution over taking Texas can hardly seem anything but pathetic. It was Calhoun who was, in many ways, the truly tragic and moving figure of the age. There may well have been, among his close associates such as Duff Green, a conspiracy of sorts to acquire Texas, and perhaps even more than Texas, but Calhoun himself was open about his desire to annex the republic. The vital consideration is that he seems to have wanted to call a halt at that point: Texas would provide the south with political parity, economic surety, and a buffer against English abolitionism and commercial expansion. Given these hedges against the immediate future, he was willing to count on constitutional revision, political compromise, and the amelioration brought about by American development. But his blatant defense of slavery in April, 1844, in which he vigorously asserted that the slave enjoyed a better life than the free Negro, only played into the hands of his opponents in the north.

Justly emphasizing that free Negroes were physically and psychologically free, and sliding over the embarrassing facts that such Negroes were only rarely granted citizenship or allowed to place a foot on the ladder of laissez-faire success, many northerners and westerners misread Calhoun's argument against the British as proof of a general southern conspiracy to extend slavery indefinitely. Calhoun actually opposed the war with Mexico when it came, viewing it as a danger to the Union and republican government. And he attacked Polk's reassertion and extension of the Monroe Doctrine, which openly challenged all European influence, as a "broad and dangerous principle, truly." He thought it guaranteed an indefinite number of future wars.

As one who had recognized the dilemma even before 1820, Calhoun was by the 1840s struggling ever more desperately to find some way of preventing expansion from tearing the country apart into antagonistic sections. He understood that empire might easily subvert republicanism rather than preserve it. His opposition to the quick annexation of Oregon, for example, was part of that concern rather than a betrayal of the south's bargain with the west. Calhoun's argument was quite straightforward: before any more territory was added, the whole relationship between expansion and republicanism had to be resolved in a way that would guarantee self-government for *all* sections of the country. Whether or not his solution through a veto by each major section over legislation by the others would have worked in practice, the main point is that he cannot be understood as merely a fanatic southern slaver. But in their acquisitive drive to take Oregon and Texas, the expansionists discounted the dangers that Calhoun saw and pointed out so clearly. The final result was a bitter struggle over the spoils of victory.

PRESIDENT POLK AND A WAR FOR LAND AND COMMERCE

Polk had come into office in 1845 opposed to internal improvements and the tariff and almost fanatic about the acquisition of most of Oregon and all of Texas and California. His aggressive impatience was typical of Jacksonian laissez faire, and his intrigues, pressures, ultimatums, and provocations gave Mexico no chance to first settle its own internal problems and then gradually accept the loss of its northern provinces. Aware of the earlier debate over the relationship between expansion and republicanism, and calling explicit attention to it, Polk made his own position clear in his inaugural address. Recalling that "the opinion prevailed with some that our system . . . could not operate successfully over an extended territory," Polk judged this view "not well founded." Anxious to further the "extensive and profitable commerce with China, and other countries of the East," as well as to get Texas and Oregon for the agrarians and businessmen, Polk was "confident" that such diplomacy would provide "additional strength and security." "It is confidently believed," he concluded, "that our system may be safely extended to the utmost bounds of our territorial limits, and that as it shall be extended the bonds of our Union, so far from being weakened, will become stronger."

In sending the army south to the Rio Grande into territory long claimed by Mexico, Polk committed an openly provocative act. Convinced that the loss of Texas would "inevitably result in the loss of New Mexico and the Californias," Mexican officials were further antagonized by the racial arrogance of Americans both north and south. "The haughtiness of these republicans," remarked one Mexican leader in sorrow as well as bitterness, "will not allow them to look upon us as equals, but merely as inferiors." Finally, after American forces blockaded the river, Mexico attacked just as Polk was ready to start the war on his own initiative.

Blossoming under the hothouse effects of the outburst of war enthusiasm and easy victories, a movement to take all of Mexico swept the west and parts of the northeast, particularly New York. "It is a gorgeous prospect," judged the *New York Herald*, "this annexation of all Mexico. . . . Like the Sabine virgins, she will learn to love her ravishers." And spokesmen of the "western spirit" began to talk of taking everything from the Arctic Circle south to the Isthmus of Panama. But less than a week after the war started, Polk compromised with Britain over Oregon. Clearly a realistic move, and one supported by some agrarians and businessmen looking for markets in England, it nevertheless antagonized many expansionists in the west and the north who concluded that the southerners were going back on their bargain to reoccupy Oregon as well as reannex Texas. Polk added to his troubles by vetoing an internal improvements bill with the arrogant remark that such laws represented a "mischievous tendency."

Confronted by that time with the challenge of the Wilmot Proviso, which proposed to exclude slavery from any territory won from Mexico, and which a coalition of westerners and northerners could pass at will in the House of Representatives, Polk and other advocates of expansion were knee-deep in the poisonous harvest of Manifest Destiny. "The North can and will be no longer hood-winked," screamed a Chicago newspaper that accurately reflected western feeling. "If no measures for protection and improvement of anything northern or Western are to be suffered by our Southern masters . . . a signal revolution will inevitably ensue." Similar anger erupted in Indiana and Ohio.

Clearly enough, the effort to extend the market place of laissez faire and thereby resolve its tensions was in reality intensifying the conflicts within the system as well as producing a war with Mexico. The developing nature of that competition was revealed in a fiery speech by Joshua Giddings of Ohio, who had already antagonized the south by his speeches against the evil slaveholders. "Are the farmers of the West, of Ohio, Indiana, and Illinois, prepared to give up the sale of their beef, pork, and flour, in order to increase the profits of those who raise children for sale, and deal in the bodies of women?" As an abolitionist, Giddings was indicating the limits of that specific religious appeal by extending his arguments to include economic issues as part of his attack on the planters.

This marked a turning point in the Age of Laissez Nous Faire: the separate moralities of laissez faire—political, economic, and religious—were beginning to converge in a campaign to change the basic rules of the game as they were set forth in the Constitution. To be sure, abolitionists such as Garrison (and, until later, even Phillips), whose politics might be compared to the undeviating and unsleeping, self-contained, migratory flights of the Arctic Tern, had not given up the struggle. They were even strengthened by the conversion of such men as Henry David Thoreau. And in going to jail in opposition to the war with Mexico, Thoreau effectively dramatized the issue (though he weakened his protest by leaving jail when somebody else paid the fine).

But as a philosophy which asserted that "any man more right than his neighbors constitutes a majority of one," Thoreau's transcendental individualism shared at least one weakness with Garrison's abolitionism: neither could have sustained the antislavery crusade by itself, nor could both together have done it. More important than Thoreau's private crusade, the Mexican War served as a catalyst in crystallizing three major conflicts within the general system of laissez faire. The most general was the rising opposition between the antislavery elements and the south. Methodists, Baptists, and Presbyterians, for example, had divided over the issue. But the various tensions and clashes within each group of primary antagonists were of great importance in determining the outcome of that struggle.

Agrarians, laborers, and businessmen had many differences with each other and within their own groups. Conflicts of function and interest were supplemented, for example, by clashes between the small and large entrepreneurs and between the banker and the industrialist. Westerners were so upset by Polk's opposition to internal improvements that nearly 20,000 attended the Rivers and Harbors Convention held in Chicago in 1847. They were also determined to keep the undeveloped western territories open for their particular, if not exclusive, benefit. And they were increasingly interested in the expansion of their markets to the Pacific coast and even to Asia. Steadily increasing in population, wealth, and political strength, the western states wanted all kinds of help from a government favorable to their interests. "Land to the landless and homes to the homeless!" was a cry heard increasingly often and with rising insistence. Coming to view the southern slaveholder and eastern business interests as almost equally antagonistic to their welfare, westerners were angry and on the prowl for allies.

They quickly found two important ones. Having joined with many eastern laborers to oppose Polk's war tax on tea and coffee as unfair "to all free laborers," the western farmer was soon repaid with interest. Rather mistakenly concluding that its campaign for the ten-hour day was generally successful (enforcement was very lax for many years), labor was turning to other programs. Some elements were attracted by the idea of organizing coopera-tive enterprises as a way to become entrepreneurs in the market place. Starting in Cincinnati in 1847, the movement had spread eastward to New York, Philadelphia, and Boston by 1850. Almost from the outset, however, the problems of raising enough capi-tal and commanding enough experience weakened the effort. Others launched a campaign for consumer co-ops. Designed to increase wages by lowering living costs, the first Protective Union was organized in Boston in 1845. There were 40 branches in Massachusetts within two years, and people in Illinois, Wisconsin, and Michigan responded almost as fast.

But the most important tie between the western agrarian and the eastern laborer grew out of the workers' renewed interest in free land and territorial expansion. A key figure in that revival, the editor of the *Workingman's Advocate*, George H. Evans, had been demand-ing free land ever since 1834, and without much success. But in the context of the war with Mexico and the Wilmot Proviso, his motto of "Vote Yourself a Farm" was picked up by three groups. Westerners liked it for the obvious reasons. So did agrarian politicians. Some of them, like Andrew Johnson of Tennessee, knew first-hand what it meant to be a small, hard-pressed yeoman. Others among the poli-ticians saw it as a way to appeal to the farmer and to businessmen interested in western development. Eastern labor (along with its spokesmen and would-be leaders) composed the third group.

EASTERN LABOR ACCEPTS THE FRONTIER THESIS AND THEREBY INTENSIFIES THE SECTIONAL CONFLICT

The crucial fact about labor's interest in landed expansion was that labor took it up with the idea of reducing the size of the growing working-force in the east. The westerner wanted land for himself (or for his sons and neighbors), but the laborer wanted it primarily for his next-door competitor and for the increasing number of immigrants. Hoping to create a labor shortage (and thereby ease the housing pressure and lower the rent levels), they launched Evans on a second career. Organizing the National Reform Association, they petitioned Congress, cornered candidates, and generally upset the existing pattern of political affairs.

And having thus embraced the expansionist thesis of democracy and prosperity in what might fairly be called an affair of the pocketbook, they straightway began to manifest noticeably stronger doubts about the morality of letting the slaveholder— *or the free Negro*—share in the bliss. In what a psychiatrist might term a revealing act, some of them began calling the abolitionists hypocrites who used morality to cover their economic interests. But others became antislavery (though not abolitionist) in their rhetoric and politics. And James Wilmot of Pennsylvania, whose name became the symbol of proscribing slavery from the land taken in the Mexican War, provided a clear indication that the general antislavery drive was not motivated by any particular concern for the Negro. "I plead," he remarked quite bluntly, "the cause and the right of white freedom."

Labor's acceptance of the free-land or frontier thesis of prosperity and democracy established the basic foundation for an alliance with the expansionists of the west. Whig politicians Seward and Weed, the one wanting expansion as a program for laissez faire and the other for the votes it pulled in, tried hard to establish and control such a coalition. Hiring Horace Greeley, an itinerant newspaper man who had coined the famous advice "Go West, Young Man!" as early as 1837, they started the *New-York Tribune* in 1841 as a propaganda vehicle. Greeley soon became an uninhibited advocate of expansion, arguing that it would control the labor market and also provide orders for eastern businessmen. Though Seward and Greeley thus laid the foundation for what was to become the Republican Party, they could not outmaneuver Van Buren in the short run.

Organizing under the leadership of Van Buren, and taking the accurate and appealing name of Free Soilers, easterners of this persuasion entered the political arena in 1848. Attracting some upperclass conservatives who were also integrating their economic, political, and religious morality into an antislavery, probusiness outlook, the new party campaigned vigorously under the banner of "Free Trade, Free Labor, Free Soil, Free Speech, and Free Men." The party offered internal improvements, free homesteads, and tariff protection along with denunciation of southern slave leaders. It thus defined laissez faire in terms that excluded the south. That was the most portentous development in American history since the 1760s when Samuel Adams had done the same thing in excluding England from colonial mercantilism. For should that definition of laissez faire be accepted by a plurality or majority that won control of the national government, then either it might attack the south or the south might revolt of its own accord.

Electing 13 congressmen (enough to exercise considerable influence in the Congress) and utterly disrupting the campaign between the Democrats and the Whigs, the Free Soilers advanced a statement of laissez faire that was at once almost pure abstract doctrine and yet practical enough to satisfy the dirt farmer. Despite being often considered insignificant if not unimportant before the time of Samuel Gompers, or before outbreaks of violence such as those in 1877, labor thus played a crucial role in American history when it took up the expansionist outlook. Nothing dramatizes this more effectively than the realization that it took three weeks and 63 ballots to organize the House of Representatives in 1849. Already antagonized by the Wilmot Proviso, the program and the effectiveness of the Free Soil campaign intensified the south's concern and bitterness. "The madmen of the North and Northwest," concluded the editor of the *Richmond Enquirer*, "have, we fear, cast the die, and numbered the days of this glorious Union."

Already embarked upon a program of self-conscious reform, the south began to think of itself as a besieged society that not only could create a balanced political economy including industry, but as one that might have to embrace that program in order to survive. Beginning in the 1840s, the region started to improve its agricultural methods, liberalize its state constitutions and extend the suffrage to more white men, build factories and railroads, develop an educational system, and carry through various social reforms. Fully aware of these efforts, many southerners felt northern attacks were doubly unfair. Not only was the antislavery campaign "a direct and dangerous attack" just as Calhoun had said it was in 1847, but it threatened to make "a fixed, dreary, hopeless minority" out of a

people who were trying to improve their society. "We do not intend
to stand still," cried Jeremiah Clemens of Alabama, "and have our
throats cut." "No, Sir," Calhoun added, "the Union *can* be broken."
And extremists like Robert Barnwell Rhett of South Carolina, who
had been talking about seccession ever since 1845, made it clear
that the south could at least manufacture its own version of the
Garrison repealer.

Supposedly a power that adjusted the myriad of competing
self-interests into the general welfare, Adam Smith's Hidden
Hand was instead beginning to trace a vicious circle. "Here it is,
this black question," cried Benton in anguish as the Free Soilers
revealed their strength, "forever on the table, on the nuptial
couch, everywhere!" Sustained by the energy that came to him
as he ceased chasing the Presidency (he was 63 and physically
very weak), and driven by his deep concern for the nation, Clay
returned to the Congress for the last time to make a valiant effort
to work out a peaceful adaptation of laissez faire to the American
realities. It was truly a noble effort. In contrast, Daniel Webster's
attempt to rally national feeling by an arrogant intervention in
the Hungarian Revolution (fire-eaters in Massachusetts wanted
to send troops) was a callous and dangerous application of the
expansionist solution to domestic problems. Webster thought
territorial expansion "very dangerous," but he had no qualms
about whipping up public enthusiasm for foreign revolutions—or
for overseas economic expansion.

By admitting California as a free state, leaving the remainder of
the newly acquired west to be organized by the actual settlers, and
abolishing the slave trade in the District of Columbia, Clay sought
to satisfy the north. He did—barely. But there was little left to offer
the south except a stronger Fugitive Slave Act. Hence the compromise was accepted only by the narrowest of margins over the opposition of New York's Seward and South Carolina's Calhoun. Both
thought it evaded the central issue, and each had drastically different solutions to offer. Seward appealed to a law which stood beyond
the Constitution, a code which justified war or else meant nothing. Calhoun asked constitutional limits on the power of the north.
The weakness of Clay's compromises, which in the later stages were
guided through the Congress by Senator Stephen A. Douglas of
Illinois was not that they took a risky course between those two

views, but that they followed an even more dangerous path around both of them.

Perhaps the most remarkable aspect of the whole settlement is the measure of the south's acquiescence in an unfavorable result. Extremists failed to rally significant strength for their convention at Nashville, and Georgia announced that it would abide by the terms so long as the north observed them. But the dynamic spirit of laissez nous faire rose like a phoenix from the Compromise of 1850 and demanded fulfillment. Its chosen instruments were Senators Seward and Douglas, and a mystic young corporation lawyer from Illinois, named Abraham Lincoln.

CHAPTER FOUR

The Transformation of Reality and the Inception of New Ideas

Democracies are prone to war, and war consumes them.

Senator William H. Seward, 1851

Come on, then, Gentlemen of the slave States. . . . We will engage in competition for the virgin soil of Kansas.

Senator William H. Seward, 1854

Fellow citizens, we cannot escape history.

President Abraham Lincoln, 1862

I don't know nothin' 'bout Abe Lincoln 'ceptin dey say he sot us free, an' I don't know nothin' 'bout dat neither.

Alabama Negro, 1864

Times are *hard.*   *American Agriculturist,* 1869

I won't call employers despots, I won't call them tyrants, but the term capitalist is sort of synonymous and will do as well.

Pittsburgh millworker, 1877

It's a question of bread or blood, and we're going to resist.

Railroad flagman Andrew Hice, 1877

You are already the great continental power of America. But does that content you? I trust it does not. You want the commerce of the world. . . . The nation that draws most from the earth and fabricates most, and sells the most to foreign nations, must be and will be the great power of the earth.

Senator William H. Seward, 1853

THE WELTANSCHAUUNG OF LAISSEZ FAIRE
ENGENDERS A CIVIL WAR

Long after it has ceased to be an effective weapon of personal recrimination or political strategy, Americans remain haunted by the Civil War. One is sometimes tempted to conclude that never have so many said so much about the same thing that is redundant or irrelevant. Underlying that persistent involvement is the realization that the war undercuts the popular mythology that America is unique. Only a nation that avoided such a conflict could make a serious claim to being fundamentally different. In accordance with the logic and psychology of myth, therefore, it has become necessary to turn the war itself into something so different, strange, and mystic that it could have happened only to the chosen people.

Whatever the appeals and sublimations of that approach, it seems more pertinent to history as a way of learning to examine the Civil War through the convergence of the three moralities of laissez faire that began in the late 1830s and reached an early climax in the Free Soil movement. As they merged in a consolidated system, the religious, political, and economic ethics were also distilled into a few key symbols. These handholds of thought, discourse, and judgment became the most potent and yet inclusive words of the age: *expansion, antislavery, freedom.* As indicated by their use as early as Jackson's time, as well as by their more formal denotations and connotations, they implied that the integrated value system of laissez faire was almost wholly negative. Freedom was defined as release from restriction. Expansion and antislavery were but the two sides of the coin that bought such liberty. But while the defining of evil is a vital function, it is no more than half the responsibility of any philosophy. Lacking a creative vision of community, laissez faire was weak in an essential respect: it provided no basis upon which to deal with evil in a nonviolent way. Its solutions were persistently aggressive and acquisitive.

For these reasons, the northern critics of the Compromise of 1850 were more influential than the southern extremists whose first fuse sputtered out at the Nashville Convention. While many of these northerners were ostensibly anti-expansionists, their position was in reality far more complex. They favored overseas economic expansion and defined the rest of foreign policy largely in terms of the trans-Mississippi west. Most westerners and eastern would-be capitalists shared the latter part of this outlook, and on the issue all of them were vigorous expansionists. Since that region was in fact America's colonial (i.e., underdeveloped) empire, their view was realistic.

But it was also extremely provocative because it defined the issue in very severe terms: would expansion into the trans-Mississippi west be undertaken within the framework of the Constitution, or would that basic law be rewritten in accordance with the abstract principles of laissez faire? The compromises under which the Constitution was adopted, the clauses of that document pertaining to representation in the Congress (which counted three-fifths of each slave) and the rights of states, and the pattern of legislation, and the decisions of the Supreme Court all pointed to a choice between two ways of handling the western territories. Either they would be opened to slaveholders as well as nonslaveholders, or the region would be divided into slave and nonslave areas. Southerners were willing to accept either of these solutions. So were a good many northerners.

But the advocates of antislavery laissez faire insisted that no one who did not accept their version of the axioms of laissez faire should be permitted to share the territorial empire. And as far as they were concerned, slavery was a violation of those principles. For them, at any rate, the arrival of the Age of Laissez Nous Faire meant that the Constitution had to be interpreted—that is, rewritten—in the light of this outlook. Since the divergence of opinion ultimately defined *the* question, the basic cause of the Civil War was the *Weltanschauung* of laissez faire. Unwilling to compete within the framework and under the terms of the Constitution, northern antislavery advocates of laissez faire finally undertook to change the rules in the middle of the game—and in the middle of the continent—by denying the south further access to the expanding market place.

In the meantime, from 1851 to 1861, the nation and its politicians fruitlessly sought a way to reconcile laissez faire with the Constitution. But since all their proposals hinged on expansion, they never broke free of the impasse. Seward had the keenest insight into this determining factor. "I cannot exclude the conviction," he concluded as early as 1846, "that the popular passion for territorial aggrandizement is irresistible." Small wonder, therefore, that he later called the struggle between north and south an "irrepressible conflict." Nor is it surprising that most leaders of the decade offered little more than Polk's strategy of balancing the gains between competing expansionist elements. Any more positive approach was almost discredited. One congressman with a sense of history expressed the attitude with great perceptiveness: any efforts to coordinate and balance the country's development "should be expunged as a disgrace to the country and to the nineteenth century." President Franklin Pierce vented the same spirit in his inaugural assertion that he would "not be controlled by any timid forebodings of evil from expansion." President James Buchanan put it even more bluntly. "Expansion is in the future the policy of our country, and only cowards fear and oppose it."

Thus the issue became dangerously oversimplified: expansion for whom? Throughout the 1850s, moreover, the debate took place against a backdrop prepared by America's first female primitive artist in words and ideas. *Uncle Tom's Cabin*, Harriet Beecher Stowe's landscape of slavery, was published in March, 1852. Though the form had not really been established (Erastus Beadle launched it in 1860), it might fairly be called the first dime novel. It was a crude, jerky, inaccurate, and violent morality play based on the manipulation of a few type-cast characters in one black-and-white situation.

By populating the south exclusively with evil slaveholders and Negroes, Stowe stereotyped the south as evil. There was nothing of the anxiety and hesitance of the area, let alone its initial propensity to accept the Compromise of 1850. The moral was provided by her misleading picture of the Negro as a man who could in "one generation of education and liberty" take his place in society as a fully matured and developed individual. An application of the principles of laissez faire would enable everyone to live happily ever after. Many southerners thought Stowe no more than a typical emancipated female—"part quack and part cut-throat"—and initially discounted the importance of the book. But the polemic became a guidebook to an enemy—the south—that had already been defined by the value system of laissez faire as it emerged in the program of the Free Soilers and the generalized antislavery spirit. Perhaps nothing defines the essence of laissez faire quite as well as the parallels between the Jacksonian campaign against the bank and the antislavery agitation. Both were negative. Both defined the enemy in secular moral terms. Both were closely tied to economic objectives. Both lacked any positive program for dealing with the problem. And both were undertaken in the name of expansion and freedom.

Even President Millard Fillmore's administration revealed itself as merely cautious (and a bit pro-northern) instead of fundamentally anti-expansionist. Fillmore allowed Commodore Matthew Perry to write his own militant instructions for opening Japan to American commerce, indicated considerable interest in Hawaii, and refused to sign a temperance pledge guaranteeing Spanish control of Cuba. Having argued in 1829 that expansion was "the *principle* of our institutions," Secretary of State Edward Everett in a more fully developed theory anticipated some features of Charles Darwin's theory of evolution. While overrated by the congressman who called it "the most 'manifest destiny' document that ever emanated from the State Department," Everett's long despatch refusing to guarantee the *status quo* in Cuba was a manifesto for empire. Once out of office, he was less verbose: "The pioneers are on the way; who can tell how far and fast they will travel?"

This vigorous spirit also infused a loose association of expansionists known as the Young Americans. Calling for commercial, territorial, and ideological expansion, they wanted to make the United States the hub of the hemisphere, the crossroads of the world, and the patriarch of global republicanism. Other expansionists followed the same general line on their own initiative. Though they ultimately failed, southerners had significant support from politicians and commercial groups in the northeast and the upper Mississippi Valley in their drive to acquire Cuba. And a similar combination of New Englanders, New Yorkers, and southerners almost turned Nicaragua into a Central American Hawaii; Buchanan even recognized their government before internal dissension and armed attack from other isthmian nations ended the colonizing venture.

Despite such involvement in southward territorial expansion, most northerners were primarily interested in overseas economic expansion, ideological empire, and control of the trans-Mississippi west. Their views won out in the Clayton-Bulwer Treaty of 1854, which facilitated trade developments in Central America while checking further territorial annexations by either Great Britain or the United States. Even so, some southerners supported the commercial push across the Pacific. Their trade interests were reinforced by the idea that such a move would help them hold their own in the territorial west, both directly and as a political *quid pro quo*. The result was a China policy designed for "maintaining order there" so that the nation's great economic opportunities would not become "the prey of European ambition."

Convinced that they were the "only powerful race" on the Pacific, some farsighted northerners like Perry McDonough Collins and Asa Whitney concentrated on plans whereby "American commercial enterprise [could] penetrate the obscure depths of Northern Asia." Backed by President Pierce and Senator Seward, and of course the Western Union Company, Collins proposed a telegraph system reaching across to Siberia and thence south to India and west to Paris, Berlin, and London. It was a vision of a vast, global funnel with the spout (and the profits) opening into the Mississippi Valley. Whitney stressed a transcontinental railroad to consolidate the opportunity. "Here we stand forever," he exulted; "we reach out one hand to all Asia, and the other to all Europe, willing for all to enjoy the great blessings we possess . . . but *all* [of them] tributary, and at our will subject to us."

Nor was this an irrelevant flight from reality. Not only were large agricultural surpluses being exported, but by 1860, manufactured goods, including iron, amounted to nearly 20 per cent of America's direct exports. But the south received few benefits from the developing subsidizing of such railroads by cash appropriations and massive land grants (approximately 3.75 million acres in 1850, 35 additional projects between 1852 and 1857, and 174 million acres gross between 1850 and 1871). A Mobile-Chicago connection was the most significant offering to the south, and that came too late to alter the established pattern of east-west routes. Land was acquired for a southern route to the Pacific, but such a gulf-coast transcontinental line was never built, at least not for *that* south.

Whatever their serious internal and sectional differences, the north and the west came to define expansion ever more clearly in terms of an interrelated industrial system based on manufactures and food. Despite Buchanan's defense of it as the policy of the "good neighbor" offering a "helping hand," they opposed his plan to snip off a bit more of northern Mexico while that country was preoccupied with internal difficulties, preferring to encourage overseas revolutions that promised commercial advantages. Seward candidly referred to such governments as "the outworks of our system of politics." "We have a direct interest . . .," agreed a westerner, "in the benefits of commercial intercourse. . . . All we want is that freedom should have a fair battlefield."

SENATOR DOUGLAS AND THE ATTEMPT TO
RECONCILE LAISSEZ FAIRE AND THE CONSTITUTION

Without too much exaggeration, it could be said that the key to understanding the coming of the Civil War lies in the westerners' definition of that term "fair battlefield." Viewing the undeveloped territories of the colonial west through the same laissez-faire spectacles, a coalition of rising capitalists in the west and northeast demanded a favorable settlement of this issue in its domestic form. Was the competitive market place of laissez faire to be defined within the framework of the Constitution (in which case slavery could enter the territories), or was it to be done according to the abstract principles of laissez-faire theory (in which case it should not)? Taking command of the issue, Senator Douglas provided a magnificent example of the rise of the politician under laissez faire. A schoolteacher and lawyer who had gone west and worked his way up through various state offices to the Senate and a leading position in the Democratic Party, he wanted to be President. But to realize this natural and legitimate ambition, Douglas had to resolve a predicament of laissez-faire politics based on expansion and at the same time honor his commitments to a free economy and local self-government.

Douglas had considerable insight into this dilemma because he was confronted in Illinois by a remarkably accurate microcosm of what was happening across the northern half of the United States. Read Chicago for New York (and the rest of the eastern urban complex), and McHenry County for the agrarian north, and the analogy reveals the political pressures and problems that Douglas faced. Farmers who could shift into specialty production for the city (as milk and poultry) benefited from the changeover from commodity crops, but the majority were growing increasingly fidgety. Neither preemption laws nor special relief acts had checked the rise of tenant farming. Second-generation farmers and fresh immigrants increased the competition, as did the large operators who held huge acreages. Land prices were beginning to rise, and still more capital was required to buy the new machinery produced by companies like Cyrus McCormick's firm in Chicago.

Periodically the victim of malaria, dysentery, or typhoid, and eternally tired (one wonders how Emerson or Thoreau would have made out with the solitude of 160 acres), the farmer was on edge. He was in no mood for irrelevant harangues or supercilious advice from easterners. He wanted help: internal improvements (including educational institutions), the opening of more land in the colonial west, and vigorous action against the Indians. Whatever his religious or secular concern for the slave, therefore, the farmer was not an abolitionist. He was against slavery on practical grounds: it was tough competition. Therefore he had no desire to check it in a way that would only multiply his troubles. Hence Free Soil meant a land free of liberated Negroes as well as slaves, and a free homestead for himself—or his local competitors.

Many urban groups, in the east as well as in Chicago, reacted in a similar way. Their morality was that of the aggressive enterpreneur or would-be businessman of laissez faire. They were, indeed, the personification of the Arminian heresy that defined Man's secular free will as God's chosen instrument. Viewing the south far more as a section that blocked their own success than as a society to be liberated, their antislavery enthusiasm resembled the attitude of the farmers. The farmers wanted liberty and were against southern leadership, but mainly they were concerned with their own freedom of action. This spirit ultimately provoked many eastern labor groups to conclude that the antislavery campaign served (if it was not designed) to distract men from the primary struggle between the owners and the workers. In that sense, their outlook was but another example of the primacy of the laissez-faire spirit over the abolitionist morality.

Acting at once as a politician with such a constituency and as a political philosopher, Douglas held that the Constitution should be honored as the framework for competition under laissez faire. Insisting that "the people shall be left free to regulate their domestic concerns in their own way," and that self-restraint in the face of extremists was the only way to make democracy work, he argued that if self-determination was to mean anything at all, it had to be preserved at the local level. Slavery as well as antislavery groups should have equal access to the market place of the trans-Mississippi west. Exemplified in the slogan "popular sovereignty," this approach, after three months of bitter debate, was written into law as the Kansas-Nebraska Act of 1854.

Douglas was not proslavery. He opposed slavery, and broke with southern Democrats after they abused the principles of the Kansas-Nebraska Act. But he did believe that the Constitution had priority over the abstract principles of laissez faire, *and he was confident that the system of free labor would prove superior in competition.* His critics can be divided into three groups: those who might fairly be called revolutionaries for their insistence in ranking the abstract principles of laissez faire above the Constitution; those who lacked his faith in the competitive power of free labor; and those whose position was principally determined by political considerations. Their combined opposition defeated Douglas. It also checked Seward and opened the way for Lincoln.

Though he preferred to contain slavery within its existing bounds, Seward accepted the challenge of Douglas's approach. The key to the contradiction between Seward's rhetoric and his policies lies in his conscious emulation of John Quincy Adams in an age that lived by different principles. Describing Adams as "this wonderful man," Seward movingly called him "a father and a guide." Not too surprisingly, therefore, Seward's central vision was an American empire embracing the world through the revolutionary power of its economy and ideas. His emotional nationalism was anchored in hard economic analysis. Disturbed as early as 1842 by signs of "decaying enterprise" and stagnation, he insisted that America's economy of manufactures and commercial agriculture had to have a constantly expanding market.

But since he also concluded that "democracies are prone to war, and war consumes them," Seward was reluctant to rely on force for such expansion, and a civil war would threaten an empire so formed even more directly. Despite his problems as a politician in a free-soil state, therefore, and his own antislavery sentiments that were determinedly played upon by his abolitionist wife, Seward persistently preferred a compromise that would allow the rising industrial economy to subvert slavery in a peaceful process as it went on to greater victories throughout the world. Seward's strategy seems to have been to bring in the old world of mercantilism to redress the imbalances of the new world of laissez faire.

Willing to assert the laissez-faire axiom that "the abstractions of human rights are the only permanent foundation of human society," he nevertheless realized that men had to control those abstractions lest they destroy society. Accordingly he stressed the responsibilities of God's trustees and stewards, and insisted that the government had clear duties connected with the "paternal care" of society. Such men had to use the state to restrain the extreme advocates of the rights of private property and moderate the harsh results of unrestrained competition. In many significant ways, therefore, Seward was the prophet of the corporation capitalism that was to triumph at the end of the 19th century. He combined the axioms of laissez faire with an acceptance of the large corporation and sought to cement the union by reasserting a version of the old corporate ethic of a Christian mercantilist commonwealth.

Buoyed up by that vision and the confidence it inspired, Seward could accept the challenge of competition with the south even though it was not his ideal solution. "Come on, then, gentlemen of the slave States," he sang out in one of the great moments of the Age of Laissez Nous Faire: "Come on, then. . . . Since there is no escaping your challenge, I accept it in behalf of the cause of freedom. We will engage in competition for the virgin soil of Kansas, and God give the victory to the side which is stronger in numbers as it is in right." But as that competition turned the political market place into a frightfully accurate copy of the economic market place, Seward found it ever more difficult to confine the struggle within constitutional limits.

Some groups did support such efforts. Deeply involved in transforming the commercial-agrarian economy into an industrial-financial system, the majority of large and established businessmen opposed policies that pointed toward war. And, watching their wages increase but 4 per cent while the cost of living went up 12 per cent during the decade of the 1850s, laborers concentrated on organizing national labor unions and on strikes (such as the successful shoe walk-out in New England of 1860). But the farmers, smaller entrepreneurs, and mechanics with a vision of themselves as employers—in short, the rising bourgeoisie of America—increasingly demanded protection in an expanding market place against the competition of slavery. Responding to this pressure in order to maintain their influence, the abolitionists became increasingly secular, and the two disseparate groups converged in a crusade to rewrite the Constitution according to the gospel of laissez faire.

Walt Whitman sang the essence of this new and far more generalized morality in a dramatic outburst of 1856. "You young men! American mechanics, farmers, boatmen, manufacturers, and all work people of the South, the same as North! You are either to abolish slavery, or it will abolish you." Whitman's either-or definition of the problem was reinforced within a year by Chief Justice Roger Taney's reassertion, in the *Dred Scott* decision, that the south had equal rights as a competitor, and that the market place included the trans-Mississippi west. This decision was but a counterpart of his earlier judgment that corporations were legal individuals competing in the market place. And both were quite within the limits of his conception of Jacksonian Democracy as a system resting on the liberties and sanctity of private property.

But by this time many congressmen were carrying revolvers and other weapons during working hours. As their armament symbolized, politicians had been taken over by politics much as admirals and generals are taken over by a war. Originally responding to popular pressures, their proposals influenced the voters who again increased the tension by further abstracting alternatives that were already extreme. This cycle of interaction was fully established by 1854. "I am in politics," explained one New England leader in supporting a policy of which he personally disapproved, "and I must go on." Seward also understood what was happening. "I know and you know," he admitted in 1858, "that a revolution has begun. I know, and all the world knows, that revolutions never go backward."

John Brown concurred in his own insane way with this hypothesis. His attack on Harper's Ferry was an effort to turn Virginia into another Kansas and thus free all the slaves of the nation. Dying with the easy indifference of all men who are already living in another world, Brown failed to end slavery but did succeed in further narrowing the range of debate about it. Those who argued for compromise within the Constitution lost ground, and men who questioned the entire outlook of laissez faire were almost literally ignored. A literary masterpiece of the time which probed the implications of this self-reliance that can ultimately become self-righteous fanaticism was Herman Melville's *Moby Dick*. Yet the book was hardly noticed; certainly it was not read and acted upon.

Perhaps the greatest natural talent in the nation's literary history, Melville grappled with the central issue of the need for some resolution of the tension between the individual and society. Though he offered no answer in *Moby Dick* (that came, at the end of his career, in *Billy Budd*), Melville did make it clear that the individualism of Ahab led only to a horrible and terrifying compulsion to control everything in the universe. Emerson's credo of relying only on oneself produced in the end an almost complete distortion of man and society. Though quite different from Melville in background, temperament, and ability, Richard Henry Dana's similar doubts about laissez faire lost him his audience among New England intellectuals. "The whole modern system," Dana concluded in 1853, "seems to me to be grounded on a false view of man . . . as acknowledging no God, nor the need of any. . . . There is a spirit of self-confidence in it, which, left to its natural tendencies, will inevitably bring a deeper and wider woe upon man than earth has ever yet known."

ABRAHAM LINCOLN AS THE PHILOSOPHER AND POLITICIAN OF TRIUMPHANT LAISSEZ FAIRE

Though neither the abolitionists nor the free-soilers gave much thought to such somber estimates of their *Weltanschauung*, Seward clearly tried to counter them with his concept of stewardship. And even the man who displaced Seward and Douglas as the philosopher king of laissez faire ultimately tried to meet the criticism by embracing a mystic Christianity that defined God as the hidden author of all forces and events. In his earlier years, however, Lincoln appeared more akin to one of Friedrich Nietzsche's supermen who believed himself an instrument of the hidden forces of History. "I always was superstitious," he later remarked, and did not indicate that he had changed. But the myth which presents Lincoln as emerging complete in wisdom from somewhat obscure origins does him (and his society) a serious disservice. It denies him his greatest virtue—the capacity to mature and ripen and transcend the limits of his earlier outlook. For there were two Lincolns; the young, aggressive man of laissez faire and the older, more humble Lincoln who sensed the weaknesses of that philosophy and tried to lead its triumphant advocates toward a more humane and responsible conception of man and society.

Lincoln's progress from a log cabin through the practice of corporation law to regional political leadership was not particularly unusual for his time. And his law partner's characterization would have served for countless young Americans of that age: "His ambition was a little engine that knew no rest." As with his jokes and stories, those aspects of his career have been inflated far beyond their significance. (But for what it is worth, most of his humor concerns the defeat of a poor competitor.) Lincoln set himself apart by the masterly way in which he used his great native intelligence. The combination was so commanding that even under adverse circumstances he could, and at one time or another did, outmaneuver any and all of his rivals and critics. He did not *win* all the time. No man can. But his record is amazing when the odds are computed, particularly so when it is realized that Lincoln very probably understood that his tactics would lose him the famous Senate race with Douglas. He accepted that risk as an investment in a bigger prize.

This ability to abstract himself from himself and the immediate situation yet all the while keeping himself in icy focus was probably the determining element in his success. He could estimate, analyze, and act with the calculated and impersonal ruthlessness of a clinical performer. This persistent pattern of operating is what makes his early definition of himself in the context of the rising antislavery and expansionist fervor so eerie, even chilling, an aspect of his career. For having defined himself as a politician, he clearly set out to determine and exploit the issue of his time. Although he praised the Founding Fathers for their genius, he denied that his generation of Americans could find "gratification" for their "ruling passion" in "supporting and maintaining an edifice that has been erected by others." "Most certainly it cannot," he flatly asserted. As for his own conception of leadership, it emerges clearly from his favorable analysis of John Locke's definition and praise of the strong king.

Lincoln also accepted Locke's labor theory of value and extended it into full advocacy of laissez faire. "I take it," he explained, "that it is best for all to leave each man free to acquire property as fast as he can. Some will get wealthy. I don't believe in a law to prevent a man from getting rich; it would do more harm than good." In his philosophy as well as in his own life, Lincoln emerged as the grand figure of antislavery laissez faire. Even his attitude toward the

Negro manifested that spirit: "All I ask for the negro is that if you do not like him, let him alone." He was, at least until the war started, the philosopher of the market place as well as the humorist of the crossroads.

He was also, as a rising politician, a bit of a demagogue. For all his emphasis on principle in his debates with Douglas, for example, he nevertheless appealed to southern democrats on the ground that they should vote against Douglas because he said slavery could be excluded from a territory. Yet Lincoln not only said it could be excluded, he insisted that it must be excluded! Nor is there any question that Lincoln was the first *national* political figure to cast the issue in either-or terms. His House-Divided Speech—"It will become all one thing, or all the other"—came months before Seward's famous remark about an "irrepressible conflict."

Thus Lincoln's assertions that he would not touch slavery where it already was failed to carry much conviction in the south. He had created an image of himself as an infuriatingly patient and persistent executioner of slavery. Spurning popular sovereignty as well as abolitionism, he argued that free labor and free entrepreneurs could triumph by denying the south any chance to expand. This did not make him an anti-expansionist; it merely made him a northern expansionist (as did his open interest in the commercial possibilities of overseas colonies founded for slaves who had achieved their freedom). Enough northerners understood this and his anti-abolitionist position regarding the Negro to elect him. Enough southerners understood it to turn his election into the signal for secession.

THE SOUTH REFUSES TO ACQUIESCE IN LINCOLN'S POLICY OF CONTAINMENT

On November 8, 1860, a southern gentlewoman summed it up succinctly. "That settles the hash." Since it did indeed, the reasons are important. In the broadest sense, and speaking as the heirs of the physiocratic forefathers of laissez faire, southerners insisted that the Constitution guaranteed minimum protection against *any* political economy. Its leaders interpreted Lincoln's election quite accurately as the victory of a movement to alter the Constitution and abrogate that compromise, literally in the sense of ending southern expansion, and philosophically in the sense of applying *all* the principles of a political economy in *all* the country. The south was correct about it.

Lincoln's election did symbolize the coming to power of a revolutionary coalition.

"Let there be no compromise on the question of *extending* slavery," he sharply reiterated after being elected. "Have none of it. Stand firm. The tug has to come, and better now, than anytime hereafter." Perhaps Lincoln expected war and preferred to wait patiently until it came. But perhaps his law partner's estimate of Lincoln's mind was absolutely correct: "he failed to see what might be seen [in his own position or a general situation] . . . by other men." Perhaps his mind was so "cold, calm, precise, and exact" that it lacked the ability to imagine how things appeared to others. If so, and not planning war himself, he may simply have assumed that the south would not act either. Possible, yet not probable. As that word "tug" suggests, Lincoln more probably thought a firm stand would bluff or cow the secessionists and produce an acceptance of defeat throughout the south.

Certainly he argued this logic very clearly in his inaugural address, pointing out that the south would have to face the demise of slavery even if it went to war. Lincoln's simultaneous reassertion that slavery would not be allowed to compete in the territories meant to the southerners that they had no choice but to fight. They thought they had both the legal right and the practical need to expand their system. And enough of them had come to agree with Jefferson Davis's estimate of 1850—that they were faced with "the steady advance of a self-sustaining power to the goal of unlimited supremacy"—to enable their extremists to muster sufficient active support, and acquiescence, to carry secession.

Some southern leaders had seen the Supreme Court's definition of the corporation as a legal person as one of the turning points. They understood that it favored northern interests in the market place. "No offering could be made to the wealthy, powerful, and ambitious corporations of the populous and commercial states of the Union so valuable," concluded a Georgian in 1853, "and none which would so serve to enlarge the influence of those states." Others stressed the nonterritorial side of the antislavery campaign as being misguided and in fact serving to unite the south. "If the north had directed its strength against the evils of slavery instead of assailing it as a sin per se," concluded one slaveholder in 1854, "it could not have survived to the present day." While probably pushed too far,

THE TRANSFORMATION OF REALITY   299

the argument made one irrefutable point. A crusade of this nature would have *changed* chattel slavery and created a nonviolent momentum toward freedom for the Negro.

As the planter's reaction suggested, the role of abolitionism in causing the war was much larger in the south than in the north. The north's developing antislavery outlook prepared it for a show-down. But neither Lincoln nor the majority of northerners entered the war in an abolitionist frame of mind or entertaining abolition-ist objectives. The south, on the other hand, had defined the enemy in the image of the abolitionist. Thus it reacted violently when a southerner named Hinton Rowan Helper argued in a coldly factual way (*The Impending Crisis of the South: How to Meet It*, 1857) that middle- and lower-class southern whites should abolish slavery in their own interest. Yet his argument had been advanced by Washington and Madison and seriously debated as late as 1832.

Considering themselves under assault, southern leaders had begun in 1853 and 1854 to look back over their history to the political economy of mercantilism as a guide for overcoming their comparative economic weakness in the face of northern power. "Throw to the winds the erroneous theories of ADAM SMITH," cried a typical critic. Decrying the "glittering bauble of an imprac-ticable free trade system," others emphasized the importance of "commercial independence," and of "bringing up the rising genera-tion to MECHANICAL BUSINESS." A diversified and improved agriculture combined with "the manufacture of her own products" would place the south "as far as is now possible above the malign influences of Congressional aggression and despotism."

While this attitude did not produce dramatic statistical results by 1860, it did help to create an atmosphere in which secession seemed not just desperately necessary but also feasible and fruitful. Had it actually produced extensive material results, it might have changed the nature of the war. But perhaps the greatest, if unplanned, strate-gic triumph of the laissez-faire antislavery campaign was its making the slave system a hero in the eyes of southerners. For this gave the conservatives rather than others with new ideas the control of the Confederacy. Not even the superb and noble leadership of General Robert E. Lee could save it under these circumstances. No northern general matched him man for man in the field, and not even Lincoln spoke a line more moving than Lee's judgment on the

Battle of Gettysburg. "It's all my fault. I thought my men were invincible." But no army wins a war on the defensive, and the strategy of Davis and other top Confederate leaders was a defense strategy.

Even so, it took Lincoln's revolutionary coalition four years to subdue an enemy that was statistically no match for it. It seems doubtful that Lincoln grasped the full significance of what the war would become until after it started. For not only did he then confront the social problem of the Negro, which he had admitted he did not know how to solve, but he came full-face with the harsh reality that there was no Union to save. He had to create a nation in the north in order to enforce a union with the south. That he succeeded as far as he did is the monument to his political genius—and ruthlessness. As he did so, however, he accelerated a pattern of development that changed the very structure of the north's revolutionary coalition. For in mustering the forces of victory he also pushed along the industrialization of the north, and its concurrent organizational changes, to such an extent that the conflicts within the coalition became strong enough to prevent any real program, revolutionary or moderate, from riding into law and institutions on the crest of victory.

RECONSTRUCTION AS A NATIONAL PHENOMENON

In some important ways, therefore, the Civil War did not produce an unconditional defeat of the south as is so often assumed. The south was beaten in the field, occupied and ruled in surrender, and in some respects treated as a colony. But counterattacking with the Negro problem and with the subversive weapon of economic opportunity, it found weak spots in the north's main line. For if there was an era of reconstruction in the south presided over by the north, there was just as certainly an era of reconstruction in the north that was not really presided over by anybody; it was a bitter and violent struggle among the major elements of the new industrialism, the older entrepreneurs and bourgeoisie, and the agrarians and laborers. The old sectional alignments and economic structure were disrupted by the railroads, the rising financiers, the factory, and the institution of the corporation.

Hence the conservative and radical wings of the revolutionary laissez-faire coalition that supplied the dynamic power of the Civil

War found themselves not only at odds with each other and the south, but beset by new opponents within the north. As in all revolutions, the hard core of radicals offered the most nearly integrated set of attitudes and policies. Thoroughgoing advocates of classic individualistic and entrepreneural laissez-faire capitalism, men like Benjamin F. Wade of Ohio, Benjamin F. Butler of Massachusetts, William D. (Pig Iron) Kelley and Thaddeus Stevens of Pennsylvania, and John A. Griswold of New York, had four primary objectives.

They wanted to establish the long-term predominance of the Republican Party throughout the south and the north, with themselves in control of it. To that end, and also because they were willing and even anxious to apply the principles of pure laissez faire across the board *at home*, they wished to free the Negro and then establish him as an element in the political economy. While not all the radicals accepted it as a program, the cry of "40 acres and a mule" for the Negro caught the spirit of this approach. Entrenched in power and having humbled the south, they could enact legislation that would establish the framework for their kind of capitalism.

"Get the rebel States into a territorial condition," Stevens advised, "and it can easily be managed." To acquire and hold the necessary voting strength, the radicals offered a high tariff for manufacturing, free land for dirt farmers, land and other subsidies to the railroads, soft (or inflationary) money for all expanding entrepreneurs, jobs or land to workers and immigrants, control of the cotton market and domestic trade to New Englanders, and the south as a new frontier to northern entrepreneurs and politicians. With this strategy in mind, the radicals badgered Lincoln incessantly for an edict of emancipation, fought him on other issues, and used the northern army to control the south while they sought to remake it in their image of laissez faire.

But the radicals lacked the power to transform their vision of the true laissez-faire society into reality. Hence, though the Civil War was brought on by revolutionary coalition, it did not become a truly revolutionary war. In the language of the French Revolution, the Thermidorian reaction proceeded concurrently with the revolution itself. The result was a society trying to deal with the circumstances of maturing institutional industrialism by using the ideas and the ethic of individualist laissez faire.

Property rights and anti-Negro prejudice were the reefs that ripped open the frigate Revolution. In a fundamental sense, of course, the conflict between property rights and a laissez-faire revolution was built into the *Weltanschauung*, just as was a similar dilemma into the mercantilist's outlook. For private property was (and is) the cornerstone of the laissez-faire system, and hence revolutionaries who proposed to act on the principle of domestic confiscation of property in order to establish the prerequisites of the system put their hand on the lid of Karl Marx's Box.

The trap was apparent: if it was permissible to take private property in order to establish or maintain laissez faire, then no sophistry could deny the equal right to take it in order to construct socialism. Only a few of the radical leaders—Wendell Phillips was one of them—proved willing to follow their ideals and their logic to a candid realization that socialism rather than capitalism would provide the kind of society that they wanted. Most radicals saw the danger and drew back. Conservatives never considered the idea. Nothing illustrates the triumph of property rights more clearly than the subsequent practice of pinning the label "communist" on even those merchants and wholly bourgeois dirt farmers who in the 1870s, and later, wanted to regulate the railroads in order to restore competition in the market place. And on the Negro issue, the problem of property rights was further reinforced by general economic and social considerations. As it was in the beginning, so did the antislavery coalition remain predominantly anti-Negro.

Lincoln grasped the troubles of a laissez-faire revolution that was caught, on the one hand, in the contradictions of its theory and, on the other, between those ideas and the reality of the changes that were taking place. "The dogmas of the quiet past are inadequate to the stormy present," he flatly announced in his intense argument of 1862 for compensated emancipation. "We must think anew and act anew. We must disenthrall ourselves, and then we shall save the country." But neither Lincoln nor anyone else made this vital breakthrough. Hence the soul of laissez faire went marching on into a world of vastly different substance and proportions. This dichotomy provides the fundamental insight into American history after Fort Sumter.

Lincoln's failure to present a postwar program meant that he simply did not have one. But admittedly it was difficult to develop policies that combined antislavery and prowhite attitudes without at the same time classifying the Civil War as a traditional political and economic conflict. Liberal historians have been trying ever since to square this circle. Lincoln's own approach to reconstruction in the south pointed toward the kind of compromise that was ultimately made between 1874 and 1880. Lincoln's death opened the way for the radicals, but they lacked the power to execute fully even that part of their program based on honoring private property. Never more than a bare plurality in the north even at the height of their influence, southerners proved masters of political guerrilla warfare, and the dynamic development of the north during and after the war so mangled the old political economy that the radicals could not muster a new coalition on any grounds.

These northern developments gave the southern conservatives the opportunity to reassert their power. They did so, however, in a society where industry, and especially the railroad corporation, was playing an increasingly important role. The Civil War was not the first modern or industrial war. It was the last merchant-agrarian war. It produced an industrial system rather than being fought with one. While there is a basic timelessness, for example, about the situation and the human crisis in Stephen Crane's *The Red Badge of Courage*, no one who has known combat in a modern war would seriously maintain that the story delineates the problem of bravery, or even captures the sense of what Crane's protagonist called "the great death," in the context of modern war where machines define men as wiggles in a line on a radarscope.

As railroads played an increasing role in northern logistics and troop movements, they also announced the coming of a new order. They extended and integrated the market place and so made it possible to specialize and consequently accelerate other economic activities. This was a tremendous boost for cities, and by the 1870s the pattern of industrial urbanism was firmly established. Railroads symbolized the steady rise of the corporation as a form and way of organizing economic activity, and revealed the depersonalizing of labor that went with this institution. By the 1870s, for example, 520 of 10,395 businesses in Massachusetts were incorporated. But the 520 held $131,182,090 of the $135,892,712 total capital, and employed 101,337 of the 166,588 workers.

The accumulation of capital for such corporations being a major

task, the financier became more important both as an active entrepreneur and as a supplier of commercial services. Railroads not
only developed close connections with such investment firms, but
generally reintroduced the idea of thinking about the economic
life of the country as a system. Yet they did so, not as public leaders as in the days of mercantilism, but as private leaders of one
of the functional groups and institutions that were becoming the
competing units of laissez faire. Hence the individual began losing
his effective power and sense of relevance at an increasing rate.
Yet at the same time the wide powers of private leaders began to
create a kind of harmony in the system which tended to reinforce
the ideology of laissez faire even though it ultimately became irrelevant to the reality of the system.

Clearly enough, these aspects of the railroad did not mature
immediately. It is vital to recognize, however, that they did have
an immediate impact. Given a national transportation system, for
example, general advertising became feasible. A New York firm
promptly responded and in 1879 began making market analyses
and supplying plans, writers, and artists for advertising campaigns.
Functional groups—such as the American National Steel
Manufacturers, the Iron Founders Association, the National Board
of Trade—formed their own organizations. The basic pattern is well
exemplified in the American Bar Association, organized in 1878.

In the narrow sense, the lawyers staunchly upheld individualism,
private property, and laissez faire. "The great curse of the world,"
they declared, "is too much government." But they also accepted
the individual's shift to corporate organization and the concurrent
restriction of the market place. Defending monopoly as "often a
necessity and an advantage," they justified trusts as "a defensive
weapon of property interests against the communistic trend." And
some members were even then, like Samuel J. Tilden, corporation lawyers who had gone into politics with this more inclusive
and systematic view of political economy. Such men personified
the beginnings of a new gentry composed of economic giants and
professional politicians who would ultimately assert their power
over national life.

But the combination of Lincoln's death and the determined and
traditional agrarian conservativism of President Johnson gave the radicals an opportunity to extend and consolidate their power. Johnson

might have effected a moderate compromise with the south, for there was considerable sympathy, both active and latent, for such a reconciliation, but his unyielding position played into the hands of men like Stevens and Sumner, and William Pitt Fessenden of Maine. Rallying support by calling up the specter of a southern victory-in-defeat, and stressing the survival of the Republican Party and the new industrialism, the radicals effectively defeated the President. Their effort to impeach him failed, but it was in all essential respects an unnecessary attempt. In dramatizing the power of the legislature as against the executive it provided a classic manifestation of the spirit of laissez faire.

The more important failure of the extreme radicals (or revolutionaries) was their inability to handle the issue of providing the Negro with property. Once that objective was abandoned, the radical program consisted of three contradictory pairs of policies and attitudes: high tariffs and low land costs; great malice and little restraint; soft money and hard politics. Hence the radicals were successful only as long as they could sustain wartime and political emotions, as long as westerners were primarily concerned with real estate, until southern whites reasserted their power, and until a new combination of financiers, merchants, and farmers established itself as a competing alliance in the north.

CROSSCURRENTS OF RECONSTRUCTION

Having passed the tariff of 1864, given the farmer the Homestead Act of 1862 (along with formal representation in the government and educational aid), and subsidized the railroads, the radicals occupied the south and jammed through the 13th, 14th, and 15th Amendments which ostensibly ended slavery, defined the Negro as a citizen and asserted his right to vote. Though they were not in any sense guiding a mass movement to liberate the Negro and remake the south, the radicals had considerable support for their program. In the negative sense, which may have been the most important, many Americans were preoccupied with the exploiting of their own opportunities and simply acquiesced. Yet as indicated by the frequency with which various individuals and groups in the north used the term "imperialism" to describe their own operations as well as those of their competitors, a good many participated actively in the reconstruction program. And a surprising number of

306 THE CONTOURS OF AMERICAN HISTORY

westerners, like the wool growers and others who hoped to industrialize the upper Mississippi Valley at a faster rate, even supported
the tariff.

Financial leaders, on the other hand, were less enthusiastic about
the radical policy of soft money. Bankers did not like having the
government in the money business, and had opposed the National
Banking Act of 1862. Their gains from inflation were small. Along
with a good many of the rising corporation industrialists, such
financial spokesmen were likewise cool to any wholesale equality for the Negro; the other side of that attitude was a desire,
particularly strong among New York merchants, to restore their
prewar economic connections with the south. And in addition
to the merchants, who were always inclined toward low tariffs or
free trade, some manufacturers and politicians were shifting away
from high rates. Some of them had been frightened by the Panic
of 1857 or had supported increases as a war measure. But others
began to argue that the new industrial system would need foreign
markets for its surpluses; hence high tariffs would only invite retaliation abroad. In the first years after the war, however, these various elements were too weak to disrupt the radical program once it
was put into operation.

Radical difficulties began with the collapse of the alliance
between Pennsylvania entrepreneurs and New England textile and
manufacturing interests. Originally the product of a happy union
between laissez-faire idealism and self-interest, the coalition
agreed on support for the iron industry and a project involving the
organization of the Negro to produce cotton on Gargantuan plantations managed by the Freedman's Bureau. Cotton would then be
taxed if exported. The anticipated result, in conjunction with the
Bureau's political and educational projects, was cheap cotton for
New England, general business control of the south, and a solid
Republican vote from the Negro. But southern devastation, poor
weather in the year of the crucial crop, and Britain's ability to find
cotton elsewhere combined to defeat the plan.

Boston bounced back with a low-tariff strategy designed to win
western support and replace New York as the financial and mercantile center of the country. In a completely logical way, therefore,
the radical coalition was disrupted by the loyalty of its members to
the laissez-faire axiom of following their own particular interests.

New England stressed trade and textiles while Pennsylvania emphasized iron and steel. Boston's switch was important, but the radicals were also weakened by the south's increasing ability to resist outside control, by other divisions in the north, and by a fortuitous food shortage in Europe.

Western manufacturers like Cyrus McCormick responded favorably to the New England return to low tariffs. McCormick concluded that he would reap more profits indirectly through expanded foreign markets for the farmers' crops than he would by being protected against imported machinery. Farmers wanted the overseas sales, and also remembered the south as an old customer and political ally with whom they might again do business. And western merchants and other businessmen were anxious to restore their prewar trade with the south, or to enter it for the first time. The merchants took the lead. "Commerce must bear the burden of taxation and businessmen are the best judges of their own wants, and what will most conduce to their prosperity," they declared at a national meeting in Detroit in 1865, adding that it "behooves them to take a deeper interest in governmental affairs."

After organizing the National Board of Trade in 1868, the merchant alliance then obtained a direct import law (1870) that made it possible to ship goods directly to inland cities before paying customs. This effectively bypassed New York in many transactions and gave Boston and the western merchants a strong competitive position in the southern and territorial markets. Coinciding with the south's lack of capital with which to regenerate and diversify its economy, and with the Negro's difficulty in finding employment at anything but agricultural labor, this northern businessmen's coalition consolidated the new economic slavery of tenant farming, share-cropping, and the planter store. Shackled to the cotton crop, the Negro (and his white counterpart) became perennial debtors to their new overseers. While it exaggerates the reality, there is a significant measure of truth in the idea that the Civil War gave more freedom—at least in the short run—to the white upper class of the south than it did to the slave. Both were liberated, but the one group far more effectively.

As should be apparent, the merchant-planter-store system involved the railroads and the monetary system in every transaction. Consequently one group of businessmen and farmers joined the financial interests in favoring a deflationary money policy; they concluded that inflation hurt them more than it helped. A similar coalition, led by radicals like Stevens, and generally based on the expanding iron and steel industry, preferred to keep the wartime greenback paper-money system and even to expand it. They argued vigorously that contraction would retard economic development ("Businessmen are hungry for money."), operate unfairly against everyone except bondholders, and hurt domestic manufacturers by undercutting the tariff. Since the per-capita money supply had declined from $30.35 in 1865 to $17.51 in 1876, the argument had considerable relevance. But the vote in the Congress on contraction revealed that the west was almost evenly divided (36 yes to 35 no), and the combination of a good harvest and foreign-crop failures temporarily damped the farmer's insurgency.

Thus sustained, the alliance between eastern and western businessmen, including farmers, turned away from the money issue to the question of railroad abuses. As much opposed in their own way to railroad policies as the western farmers, the merchants not only helped to initiate the attack on the lines in both sections of the north, but the New York group joined forces with their Boston and Chicago competitors on the issue. Anger against the roads had appeared as early as 1863, and the House of Representatives had passed regulatory laws in 1874 and 1878 only to have them ignored by the Senate.

REGULATION AS AN ESSENTIAL FEATURE OF LAISSEZ FAIRE

Though a first impression might indicate otherwise, the farmers, and merchants, remained within the framework of laissez faire in making their attack on the railroads. They wanted to become more effective (and profitable) entrepreneurs within the system, they did not want to change it. Their logic followed that of the master himself. For as Adam Smith reiterated *ad nauseam*, the key element in laissez-faire theory was the market place. As long as it expanded, and as long as individuals had free access to it, unrestrained competition produced both individual freedom and the general welfare. When some part of it ceased to expand, however, Smith explicitly called for regulation to preserve competition.

Not only were the railroads by their very nature part of the structure of the whole *system's* market place, but they demanded such tremendous investments that the market place in which they could be constructed (i.e., the railroad industry per se) was very small. Entrance into it was anything but free. Furthermore, the market place for railroads had a saturation point beyond which it was irrational and unprofitable to build any more. On all these counts, but especially that concerning the railroads as a structural part of the system's general market place, the first principles of laissez faire justified regulation, even demanded it. The market place had to remain neutral, or as nearly so as possible, so that the various interests would be afforded the famous "open field" for competition. A monopoly of the market place itself was simply indefensible under laissez faire.

Quite rightly, therefore, the farmers demanded that the structure of the market place be stabilized so that competition could continue to their greater benefit. To this end they concentrated on establishing rules and limits for the railroads and on initiating cooperative enterprises to produce or buy certain necessities. Thus, though it started as a fraternal society generally but vaguely interested in benefits for agriculture, the Grange movement began in 1869 to concern itself more directly with the state of the political economy.

It shifted its approach for two reasons: the farmer found it impossible to sublimate his real difficulties in social functions and lecture meetings, and other farm organizations came forward with more vigorous economic and political proposals. Grangers in Iowa organized cooperatives as early as 1872 in order to harvest the benefits of mass purchasing and insurance programs. Two years later they were manufacturing their own harvesters and selling them at about half the market price. Californians even started their own banks. Such enterprises failed because of the lack of sufficient capital, prices that were too low, litigation and price-cutting by their competition, a lack of the cooperative spirit among the farmers themselves, or because the agrarians became manufacturers (and raised their prices).

Collaboration with the merchants in an antirailroad campaign proved more effective. Nor were the merchants slow to see the advantages of an economic liaison with the large agrarian market. Montgomery Ward and Co. was founded in 1872 as the direct result of discussions between the Grange and urban businessmen. Spearheaded in Illinois by the Chicago Board of Trade as well as by farmers,

310 THE CONTOURS OF AMERICAN HISTORY

the alliance produced on the political side a warehousing law of 1867
that required railroads to load grain from nonrailway elevators, pushed
through a constitutional amendment authorizing regulation in 1870,
and fixed maximum freight and passenger rates in 1871. A similar
coalition in New York effected the famous Hepburn Investigation
of 1879. Other states followed all such examples. Attacking exces-
sive rates, discrimination in charges between short and long hauls,
personal favoritism, and the general arrogance and corruption of the
system, the assault put the railroads temporarily on the defensive.

Less encouraging was the revelation that outsiders lacked the
experience and knowledge to dig out the full story of corporation affairs so that the general public could help to formulate
and then choose between alternate plans for enforcing equitable and responsible business conduct. Georgia and California
reacted to this serious problem in 1879 by establishing permanent commissions staffed by experts to keep a running check
on the lines. This was the beginning of an approach that gained
national acceptance and application in later years. In two major
cases, meanwhile, the Supreme Court upheld the axiom of
public accountability in a way that revealed the paradox of an
uncompleted revolution.

By way of validating an Illinois regulatory law in the case of
Munn. v. Illinois (1877), Chief Justice Morrison R. Waite explicitly invoked mercantilist precedents. Citing the English common
law as enunciated by Lord Chief Justice Hale during the period of
Shaftesbury's influence in the 1670s, and examples taken from the
era of Madison and Monroe, Waite reasserted the principle that
"property does become clothed with a public interest when used in
a manner to make it of public consequence, and affect the community at large." He also reiterated a cardinal principle that had been
vigorously defended by Madison and Marshall. "For protection
against abuses by legislatures, the people must resort to the polls,
not to the courts."

Waite thus reopened the issue that had plagued the mercantilists: how can the public welfare be advanced and protected if private
property is allowed to stand above other values? He boldly asserted
that it could not, and also reaffirmed the principle that the courts
were bound to respect the judgment of the people in such fundamental questions. But while his reference to English common law

of the mercantilist era was valid in the broad sense, his use of Lord Hale's judgments was open to serious criticism. For that law concerned property which had been endowed with public interest by law. Technically, at any rate, the railroads stood outside this category. Hence his decision (as he probably realized) rested on shaky ground.

The state laws also begged a second important part of the railroad question. As the connecting links in a national system, veritably the nervous system of Adam Smith's expanding market place, the railroads could not be broken into arbitrary fragments along political boundaries without causing serious consequences. Though their underlying purpose was both equitable and relevant within the *Weltanschauung* of laissez faire, in operation such particularistic regulations were both illogical and inefficient. This was especially the case so long as the central question concerning private property was not resolved; such laws could not only disrupt service, they could actually cause serious economic dislocations.

Waite and his court knew that it was a touchy issue. For in upholding the law of a postwar Louisiana legislature that regulated the place and circumstances of slaughtering for public consumption, the majority placed considerable emphasis on the point that any butcher could use the facilities. They thus revealed the basic ambivalence and dilemma of the entire war and reconstruction era: on the one hand, the ideology of the revolution was laissez faire for private property; on the other, considerations of public welfare and the changes in the economy created the necessity for a corporate outlook that would place equal stress on social property.

But the Louisiana law does clarify one vital issue: the exercise of northern power in the south was by no means wholly absurd or selfish. Therein lies the real tragedy of reconstruction in the south. For it was the north's inability to resolve the conflict between its antislavery ideals and its commitment to private property that subverted the originally revolutionary objectives. That failure made it much easier for the Ku Klux Klan and the Red Shirts to succeed as the advance guards of a counterrevolution based on self-interest, on personal, rather than social, property rights, and on race hatred. Yet even the southern whites paid a backhanded tribute to the greater ideal by presenting themselves as men who would restore the paternalism of the region's lost gentry.

PARADOXES OF SOUTHERN REHABILITATION

Supported by the power of the Congress and the Presidency and backed by the Union Army, the freed Negro dominated the early phases of reconstruction. The Negroes were in themselves half the issue, and their legislative program was the other half. They were poor, and they had a vague image of the north as the good society. Hence they demanded relief acts, educational programs, basic public investments and improvements, and political reforms. Both the victorious northerners and the new southern leadership, which was industrial rather than planter, had to operate within this context.

Too often lumped together under the title Carpetbagger and described as corrupt politicians and economic grave diggers, the northerners who went south actually composed a varied contingent. It included a sizable quick-profit brigade, dedicated revolutionaries trying to make the south "identical [with the north] in thought, sentiment, growth, and development," and honest politicians who reformed where they could and did a great deal to encourage southern recovery and improvement. A good many others, perhaps the plurality, were simply men who found southern reconstruction an underground railway along which to escape from their wives, the law, or poor pickings in the north. But consciously or unconsciously, all of them saw reconstruction as what some Wisconsin veterans called the new frontier. To many, at any rate, it seemed to offer more opportunities with less labor and risk than the forbidding prairie, the western mountains and desert, or the business market place.

As it did in the north, reconstruction produced waste, debts, and corruption in the south. But not only is it factually wrong to blame the Negro for all the weaknesses and failures, but the indictment is a double-edged sword. After all, the Negro in the postwar era was the product of American civilization, and his northern and southern masters were reaping their own harvest. In reality, the Negro did amazingly well. To cite but one example, the Negro-based reconstruction governments in South Carolina provided public schooling for 500 per cent more children.

Southern whites initially divided on how to cope with the rise of the Negro. Upper-class leaders either joined the Republicans (and won the epithet Scalawag), or tried to organize new parties based on the

Negro vote. Despite their race prejudice, they were willing to trade a significant measure of equality for political and economic leadership. "Go in for the niggers," exclaimed one of them bluntly, meaning buy the Negro vote by letting them hold office and relaxing some social taboos. Many changed their strategy when confronted with the taxes required to finance the Negro legislative program. Some were willing to let "every office in the State [of Louisiana], from Governor to the most insignificant constable, [be] filled by a negro" in return for lower taxes. But the northern white could always outbid them in that game, and lower-class white southerners withheld their support.

Though the racial attitudes of the poor whites probably played the largest part in their opposition to collaboration with the freed Negro, it is misleading to discount economic and class considerations. Such collaboration did after all occur a relatively short time later. During the immediate postwar period, however, a good many poor whites clearly viewed the Negro as a lower-class citizen who was leap-frogging over himself—a competitor enjoying special and unfair advantages. Hence it seems far more likely that economic, class, and racial antagonisms reinforced each other. Joining their upperclass rulers, the poor whites formed a political and extra-legal alliance that ultimately defeated the Negroes and the Republicans.

But once again in keeping with northern reconstruction, the southern white party was pro-industrial and fundamentally conservative. Hence the irony of the disputed election of 1876. As the prewar defender of the individual entrepreneur, the Democratic Party nominated in Samuel J. Tilden a corporation lawyer who symbolized the cutting edge of the new industrialism. And the Republicans, coming more and more to be dominated by giants of the new society like Roscoe Conkling, selected in Rutherford B. Hayes a personification of the older capitalism. Neither candidate was particularly solicitous for the Negro. The compromise that put Hayes into the White House was based on a common ground; had the two parties differed on fundamentals, the deal would have been impossible.

DEPRESSION AND CRISIS IN THE NORTH

In the broader sense, however, the compromise has to be understood as part of laissez-faire capitalism's reaction to the onset of grave economic troubles in 1873. It was a closing of ranks against the general difficulties of the system, against the agitation of farmers and laborers, and against a general increase in lawlessness and dissatisfaction. Far from being the culminating embrace of reconstruction (that came in the routine election of 1880), the compromise of 1876 was only the first scene of the final act. The real climax came with the great railroad strike and associated industrial disorders between 1876 and 1878. Having destroyed the old planter aristocracy and come to terms with its industrial successor, the leaders of northern laissez faire had to consolidate their power within their own coalition.

For despite its extensive contributions to the victory, the labor movement never fully overcame a skepticism about the purposes and consequences of the war. Draft riots in New York revealed that underlying resistance and at the same time typified, and were in part caused by, anger over inflation and unemployment. Labor also fought the Contract Labor Law of 1864 which increased the influx of cheap and manageable immigrant labor, the repression of strikes, and the attack on the apprenticeship system. It also maintained a campaign for the eight-hour day; and some groups still agitated for land and monetary reforms that would enable the worker to save enough to become an entrepreneur.

While it declared for all these objectives, the National Labor Union's noble and egalitarian willingness to admit women and Negroes and to organize the unskilled along with trade craftsmen only compounded its other difficulties. The trouble was not so much that the Union's reform goals contradicted its more narrowly economic objectives, but rather that its *Weltanschauung* of laissez faire made it extremely hard to pursue both in any integrated fashion. While ostensibly against the wage system, and therefore concerned to establish cooperative production units, the Union also wanted small capitalists to expand and thereby hire more workers, fought for more rigorous apprenticeship regulations, and favored arbitration over strikes.

As with the farmers who turned to cooperatives, the labor approach to such organizations did not signify any fundamental break with capitalism and private property in favor of socialism. However unrealistic it may seem a century later, labor's conception of a cooperative was entirely within the logic of laissez faire: it was the idea of an association of petty capitalists joined in a legitimate trust. The object was to restore and extend their competitive power in a more balanced and equitable market place. Although disrupted by economic and racial opposition to the Negro, and by the narrow conception of self-interest held by the leaders of the movement to emancipate women (who were willing to serve as strikebreakers), the National Labor Union was basically divided and perplexed over how to cope with the new industrialism. It disintegrated into groups that concentrated on functional or local issues, or joined various political movements such as the Greenback campaign for an inflationary money policy. Negroes formed their own union in 1869, and women, after their brief regression into heterosexual alliance, climbed back onto the high road of emancipation to a position of separate and unequal standing.

During the depression's worst years, therefore, the labor movement declined to approximately 50,000 members (about 1 in 100 workers). But that figure is misleading on two counts: among those in the labor group were the iron, steel, and railroad workers, who were organized and militant, and the seemingly small number was supplemented by large numbers of unemployed adults and aimless youths. With new jobs almost nonexistent and wages in 1875 down to $1.50 for a ten-hour day, the crisis had become the most general breakdown of capitalism in American history. A major riot erupted in New York in 1874. Elsewhere great numbers of parvenu tramps roamed the country. Boston leaders compared the situation to "some great fire or more serious calamity." But even when measured against the Chicago fire, the depression was far worse both in its immediate impact and the time it took to rebuild the community. A sizable number of upper-class leaders throughout the country sensed that they were threatened with a fundamental challenge to the existing order.

"I won't call employers despots, I won't call them tyrants," remarked one steelworker, "but the term capitalist is sort of synonymous and will do as well." Even the Governor of Massachusetts admitted in 1874 that the state's textile workers were "becoming exhausted, ... growing prematurely old, and ... losing the vitality requisite to a healthy enjoyment of social opportunities." Coal miners struck in 1875 only to be defeated and lose their union as well as 20 per cent of their wages. Other employers were from one to four months tardy in paying wages. And a major strike at the Cambria Iron Works in Pennsylvania, which had integrated its operations from ore to blast furnaces and a company town for its workers, failed with pathetic human consequences.

Then in a move that could hardly have been more remarkably symbolic, railroad workers refused in 1877 to take a further pay cut and touched off an industrial war in West Virginia that soon spread to other states. "It's a question of bread or blood," explained a Pennsylvania Railroad worker, "and we're going to resist." Blood it was. Ordered into Pittsburgh by President Hayes, federal troops confronted an unorganized alliance of railroad strikers, unemployed steelworkers, and juvenile and adult delinquents. Stones from the kids provoked rifle fire from the adults and that begot carnage and arson by everyone. Parts of the city became a shambles. Other outbreaks followed in Baltimore, Chicago, and St. Louis. But lacking any clear leadership, even from the tiny group of socialists and communists who belatedly discovered the crisis, the riots passed away in what might be called a euphoria of bourgeois second thoughts.

Though labor won some immediate gains (the railroads gradually restored the pay cuts), the long-range results are more difficult to estimate. Erupting out of agitation against Chinese labor imported for railroad construction, riots in San Francisco led to the forma- tion of the Sand Lot Party which enjoyed considerable influence in California for a few years. But as that episode suggests, labor's vision was certainly limited and clearly inclined to be bigoted. Most of its rising leaders, like Samuel Gompers and Adolph Strasser of the cigar workers, turned away from any program that envisioned a different and better system outside the confines of laissez faire to concentrate on strengthening labor's position in the existing order. And although it polled over a million votes in the election of 1878, and advocated other reforms as well as monetary inflation, the Greenback campaign soon lost its verve and support.

In the broader sense, the conservative response to the crisis of 1877 was accepted by a plurality of Americans. Chaos and violence crystallized the existing anxiety of the middle class that it was being squeezed between those who would destroy the rights of property and others who abused them. But forced to choose, its members clearly preferred the chance to exploit the liberties of the entrepre- neur. And upper-class leaders became even more determined to consolidate their control over the system. A federal judge named Walter Gresham who followed Tilden into the Democratic Party was a bit more extreme and outspoken than most, but he nevertheless typified the general attitude of his stratum of society. "Democracy is now the enemy of law and order and society itself," he concluded, "and as such should be denounced." Gresham's private attitude was given public exposure by a young middle-class entrepreneur from Indiana named John Hay, who had been one of Lincoln's secretaries and who aspired to leadership for himself. Hay's book, *The Breadwinners*, was a fictional polemic against labor. As a novel it was feeble art, but it outsold by a wide margin a rival interpretation of the crisis of 1877, Henry F. Keenan's *The Money Makers*.

SECRETARY OF STATE SEWARD AND THE ADAPTATION OF THE FRONTIER THESIS TO INDUSTRIALISM

Hay and Gresham also came to personify a developing bipartisan consensus on foreign policy. Both saw overseas economic expansion as the long-range solution to such dangerous unrest and the malfunctioning of the system that caused it; Gresham's performance later as Secretary of State under President Grover Cleveland, and Hay's actions in the same post under President William McKinley were to show this outlook in its matured form. Though they were not in a position to deliver the dramatic results produced by Gresham and Hay, the same basic approach guided key foreign-policy leaders during the postwar era.

Expansionists of the reconstruction period faced several handicaps. Seward explained the most important of them very simply, remarking that the public "refuses to dismiss" the issues of readjustment in order to pursue world power. This attitude magnified the impact of the overt opposition. Such critics were afraid that more expansion would reopen the question of slavery or that it would undercut the political and economic functioning of the laissez-faire system. Carl Schurz neatly combined all such arguments in his opposition to taking any Caribbean islands. "Have we not enough with one South? Can we afford to buy another one?" But the expansionist coalition was only checked; it was not disrupted, nor was it replaced by a new alliance of anti-expansionists.

"I chant the new empire, grander than before. I chant commerce opening," sang Walt Whitman in praise of the American who "colonizes the Pacific." William Gilpin, a friend of President

Jackson who had supported the Mexican War with great enthusiasm, returned to the campaign by reissuing (1873) his treatise on *The Mission of the North American People.* "The *untransacted* destiny of the American people," he cried, ". . . is to . . . rush . . . to the Pacific Ocean . . . to establish a new order in human affairs . . . to regenerate the superannuated nations." Businessmen joined in with petitions "to establish and maintain our ascendancy in Asia," and to "*manage it so that the whole world would be tributary to us.*" And in his annual message of 1868, President Andrew Johnson curtly dismissed the old argument "that our political system cannot be applied to an area more extended than our continent." The principle and the system were "of sufficient strength and breadth to comprehend within their sphere and influence the civilized nations of the world."

Although he was an expansionist, Johnson's remarks plainly bore the imprint of Secretary of State Seward. Still concerned to construct "such empire as the world has never before seen," Seward understood the need to change the nature and purposes of territorial expansion as the economy became more industrial. While retaining some of his earlier belief that Latin-American countries would eventually apply for statehood, and speaking openly of "our" Panama isthmus, he clearly realized that commercial expansion was the key to making America "the master of the world." Instead of needing territory for colonization, the new kind of economic expansion required key land bases for the projection, development, and protection of trade and investment.

Internal improvements were needed to insure "diminished cost[s] of production," and wars should be avoided because the United States was "*sure* to be aggrandized by peace" because it would control world commerce. As Lenin was to argue more than two generations later, Seward maintained as early as 1853 that the key to overcoming British supremacy was to be found in Asia. "France, and England, and Russia," were the rivals: "Watch them with jealousy, and baffle their designs against you." "You are already the great continental power of America. But does that content you? I trust it does not. You want the commerce of the world. This is to be looked for . . . on the Pacific. . . . The nation that draws most from the earth and fabricates most, and sells the most to foreign nations, must be and will be the great power of the earth."

Seward's accomplishments fell shy of his desires. France was already on the way out of Mexico when he intervened, and his full-handed shove only accelerated the retreat. He failed to acquire either the Danish West Indies or Hawaii. But in the 1960s there was to be no need to belabor the significance of his Alaskan success; even at the time, some Americans understood its role in outflanking the British in North America and in giving the United States a strategic bridge across the top of the Pacific basin. "It seems inevitable," commented *The New York Times*, "that all that commerce should be American." And today Seward's vigorous effort to penetrate the Asian mainland by establishing a foothold in Korea seems eerily prescient. Seward confounds the view that America had world power "thrust upon it" by external force of circumstance.

Much the same is to be said of President Ulysses S. Grant, whose desire to push overseas expansion was a central theme of his two terms in the White House. Grant was persistently concerned for "new markets for the products of our farms, shops, and manufactories." Indeed, one of his strong reasons for seeking the nomination for a third term was to help American investors expand their overseas operations. With the tutoring that he and Seward provided, other industrial nations recognized that a new competitor had entered the world arena. Britain astutely realized that the turn of the trade balance in 1877, when America began regularly to export more than it imported, was more important than the violence in Pittsburgh. The evidence was irrefutable, explained the London *Times*, because American tools and machinery were cutting into the market in England itself, as well as in Australia and Canada.

For that matter, England had already provided in 1871 the single most dramatic symbol of America's rise to world power. Worried about Bismarck's unification of Germany through the defeat of France, and concerned about Russia's renewed push into the Black Sea region, Great Britain apologized for having allowed its shipbuilders to aid the Confederacy. It formally expressed, "in a friendly spirit, the regret felt by Her Majesty's Government." Buoyed up by that candid recognition of their power, and having checked the laborers and the agrarians, the leaders of America's Age of Laissez Nous Faire moved on to the fulfillment of their self-interests and the maturation of the system's contradictions.

CHAPTER FIVE

The Fulfillment of the Passing Order

"Cast down your bucket where you are." . . . *Cast it down in agriculture, mechanics, in commerce, in domestic service, and in the professions.*
Booker T. Washington, 1895

The Fourteenth Amendment . . . means freedom to go where one may choose, and to act in such a manner, not inconsistent with the equal rights of others, as his judgment may dictate for the promotion of his happiness; that is, to pursue such callings and avocations as may be most suitable to develop his capacities, and give to them their highest enjoyment.
Supreme Court Justice Stephen J. Field, 1877

We declare the true purpose of government to be the maintenance of that sacred right of property which gives to everyone opportunity to employ his labor and security that he shall enjoy its fruits.
Henry George, 1886

It was wonderful to find America, but it would have been more wonderful to miss it.
Mark Twain, in *The Tragedy of Pudd'nhead Wilson*, 1894

We say to you that you have made the definition of a business man too limited in its application.
William Jennings Bryan, 1896

The world should be open to our national ingenuity and enterprise.
President Grover Cleveland, 1893

A BALANCE SHEET FOR LAISSEZ NOUS FAIRE

Given the dilemmas and contradictions inherent in their outlook, and granted their failure to complete the revolution implicit in the antislavery campaign, the leaders of the Age of Laissez Nous Faire fulfilled their *Weltanschauung* to a remarkable degree. For by 1897, when they formally surrendered power to the spokesmen of a new conception of the world, they had begun to recover from their third major depression, were underselling England and Germany in the world steel market, and had provided major testaments to the importance and the dignity of the individual human being. And despite the dangers in the romantic exaggerations of Emerson and Thoreau, that emphasis on individual men and women could be dismissed as merely an agrarian myth only at the price of accepting a substitute conceived of statistical data and born of computing machines.

As suggested by the conflict between private and social property in the Age of Mercantilism, the word and concept *fulfillment* have two different meanings that are usually combined in using the term. The denotation bespeaks the culmination of a given logic or pattern of development. But the connotation adds a favorable judgment. It is particularly important to keep these two aspects separate in evaluating the Age of Laissez Nous Faire. For while its advocates stressed individual liberty, opportunity, and achievement, some of their actions which represented a fulfillment of the axioms and logic of the system did not, even by their own standards, warrant the favorable connotation of the term.

This was apparent, for example, in the way that Andrew Jackson's attitude and policy toward the Indians culminated during and after the Civil War. That bitter and violent antagonism produced one general western war which cost $223,891,264, and did not end until 1882. As one of the commanders who defeated the natives, General Philip F. Sheridan left a harsh judgment of the enterprise. "In other words," he reported to the Secretary of War in 1878, "we took away their country and their means of support, broke up their mode of living, their habits of life, introduced disease and decay among them. . . . It was for this and against this," he added, "that they made war." Chief Joseph of the Nez Percé tribe, after having narrowly failed in 1877 to escape across the Canadian border, provided a moving epitaph for all Indians. "I want to have time to look for my children and see how many of them I can find. . . . My heart is sick and sad."

President Chester A. Arthur candidly acknowledged in 1881, "the appalling fact" that even then the problem remained unsolved. Mercantilists viewed the Indians as men with an organized society, and had hoped to resolve the conflict by giving them land as a tribal unit and then encouraging and helping them to shift over to a fixed agricultural economy in which they would work out their own compromises between the two cultures. Laissez-faire leaders pursued a fundamentally different policy. Dramatized in 1871 by the formal decision to destroy tribal society and culture, their approach was to force the Indian to accept the institution of private property and ultimately enter the market place as an individual entrepreneur. Congress acted on that axiom in 1887, after Indian resistance had collapsed, and opened up an era of more subtle but hardly less effective economic warfare.

Though it produced a different *policy*, the same classic concern with the market place manifested itself in connection with the immigrant. Maintaining their own great fecundity (population increased 25 per cent between 1860 and 1890), and confronted with the economic and social problems of a prolonged depression, Americans began to restrict the foreigner's entry into competition. "The nation has reached a point in its growth," observed a citizen in a letter to the editor of the New York *Tribune* in 1881, "where its policy should be to preserve its heritage for coming generations, not to donate it to all the strangers we can induce to come among us."

Religion continued to play a part in such antagonism, but the immigrant's role in the economic and social market place became the focus of attack. Native labor opposed the competition and at the same time agreed with upper-class spokesmen on the immigrant's inferiority. Both groups resolved the non sequitur by invoking the central laissez-faire argument about the danger of class conflict. Since they accepted the promises of laissez faire, neither the higher orders nor the workers wanted such social war and feared that the immigrant might precipitate it. That specter of devolution into social violence became one of the strongest themes of the era and strongly influenced the first restrictive legislation of 1882 and the organization of the American Protective Association in 1887.

Both the treatment of the Negro *and the Negro's response* also developed within the *Weltanschauung* of laissez faire. Since 90 per cent of the Negro population remained in the south until the era of the First World War, and because the northern antislavery coalition had never been vigorously pro-Negro (and had collapsed), the Negro confronted and grappled with his fate as a freedman within that region. He also did so primarily as an agrarian. As they reestablished their authority, white southerners did not immediately exclude the Negro legally from political action. The black man was lynched, threatened, bullied, and cajoled, and tricked, foxed, and hoodwinked; but he was also voted at the appropriate times and places as a pawn in the white man's game.

Negro reaction was appropriate to the environment: Negroes accepted the self-interest philosophy and its definition of success and began to build a parallel society. Negro newspapers declared, for example, that high income was "real success," and the class of 1886 at Tuskegee Institute chose the slogan "There Is Room at the Top" as their motto. The Negro community rather quickly stratified itself in replicas of the wealthy white entrepreneur and his aspiring competitors. At the bottom were the miserable and maltreated convict laborers leased out to such gigantic white firms as the Tennessee Coal, Iron and Railroad Company for even less than their keep, which was literally infinitesimal. At the top were Negro professional men and capitalists whose incomes were far greater than those of many whites in any section. Within a short time, the latter group developed a vested interest in segregation that was only very slowly overcome.

Yet the Negro was potentially dangerous to white leaders because he could vote. This reservoir of power and trouble was tapped in the late 1880s as the agrarian *interest* and to some extent the lower *classes* (fearing a lowering if nothing else) began to collaborate across the color line. Keeping well within the perimeter of laissez-faire politics in which interest was the benchmark of decision, the Negro saw that he held a potentially winning hand as a minority capable of delivering a bloc vote to the highest-bidding white faction. Neither the whites nor the Negro offered any strong corporate or commonwealth sentiment or program. It was classic laissez-faire interest and class politics, and the result was the fulfillment of that logic. Southern whites, whipped up by such demagogues as Baptist minister Thomas Dixon of North Carolina, or candidly lectured on their interests by upper-class spokesmen like Carter Glass of Virginia, collaborated in a drive that *legally* segregated and disfranchised the Negro. Southerners searched their souls and found their interests.

The dominant group of Negro leaders did likewise. Accepting their minority position, they argued that it was necessary to rise to a competitive position within the system in order to extend their rights and opportunities. Coming from Booker T. Washington, who enjoyed entré into the society of Standard Oil executives, rail-road magnates, and Andrew Carnegie, the strategy was persuasive. Washington avowed his loyalty to laissez faire, took his stand in the south as a southerner, and accepted social inequality for the forsee-able future. Blocked by the power of the whites and told by their own spokesman that "white leadership is preferable," most Negroes followed the advice to start climbing up a separate and identical but longer competitive ladder of laissez faire. Only much later did other Negro leaders effectively challenge Washington's influence.

In the meantime, Washington's position was made almost impregnable through the generosity of northern white philanthro-pists who liked his ideology (which included a code of labor quiet-ism and even strikebreaking). Offered within the broad framework of a humanitarian and extremely hard-headed desire to prevent social upheavals by directing and controlling reform, their help established such educational centers as Howard University and Tuskegee. Judged within its own assumptions, the gravest weakness of such philanthropy was that it was a poor and ineffective second-best for the wholly legitimate (if for the time revolutionary) lais-sez-faire principle of giving the freed Negro a property stake in the system. For granted the premises and the logic of laissez faire, the periodic redistribution of property is the most internally consistent approach to sustaining that political economy. Though unquestion-ably noble, philanthropy is a feeble and wasteful substitute.

A modified version of such redistribution was first outlined in 1871 by Henry George in the form of his single-tax program. But it did not stir any great response for almost a decade. During that inter-lude, the competitive drive, ability, wiles, and chicanery of tremen-dously wealthy and powerful entrepreneurs put them in a position to destroy or severely limit competition in the major areas of the economy. While men like Carnegie (iron and steel) and Gustavus Swift (processing, packing, and refrigeration of meat) have with some reason come to symbolize the laissez-faire capitalist, the issue is actually far more complex. For one thing, some entrepreneurs shifted over to the corporation outlook and thus became the architects of a new era as well as the heroes of the passing age. Other giants, men like Jay Gould ("The Spider"), James Fisk ("The Hatchet Man"), and Daniel Drew ("The Spoiler") were ruthless and predatory, and incapable of being defended within the standards of laissez faire (or any other philosophy outside the jungle).

Finally, the bulk of economic activity was carried on by small-to-medium-sized capitalists whose businesses were undramatic and even unimportant when considered individually. But they were often the first to introduce and perfect key innovations (as the refinement of iron into steel) which were then taken over by the big operators who proceeded to put many of the real innovators out of business. Most of them died unknown and have remained so, yet they carried the burden of industrialization and commercial development. They also applied the principles of the laissez-faire market place to sports, as with baseball and prizefighting. This processing of games into enterprises was in some respects the classic proof of the triumph of business in America.

The undeniable achievement of the laissez-faire entrepreneur, from Carnegie to the Wyoming dry goods merchant, is that he sustained the momentum of economic development through a long-wave depression (and an era of steadily falling prices) that lasted from 1873 to 1898. Up to 1893, at any rate, per capita income, real wages, and gross national product all continued to increase. That tremendous surge of industrial strength changed the face, the food, and the ideas of America and provoked serious reevaluations of diplomacy in European and Asian capitals. It also extracted a terrible cost in death and physical injury, in psychic and emotional wounds, and a process of moral leaching that carried away a great amount of American idealism. Judged against the facts that the nation was completely free from any danger of foreign attack, and further graced with fantastic natural wealth and skills, the relative and absolute cost of those economic gains can only be described as exorbitant. Had America been truly unique, it would have pared the social and personal costs of free enterprise to a fraction of their actual total.

The men who directed and sustained that ruthless and expensive accumulation of capital and industrial construction were for the most part young men of the east between 45 and 50 years of age whose fathers were business or professional leaders. Very, very few of them were really self-made in the narrow sense, and all of them were provided a fantastic and public subsidy by the Civil War (which even their most ardent admirers have not yet defined as private enterprise). The most important and revealing aspect of the self-made myth lies in its symbolism of the age and in its influence on later generations that were to live in a vastly different world.

Carnegie was nearest to being the pure laissez-faire entrepreneur. Even when he formed a limited partnership to expand and integrate his holdings, as with coke fields in 1882, he retained tight control. He would shade prices with childish glee, but he hated pools and other combinations. "Only let them hold firmly to the doctrine of free competition," he demanded. "Keep the field open." Along with John D. Rockefeller, he personified the spirit of pursuing one's self-interest. "Whatever I engage in," he admitted, "I must push inordinately." Frankly admitting that he was an entrepreneur rather than a steelworker, he hired that talent in Captain Bill Jones. A brilliant and dedicated individual whose essays on the craft of steel-making were read before the Royal Society in London, Jones had the typically laissez-faire goal of a salary equal to that of the President of the United States. Carnegie astutely and happily gave it to him. Together they represented in almost classic form the complementary halves of laissez-faire capitalism.

In addition to his philanthropy, which was clearly (and somewhat subtly) conceived to sustain the system, Carnegie made two other significant contributions to the ideology of laissez faire. He took Adam Smith's insistence upon expanding the market place and translated it into a rule of practical operation that might be called Carnegie's law of the surplus. Maintaining steady production was cheaper than shutting down part of the operation, he explained, even if the going price fell below cost. "The condition of cheap manufacture is *running full.*" Exports were the answer. They would undercut foreign competition and ultimately create a larger market at profitable prices. Carnegie also played a key role in developing the single price (not rate) system whereby final costs to the buyer were computed by adding the freight from Pittsburgh, even though the consumer might be ordering from a local plant. While the basing-point system was refined in a later era, it originated as part of laissez faire's concern with regularizing the market place and increasing profits.

In the early stages of their careers, both John D. Rockefeller and J. Pierpont Morgan also operated as laissez-faire entrepreneurs. Indulging his mania for handling details—"Work by day and worry by night, week in and week out, month after month"—and even in the midst of the Civil War talking oil until his sister was "sick of it," Rockefeller captured approximately 90 per cent of the domestic petroleum business between 1870 and 1880. He also entered the export market with the same drive for dominance. "I believe it is my duty to make money and still more money," he explained (if he needed to), "and to use the money I make for the good of my fellow man according to the dictates of my conscience." He did both. That outlook indicates why his firm retained, at least until 1889, most of the characteristics of an individual capitalist even after he reorganized it as a trust in 1882. Given his highly personalized pattern of behavior prior to 1882, it seems probable that he was being both candid and accurate in denying any great revolutionary intent when he changed to the trust form. "I discovered something that made a new world," he told upper-class associates in later years, "and I did not know it at the time."

Morgan, on the other hand, was unquestionably conscious of broadening the outlook of the individual capitalist into the inclusive, corporate view that later came to be called financial capitalism. He even dreamed about the horrors of competition. Even so, the persistence of the *Weltanschauung* of laissez faire was clearly revealed in the nature, as well as the failure, of Morgan's first effort in 1888–1889 to coordinate and consolidate the railroads. It was a gentleman's agreement that quickly broke down in a renewed outburst of competitive mistrust and self-interest. For though they were using the form, and exhibiting some of its mature characteristics, the railroads were not yet thinking within the framework of a political economy defined and based on the institution of the corporation. In a remark that revealed the difference, Leland Stanford boasted in 1887 that as corporation president he kept "only such papers as, in case I never returned, I cared that other people might see." And like Morgan's early attempt, most other efforts at combination or coordination collapsed when one member saw a chance for a coup in the market.

Though the corporate holding company was making its appearance and would ultimately dominate the political economy with a different outlook and pattern of organization, the spirit of laissez faire remained supreme through the 1880s and well into the 1890s. Whether offered by Supreme Court justices or artists, academic philosophers or crusading reformers, and varied and clashing though they often were, the major intellectual and political testaments of the time originated within that *Weltanschauung*. One of the most striking and influential statements was the work of Justice Stephen Johnson Field, who had lived a typical career of laissez-faire individualism (including a sojourn on the frontier) before being appointed to the Supreme Court by President Lincoln.

Field recognized very clearly the central importance of the market place as the mechanism for adjusting the conflicts of self-interest between the many units of private property. Competition in the market place produced individual well-being and the greatest happiness for the greatest number. Field's objective was to strengthen that institution without undercutting the principles of laissez faire by going back to mercantilism and thereby reintroducing the idea of social property. He stressed the "privileges and immunities *which of right belong to the citizens of all free governments*." Once a state legislature established a unilateral right to regulate railroad rates, he angrily pointed out, the door was open for fixing "the prices of everything from a calico gown to a city mansion." Had he stopped there, Field could be dismissed as a monomaniac on the subject of private property, as a man who would tolerate no limits on its rights. But as he had indicated during his tenure in the California courts in upholding the rights of Chinese immigrants, he honored the ideals of laissez faire as well as defended its materialistic base. He was at once sophisticated and dedicated, and understood that the market place was going to be regulated by some agency for the simple reason that it did not work either automatically or perfectly.

Field's strategy was to define the market place as a national rather than a state problem and then insist that the due process clause of the 14th amendment gave the Supreme Court the power and the duty to review all restrictions on private property. That meant that the market place of the system would remain one unit instead of becoming a wild and uneconomic conglomeration of many different (state) market places. It also meant that regulation would be milder because of the weaker position of the reformers in the Congress. His first victory came when the New York high court accepted his dissenting argument against Justice Waite in the Munn Case as its majority view. In a test (*In re Jacobs*, 1885) of the state's right to regulate the atrocious conditions of cigar manufacturing, New York judges explicitly raised the specter of a return to mercantilist doctrine on social property. Such ideas—"from those ages when governmental prefects supervised . . . the rate of wages, the price of food, and a large range of other affairs"—were declared archaic. They disturbed the "normal adjustments" of the market place, and also violated the due process clause which protected "personal liberty and private property."

During the next two years, moreover, even Waite agreed that the "right of continuous transportation from one end of the country to the other is essential," and admitted that the corporation was entitled to "equal protection" as an individual under the due process clause. Field's triumph was announced by his ideological colleague, Justice Rufus W. Peckham, in 1889 with a direct reference to Waite's earlier citation of English mercantilist law: "no reason exists for . . . [going] back to the seventeenth or eighteenth century ideas of paternal government." It was further consolidated in 1897, in the *Allgeyer* v. *Louisiana* case, when the court stressed the "right of the citizen to be free in the enjoyment of all his faculties" and tied that principle to the "pursuit of happiness" clause in the Declaration of Independence.

Another brick in the ideological monument to laissez faire was made with straw from the natural sciences. Because it was a relatively obvious and easy comparison to make, the system was often explained and favorably presented as the human counterpart of the Darwinian mechanism of evolution in the world of nature. Competition produced the changes that were necessary for survival and desirable for progress. Most arguments of this kind were taken second-hand from the English adaptation provided by Herbert Spencer and showed little imagination or subtlety. But since it was often presented in an articulate and stylish form, this pseudo-theory often gives the impression of having established something of a monopoly in the ideological market of the time.

While some entrepreneurs like Carnegie and a few railroad executives appear to have thought at the time about their operations within this framework, the Darwinist analogy was actually used by intellectuals, reformers, and some capitalists more in talking about the system either to explain their actions after the fact or to place invidious connotations of the jungle upon its protagonists. Even Carnegie, as in his law of the surplus, relied more upon the ideas of classical economists such as Adam Smith, Jean Baptiste Say, and John Stuart Mill. And a closer reading of such supposedly pure Spencerians and Darwinists as the Yale sociologist William Graham Sumner suggests that Adam Smith's principles of self-interest and an expanding market place provided the muscle which moved a face of Darwinism and Spencerianism.

Laissez-faire intellectuals and ideologists relied more upon their own resources in confronting the moral dilemma of their system. Whether it appeared as the dichotomy between the private morality of the individual and his ethics as an entrepreneur in the market place, in the fantastic discrepancies and inequities in economics and politics, or in the treatment of the freed Negro, this moral issue became the central theme of the major writers of the Age of Laissez Nous Faire. Though displaying quite different styles and perspectives, and using radically different subject matter, Mark Twain and Henry James were alike in accepting this challenge.

FUNDAMENTAL CRITICISM FROM WITHIN THE SYSTEM

While a great deal can be, and has been, read into James's novels beyond what he put there, it is clear that his central theme is the abuse of human (and American) values by the protagonists of the age. "I see what you are *not* making," he cried out in 1905, "oh, what you are so vividly not!" Laissez faire had been "a colossal recipe for the creating of arrears" that future generations would have to pay—if they were left the intellectual, moral, and physical resources. Thus James agreed with Melville on the failure of a romantic or transcendental definition of self to supply a viable standard even for coming to terms with reality, let alone for living in a society with other human beings.

While James never offered a formal philosophical or programmatic resolution of the problem, he defined and stated the issue in unmistakable terms and with great courage, sophistication, and style. The greatness of James lies in his refusal to retreat. He stood his ground even though he realized that the coming corporation order would institutionalize the very individual characteristics that appalled and worried him so deeply. Often misunderstood as a running away, his long sojourns in Europe were voyages in search of perspective on America: "I have always my eyes on my native land."

And despite more than a half-century of further, and supposedly more brilliant, inquiry, neither sociologists, psychologists, nor historians have added much to the analysis and insights that James provided in *The American Scene* (1907). The extremely perceptive novelist Wright Morris is probably correct: the reason Americans prefer analyses by foreign aristocrats like the Frenchman Alexis de Tocqueville or the Englishman Lord Bryce is that James "is simply too much for us." He is not mildly critical while holding out the assurance that everything will turn out just dandy. James is devastating while warning us that there is no universal law of happy endings.

America had matured under laissez faire, he insisted, as the creation of a business approach to life. Hence its men were "thoroughly obvious products of the business-block, the business-block unmitigated by any other influence definite enough to name." As for the women, he realized that by defining emancipation in terms of becoming the equals of men, they were very apt to define themselves out of their only existence. Granting the liberty of laissez faire and the western frontier, he refused to pretend that it was a meaningful or worthwhile end in itself. Instead, he recognized that such liberty produced an inability to face solitude, let alone seek it as a necessary part of human life. Yet neither did it create a society based on a sense of community. The pursuit of the kind of freedom found on the frontier would lead—if it had not already led—to a situation in which the "freedom to grow up blighted" would be "the only freedom in store for the smaller fry of future generations." By itself, that insight does more to account for later juvenile delinquency among upper-income families than 99 per cent of modern explanations.

James was even too much for his admirers. Edith Wharton, who wrote of the moral decay in the new industrialists and financial capitalists, and Willa Cather, who shifted the locale of the drama to the prairie, ultimately retreated to an earlier and more simplified world. That was where Mark Twain began, but he moved in the other direction, *toward* the courage and insight of James. In his first books, such as *Tom Sawyer* and *Huckleberry Finn*, Twain preferred to "light off to the territories" (always with another man, not a woman), or to drift down the river to a romanticized version of the old south's corporate society. And William Howells too, whatever his horror and dismay over the results of laissez faire, defined his solution in terms of Silas Lapham, a traditional businessman whose personal and market-place code happily coincided. Yet in another sense both Howells and Twain went further than James and to some degree reasserted the ideal of a Christian commonwealth in secular logic and rhetoric. In the end, however, their limited socialism was of the heart only, rather than of the heart *and* the mind *and* the will.

But Twain's later story of *The Tragedy of Pudd'nhead Wilson* does confront the moral dilemma just as effectively as James. He first denies his protagonist the chance to go off down the river or into the west. Thus confined—and that refusal to duck off into the frontier was a great triumph for Twain—the issue is presented in terms of relations between the white man and the Negro. Twain never really answered the challenge, at least not by presenting a direct solution. But what he did may have been more significant: he said that the idea of total liberty to pursue happiness was a myth. All men were in effect slaves to each other, and the important thing was to recognize this truth so that the slavery could be defined in human and creative terms.

At the end of the book, Twain's protagonist remarks that it was wonderful to see America confront and grapple with this crucial issue, but that it would have been more wonderful to have missed the encounter. By floating down the river or scampering off to the territories, America had evaded the central question. It took moral courage for a man who loved his country as much as Twain to admit this to himself and then declare it to the public. In passing the judgment, Twain was also implying a momentum toward some catastrophe. That pattern of thought became increasingly evident after 1880 as conservatives no less than reformers persistently argued that social violence and chaos would result unless the imbalances and malfunctioning of the laissez-faire system were corrected.

A contributor to the *Atlantic Monthly* in 1882 wrote that America's "happy immunity from those social diseases which are the danger and the humiliation of Europe is passing away." And no doubt thinking of such outbreaks of violence as the Haymarket Massacre of 1886 in Chicago and other urban riots, a local Kentucky politician fretted that "the times are strangely out of joint. . . . The rich grow richer, the poor become poorer; the nation trembles." The same either-or theme is at the heart of Henry George's power-ful analysis of the paradox of *Progress and Poverty*, which became a best-seller in the 1880s. Desperately concerned over the decline of democracy, and aware of the "widespread feeling of unrest and brooding revolution," George concluded that the tendency to barba-rism "is an increasing one." Ignatius Donnelly, a leader of the agrar-ians, emphasized the same danger of "terrible social convulsions." So did Henry Demarest Lloyd, a newspaper writer who became a reform (and ultimately a radical) publicist. But conservatives like Presidents Harrison and Grover Cleveland commented on the same possibility, as did Senator George F. Edmunds of Vermont, Federal Judge Gresham, and William T. Harris, who was national commissioner of education and an influential writer.

REFORMERS ATTEMPT TO SUSTAIN THE SYSTEM

This broad consensus affords an insight into the upsurge of social and political agitation that climaxed the Age of Laissez Nous Faire. However haltingly, and despite great mutual suspicions and bitter conflicts of interest, the conservative and the liberal defenders of laissez faire cooperated in a belated and unsuccessful effort to save that system. Other conservatives, along with their enemies the radi-cals, agitated each in his own way for a new system. In the crisis, of course, all conservatives and liberals stood fast against the radicals, but the differences within the coalition against the left provide the fundamental explanation of the political ferment of the era.

As one whose idea of taxing the unearned increment of land values had its roots in physiocratic doctrine, George made no sweeping attack on private property. "We declare the true purpose of govern-ment," he explained in 1886, "to be the maintenance of that sacred right of property which gives to everyone opportunity to employ his labor and security that he shall enjoy its fruits." He argued in classic laissez-faire logic that the decline in propertyholding would create a mass of men "who feel no direct interest in the control of government." That would facilitate the rise of demagogues who would destroy political democracy. George was offering a way of maintaining the circulation of property to avoid such devolution. It appealed to a number of middle-class property owners as well as laborers, and for a time undercut the strength of the currency inflation movement. While George was not a radical in the sense of attacking the system itself, his program to purify and thereby preserve it was both extensive and rigorous. It is very misleading and rather supercilious to call such men (including the Populists) either backward or reactionary. They were vigorous reformers acting on the first principles of laissez faire.

The fulfillment of the laissez-faire labor movement came with the subsequent organization of the American Federation of Labor and the Knights of Labor. In opening its membership to all but a tiny minority of so-called workers (bankers, lawyers, doctors, and men of the liquor trade were excluded), to the unskilled as well as the skilled, and to Negroes along with the whites, the Knights offered moral leadership of a high order. Accepting the principles of laissez faire, leaders like Grand Master Workman Terence V. Powderly recognized the reality of class conflict and labored to end it. His opposition to the wage system was not an attack on laissez faire; it was merely a kind of hard-headed idealism about the market place.

He argued that an interim improvement in working conditions through various reforms such as an eight-hour day and the arbitration of disputes with capital would prepare the way for the worker to become a property owner in the market place through the organization of producer cooperatives. Far from being an adaptation of socialism, the Powderly program was a premature and fuzzy vision of later profit-sharing plans. As the basis of his ultimately successful competition with the Knights, Samuel Gompers offered a more routine laissez-faire objective: accept the system and get as much as possible within it. Concentrating on the skilled elite of the labor force, his early views and programs developed wholly within the assumptions of individual private property and the market place.

Despite certain indications to the contrary, the agrarian protest movement also developed within them. Like many vigorous reformers who operate within a given system, the Populists accentuated certain weaknessess of the existing order. Some of its leaders combined the prejudices and demagoguery of the Jacksonians with others borrowed from aristocratic bigots in the east. Thus foreigners and Jews were attacked for irrelevant reasons. Yet much criticism of the Populists on these counts is grossly exaggerated and distorted because it derives from the narrow and anemic modern definition of tolerance. Hence it misses or obscures the important point that the target of their anger was the wholly real malfunctioning of the system itself. Jews and immigrants became symbols of that failure; and though the syllogism was mistaken and unfair, it was nevertheless quite a different matter from attacking these groups as such.

Farmers caught the full impact of the declining *rate* of economic growth that became apparent in the late 1880s. They observed the ground rules of laissez faire, applied the new technology, used the new machinery, specialized in regional crops, and produced more—yet their share of the system's income decreased. Freight rates and other industrial prices fell about 67 per cent between 1865 and 1896, but farm prices dropped about 75 per cent. During the same years, moreover, the exportable surplus of wheat jumped 16 per cent. And by 1885, even the Federal land commissioner acknowledged "that the public domain was being made the prey of unscrupulous speculation and the worst forms of land monopoly through systematic frauds."

Farmers were bedeviled by the patent racket (as in barbed-wire fencing), losing money on cows as well as on wheat and corn, and reduced to making chattel mortgages at up to 35 per cent interest to secure capital for machinery and land that in some states was doubling in price in less than a decade. With considerable justification, they reacted negatively to supercilious lectures from easterners whose knowledge of dirt came from formal gardens and croquet lawns or from city parks and summer estates. In an analogy with colonialism, the farmer accurately charged that a sizable share of his agricultural production ended up as locally undistributed profits that went east to banks and other absentee landowners. Farm tenancy was rising steadily, as was the consolidation of holdings into large farms. Even those great individualist craftsmen of the age, the cowboys, resorted to strikes in Texas. And their will finally broken by a run of bad weather in the late 1880s, thousands of farmers in Kansas and Nebraska gave up their land.

As that reverse migration of the failures suggests, the Populist movement was in large measure an uprising of *surviving* farmers against existing leadership. However tenuously, they still held on to their land. Cleveland's pious invocations in behalf of "a healthy and free competition" struck them as arrogant nonsense, and they equated the Republicans with Carnegie. Beginning with a revival of the Southern Farmers Alliance (it had originated in Texas in 1875 as a protest against absentee capital in ranching), the agitation spread rapidly into the north and west. Employing the ideas and invoking the names of Jefferson and Taylor, Jackson and Benton, the farmers developed a program that consolidated the general antagonism against railroads and other giant entrepreneurs.

Conservatives as well as reformers began to act. After extended hearings around the country in 1886–1887, a Senate committee reported "that upon no public question are the people so nearly unanimous as upon the proposition that Congress should undertake in some way the regulation of interstate commerce." The Interstate Commerce Act of 1887 was the result. Avowedly a serious compromise effort to adjust and stabilize the framework of the market place within the assumptions of laissez faire, it attempted to remove existing abuses and prevent future inequities in the railroad system.

During the next three years, moreover, four agrarian states were admitted to the union, more funds were provided for agricultural science and education, and a cabinet post was added for agriculture. Rapidly gaining strength and confidence, the farmers began, as in their St. Louis meeting of 1889, to work out an alliance with the Grange, the Greenbackers, and some elements of labor. Before their full program was settled, but as their power was becoming apparent in the enactment of laws against trusts and monopoly in southern and western states, men like Senator George F. Edmunds of Vermont and George F. Hoar of Massachusetts, who feared grave social disorders if the system were not put back in balance, joined with reformers to write and pass the misnamed Sherman Anti-Trust Act of 1890. Whatever its weaknesses (it did not offer definitions of trust or monopoly, for example), and however it was emasculated and abused in later years, the law was one of the major symbols of the fulfillment of the Age of Laissez Nous Faire. It represented as law the essential principle of that *Weltanschauung*—competition throughout a national market place.

Populists also demanded broad educational assistance, for the south as well as for other sections, and free trade to expand their exports and strengthen competition in the home market for manufactures. They also proposed a commodity credit plan that would regulate marketing throughout a given crop-year and facilitate the sale of surpluses while giving the farmer short-term loans. And in their most dramatic, and generally misunderstood, proposal, they called for the nationalization of the commercial arteries of the market place. Far from becoming agrarian socialists, the Populists were in this plan to nationalize the railroad, telegraph, and telephone systems merely carrying the logic of laissez faire to its classic fulfillment. Given the absolutely essential role of an open and equitable market place in the theory and practice of laissez faire, they concluded that the only way to guarantee the cornerstone of the system was by taking it out of the hands of *any* enterpreneur. "It is simply a battle for liberty," explained Populist presidential candidate James B. Weaver of Iowa in 1892. "Having secured the power we will work out the details." While some of the reformers ultimately became true radicals, the movement itself was radical only in the sense that it reasserted and attempted to act on the basic axioms of the existing order.

The party's decision to endorse William Jennings Bryan of Nebraska for President in 1896 underscored its fundamental attachment to laissez faire and the existing political system. So did their argument that the unlimited coinage of silver at 16 to 1 would create more economic opportunity; this was the same kind of inflationary logic that antislavery radicals like Thad Stevens had used in the 1860s. Citing Jackson and Benton as reliable guides, Bryan reiterated the axioms of laissez faire and infused them with the righteous emotional ardor of the early Jacksonians. "We say to you," he thundered in his famous Cross of Gold Speech, "that you have made the definition of a businessman too limited in its application." By Bryan's criteria, almost everyone was a businessman. "The man who is employed for wages . . . the attorney in a country town . . . the merchant at the cross-roads . . . the farmer . . . the miners . . . are as much business men [as others]. We come to speak for this broader class of business men."

Bryan and the Populists were attempting to restore and sustain the system of laissez faire in the same way that Jackson had made clear he would maintain the framework of the system. Jackson had attacked South Carolina planters and New England speculators; Bryan assaulted eastern industrialists and New York financiers. But having defeated the mercantilists by splitting the shield of social property with the sword of private property, the true believers of laissez faire found themselves naked on the battlefield. Their attempt to use liberty and private property to attack private property and liberty was doomed from the outset. Such proposals as the nationalization of the communications network appalled the privates in their own ranks. Only a new and at least in part more social basis of criticism could make any headway against the power of laissez faire.

THE PERSISTENT DILEMMAS OF EXPANDING THE MARKET PLACE

This became apparent as the advocates of a reformed laissez faire confronted the dilemmas of their system in foreign policy and philosophy. Since the continuing expansion of the market place was the *sine qua non* of laissez faire, President Rutherford Hayes explained in 1877, the "long commercial depression . . . directed attention to the subject" in a concerted manner. For that matter, some entrepreneurs had already been talking to Grant's Secretary of State Hamilton Fish about foreign policy as a way "to relieve business distress." Some companies had begun to expand into Canada in 1870, and by 1887 their total was 48. Others were increasing their holdings, or entering the market in China or, like the Singer Sewing Machine Company, moving into Great Britain and other European nations.

Politicians responded quickly. Persistently reminded of the importance of expansion and the necessity of government assistance by such men as Charles Dalton of the textile industry and H. K. Slayton, a dry goods merchant, Senator John T. Morgan spoke for a growing consensus of congressmen as early as 1882. "Our home market is not equal to the demands of our producing and manufacturing classes and to the capital which is seeking employment. . . . We must enlarge the field of our traffic," he concluded in a typical either-or warning, "or stop the business of manufacturing just where it is." Numerous congressmen offered similar analyses and spoke increasingly of China as "our India," and of the nations to the south as "twenty American Indies, if only we shall do our duty toward grasping their trade." This explicit analogy with Britain's empire is one of the most revealing aspects of the mature foreign policy of laissez faire.

As for India itself, American attitudes revealed the steadily growing interest in overseas economic expansion as a solution for domestic troubles. Reporting that he had received "hundreds" of inquiries from American firms, one State Department official in India urged his countrymen to exploit the opportunities for "great" and "huge" profits. And though challenged by Russian products, the Standard Oil Company dominated the oil market through the 1890s. In Africa, meanwhile, American businessmen and officials struggled to establish the principle of equal opportunity. Concluding that it was "futility" itself to negotiate individually with the empire mother countries, and an "abdication of present duty" to acquiesce in European control of the continent, American leaders like President Chester A. Arthur and Secretary of State Frederick T. Frelinghuysen made vigorous efforts to secure "equal commercial rights" in the Congo. Concerned with "our business men who are suffering from the depressed condition of our export and import trade," they won the basic objective in the Berlin Conference of 1884–1885. Even though the opportunity was not immediately exploited, both the general outward push and the specific policy provided a revealing preview of the evolution of a vigorous open door policy a decade later.

Viewing the navy as the key to such expansion, Congress began to debate a large construction program and in 1884 established the Naval War College. Senator John F. Miller of California, Chairman of the Senate Foreign Relations Committee, provided a neat summary of the outlook. "The time has come when . . . new markets are necessary to be found in order to keep our factories running. Here lies to the south of us our India. . . . If we reach out and attempt to secure this great prize of commerce we shall excite the jealousy of other peoples, and we shall be led, perhaps, into complications, which we shall extricate ourselves from if we are prepared to meet our enemies." And Cleveland's Secretary of the Treasury, John C. Carlisle, constantly reiterated the argument that "prosperity . . . largely depends" on the ability to sell "surplus products in foreign markets at remunerative prices."

While all laissez-faire leaders wanted the markets, some of them saw dangers in such commercial empire. Men like Cleveland, Bryan, and liberal Republicans such as Carl Schurz understood that the dilemma of empire was in a real sense *the* dilemma of laissez faire. Without the markets, so their logic and interests told them, depressions and class conflict would follow; but getting the markets would lead to moral degradation, big government, and militarism at home. "It *is* possible," Schurz cried out again and again, "to demoralize the constitutional system and to infuse a dangerous element of arbitrary power into the government without making it a monarchy in form and name."

Down to the spring of 1897, such men effected an ambivalent and unstable resolution of their dilemma. They blocked formal colonial annexation of Hawaii while taking a militant stand against any extension of Britain's sphere of colonial influence in South America, yet they also retained effective control of Hawaii and used the American navy (steadily being built up to modern battleship strength) to further American economic objectives in Brazil and the Caribbean. While magnificently outraged by the coup staged with the assistance of the navy by American nabobs in Hawaii (their revolution was a product of the same kind of colonization that had won Texas), and though refusing the resulting bid for annexation, Cleveland nevertheless accepted the American predominance that the revolution established and did nothing to return the native rulers to power.

But perhaps the most revealing illustration of laissez-faire expansion came in Cleveland's successful armed (naval) intervention in a Brazilian revolution in 1894–1895 that threatened America's developing trade with that country. Vigorous pressure for action from such firms as Standard Oil, and W. S. Crossman and Brothers, intensified Secretary of State Gresham's already strong fears that the depression would cause a social upheaval, and brought prompt and effective countermeasures. Replacing a naval officer who was less than enthusiastic about the undertaking, Gresham and Cleveland then used the navy to check the rebels. They kept the American task force on duty in Brazilian waters through the height of the yellowfever season to prevent any renewed outbreaks.

Cleveland's subsequent vigorous support for Venezuela in its boundary dispute with Great Britain should be judged against the background of the Brazilian episode. Taken together, they made it clear that the positive, assertive side of the Monroe Doctrine had become fully ascendant. "To-day," cried Secretary of State Richard Olney (Gresham having died), "the United States is practically sovereign on this continent, and its fiat is law upon the subjects to which it confines its interposition." Cleveland added that "we have determined [that the territory in question] of right belongs to Venezuela." In a move that gave added and unmistakable meaning to its earlier apology over Civil War disputes, England backed down.

In the case of the Cuban Revolution which erupted in 1895, however, the exponents of laissez faire found it more difficult to further economic expansion without falling into the quicksand of colonialism. Cleveland's strategy was "pacification of the island" under a weakened Spanish rule that would safeguard the extensive American interests in the island and facilitate their continued growth. But the difficulties of this approach ultimately involved the leaders of the new corporation order in the first of the many wars they found it necessary to fight. Perhaps even more than those who led the agrarian protest movement (many of whom favored such expansion), the advocates of laissez faire who stood out to the end against the growing drive for territorial and administrative empire represented the finest fulfillment of that *Weltanschauung*.

As in many ways the symbol of the best that laissez faire could produce, William James offered leadership in the anti-imperialist movement, made fundamental contributions to the theory of individualist psychology, and offered an appropriate statement of the laissez-faire outlook in his pragmatic philosophy. Along with his friend, William Graham Sumner, James pushed the axioms of his age as far as they would go. On the one hand, his basic assumption that the world is chaos, and that the mind serves only to guide the will, led him to attack science and to assert the anti-intellectual claim that contemplation was unhealthy. By that standard he proclaimed that "truth is what happens to an idea." Hence the "cash values of ideas" was their final determinant. And his appropriately "tough-minded" man, who could survive and flourish in such a cosmos, exhibited many traits of the driving entrepreneur, or what later social psychologists have called the authoritarian personality. As James implied in some of his own comments, this side of his pragmatism offered a way to get rich and reform the world in one's own image.

"We seem set free," he proclaimed, "to use our theoretical as well as our practical faculties . . . to get the world into a better shape, and all with a good conscience."

On the other hand, James realized that what he called the "bitch goddess SUCCESS" did not always let the truth happen to the best ideas. Hence he had to admit that error, or evil, did exist. Drawing upon the transcendentalist version of the Romantic Movement's assertion that the individual could separate truth from evil through one of what James called the varieties of religious experience, he was then able to offer the individual a way out of the dilemma. Yet in society at large, and particularly in foreign affairs, James understood that violence or war was the usual way that truth happened to an idea. His answer—find a moral equivalent for war—was a magnificent and moving plea against imperial expansion and its consequences. But it also revealed the central weakness of laissez faire; for war was a social phenomenon, and James was attempting to resolve it on an individual basis. The circle could not be squared.

As one of James's major opponents who saw the danger of the romantic and transcendental conception of the individual, Josiah Royce argued that men had to commit themselves to something bigger than themselves. Such idealism was essential; otherwise the "cash value of ideas" would always win out. Yet he also understood that idealism could be the spur to the most virulent kind of aggression. His solution, which he never thoroughly worked out, was a creative regionalism in which men could work together to build a truly human society. But both James and Royce were spokesmen of a passing era. The men who took charge of the effort to resolve the dilemmas of laissez faire were aware that it had to be done around some idea of a corporate system, yet they were determined to avoid the pit of social property as well as the pendulum of class war. Their proposals, and the momentum of their institutions, created a system based on the political economy of the large corporation and a more active government charged with the task of maintaining some check on the increased power of private property.

The Age of Corporation Capitalism

1882–

> *The modern stock corporation is a social and economic institution that touches every aspect of our lives; in many ways it is an institutional expression of our way of life. . . . Indeed, it is not inaccurate to say that we live in a corporate society.*
>
> William T. Gossett, Ford Motor Company, 1957

> *Lords Temporal rarely if ever make good Lords Spiritual.*
>
> Adolf A. Berle, Jr., 1959

CHAPTER ONE

The Triumph of the Rising Order

Independent capital persists as a force, but the units that compose it melt like bubbles in a stream.

William J. Ghent, 1903

A man who won't meet his men half-way is a God-damn fool.

Mark Hanna, 1894

Mr. Bryan said just one thing in his big [Cross of Gold] speech . . . that strikes me as true. He said that farmers and workingmen are business men just as much as bankers and lawyers. Well, that's true. I like that.

Mark Hanna, 1897

Mr. McKinley. . . . undertook to pool interests in a general trust into which every interest should be taken, more or less at its own valuation, and whose mass should, under his management, create efficiency.

Henry Adams, 1918

We have a record of conquest, colonization and expansion unequalled by any people in the Nineteenth Century. We are not to be curbed now.

Henry Cabot Lodge, 1895

The extraordinary, because direct and not merely theoretical or sentimental, interest of the United States in the Cuban situation can not be ignored. . . . Not only are our citizens largely concerned in the ownership of property and in the industrial and commercial ventures . . . but the chronic condition of trouble . . . causes disturbance in the social and political conditions of our own peoples. . . . A continuous irritation within our own borders injuriously affects the normal functions of business, and tends to delay the condition of prosperity to which this country is entitled.

The United States to Spain, 1897

It is frequently asserted . . . that the output of factories working at full capacity is much greater than the domestic market can possibly consume, and it seems to be conceded that every year we shall be confronted with an increasing surplus of manufactured goods for sale in foreign markets if American operatives and artisans are to be kept employed the year round. The enlargement of foreign consumption of the products of our mills and workshops has, therefore, become a serious problem of statesmanship as well as of commerce.

The Department of State, 1898

Dependent solely upon local business we should have failed years ago. We were forced to extend our markets and to seek for export trade.

John D. Rockefeller, 1899

In the field of trade and commerce we shall be the keen competitors of the richest and greatest powers, and they need no warning to be assured that in that struggle, we shall bring the sweat to their brows.

Secretary of State John Hay, 1899

THE NATURE AND THE POWER OF THE LARGE CORPORATION

Powerful and productive in the world of things, and capable of sustaining and strengthening the oligarchies that created them, the large corporations (and their leaders) dominated American history from 1896 until past the middle of the 20th century. In its industrial and financial forms, the corporation transformed the fears of men like Madison and Jefferson, and the expectations of others like Seward, into a reality that crossed every economic, political, and social boundary, affected every branch of government, and permeated every aspect of the individual citizen's life. Ostensibly created to facilitate the rational and efficient production of goods to meet the needs of men, the corporation (like the sorcerer's apprentice) ultimately began creating in men the demand for goods they had never seen, observed in use, or even known they needed. And in many cases the original judgment had proved correct—they did not need them.

Undertaking a shopping trip in pursuit of an item first seen on the television screen produced by a corporation that very probably also provided the air time for the program, a housewife in the 1950s could easily have put on a dress made of synthetic fibers made by a corporation that exercised a large influence in the corporation that built the car (or bus) that she used for transportation. The insurance company that underwrote her trip may very well have financed the car itself, the garage in which it was parked, and the city streets upon which she drove. The gasoline that powered the car might have been produced by a corporation that could easily have had some share in the supermarket where she shopped. If not, the vegetables she purchased could have been grown on a contract farm owned by the corporation that also made the detergent or soap with which she washed the dishes from which the vegetables were eaten.

Even if he were, superficially, an independent businessman, her husband was still more intimately involved with these same, or similar, corporations. Most of the couple's entertainment was provided by corporations, as was the news they read in their newspapers and magazines, or heard and viewed over the television set that provided the starting point in the entire web of relationships. The political and economic issues in this news were defined largely by the policies and the programs of the corporations and their leaders. As man and wife, their own efforts to organize or participate in other functional groups that attempted to check or balance this power of the corporation were at best productive of little more than occasional minor victories, and more generally of an uninspiring and enervating stalemate that left the large corporation in its position of predominance.

The couple's fears for the future were centered on one of three major issues: upon their inability to break out of the pattern of installment living produced, packaged, and promoted by the advertising and public relations adjunct of the corporations; upon the possibility that the corporation economy might falter and flatten them along with its dividend payments; or upon the tension in foreign affairs that was very largely the result of the conflict between the expansion of those corporations and the opposition to them manifested by vigorous and militant rivals. With overseas direct investments of 29 billion dollars, sales of overseas agencies of 30 billion dollars (with an average profit of 15 per cent), and direct exports of between 15 and 20 billion dollars, the overseas economic empire of the United States in 1957 amounted to a total stake of twice the gross national product of Canada and was larger than the same total for the United Kingdom.

348 THE CONTOURS OF AMERICAN HISTORY

The problems of that empire provided most of the national head-lines in the 1950s, just as very similar foreign fears and antagonisms had greeted the new corporation system at the turn of the century. Writing in 1902 of *The Americanization of the World*, William Thomas Stead of England termed it the "greatest political, social, and commercial phenomenon of our times." "In the domestic life," echoed his countryman Fred Mackenzie in the London *Daily Mail*, "we have got to this: The average man rises in the morning from his New England sheets, he shaves with 'Williams' ' soap and a Yankee safety razor, pulls on his Boston boots over his socks from North Carolina, fastens his Connecticut braces, slips his Waltham or Waterbury watch in his pocket, and sits down to breakfast. There he congratulates his wife on the way her Illinois straight-front corset sets off her Massachusetts blouse, and he tackles his breakfast, where he eats bread made from prairie flour (possibly doctored at the special establishments on the lakes) . . . and a little Kansas City bacon. . . . The children are given 'Quaker' Oats. . . ."

"He rushes out. . . . [And] at his office, of course, everything is American. He sits on a Nebraskan swivel chair, before a Michigan roll-top desk, writes his letters on a Syracuse typewriter, signing them with a New York fountain pen, and drying them with a blot-ting-sheet from New England. The letter copies are put away in files manufactured in Grand Rapids. . . . At lunch-time he hast-ily swallows some cold roast beef that comes from the Mid-West cow . . . and then soothes his mind with a couple of Virginia ciga-rettes. To follow his course all day would be wearisome. But when evening comes he . . . finishes up with a couple of 'little liver pills' [that were] 'made in America.' "

Germans and Frenchmen revealed similar uneasiness about American expansion, and the high Russian newspaper *Novoye Vremya* expressed its concern by pointing specifically to the example of Great Britain. "Everything," it lamented, "proves that Great Britain is now practically dependent upon the United States, and for all international intents and purposes may be considered to be under an American protectorate. . . . The United States has but just entered upon the policy of exploiting the protected kingdom." While such estimates were obviously exaggerated as of 1900, the reality moved ever closer to them throughout the 20th century in the Western Hemisphere, in Europe, and throughout the rest of the world. Very candidly, and with considerable forethought, America pushed its way into the struggle for economic empire between 1895 and 1898. This involvement was dramatized and extended by the war with Spain, and in 1899 and 1900 culminated in the famous Open Door Notes which demanded equal opportunity for America's tremendous economic power, a weapon that the nation's leaders felt confident would produce world economic supremacy without the limitations and dangers of old-fashioned colonialism.

Likewise, even as the nation emerged from the bloody strife and suffering of the depression of the 1890s, the inclusive nature and extensive power of the corporation was clearly revealed at home. Its triumph established a new political economy, a system of organized and controlled interrelationships and influence that was developed and put in operation during the presidential campaign of 1896. Whereas laissez faire had required at least two elections to establish its primacy under Jackson, the leaders of the age of the corporation scored an impressive victory in their first test. Organized and managed by Mark Hanna, one of the new order's more perceptive and effective spokesmen, this victory established the modern pattern of politics as an expensive, extensive, and centrally coordinated, high-pressure effort.

Despite the flamboyance and extremism of the rhetoric on both sides (itself a reminder of the campaign of 1828), and the emotional ardor of his supporters, Bryan never seriously approached victory in the election of 1896. The rise of the large industrial corporation had given the urban manufacturing and commercial centers and their spheres of influence in the surrounding agrarian areas a predominance in the political economy that would never be successfully challenged by a purely and narrowly laissez-faire interest party such as the Democrats were under Bryan. For that matter, many western farmers responded to the Republican argument that overseas markets for surpluses would solve their particular problem while bringing general prosperity. The real issue was not whether the new order would triumph, but who was to control and direct it; that is, how it was to maintain an internal balance, accomplish the necessary domestic and overseas expansion, and in what way meet and master its political, economic, and philosophic competitors at home and abroad.

With considerable exaggeration, the beginnings of the age of the corporation might be dated from the first textile-mill town (complete with minister and teacher supplied on contract by the owner) established in New England early in the 19th century. But the foundations of the new system were actually started by the post-Civil War operations of men like James J. Hill in railroads and associated enterprises, the integrated organization of the Cambodia Iron Works near Pittsburgh, and the development of the Rockefeller and Carnegie empires during the 1880s. After the adoption of favorable holding-company legislation by Delaware, Maryland, and New Jersey during the same decade and the concurrent consolidation of the House of Morgan, the rise of the large life insurance companies and such firms as the American Telephone and Telegraph Company made it clear that the corporation had moved rapidly into a position of predominance, a position that has never been challenged in a fundamental way.

None of the early firms, however large, revealed all the basic features of the corporation either in their specific organization and operations or in their impact upon the society at large. And in the case of Carnegie, of course, the overall characteristics represented a culmination of the laissez-faire entrepreneur. For this very reason, however, he and Rockefeller, along with Hill, offer apt illustrations of how the corporation economy emerged as a function or consequence of laissez-nous-faire competition. But each of these enterprises did develop one or more of the essential aspects of the corporation that enabled it as an institution to create a distinctive new order once it came to control the key elements of the system. While the secondary characteristics and indirect ramifications of the corporation are numerous, even today not wholly known, its central features are clear.

Beyond the obvious fact of size, of authority and power as *one* unit over the rest of the economy, perhaps the main element introduced by the large corporation was a fundamental change in ideas about economic activity itself. Laissez-faire operators and spokesmen thought of the market place as a scene of individualized and somewhat random activity. But the spokesmen and directors of the new order, though they accepted the traditional premise of private property and the vital role and necessity of an expanding market place, defined economic activity as making up an interrelated *system*. It was not just the sum of innumerable parts operating in an essentially casual and *ad hoc* fashion. The political economy had to be extensively planned, controlled, and coordinated through the institution of the large corporation if it was to function in any regular, routine, and profitable fashion.

This view developed in part from the narrow or interest drive of the corporation entrepreneurs to rationalize and control as much of the market place as possible—to make it *their* system. But it was soon generalized as the result of observation and reflection on broader issues. They concluded that Adam Smith's Hidden Hand was often so hidden that it failed to provide the guidance which should have prevented individual and general crises. Also, competition proved in practice to be inefficient, redundant, and wasteful. Finally, from being directly associated with both of these considerations, they grew more and more fearful that the end result of laissez faire would be economic breakdown and social revolution. "The panic of last year is nothing," warned Hill in 1894, "compared with the reign of terror that exists in the large centers. Business is at a standstill, and the people are becoming thoroughly aroused." Like the advocates of laissez faire, the corporation leaders feared social upheaval, but they provided a different answer to the question of how to avoid it. In their way, therefore, the proponents of a system based on the large corporation were capitalists who accepted, on the evidence of their own experience as well as their casual and distorted knowledge of his ideas, the analysis made by Karl Marx, and set about to prevent his prophecy of socialism and communism being fulfilled.

These broad ideas provided the background for understanding the nature and the ramifications of the corporation itself. It was and remains a form of organization designed to accumulate large amounts of capital, resources, and labor and apply them to the rational, planned conduct of economic activity through a division of labor and bureaucratic routine. Acting within this framework, corporation leaders directly and indirectly exerted several major influences on the political economy. They consolidated the main elements and processes of the economic system in a small number of giant firms. By the end of World War II (1947), for example, when the United States produced approximately 50 per cent of all manufactured output in the world, a mere 139 corporations owned 45 per cent of all manufacturing assets in the country. These behemoths further centralized power within their own group and within specific corporations. Such centralization meant that the rights of the participants (directors and managers, as well as stockholders) were limited in a hierarchical fashion so that control over many units might be maintained with a comparatively small investment and a few firms dominate the general consolidation of the political economy.

In striving to achieve their various objectives, corporation leaders produced two kinds of integrated organization. One was horizontal, pulling together a number of operations at the same stage of production or service. Its purpose was to control the market. The other was vertical, several levels of production (from raw materials to distribution) being acquired and coordinated for becoming independent of the market. In later years, particularly after World War I and the Great Crash of 1929, such power was extended even further as giants like the House of Morgan, Procter and Gamble, and insurance companies began to acquire and operate various real estate (including farm) holdings.

In all its manifold features and enterprises, and in finance as well as in industry, the corporation operated within an oligarchic framework. Individual propertyholders (today stockholders) no longer enjoyed the kind of direct authority they had wielded in the age of laissez faire. And the labor unions neither sought nor received such power in the area of basic investment or operational decisions. This separation of literal ownership from practical control became progressively greater during the 20th century. As it did so, some observers concluded that corporation leaders were no longer guided by the philosophy and ideology of private property, but had in effect become dehumanized managers who abstractly kept the system going for its own sake. Another argument maintained that the managers had become public servants driven only by a desire to create the good society.

In the narrowest sense, these interpretations overlook two relevant factors. Up to World War I, and even later in specific cases, a bloc of voting stock large enough to sway key decisions was often held by one or two individuals. And in subsequent years the evidence has suggested strongly that however small their personal holdings, the directors and managers who staff the corporation still *think* and *act* as though the firm belonged to them. In an even more fundamental way, they have continued to define the system created and ordered by the corporation as one based on private rather than on social property. A typical sector of the corporation economy— say the automobile industry—would be a different phenomenon if it were organized and operated as a socialized enterprise. Such features as built-in obsolescence, indifference to safety factors, and redundancy of design would be avoided. For that matter, automobile production might be cut back very sharply in favor of a social investment in modern public transportation systems.

Though it may seem strange in view of the later inefficiency of the corporation system, the drive for efficiency was one of the motives that powered the merger mania of the period between 1889 and 1903. Capitalized at 25 million, for example, the Illinois Steel Company of Chicago was organized with the claim of having a plant more efficient as well as larger than that of Carnegie. Rockefeller's Standard Oil Company abandoned the ambiguous partnership-trust form it had used after the reorganization of 1882 and became a gigantic holding company with clearly apparent corporate characteristics. And J. Pierpont Morgan successfully corralled the skittish and maverick railroad entrepreneurs in a consolidated and centralized railroad system in the east. "The purpose of this meeting," he bluntly told them, "is to cause the members of this association to no longer take the law into their own hands . . . as has been too much the practice heretofore. This is not elsewhere customary in civilized communities, and no good reason exists why such a practice should continue among railroads."

"Consolidation and combination are the order of the day," judged Walker Hill, president of the American Bankers Association in 1899; and the chief statistician of the Census Bureau verified this estimate in 1900. "A startling transformation" had occurred in the previous decade, he reported, one which "set at naught some of the time-honored maxims of political economy, which must readjust many of our social relations, and which may largely influence and modify the future legislation of Congress and the States." Joined by such men as August Belmont, and such firms as Lee, Higginson of Boston and Kuhn, Loeb of New York, Morgan's crusade for what he called a "community of interest" produced more than 300 consolidations between 1897 and 1903.

Morgan's own formation of the Gargantuan United States Steel Company symbolized the entire epoch, but the appearance of the

Amalgamated Copper Co., the American Tobacco Co., the Standard Distilling Co., the National Biscuit Co., the International Harvester Co., and the reorganization of the du Pont firm were just as important. And by 1900, the year after 1,028 firms had disappeared, the American Telephone and Telegraph Co. had become a $250 million corporation. Similar expansion and coordination completed the integration of such firms as Macy's, John Wanamaker's, and Woolworth's into the new political economy. Marshall Field and Sons exemplified the pattern with its wholesale purchasing, functional organization of the store, ownership of some supplying factories, and even in its benevolent creation of the Chicago Manual Training School.

THE CRISIS OF THE 1890S AND THE SPECTER OF CHAOS

Not only did the many business failures of the 1890s create circumstances favorable to such consolidation and centralization, but the crisis convinced most remaining doubters that laissez faire was unable to cope with the tensions and problems of mature industrialism. Beginning with Black Friday, the Panic of 1893 initiated an intense and double-cycle depression that lasted until 1898. Signifying the end of the easy investment opportunities and massive profits that had been provided since 1789 by the dramatic and once-over development of the continental west, and signifying also the completion of the basic steel, transportation, and power segments of the industrial economy, the depression of the 1890s profoundly shocked even the advocates of the new system.

Following upon the Haymarket Riot of 1886, the sequence of a general strike of Negro and white workers in New Orleans and bread riots and other disturbances throughout the south and the north reached a portentous peak of violence in the bloody and prolonged strike against Carnegie's Homestead plant in 1892. While willing to use troops in such emergencies, most capitalists realized that the economic system could not be operated on the basis of private and government soldiers maintaining production. Nor was the trouble limited to the east. Army units were also used during the same summer in the Utah copper strike. Then, coming after the depression had started, and seeming to verify the worst of the nightmares produced by the Homestead affair, the even more violent and extensive strike against the Pullman Company and the railroads in 1894 dramatized beyond any question the need for a new approach.

Though in many ways the culmination of the old 19th-century pattern of company towns originated by textile mills, the circum-scribed community and society founded and controlled by the Pullman Company was widely regarded before the upheaval as a model of, and for, industrial relations. More perceptive architects of the emerging corporation system such as Mark Hanna, the Ohio entrepreneur and politician, understood its weaknesses, but they did not immediately alter that general impression of the company. "Oh, hell! Model——!," he thundered to a group of industrialists and bankers. "Go and live in Pullman and find out." But most of his associates initially mistrusted him rather than the supposedly ideal solution to labor problems, and they did not begin to modify their opinions until the continuing crisis forced them to admit the need of a broader outlook. Hence their fears were further intensified by what they thought was a revolutionary march on Washington by Coxey's Army. The army was actually a rather pathetic and motley band of unemployed men who wanted relief rather than revolution.

Already prone to interpret such events in either-or terms, however, American leaders responded to the economic depression and its asso-ciated social unrest by intensifying their efforts to formulate ideas that would account for the crisis and provide practical solutions. As they developed such explanations and recommendations, they empha-sized increasingly the role of foreign policy in solving domestic trou-bles and consciously initiated a broad program of sophisticated impe-rialism. For that matter, the triumphant corporation system rode in on the crest of what John Hay, in a revealing if indiscreet moment, called "a splendid little war." Underlying that expansion, and sustain-ing it on into the 20th century, was the central idea that overseas economic expansion provided the *sine qua non* of domestic prosper-ity and social peace. Gradually transforming this initially conscious interpretation of the crisis of the 1890s into a belief or article of faith—an unconscious assumption—Americans by the middle of the 20th century had established a network of investments, branch factories, bases, and alliances that literally circled the globe. Just as the sun had never set on the British Union Jack in the 19th century, neither did the Stars and Stripes know any darkness in the 20th century.

Also starting in the 1890s, Americans concurrently evolved a set of attitudes and ideas to rationalize and reform the political economy created by the large corporation. But even though they began with the urge to reform themselves, by 1917 they had concluded that such domestic progress depended upon first reforming the rest of the world. And despite periods of enforced preoccupation with domestic failures, this propensity to link improvements at home to conditions overseas remained an axiom with American reformers. Though the full development and convergence of these domestic and foreign programs did not occur immediately, it is nevertheless useful to preview the underlying assumptions and basic features of such new ideas.

For example, it is almost impossible to overemphasize the importance of the very general—yet dynamic and powerful—concept that the country faced a fateful choice between order and chaos. Not only did it guide men in the 1890s; it persisted through World War I, the Great Depression, World War II, and emerged more persuasive than ever in 1943–1944 to guide the entire approach to postwar opportunities and problems. Only the anarchists and a few doctrinaire laissez-faire spokesmen seemed willing to accept the possibility of chaos. Arguing that it was both necessary and possible, most Americans reformulated and reasserted their traditional confidence in their ability to choose and control their fate. This Romantic axiom had been a central theme of American history ever since the 1820s, and it carried over into the new age. But given a consensus on the sanctity of private property, and confronted by the increasingly obvious failure of laissez faire, this faith could be verified only by controlling the market place. While this tangle of ideas produced enough ideological rope for many a tug-of-war over who was to control the system and by what standard it was to be done, all such contests found the victors basing their program on overseas expansion.

THE INCEPTION OF AN AMERICAN SYNDICALISM

Within this framework, and originating largely as a reaction within the ministry against the failure of the church to sustain its old relevance and appeal as the source of values and inspiration, the idea of religion as the guide for creating an ordered and balanced system produced a movement known as the Social Gospel. Protestants as well as Catholics were influenced in such thinking by Pope

Leo XIII's famous encyclical *Rerum novarum* (1891) on the nature and role of labor in an industrial society. Recommending the renewed study of St. Thomas Aquinas, and stressing the ideals of cooperation and equity between capital and labor, his ideas were particularly relevant to the political economy of the large corporation.

Even though in stressing the role of the Church it offered a different kind of unifying theme, such a fundamentally functional and syndicalist approach reinforced similar analyses provided by sociologists and industrial spokesmen. It also influenced the large number of American labor leaders who were Catholics, for it reinforced their preference for improving labor's position without attacking private property. Yet just as in earlier centuries, the advocates of a Christian solution for the problems of society divided over whether the commonwealth should be based on private or social property. While a minority asserted the stronger logic and the greater equity of Christian Socialism and exerted some influence in the early years of the century, the great majority in the Social Gospel movement favored Christian Capitalism.

Even within the ministry, such Christian Capitalists soon accepted the necessity and wisdom of American expansion and played a crucial role in reinvigorating the missionary movement. Arguing that it was necessary for effecting Christian reforms and for creating the circumstances in which men would turn to Christ, they also supported economic expansion. Reverend Francis E. Clark thought missionaries played a key role in "the widening of our empire." Robert E. Speer, secretary of the Presbyterian Board of Foreign Missions, reported that his church accepted commercial expansion and "welcomes it as an ally." And Henry Van Dyke of Princeton presented an argument that sounded like the expand-or-stagnate thesis of industrial prosperity. "Missionaries are an absolute necessity," he explained, "not only for the conversion of the heathen, but also, and much more, for the preservation of the Church. Christianity is a religion that will not keep."

Another persuasive idea was different in being a secular thought that became a religion, and in initially placing little weight on overseas expansion as such. Clearly arising out of the needs and desires of various interests to strengthen their own position within the corporation political economy, the idea that efficiency was crucially important to prosperity and the socially tolerable functioning of the system soon gained wide acceptance. Though some businessmen had stressed the axiom earlier, the general discussion was launched by engineering and scientific journals in the 1880s. Then it was adapted by Frederick W. Taylor to the needs of management. That in turn opened the way for a theory (and ideology) of rationalizing the political economy under the direction of the corporation that was evolved under the general leadership of Elton Mayo of the Harvard Business School. An initial stress on efficiency thus led to the view that the corporation was the feudal lord of a new corporate society.

Finally, and in a way that provided the foundation for all such thought and discussion, Americans came increasingly to see their society as one composed of groups—farmers, workers, and businessmen—rather than of individuals and sections. Almost unconsciously at first, but with accelerating awareness, they viewed themselves as members of a bloc that was defined by the political economy of the large corporation. Perhaps nothing characterized the new *Weltanschauung* more revealingly. For given such an attitude, the inherent as well as the conscious drift of thought was to a kind of syndicalism based on organizing, balancing, and coordinating different functional groups. In part a typical example of the way interests and experiences influence thought, but also the product of abstract analysis and interpretation, that kind of corporation syndicalism became by 1918 the basic conception of society entertained by Americans. That outlook provides the underlying explanation of the persistent conflicts between the units, and of the continued difficulty of developing any broad truly inclusive program for balancing and directing the system. In one sense, the corporation was merely one of the functional units. But it exerted more power and influence than the others, and its approach to organizing and balancing the political economy remained an interest-conscious conception even though it did become progressively more sophisticated.

One of the best, as well as earliest and most widely read analyses of the syndicalist nature of mature industrialism and of the natural predominance of the large corporation within it, was provided in 1902 in a wry but essentially fatalistic study, *Our Benevolent Feudalism*, by William J. Ghent. Ghent thoroughly understood the essential feature of the new order: through its coordination of technology, capital, and labor, it could produce enough to provide plenty for everyone. But with the insight that provided the imagery of his title, he also realized that an economic, or political and social, decision by the giants would affect every citizen to a sizeable degree. While he concluded that the new system was too powerful to be destroyed and supplanted, and was likely to be moderately benevolent, he nevertheless pinpointed a central problem suggested by his analogy with feudalism: How were the vassals and the serfs of the new system to enforce the reciprocal obligations of the lords? This became a major issue that was never satisfactorily resolved.

In the meantime, several concurrent developments exemplified the kind of organization that Ghent anticipated would arise within the political economy. Often called by its advocates the "business form of government" the commission form of city rule was initiated in Galveston, Texas, in 1901. Devastated by a tidal wave, the city was reestablished in line with the theory that "a municipality is largely a business corporation." Designed to break down the division between legislative and administrative functions, and thereby provide a way to plan and coordinate urban development, the commission system was opposed by special interests that wanted government amenable to them rather than responsible for a broader conception of the community. But mounting debts, inefficiency, and graft prompted reformers as well as corporation leaders to turn to various variations on the city-manager form, and by 1960 almost half of America's cities were organized on this plan.

In a similar way, trade associations became more active and extensive in coordinating various branches of the system and in exerting influence on the government as well as on the market. And rapidly expanding as a part of the general process of controlling the economic market place, advertising firms began to extend their services into the area of public relations. Men like Ivy Lee approached the ultimate objective by creating a favorable image of the corporation and fixing it in the mind of the general public. One of his early successes presented John D. Rockefeller as a man who distributed corporation profits by handing out dimes to children. By thus manufacturing a certain kind of news and organizing its mass distribution, the advertisers created a special function for themselves and at the same time began the now familiar process of defining the good society in terms of the corporation and the corporation in terms of benevolent efficiency.

Accepting the new system, Samuel Gompers assumed leadership

of its labor sector. In theory, at any rate, Gompers could have dealt with the corporations in one of five ways. He could have ignored them (or gone along with the idea of company unions), tried to break them up through agitation for strong enforcement of the anti-trust laws, attempted to regulate them, turned to socialism (or cooperatives) and tried to change the property base of the whole political economy, or simply concentrated on organizing them while not challenging their basic predominance. He chose the last option. Then, in an act that was even more revealing of his outlook, he and his fellow labor leader John Mitchell of the coal miners joined Mark Hanna, Ralph Easley, August Belmont, J. Pierpont Morgan, George W. Perkins, and other corporation leaders on the board of directors of the National Civic Federation.

MARK HANNA AS THE ENTREPRENEUR OF THE CORPORATION SYSTEM

Conceived as a forum and institution for resolving industrial conflict through the cooperation of capital and labor, the NCF was organized by men who stressed the necessity of coordinating the various syndicalist elements to prevent crises (which would lead to socialism) or government intervention (which would lead to tyranny). As typified in his wholehearted acceptance of the axiom that "organized labor cannot be destroyed without debasement of the masses," Hanna provided the new political economy with a vigorous, talented, and perceptive corporation leader. A businessman who took a Senate seat as his just reward for engineering the political victory of 1896, Hanna understood both the nature and the power of the new system. Exploiting both, but trying to do so in a way that took into account his awareness of the need for an attitude and an ethic that would promote a positive consensus among its various elements, he emphasized the need for order, for give-and-take, and for the necessity of running the system as precisely that, a system.

His superior understanding and sophistication prompted many economic giants of his own time to conclude that he was too liberal. They never bothered to hear him out, or simply could not follow him, on such issues as his candid evaluation of the Populist demand for nationalization of the railroads. Acknowledging its economic relevance in stabilizing a crucial element of the private-property market place, he merely commented that it was perhaps a good idea—provided it was not done until the corporations had extracted the first-run profits from building and establishing them. His calm estimate was based on economic logic and an astute perception of the basic loyalty of the reformers to private property—they were "useful citizens." His analysis also anticipated by half a century the reaction of British conservatives to the nationalization of the coal mines in England after World War II. Hanna understood that the same people would very probably run the railroads, and in all probability would hold a large share of the government securities that financed them.

Accepting the demise of the ruthless and callous individual entrepreneur, Hanna seems clearly to have realized that the "harmony of interests" which he sought depended upon the corporation executives, himself included, rising above interest-conscious leadership to the class-conscious outlook of an industrial gentry. For his background, time, and circumstances (which included opposition from reformers that was just as bigoted as that from interest-conscious corporation leaders), he progressed a long way up that difficult emotional and intellectual slope. As with mercantilists like Shaftesbury or the Adamses, Hanna understood that a system based on private property needed class-conscious leadership just as much as does a revolutionary movement. And he realized the crucial weakness of corporation leaders with an interest-conscious outlook. For even though the interest was a corporation which embraced much of the political economy, such men still viewed society from that interest base—stressing immediate opportunities or problems—rather than from the outside and with primary emphasis on its long-run, inclusive needs and equities.

In many cases, moreover, he revealed such class-consciousness in his actions. As a coal operator, he damned the militia for shooting a worker involved in a strike against his plant, and was immediately attracted to William McKinley, the young lawyer-politician who defended the union. Later, he played a major part in settling the bitter anthracite strike of 1900. Feeling that vigorous rivalry between various elements of the syndicalist system helped balance them, he encouraged the farmers to stand up for their rights. "Anybody abusin' you people now?" he would ask western audiences that were prepared to be critical. "All right, combine and smash 'em!" He was in turn capable of fighting with all the great power at his call to protect corporations when he thought they were being treated unfairly or limited to an extent that threatened their fundamental role in the system. And in some cases of that kind, his judgment was narrow and mistaken. Thus he never became fully class conscious.

But he did recognize the basic issue and did educate a good many leaders of his time, even though few of them ever admitted it. His courage and wisdom helped Theodore Roosevelt as well as McKinley, and his astute political sense put both of them into the White House. As might be expected, he organized political action as though it were a corporate enterprise. From collecting funds from corporations (and returning any that were given in anticipation of special favors or that were not used) to paying individuals to wear McKinley buttons for the bandwagon effect, Hanna established the modern political operation. He used carloads of Civil War veterans instead of bevies of titillating females, and dinner pails instead of straw hats, but his latter-day imitators added nothing essentially new. The politician as organizational man came in with Hanna.

But McKinley was far from the weak figure some have thought him. Even before he met Hanna, for example, he grasped the essentials of an equitable relationship between capital and labor and sensed the idea of the Presidency as the directorship of a corporate society. Hanna's tutoring strengthened and extended these insights and provided support and organization, but McKinley's reputation played a crucial role in winning labor to Republicanism in the 1890s. He was President in his own right and brought to the White House a firm conception of an integrated and balanced society based on private property and the large corporation.

In approaching the problems of the new political economy, McKinley laid great stress on ending social unrest and on the relationship between overseas economic expansion and domestic prosperity. Hence it is misleading to view him as a weak man who was pushed into expansion and war against his will by popular excitement and special interests. The issues were far more complex than that, as was the history, and revolved around the questions of how internal stability could be restored and how the most efficient kind of expansion could be initiated and sustained. Those were the basic issues. Spain's inability to restore order and routine government in Cuba was the catalyst in a dynamic equation formed of several potent elements.

THE REASSERTION OF THE EXPANSIONIST THEORY OF
AMERICAN HISTORY AND THE WAR WITH SPAIN

Clearly the most significant of the factors was the consensus among business leaders on the absolute necessity of overseas expansion. Even before he had become a presidential candidate, for example, the National Association of Manufacturers chose McKinley to keynote their organizational meeting in 1895 of "the large manufacturers who are engaged in foreign trade." Acting on the axiom that such overseas economic expansion offered the "only promise of relief" to the now perpetual existence of vast surpluses, the N.A.M. stressed the need of vigorous government support and the usefulness of reciprocity treaties in obtaining cheap raw materials as well as new export markets. McKinley had modified his support of high tariffs in line with the more sophisticated views of former Secretary of State James G. Blaine as a way of satisfying Ohio businessmen who demanded access to overseas markets. "It is a mighty problem to keep the whole of industry in motion," he explained in 1895, and concluded that it "cannot be kept in motion without markets." Moving vigorously once it was organized, the N.A.M. established its own warehouses and agents in Asia and Latin America and began an ultimately successful campaign for government assistance in entering and developing such markets.

McKinley gave the featured address at the 1897 meeting of the Philadelphia Commercial Museum, also organized to push overseas economic expansion. "No worthier cause [than] the expansion of trade," he asserted, ". . . can engage our energies at this hour." Flour millers, wool manufacturers, the National Live Stock Exchange, and the Committee on American Interests in China (which soon became the American Asiatic Association) added their enthusiastic agreement—and their vigorous pressure on the government. Journals like *Scientific American, Engineering Magazine,* and *Iron Age* asked for relief in the same form. But McKinley himself provided the most succinct summary of the whole movement. "We want our own markets for our manufactures and agricultural products"; he explained in 1895, "we want a foreign market for our surplus products. . . . We want a reciprocity which will give us foreign markets for our surplus products, and in turn that will open our markets to foreigners for those products which they produce and which we do not."

Other politicians and intellectuals extended the expand-or-stagnate approach to the American economy to include all aspects of American life. Church leaders resolved the conflict between pseudo-science and religion by merging and transforming them in a supercharged reforming imperialism. Congregationalist Josiah Strong thought it "manifest" that the American branch of the Anglo-Saxon family would move out into the new frontiers of the world with righteous benevolence. "It would seem," he concluded, "as if these inferior tribes were only precursors of a superior race, voices in the wilderness crying: Prepare ye the way of the Lord." In his view (shared or adapted by others like John Fiske), America was the chosen instrument of a white, Protestant, Anglo-Saxon Jehovah whose master plan was an earlier version of Darwinism.

Several historians presented secular versions of the same basic argument. Though originally an anti-imperialist, naval officer Alfred Thayer Mahan was converted to empire by a combination of the Navy's own interest and his reading of (and borrowing from) English and French mercantilists. Though his influence has often been exaggerated, Mahan's neat formula for producing domestic wealth, welfare, and morality through exports protected by a big navy did enjoy wide popularity and provided a convenient way of talking about empire in terms of ethics and defense.

Though he was almost unknown to the general public, Brooks Adams was more original than Mahan and also exerted considerable influence on foreign policy leaders like Richard Olney, John Hay, Henry Cabot Lodge, and Theodore Roosevelt. Arguing from his study of history that great civilizations were created by conquering, organizing, and integrating huge slices of the world's western frontier, Adams concluded that the center of empire had in the 1890s reached the United States. In order to maintain that position, the nation had therefore to abandon laissez faire, accept the corporation political economy, organize it rationally and effectively, and expand it by tightening up control of the Western Hemisphere and winning economic dominance of Asia. Desperately concerned to avoid a revolution that would bring socialism, or perhaps simply anarchy, Adams openly avowed his imperialism. "I take it our destiny is to reorganize the Asiatic end of the vast chaotic mass we call Russia." He enthused at the prospect. "And, by God, I like it."

Far less openly imperialist, though by no means opposed to expansion, Frederick Jackson Turner developed a narrower and more specifically American version of the frontier thesis. Expansion had made Americans democratic and prosperous. The implication was clear: no more frontiers, no more wealth and welfare. Though Turner remained primarily a historian and seldom entered the arena of public debate or the dens of private influence, many public figures immediately recognized that he was saying the same thing as the corporation leaders, even though he was phrasing it in the rhetoric of the middle class. Men as different as Theodore Roosevelt, who had also written about the conquest of the west, the editors of the *Atlantic Monthly*, and a young intellectual named Woodrow Wilson who aspired to political power saw this meaning and significance in Turner's interpretation and adopted it as their own. And in subsequent decades, the idea that new and expanding frontiers provided the solution to America's difficulties became one of the nation's basic and persuasive assumptions. It influenced the outlook of men as different as Nelson Rockefeller and Henry Wallace as well as their respective peers, together with less famous but none the less important policy-makers.

Each of these major ideas, from the conception of the new system as depending upon an expanding market place to Turner's frontier thesis, reinforced and extended the others, and taken together they made sense out of the multiplicity of particularistic demands for expansion. *Given this expansionist theory of prosperity and history, the activities of foreign nations were interpreted almost wholly as events which denied the United States the opportunity for its vital expansion. A different explanation of the nation's difficulties would have produced a different estimate of foreign actions, for not one of the countries actually threatened the United States.*

But when European nations like France, Germany, and Austria raised tariff barriers against American surpluses, the act was viewed as threatening American wealth and welfare. Not even England escaped a share of the blame. For though it was clearly deciding that it would be wise to work out an underlying entente with America, England gave no evidence that it would cease to compete with the United States within that framework. And in Asia, where China was rapidly coming to be defined as the vital new frontier of American prosperity and democracy, Japan and Russia were seen as joining England and France (and even Germany and Italy) in dividing the opportunities among themselves and thereby excluding the United States. McKinley agreed with Cleveland's conclusion that the Asian crisis "deserves our gravest consideration by reason of its disturbance of our growing commercial interests." And both were intimately familiar with the requests from corporation leaders for "energetic" action "for the preservation and protection of [our] important commercial interests in that [Chinese] Empire."

Up to the spring and summer of 1897, therefore, American foreign policy was largely taken up with an expansionist drive directed toward Asia. Spain's difficulties in Cuba were a matter of official concern and sporadic popular interest, but not even Joseph Pulitzer and William Randolph Hearst managed to whip up any sustained excitement or pressure for intervention. As they later admitted, both newspaper publishers were acting as narrow interest-conscious operators concerned with their circulation figures (and hence advertising revenues). They were classic examples of the irresponsibility of the new mass-merchandizing approach to infor-mation. While they undoubtedly created an emotional concern in the winter and spring of 1897–1898 to save Cuba, neither they nor their readers made the decision to go to war.

That was done by McKinley and a few close advisors on the grounds that specific and general American interests could not be satisfied by any other course. Hence to explain the Spanish-American War as inevitable is to engage in an intellectual and moral evasion of the entire problem. America was vastly more powerful than Spain. And the definition of America's needs made by its own leaders produced the war. To conclude that such a definition was also inevitable is to resort to nonhistorical reasoning. For being able to explain how that outlook arose in the minds of American leaders is not at all to prove that no other view could have developed.

Against the background, and in the context of the consensus on expansion, several factors combined to shift primary attention from China to Cuba. American corporations with direct economic inter-ests in the island launched a vigorous campaign for intervention. At the same time, many people who had favored the revolution began to change their minds. Becoming skeptical of its nature and purposes, they preferred intervention to support moderate and conservative elements. By the late fall of 1897, moreover, many large corporation leaders who had opposed war up to that time began to feel that the situation had to be stabilized so that domestic recovery and overseas expansion could proceed without further delay and interruption.

Sharing this estimate, the McKinley Administration had already advised the Spanish as early as November 20, 1897, that "peace in Cuba is necessary to the welfare of the people of the United States." Having defined the problem in those terms, McKinley on December 6, 1897, graciously gave Spain "a reasonable chance" to do what he told them. But in complying with American pressure to replace a military commander who was in fact restoring order, Madrid only made it impossible for itself to comply with the basic demand. For less determined military operations allowed the rebels to recoup some of their losses. Stalemate was the result. America had thus irresponsibly demanded results while denying Spain the right to use effective means. Impatient of further delay, and cavalierly depreciating Spain's continued efforts to meet his demands, McKinley went to war to remove the distraction, establish firm control of the Caribbean, and proceed with expansion into Asia.

Ordering troops into the Philippines on May 4, 1898, even before he had official word of Commodore George Dewey's victory over the Spanish fleet in Manila Bay, McKinley dramatized the broader context of the war and opened a vigorous debate over what kind of empire the United States should establish. Opposed to colonialism on the grounds that it was unnecessary (and even harmful) to economic expansion, and because it would weaken political democracy and public morality by strengthening the influence of the military and increasing taxes, some leading politicians and intellectuals like Carl Schurz advocated a more sophisticated kind of empire based on economic power. Quite logically, in view of his own law of surplus disposal whereby exports could be extended and then sustained by underselling, Carnegie, and some other businessmen, supported this view. Pointing to the Philippine Rebellion against American forces (and to the way that the Army crushed it with a ruthlessness equal to similar European actions) as proof of their argument against colonialism, such anti-imperialists raised a great ruckus and caused the McKinley Administration some political embarrassment.

For the most part, however, McKinley and his advisors actually agreed with the anti-imperialists. Bryan, for example, opposed colonialism but assumed that America would crush the Philippine revolt, keep an economic and naval base in the islands, and go on to economic predominance in Asia. But McKinley advocated that very policy. Extremists like Theodore Roosevelt either missed or ignored, and thereby obscured, this vital convergence of thinking. Even in the short run, for that matter, it would seem that the anti-imperialists took the crucial line in the argument. For while the United States annexed Hawaii (with the votes of many anti-imperialists, who admitted their concern for the Asian trade), and took temporary title to the Philippines, it based its strategy of empire on economic rather than territorial expansion. In view of this, McKinley roundly trounced Samuel Gompers in a debate before a labor audience by candidly explaining the connection between overseas economic expansion and a full dinner pail on the job.

In a real sense, therefore, the anti-imperialists kept on arguing about an issue they had won while the expansionists moved on to deal with the next problem. "Whatever difference of opinion may exist among American citizens respecting the policy of territorial expansion," wrote former Secretary of State John W. Foster in 1900, "all seem to be agreed upon the desirability of commercial expansion. In fact it has come to be a necessity to find new and enlarged markets for our agricultural and manufactured products. We cannot maintain our present industrial prosperity without them."

Corporation leaders and intellectuals like Brooks Adams quite agreed that the nation's tremendous economic strength would underwrite a tremendous empire. Writing bluntly about *America's Economic Supremacy* in 1899–1900, Adams concluded that victory in the Spanish-American War was merely a prelude to triumph in the main contest for world predominance. Influenced by corporation directors (and politicians who followed the same line), and by friends and advisors like Adams, Secretary of State John Hay evolved a basic strategy of expansion. Demanding equal access and fair treatment for American economic power in China (1899), and then asserting America's direct interest in maintaining the territorial and administrative integrity of that nation (1900), his famous Open Door Notes defined the framework within which the United States entered—ultimately to dominate—the competition for empire.

As revealed in McKinley's use of the phrase "open door" to define his approach as early as 1898, the basic idea was broadly understood and accepted. It was *not* an English policy. Advisor William Woodville Rockhill pointed this out very emphatically during his discussions with Hay: "the policy suggested as that best suited to our interests is not a British one." London's version of the open door policy acknowledged spheres of influence, whereas (again in Rockhill's language) the United States insisted on "absolute equality of treatment." Convinced of the necessity to expand, and yet wanting to avoid the pitfalls of a formal colonial empire and of having to fight periodic wars with such rivals, American leaders saw in the policy and the strategy of the open door the perfect way to deploy and exploit America's economic predominance. This outlook guided their actions for more than half a century.

Combined with Morgan's organization of the United States Steel Corporation and the founding of the National Civic Federation in 1901, the Open Door Notes capped and symbolized the triumph of the new order of corporation capitalism. The concurrent publication of Adams's essays on the nature and strategy of using *America's Economic Supremacy* to build an empire (1900), and Ghent's perceptive analysis of the domestic features of *Our Benevolent Feudalism* (1902) provided appropriate intellectual statements. And the sudden rise of Theodore Roosevelt to the Presidency by virtue of an anarchist's assassination of McKinley added an eerie climax. Given the nature of the new order, Roosevelt as a class-conscious descendant of the old New York feudal aristocracy provided a supremely appropriate leader. And as he asked Adams for advice on his first annual message to Congress, the political economy of the large corporation confronted many difficulties and problems that demanded the best it could produce.

Granting the assumptions of the system, Roosevelt most certainly dealt with those difficulties from the most relevant and potentially most successful point of view. His conception of leadership derived from the agrarian gentry, a group that had wielded power in an earlier society also characterized by consolidated economic power (in land), and by a similar vast and interrelated network of authority, influence, and responsibility. Hanna understood the modern industrial system based on centralized power in the corporation, but lacked the tradition of class-conscious leadership. His significance lies in his recognition of that lack, and his effort to overcome it. It was a great achievement that has been too little understood and acknowledged.

Roosevelt did not fully comprehend the industrial system, but he did have the image and ideal of class-conscious leadership. That was crucial. The political economy of the large corporation could not be run either effectively or equitably by men who made decisions on the basis of an interest-conscious outlook. Roosevelt did not fully effect the transition to the industrial age. Nor did he really master the working of the system. He also made errors of execution, some of which patently stemmed from his view of the leader as a feudal knight. The question whether the greater personal achievement was not made by Hanna since it involved more of a change in fundamental point of view is largely one for debate and each individual's resolution. In the broader sense, the important consideration is that Roosevelt provided a relevant model for later leaders. In that fundamental sense he was progressive even though the model was in the explicit sense archaic.

CHAPTER TWO

A New Reality for Existing Ideas

The tremendous and highly complex industrial development which went on with ever-accelerated rapidity during the latter half of the nineteenth century brings us face to face, at the beginning of the twentieth, with very serious social problems. The old laws, and the old customs . . . are no longer sufficient.
Theodore Roosevelt, 1901

We are facing the necessity of fitting a new social organization . . . to the happiness and prosperity of the great body of citizens. . . . But we can do it all in calm and sober fashion.
Woodrow Wilson, 1912

But here is the challenge to our democracy: In this nation I see tens of millions of its citizens—a substantial part of its whole population—who at this very moment are denied the greater part of what the lowest standards of today call the necessities of life.
Franklin Delano Roosevelt, 1937

The ordeal of the Twentieth Century—the bloodiest, most turbulent era of the Christian age—is far from over.
Adlai E. Stevenson, 1952

An additional reason for caution in dealing with corporations is to be found in the international commercial conditions of today. . . . Business concerns which have the largest means at their disposal and are managed by the ablest men . . . take the lead in the strife for commercial supremacy among the nations of the world. America has only just begun to assume the commanding position in the international business world which we believe will more and more be hers. It is of the utmost importance that this position be not jeopardized, especially at a time when . . . foreign markets [are] essential.
Theodore Roosevelt, 1901

We cannot go through another 10 years like the 10 years at the end of the twenties . . . without having the most far-reaching consequences upon our economic and social system. . . . When we look at that problem, we may say it is a problem of markets. . . . We have got to see that what the country produces is used and is sold under financial arrangements which make its production possible. . . . You must look to foreign markets.

Dean G. Acheson, 1947

We delude ourselves if we do not realize that the main power of the Communist states lies not in their clandestine activity but in the force of their example, in the visible demonstration of what the Soviet Union has achieved in forty years, or what Red China has achieved in about ten years.

Walter Lippmann, 1959

VARIOUS APPROACHES TO THE PROBLEMS OF THE CORPORATION POLITICAL ECONOMY

As they emerged from the Depression of the 1890s and the Spanish-American War into an era of peace and greater domestic prosperity, Americans faced several problems in organizing and institutionalizing the new political economy of the large corporation. Some concerned domestic affairs and would have existed even if the new political economy had never been criticized by domestic radicals or foreign rivals. Others were more directly related to the difficulties of maintaining the overseas economic expansion which began in the late 1890s (playing an important part in recovery from the depression) and was considered vital to the system. Part of those foreign policy problems were endemic to the expansionist effort itself. The rest grew out of the opposition to American expansion manifested by conservative and liberal— as well as radical—leaders of foreign countries. Since all of those aspects of reality continued to exist past the middle of the century, it is apparent that any discussion of them has to be conceived in terms of decades rather than years (or a few special events).

At home, Americans had to devise ways of maintaining the sustained functioning of the large corporation; not only was it *the* unit of economic production, and hence of welfare, but because of its vast interconnections throughout the rest of the system its failure would mean social and political crisis. They also had either to develop a pattern of politics that would institute and maintain a

democratic process of decision-making among the various functional and syndicalist elements of the system (*and within them*), or
they had to evolve and accept a sophisticated class-conscious leadership that would take command of the system and run it on the
principles of equity and long-range objectives. Finally, and regardless of the choice between these alternatives, the society faced the
necessity of constructing a philosophy appropriate to an interrelated system in which the individual was clearly not the key figure
that he had been during the age of laissez nous faire.

Despite many assertions to the contrary, these features of the new
reality were not unique to the United States. Nor were American reac-
tions as different as observers have claimed. Some Americans became
reactionaries who wanted to restore laissez faire as it had existed in the
1850s or 1870s. Radicals of various persuasions proposed socialism,
labor syndicalism, or anarchism. Interest-conscious corporation leaders,
who composed the largest bloc of conservative spokesmen, accepted the
new system and argued, in keeping with the precedents of their outlook,
that the corporation should be allowed to run its world within broad
limits. Liberals (reformers, as they will subsequently be called) likewise
accepted the basic features of the new order and sought to balance its
various elements and moderate its inequities. And a small coalition
composed of descendants of the colonial feudal gentry, others who
identified with that tradition and heritage, and a small group of corporation leaders who very slowly developed the class-conscious outlook of a
new industrial gentry sought to balance and sustain the system through
control of the new corporation economy and the national government.

Though this political and philosophical spectrum is anything but
novel, it might be argued that American reformers have been almost
unique in the intensity of their commitment to private property.*
To an extensive degree, the reformers—like the conservatives and
reactionaries—have defined Man, and individual men, as creatures
of, and dependent upon, property. More property rather than more
thought has been the key to wealth and welfare in their world. They
have not been callous, and their efforts have improved society. The

---

* The development of Western European socialists raises doubts about the
uniqueness of even this attitude. They have steadily moved toward the position
taken up by American reformers at the turn of the century. Even Britain's Labour
Party has produced little beyond the American warfare-welfare state.

nature of their position, not a judgment of their accomplishments, is the issue. And to borrow the wonderfully perceptive term of Professor George Mosse, American reformers have been socialists of the heart. They have tried to take for their own purposes Marxian Socialism's magnificent reassertion of the ideal of a Christian commonwealth, and a few of its practical tools, without taking its commitment to social property. Therein lies the most persistent and persuasive influence of the frontier experience itself, and of the frontier thesis of American (and world) history advanced in the 1890s. It was fundamentally and extensively anti-intellectual in its direct impact and long-range results. Having defined everything good in terms of a surplus of property, the problem became one of developing techniques for securing more good things from a succession of new frontiers. The alternative, that of defining the good society in nonproperty terms, was dismissed as leading to the horrors of socialism in which the individual is destroyed because he has no property. Walter Lippmann caught the essence of such socialism of the heart as early as 1914. "There has been no American policy on the trust question," he explained: "there has been merely a widespread resentment."

Despite all the assertions about old and new orders, and about various fundamental changes that are claimed to have occurred, the essence of American history throughout the twentieth century has been the continuing attempt to resolve the dichotomy between a set of ideas developed in the 1890s and a reality to which they have proved ill-adapted. American leaders have been grappling with one central issue: how to transform a political economy created and dominated by the large corporation into a true social system—a community—without undercutting private property, without destroying the large corporation, and while further handicapped by the anti-intellectual consequences of the frontier experience (and the frontier interpretation of history) which offered a surplus of property as a substitute for thought about society. Having at bottom not much more to guide them than the frontier conception of democracy as a bundle of rights, and lacking any rigorous and sophisticated theory of mutual and interrelated duties, obligations, and responsibilities which combine to make a society, Americans have been repeatedly confronted by the harsh fact that the corporation leaders know more about managing the central and dynamic element of the system than any other group.

By and large, therefore, leaders of the large corporation have exerted a preponderant influence in the nation's basic decisions. But even this group has been severely limited in its grasp of the mechanics of the system and by the narrowness of its interest-conscious outlook, which emphasizes the importance of private property in its corporation form. The resulting pattern of unstable, lurching, oscillating, and inequitable development was a poor performance judged even by the assumptions, criteria, and claims of the system, to say nothing of the organization and results that would have been possible if the effort had been directed more rationally according to priorities set by a different scale of values. This inferior record benefited the reformers and the class-conscious gentry in two principal ways. It provided them with after-the-failure chances to moderate some of the more glaring weaknesses. And this caretaker function placed them in a relatively more favorable light and at the same time created the impression that they had a dynamic and basically effective philosophy and program. But in fact they have *on their own* never done more than restore the system to a level of performance that existed before the periodic crises. In every instance, further development has been achieved only with assistance from the interest-conscious corporation community, and through the kind of hot-house economic boom that always accompanies a war in which a country suffers neither serious indirect losses nor direct physical damage.

In the case of the reformers, at any rate, the extent of their differences with the conservatives has been, on the one hand, a more sophisticated version of Bryan's charge that the conservatives made the definition of businessmen too narrow and, on the other, a progressively more vigorous effort to extend the frontier and solve the problems of the system in that manner. This approach has unquestionably given more people more things on a combination of private and official installment plans, but there is not much evidence that such property gains have been matched in other areas of human activity. Faster cars, wider roads, and fancier fires do not make better picnics. Nor do cold wars produce warm hearts.

More than a few reformers recognized this fundamental

weakness in their own outlook. David Graham Phillips, who prepared what was unquestionably the single most devastating analysis of the narrow interest-conscious corporation leaders and their political agents and allies in *The Treason of the Senate* (1906), did so very early. "I am so sick of fraud and filth and lies, so tired of stern realities," he cried out in 1902 over the nature of the system and the limited horizon of the reformers. "I grasp at myths like a child." Thirty years later, after one war and several economic crises culminating in the Great Depression, Lincoln Steffens was more detached but his judgment was no less devastating. "The ideals of America . . . are antiquated, dried up, contradictory; honesty and wealth, morality and success, individual achievement and respectability, privileges and democracy—these won't take us very far."

For just such reasons, many reformers ultimately identified with the survivors of the old feudal gentry that asked the right questions even though its agrarian tradition was not essentially relevant to mature industrialism, or with the sophisticated corporation leaders who were trying to evolve the outlook and the policies of an industrial gentry. As the men in effective possession of giant chunks of private property that dominated the social and political economy, such corporation spokesmen had either to find and open up new frontiers or to transcend their interest viewpoint and transform it into a class-conscious outlook if the system were to have any chance of surviving as a social system based on private property. And by the end of World War II there was evidence to suggest that a small group of corporation leaders, and a handful of reformers, had managed the difficult task of raising themselves by their own philosophic bootstraps.

THE UNDERLYING RELATIONSHIP BETWEEN EXPANSION AND REFORM

But not even these men seemed fully to understand the significance of the fact that they had progressed toward that objective *only when their frontiers of expansion were closed by foreign opponents or severe domestic economic crisis.* Such periodic shutting down of the frontier forced them to turn in upon themselves, face up to reality, and begin defining and analyzing the central issues in realistic terms and developing some tentative answers. Failing to see the connection between the two processes, or seeing it and turning away because of the fear that such an approach would end in the substitution of social property for private property, they repeatedly turned back toward expansion of the frontier.

That kind of closing of the frontier happened four times after the wave of expansion at the turn of the century. The first, defined by the beginnings of a serious depression in 1913 and the outbreak of World War I in 1914, was dealt with by organizing to win the war and then using that power to extend America's overseas economic empire. Next came the Great Depression. That produced more extensive internal changes and did much, despite the myth that they had learned nothing, to generate a broader outlook among corporation leaders. But the lesson was interrupted by another, even stronger, foreign challenge—World War II. The corporation community slipped back into the old response, not merely of defending the society that existed, but of proceeding again to extend the frontier. Unconditional surrender is a doctrine clearly connected with the frontier conception of conflict. But between 1949 and 1956 the frontier was again limited, that time by the radical challenge of a rigorous anti-imperialism, socialism, and communism armed with nuclear weapons.

Striving once more to open the frontier, and giving even less attention than in earlier instances to other possibilities and problems, American leaders seemed surprised to discover in the late 1950s that the substance and tone of the nation's life had suffered from such concentration on externals. Yet even then few Americans began to explore the possibility that the frontier took men away from the essentials. Very few began, that is, to ask if they had not been using the frontier as precisely what Turner in a deeply revealing metaphor said it was—"a gate of escape."

As with other Americans who had acted upon the principle without turning it into a theory, Turner and those who accepted his analysis of American history welcomed the frontier as a "gate of escape from the bondage of the past." That was what had made America democratic and what would keep it that way. But while it included unhappy and inequitable features, that "bondage of the past" also included man's acceptance of the fact that he was human only when he lived with other men in society, not when he was away from them on the frontier. To seek an escape from that, whether in the 1750s, the 1850s, or the 1950s, was to seek to become a world unto oneself. Democracy of the frontier variety was really a minor achievement. Even Turner called it "a kind of primitive organization." Whether Americans at mid-century would candidly examine such aspects of the frontier outlook was a nonhistorical question. History could raise it; but history could not answer it.

THE BEGINNINGS OF AN UPPER-CLASS LEADERSHIP

Even though they accepted and acted upon the frontier thesis, however, Americans in the years before World War I also devoted their attention and energy to domestic affairs per se. The reformers, the old feudal gentry, and the more sophisticated corporation leaders made valiant and partially effective efforts to resolve the problems of the system. One of the most obvious difficulties lay in the limited outlook of the narrowly interest-conscious corporation leaders and their political representatives. Coal operator George Baer was one of the more arrogant, bigoted, and condescending owners whose philosophy began and remained with the rights of private property. Though personally more suave and less extremist, Henry O. Havemeyer of the sugar refining industry was another such giant whose vision was limited by cataracts of profits. One remark by Representative Joseph G. (Uncle Joe) Cannon, who dominated the House of Representatives with a deeply conservative outlook until 1910, caught the essence and the spirit of their attitude and at the same time provided an unintentional commentary. "This country," he was fond of repeating, apparently in the conviction that it answered all criticism: "This country is a hell of a success." Even the more moderate members of that group revealed a negative outlook. "What we want is stability—the avoidance of violent fluctuations!" thundered Elbert H. Gary, a judge who became head of U.S. Steel.

But these leaders did not produce stability, and critics attacked both the imbalances of power and its distribution, and the periodic crises that worked great pain and misfortune on millions of citizens. Although the reformers were vigorous in pointing out such failures, and hence created an image of themselves maintaining a lonely vigil at the gates of catastrophe, many of the more sophisticated corporation leaders also recognized and acknowledged such weaknesses. They placed particular stress on the imbalance between industry and agriculture. And, until a very late date, even the reformers were reluctant to come to terms with the fundamentals of the labor question. Along with the gentry and the more perceptive corporation leaders, as well as the narrow-minded economic giants, the reformers feared that labor threatened private property almost as much as did the corporation itself.

Most reformers did not, of course, exhibit so thoroughly negative an attitude as did those conservatives who, between 1903 and 1905 under the national leadership of David M. Pary, reversed the early emphasis of the National Association of Manufacturers on overseas economic expansion in favor of a militant anti-union campaign. But though they approved humanitarian reforms such as legislation limiting hours of work, they moved very slowly in strengthening the relative power of labor in the political economy. In keeping with their emphasis on private property, and in some cases their own backgrounds, they were more inclined to help agriculture. For that matter, some large corporations probably did more to initiate a more equitable approach to labor that was ultimately extended to the entire system.

Such firms, beginning with the National Cash Register Company in 1899, slowly developed a kind of paternalism designed to solve what many leaders felt were the crucial problems of "the class struggle and the question of proper distribution of wealth." Installing civilized rest rooms and providing free lunches, entertainment, and a library supplemented by lectures, that particular company inaugurated the typical program to encourage the worker to think of himself as a property owner despite his lack of any effective stake in the political economy. For what property he did own, other than his own muscles and skills, provided no direct, and very little indirect, leverage in the productive process. It was composed of objects that he bought and used as a consumer. They were necessary and pleasurable, and in no sense to be disparaged, especially in a system characterized by low efficiency and inequities in distribution, but they were not the kind of property that gave men any say in fundamental decisions. The worker simply could not obtain such a participating share in basic decisions unless and until he was willing to use his labor as the means. Neither he nor his leaders were primarily concerned with such objectives, and that in itself was one of the new realities which made it more difficult to balance the system. Indeed, labor's share in the malfunctioning of the system was by no means inconsiderable. As with the outlook of the reformers, the point is not to blame labor but only to realize that the interest-conscious corporation leaders did not bear all the responsibility. Labor was content with middle-class objectives and finally achieved them.

Another troublesome aspect of the new reality was the struggle between industrial and financial corporations for primary influence in the system. And though in no sense did they become emotional reformers, the industrial leaders did manifest a progressively more tolerant and intelligent attitude as they slowly gained control of the system during and after World War I. The conflict between financiers and industrialists was revealed, personified, and symbolized in Henry Ford's suspicions, fears, and hatred of bankers. Though one of the most complex and even yet imperfectly understood antagonisms of the age, its main features are clear enough. It arose out of the hiatus between the completion of the first rush across the continent and the requirements of an intensive development of that great wealth and further expansion overseas. In the basic sense, therefore, it was a product of the problem of accumulating, organizing, and allocating capital. Only a small group of the giant industrial corporations produced by laissez faire had the capital available in the context of the depression of the 1890s to make that transition.

Carnegie, Rockefeller, and Ford typified the reaction of the tiny minority that did. In a decision that revealed his understanding of his own place in the old order, Carnegie sold out and retired to his castles. Rockefeller became a financier. Ford remained an industrialist. The great majority became temporarily dependent upon the large investment bankers (or finance capitalists) headed by Morgan, but including such other firms as Rockefeller; Lee, Higginson of Boston; the Seligman Brothers; and the Kuhn, Loeb-Harriman alliance. Such providers of capital had several important sources of largesse: (1) their experience and reputation in the securities markets, both at home and abroad; (2) their own and connected banking operations; (3) the premium (and other) receipts of the large life insurance companies which provided centralized depots of capital accumulation on an ever-increasing scale; and (4) the security and profits from the industrial plants (such as U.S. Steel and Standard Oil) which they controlled. They used such capital to continue building and extending the system and to provide trouble-shooting services in times of crises—as in 1903, 1907, and, unsuccessfully, between 1929 and 1932.

One of the more dramatic aspects of the operations of the bankers which was the focus of a great deal of public comment and some action, was the extent to which they violated the law in both its letter and its broader moral context. Their lawbreaking was of two kinds. One stemmed from the fact that the new system could not operate according to the standards of laissez faire, and the older regulations and codes were simply evaded or bypassed. Personal and collusive corruption was another type of misbehavior. There was, and continued to be, a great deal of it, but it is important to realize that the power of firms like the House of Morgan was not based on that kind of self-provided subsidies; they overpowered their competitors quite impeccably. Other promoters were by no means as honest, yet the issue of honesty was not what really weakened the financiers.

Ultimately they simply proved incapable of supplying enough capital to maintain the system, to put all of what they had into profitable production, or to retain control of the industrial corporations which they had done so much to coordinate and consolidate in the early years of the century. They had in the end to turn to the government to provide, through taxes on non-stockholding and non-bondholding citizens, the resources that were needed. While that development pushed them into the government, it also sharply delimited their independent power as financial capitalists. Thus it lowered them toward a position of parity with top-level national politicians and leaders of the industrial corporations. The result was a merging of financial and industrial leadership similar to the kind of interrelated and coordinated operation that Rockefeller had established at the outset.

In the meantime, however, industrial leaders sought to reassume strategic as well as tactical, or managerial, control of their own firms and the system. Ultimately they did. Their own operations produced much of the capital they needed, and once the government was brought into the new system as a purchaser of goods and services on a large and routine scale, they could and did deal directly with this new source of capital. Though it was certainly a significant part of their victory, especially in the period between 1918 and 1924, the extent to which the industrial leaders freed themselves of the economic need for bankers and provided their own capital from current operations and long-term reserves is not the whole explanation of the change. Routine, daily demands and experiences in decision-making inside the firm were also important. The system was an industrial one, and bankers functioning as industrialists moved slowly but none the less significantly toward the outlook of industrialists per se. As one banker explained in a personal interview: "Well, you simply can't run a factory like an investment house." But all such factors operated within the basic framework of the inability of the financiers to accumulate enough capital and the resulting turn to the government (and therefore to the taxpayer) for assistance.

Financiers and industrialists also disagreed over how, and by what philosophy, the political economy should be managed. They of course were in agreement on many fundamentals; and as in the instance of supplying capital, where they ultimately came together inside the government and worked out a basic (if sometimes strained and acrimonious) compromise, the final outcome was a confluence of thinking. But while the industrialists could be as impervious as basalt to the demands of labor or other groups when they thought it necessary, the difference in outlook was indicated by the early disagreements within the U.S. Steel Corporation.

Bankers and their lawyer spokesmen revealed a strikingly firm conception of a benevolent feudal approach to the firm and its workers. Both were to be dominated and coordinated from the central office. In that vein, they were willing to extend—to provide in the manner of traditional beneficence—such things as new housing, old age pensions, death payments, wage and job schedules, and bureaus charged with responsibility for welfare, safety, and sanitation. Though he was not the most sophisticated of the industrialists, Charles M. Schwab of Bethlehem Steel revealed the essentials of a different outlook at an early date. Concluding from the Homestead Strike that labor "had some rights, whether others were willing to recognize it or not," Schwab also understood the necessity of making periodic, on-the-spot accommodations with labor in order to maintain steady production. Financiers, he complained, were "always ready to treat the men fairly as individuals and give them good liberal wages," but they did not grasp the value of unions either to the laborer or to the corporation itself.

Neither did they sense the role of unions in managing what the industrialist James J. Hill called "this great economic corporation known as the United States." Thus it is not as surprising as it might at first appear to find Samuel Gompers praising a man like George

W. Perkins of International Harvester for his "broad human under-standing of the problems of industrial relations." Later, between 1918 and 1935, John P. Frey of the International Molder's Union drew the same kind of distinction between bankers and industrial-ists. As one who worked hard, and with considerable sophistication, to establish an alliance between labor and capital, Frey reluctantly concluded that the government would have to be brought into the coalition because the financiers refused to accept the broader view of men like Gerald P. Swope of General Electric.

Still other aspects of the financial-industrial divergence appeared in connection with the generally agreed upon program of overseas economic activity. Since the poor countries had to have money to buy American exports of goods and services, they had either to accumulate it by increasing their exports of raw materials or by borrowing from abroad. At the turn of the century, when the bankers were organizing the new industrial complexes, they were fully in accord with the basic strategy of the Open Door Notes, which emphasized the importance of access for American exports and industrial operations. While Hay's dispatches did not specifi-cally ask guarantees for financial penetration, the omission should not be interpreted as indicating ignorance or indifference. The basic, as well as the immediate, objective was markets.

Dollar Diplomacy, as it was openly referred to by President William Howard Taft and other government officials, developed as a technique of implementing the Open Door Notes, not as a change in interest or definition. Backward countries needed capital, yet American financiers needed help at home. They wanted "effec-tive co-operation," as they put it, in corralling what they called the "scattered cash reserves" throughout the country. They also needed assistance in breaking into the market heretofore dominated by European nations. The Panic of 1907, for example, forced Harriman to delay a major project in Northeastern Asia. Circumstances changed, and whatever opportunities it offered were lost.

Even more significantly, the bankers needed open government support in order to attract capital from the great number of individ-ual savers who were unfamiliar with foreign operations and hence rather skeptical of their economic value and security. That also made the bankers particularly desirous of winning firm guarantees of repayment from the poor nations. But that in turn antagonized the foreigners and, as those who took a broad view realized, threatened the entire strategy. Finally, some bankers like the House of Morgan were inclined to favor cooperation with England, Japan, and even France. They had connections in those countries, and were more concerned with the narrow financial side of overseas expansion. Industrialists argued that such an approach favored competitive exports and thereby seriously hampered the construction of an *American* system.

THE FURTHER DEVELOPMENT OF AMERICAN SYNDICALISM

As such functional differences suggest, another aspect of the new reality that confronted American leaders, and caused them great difficulties, was the strong propensity of the system to develop in a syndicalist pattern. Now syndicalism is usually thought of in connection with revolutionary labor movements and assumed to be a violent proletarian outlook. This interpretation confuses the group in modern industrial society which has usually, though by no means always, or even most effectively, embraced and acted upon the idea with the outlook itself. Syndicalism is in essence a philosophy derived from two basic values: function and efficiency. Arguing that an industrial system operates through a division of labor organized by function and in groups rather than through individuals who handle many jobs, syndicalists conclude that such a pattern should be accepted, encouraged, and rationalized. Political representation should arise within each segment and be coordinated at the top in the national government. Individuals would thus participate in the relevant decisions and at the same time enjoy a sense of community and purpose within their particular group that would replace the alienation of an individual lost in a highly organized society.

As in Europe, overt syndicalism first appeared within the ranks of labor. Founded in 1905 under the leadership of Daniel DeLeon, William Haywood, and Eugene Debs (who resigned two years later), the Industrial Workers of the World presented a militant challenge to the established leadership of the corporation system. Organizing western miners, itinerant workers in agriculture and construction, and eastern textile laborers, it practiced a tough, violent kind of unionism dedicated to changing the existing order. The fear that it might penetrate the automobile industry seems to have played a part in Ford's introduction of the Five Dollar Day. On a more general level, the I. W. W. unquestionably served as a spur to corporation leaders and business union spokesmen to evolve some pattern of accommodation within the established system.

While they were openly scared of and antagonistic toward the I.W.W.'s kind of labor syndicalism, American leaders nevertheless adapted the principles of that philosophy to their own conservative objectives. Theodore Roosevelt repeatedly analyzed society within that framework, as did Herbert Croly and later Progressives whose slogans, the New and Fair Deals, were merely rather unimaginative variations of the Square Deal. Even more significantly, the corporation leaders who struggled to transform their interest-conscious outlook into a class consciousness developed their thought almost wholly within the syndicalist approach. Hanna was merely one of the first to use the tool, as in his advice to the farmers to organize trusts of their own.

In later years, men like Bernard Baruch, Owen D. Young, and Swope developed and extended the same analysis. But Herbert Hoover was the crucial figure in the evolution of the approach. Describing society as composed of three major groups—labor, capital, and the government—he struggled to balance and control the units so that they would not drive the system toward fascism (business control), socialism (labor dominance), or the tyranny of bureaucratic government. All such men, from Theodore Roosevelt through Hoover and later theorists, recognized that the central problem was to find some ideal that would generate the self-discipline and public spirit essential to maintaining equity.

To some extent, the theologian Reinhold Niebuhr ultimately provided a philosophy appropriate to the need. Combining selected portions of Catholicism and Calvinism, and then adding a generous leaven of Freud, pragmatism, and the frontier interpretation of American history, Niebuhr constructed a *Weltanschauung* that explained and justified the limited achievement of the Progressive Movement on the grounds that utopia was impossible, and that a more dynamic outlook would in any event produce one of the dangers outlined by Hoover. But nationalism was the main driving force of whatever unity and purpose the system exhibited, and it was largely the negative kind of nationalism directed against other countries and ideas.

One such foreign challenge was itself syndicalist in nature. As a basic component of both the fascist movement in Italy and the hard core of National Socialism in Germany, syndicalism provided the leaders of both parties and countries with many of their central ideas and programs. Since they resorted to terror in establishing and maintaining the approach, and distorted it in other ways, the essential characteristics common to American and European syndicalism are generally missed or discounted. Although there was widespread use of intrigue and violence against American labor, the foreign methods created a difference of degree that in the end produced a difference in kind. The Progressive Movement did not become fascist or Nazi. The initially favorable response to Mussolini, and even to Hitler, manifested by many corporation leaders and other Americans should not be interpreted in that light.

What is significant, however, is the extent to which a syndicalist analysis and approach underlay the programs of all three countries. Even American labor, which vigorously criticized fascism from the outset, did so on the ground that it favored business almost exclusively, not that the syndicalist approach was wrong. And not only did it support the National Industrial Recovery Act, which was openly compared to Italian fascism by New Deal spokesmen, but it continued to frame its own programs within the syndicalist outlook. In the end, of course, the particular nationalisms which were used to coordinate and unite each respective system in a corporate whole came into conflict and produced American involvement in World War II.

THE CHALLENGE OF DOMESTIC RADICALISM

Though it seemed to have disappeared by the end of that conflict, domestic radicalism had nevertheless posed a significant challenge to the leaders of the corporation society down through World War I. Radicalism's international manifestations appeared about that time in the Mexican Revolution that began in 1910–1911, and were focused and extended in the Bolshevik Revolution in Russia (1917–1918), and the Chinese Revolution that renewed itself in the same years. Radicalism sustained that momentum through World War II and reemerged in Asia and the Middle East, in the revolt against white rule in Africa, and in the Cuban Revolution of 1958.

Even before the Cuban uprising of 1895, however, Edward Bellamy's vision of a neo-socialist Utopia presented in the novel

Looking Backward (1888) attracted thousands of Americans. Bluntly assaulting the waste of "mistaken undertakings" and "idle capital and labor," "the competition and mutual hostility of those engaged in industry," and "the periodic gluts and crises" of capitalism, Bellamy offered socialism as an alternative to the consolidated corporation order that he recognized would be the successor to laissez faire. His novel no doubt helped prepare the way for the socialist movement that began to appear at the turn of the century under the inspiration and leadership of Debs.

So, too, did the writings of Henry Demarest Lloyd, a newspaper writer on the staff of the *Chicago Tribune* who became a reform publicist and ultimately a socialist. Though he offered no dramatic Utopia, Lloyd's analysis of corporation capitalism was perhaps even more influential in changing the minds of men and women who in the beginning took for granted their commitment to private property. Attacking Standard Oil and at the same time commenting on the general character and consequences of corporations per se, Lloyd explained how the new system was alienating men from their own labor.

"Nothing is any longer made by a man"; he explained in *Wealth Versus Commonwealth* (1894), "parts of things are made by parts of men, and become wholes by the luck of a good-humor which so far keeps men from flying asunder." And he astutely analyzed the weakness of trying to build a commonwealth on the foundation of private property with the corporation as a cornerstone. "The possibility of regulation," he concluded, "is a dream. As long as this control of the necessaries of life and this wealth remain private with individuals, it is they who will regulate, not we."

As can be seen from the writings of Bellamy and Lloyd, the essence of the radical challenge was contained in two principal ideas. First, it secularized and then reasserted with tremendous vigor the positive theme of early Christianity. To be a good world man's world had to be built as a commonwealth in which men were brothers first and economic men second. They gained their individuality from association with other men as equals as well as from proving their differences. Very simply, the radicals argued that true individuality derived far more from the development of an integrated personality and its relationships with others than from external achievements or overt and superficial superiority. Indeed, they insisted that a human individual could not develop under circumstances which based the survival of the person upon his competitive success in economic affairs.

Hence their second thesis: private property, since it emphasized and encouraged all the negative aspects of acquisition and competition, could not provide the basis for such a commonwealth. It would therefore have to give way to social property as an a priori basis for a humane society. What was often misunderstood about the socialist position was that economic welfare, meaning very high level subsistence achieved in a routine manner, was considered the basis for socialism, not the full definition of socialism. It was the necessary foundation for the creation of the commonwealth and for the emergence of a creative individualism which would enable men to live as human beings for the first time in their history.

No radical ever understood, let alone captured in words, that deep sense of the radical challenge better than Eugene Debs. "When the bread and butter problem is solved," he explained in 1908, "and all men and women and children the world around are rendered secure from dread of war and fear of want, then the mind and soul will be free to develop as they never were before. We shall have a literature and an art such as the troubled heart and brain of man never before conceived. . . . We shall have beautiful thoughts and sentiments, and a divinity in religion, such as man weighted down by the machine could never have imagined."

Radicals also stressed the necessity of planning and directing the economy in order to achieve and maintain a high level of material welfare. Such self-discipline and sharing would remove the necessity of imperialism and make it possible to end war and the exploitation of weaker societies by the advanced industrial nations. Hence in every vital respect the radicals confronted the advocates of the new corporation order with a fundamental challenge. And despite the abuses and violations of their own values that were apparent in the Russian and Chinese Revolutions, the radicals offered *the* challenge. Their weaknesses notwithstanding, they had asserted and acted upon the very ideas and values that the new corporation order, both from interest and from its own concern for a human society, had finally to assert in its own name. In the end, three centuries after their great debate within Cromwell's Revolutionary Army, the liberal heretic and the radical fundamentalist stood face to face before the ancient altar of a Christian corporate commonwealth asserting their respective rights to the grail.

Given such an array of practical difficulties, confronted with such challengers, it should be clear that the process of adaptation for the corporation order was both complicated and prolonged. Just as the corporation itself merged and consolidated the political economy, so were the various phases of the development of its society blurred and run together. This only served to dramatize an aspect of life—and hence of history itself—that hopefully may have become apparent through the organization of this essay. To employ the very simple analogy of time zones across the country, history is made in such different but concordant eras. Two or more events which occur at precisely the same moment may easily happen in zones that are different. One may be in an age that is dying, another in the age of the dominant system, and a third may be a harbinger of a new order. This is particularly true of 20th-century American history, and should be kept constantly in mind when considering the next two sections of this essay.

CHAPTER THREE

The Adaptation of the Existing Order

The truth is, we are all caught in a great economic system which is heartless.

Woodrow Wilson, 1912

What this country needs above everything else is a body of laws which will look after the men who are on the make rather than the men who are made.

Woodrow Wilson, 1912

We shall deal with our economic system as it is and as it may be modified, not as it might be if we had a clean sheet of paper to write upon.

Woodrow Wilson, 1913

The antagonism between business and Government is over.

Woodrow Wilson, 1914

THE KEY ROLE OF THE PROGRESSIVE MOVEMENT

As the combination of ideas and organizations through which Americans adapted themselves to the political economy of the large corporation and that system to the realities of the 20th century, the Progressive Movement symbolized many of the essential characteristics and provided much of the continuity of American history after 1900. To some extent, moreover, its fund of rhetoric, images, heroes, and ideas will play a role in the transition to whatever new society emerges from the present era of flux and travail. While periodically overshadowed by more conservative groups, some combination of Progressives has guided American policy during most of the century irrespective of whether Republicans or Democrats have been in control of the national government.

Struggles for political power, within and between the parties, have of course existed and been important. But several factors suggest that it is more helpful to approach the politics of the period, as well as its general history, in a less traditional way. For one thing, the functional-syndicalist organization of the economy led most political groups to play both sides of the street. Corporations, for example, contributed money and leaders to both parties; and despite the picture of labor union leaders and the rank and file being exclusively Democrats, both elements of the labor movement have supported Republicans on many occasions. In the same way, both political parties have shared a broad range of basic assumptions about such fundamental issues as private property and the relationship between prosperity and overseas economic expansion. Finally, the essentially bipartisan nature of the Progressive Movement itself, as symbolized by the two Roosevelts, makes it more accurate to view the major elements and ideas of that shifting coalition as landmarks of the entire century.

THEODORE ROOSEVELT AND THE RISE OF AN INDUSTRIAL GENTRY

Although it was numerically the smallest, the group of Progressives that came from the dwindling descendants of the old feudal and neo-feudal gentry supplied crucial leadership for the movement. Drawn for the most part from the Hudson River Valley and the south, that class-conscious gentry also included New Englanders who considered themselves, with more or less warrant, as the heirs of men who honored the political economy of Calvin and the mercantilists. Supplying Theodore and Franklin Delano Roosevelt as Presidents, and such men as Henry L. Stimson and Brooks Adams as official and unofficial advisers, this gentry performed a vital function in sustaining and trying to adapt the ideas and policies of an agrarian *noblesse oblige* to the industrial system.

Fearing the "terrible convulsion that might be produced" if poor leadership ran the country aground on "the rock of class hatred," Theodore Roosevelt viewed the Presidency "as the steward of the public welfare"—"of the commonwealth." Candidly aware of the "real and grave evils" of the corporation system, and of the "arrogant stupidity" of some of its leaders, he nevertheless shared Stimson's view that "the interest of the public is inextricably bound up in the welfare of our business." Labor was thus bound "not only by self-interest, but by every consideration of principle and duty" to stand with capital on "matters of most moment to the nation."

But corporation leaders needed education and "a constantly increasing supervision . . . and control." The lesson was the traditional sermon from the lord of the manor to his less sophisticated but nevertheless powerful vassals. "The friends of property must realize," Roosevelt was fond of repeating, "that the surest way to provoke an explosion of wrong and injustice is to be short-sighted, narrow-minded, greedy and arrogant." Fully accepting the idea that private property was essential to society and individual identity, he took a long-range view of preserving the property by making its human aspects more equitable and its economy more efficient.

For a good many years, a large number of reformers and rank-and-file property owners followed Roosevelt like lieges of the lord in the days of feudalism. So did a number of men who (like Perkins) were anxious to identify with such an upper-class outlook even though they were not wholly legitimate heirs of the tradition. Moved by a multiplicity of motives, they became administrators (like Gifford Pinchot and George B. Cortelyou) and intellectual leaders who labored long hours in the vineyard that ultimately produced a small but vintage crop of men who could legitimately be termed America's industrial (or modern) gentry. Probably the most famous of the intellectuals was Herbert Croly. His estimate of *The Promise of American Life*, and his journal of analysis and opinion, *The New Republic*, brought together some of the best Progressive thought.

Though by no means wholly derivative, Croly is often given credit for ideas that were advanced much earlier by people like Brooks Adams and even Roosevelt himself. Croly provided a synthesis that appealed to many Progressives because he organized and stated their explicit and latent ideas with verve and power. Calling for "a new national democracy" based upon an acceptance of the corporation and other "well-organized special interests" within a syndicalist framework, he openly feared a syndicalist revolution staged by labor and therefore stressed the importance of moderating "existing inequalities in the distribution of wealth." But like Roosevelt and other Progressives, Croly had difficulty in developing any new philosophy to provide the cement and the élan that Christianity had supplied in earlier centuries. Falling back on the ideas of militant nationalism and expansion, he rather lamely asserted a belief that "somehow and sometime" the problem would be solved.

Walter Lippmann and Walter E. Weyl grappled with the same issues. Nobody asked the basic questions about the corporation political economy better than Lippmann did in his essay on *Drift and Mastery* (1914), but having abandoned even a socialism of the heart, he matured as a keen analyst of the system and a sophisticated missionary preaching the need of a corporate ethic. Though not as famous as Lippmann or Croly, Weyl was in many respects the most rigorous thinker of the group. While he obviously learned much from his friend Ghent's outline of *Our Benevolent Feudalism*, and from his association with Mitchell of the miners' union, he went beyond that analysis and the ideas of the National Civic Federation.

Starting from the assumption that as far as capital and labor were concerned, "the interest of one is the interest of the other," he tried to evolve an approach whereby the syndicalist nature of the system could be coordinated in a corporate unity that would produce a "new individualism." Accepting the importance of overseas economic expansion, he also realized that the poor countries would have to be given an "integrated economic solution" for their problems if the empire were to be either efficient or defensible. In a similar way, he recognized that an "association of consumers" was needed to balance the other syndicalist units and at the same time cut across them. He understood, probably more clearly than any other Progressive, that the problem was to provide a base for socialism of the heart without subverting private property. He admitted, finally, that it could not be done and became a socialist.

Moving in just the opposite direction, John H. Reagan was a politician and reformer who began his career as something of a socialist of the heart and concluded it as a defender of the corporations. As the co-author of the Interstate Commerce Act of 1887, Reagan's intellectual and philosophical journey symbolized the power of a second major group within the Progressive coalition. Indeed, the role of such sophisticated corporation spokesmen ultimately provoked a good many middle-class members of the Progressive Movement to leave what they disgustedly concluded was a "millionaire's reform movement" either using Roosevelt or offering support which Roosevelt would not repudiate. After discovering the same kind of men in Wilson's entourage, and being in the end unwilling to build a new party behind the leadership of Wisconsin's Robert M. La Follette, they oscillated between the two major parties as a so-called independent vote. They might more aptly have been called the dependent vote because they evolved no program of their own, and their steadily increasing numbers documented the bipartisan nature of the Progressive Movement's leadership.

Hanna was of course the precursor of all sophisticated corporation leaders who were to become ever more important to and within the Progressive coalition. He not only lectured Roosevelt on the absurdity of thinking that agrarian reformers were wild revolutionaries and scared him by the measure of his own political support outside business circles; he also educated the corporation community in the art of discriminating between short-run and long-range interests. Charles G. Bonaparte of Baltimore, George W. Perkins of the House of Morgan, and Hazen S. Pingree and James Couzens of Detroit were other leaders in extending the interest-conscious outlook of their associates. Even before World War I, for that matter, some of them were clearly approaching a class consciousness that saw the corporation as merely the key institution of the system rather than as the system itself.

The essence of this evolution was caught in one sentence by publisher Frank Munsey in his obituary of Perkins. "George W. Perkins is dead at 58," he announced in 1920. "In this span he lived 400 years." Influenced by his father's missionary approach to various reform movements, Perkins first developed an almost classic kind of 16th-century paternalism in his early years with the New York Life Insurance Company and the House of Morgan. Like the directors of U.S. Steel, Perkins thought it was sufficient to treat the individual worker fairly. But he gradually accepted organized labor and realized the necessity, if the system was to be sustained, of a partnership between the two interests. Men such as Perkins did not become vigorous advocates of a labor movement organized to preempt the prerogatives of capital. Their actions often belied or severely modified their rhetoric. But the stereotype of them as merely interest-conscious leaders is gravely distorted. That they modified the traditional outlook as much as they did within their own lifetimes is persuasive evidence of the developing ideas of a corporate system.

Others of the same group, like James D. Phaland, a wealthy San Francisco industrialist and financier, grasped the point of Hanna's argument about the railroads and came to advocate public ownership of all municipal services. Samuel M. (Golden Rule) Jones was a manufacturer who favored, and practiced, such class-conscious reforms as profit-sharing, the eight-hour day, minimum wages, and paid vacations. And as an editor of *The Wall Street Journal* who helped develop its broad-gauged outlook, Sereno E. Pratt was another such figure. Many reformers would have been (and would still be) thunderstruck at the contents of the paper. Many interest-conscious corporation leaders were (and continue to be) outraged by its ideas, as when in 1902 it advocated giving the government full authority to set rates for the railroads. And though it would be erroneous to call him a Progressive, so basically conservative a figure as Senator Nelson W. Aldrich illustrates the main point. For Aldrich's deep and persistent concern with the problem of accumulating and allocating capital for the system produced a series of investigations, studies, and preliminary laws that provided much of the foundation for the Federal Reserve System.

THE INTERESTS AND THE IDEAS OF THE REFORMERS

Aldrich was of course, and not without reason, damned generally by the conglomeration of middle-class reformers who composed the third and by far largest portion of the Progressive Movement. They were principally small and middle-sized businessmen or farmers who as individuals had no effective stake in the new corporation order. Taken singly, their property was irrelevant economically and ineffective politically and socially. They were declining in prestige and status, but these losses were secondary and derived from their economic impotence. Yet they were realistic enough to realize that their commitment to private property forced them to accept the system. They sought, by organizing politically (and to some extent in economic cooperatives), to win some semblance of parity or equity in the system. Implicitly, at any rate, they acted on the same kind of syndicalist logic that more explicitly guided the gentry and increasing numbers of corporation and labor leaders.

Hence it may be useful as well as fair to rechristen them conservatives, as some commentators have done, but it is grossly inaccurate (as well as supercilious) to call them reactionaries. After all, a good many of these people turned to Eugene Debs and socialism between 1900 and 1920 as they came to understand what they felt were the structural weaknesses and lifeless character of a syndical-ism dominated by the interest-conscious large corporation. Even the attitude toward labor of those who remained reformers within the Progressive Movement revealed a kind of shrewd perception. They were sympathetic, and willing to support labor in some ways, but they also had a very real fear that the unions would reach a basic accommodation with the corporations. In their view, that would transform the political economy into a kind of mortar-and-pestle syndicalism that would reduce them to insignificance. They flatly called it "a dangerously oppressive partnership." But to blame them for some skepticism about the results of labor's business unionism is rather to miss, or ignore, one of the central developments of the era.

The essence of the middle-class reformers' program, and the grounds for their on-again, off-again liaison with the gentry and the more sophisticated corporation leaders, lay in two broad objec-tives. They wanted to hold the large corporation at its existing level of power while raising other groups to positions of relative balance. They also sought minimum standards of equity and moral behavior. As should be obvious, the reformers were largely interest-conscious leaders united in a loose, and often mutually suspicious, alliance to check the dominant interest. Their greatest weakness was the lack of any broad and dynamic conception of how the system was to be coordinated and sustained. They did not like the large corporation but they did not have anything to put in its place.

Had the reformers actually been reactionaries, as they are peri-odically labeled (Roosevelt once called them rural Tories), they would have gone all out to use the anti-trust laws to restore laissez-faire capitalism. But they were caught in the same kind of dilemma that had faced the radical antislavery men during the Civil War and reconstruction. When it came down to cases, they were unwilling to tamper with the anchor of the system—the legal interpenetration of the rights of private property and the corporation form of organi-zation—for fear of damaging the former in weakening the latter. Hence they had little choice but to concentrate on political reforms. Yet the system was as much an integrated economy as a pattern of politics, and their efforts never produced the results that they antici-pated. For while their reforms were certainly understandable and defensible, and not wholly ineffective, they did not cut into the power structure of the corporation system. Strong on criticism, and on proposals to strengthen their particular interests, the reformers were weak on ideas appropriate to the entire political economy.

This aspect of reform thought was particularly apparent in the muckraking literature. Its very negative and outraged nature had much to do with infusing the movement with enthusiasm and righteousness. As a big business itself, the industry of the exposé typified the extent to which information had become a commodity handled much like any other product. Advertisers and public-relations men were engaged in the same kind of operation, and when the three sides of this approach to news as prepackaged merchandise converged, the system had a tool which could be used to create and sustain images that distorted reality as much as they illuminated it.

For that matter, even the muckrakers suffered from the one-sidedness of their analysis of the system. Corruption and central-ized power did exist, but they were symptoms rather than causes. Being basically a movement against symptoms rather than for a clearly delineated program of action on causes, the crusade ended in indifference or disillusionment when the reformers discovered that the system exhibited a tremendous inertia that resisted their changes in administrative and electoral procedures. Efforts to use such instruments as the initiative, the referendum, and the recall proved so expensive and involved, and so limited in results, that they were soon abandoned.

Though not usually considered among the muckrakers, Thorstein Veblen was one of the few members of the group who moved beyond the limits of that approach. His first and only generally read book, *The Theory of the Leisure Class* (1899), was the earliest and clearly the most witty and sophisticated of the entire genre. In many ways Veblen was to the age of the corporation what John Taylor had been to the era of industrialism itself. Both men criticized new ways and institutions from a point of perspective located far back in an earlier time when Veblen's "instinct of workmanship" was a highly personal affair based on each man doing all of his particular job. Yet Veblen did extend his analysis and thereby helped to estab-lish among American intellectuals the institutional approach to political economy. He also recognized the great significance of the

Bolshevik Revolution, and understood that it dramatized the need for an American program that would transform the corporation into an instrument for building a true commonwealth. On the one hand, his institutional economics assisted later reformers and other Progressives who were trying to make such a change. But on the other, his emphasis on efficiency was an intellectual sword that cut for the corporation as well as against it. Efficiency was not really the central issue, and hence reformers who criticized the corporation system on that basis were left without much to say when the corporation became more efficient and with great effectiveness used the argument in its own behalf.

Another negative aspect of Progressive thought derived from its ethnic consciousness. The gentry and the reformers, corporation directors and labor leaders, and farmers and small-town businessmen had a common pride in their Anglo-Saxon heritage. It was an integral part, for example, of the gentry's class consciousness. Such cultural self-respect and pride of achievement are normal and healthy, even creative, forces; but under the stress of foreign competition and domestic troubles, the Progressive coalition, along with its conservative opposition, pushed it into bigotry against other ethnic and religious groups. Woodrow Wilson, for example, did not include the Negro in his New Freedom or in his crusade to make the world safe for democracy. This attitude toward the Negro was characteristic of most Progressives until after World War II. Other ethnic minorities and Jews suffered similar discrimination (although Zionists often and with equal unfairness interpreted as anti-Semitism the opposition to their agitation for a Jewish state created on territory claimed and occupied by Arabs).

Without much question, domestic and foreign radicalism played the most important part in weakening such discrimination. Negro leaders William E. B. Du Bois and Paul Robeson symbolized such militant insistence that every American was a citizen until his conduct proved otherwise. Though few of the other leaders, or members, shared the across-the-board radicalism of Du Bois, the National Association for the Advancement of Colored People (founded in 1909) based its entire approach on the simple demand for equal rights. But given that opportunity, most Negroes wanted only to become like white Americans. That ironic tribute to their overlords provided one of the main reasons for the slow rate at which the campaign for desegregation moved throughout most of the era.

From the time of the Bolshevik Revolution, however, foreign radicalism exerted an ever-increasing pressure against the more overt kinds of discrimination. Ethnic equality, for example, was a strong theme in the socialism of the heart that came to a climax during the Great Depression. Even so, not many basic gains were made until the Soviet Union emerged from World War II as a major power and effective competitor for world leadership. And as in the crisis over integrating the schools in Little Rock, the response was implicitly negative though explicitly positive: discrimination was held to be bad because it hurt the United States in the Cold War. However else it had failed, foreign radicalism certainly played a significant role in subverting at least that American tradition. But since the Progressives had little positive conception of community or commonwealth, the result was a crippled, negative kind of tolerance.

At the same time, the achievements of Negro and other minority representatives also helped to improve the general standing of their groups. So, too, did the slowly increasing demand by the corporation for a homogenous supply of talent and labor, and the same kind of market. In that instance, at any rate, the Progressive emphasis on efficiency had a positive social consequence. But the basic weakness, and paradox, of the Progressive attitude toward discrimination appeared even more clearly as part of another general idea that it embraced. Called "Reform Darwinism" by Professor Eric Goldman, this clever intellectual maneuver consisted of emphasizing the environmental side of Darwin's theory of evolution as against the stress placed on competition by conservatives.

By changing the environment, so ran the argument, men could create positive changes without tooth-and-fang competition. Unfortunately its advocates overlooked or discounted, in a most unscientific way, two things. Competition was necessary to change the environment, and competitors needed a clear conception of what they wanted if the effort was to produce any significant changes. As a result, such Progressives were perpetually surprised, and many of them disillusioned, by the difficulty even of holding their own against the corporation, to say nothing of effecting fundamental modifications in the political economy. Yet such environmental Darwinism did suggest that the Negro or the tramp or the prostitute (or the foreigner) was primarily a creature of circumstance who could be transformed by changing his habitat. Then the paradox turned in upon itself, for of course the Progressive assumed that American industrial society was the best kind of environment. For narrow ethnic prejudice in America, therefore, the Progressives tended to substitute an ideological and nationalistic bias that was in some respects even more invidious. People were capable of improvement, but improvement was defined as becoming more like Americans.

Because of its usefulness in reconciling science and religion, there was a good bit of such environmental Darwinism embedded in the assumptions of the Social Gospel movement. But some religiously oriented reformers also used it as a general framework within which they developed other ideas. Attracted in many cases by the land of their ethnic origins, as well as by intellectual excitement, students like Richard T. Ely had studied in Germany during the 1870s and 1880s. Stimulated by Germany's effort to integrate and unify an industrial system after its victory over France in 1870, they had been impressed and influenced by the kind of neo-mercantilism that German industrialists, politicians, and conservative intellectuals developed as a counter to socialism. Germans had been responsive to the ideas of the American mercantilist Francis List after he had returned to Europe earlier in the 19th century, and their own scholars like Gustav Schmoller extended that approach into a major analysis and interpretation of that earlier epoch in history. Concluding that the mercantilist approach was relevant to their own later problems, Germans openly borrowed many specific ideas as well as adapting much of the general outlook.

Along with Ely, such men as John Bates Clark, Edwin R. A. Seligman, and Washington Gladden took up such ideas and evolved the related concepts of a quasi-collective Christian ethic and greater government participation in the economy. Such an approach, they concluded, would prevent class war. Thinking along functional and syndicalist lines, they advocated "unified efforts, each in its own sphere," the unification to be provided by the religious outlook and the "positive assistance" of the state. "The true ideal," Ely explained, "lies midway between anarchy and socialism, and may be termed the principle of social solidarity."

In founding the American Economic Association, but even more in developing their own institutional and Christian Capitalism, Clark, Ely, and the rest started an intellectual movement that ultimately converged with the growing group of sophisticated corporation leaders. Having begun as "rebels . . . fighting for our place in the sun," as Ely put it, they gradually became (and inspired and trained other) men who played roles similar to the one that Locke had filled in his relationship with Shaftesbury. To an even greater extent than did Mahan, they reintroduced and adapted certain aspects of mercantilist thought into American development. In later years, their approach merged with that of the British economist Lord Keynes. But Keynes himself was avowedly influenced by the mercantilists, and so the heritage was reinforced once more, albeit in a more sophisticated manner.

Like the Christian Capitalists, many other Progressives were inclined to break into a rousing chorus of "Onward Christian Soldiers" at moments of outrage or elation. A tiny group followed the tradition back to its early emphasis on social property; led by Walter Rauschenbusch, whose *Christianizing the Social Order* (1912) applied that doctrine to industrial society, they attacked the corporation system at its very roots. "If we can trust the Bible," Rauschenbusch concluded as early as 1907, "God is against capitalism, its methods, spirit and results." But though they influenced some individuals, they never threatened to socialize the Social Gospel. The great majority remained loyal to private property and accepted the basic features of the corporation order.

So, too, did the leaders of the labor movement like Gompers and the John R. Commons school of labor historians and economists. While often developed cautiously and conservatively even within the school's own assumptions, their approach was never as feeble or irrelevant as its critics have charged. The A.F. of L.'s gravest weakness was in refusing to apply its own functional and syndicalist logic in a thoroughgoing manner and organize unskilled workers. But given its organizational difficulties, the competition offered by Debs and the socialists (and the I. W. W.), the great strength of the corporations, and the skeptical and even antagonistic attitude of many members of the Progressive Movement, Gompers and Commons accomplished a great deal. Having accepted the system, labor had logically to organize its own segment of the syndicalist political economy before it could exert much effective pressure to be accepted as a full member in good standing. Gompers and Commons were far more astute than the muckrakers and far more realistic than many of the reformers who embraced environmental Darwinism. Gompers was hard at work changing the environment whereas they tried, rather illogically, to regulate it from the outside.

JOHN DEWEY AND THE ROLE OF PRAGMATISM IN THE ADAPTATION TO CORPORATION CAPITALISM

As such a review of some of their principal ideas may have suggested, several factors help to explain the propensity of the rank-and-file Progressives to roll with the system. Their commitment to private property, and the difficulty of organizing and applying pressure through such groups as the Consumers League reinforced the limited nature of most of their proposals. By 1910–1912, however, the Progressives were adopting a philosophy that provided a positive defense for their restricted, ad hoc approach. Probably the single most powerful influence on the Progressive Movement between 1910 and 1940, and hence upon American society itself, was the relativistic pragmatism and instrumentalism developed by John Dewey.

Perhaps the most cheerfully eclectic thinker ever to be taken seriously as a philosopher, Dewey borrowed from Emersonian transcendentalism, evolutionary Darwinism, Marxian socialism, functionalism, and Christian Capitalism with a fine and even exciting disregard of logic and consequences. Given such an approach and technique, it is hardly surprising that he has upon occasion been praised or damned for almost everything that happened in America after the publication of his first pamphlet on education at the turn of the century. Though there is some validity in defending him on the grounds that his followers misunderstood and hence distorted his thought, the followers deserve a word in their behalf. There is a fundamental truth in the old cliché that to write clearly one must think clearly, and hence they faced an extremely difficult task in deciphering precisely what Dewey did mean. His writings are filled with conflicting and contradictory judgments and recommendations that are nowhere resolved. After one particularly crucial paragraph which is none the less very, very murky, Dewey admits candidly: "This is a vague statement." But he makes no attempt to clarify the presentation.

This aspect, as well as the more fundamental nature, of his philosophy was once caught by one of his followers in the revealing remark that Dewey's pragmatism was "Calvinism on the frontier." While his attempt to break through traditional forms and reconcile those two outlooks on life is the measure of Dewey's greatness and influence, the results fell considerably shy of the objective. For in his concern to attack the old outlooks he denied the validity of *any* formal, rigorous definition of a desirable order. Asserting that "the hypothesis that works is the *true* one," he was willing to do what seemed best at any particular time and "trust the rest to fate, fortune, or providence."

Despite all Dewey's concern with becoming—with growth, as he put it time and time again—he was weak on what growth really amounted to when a rigorous answer was demanded. Perhaps his greatest contributions were in opening out the education of the child, and in stressing the idea that the new order was intrinsically a society rather than a conglomeration of individuals. But there was considerably more of the frontier than of Calvinism in his ideas on both those issues. He transferred the romantic view of the adult to the child, for example, and thereby provided an exceedingly undemocratic definition of human relationships. For by taking the child very largely at its own valuation, Dewey implicitly, and often explicitly, discounted the adult.

Granted that adult control of the child has a propensity to become confinement, and granted that Dewey was everlastingly justified in trying to check and limit that tendency, it nevertheless is true that to accept the child's judgment of himself is to make the child more important than the adult. But the present is just as important as the future. At most, and in equity, the child is *as* important as the adult. But no more. And in many respects, the adult is more important for the simple reason that he has responsibility for the present. Indeed, Dewey's emphasis on children amounts in many ways to a frontier that enables the adult to escape the hard realities of the present by living in the child's future.

As for industrial society, his definition of the "newer morale" and "ethics" was somewhat fulsome in its praise of the corporation.

"Wherever business in the modern sense has gone," he judged, "the tendency has been to transfer power from land to financial capital. . . . The change in the political center of gravity has resulted in emancipating the individual from bonds of class and custom and in producing a political organization which depends less upon superior authority and more upon voluntary choice." And since he never offered a City of Pragmatism, Dewey's future was at best no more than "the projection of the desirable in the present." Beyond limiting its advocates to the rectification and adjustment of present difficulties, this would seem to be for a philosopher a significant failure of social imagination.

Persistently failing to define any standard for discriminating between subjective desire and objective desirability, Dewey had no alternative but the undefined concept of growth and what he called the "perpetual open frontier." His rather pathetic efforts to define the scientific method as rational problem-solving, and thereby escape the dilemma, led him into such wild conclusions as the remark that "science rests upon opinion." Dewey might far more fruitfully have explored and extended his idea (probably borrowed from Marx) that a mixture of intellectual and manual work produced a whole man whose sense of human and social values was strong as well as balanced.

But his concept of growth means all things to all men, and without any more than the accomplishments of the business community or the opportunities of a "perpetual open frontier" to guide it, such a standard comes down in the end to meaning that the new order can be kept open and free only by never being forced to confront itself directly and rigorously. And in that sense, Dewey's relativist pragmatism had much to do with the distortions of Sigmund Freud's doctrines in America. For Freud's objective was to know the irrational in order to discipline and control it, but Dewey's approach led to knowing the irrational in order to adjust to it.

A philosophy without a Utopia is like the sky without the stars. It is very inspiring until it gets dark. Randolph Bourne, a left-wing Progressive originally attracted to Dewey's approach, raised that issue in a dramatic way at the time of America's entry into World War I. He argued that if Dewey, despite his great humanitarianism, could justify that course by pragmatism, then anyone could justify anything by the same logic. It offered no benchmarks of judgment.

Hence it was at best an amoral if not actually unmoral philosophy, and was further and deeply permeated by the traditional antiintellectualism of the frontier.

Despite its positive features, the critics of Dewey's philosophy made a fundamental point: whatever Dewey's *personal* history, his philosophy of relativist pragmatism provided in its general impact an encouragement for ameliorative adjustment to things-as-they-are. External success was thus strengthened as a standard for judging intrinsic value. And as Dewey himself implied rather clearly, trusting the rest "to fate, fortune, or providence" meant under the circumstances of 20th-century America trusting it largely to the corporation.

Supreme Court Justice Oliver Wendell Holmes probably did as much with pragmatism as it is possible to do, but he very clearly employed it *within* the limits of a more basic philosophy of humanistic common law that also controlled his personal preference for laissez-faire economics. Enjoying the confidence rather typical of such class-conscious leaders, Holmes was willing to relax in his faith that, short of a clear, present, and major danger, the system would survive any reasonable legislation that did not explicitly violate the Constitution. Measuring corporations as well as radicals against that yardstick, Holmes left a body of literate and cogent opinions that, together with his study of *The Common Law* (1881), offered the basis for an American philosophy of the law that was appropriate to the ideal of a commonwealth. While not a Progressive in any formal sense, and most certainly not in many of his personal judgments on reform legislation, Holmes nevertheless provided that movement with key elements of the kind of a broad-gauged outlook it needed.

In a very revealing way, however, most Progressives were more attracted by the way that lawyer (and later Justice) Louis D. Brandeis used efficiency as a standard by which to win approval for various reforms. Originating in the engineering community as an extension of its neo-scientific and inherently functional approach, the emphasis on efficiency was expanded by men like Charles R. Taylor under the general idea of Scientific Management. Taylor himself worshiped production as such. But corporation leaders took his ideas and used them (as in rationalizing and speeding up production and in setting wages) as a tool for maintaining and increasing their profit margins. While it opposed the approach in these early forms, labor gradually adapted the idea and used it as an argument to win returns for itself from higher productivity. And as early as 1901, Theodore Roosevelt's own stress on efficiency prompted him to call for handling the tariff problem through "scientific management."

As such examples suggest, efficiency was a standard that almost any group could use. Like the reformers who turned Darwinism around, Brandeis merely applied it in defense of social legislation. Women were different and in some respects weaker, therefore it was inefficient to work them as long or as hard as men (*Muller* v. *Oregon*, 1908). In the same way, lowering wages below a certain point was inefficient and harmed the functioning of the system— hence wage legislation was necessary and legal (*Stettler* v. *O'Hara*, 1917). Brandeis had a strong moral sense, and was deeply humanitarian, but he nevertheless relied upon the logic of efficiency to win his reform battles. He did the same in dealing with the problem of regulating corporations. Far less of a laissez-faire thinker than he often appeared to be, Brandeis was primarily concerned to judge the size of corporations by the benchmark of efficiency. But as he and other reformers discovered, corporation spokesmen were quite capable of winning an argument on those terms.

THE PROGRESSIVES TURN BACK TOWARD THE FRONTIER THESIS

Although it suffered that kind of defeat, or stalemate, in many instances, and certainly did not make any dramatic changes in the system, the pre-World War I efforts of the Progressive Movement did effect several gains. Especially at the local level, it extended popular government, established some checks on the more blatant kinds of corruption, and reinvigorated and increased various kinds of individual and social welfare programs. Its reformers also helped to rationalize the political economy of the large corporation in a way that was ironic in view of their emphasis on equity and morality, and in a way that interest-corporation leaders were very slow to acknowledge. Many such corporation leaders opposed the reformers despite the fact that many of the reforms, undertaken in a spirit of hostility and righteousness to remove inequities, actually had little effect on the moral flaws but did improve the functioning of the existing system.

Many reformers approached conservation, for example, largely in terms of emotional, aesthetic, and moral values. But Roosevelt and the more sophisticated corporation leaders who played a large part in initiating the program supported it for rather different reasons. As Roosevelt remarked, "conservation means development as much as it does protection." Some agrarian groups that supported other Progressive reforms fought conservation just as bitterly as did interest-conscious operators in industry. Both wanted the land and resources for immediate exploitation. The same kind of paradoxical and complex alignments helped Roosevelt to establish the Department of Commerce and Labor with a special Bureau of Corporations to keep watch on the giants. Efficiency also emerged from the morality that motivated many of the votes for the Elkins Act against rebates (1903), and for the Hepburn Act of 1906, which increased the power of the Interstate Commerce Commission and extended its authority over pipe lines and other modes of transportation.

The evidence suggests that the reformers improved the existing system more by making it work better than by changing it in any significant ways. The corporation remained dominant, and the Progressives did very little to strengthen even the relative position of labor or agriculture. In an important sense, therefore, the greatest accomplishment of the early reform drive of the Progressive Movement was in its educational effect. Americans became more conscious of the system, learned something about its nature and weaknesses, and began to think more explicitly about how it could be improved, operated, and controlled. Along with the intellectuals who followed one or another variant of the Christian Capitalism that evolved out of the new economics and the convergence of science and religion in environmental Darwinism, the group of Progressives that gained the most was composed of the more sophisticated corporation leaders who began to recognize the practical limitations and social dangers of an interest-conscious approach.

This was of crucial importance, for without the gentry the Progressive coalition did not prove to be very dynamic until such corporation spokesmen gained positions of leadership. Theodore Roosevelt not only outlined between 1907 and 1910 every piece of Progressive legislation that was passed before World War I and most that came afterward, but some of his ideas, such as federal control of corporation prices in time of peace, have never been enacted. He also accomplished most of his victories before the reformers were organized as an effective force. By working first with the more broad-gauged corporation men like Hanna, Morgan, and Perkins, and then with the influence he could win by appeals to the public, and through tough, shrewd deals with interest-conscious politicians like House Leader Joseph G. Cannon, Roosevelt managed such triumphs as the stabilizing of the economy during the Panic of 1907 and the passage of the Hepburn Act.

Granting those achievements, and the relative sophistication of his conception of the political economy, the underlying weakness of even Roosevelt's outlook became very apparent by the time he left the White House. In the famous coal strike of 1902, for example, the lack of any positive, creative philosophy forced him to threaten nationalization of the mines. While no doubt effective as an occasional threat, or even as a serious proposal in the case of declining industries, that kind of approach offered nothing in the way of a long-range, routine way of coordinating the system. Nor was the settlement itself anything more than an evasion of the entire issue that set a precedent for the entire Progressive Movement. It was the kind of syndicalist and inflationary-expansionist solution that has now become traditional: the miners got a 10 per cent raise in wages, the operators increased their prices 10 per cent, and the consumer paid 10 per cent for the privilege of again buying coal. Two syndicalist units of the political economy simply divided more on the same basis instead of working out a more equitable and dynamic settlement.

Though he entertained far more of an interest-conscious outlook, and was in any event a lazy man not much given to thought, President William Howard Taft nevertheless had a rough insight into the dangers in the way that Roosevelt's feudal *noblesse oblige* turned into a nationalistic, conservative syndicalism when applied to an industrial society. As the imagery of the Square Deal suggested, it was no more than a promise that each interest would get an honest card each time around. Not even that part of the commitment was fulfilled, and it was not even implied that the cards would be equal. Nor could they be, given the rules of capitalism or the nature of the corporation economy.

Worried by the implications of what he mistakenly termed Roosevelt's "tendency to socialism"—it was really a rather rudimentary

approach to state capitalism—Taft felt safer with a straightforward interest-conscious strategy. His great enemy was the railroad, and the Mann-Elkins act of 1910 strengthened the Hepburn
Act by further extending the power of the Interstate Commerce
Commission. He also favored a corporation income tax, and
initially encouraged the reformers in their attack on Cannon's
autocratic control of the House of Representatives. But his real
answer to the problems of the system was overseas economic
expansion. He offered the argument, by then standard, that such
an extension of the market place would provide prosperity, and
added that it would do so without Roosevelt's dangerous domestic
policies. Hence he vigorously pushed a policy of "active intervention to secure for our merchandise and our capitalists opportunity
for profitable investment."

In that ironic way, therefore, both Taft the conservative and
Roosevelt the Progressive fell back on nationalism and overseas
economic expansion as the only ideas that would unify or sustain
the system. So, too, did Woodrow Wilson, though at the time of his
rapid rise to the Presidency he seemed to offer something else. That
impression, which has influenced a good many later commentators
just as it did many Progressives at the time, derived from the fact that
Wilson was the first (and only) representative of the intellectual and
Christian Capitalist wings of the Progressive Movement to win top
political leadership. As might be expected, one of the major elements
in that triumph was Wilson's *very* strong drive for personal power. "I
should be complete," he wrote in his early years, "if I could inspire a
great movement of opinion." And in his intimate conversations with
Frederick Jackson Turner, whose frontier thesis of American democracy and prosperity he accepted whole-heartedly, Wilson talked
often "of the power of leadership; of the untested power of the man
of literary ability in the field of diplomacy." As Turner put it, Wilson
"mentioned his ambition to get into political life."

As perceptive as he was determined, Wilson cultivated three
sources of such power that would help one who lacked any functional base of operations. He identified with the traditions of the
Christian trustee *and* the southern neo-feudal gentry, and he
analyzed American society to the conclusion that large business
enterprise was the most powerful interest. Entering politics through
a very direct alliance with that interest, Wilson then stepped forth

as the Christian Capitalist who would balance and unify the system according to the true gospel. Wilson was an effective political leader by virtue of his willingness to strike compromises with the large corporation community and his exceptional ability to dramatize himself and Christian Capitalism in highly righteous rhetoric. Yet it is often forgotten or overlooked that he won his first election only through a split in the Republican party, and squeaked through in the second only by a *very* narrow margin. Actually, Wilson became the symbol of Progressivism only as and after he began to emphasize foreign policy.

Neither Wilson nor his early advisors offered any new ideas or programs. The Federal Trade Commission Act was an old recommendation that Wilson got credit for because the reformers had won control of many states and thereby increased their power in Congress. Along with Representative Oscar W. Underwood, the party's tariff spokesman since the 1890s, Wilson and other Democrats candidly admitted that their low tariff bill was designed to extend overseas markets more effectively than the reciprocity approach advocated by Republicans. And the conservative, basically interest-conscious Republican Senator Aldrich had either done himself or directed most of the research that finally matured as the Federal Reserve Act.

Wilson's role in securing that legislation was of course significant. He checked the narrow-minded corporation leaders who failed to grasp the virtues of such a centralized banking system, and pacified the reformers who, like Madison and Calhoun in an earlier age, wanted it more directly controlled by the government. It was in many respects the single most important piece of legislation of the prewar era, for it reestablished in a more sophisticated and effective form the badly needed institution of a national bank. Wilson deserves all credit for his part in rationalizing the financial basis of the political economy. But though he could have appointed men of a different background and outlook—a few economists of the Christian Capitalist view, for example—Wilson selected men from the banking community to direct the powerful central board of the Federal Reserve Banks.

As he had spoken in 1912, so Wilson acted in 1914: "the truth [is] that, in the new order, government and business must be associated." Having successfully appealed to the reformers for election, he showed little more sympathy for, or interest in, labor than he had when he opposed the unions in the coal strike of 1902. Nor was he in favor of assisting farmers through government credit facilities; that would be class legislation. With considerable justification, therefore, he sought even before the outbreak of World War I to counter the impression that he was against business. "It would be particularly unfair to the Democratic Party and the Senate itself," he remarked, "to regard it as the enemy of business, big or little." Quite properly for a Christian Capitalist, Wilson announced in 1914 that "the antagonism between business and Government is over."

Wanting only to improve and sustain the system, Wilson and other Progressive leaders were by that time very seriously upset by the depression that had begun as a financial downturn in 1913. They simply did not have any more ideas about how to maintain the even moderately successful functioning of the economy. For that matter, their record up to 1912 was not very exceptional. Manufacturing production had almost doubled (from 100 in 1899 to 199 in 1913) but real wages had improved over the 1890–1899 average in only three years of that decade. During the winter of 1914–1915, Massachusetts labor unions reported that 18.3 per cent of their members were out of work; and a random check in New York revealed that 23.7 per cent of 115,960 families had working members who were out of work. As for agriculture, commodity prices had been leveling off since 1912, and many farmers feared that the depression would hit them next.

Wilson's solution was to maintain official silence about the depression while turning to a vigorous program of overseas economic expansion. Though this is often interpreted as a drastic new aspect of Wilson's leadership, it was actually only the reemergence of a very old, pronounced, and persistent theme in his basic outlook. Having accepted Turner's frontier thesis about democracy and prosperity even as Turner was working it out, Wilson applied it almost literally to the problems of the new corporation order. Attributing the "tense and difficult" crisis of the 1890s to the closing of the frontier and the ending of "the days of glad expansion," he defended further expansion as a "natural and wholesome impulse" and described the Philippines as offering "new frontiers." And he interpreted Washington's Farewell Address in the same way, but with even less restraint than had men like John Quincy Adams.

Washington "would seem to have meant," Wilson explained in 1900, " 'I want you to discipline yourselves and . . . be good boys until you . . . are big enough . . . to go abroad in the world.' " Wilson clearly thought America was big enough.

Having warned bankers to prepare for a "day of reckoning" as early as 1910, and decried "our provincialism" in international finance early in 1912, Wilson then offered a full-scale analysis to a group of labor leaders and other reformers during the presidential campaign itself. "Almost by inevitable consequence," he explained, prosperity "consists in the growth of enterprise and the growth of commerce." America's "domestic market is too small," he continued. "We have reached, in short, a crucial point in the process of our prosperity. It has become a question with us whether it shall continue or shall not continue." "If [America] doesn't get bigger foreign markets, she will burst her jacket. There will be a congestion in this country which will be more fatal economically than any wider opening of the ports could be."

Wilson's renewed emphasis in 1914 on overseas economic expansion sustained the policies of Roosevelt and Taft, as well as giving practical meaning to his own earlier analyses. That expansion represented even more obviously the kind of consolidation and cooperation that was developing between business and the reformers in domestic affairs. It also provided the basic context of America's ultimate involvement in World War I. For along with many other leaders concerned with the problem, Wilson in 1912 had seen Germany as the main competitor for economic empire.

CHAPTER FOUR

The Transformation of Reality and the Inception of New Ideas

If the American public is to be educated to the point of financing the sale of our materials abroad—and that is the question of foreign trade and foreign loans—the American Government must make some statement which will reassure the public and give them the thought and the belief that in case of default, or in case of difficulty . . . that the Government will act as the advocate of the public and in the international courts of diplomacy.

Willard Straight of the House of Morgan (and formerly of the Department of State), 1914

Our prosperity is dependent on our continued and enlarged foreign trade. To preserve that we must do everything we can to assist our customers to buy. . . . To maintain our prosperity, we must finance it. Otherwise it may stop and that would be disastrous.

Secretary of the Treasury William G. McAdoo to President Wilson, 1915

We are passing from a period of extremely individualistic action into a period of associational activities.

Herbert Hoover, 1922

The participation of American corporations in the development of Latin America involves an incalculable corrective to existing trade figures and implies a distinct and direct American influence in Latin American policies. Irrespective of the policy at Washington and the personality of statesmen, the operations of such enterprises as the United Fruit Company or the several American oil companies create independent political interests in the territories subject to their economic operation which supplement and often determine official policy both at Washington and in the various Latin American capitals.

The Department of State, 1930

Our productive capacity today is 25 per cent in excess of our ability to consume. . . . These glaring facts and conditions soon will compel America to recognize that these ever increasing surpluses are her key economic problems, and that our neglect to develop foreign markets for surpluses is the one outstanding cause of unemployment.

Representative Cordell Hull, January 3, 1929

There is mean things happenin' in this land;
There is mean things happenin' in this land.
Oh, the rich man boasts and brags,
While the poor man goes in rags,
There is mean things happenin' in this land.

Depression Chant of Negro Sharecroppers, 1934

Boys—this is our hour. We've got to get everything we want—a works program, social security, wages and hours, everything—now or never.

New Deal Reformer Harry Hopkins, 1934

I see millions of families trying to live on incomes so meager that the pall of family disaster hangs over them day by day. . . . I see one-third of a nation ill-housed, ill-clad, ill-nourished.

President Franklin Delano Roosevelt, 1937

With 12 millions unemployed, we are socially bankrupt and politically unstable.

Secretary of Commerce Harry Hopkins, 1939

We can no longer be sure that unemployment is a cyclical problem appearing and disappearing as the economy alternates between depression and prosperity. Unemployment may be an enduring problem arising from a continued diminished volume of private investment.

New Deal Political Economist John K. Galbraith, 1940

THE APPLICATION AND SIGNIFICANCE OF THE OPEN DOOR POLICY

Although dramatic and important events that offer obvious landmarks, neither the First and Second World Wars nor the Great Depression provide wholly satisfactory points of perspective for understanding and interpreting American history in the 20th

THE TRANSFORMATION OF REALITY

century. Both the nature and direction of American thinking and development are more fully and accurately comprehended within a slightly different framework. Wilson's decisions in domestic economic affairs and foreign policy between his inauguration and the outbreak of the war represented not only the Progressive Movement's adaptation to the corporation, but also marked the beginning of a period of transformation that continued on through the Crash of 1929 to 1938, when the reforming social worker Harry Hopkins was appointed Secretary of Commerce and reiterated Wilson's argument that any future gains would have to come through overseas economic expansion.

As far as domestic economic affairs are concerned, the era between the depression of 1913–1914 and the severe recession of 1937–1938 offers a far more accurate and revealing unit than the Great Depression itself. For that period was in reality one long, coherent cycle in which the economy suffered four significant downturns. As with the first, so with the last: recovery came only through the boost provided by involvement in war. During the same years, moreover, the corporation community produced a small core of leadership with extended and deepened economic and social perceptions that ultimately matured as what was in almost every respect a class-conscious gentry. Herbert Hoover was the key figure of that achievement, offering economic proposals such as public works as early as 1920, and making analyses of the fundamental political and social issues that remain illuminating more than 40 years later. Working in their different but converging traditions, other Progressive intellectuals concurrently evolved economic and philosophic concepts and systems appropriate to that new leadership, and to the mature political economy of the large corporation.

At the same time, some of the weaker elements of the economy, particularly labor and agriculture, organized more effectively and achieved a rough parity with the corporation that was later extended and consolidated. Through the same period, moreover, the fundamental role of the government as *the* accumulator of capital (through taxes) for the corporation economy was gradually institutionalized. And finally, a firm intellectual and moral challenge to the frontier and expansionist ideology of American history, and policy, was developed and offered as an alternate *Weltanschauung*. In sum, entry into World War I was part of the transformation of

American society that had already begun, whereas involvement in World War II was the first phase of an era of fulfillment for the corporation society.

In both situations, American leaders had turned to overseas economic expansion as the strategy of recovery and future prosperity *before* the United States became involved in the conflicts as either a non-fighting belligerent or an active military protagonist. Neither the New Freedom nor the New Deal sustained their outbursts of self-contained confidence and élan or maintained the atmosphere of a commonwealth that characterized them for brief periods. In each case, therefore, the system began to produce welfare and a sense of community only as a by-product of warfare. Neither the Progressives nor their conservative critics went to war because they wanted to. But their ideas and their interests produced programs and actions that led them into situations in which war became the only policy that seemed practical—or moral.

This convergence of the morality and practicality of expansion had, of course, begun with the mercantilists, had been sustained through the 19th century by Jacksonian Democrats and Lincoln Republicans, and had emerged with renewed vigor at the turn of the 20th century. Quite in keeping with the traditional outlook of the gentry and with his personal estimate of the opportunities and difficulties facing the United States, Theodore Roosevelt defined the foreign policy problem in broad terms: to establish, maintain, and exploit an open door for the economic expansion of the corporation political economy. "I regard the Monroe Doctrine," he explained in a classic summary of his policy, "as being equivalent to the open door in South America."

Bluntly staking out the preserve in the Western Hemisphere, Roosevelt told each Latin American nation that it could count on the "hearty friendship" of the United States if it acted with "reasonable efficiency and decency in social and political matters," and "if it keeps order and pays its obligations." If the nations behaved, "prosperity is sure to come to them." If not, then the United States would intervene: on the one hand, to chastise wrongdoing and establish minimum conditions for profitable enterprise, and on the other, to keep other industrial powers from weakening America's position. Violating his own pledge against territorial intervention, he took the Panama Canal Zone from Colombia in as brazen a bit of imperial

THE TRANSFORMATION OF REALITY   417

land-grabbing as is recorded in modern history. Given the strategy
of the Open Door Policy, the act could of course be justified. In view
of the bitter competition for empire, the United States could wait no
longer for rapid commercial and military transit to and from Asia.

But it was not the want of a canal that kept Roosevelt from
being effective in Asia. America lacked the relative predominance
of power it enjoyed in the Western Hemisphere, and was belatedly invading an area already claimed by other powers. Thus a full
commitment for a major push into China implied war with Japan,
and perhaps with others. But the Open Door Policy was conceived
as a way to win the economic battle without a war, and even had
he decided to use force as well as talk about it, Roosevelt knew that
it would be very difficult, if not impossible, to obtain the necessary
public support at that time. For the "splendid little war" was too
fresh a memory, and the public had accepted the victory-without-
war logic of the Open Door Policy.

Another alternative was to work with the Russians, probably sharing in the development of Siberia as well as of China.
Encouraged by the Russians, who saw such an entente as protection against Japan, a group of railroad leaders and other businessmen headed by James J. McCook had tried to swing McKinley to
this plan in the 1890s. At that time, Roosevelt seemed to agree.
But Standard Oil opposed the move, and Morgan was very
cautious, preferring his traditional ties with England. And by
1903 Roosevelt and Hay had themselves become strongly anti-
Russian. Their strategy was to support Japan (ostensibly the
weaker power) in the thought that the result would be a stalemate between Tokyo and St. Petersburg. They argued that this
would enable America to consolidate and extended its then
(1903) very strong—if not predominant—position in the trade
and commerce of Manchuria.

Japan's subsequent victory over Russia ended that rosy prospect.
Tokyo pushed American corporations and traders out of Northeastern
Asia and firmly closed the open door. Spurning the advice of
several high officials who recommended a favorable response,
Roosevelt ignored new Russian overtures. Instead, he took the only
remaining alternative. Accepting Japan's predominant position in
Manchuria, he launched the United States on a Far Eastern policy
that it was to follow until Pearl Harbor. Reemphasizing the Open

Door Policy, and its own commitment in China, America chose at the same time to gain what direct and indirect benefits it could through economic ties with Japan, including Tokyo's projects on the mainland. Coupled with political and military pressure, as in Roosevelt's dispatch of the Great White Fleet to Japan in 1907, the United States anticipated that such economic ties would enable it to control Japan's penetration of China proper.

Roosevelt also concerned himself with a certain kind of reform in the underdeveloped countries into which America's expansion was directed. As in his manifestoes to Latin America, this approach was revealed very clearly in his intervention in the scramble between France, England, and Germany for African colonies and spheres of influence. Determined to obtain "an equal share in whatever priveleges of residence, trade, and protection" were given up by the Moroccan Empire, Roosevelt and Secretary of State Elihu Root also exerted strong pressure for internal changes. They wanted "far-reaching reform" that would guarantee "security of life and property; equality of opportunities for trade with all natives [regardless of religion or class] . . . orderly and certain administration of impartial justice; rigorous punishment of crimes against persons and property . . . and the power to repress subversive disorder and preserve the public peace." They demanded, in short, reforms that would create such conditions "that the door, being open, shall lead to something; that the outside world shall benefit by assured opportunities, and that the Moroccan people shall be made in a measure fit and able to profit by the advantages" of the new relationship with the United States and other industrial powers.

President Taft sustained that policy, as in Latin America, and in his personal pressure on the Prince Regent of China to win American participation in a large multi-nation loan. But Taft encountered a fundamental (and ironic) difficulty: America needed at least one major reform at home before it could exploit the Open Door Policy that it had embraced. It was simply an unhappy but undeniable fact that, though overseas investments had jumped from $700 million in 1897 to $3.5 billion in 1914, the corporation political economy could not itself accumulate all the capital it needed to finance the exports that were considered vital to prosperity and social peace. Such crises as the Panic of 1907, which aborted Harriman's grandiose plan to collaborate with the Russians in Asia, effectively dramatized the problem.

So did Willard Straight, who served as an advisor to Harriman as well as filling a similar role in the State Department before shifting over to the House of Morgan after Harriman's death in 1909. As a close student of what he called former Secretary of State Seward's "prophetic words" about expansion, Straight understood that the government had to help accumulate the capital as well as protect the investment itself. As he put it, the public had to be "educated" concerning its vital role in financing corporation exports. Taft was willing to supply such aid in the form of an official endorsement of the China loan. But his defeat by Wilson, followed by the onset of the depression in 1913, reopened and intensified the problem.

In a move that has often been misunderstood, Wilson refused the request of the bankers for a new and public display of support. The key to that rejection lies in two remarks. Secretary of State Bryan commented that the administration disliked such multi-nation loans because the American banking group "could not have a controlling voice" in the operations. For his part, and speaking to a session of the National Foreign Trade Convention assembled in the East Room of the White House for a special audience, Wilson stressed his concern for the "righteous conquest of foreign markets." As "one of the things that we hold nearest to our heart," he assured the businessmen that he and his administration would "co-operate in the most intimate manner in accomplishing our common object."

Wilson was simply being true to his conception of Christian Capitalism, to his understanding of the frontier thesis of American history, and to his view of himself as the agent of world reform. The discrepancy between his public moral lecture to the bankers and his private reassurances to them (Straight called them "very satisfactory") was neither unique in American politics nor particularly surprising for a conservative who had won the election by appealing to the reform vote. Like Roosevelt and Root, Wilson wanted an *American* economic empire and understood the importance of reforms of a certain kind if the open door was to lead to prosperity. As Bryan explained to the businessmen, Wilson had a very broad approach: he "contemplates the formation of an environment which will encourage" such expansion.

The President anticipated that an independent moral posture would improve America's standing, and hence America's influence, in China. Nor is there any question of his sincerity: he was simply a Christian Capitalist who took a sophisticated view of the relationship between reform and profits. As he made clear, he intended the United States to "participate, and participate very generously, in the opening to the Chinese and to the use of the world the almost untouched and perhaps unrivaled resources of China." To that end he went on to initiate a broad range of studies, proposals, and laws designed to extend the Open Door Policy, to exempt expanding corporations from anti-trust prosecutions, and to provide American operators with "the banking and other financial facilities which they now lack and without which they are at a serious disadvantage."

THE PROGRESSIVE COALITION GOES TO WAR

Wilson's vigorous economic and even military intervention in the domestic affairs of several Caribbean countries and in the Mexican Revolution was generated and guided by the same practical morality of his Christian Capitalism. That outlook also explains why his famous phrase—"The world must be made safe for democracy"—accurately summarized all the elements bearing on America's entry into World War I. Underlying that involvement was the fundamental reality that between 1895 and 1914 the United States had developed a corporation political economy, and had defined its immediate and future wealth and welfare in terms of imperial economic expansion. Already wobbly from internal malfunctioning, the economy was stunned by the outbreak of the war in Europe which subjected it to major deflationary pressures. Hence the central decision came very early and was very clearly defined: How would the country reestablish its vital relationship to the world economy, and particularly with the belligerents and their colonies who purchased 77 per cent of America's exports and were intimately involved in its financial affairs?

Frank A. Vanderlip of the National City Bank and a key man in the formation in 1914 of the American International Corporation designed to undertake major overseas development projects, summarized the situation very candidly. "You must remember that at the time of the war's beginning, the country was not in a prosperous condition. . . . We had the idea very much of keeping up our foreign trade throughout the world." Morgan offered a similar analysis. "The war opened during a period of hard times that had continued in America for over a year. Business throughout the country was depressed, farm prices were deflated, unemployment was serious, the heavy industries were working far below capacity, [and] bank clearings were off." For that reason, as well as because nobody wanted to go to war, the idea of true neutrality elicited a favorable response. But though the words were used, the actions of American leaders did not follow such neutrality for the simple reason that Germany was from the beginning considered a dangerous economic rival and an enemy of Progressive values.

That ideological orientation of the Progressive Movement, and of Wilson in particular, came to provide the basic rhetoric of American involvement. It was expressed very pointedly as early as the summer of 1915, for example, by Robert Lansing, a deeply religious corporation lawyer who became Secretary of State after Bryan resigned in opposition to Wilson's ever firmer stand against Germany. Lansing thought a German victory would "mean the overthrow of democracy in the world . . . and the turning back of the hands of human progress two centuries." Ethnic ties, and ideology, that connected the great majority of Americans to the Allies extended and intensified such philosophical favoritism.

Those factors, as well as past business associations, reinforced the specific economic connections that such firms as Morgan and du Pont quickly developed with the English and French war effort. Far more important than those interest bonds, however, was the way in which the entire political economy of the large corporation in its every functional element became intimately involved with the Allied war economy. Wilson understood the implications of that interpenetration, and it was discussed throughout the government and in general as well as in high public forums. In all probability, the crucial debate occurred among the central directors of the Federal Reserve Board.

One group, led by investment banker Paul M. Warburg, offered two strong arguments against further commitment of the economy to the Allied war programs. It risked serious economic consequences because the prosperity was artificial and it would weaken the efforts of the United States to build its own economic empire. Others, including Secretary of the Treasury William G. McAdoo, favored all-out exploitation of the opportunities. He appealed directly to Wilson on the grounds that "great prosperity is coming." "To preserve that," he bluntly told the President, "we must do everything we can. . . . Otherwise it may stop and that would be disastrous."

Late in 1915, Wilson made the crucial decision to support the McAdoo group. It signified the Progressive Movement's commitment to that strategy for sustaining current economic development, and tied existing prosperity, and Democratic Party fortunes, to further involvement with the Allies. It also signaled the onset of a fundamental drift in the thinking of American leaders on the issue of sustaining the private property economy of corporation capitalism. Together with his decision, also in 1915, to support and lead the preparedness movement, Wilson and his associates had involved the government in helping the corporation economy accumulate capital—through war orders and later war loans—under a banner of Christian Capitalism that did not challenge property rights.

Even as late as 1916, Wilson still hoped, along with most Americans, to accomplish the defeat of Germany and thereby establish the framework of a Progressive and Open Door world without recourse to war. But neither Germany nor Great Britain was willing to permit America to dominate a negotiated settlement or to allow the other to win by default. Germany's recourse to all-out submarine warfare threatened to defeat the allies and thereby end Wilson's pious hope to apply the principles of Progressive Christian Capitalism to the world. Just as English, French, and German leaders, Wilson chose to fight rather than modify or abandon his objectives.

WILSON'S DIFFICULTIES WITH THE RADICAL CHALLENGE TO CORPORATION CAPITALISM

Quite in keeping with his entire career, Wilson's program for peace was a potpourri of Progressive ideas and policies transferred to the international scene and infused with the emotion and righteousness of Christian Capitalism. Its basic purpose as he later explained, was to survey, grade, and build "The Road Away From Revolution." It thus involved establishing a set of rules (such as the principle of the open door, the freedom of the seas, and political boundaries coinciding with ethnic distribution); providing for enforcement (as in Articles X and XVI of the League of Nations

Covenant which outlawed territorial changes and provided for enforcing that provision); effecting compromises between advanced powers and the underdeveloped countries that insured continued economic expansion by the former (as in the mandate system); arranging compromises between industrial powers (as between Japan and the United States in Asia); and inaugurating a system of future control to be dominated by the United States, Western European nations (ultimately including Germany), and Japan. Having vetoed the bank's consortium in China, Wilson proposed a consortium of advanced industrial nations led by the United States as the first and most powerful among equals that would regulate and reform the development of all the Chinas of the world. He asked for no reparations except the acceptance by the rest of the world of America's Progressive *Weltanschauung.*

Wilson's grand effort was defeated by a strange coalition of three groups that cut across all domestic political as well as international boundaries. Radicals and left-wing reformers abroad offered the most fundamental criticism and, through the impact of the Bolshevik Revolution in Russia, probably turned the balance against Wilson. Whether through Marxism, as in Russia and other European countries, through native traditions, as in Mexico, or both, as in China, such radicals had sustained and now reasserted the ideal of a self-defined and controlled commonwealth based on social property that had characterized one wing of Christianity and the English Revolution.

Wilson understood the nature and the significance of that challenge to American expansion and influence, and to his own Christian Capitalist wing of the Progressive Movement. Since the complaints against the abuses committed with the power and in the name of private property were justified, and since the Progressive tradition upheld the right of protest, Wilson admitted that "it certainly was a cruel dilemma." But he favored "a slow process of reform" and hence used American power against the radicals in Russia, central and eastern Europe, China, and Mexico. That decision very probably turned a crucial handful of Progressives like Hiram Johnson of California, William Borah of Idaho, and Robert M. La Follette of Wisconsin irrevocably against Wilson's League of Nations Treaty. Wilson's action also dramatized the impossibility of preventing change without a constant recourse to force, and this became the basis of opposition by members of the gentry like Henry L. Stimson, sophisticated corporation spokesmen like Herbert Hoover and Elihu Root, and interest-conscious leaders like William Boyce Thompson of the House of Morgan. Joining with vigorous expansionists like Henry Cabot Lodge and disgusted corporation leaders who were impatient with the delay in getting on with what Vanderlip called the commercial "war after the war," these groups mustered enough votes to defeat Wilson and the treaty.

This reversal was paralleled by the failure of Wilson (or the reformers) to offer any concrete proposals to sustain the economy after the war boom. Neither did they implement his vague idea of "some sort of partnership" between capital and labor and thereby provide some beginnings of community within the functional and syndicalist system. These moral and practical failures ended the power, appeal, and direct influence of the Christian Capitalist wing of the Progressive Movement. The collapse produced a shock of disillusionment that converted many reformers into cynics disguised as realists, and turned many Americans against extensive reform. In later years, particularly after World War II, many Progressives used the rhetoric of Christian Capitalism as part of their ideological warfare against radicalism at home and abroad. And in many respects, Secretary of State John Foster Dulles was a displaced missionary of this outlook. But as a politically significant effort to synthesize a Progressive *Weltanschauung* for the corporation system, this movement ended with Wilson. Its last and appropriately grotesque influence resulted from atmosphere that it had created, for this was distorted and misused by the Christian Temperance movement to jam through a prohibition law in 1919 which, by dint of further bigoted crusading, was to be sustained until 1933.

Since domestic radicalism had been defeated by a combination of the Wilson Administration's vigorous physical and political repression, and its own internal divisions over the meaning and authority of the Bolshevik Revolution, the Progressives had two sources of leadership. One was the possibility that La Follette could rally the reformers, form a coalition with labor and agriculture, and run the country along the lines of prewar policies and programs. Though providing for effective leadership at the state level, such a program was inappropriate and insufficient for the national political economy. Either it veered so far toward socialism in order to become relevant and effective that it lost support as an attack on private property, or it simply lacked any dynamic appeal because it had been tried and found wanting. La Follette tried both approaches and was defeated each time.

THE CENTRAL ROLE OF HERBERT HOOVER IN THE MATURATION OF AN INDUSTRIAL GENTRY

As a result, the sophisticated corporation leaders moved into authority within the Progressive Movement. They faced four major problems. Most troublesome, at least in the overt sense, was their running fight with narrow interest-conscious members of the corporation community. Those men neither understood, nor wanted to learn, the broader approach of men like Herbert Hoover and Owen D. Young. Hoover and his allies faced similar, and sometimes even more irrational, opposition from the reformers. At the same time, the Hoover group struggled to transform their sophistication into the true class consciousness of an industrial gentry and to evolve a program that would sustain and improve the functioning of the system. And finally, Hoover and his associates needed desperately to increase the numbers of their own group and, if possible, effect a liaison with the remaining members of the earlier agrarian gentry. Without those gains, they had no hope of assuming leadership of the Progressive Movement on a routine and bipartisan basis.

Along with other such corporation spokesmen, Hoover had moved beyond the interest-conscious approach prior to the war. The idea of coordinating industry at the national level, for example, was discussed seriously as early as 1907. In addition to the heated debate over the Federal Reserve System, Wilson's emphasis on overseas expansion had produced further interest as a part of the investigations and studies of the Federal Trade Commission, the U.S. Tariff Commission, and various Congressional inquiries. But it was, of course, their war experiences that affected these men most deeply. "What was done in those war years," commented speculator and financier Bernard Baruch, "was never to be completely forgotten." They learned and practiced "the co-ordination of industries and resources," recognized the relationship between such planning and high profits, and saw the concrete benefits of organizing and stabilizing labor relations within the corporation framework. As a result, such men as Young, Charles G. Dawes and Dwight Morrow (of the House of Morgan), Julius

Rosenwald (of Sears, Roebuck), Howard E. Coffin (of Hudson Motor Co.), Gerald P. Swope (of General Electric), Theodore N. Vail (of Bell Telephone), and Daniel Willard (of the Baltimore and Ohio Railroad) emerged from the war determined to manage the system more effectively, efficiently, and equitably.

Though men like Rosenwald and Morrow, Swope and Young, and Dawes and Willard were very important figures, the key leader among those Progressive and sophisticated corporation executives was Herbert Hoover. But Hoover was smeared and defamed by the Democrats in 1932 as the callous, incompetent, and autocratic cause of the Great Depression. As a result, he is very seldom recognized and acknowledged for what he is: the keystone in the arch that leads from Mark Hanna and Herbert Croly to such later figures as Nelson Rockefeller and Adolph Berle.* Hoover came very close to being, perhaps he was, the first truly class-conscious corporation leader produced by the system. While two wrongs do not make a right, there is a kind of poetic justice in the way that Democrats who helped to smear Hoover were later and with equal injustice smeared by Republicans as men who sold China down the river to the communists after World War II. If nothing else, the episodes reveal the thoroughly bipartisan nature of demagoguery in American politics. Hoover no more had the depression to give to the American people than Harry Truman or Dean Acheson had China to give to Mao Tse-tung.

---

* Several comments may be relevant for the reader in considering the following analysis and interpretation of Hoover, since it is somewhat different from the routine estimate. Hoover offers a classic example of the necessity for historians to break out of their own frame of reference if they are to understand the past. More than any other 20th-century American's, Hoover's reputation is the product of misinformation and distortion. He is also a notable example of the man whose ideas are borrowed by others without acknowledgment, and of the man whose analyses and insights are proved valid after an unfavorable stereotype has been established. For that reason it is easy to overlook them, and to assume that his failures comprise the whole story. This estimate of Hoover is based on extended research in his correspondence that can be found in the manuscript collections of other people; in his published books, testimony, and miscellaneous writings; in the government archives during his long official service; in the mass of secondary accounts of his activities (which include many quotations); and through interviews with 27 persons who either worked with him or opposed him vigorously. The writer's opinion of Hoover changed considerably as a consequence of research in these materials.

Beyond the fact that he contributed to the founding fund of Croly's *New Republic* in 1914 and became one of Wilson's closest advisors after 1916, perhaps the most effective testimony to Hoover's progressivism comes from the Democrats. They very seriously approached him to accept their nomination for the Presidency in 1920. "He is certainly a wonder," exclaimed Franklin Roosevelt when Wilson's Assistant Secretary of the Navy, "and I wish we could make him President of the United States. There could not be a better one."

Though that wish was not fulfilled until 1928, and then by the Republicans, Hoover exercised great power and was a key figure in American history during his service as Secretary of Commerce under Presidents Warren G. Harding and Calvin Coolidge. Throughout those years, Hoover was quite aware that the American economic system was not functioning satisfactorily at a time when it faced stiff competition from capitalist rivals and the across-the-board radical challenge symbolized by the Soviet Union. He also realized that the outbreak of radicalism stemmed from "the great inequalities and injustices of centuries." Hence any return to "individualism run riot" would only increase "social ferment and class consciousness" among the lower classes and thereby accelerate the "drift toward socialism."

Convinced that "the failure and unsolved problems of economic and social life can be corrected," and that the crucial element of that success "must be a high and growing standard of living for all the people, not for a single class," Hoover analyzed the corporation economy and offered an exceedingly thorough program to correct errors and underwrite future prosperity. In a way that was strikingly similar to the prewar efforts of Progressive intellectual Walter Weyl, Hoover sought an approach that would preserve private property and the large corporation yet at the same time create the conditions for the flowering of a "new individualism."

Studying the corporation political economy, Hoover concluded that it was composed of three basic functional and syndicalist elements: capital (including agricultural operators as well as industrialists and financiers), labor, and the public at large, represented institutionally by the government. Each citizen was a member of two of those groups. Arguing that "Progress is born of Cooperation," Hoover proposed three fundamental strategies for achieving that goal. Within capital and labor, cooperation in trade associations, agricultural cooperatives, and unions was necessary and legitimate and should be encouraged by the government. Between capital and labor, collective bargaining played a similar role. Led by sophisticated and responsible men, that is, by a class-conscious industrial gentry, and ultimately controlled by the citizen through his vote, the national government assumed the task of coordinating and balancing each of those major elements of the political economy and of providing the assistance needed to sustain economic development.

With great perception, Hoover saw the dangers inherent in such a political economy. He also had the courage to face them openly and squarely. There were four of them. "Where dominant private property is assembled in the hands of the groups who control the state," fascism resulted. In other words, interest-conscious corporation leaders would produce fascism if not controlled and educated. Without any doubt, Hoover analyzed and specified the danger of fascism long before the reformers within the Progressive Movement did. Second, labor could acquire the same kind of power and produce socialism. Or, third, if the government itself came to extend its power under the leadership of purely political leaders as narrowly interest-conscious in their way, and for their careers, as their opposite numbers in the capital group, the result would be bureaucratic tyranny. And finally, in what proved to be an uncanny insight into what actually happened, Hoover saw the danger of "a syndicalist nation on a gigantic scale" in which power was controlled and exercised by a relatively few leaders of each functional bloc formed and operating as an oligarchy.

In all cases, therefore, Hoover concluded that the essential safeguard against danger was to prevent the government from becoming the dominant element in the system. Its function was to help individual units and to coordinate and regulate their interrelationships. But if it became *the* element, not only could one syndicalist unit take over the government and thereby dominate the system, but Hoover was both morally and practically opposed to having the government accumulate capital for the corporation. Such action placed the citizen in double economic jeopardy; for in addition to the profits taken by the corporation, or by other capitalists, from the price paid by the consumer, the consumer as citizen contributed another profit in the form of taxes that were paid to the government which then funneled them to the corporation through loans, contracts, or other subsidies. Hoover thought that this was immoral behavior toward future generations as well as toward the living. He also doubted that even that method of sustaining the system would work without ultimately involving the nation in wars undertaken either in defense or in extension of such investments.

At that point, Hoover came face to face with the traditional capitalist emphasis on expansion of the market place, and the frontier interpretation of American history which explained democracy and prosperity as a result of the same kind of expansion. He made a valiant effort, certainly the most courageous and rigorous one undertaken by any American in power after John Quincy Adams and Henry Clay, to evolve a way of having and eating the expansionist cake without paying for it by imperial wars. Thus he began by defining overseas economic expansion as the *sine qua non* of American wealth and welfare. It was "part of our domestic progress, both socially and economically" because it was "of peculiar importance to us in maintaining a stable and even operation" of the system, and because it brought recovery from setbacks "faster and more effectively." Nothing captures the nature and intensity of Hoover's emphasis on such overseas economic activities as succinctly as his remarks about the role of that expansion in America's developing relations with the Soviet Union. They were written on December 6, 1921, in answer to Secretary of State Charles Evans Hughes's suggestion, in line with the proposals of some financiers, to allow Germany to serve as middleman in trade with Russia.

"The hope of our commerce," Hoover tersely replied, "lies in the establishment of American firms abroad, distributing American goods under American direction; in the building of direct American financing and, above all, in the installation of American technology in Russian industries. We must, of necessity, in the future finance our own raw materials into Russia and if our manufactured goods are distributed through German hands it simply means that when Germany has established trade of sufficient distribution to warrant her own manufacture we shall lose the market."

At the same time, Hoover was aware that "a large part of the world has come to believe that they were in the presence of the birth of a new imperial power intent upon dominating the destinies and freedoms of other peoples." That could provoke war. In response, Hoover formulated three rules for America's expansion. "We should be mainly interested," he emphasized, "in development work abroad such as roads and utilities which increase the standards of living of people and thus increase the demand for goods from every nation, for we gain in prosperity by a prosperous world [and] not by displacing others." Such "development of backward or crippled countries" would blunt the jealousy and fear of America's power. A second kind of authority that he wanted, but failed to secure because of the fear that it would subvert the rights of private property, was full power to prevent loans being made for armaments or other non-developmental uses. Interest-conscious financiers blocked that move, though Hoover did win some control over their operations. And finally Hoover asserted, and honored, a strong disinclination to use threats—or actual violence—in defense or extension of the American empire.

In general and in particular, Hoover won support from three groups: the voting public, many industrial corporation leaders, and a significant part of the labor movement. Most importantly, the general public came to trust and respect his abilities and his integrity. He was never a popular leader in the sense that both Roosevelts were, but neither was he merely accepted. Hoover was also backed by the small but growing community of more perceptive corporation leaders. As vital figures in a political economy that by 1920 had more of its people in cities than on the land, and more employed in manufacturing than in agriculture, they were of crucial importance. By the end of the war, 31 per cent of all manufacturing concerns were corporations, and that group employed 86 per cent of all manufacturing labor and produced 87 per cent of manufactured products.

Manufacturing corporation leaders also gradually reasserted their control over the financiers and took more direct command of the industrial system during the 1920s. And even in the early part of the century, such men had been more inclined to take a broader view of labor relations and the political economy in general. Owen D. Young was one of the most sophisticated of that group. Deeply concerned by what he termed the loss of confidence by Americans since the closing of the continental frontier, he fully shared Hoover's concern with overseas economic expansion. He very bluntly (and authoritatively) explained why exports were so vital. They were "a most material contribution to our prosperity. The dividing line between prosperity and the want of it is so sensitive that all our surpluses vitally affect it." And like Hoover, he felt that the system would fail if it could not handle the surplus problem in a creative manner. "If America starts to burn surplus wheat or cotton, or what have you please, when people are hungry elsewhere in the world, that fire will start a conflagration which we cannot stop."

Young also worried about the increasing alienation of the worker in modern industry. He saw the "lack of zest," the deterioration of community, and tried to improve management policies accordingly. His fellow industrialist, Gerald Swope, even pleaded unsuccessfully with the A.F. of L. to organize the unskilled industrial workers at General Electric. Such men of course thought in terms of unions operating within the limits of the company structure, and were not advocating organizations that challenged management's prerogatives. But most union leaders were like-minded; indeed, the decade of the 1920s was marked by a distinct lack of militant labor activity. Hence it is not surprising to find that the key figures of the A.F. of L. shared most of Hoover's views.

Spurred on, though not formally led, by John P. Frey of the International Molders Union, the A.F. of L. operated on the assumptions that productivity was the key to prosperity and that "productivity can be enhanced through the cooperation of management with trade union activities." Wanting primarily to be accepted as a "partner" in the system, labor feared government intervention for the same reasons that Hoover did. Thus, while ambivalent about the importance of overseas economic expansion because it seemed to benefit the few much more than the many, labor opposed it vigorously only when it resulted in military intervention.

In an even more dramatic way, the railroad unions revealed the kind of conservative syndicalism that guided labor's thinking. Their Plumb Plan for rehabilitating and rationalizing the railroads proposed to consolidate them in a giant corporation run by a board composed of representatives from management, the unions, and the government. Often misunderstood or misconstrued as a socialist scheme, and very probably defeated on those grounds despite the support given to it by many corporation leaders, it was in reality an intelligent and thoroughgoing application of syndicalist principles to one particularly weak sector of the economy. And the Transportation Act of 1920, which further extended the powers of the Interstate Commerce Commission, was based on the same logic.

In another area, labor's commitment to cooperation with capital produced an undramatic result that nevertheless became very
important in later years. Joining with academic and corporation
economists, with industrial and financial corporation executives, and
with farm spokesmen, Frey helped to organize the National Bureau
of Economic Research, becoming its chairman from 1922 to 1928.
Along with the Brookings Institution, which evidenced a somewhat
narrower and more conservative outlook, the N.B.E.R. provided an
intellectual forum for the various functional elements of the economy.
Such groups were in many ways the most intelligent and productive
kind of philanthropy ever financed by the corporations. For they not
only provided a body of information and analyses from which effective policy could be developed, but they offered the circumstances in
which the leaders of the political economy could, and did, gradually
evolve a basic consensus on how to run the system.

In the meantime, Hoover had to take much of that responsibility on his own shoulders, during the postwar depression that staggered the economy in 1921–1922. On the basis of an index number
of 100 for 1915, wholesale prices fell from 227.9 in 1920 to 150.6
in 1921. Agricultural earnings dropped from 100 (based on the
1910–1914 average) to 75 in 1921. Real wages, on the other hand,
jumped from 100 in 1914 to 105 in 1919, 113 in 1922, and 132 in
1928. Along with the tremendous expansion in the automobile and
utility industries and in consumer appliances and chemicals, these
statistics do a great deal to explain labor's relative quiescence. But
the depression itself was a serious blow, and an insider once esti-
mated that Hoover held 900 separate conferences and organized
200 committees in his efforts to check the fall and organize recovery
on an effective, efficient, and sustained basis. In the course of those
efforts, he helped establish the principle that public works should
be used "as a powerful stabilizing influence" in future crises on the
grounds that "public construction is better than relief." Strongly
backed by Hoover, the Congress passed one such law in 1921.

Hoover ran into several kinds of opposition and difficulties in his
efforts to extend the recovery from the depression. Hurt far more
seriously by that downturn than labor (453,000 farmers lost their
stake in the system), and failing to make a full recovery, agriculture
demanded direct government aid. Long before 1925, when 36 per
cent of owner-operated farms were mortgaged to an average of 42

per cent of their value, the farmers began agitating for export subsidies and government credit facilities. And they were organized. Through the National Farm Bureau Federation, largely representing the big, successful operators, the National Farm Union, speaking for smaller farmers, and such more openly political associations as the Non-Partisan League, they exerted tremendous pressure.

Striving to maintain their favorable prewar position and thus remain on a roughly comparable level with the industrial corporations within the syndicalist system, agricultural leaders openly demanded "equality" as a way of preventing "state socialism." Nor was their stress on foreign markets unconnected with the same program pushed by the corporations. One of the farm bloc's key leaders was George N. Peek, an implement manufacturer who had learned the "benefits of proper co-operation" and the key role of exports while serving on the War Industries Board. He argued very openly that his implement business depended upon export markets for the farmer.

Hoover agreed that "the farmer is in a position of inequality in purchasing power as compared with other industries." And he understood that the imbalance was "digging a grave of unemployment for the other industries." But he was not willing to put the government into the export subsidy business. That would open the way for similar demands by the other functional units of the economy. And this in turn would very quickly establish the "syndicalist nation on a gigantic scale" that he feared as creating an oligarchy and subjecting the citizen to double, or triple, economic jeopardy. Instead, Hoover offered two solutions. He persistently encouraged smaller farmers to organize cooperatives, arguing that they could thus compete more efficiently and effectively with the quasi-corporation units in agriculture and at the same time control their production and their marketing to coincide with the domestic and international supply. The farmers did not respond. Hoover's second proposal was to win "the cooperation of our bankers and our industry" in financing agricultural exports. And in large measure the Dawes Plan for financing the recovery of Germany, and thereby the rest of Europe, was the product of such cooperation and coordination.

Indeed, the Dawes Plan was in reality a combination of an American peace treaty in Europe and the first coordinated effort to underwrite the wealth and welfare of the corporation political economy through overseas economic expansion. Secretary of State Hughes, who handled the formal negotiations with the businessmen and financiers as well as with the foreign countries, shared Hoover's views. Concerned to find "the antidote to Bolshevism," and believing that the "businessman has the most direct interest in the conduct of foreign relations," Hughes saw the answer in "the enlarging of the opportunities for industry and commerce by the recognition and extension of the policy of the Open Door." In that vein, the Dawes Plan was viewed as a way to finance the recovery of Germany, check the more aggressive policy of France, and thereby create markets for America's industrial and agricultural surpluses.

Though Hughes and Hoover finally won the cooperation of the House of Morgan in connection with the Dawes Plan, their difficulties in doing so dramatized the persistent trouble Hoover had with some financiers. The Morgan group was less intensely interested in a balanced system, or even in an *American* empire. Their concern was in maintaining their connections as middle-men in the British system, taking advantage of any opportunities elsewhere, and if possible pressuring the government into using the taxpayer's money to make foreign loans which they would handle. Hoover opposed them on all those counts and found it much easier to work with industrial leaders.

In their stress on development projects and in their willingness to compete vigorously with the British, for example, the National City Bank, the Rockefeller interests, and Vanderlip came much closer to Hoover's outlook. So did the corporations that were establishing branch factories in Eastern and Western Europe and in Latin-American countries. In a similar way, Hoover and Hughes backed Firestone Tire and Rubber Company's economic invasion of Liberia, a move calculated to provide an American source of rubber. The same view explains why they favored having American industrial corporations penetrate the Soviet economy, even though at the same time they refused to recognize the government and persistently opposed its efforts to float bonds in the United States. Formal political or financial recognition would link improvement in Russian conditions to the communists, whereas they thought, and hoped, that independent American operations would help prepare the way for the downfall of the Soviets and the restoration of the rights of private property.

Hoover and Hughes also had trouble with financiers like Morgan's Thomas Lamont in connection with the Open Door Policy in Asia. Both government officials were willing to go, and did go, a considerable distance along the road of compromise to reach a *modus vivendi* with the Japanese. Having done a great deal to block Tokyo's wartime efforts to penetrate China and Siberia, they wanted an understanding among the industrial powers that would undercut Chinese radical nationalism and at the same time control and limit Russian influence. That accommodation, achieved during the Washington Conference of 1921–1922, was based on a simple *quid pro quo*: America recognized Japanese influence in Manchuria in return for Japan's reaffirmation of support for the Open Door in China and the Far East half of Russia. On that basis, all powers agreed to hold their naval armaments at a balanced level.

Thus the Hughes-Hoover resistance to Lamont's desire to float Japanese loans was not indicative of a blanket opposition. They wanted the business, and quite understood that such ties would help influence Japan's actions. On the other hand, they did not want Americans to finance Japan's complete domination of Manchuria. Though they finally acquiesced in the banking connection, therefore, they tried to strengthen their own position in China. They were moderately successful, if only in sustaining the turn-of-the-century view that China was the American frontier of the future.

Exports to China increased steadily (from $26.1 million in 1913 to $190 million in 1930), and some industrial projects were undertaken. Perhaps even more indicative of the American strategy was the large industrialists' use of Red Cross Relief and other philanthropies to prepare the way for future gains. As it candidly admitted in its own reports, the Red Cross "is a creature of the Government of the United States." And an on-the-scene report of January 18, 1930, made it clear that Red Cross "relief funds raised abroad and in China are utilized for the creation of a sort of revolving fund that could be used for financing irrigation projects, road construction, etc." One such operation involved grading a highway on the route laid out for a projected U.S. railroad.

American economic expansion was even more sophisticated and extensive in Latin America. "We have advanced from the period of adventure," explained Leo S. Rowe, Director General of the Pan-American Union in 1928, "to the period of permanent investment."

As that pattern evolved, Hoover and other like-minded American leaders moved away from the traditional kind of vigorous diplomatic or military intervention. Seeking themselves to avoid revolutionary upheavals, and to help the poorer countries, as well as being responsive to criticism from reformers like La Follette, Johnson, and Borah, a good many corporation leaders and government officials tried very hard to rationalize the economic empire south of the Rio Grande. One of the key figures in that effort was Dwight Morrow of the House of Morgan (a fact that illustrates the fallacy of lumping all bankers together). His approach was typified in what he called an Eleventh Commandment that he offered to help all corporation leaders move beyond an interest-conscious outlook—"Take not thyself too seriously."

Morrow negotiated a *modus vivendi* with the Mexican Revolution that eased, though it did not resolve, the tension arising out of its effort to control its own land and resources, and the counterdetermination of American oil, mining, and agricultural interests to retain their property rights. In that and similar negotiations, Hoover and other American officials actually initiated much of both the spirit and the practice of what Roosevelt and Hull later received credit for under the name of the Good Neighbor Policy. But in both cases, American leaders reasserted their determination to view outside economic challenges as a danger to be opposed and ultimately resisted with force. The Hemispheric Empire was to be rationalized and reformed, not abandoned.

Despite such expansion, and with parallel development in many domestic industries, the corporation political economy did not generate sustained development. As early as 1926, for example, steel and automobile spokesmen were warning of the need for still more and bigger overseas markets. And neither the coal industry nor agriculture were prosperous. Nor was the wealth of the system distributed equitably. Before the crash in 1929, only 2.3 per cent of the nation's families enjoyed incomes of over $10,000, while 60 per cent received only, or less than, $2,000, the figure needed "to supply only basic necessities." Recognizing the danger of a continued agricultural depression, Hoover moved quickly after he took office as President in 1929. The Agricultural Marketing Act of June, 1929, created a Federal Farm Board empowered to loan money to cooperatives or established agricultural corporations. Even had it come earlier, it is extremely unlikely that the action would have prevented the crash. Riding a wave of expansionist and speculative enthusiasm, the political economy of the large corporation simply collapsed. It proved incapable either of generating the necessary capital for continued investment, or of distributing its wealth in a way that maintained sufficient purchasing power.

Hoover's failure to act more decisively and extensively to halt and reverse the failure was largely the result of his own analysis of the system and the way this interpretation seemed to be verified by concurrent developments in Italy, Germany, Japan, and Russia. Entertaining a fundamental confidence in the system and its capacity to recover, he did not want by government action to drive it toward fascism, socialism, or oligarchy. Nor did he wish to stop Japan's invasion of Manchuria (1931) by taking a stand that he thought risked the great probability of war; that, too, would push the United States toward oligarchy (or even tyranny), and would also strengthen Russia and radicalism in China.

The disagreement that developed between Hoover and Secretary of State Henry L. Stimson over that crisis serves to dramatize a crucial aspect of the entire era. For in a way that offered a broad analogy with James Monroe's selection of John Quincy Adams as his Secretary of State, Hoover's choice of Stimson symbolized an important convergence of a rising new industrial gentry with the remaining heirs of the colonial feudal gentry within the Progressive Movement. Stimson had modeled his career and ideas on those of Theodore Roosevelt, and in the Manchurian Crisis he advocated an appropriately strong stand calculated to shock the Japanese and put them back on the high road to becoming Western gentlemen. In fine feudal style, he discounted or dismissed, or perhaps even accepted, the risk of war. In an even more striking illustration of that outlook, Franklin Delano Roosevelt, himself a clear and conscious (and more legitimate) descendant of the New York agrarian gentry, thought the only thing to fear was fear itself. He shared Stimson's views on standing up to the Japanese and reasserting the Open Door in China.

But while the old feudal gentry took a much more vigorous stand in foreign affairs, they turned to the more sophisticated corporation leadership in domestic affairs. If there was any new development connected with the events of the Great Depression, it appeared in Hoover's hesitant, partial retreat from the frontier expansionist approach to foreign policy—*not* in the domestic policies of the New Deal. The policies that Hoover did finally employ in his efforts to halt the depression provided the rudiments of Roosevelt's program. And Hoover's analysis of the propensity of the corporation political economy to produce "a syndicalist nation on a gigantic scale" was ultimately verified by the results of Roosevelt's New Deal.

Hoover's handling of the depression can in truth be criticized upon only one basis. He refused to save the system through means that he considered destructive of its values and potential. The American people proved willing to use, or to acquiesce in the use of, those means in order to preserve a sense of identity that rested upon private property. They were thus willing to pay a political, social, and even economic price that Hoover judged at the time to be exorbitant. He was judged by the voting public in the election of 1932. Having taken a stand, he accepted the consequences. Most of the subsequent commentary on his performance has ignored both the issues that he raised and the nature of later American development.

Before that defeat in 1932, however, Hoover had pulled out every antidepression tool the Progressives ever owned. He first tried, as had Theodore Roosevelt in the Panic of 1907, to coerce and whee-dle financial leaders such as Andrew Mellon and Thomas Lamont into underwriting the stock market and thereby stopping the downturn. They lacked both the will and the capital. Hoover then recommended or approved a wide spectrum of recovery meas-ures. The Norris-La Guardia Act of 1932 established the principle of collective bargaining as the law of the land. The Reconstruction Finance Corporation provided the model as well as one of the key instruments of most New Deal financing of domestic production and overseas economic expansion. Hoover asked also for a signifi-cant tax cut to encourage investment, a $423 million public works program, more credit for farmers, new guarantees for bank deposits, more liberal bankruptcy laws, and direct-relief appropriations. But whatever the value of Hoover's recommendations, the Democrats were by that time refusing to support them and Roosevelt entered the White House only to confront a very grave crisis.

THE NEW DEAL AS THE CONVERGENCE AND CONSOLIDATION
OF OLD TRADITIONS—NOBLESSE OBLIGE AND REFORM,
SYNDICALISM AND EXPANSION

Though its own leaders admitted that it lasted barely five years (1933–1937), and though it ended with candid admissions of failure from its major protagonists, the New Deal is often viewed as a major turning point in American history. A bit more perspective suggests that it represented a reaction to a severe crisis in which most of the elements, attitudes, and policies of the Progressive Movement were finally consolidated in one short period under the leadership of a particularly dramatic politician. The New Deal saved the system. It did not change it. Later developments and characteristics of American society which suggest an opposite conclusion are no more than the full extension and maturation of much earlier ideas and policies that were brought together in what a high New Dealer called a shotgun approach to dealing with the depression.

For that matter, such fulfillment of the age of the large corporation did not actually begin until the New Deal had collapsed in the Recession of 1937–1938. New Deal reformer Harry Hopkins made that clear in his more-than-a-little-desperate remarks of 1939. "This country cannot continue as a democracy with 10,000,000 or 12,000,000 people unemployed. It just can't be done. We have got to find a way of living in America in which every person in it shares in the national income, in such a way, that poverty in America is abolished." The same point was made by presidential advisor Adolph A. Berle in a warning to Roosevelt on August 16, 1938. "The paramount necessity now is to do some thinking at least one lap ahead of the obvious financial and industrial crisis which is plainly indicated within the next few years."

Although the New Deal is often characterized by three Rs—relief, recovery, and reform—and even divided into chronological eras ostensibly coinciding with those different emphases, such an approach is misleading on at least three important counts. First, the economic system did not recover and sustain its predepression performance, let alone surpass those levels of employment and production, until domestic and foreign war orders (and investment) pulled it out of the condition of barely tolerable stagnation—with between

9 and 10 million unemployed in 1939—to which the New Deal had temporarily lifted it from the abject depths of 1932–1933. After all, it was Roosevelt himself who remarked even before the Recession of 1937 that one-third of the nation was ill-housed, ill-clothed, and ill-fed. And it was. Second, instead of providing recovery, the New Deal promoted the rationalization of the existing syndicalist political economy based on the large corporation. And third, the main efforts of relief, rationalization, and reform actually occurred in a jumble rather than proceeding in any step-by-step order or neat plan of development. Pragmatic to the core, the New Deal was not so much misdirected as it was undirected.

Paradoxically, in view of his magic with the voters, much of that was due to the character of Roosevelt's approach. Fundamentally he was the last and certainly one of the most conservative representatives of the American feudal gentry to hold the Presidency. He manifested, among other characteristics of that tradition, its spirit of *noblesse oblige* and disinterested humanitarianism to a high degree. A North Carolina worker recognized this in a moving remark of 1934 which also illustrates why Roosevelt commanded such a broad and intense personal following. "I do think," concluded the mill hand, after making some criticisms of the New Deal: "I do think Roosevelt is the biggest-hearted man we ever had in the White House." Roosevelt also symbolized the buoyant confidence of such an aristocracy, and that, too, was an important element of his success.

Yet that old gentry was nearing the end of its tenure in American society, and the signs of enfeeblement in such a declining tradition also appeared in Roosevelt. His confidence was very prone to slip over into arrogance and, perhaps as a result of his victory over polio, into a kind of recklessness that came very close to being irresponsibility. He also rather liked power for its own sake. Yet the gravest weakening of the tradition was revealed in Roosevelt's failure to study, know, and master the political economy in which he held such an initially high place. He just did not know very much about the workings of an industrial system. Since the ideal of informed and responsible power was in essence the crucial definition of the gentry, Roosevelt fell short of the mark on both counts. To make up for the discrepancy, he substituted and relied upon a thoroughgoing pragmatism and an almost fantastic political skill.

The combination served to save the system and produce a kind of ad hoc balancing of forces in society, but it neither offered nor institutionalized any lasting and dynamic direction to the country.

Roosevelt's greatest contributions in the crisis, and to the New Deal as such, were his élan and his determination to relieve suffering at any cost. Americans were so numbed by events and by the discrepancy between reality and their Progressive faith in a succession of frontiers, that they did not rally from the crash for three years. That failure to throw up leaders with new ideas or with vigorous adaptations of old ones is so awesome and devastating a comment of American education and the anti-intellectual nature of the frontier-expansionist theory of history that it defies comment. It also indicates in an equally persuasive manner the fundamental weakness of John Dewey's pragmatic relativism.

As for the need for relief, it is poignantly caught in a letter of June 14, 1933, from a railroad worker to a member of Roosevelt's cabinet. "We are wearing rags and using flour and feed bags for towels and pillow slips ... We go to market once in a while to look at the nice vegetables then go home and eat macaroni and oatmeal." Others were not that fortunate. They munched along on wild berries and roots. And some, no one really knows how many, died of malnutrition or the host of diseases which feast upon weakened bodies. Beginning with the establishment of the Civilian Conservation Corps and the Federal Emergency Relief Administration (1933), and expanded under the pressure of need and social-worker Harry Hopkins, the New Deal relief measures culminated in the Works Progress Administration of 1935. By that time, the Public Works Administration, established in 1933, had also begun to employ significant numbers of men through its contracts with private construction corporations. On balance, the relief efforts of the New Deal were very probably its most notable and noble contributions to American life.

Beyond the psychological triumph of restoring confidence, and the humanitarianism of relief, the New Deal ultimately brought the main functional and syndicalist elements of the political economy into a rough kind of legal and practical balance. Four of its first laws, for example, represented government action to save the banking system and to establish rules and procedures of honesty and safety for the securities market. For leadership in those matters, as well as in subsequent industrial legislation, Roosevelt turned to the corporation community and its political allies and associates. Such spokesmen responded with the National Industrial Recovery Act (1933) and an expansion of the powers of the Reconstruction Finance Corporation established by Hoover.

Hoover had been offered several plans like the N.R.A., but had turned them down on the grounds that they all pointed the country toward some kind of fascism. And a good many observers in and out of the New Deal called attention at the time to the fact that the N.R.A. did have many parallels with the kind of corporate syndicalism developed in Italy. Bypassing the anti-trust laws, it empowered businessmen (meaning in practice the large corporations) to manage the economy on condition (Section 7a) that they recognized "the right [of workers] to organize and bargain collectively through representatives of their own choosing." While that seemed equitable, the law did not provide any effective way of enforcing labor's rights. At the same time, agriculture was assisted through such measures as the Federal Farm Loan Act and the Agricultural Adjustment Act which initiated the now standard practice of using federal funds to pay farmers for reducing their production. Beyond relief, the most direct aid to the unorganized consumer came in the Home Owners Loan Corporation, which used government funds to underwrite, and thereby save, over a million residential mortgages from foreclosure.

The failure of those and associated efforts to produce a rapid and general recovery of the economy provoked a general restlessness throughout the country that opened the way for the reformers to reestablish their influence in the Progressive Movement. "Boys," cried Hopkins, "this is our hour. We've got to get everything we want—a works program, social security, wages and hours, everything—now or never." Hopkins was probably correct. Had the N.R.A. succeeded in restoring a significant momentum toward recovery, Roosevelt's conservatism might very easily have blocked many reforms that were finally written into law. As it was, he persistently resisted some of them—such as a more effective charter for labor—until it became politically risky to balk any longer.

Five broad groups provided the ideas and the pressure that forced Roosevelt to veer toward the reform side of the Progressive tradition. The reformers themselves provided many of the ideas and the sustained pressure inside the government. A small group of sophisticated corporation leaders, including politicians and business economists, was associated in a loose way with the reform bloc, but most reformers were socialists of the heart. Without them and their devotion to improving conditions for the unorganized citizen, much less would have been accomplished by the New Deal. They were not revolutionaries, nor even particularly rigorous critics of the essential political economy of the large corporation, and only a few attacked the institution of private property. A tiny number accepted communist leadership. But even they failed to offer any revolutionary proposals. For the most part, they contented themselves with trying to adapt Russian ideas and forms to the United States, or to fit 20th-century facts into 19th-century Marxian analyses.

In later years, after Germany, Italy, and Japan turned to military expansion in Spain and China, such communists and associated radicals tried to influence the government into a close and active tie with the Soviet Union. So did a number of non-communist leaders. But a few of the communists went further and tried to help the Russians by illegally giving them information which the United States had gathered about the Axis powers. Since the Soviet Union and the United States were not nations that had openly declared themselves enemies or that were at war, the action was not treason. For according to the Constitution, at any rate, the United States cannot declare war against an idea. Often unfairly deprived of hard-earned credit for having helped bring about the reforms of the New Deal, such radicals should not, by an inverse logic, be blamed for all America's later difficulties. American communists in the 1930s no more imperiled the United States than they saved the Soviet Union.

Another significant, though more diffuse, influence was the program for old age and retirement benefits developed and agitated for by Francis E. Townsend of California. Joined or supported by others who demanded unemployment compensation and similar relief on a routine basis, Townsend rapidly became a significant political force that threatened even greater influence. Still another and more difficult pressure to estimate came from Louisiana in the appeal and approach of its Governor Huey Long; originating in the south, but quickly winning support in the west and even the upper Mississippi Valley, Long's "Share the Wealth" program caused the same kind of concern in Washington.

Long was the shrewd and demagogic leader of what was in many respects a grass-roots revolt throughout the south and west against what those regions felt to be their colonial position within the domestic empire of the large corporation. It had a good many of the features, rational and emotional, of the kind of activity that came in later years to be called anti-imperialism, anti-colonialism, and colonial nationalism. Its more moderate wing included businessmen and ranchers as well as poor whites and reformers. And in Texas historian Walter Prescott Webb's study of the corporation economy, *Divided We Stand: The Crisis of a Frontier-less Democracy* (1937), it offered so trenchant a criticism of the system that one corporation forced it to be withdrawn from the public market.

The conditions which produced Long also provided the raw material for an essay on the South in prose and photography by writer James Agee and cameraman Walker Evans that was one of the nation's true artistic and human masterpieces. A corporation also refused to publish the essay, even though having in 1936 commissioned its preparation. Finally appearing during World War II under the ironic title of *Let Us Now Praise Famous Men*, it provided an enduring reminder of the failure of the New Deal in the very region in which one of its most favorably famous monuments, the Tennessee Valley Authority, was located.

Long's excesses are neither excused nor justified by such factors. But Long also made good on many of his promises (as in the instance of a state university), a fact often overlooked by the critics of his demagoguery. It is worth pointing out, furthermore, that most opponents of Long have proved peculiarly blind to similar exaggerations, dishonesty, and pie-in-the-sky promises offered by more respectable reformers and their associates in the corporation community. Whatever the nature of one's judgment of Long today, however, the vigor of his leadership and the relevance of his criticism worried New Deal leaders at the time.

With a deeply conservative point of view and even more demagogic characteristics than Long manifested, Father Charles Coughlin led a fourth section of opinion. His blatant advocacy of a crude fascist kind of corporate and syndicalist government for the industrial system attracted a sizable and fanatic following. By and large it was a following that paid little heed to his Catholicism, and he may have been the first 20th-century politician to break through that barrier in American politics. His fuzzy, almost incoherent program for a corporate state that would soak the rich and dunk the radicals to the everlasting security and glory of private property and the middle class worried all national leaders—radical and conservative.

But the most important and influential uprising came from labor. Leading the way was the Congress of Industrial Organizations, initially a subdivision of the A.F. of L. that concentrated on assembly-line and other unskilled workers in large industry. Erupting in 1934 in a series of strikes throughout the industrial sections of the country, and at the same time in a fight for control of the A.F. of L., the more militant unionism of the C.I.O. infused the entire labor movement with a determination to win recognition, higher wages, better working conditions, and a parity of representation and power within the functional and syndicalist organization of the system. Though violently opposed by many corporations, the bitter organizational drive of the C.I.O. led by such men as John L. Lewis (coal), Philip Murray (steel), and Walter Reuther (automobiles) succeeded in what was in reality a very short time.

Joining in an alliance with such key reform leaders as Senator Robert F. Wagner of New York, and indicating that their new power would be used in politics, they won a significant victory in the Wagner Labor Act of 1935. That law defined and established labor's position in the syndicalist system and provided, in the National Labor Relations Board, an institution for adjudicating its basic relationships with capital. Labor also influenced the Social Security Act of the same year, and generally injected more verve and drive into the New Deal. Despite that vigor, and its gains and influence, the labor movement rather rapidly settled down into the syndicalist pattern that was by then clearly emerging from the excitement and flux of the New Deal.

Dramatized by their role in Roosevelt's steamroller victory in the election of 1936, the reformers and labor had played a vital role in rounding out the essential features of the syndicalist organization of the system. Along with the great majority of corporation leaders and farmers, those groups had also accepted the principle that the government should accumulate and allocate capital to sustain the system. They also proved willing to employ that strategy on a grander scale than had been the case with early American mercantilists, or 20th-century leaders like Hoover. The reformers and a growing number of corporation leaders also developed a more sophisticated approach to the mechanics of such investment, as in its timing, the sectors of the economy to be assisted, and the amount needed. Though the economic theories of England's John Maynard Keynes influenced such men, they also learned a great deal from their own experiments and study. Those latter considerations point up an elementary aspect of the whole development: neither the principle nor the practice was new in America. As Keynes himself acknowledged, he had learned a great deal from the mercantilists, and their tradition had entered the Progressive Movement at an early date.

Those two issues, the role of the government as accumulator of capital and the maturation of a syndicalist pattern of organization for the political economy, were the crux of the New Deal's struggle with the Supreme Court. Between 1934 and 1937, in a series of decisions based on the rights of private property and on the unconstitutionality of consolidating and centralizing great power in the Executive Department, the Court invalidated many early New Deal laws. Though a good many of them were modified and reenacted, New Deal leaders needed final legal sanction for the policies and institutions they had established. Roosevelt obtained that; for though he lost his dramatic assault on the structure of the Court itself, he won the war against its reluctance to accept syndicalism.

The Court gave way in the face of Roosevelt's election triumph, and in view of the apparent necessity to legalize the means that seemed to be saving the corporation economy. In April, 1937, in the case of the *National Labor Relations Board* v. *The Jones and Laughlin Steel Corporation*, the Court upheld the Wagner Labor Act. By explicitly sanctioning unions because they were "essential to give laborers opportunity to deal on an equality with the employer," Chief Justice Hughes implicitly authorized the government to intervene in the political economy to establish, maintain, and institutionalize a rough kind of parity between the various functional units. Furthermore, the Court held that the corporation economy was a system that could not be broken up and dealt with in smaller units. Those two aspects of the decision established the central principle of a functional and syndicalist organization of the political economy on a national basis.

The Court's decisions upholding the Social Security Act and the State of Alabama's Unemployment Compensation Act were perhaps even more necessary to the functioning of that system. Holding that social security deductions were justified as an excise tax, and further in being used for "the general welfare," the judges underwrote that approach to old age and retirement benefits. The Court went even further in the Alabama case. For in that instance the plaintiff charged that the taxes returned no benefit to those who paid them, thereby raising the question posed by the role of the government in accumulating capital from the taxpayer and allocating or investing it without his direct participation in the decisions. To avoid any misunderstanding, it seems wise to emphasize very strongly that the questions of social security protection and unemployment compensation are not in themselves the fundamental issue. Both are necessary and desirable.

The crucial point is quite different: In a syndicalist system composed of interest-conscious functional groups which exert extremely powerful and effective pressure on political leaders, how does the citizen-taxpayer either participate to any significant extent in the formulation of proposals or protect himself against decisions taken in his name which subject him to double jeopardy in matters of economics or civil rights? The meaning of the decision in the Alabama case was very simple and very blunt: he does not. "The only benefit to which the taxpayer is constitutionally entitled," the Court pronounced in the words of Justice Harlan F. Stone's opinion, "is that derived from his enjoyment of the privilege of living in a civilized society, established and safeguarded by the devotion of taxes to a public purpose." That meant that the citizen elected a representative who was his agent, but over whose actions he had no substantial control. For electing a different man did not even modify the basic features of the system, let alone change them.

Thus the Alabama case sanctified a system and procedure of defining the "public purpose" which not only left the citizen far removed from final decisions, but denied him any grounds for appeal through the courts. An ad hoc syndicalist system was thus formally held to be democratic in domestic affairs. In later years, during and after World War II, such vast powers of the government were further extended. Japanese-American citizens who were abruptly, arbitrarily, and forcefully uprooted from their homes, and property, and confined in concentration camps were told by the Court that the government had the right as well as the power to act in that fashion. But since the Court had validated acts connected with foreign policy (however questionable or debatable) ever since the era of John Marshall, the Alabama case was more important. It upheld such power in wholly domestic affairs. As a result, the individual has three choices: he can acquiesce, he can go to jail, or he can initiate a national campaign to change the policy.

It is of course essential to evaluate the combined significance of these decisions within the framework of the syndicalist approach that had been present in the Progressive Movement from the very beginning of the 20th century, and which the New Deal consolidated. *Granted those assumptions*, what the Court had done was to legalize a system created by the large corporation and the Progressive Movement. In that system, the citizen was almost wholly dependent upon the definition of public welfare that emerged *inside* the national government as a consensus among the leaders of the various functional-syndicalist elements of the political economy. The possibility that Hoover had projected in 1921–1922 had emerged as reality: the United States was "a syndicalist nation on a gigantic scale."

Yet the citizen's political activity was carried on within a framework that was organized on an entirely different basis: i.e., geographic boundaries which had only the most casual and accidental relationship to the syndicalist structure of the political economy. That discrepancy left the citizen without any effective, institutionalized leverage on the crucial and centralized decisions affecting every phase of his life.

Hence the citizen, and the public in general, had two options that were appropriate to the circumstances and that did not challenge private property in any fundamental way. The public could demand a convention to revise the Constitution, a reorganization of the nation's political system to fit the syndicalist political economy. Depending upon the extent of the democracy within each syndicalist unit, that would give the citizen some meaningful role in framing alternatives and choosing between them. Even so, the result would be far more oligarchic than democratic, for the final decisions would still be made through compromises among the leaders of each element.

Or, on the other hand, the public could hope that a truly class-conscious industrial gentry would arise and, by dominating both parties, provide a basic definition—national and equitable—of the public and the general welfare for which taxes would be spent. That would offer the citizen some measure of choice, as between differences of emphasis and means to achieve such objectives, within the existing political system. In return for accepting the loss of any significant part in evolving alternatives for the present and future, the citizen would be assured of having an interest taken in him by the new gentry.

Recognizing the devolution of the system toward that choice as early as 1935, Walter Lippmann tried to dramatize the issue within the *Weltanschauung* of the Progressive Movement. "We cannot begin," he explained, "until we have said farewell to the assumption that Utopia is in the old American frontier." In that one brilliant sentence, Lippmann cut through to the failure not only of the New Deal, but also of the entire Progressive Movement. For despite its consolidation in the New Deal, it had provided neither a class-conscious industrial gentry nor a bold approach to a fundamental reorganization of the constitutional and political framework.

At the same time, of course, Lippmann understood the importance of being so explicit in pointing out that the frontier-expansionist solution was no longer relevant. For he realized that Americans had a very strong tendency to view that as a way of resolving their difficulties without having to change their traditional habits and outlook. Further overseas economic expansion, that is to say, would enlarge the pie and thereby enable each functional-syndicalist element to enjoy a larger piece even though the relative sizes of the pieces remained the same. And the traditional forms of democratic politics could continue to be observed without upsetting the syndicalist oligarchy that actually controlled the system. Given the anti-intellectualism of the frontier thesis, in which property was defined as the source of wealth, welfare, and democracy, the system exhibited a powerful propensity and momentum to follow that line of development.

And it was precisely to such expansion that the New Deal turned in the crisis of the Recession of 1937–1938. It did not undertake an imaginative program of building more TVAs, thereby laying the foundation for a regional and syndicalist reorganization of the political economy. Had it been coupled with a new Constitutional Convention (instead of an attack on the Court), it is conceivable that such an approach might have transformed Josiah Royce's ideal of regional communities into an exciting and humane society. If that alternative was to be derived only from axioms outside the assumptions of the New Deal, then it would of course be unfair criticism.

But that is not the case. For the syndicalist approach had been an inherent part of the Progressive Movement ever since the days of Mark Hanna, Theodore Roosevelt, and Herbert Croly. And given the nature of the political economy by 1936, such a solution would clearly have qualified within the limits of Dewey's pragmatism. For that matter, the idea of more TVAs was discussed by many New Dealers, including Franklin Roosevelt himself. But no legislative program was evolved and introduced. The criticism is incidental: the crucial point is that the frontier-expansionist outlook proved to be the strongest element in the Progressive *Weltanschauung*. By 1938, the New Deal was wholly committed to a further extension of the frontier of overseas economic expansion. Roosevelt's act of shifting reformer Harry Hopkins over to the job of Secretary of Commerce symbolized that decision. As Hopkins made clear during dinner conversations with top corporation executives at the White House, it meant that the New Deal was undertaking an even more vigorous implementation of the strategy that Hoover had outlined when he had been Secretary of Commerce—the internationalization of American business.

CHAPTER FIVE

The Fulfillment of the Passing Order

National self-containment has no place in the economic policy of the United States.
National Foreign Trade Council, 1935

Foreign markets must be regained if America's producers are to rebuild a full and enduring domestic prosperity for our people. There is no other way if we would avoid painful economic dislocations, social readjustments, and unemployment.
President Franklin Delano Roosevelt, 1935

We're just going to wake up and find inside of a year that Italy, Germany, and Japan have taken over Mexico.
Secretary of the Treasury Henry Morgenthau, 1937

After ten years of struggle America still has 8 million unemployed. Unemployment is a social disease gnawing at our vitals.
Paul Hoffman, 1941

The greatest danger that our nation faces, not only in the transition period, but also in the long-time future, is the tendency for people to become broken up into blocs and segments, each organized for the narrow interests of the moment.
Bernard Baruch, 1944

In the profit-sharing scheme we're trying to find a rational means by which free labor and free management, sitting at the bargaining table, can attempt to work out in their relationship practical means by which you can

equate the competing equities—in workers, stockholders and consumers.
Walter Reuther, United Auto Workers, C.I.O., 1958

We are just beginning to begin in the development of an American frontier we have only touched upon, relatively speaking, in previous years— the limitless frontier of foreign trade.
Eric A. Johnston, 1943

We cannot possibly maintain full production and full employment unless we have a world pool of free and prosperous consumers.
United Auto Workers, C.I.O., 1945

I have considerable sympathy with Herbert Hoover's problem as Secretary of Commerce.
Secretary of Commerce Henry Wallace, 1945

Dollar diplomacy is derided, although it is exactly the policy of the Government and of our exporters which Mr. Wallace himself advocates to develop foreign trade, except that it did not involve our lending abroad the money to pay for all our exports.
Senator Robert A. Taft, 1945

We are on the wrong side of a social revolution . . . and it's uphill work.
The Wall Street Journal, 1958

THE NEW DEAL AND THE EXPANSIONIST PHILOSOPHY OF HISTORY

Between 1938 and 1960, America's political economy of the large corporation fulfilled itself in several important respects. Coordinating its tremendous productive plant and its trained and skilled manpower to a unique extent, it joined with England and Russia to defeat the Axis powers. Impelled by the traumatic memories of the depression, the demands of the war effort, their own reform urges, and the necessities of meeting the challenge of radical alternatives, American leaders further balanced and rationalized the functional and syndicalist elements of the economy. They also extended and institutionalized the role of the income tax and the government as the method and the agency of accumulating capital for its operation. And as a central part of its efforts to sustain the existing order, both in overcoming its domestic tendency toward stagnation and in the face of challenges by the Axis and the Soviet Union, the United States enlarged its Open Door empire. In the course of doing so, some of the reform spirit of the Progressive Movement and the New Deal was transferred to foreign affairs. In conjunction with other influences, that attitude led to policies that in some degree mitigated the inequitable nature of the relationship between the American metropolis and the poorer and less developed members of that empire.

But in the single most crucial respect of creating a class-conscious industrial gentry capable and powerful enough to lead the system on a routine basis, the American political economy of the large corporation during those years did not fulfill either its need or its logic. Yet both as a form of consolidated private property and as the dominant element in the political economy, the 20th-century corporation did correspond to the lord of the manor in feudal society. Hence it was the institution to provide such a modern gentry, and the system clearly needed the kind of informed and responsible leadership that the tradition was capable of providing.

True enough, the beginnings of such a gentry had existed at the turn of the century and had been symbolized by Mark Hanna. It had further developed through the efforts of men like Young, Swope, and Hoover. And by the end of World War II, it had established itself as a small but permanent element in the system. Since its power to some extent offset its numerical and organizational weaknesses, it exercised important and beneficent influence upon some important decisions. But that gentry did not control the political economy. Nor had its members yet confronted without flinching the basic issues of private property, the equity of the system, and overseas expansion.

Neither had New Deal leaders at the time of the Recession of 1937–1938 done so. True enough, in extending and establishing on a routine basis the practice of capital accumulation by the government, they also increased the benefits to labor and other elements of society. That was of course a net gain for all concerned. But by no means all were concerned. Furthermore, the large corporation continued to be the most powerful element in a syndicalist system, and hence benefited in a quite disproportionate way. As far as expansion was concerned, the New Deal never seriously questioned either the axiom or the practice. New Deal leaders did briefly debate the means most effective for such expansion. They also emphasized domestic affairs during most of their first year in office. But they did not become isolationists, and they very quickly reasserted and invigorated the Progressive Movement's traditional emphasis on overseas economic expansion.

Even before Lippmann denied the validity of that orientation, historian Charles Austin Beard had challenged the New Deal to break with the expansionist tradition. Arguing in 1934 that America's troubles had their origins in domestic causes, and that they could not be solved by continued overseas expansion, he called for a Five-Year Plan to rethink and reorganize the corporation political economy. Otherwise, and even at that early date, he implied that the New Deal would become involved in another war for empire. Speaking through the National Foreign Trade Council, the corporation community opposed Beard unequivocally: "National self-containment has no place in the economic policy of the United States." But as with most of his critics, the N.F.T.C. either missed or evaded the central point that Beard was trying to make. Graced with a powerful mind that he had disciplined in business and academic apprenticeships, Beard was asking the crucial question. Could liberal internationalism be sustained without imperialism and without subverting private property? His answer was "Yes"—if the nation abandoned the frontier-expansionist theory of history and allocated its human and material resources in a more rational and equitable fashion. But neither corporation nor New Deal leaders faced up to the issue at that time. Only a generation later, after the Soviets developed the hydrogen bomb, did they begin that difficult and demanding effort.

In the formal sense, Beard was tilting with New Deal Secretary of Agriculture Henry A. Wallace, who reasserted the expansionist view in his own book announcing that *America Must Choose* (1934). Adapting the analysis that Hoover had advanced in the early 1920s, Wallace insisted that the nation would slide toward fascism (or less probably, socialism) unless it maintained and increased its overseas economic activity. While that reply was indicative of New Deal thinking, and provided an illuminating insight into Wallace's later performance as Secretary of Commerce, the expansionist outlook of President Roosevelt and Secretary Hull needed no interpretation or clarification.

In the 1920s, for example, Roosevelt shared the common view that the weakness of agriculture should be overcome by exporting farm surpluses. He applied the same approach to industrial problems and at the end of the decade organized an investment firm to facilitate such exports. And though his broad, confident view of the gentry also influenced the decision, he stressed the importance of exports (as did industrial and cotton interests) in recognizing the Soviet Union in 1933. Shortly after that move, the President made it clear that he also wanted all diplomats to have experience as consular, or commercial, officials "in order to gain administrative experience and make contacts with the business world." Secretary of State Hull had been a vigorous advocate of expanded exports, and raw material imports, ever since he entered politics in a Tennessee area which had an important export trade with Latin America. His foreign policy outlook was a model of directness. American trade should be expanded under the strategy of the Open Door and the tactic of reciprocal trade treaties whose benefits to the United States would be further extended through the most-favored-nation provision. If acted upon with vigor and determination, those policies would produce peace, prosperity, and democracy.

At the very outset of the New Deal, conservative Texas banker Jesse Jones took charge of the Reconstruction Finance Corporation and quickly expanded its role in financing exports (such as cotton). Hull concurrently chartered the First Export-Import Bank explicitly to finance surplus sales to Russia and at the same time prepared his campaign for reciprocal trade treaties. When the Soviets refused to pay pre-revolutionary debts, Hull lost interest in the Russian market. He quickly organized another Export-Import Bank and turned to the work of exploiting the opportunities created by the passage of the basic trade legislation in 1934. By that time, moreover, New Dealers were emphasizing the export subsidy provided by stockpiling gold in Fort Knox. Such purchases of bullion from overseas provided foreign nations with dollar credits. As such, the gold-buying spree operated as a continuous, non-repayable loan financed by the taxpayer for more than a decade before the Marshall Plan and other foreign aid programs were even mentioned. And in 1935, Roosevelt made it clear that he supported the expansionist approach. "Foreign markets must be regained," he asserted. "There is no other way if we would avoid painful economic dislocation, social readjustments, and unemployment."

With great enthusiasm, other New Deal leaders accepted and worked long hours to implement the traditional strategy of economic expansion. As Hull's chief assistant in the campaign, Assistant Secretary of State Francis B. Sayre candidly called the reciprocal trade treaties "an instrumentality for throwing the weight of American power and influence" against any countries that were reluctant to honor the principles of the Open Door Policy. Sayre accepted the expand-or-stagnate thesis that had been first stated by businessmen and other Progressives in the 1880s and 1890s. With him, as with others, it had become an article of faith. "Unless we can export and sell abroad our surplus production, we must face a violent dislocation of our whole domestic recovery."

William S. Culbertson, a key official who had labored to expand exports under Wilson and Hoover, continued to be influential during the New Deal era. Like Turner, Culbertson occasionally quoted Rudyard Kipling, England's bard of benevolent empire, as a footnote to the frontier thesis. According to Culbertson, economic expansion produced "material progress and a widening culture," whereas those who did not expand became "unprogressive." Assistant Secretary of State George S. Messersmith flatly declared that any change in the traditional outlook "would call for a complete rearrangement of the entire economic setup of the United States." In his opinion, as with that of the great majority, that settled the question once and for all. For that reason, he commented after the Recession of 1937 was well under way, "it would require a considerable amount of time, and perhaps a whole book, to cover in an adequate fashion the services which the Department of State is rendering to businessmen." A whole book devoted to each country would have been a more realistic estimate, as Messersmith undoubtedly knew.

But as Roosevelt explained at the end of 1937, not even that kind of assistance was sufficient unto the need. For one thing, the Mexicans were again asserting the right to control their resources and adding that they intended to set minimum standards for the labor policies of foreign corporations. In addition, American economic interests were finding that Latin-American countries were so poor and so lacking in the minimum essentials of a modern economy that they afforded limited and spotty markets. Corporations therefore asked the government for more aid and at the same time began to complain about competition. A sizable and growing number agreed with James S. Casson, Vice-President of the American and Foreign Power Co.: "Japanese and German competition" was becoming an increasingly serious problem. A National City Bank spokesman verified "our loss" to Germany, and Grosvenor Jones of the Department of Commerce openly decried the "spectacular gains" made by the same rival. Secretary of Treasury Henry Morgenthau was even more frightened. "We're just going to wake up and find inside of a year," he blurted out to his diary on December 16, 1937, "that Italy, Germany, and Japan have taken over Mexico."

A very similar reaction, though initially less intense, occurred when Japan reopened its military campaign in China during 1937. For contrary to a rather general impression, and one that remained prevalent even after World War II, American economic expansion into Asia had steadily increased after the mid-1920s. Between 1931 and 1937, for example, Asia took the following shares of American exports: iron and steel, 33 per cent; copper, 26 per cent; industrial machinery, 15 per cent; and paper products, 40 per cent. As the Department of Commerce pointed out, between 1932 and 1938 the United States "consistently held first place in China's foreign trade, in both exports and imports." In 1935, for example, America's share amounted to $102 million whereas Japan's was only $80 million. Those facts had underwritten a revival of the old idea that China was the next American frontier. An economic commission sponsored by the corporation-dominated National Foreign Trade Council (with unofficial support from the government) came back in 1935 infused with "a new spirit" for the old Utopia. And near the end of 1937, the Department of Commerce happily announced that the trade figures for the first half of that year provided even more support for this view. But Japan's renewed military attack in the same year clearly threatened the "especially bright" prospect. ·

As Roosevelt explained at the end of 1937, America's recovery-and-prosperity-through-expansion campaign was imperiled by "important trading countries not now within the orbit of our program." Despite all the efforts that have been made to prove that Roosevelt determined at that time to go to war, the available evidence (including the $1 billion naval expansion program of May, 1938) does not support such a black-and-white interpretation. It is clear, however, that the New Deal and the corporation leadership of the country began to consider and debate the likelihood that war would be neces-sary. One such figure among them, Allen Dulles of the corporation law firm of Sullivan and Cromwell, advised corporation leaders in 1937 to "dismiss the idea" that any neutrality legislation would "have any decisive influence in keeping us out of war." Perhaps a good many of the nation's leaders privately agreed, but they acted otherwise.

Indeed, the New Deal clearly followed the line of appeasement both in Europe and in Asia until after Germany made it unmistak-ably clear that it considered the Munich Pact of 1938 as a tempo-rary expedient. At the Brussels Conference of 1937, for example, the Roosevelt Administration brushed aside Russia's overture for a strong stand in the Far East and instead tried very hard, as it had at the Washington Conference in 1921–1922, to pressure China into compromising on economic issues in return for a Japanese military withdrawal. And a year later, Roosevelt went along with the Munich settlement.

In Latin America, however, the New Deal was more militant. In that sense, and it is a very significant one, American entry into World War II began with a decision in 1938 to eliminate Axis economic penetration of the hemisphere. While referring explic-itly to German and Italian competition in the airline industry, both New Dealer Berle and Pan American president Juan Trippe extended the spirit of their remarks to include all economic affairs. "We initiated a campaign," Berle told Congressmen, "to clear those lines out." Looking beyond that victory, Trippe saw a majes-tic vision: "Perhaps our role can be something like that of Britain. . . ." Secretary of State Hull had already explained how such actions could be taken in the face of an agreement with Latin-American nations that "no state has the right to intervene in the internal or external affairs of another." Hull had no more signed that pledge in 1933 than he remarked that it was "more or less wild and unreasonable."

During the same months in 1938 that Berle and others were moving against foreign airlines, corporation leaders were succeed-ing in obtaining more government assistance in Latin America. They argued very rationally that every phase of their expansion—exports, branch factories, loans, the exploitation of raw material resources—depended upon the existence of port facilities, roads, land reclama-tion, a basic minimum of public health services, and similar essentials.

In response, the Export-Import Bank in 1938 granted a loan for such projects in Haiti. Shortly thereafter, Brazil received similar consideration. Since such loans are usually thought of almost exclusively as part of the New Deal's Good Neighbor Policy, it is important to recall that the principle had been evolved during the 1890s and that the problems connected with the approach had been thoroughly aired inside the Taft Administration.

As Willard Straight had done in 1914, a spokesman for a major corporation explained the essentials of the loan to Brazil in 1938. He was equally blunt. "The people, through the Government [would] have to carry the bag, such as they are doing in the case of many other loans and subsidies." President Roosevelt unintentionally dramatized that central point on July 4 of the same year. He announced his "conviction that the South presents right now the nation's No. 1 economic problem," only he meant the southern section of the United States. Unfortunately, however, the Export-Import Bank was prevented by its charter from doing business with Alabama, Georgia, or Mississippi. Thus, even though one of its members openly compared it to the British Colonial Development Corporation, it could not finance any TVA projects in the south.

Thinking ever more wholly within the confines of the frontier-expansionist conception of history and economics, a small but influential number of sophisticated corporation leaders and New Deal reformers further refined and rapidly extended the program of the Export-Import Bank. Though their actions were of course important, it is useful to remember that they were doing little more than implementing Hoover's much earlier emphasis on helping the "crippled countries." Laurence Duggan of the State Department typified those of the group who acted within the tradition of a socialism of the heart. Duggan cared deeply about the character and consequences of America's expansion and wanted particularly to improve the lives of foreigners who composed the human resources of that economic empire. His superior in the Department, Sumner Welles, was far more conservative. But the pressure of failures like Mexico, the challenge of Axis penetration, his fundamental commitment to human standards of life, and his sense of upper-class responsibility combined to modify his earlier approach. He never ceased to emphasize the vital importance of American economic expansion, but he did modify the kind of militant resistance to change that he had manifested in preventing radicals, and even reformers, from coming to power in Cuba during 1933 and 1934.

Nelson Rockefeller and Eric Johnston represented similar thinking within the corporation community. In particular, Rockefeller symbolized those men in a new generation of corporation leaders who were on the verge of becoming a truly class-conscious industrial gentry. Extremely knowledgeable about Latin-American affairs as a consequence of his own corporation's vast enterprises in the region, and deeply aware of the responsibility of his power, Rockefeller thoroughly understood the crisis. Committed to continued economic expansion—he spoke often of new frontiers—he nevertheless realized that the empire had to be made more equitable if it was to function satisfactorily, and if it was in any sense to be justified on moral grounds. Rockefeller thoroughly agreed, therefore, with others in the corporation community who put the issue very boldly during the 1938 meeting of the National Foreign Trade Council. "The necessity of the 'have not' nations to obtain a more equitable position in the markets of raw-material-producing areas and to realize standards of living to which they have a right to aspire must be recognized."

After a long period of characteristically pragmatic ambivalence, Roosevelt finally threw his support to that approach. To some extent, his decision was influenced by Ambassador to Mexico Josephus Daniels, an old-line Progressive who had modified his views about the value of intervening to reform the poor countries. Daniels still emphasized economic expansion, but he had come to stress the importance of taking the long-range view, and of using pacific means to achieve that objective. Two other factors were more important: Roosevelt's own sense of *noblesse oblige* and the clear possibility that Mexico might shift some of its trading connections to other countries.

Roosevelt's subsequent actions were typical. On the one hand, he began in 1940 to talk (in what was a revealing commentary on the previous nature of his Good Neighbor Policy) about underdeveloped countries in terms of what he called a new approach—"Give them a share." On the other hand, he thought it a "terribly interesting idea" that England would probably have to liquidate many of its holdings in the Western Hemisphere in order to finance its war effort. He thought the United States might finance the transfer. And within a year, Hull and Welles had begun their long campaign to win free economic access to Britain's empire in return for Lend-Lease and other economic assistance.

By that time, of course, Roosevelt was engaged in battle with those at home who opposed his policies as leading America into war. Various motives and reasoning guided such opponents. The great majority shared a very simple and human disinclination to fight another war. Within that consensus, there were several major groups and arguments aligned against the President. Beard and others of his outlook insisted that the age of the Open Door Policy was over. He advocated a hemispheric system prepared for and capable of defending itself against attack. Some members of the divided corporation community shared that general view. Others were far more concerned with domestic economic and labor problems. And a final group of Roosevelt's opposition among corporation leaders thought that it would be possible to work out some division of the economic world with Germany, Italy, and Japan. For that matter, some of them were busily engaged in doing just that.

Although it had no sympathy for fascism or Japanese militarism, and despite its great emotional commitment to Roosevelt, labor was also disinclined to rush into war. Clearly aware of the heavy emphasis on overseas economic expansion that began in 1937, the steelworkers resolved that foreign policy should not be "formulated or made dependent upon the protection of the vested or property interests in foreign countries of the large corporations in this country." More concerned at that time with the fact that real income had not yet returned to the 1929 level, the C.I.O. stressed the "still unsolved grave economic questions, social and industrial maladjustments."

Labor also feared the consequences of a draft law and other mobilization measures, feeling that they would threaten its newly strengthened position in the political economy. But by 1939–1940, even John L. Lewis was beginning to be ambivalent. Arguing that "the 'Open Door' is no more" in Asia, he called for new efforts to expand trade (and the influence of American unions) in Latin America. But at the same time, the C.I.O. urged government loans "for the purpose of expanding our country's trade," and other (unspecified) action to retain America's "rightful share of world commerce." A year later, in 1940, Lewis concluded that the system faced a basic choice. "Unless substantial economic offsets are provided to prevent this nation from being wholly dependent upon the war expenditures we will sooner or later come to the dilemma which requires either war or depression." Such economic offsets were not provided. But most American leaders did not define the issue in Lewis's implacable terms. They thought more along the lines of Assistant Secretary of State Sayre's analysis. "The economic world became a battlefield," he observed in 1939, "in which the issues were sometimes political as well as economic."

Sayre's remark offers an insight of considerable value. Read against the background of the Progressive Movement's half-century commitment to the frontier thesis of prosperity and democracy, and in the context of the New Deal's additional stress on overseas economic expansion after the Recession of 1937, it suggests that American leaders viewed World War II as a war for the Open Door. As the entire history of the age of the corporation should have by now made apparent, and the evolution of the "give them a share" approach should have dramatized, the Open Door Policy had come to symbolize the overseas economic expansion that produced a prosperous, democratic, moral society based on private property. A society, furthermore, that automatically carried those benefits abroad as part of the economic expansion of the large corporation. And finally, therefore, a society and a set of values that were threatened by any assault upon the essentials of that economic empire.

On that basis, Roosevelt and other American leaders (including a strong majority within the corporation community) concluded within their own minds by 1940 that Germany presented such a challenge. Given the existing state of technology, their verdict was not open to a reasonable doubt. *For within their framework*, America could not survive as a prosperous democracy even if Germany did not attack the Western Hemisphere. And by the same logic, and for the same reasons, Japan had to be forced to withdraw from China. Within a year, the United States was involved in an undeclared war at sea with Germany. During the same period, the Roosevelt Administration made its decision to effect Japan's retreat by using the weapon of economic power.

By shutting off Japan's supplies of oil, steel, and other vital items, so ran the argument, the United States would win the classic bloodless victory of the Open Door Policy. It seems plain that American leaders simply misjudged the effect of that economic pressure because ever since 1905 they had been telling themselves that it would work. They had by 1940 come to *believe* that it would. The conscious analysis of the 1890s had become an unconscious article of faith. The United States at Pearl Harbor was not the victim of some horrible conspiracy among its high leaders, it was only the victim of having come to confuse the very materialistic logic of the Open Door Policy with Eternal Truth. Within the logic of the Open Door Policy, Japan *should* and *ought* to have retreated. Unfortunately, American leaders had never considered how the Open Door Policy looked from the other end of the empire. It left them quite unprepared for what happened.

But as Beard pointed out, and in the process earned the apparently everlasting enmity of the Progressive Movement, that was not quite the whole story. The New Deal was always defended as the culmination of Progressivism, and Roosevelt viewed as the finest product and exponent of the American gentry. Thus, while very simple, Beard's two basic questions were extremely disturbing. What kind of a gentry is it, he asked, that has so little confidence in its citizens, and so little respect for the truth, that it lies about the central issue of war and peace? And what happens to democracy, he concluded, when decisions made by a leader leave the citizenry with no effective choice? Beard himself thought the war necessary as a simple matter of national survival. Hence he was actually raising the very fundamental question as to whether the frontier-expansionist conception of history did in fact produce democracy and prosperity. In the eyes of his critics, that was his great and unforgivable transgression.

Beard was unable to force his countrymen to confront that central question. A minor part of the failure was explained by the intensity of his own emotional and patriotic involvement. He was so upset that for the first time in his career he wrote a book, *President Roosevelt and the Coming of the War, 1941* (1948), in which he tried to establish *two* basic hypotheses and interpretations. Instead of concentrating on his primary question about the results of the frontier-expansionist outlook, he also attempted to discover whether a conspiracy to go to war had existed in the highest circles of the Roosevelt Administration. That was, of course, a dramatic issue. And since the behavior of American leaders on the eve of the Pearl Harbor debacle was indeed strange, it was a defensible line of inquiry. But it almost completely distracted his audience from the far more profound inquiry as to the consequences of the frontier-expansionist outlook. Even had he proved the conspiracy hypothesis, the frontier issue would have remained more important. For it would have been a conspiracy to sustain the frontier by war.

Even so, that was not the primary cause of Beard's failure. He was unsuccessful because the great majority of Americans were committed to the frontier *Weltanschauung*. Even men such as Lippmann, who had questioned it in the mid-Thirties, turned back to its logic within a few years. Beard asked them to change the entire structure of their conception of the world. In that vital sense, Beard was more radical than most American socialists (to say nothing of the reformers or communists) despite the fact that he was a thoroughgoing defender of private property. And in that respect, at any rate, Beard, even more than Hoover, was the first American in the Age of the Corporation to make the crucial intellectual breakthrough that was absolutely essential for the full maturation of a class-conscious industrial gentry.

For as long as the would-be Founding Fathers of such a gentry defined the wealth and welfare of their projected commonwealth as a dependent variable of overseas economic empire, they would of necessity have to pay more attention to foreign policy than to building the commonwealth. And that was precisely what they did in the years after 1940. As for the bulk of the Progressive Movement's decision on that issue, Roosevelt summed it up in his famous remark that Dr. New Deal would have to be taken off the case in favor of Dr. Win The War. For while it was of course vital to win the war, the admission that the New Deal could not do it provided, albeit unconsciously, a judgment that could hardly have been more devastating.

America's continued commitment to the frontier-expansionist outlook, and to the policy of the Open Door, was the central characteristic of the war and postwar years. For within that framework, there was no way to maintain the balance and equity of the functional and syndicalist system except by sustained overseas economic expansion financed by the taxpayer. Nor was there, given their own commitment to that *Weltanschauung*, any effective appeal or issue upon which the small community of otherwise class-conscious industrial gentry could replace the syndicalist oligarchy that dominated the system. For each element of the oligarchy had always offered the frontier as Utopia. And through a combination of their consolidated political power and overseas economic expansion they were able, at least until the end of the 1950s, to maintain their position.

THE BELATED CONSOLIDATION OF A SMALL, CLASS-CONSCIOUS INDUSTRIAL GENTRY—AND ITS FUNDAMENTAL WEAKNESSES

Because they shared the view that overseas expansion was essential, the ideas and programs of the men who glimpsed the vision of a capitalist commonwealth were insufficient to establish that kind of a society. Instead, their great talents and energy served primarily to improve the functioning of a syndicalist political economy that failed to measure up to their own ideal, either in spirit or in performance. Despite that limited result of their efforts, and although they continued to accept the frontier-expansionist thesis, the men who began in 1941 and 1942 to organize the Committee for Economic Development symbolized the highest achievement of the age of corporation capitalism. Along with their colleagues on the previously established National Bureau of Economic Research and The Rockefeller Brothers Foundation, and with those who later staffed the Fund for the Republic of the Ford Foundation, the men of the C.E.D. comprised the appallingly small class-conscious industrial gentry that the corporation political economy had managed to create. There were others, of course, like financier Eugene Black, who also belonged in that community, but even when such additional figures were included, the gentry's membership was but an infinitesimal proportion of the entire corporation leadership.

Walter Reuther of the United Auto Workers and the C.I.O. represented the even smaller group from within the labor movement that slowly adopted the essential features of the gentry's view. Most leaders of the labor segment of the political economy remained wholly within the syndicalist outlook. Very probably Reuther's achievement was due to his early interest in socialism, which gave him a more inclusive sense of society as a community. But whatever his occasional lapses into the rhetoric of that approach, he had by 1940 thoroughly accepted the private-property political economy of the large corporation.

Some Progressive and New Deal reformers, most of whom had been originally socialists of the heart, also began to identify with the gentry. Adlai Stevenson was one of the few politicians of that tradition to make the transition. But as he slowly did so (his real progress came after 1956), he lost his power within the syndicalist oligarchy. Most of the reformers who extended their views were economists who derived from the Richard Ely and John Bates Clark wing of the Progressive Movement that had developed and advocated Christian Capitalism in the years before World War I. Others matured within the approach that Hoover had outlined during the 1920s. Henry Wallace was in many respects a figure who emerged from both groups, a consideration which helps account for many of his ambiguities and ambivalences, and for his later difficulties with the oligarchy that consolidated its power at the end of World War II. Neither Reuther nor Wallace were ever fully accepted by or into the gentry, but they were clearly men whose ideas converged with those of the men who composed that evolving group.

In a broader sense, Adolf Berle and Gardiner C. Means represented and symbolized all the elements that had contributed to the rise of the class-conscious gentry. They were scholars who had produced a monumental analysis of the corporation political economy in their book, *The Modern Corporation and Private Property* (1932), and in later associated studies. They had also served long periods as creative and responsible government officials during the 1930s and 1940s, and Berle was in addition a key figure in a corporation noted for its sophisticated management and social responsibility. Others, like Paul Hoffman of the Studebaker Corporation; Beardsley Ruml of R. H. Macy Co.; Ralph Flanders, Vermont banker and industrialist; and Donald Nelson of the steel industry were men who shared the same general outlook.

All those men agreed on four fundamentals. To their thinking the most crucial was the simple fact that the corporation economy seemed perpetually about to lose all its momentum and stagnate. That would of course destroy the whole system. They constantly reiterated that fear. Hoffman spoke for them all when he candidly emphasized that danger during the early meetings of the C.E.D. "After ten years of struggle," he flatly announced in 1941, "America still has 8 million unemployed. Unemployment is a social disease gnawing at our vitals."

The second crucial point in the gentry's analysis was stated very clearly in a report published in 1944 by a government committee headed by Bernard Baruch. "The greatest danger that our nation faces," it concluded, "not only in the transition period [after the war] but also in the long-time future, is the tendency for people to become broken up into blocs and segments, each organized for the narrow interests of the moment." Among others, Charles E. Wilson saw and warned of the same danger.

In that fashion, the gentry acknowledged that the wartime spirit of community had only camouflaged, not fundamentally altered, the fact that the United States was what Hoover had called "a syndicalist nation on a gigantic scale." In response, the gentry were deeply concerned to find some way of establishing and strengthening a true sense of community. Put very bluntly, they realized that the advertising industry's conception of the citizen as consumer, and the consumer as waster, was both practically and morally indefensible. And to the degree that any other functional element entertained the same view, or acquiesced in its application, it shared the responsibility for the unhappy consequences.

The gentry wanted something fundamentally different: a set of values and ideas that would not only override and thus unite the various separate syndicalist elements of the system as it stood but would generate a broad philosophy of equity to serve as a standard by which to adjust conflicts of interest between such functional groups. Despite a great deal of rhetoric about the public welfare that was supplied in equal proportions by corporation leaders and reformers, the single most relevant starting point for such a solution was actually provided by Reuther. Appropriately enough, however, its essentials had been advanced by corporation leaders at the turn of the century, and by syndicalist-minded labor and corporation leaders at the end of World War I.

As he first outlined it in 1942, Reuther proposed to combine various features of the railroad union's Plumb Plan of 1919–1920 with Gerald Swope's program of 1931 for ending the depression and then to apply the result to the automobile industry. He suggested that the industry be converted to war production and run during the war by a board composed of union and management representatives chaired by a director appointed by the government. New Deal leaders vetoed the idea. During the following years, Reuther gradually modified the plan into the profit-sharing program that he brought forward in the 1950s. His own description shows how he was trying, as a man thinking within the framework of the gentry, to provide a way of overcoming the syndicalist fragmentation and the inequities of the existing political economy. "In the profit-sharing scheme," he explained, "we're trying to find a rational means by which free labor and free management, sitting at the bargaining table, can attempt to work out in their relationship practical means by which you can equate the competing equities—in workers, stock-holders and consumers."

But along with the more formal members of the gentry, Reuther and the rest of labor based their entire approach on a continuing expansion of America's overseas economic empire financed by the taxpayer. He bypassed the problem of achieving equity in that fundamental area of the political economy. "We cannot possibly maintain full production and full employment," he concluded, "unless we have a world pool of free and prosperous consumers." Assistant Secretary of State Messersmith's estimate of how much space it would need to review the Department's assistance to corporations applies with equal force to the problem of reviewing the thousands of memorandums, letters, speeches, and excerpts of testimony before Congressional committees in which the gentry, right along with the oligarchic leaders of the syndicalist system, advocated and explained the proposition which was basic to their entire outlook.*

A few examples will indicate the essential features of their approach. "We are just beginning to begin," explained Eric Johnston in 1943, "in the development of an American frontier we have only touched upon, relatively speaking, in previous years—that limitless frontier of foreign trade." "With the closing of our own frontier," explained Nelson Rockefeller, "there is hope that other frontiers still exist in the world." Others like Hoffman and Berle preferred the more traditional economic vernacular of expanding markets for American exports. But perhaps the most characteristic and revealing remark came from Wallace as he became Secretary of Commerce in 1944–1945. "I have considerable sympathy," he told Congressional questioners, "with Herbert Hoover's problem as Secretary of Commerce." Having said in 1934 that Americans had to forget about

---

*   The reader who wishes a more detailed review of the development of American foreign policy during the period between 1941 and 1960 is referred to two earlier studies by the author: "American Foreign Policy and the Frontier Thesis," *Pacific Historical Review* (1955), and *The Tragedy of American Diplomacy* (1959).

frontiers and learn to live with themselves, he announced a decade later that economic expansion was essential: "This is the new frontier, which Americans in the middle of the 20th century find beckoning them on." An "aggressive sales campaign abroad was therefore essential."

THE TRIUMPH OF A SYNDICALIST OLIGARCHY AND
THE ONSET OF THE COLD WAR

Given that commitment to expansion, and already a minority group within the political system, the members of the gentry could have displaced the syndicalist oligarchy only by successfully advocating one of three alternatives. They could have faced the issue with complete candor and concluded that the time had come to stop blaming other countries for America's troubles. That tradition had been established when the McKinley Administration held Spain responsible for American welfare, and it had in the course of the century become an automatic explanation for all the ills of the nation. In all fairness, however, it would have demanded an almost unique combination of intellectual rigor and moral nerve for the gentry to have chosen that alternative—at least before the Russians produced their bombs (that development made it a rather obvious approach).

Furthermore, some members of the gentry did consider and even advocate a second, less rigorous, alternative that nevertheless amounted to a significant modification of existing policy. Corporation leaders like Nelson and Johnston suggested near the end of the war that the traditional commitment to private property as a prerequisite for membership in America's Open Door system might profitably be dropped. Roosevelt himself had moved in that direction, at least in Latin-American relations, and he seems to have been interested in their plan to extend the beneficence to the Soviet Union. Their idea was to respond favorably to Russian overtures and undertake a massive program of economic aid to that devastated country. By that method they anticipated creating an atmosphere in which political issues, such as the postwar settlement in Eastern Europe, could be resolved, and at the same time underwriting a postwar market that would sustain the American economy and provide a stable foundation for improving the substance, texture, and tone of American life.

After long meditation, Henry L. Stimson joined this group on September 11, 1945, and offered the most dramatic proposal ever advanced by any member of the gentry. Stimson boldly suggested that the United States should stop dealing with the Russians "having this weapon rather ostentatiously on our hip," and should instead work out a way of handling the atomic bomb through discussions with the Russians. Stimson's act not only signified that he had wrenched himself free of Theodore Roosevelt's conception of world power and of the Progressive Movement's urge to reform the world in the image of America, but came very close to qualifying as an abandonment of the frontier-expansionist outlook itself. Neither the trade plan nor Stimson's bomb proposal were accepted, however.

Henry Wallace attempted to sustain those two proposals and cautiously outlined a third—the idea of channeling American economic expansion through the United Nations Organization. Though neither Wallace nor the gentry themselves ever did much with that approach during the first 15 years after the war and the dominant political leadership opposed it vigorously, it very probably provides the gentry with a strategy suited to their needs and objectives. It would most certainly work economically, though not of course in the traditional pattern of an Open Door empire. Perhaps more importantly, it could—especially if coordinated with a serious program of disarmament—readily create a popular enthusiasm that would enable the gentry to win political power and formal leadership of the country. But to exploit that opportunity, the gentry would have to abandon the traditional frontier-expansionist outlook.

Neither the gentry nor the syndicalist oligarchy did that at the end of the war, however, and Wallace was dismissed by President Harry S. Truman in 1946. The firing of Wallace symbolized the final triumph of the bipartisan oligarchy that emerged from the Progressive Movement, the New Deal, and the wartime administration of the country. It was composed of four major groups. The first was made up of the leaders of each of the three major elements of the economy: labor, agriculture, and the industrial and financial corporations. Although their power was more hedged around with legal checks, and by the increased strength of labor and agriculture, the large corporation leaders clearly exercised the most power, authority, and influence in the system. Though a good many of those syndicalist leaders were articulate and sophisticated men, they nevertheless continued to think and act in interest-conscious terms. They lacked the breadth of economic and social vision, and the self-discipline, that were characteristics of class-conscious leadership.

For that very reason, the second broad group of the oligarchy was composed of very sophisticated professional politicians. Their role was crucial in the syndicalist system, and in some ways comparable to the functional position held by their predecessors during the Age of Laissez Nous Faire. Such leaders began to emerge mid-way through the New Deal's short life, and in subsequent years became ever more prominent. Representative Sam Rayburn and Senator Thomas Terry Connally were classic examples of the politician as coordinator. And in later years, Senator Lyndon B. Johnson ("I'm a rancher and I'm a banker") emerged as perhaps an even more thoroughly syndicalist leader.

In some respects, such politicians provided the system with a substitute for a class-conscious industrial gentry. But they were a substitute, for what they did was to arrange compromises between the various syndicalist elements of the political economy. They did not lead with a broad, dynamic outlook. While the harshness of their discipline, or the occasional arrogance of their leadership, often warranted criticism, the reformers who attacked them were often wide of the mark. For given the system, such politicians were essential. There were no parties other than those created by such politicians *after* the elections. Nor (again, within the system) could there be until and unless a class-conscious industrial gentry gained enough power and support to establish a new common denominator for the conduct of public affairs. Then parties could disagree over programs and policies designed to achieve goals that were generally accepted. In the meantime, the leadership of the syndicalist politicians was strong, for it had to be. But it was neither bold nor imaginative because by their very position it could not be.

As a result, not even the vast and significant improvement since 1940 in the nation's material standard of living was shared by all Americans. "In the wealthiest nation in the world," Adlai Stevenson pointed out, "at least 5,000,000 families still live in squalid but remediable poverty." Other estimates put the total as high as 50,000,000 individuals. In 1958, for example, the bottom 20 per cent of American families received 4.7 per cent of the nation's total personal income, while the highest 20 per cent of the families enjoyed a share

472 THE CONTOURS OF AMERICAN HISTORY

that came to 45.5 per cent. As Harvey Swados noted, automobile workers with 20 years of experience and service still earned less than the starting salaries of college graduates who nevertheless had to be educated before they were of any significant value to the same corporation. One of those very workers provided an insight into the broader weaknesses of the system that was every bit as profound as any offered by academics or other public figures.

"Ever stop to think," the worker blurted out during a lunch hour in 1956: "Ever stop to think how we crawl here bumper to bumper, and crawl home bumper to bumper, and we've got to turn out more every minute to keep our jobs, when there isn't even any room for them on the highways?" Small wonder, as Swados reported from the assembly line, that "the worker's attitude toward his work is generally compounded of hatred, shame, and resignation." That was the reality of which James Reston spoke when he called America "a system debased and out of balance," and which Stevenson had in mind when he described it as a "chaotic, selfish, indifferent commercial society" dominated by an "inner, purposeless tyranny of a confused and aimless way of life."

Not even theologian Reinhold Niebuhr's grand effort to revitalize the doctrine of Christian Capitalism offered a meaningful or inspiring guide to improve the situation. Niebuhr failed because he took the essential element of Christianity out of his philosophy. For by misreading Freud to the conclusion that men could not be moral in society, and by accepting the limited vision of Dewey's pragmatism, Niebuhr denied that men could achieve great and noble goals. He therefore denied the very Utopia offered by Christianity. Like other reformers, Niebuhr was a heretic. Like other Progressives, Niebuhr concluded that men could retain their morality only through an expanding frontier. But Christ, and Marx and Freud as well, had insisted that the only important frontier was man in society—not man on a frontier. To them, the frontier was harmful not merely because it offered an escape from difficulties that needed to be faced and resolved; that was but a minor point. To them, the frontier was harmful because it was precisely what Turner called it: an escape from even the chance to become fully human. Hence Christ and Marx and Freud quite understood the vital function of a Utopia. Unlike Dewey and Niebuhr, they put stars in their philosophic sky.

Such an ideal was essential if men were to move beyond the enervating and ultimately dehumanizing stalemate of existence.

In a curious way, Niebuhr's philosophy reasserted the frontier outlook even though it also admitted that the frontier failed to provide any real resolution of America's problems. It offered the best there was even though it was by no means all that was imaginable. For that reason, Niebuhr's philosophy attracted a good many of the reformers who made up the third group of the syndicalist system. By the 1950s, of course, most of those men and women were Progressives of New Deal vintage, although a few from the World War I era were still active in public affairs. Though they usually appeared as representatives of a given element in the economy, the group also included academicians seeking power, and various experts who moved on and off the official stage as their skills and opinions proved necessary or momentarily popular. Only a few of them could any longer be termed socialists of the heart. Quite in line with Niebuhr's philosophy, they had become ameliorative capitalists. In many instances, for that matter, their breadth of vision and rigor of thought were considerably less than manifested by the industrial gentry—or even by some of the interest-conscious leaders.

Finally, a fourth group had evolved in the form of permanent government officials who operated at lower levels of policy-making. This group had emerged as the state assumed ever larger responsibilities as a consequence of reform measures, as it had expanded to fulfill the function of accumulating and investing capital for the economy, and as the overseas economic empire continued to expand. This latter development had of course strengthened the military section of the officialdom. But in evaluating that phenomenon, many observers overlooked the point that it had been the civilian leaders of the country who had defined the world in terms that gave the military its new influence.

Like a good many other aspects of 20th-century American history, that military definition of the world was a direct product of the frontier-expansionist outlook. It had started in 1897 when American leaders assigned Spain the responsibility for America's welfare. Theodore Roosevelt, Woodrow Wilson, and Franklin Roosevelt sustained and intensified that implicit corollary of the frontier thesis. For given the basic axiom that the frontier was the source of wealth and welfare, it was but a step to the conclusion that overseas economic expansion provided the frontier to replace the continental west. But the frontier of overseas economic expansion involved established societies, both directly as areas into which America penetrated, and indirectly as competing industrial countries. Hence holding the frontier responsible for American development meant placing the responsibility on other people.

Thus in 1897 the United States told Spain that its action delayed "the condition of prosperity to which this country is entitled," and that a settlement on American terms was "necessary to the welfare of the people of the United States." Shortly thereafter, John Hay and Theodore Roosevelt extended the principle to the world at large. Woodrow Wilson applied the same idea succinctly in his war message of 1917: the United States would use force against Germany to establish "a government we can trust." Having announced in 1933, in a classic bit of frontier anti-intellectualism, that the only thing Americans had to fear was fear itself, Franklin Roosevelt had by 1936 decided that the trouble was more down to earth: "The rest of the world—Ah! there is the rub."

By the end of World War II, American leaders were thinking even more explicitly within the pattern evolved in the 1890s. Fearing another depression (or a backslide into the one of the 1930s), they turned once again to overseas economic expansion as the frontier which would make it possible to build what Secretary of State Dean Acheson called "a successfully functioning political and economic system." In that connection, Acheson explained the standard for awarding American aid within that same frontier tradition. "We are willing to help people who believe the way we do, to continue to live the way they want to live." President Truman phrased the underlying axiom even more explicitly. "The situation in the world today is not primarily the result of the natural difficulties which follow a great war," he explained. "It is chiefly due to the fact that one nation has not only refused to co-operate in the establishment of a just and honorable peace, but—even worse—has actually sought to prevent it."

As with Spain in 1897, therefore, so with Russia in 1945: each was held responsible for American wealth and welfare. Very clearly, moreover, American leaders thought that their unilateral possession of the atom bomb would guarantee the ultimate and peaceful triumph of the Open Door Policy throughout the world—in Russia and China as well as in areas already considered part of the American frontier. Indeed, the whole policy of containment was, no doubt unconsciously, the product of analyzing the Soviet Union from the assumptions of the frontier-expansionist theory of history. Denied the chance to expand, ran the doctrine, Soviet society would break down. Having assumed that their own society would collapse without an expanding frontier, American leaders made the same assumptions about Russia.

But that frontier-style definition of American welfare in terms of Soviet collapse (or of across-the-board acceptance of American conditions for peace) had several weaknesses. First, and most obviously, the Soviet Union was not Spain. The frontier had by the late 1950s become a dynamic industrial nation armed with hydrogen bombs. Second, the frontier outlook made it extremely difficult for American leaders to accept the reality of a nuclear stalemate, let alone to negotiate the kind of fundamental compromises that would make disarmament feasible and realistic. Instead, they reacted by calling for more military power to reestablish American supremacy. But supremacy in the frontier sense was no longer obtainable.

Finally, that conception of the welfare of the United States as primarily a function of Russian conduct left American leaders without any clear or firm or dynamic ideas and programs for the further development of American society. To a shocking degree, even the more generous and sophisticated definitions of democracy had devolved very far toward being philosophies cast within the confining limits of anti-communism. Senator Joseph R. McCarthy was neither the first nor the last public leader to exploit that interpretation for personal and interest group objectives; he was merely the most brazenly successful. And long after his career had ended, the strategy of anti-communism not only sustained the same kind of operations by other public figures, but had been institutionalized in government and other public affairs.

Prosperity, meanwhile, was seen very largely as little more than a high level of employment underwritten and sustained by overseas economic expansion, other government expenditures in the cold war, and time-payment consumer purchases. Full employment was of course a desirable condition. But the way it was maintained and the products of the labor were just as important. Neither of those were particularly inspiring or creative. Even the few positive achievements of the postwar era, such as the beginnings of desegregation in the south, were supported within the same negative framework. The Little Rock crisis, for example, was approached and handled as a skirmish in the cold war far more than as an approximately 100-years-overdue effort to implement the implications of the Civil War—or the literal and explicit meaning of the 13th, 14th, and 15th Amendments to the Constitution.

Those weaknesses of the frontier-expansionist outlook served to accentuate the achievements, and to enhance the appeal, of the Soviet Union beyond their intrinsic, and wholly legitimate and valid, merit. Admittedly, the comparison was unfavorable. Among the many observers who commented on that fact, no one expressed it more clearly than Adlai Stevenson. Deeply impressed, and troubled, by the "thrust and purpose in most aspects of Soviet life," he made it clear that such creative drive could not be produced by fear and coercion. He concluded that it came from an abiding faith in the ability of men to create a better present and a magnificent future. America, he feared, had "no corresponding commitment to our fellowmen."

But even more than such comparisons, and even more than the staggering accomplishments of Russia and China, the origins and course of the Cuban Revolution of 1958 provided the most illuminating example of the weaknesses of the frontier-expansionist outlook. For the Russians neither caused the Cuban Revolution nor did they occupy the country after it occurred. Neither was their influence as great in Cuba as that of America in comparable situations, say in Formosa or Okinawa. Furthermore, Cuba turned to the Soviets for help only after having been denied sympathy and assistance by America. The United States made no serious effort even to explore, for example, a very rational suggestion put forward by other Latin-American countries: Cuba would pay for the American property it nationalized through bonds to be liquidated by income from its share in a hemispheric sugar pool.

In the more fundamental sense, of course, the question of Russian influence in Cuba would never have arisen had America's Open Door Policy actually produced in Cuba the results claimed for it ever since Secretary of State Hay had announced it in 1899 and 1900. What Hay called "a splendid little war" had in the end produced the danger of a monstrous conflict. Yet that very danger was created by a situation which could shock Americans into a recognition of the failure of the frontier-expansionist outlook. For in Cuba they were confronted for the first time in the 20th century with some inkling of what the frontier—or the Open Door empire—looked like from the other side.

Not only had the expansionist outlook failed to produce wealth and welfare for the Cubans, but it had produced anything but wealth and welfare for the United States. Without any recourse to military action, relying solely on the appeal and the reality of its example, the Soviet Union had given Americans a first-hand illustration of how Russians felt when they looked across their borders and saw American bomber bases and missile-launching pads. For that matter, the situation, in 1960, at any rate, was considerably less than fully comparable. The Russians had no bombers or missiles in Cuba. Even if they had, the United States would confront only the same situation as did the Soviets, not a more difficult one.

Having defined the frontier as Utopia and lived by that ideal for most of their history, Americans had finally been faced by the harsh fact that the frontier as Utopia produced the very stalemate it had been designed to circumvent. The frontier was gone. The past could no longer be lived over again. It was done and done and done. Hence the approach to history which views it as a way of learning had proved its great value. It had provided a method of discovering the essential features of existing reality; in doing that it had provided a way of formulating the central question facing Americans in the second half of the 20th century. Could Americans define their existence without recourse to the expanding frontier that had formerly provided them with the private property they used to prove their existence? Could they, in short, define their existence and conceive grand ideas and great ideals without recourse to private property as the *sine qua non* of democracy, prosperity, and the general welfare?

History as a way of learning cannot answer that question. It can only raise it. Americans will answer it. But it is the question. And it just may be that the Age of Corporation Capitalism has created the conditions that will enable Americans to answer the question in the affirmative. In any event, American corporations had produced in the atom bomb the most radical and subversive product in their entire history. For just as the bomb had fused the sand into glass at

Los Alamos, so had it transformed the rights of private property into the responsibilities of social property. The world was no longer a series of frontiers, it was a community which would survive or perish by its own hand. If through its creation of the bomb the Age of Corporation Capitalism forced Americans to recognize that fact, then it would have fulfilled itself—and more.

Conclusion: History as a Way of Breaking the Chains of the Past

I see what you are not making, oh, what you are so vividly not. . . .
Henry James, *The American Scene*, 1907

Imperceptibly, the function of nostalgia reduces the ability to function.
Wright Morris, *The Territory Ahead*, 1958

We cannot begin until we have said farewell to the assumption that Utopia is in the old American frontier.
Walter Lippmann, 1935

I'm not concerned with the New Jerusalem. I'm concerned with the New Atlanta, the New Birmingham, the New Montgomery, the New South.
Reverend Martin Luther King, Jr., 1960

History as a way of learning has one additional value beyond establishing the nature of reality and posing the questions that arise from its complexities and contradictions. It can offer examples of how other men faced up to the difficulties and opportunities of their eras. Even if the circumstances are noticeably different, it is illuminating, and productive of humility as well, to watch other men make their decisions, and to consider the consequences of their values and methods. If the issues are similar, then the experience is more directly valuable. But in either case the procedure can transform history as a way of learning into a way of breaking the chains of the past.

For by watching other men confront the disparity between existing patterns of thought and a reality to which they are no longer relevant, the outsider may be encouraged to muster his own moral and intellectual courage and discipline and undertake a similar reexamination and re-evaluation of his own outlook. Whether the student of history follows the responses of earlier men remains a matter of his own choice, and even if he accepts their views he is obtaining his answers from men, not History. History offers no answers per se, it only offers a way of encouraging men to use their minds to make their own history.

This essay in the review and interpretation of American history has suggested that several elements have emerged as the major features of American society, and that those have in turn defined the central issues faced by contemporary Americans. One is the functional and syndicalist fragmentation of American society (and hence its individual citizens) along technological and economic lines. The personal and public lives of Americans are defined by, and generally limited to, their specific functional role. To an amazing extent, they share very little on a daily basis beyond a common duty as consumers and a commitment to anti-communism. The persistent cliché of being "caught in the rat-race" dramatizes that alienation, as does the attempt to "play it cool" in order to maintain some semblance of identity and integration.

The second theme is the persistence of a frontier-expansionist outlook—a conception of the world and past American history—which holds that expansion (or "growth," as Walter Lippmann put it in 1960) offers the best way to resolve problems and to create, or take advantage of, opportunities. A third is a commitment to private property as the means of insuring personal identity, and of thereby guaranteeing democratic politics, and of creating material well-being. And finally, Americans have displayed a loyalty to an ideal of humanity which defines man as more than a creature of property; which defines him as a man by reason of his individual fidelity to one of several humane standards of conduct and by his association with other men in a community honoring those codes.

None of those themes is unique, or even of recent origin, in American history. One example will suffice to establish that. Bernard Baruch raised in 1944 the specter of a dangerous fragmentation of American society into functional groups bent on pursuing the short-run satisfaction of their interests to the detriment of the general welfare, and his report was followed by many related or separate comments on the same problem. But Herbert Hoover had discussed the same issue at great length in the 1920s; the founders of the National Civic Federation had been motivated in large part by a similar concern at the turn of the 20th century; Abraham Lincoln had come to stress the same issue after he became President in 1861; James Madison and other Founding Fathers had grappled with the identical problem in the late 18th and early 19th centuries; and Shaftesbury had struggled to provide a resolution of the same dilemma during the Restoration Era in England. Hence it was not the issues that were new in 1944. The crisis was of a different nature, being instead defined by the progressive failure of the approach that Americans had evolved to solve the problems. That approach no longer provided a satisfactory resolution.

From Shaftesbury's time forward, the solution developed by Americans had been compounded of two conflicting themes or answers. One was the interpretation of Christianity advanced by the Levellers during the English Revolution, and later reasserted wholly within that tradition by Karl Marx in the form of a secular socialism. It held that the problems raised by faction, interest, fragmentation, and alienation could only be resolved—and man restored to a true wholeness and identity—by deemphasizing private property in favor of social property and through the cooperative building of a community rather than the mere construction of an organized collective system. Save for the first two decades of the 20th century, that outlook never played a large and direct role in American history. Indirectly, however, it did exert a sustained influence.

The other approach accepted private property as necessary and desirable. For guidance in defining and honoring the ideal of a commonwealth, its followers looked to different religious and secular traditions. One of these was Calvin's conception of a corporate Christian commonwealth in which the trustee accepted and discharged the responsibility for the general welfare; at the same time, all men were charged to honor the axiom that their choice between callings should be made in favor of the one that contributed most to the common good. Another tradition involved the ideal and practice of feudal *noblesse oblige*. That view had of course arisen within the Christian world, but by the 17th century had developed a secular life of its own. Finally, such men also relied upon a secular argument which held that expansion offered the only feasible way of underwriting private property while at the same time improving the general or collective welfare.

Put simply, the mercantilists such as Shaftesbury sought to integrate those three themes into a coherent and consistent *Weltanschauung*. That outlook on the world was, and remained, the essence of all class consciousness among upper-class groups in England and the United States from the Age of Elizabeth I. Thus Shaftesbury accepted the responsibility of those who enjoyed the possession of consolidated property for maintaining the general welfare and viewed the state as the natural and appropriate instrument for implementing that obligation. At the same time, he tried to organize political affairs on the basis of parties which included men of all functional interests (or factions) who accepted a broad conception of the general welfare and the means to achieve it. By thus coming together as men who shared an ideal of community—a Utopia—they would be able to override the tendency of functional activity to fragment and divide them—both internally (or personally)—from their fellow men.

Shaftesbury extended that outlook into foreign affairs. He accepted the necessity of expansion and acted vigorously to coordinate the various aspects of commerce and colonization. But he also sought to build such an empire as a mutually beneficial and responsible commonwealth. He had few qualms about waging war against outsiders to protect or extend the empire, and certainly intended to control its members; but he did have a strong sense of partnership that guided his actions toward the colonies. Shaftesbury and other mercantilists made many false starts, and they failed to control all factions (or to subordinate their own particular interests) at all times. It is nevertheless true that they did to a rather remarkable degree develop and act upon such a class-conscious outlook that combined a defense of private property with a belief in the necessity of expansion, and with an ideal of community and commonwealth.

That outlook was carried to America by the Puritans, by other emigrants, and by the empire directives prepared by Shaftesbury and his successors. It was thereby established, in various versions, in every colony. In many respects, moreover, it continued to mature and develop beyond its English origins and precedents. Indeed, Jonathan Edwards integrated its various themes perhaps more successfully and infused them with a more noble vision of Christian community than any English or American philosopher either before or after his time. His corporate Christian commonwealth was one of the few American visions worthy of the name Utopia.

But in any of its versions, that outlook was a demanding *Weltanschauung*. As Frederick Jackson Turner pointed out three centuries after the colonies had become firmly established (and in doing so offered a revealing insight into his own generation), the urge to escape the responsibilities of that ideal of a corporate Christian commonwealth was powerful, persistent, and without regard for the direct and indirect costs of such flight. In England, for example, expansion offered a progressively more appealing substitute for the self-discipline and fidelity to ideals that was essential in maintaining the general interest against the factional. And in America the presence of a continent defended only by weaker souls made that solution even more convenient. Americans proceeded in the space of two generations to substitute the Manifest Destiny of empire for the Christian Commonwealth of Jonathan Edwards. Thomas Jefferson was the great epic poet of that urge to escape, to run away and spend one's life doing what one wanted—or in starting over time after time. Jackson, Benton, and Polk were but the typecast protagonists of that dream, and through his early years even Lincoln was a man who charted his career by that same western star.

James Madison was the theorist of the outlook, and in offering expansion as the way of controlling faction, he articulated the guiding line of American history from the end of the 18th century through the 1950s. Yet unlike most who followed his theory, Madison recognized the grave implications of the solution; along with such men as Calhoun, Monroe, Clay, and especially John Quincy Adams, he sought to prevent the complete devaluation of the self-restraint and other ideals that Shaftesbury and Edwards had stressed. The continent was too much for them. By making escape so easy, it produced an unrestrained and anti-intellectual individualist democracy that almost destroyed any semblance of community and commonwealth. Even before the continent was filled up, the frontier had become a national Utopia and Madison's theory the New Gospel. Men largely ceased to think about problems, and merely reacted to them by reciting the frontier catechism and pushing the Indians off another slice of the continent. Following the general lines of Seward's reformulation of Madison's argument to fit the conditions of an industrial society, Hay's Open Door Notes merely restated the principle in terms appropriate to the 20th century.

Less than 60 years later, however, the open door of escape was no more than ajar. Two forces had combined to all but close it: Russian and Chinese industrial and nuclear power and potential; and the growing refusal by societies that had formerly served as the frontier to continue in the role any longer. As a result, the frontier Utopia had ceased to offer a practical substitute for the more demanding *Weltanschauung* of class-conscious leadership and responsibility. *Expansion as escape meant nuclear war.* Yet the cold war was essential to those who still, consciously or unconsciously, saw expansion as the means of adjusting and controlling factions and at the same time providing some measure of welfare. In typical frontier fashion, such people saw defeat or war as the only other solutions.

Expansion of a vastly different character and drastically more limited nature was still possible, but even that could be sustained only by strengthening the self-discipline necessary to honor the commonwealth ideal that Shaftesbury, Edwards, and Adams had tried to sustain. Expansion of any sort was only possible without war, and that is to say, only possible if the frontier were abandoned as a Utopia. Expansion of that kind would of necessity be channeled through the United Nations, without political or economic strings, in an effort to help other societies solve their own problems within their own traditions. Hence the possibility of any full maturation of the class-conscious industrial gentry that had slowly been created by the corporation between the 1890s and the 1950s turned on one very simple test. Did that gentry have, or would it manage to muster, the nerve to abandon the frontier as Utopia, to turn its back on expansion as the open door of escape?

It is of course fair to ask whether any precedents exist for encouraging such a display of intelligence and courage. For while it is helpful to find examples in the past, it is too much to ask that contemporary corporation executives and political leaders model themselves on Shaftesbury or John Quincy Adams. Very few, if any of them, are men of sufficient empathy. Nor would it be wise for them to follow such a course even if they could. Not only are the circumstances different, but it is the attitude and the ideals that are important, not the personal styles or the specific policies. But there is no need to return to the past in that sense, for some of the very Americans who restated the expansionist outlook in the 20th century also realized that there was another choice.

Brooks Adams, for example, admitted that America did not have to embark upon a program to control China and Siberia. It was merely the easier way out of the dilemma, and one which in his opinion offered more glory and riches. And as late as 1944, Dean Acheson acknowledged that he and his colleagues in government could invest an indefinite amount of energy and time in discussing alternatives to expansion as a way of building "a successfully functioning political and economic system." Acheson dismissed such approaches, however, on the grounds that they would weaken the rights of private property, require modifications of the Constitution, and limit the frontier-style liberties to which Americans had become accustomed.

Herbert Hoover and Charles Beard had more intellectual courage and imagination than either Adams or Acheson. They argued that it was possible to build a community—a commonwealth—based on private property without relying on imperial expansion. Whatever his other failings, Hoover did at least refuse to go to war for the Open Door in Asia, and did try very hard to change the character of America's overseas economic expansion. In some ways, at least, Beard advocated an even more rigorous effort to restore the ideal of a commonwealth as the American Utopia. But in its commitment to the frontier as a Utopia of escape, the American public refused to give that approach a serious or a fair trial.

Finally, the mid-century industrial gentry might draw even more encouragement from the example provided by the southern Negro. During approximately a century after the Civil War, the Negro modeled his aspirations and ideals on the white society in which he existed. Briefly at the end of the Civil War, again in the 1890s, and then with a rush during World War I, the Negro adapted the frontier-expansionist outlook to his own position. He defined northern urban centers as his frontier of escape from the conditions of survival in the south. For a generation or more, Negroes streamed into that supposed Utopia only in the end to discover that it was largely a mirage. Then, under the leadership of deeply religious and courageous men like the Reverend Martin Luther King, Jr., they broke with that traditional view of the frontier as escape and defined the south, the cities and the states where they lived, as the only meaningful frontier that existed.

Having made that magnificently courageous and deeply intelligent decision, they stood their ground and faced the issue in the present, reasserting as their solution the ideal and the practice of a Christian community or commonwealth. In a way that dramatized their abandonment of the frontier outlook, they organized themselves in such groups as "The Montgomery Improvement Association." No longer did they rally under the old slogan of the frontier, "Kansas or Bust," merely changing Kansas to read New York or Chicago or Detroit or Cleveland or Pittsburgh. They made no mention of the frontier: they simply talked about the here and the now, and set about to improve it guided by the Utopia of a Christian commonwealth. And to do so they chose the appropriate weapon—nonviolent resistance. Within one year they had effected more fundamental progress than in a century of following the white man's theory of escape through the frontier. Not merely did they begin to obtain food in formerly closed cafés: that was really a minor point. What they really won was respect for themselves as men who no longer ran away. The frontier never had and never could give a man that kind of self-respect.

But while Reverend King and the Montgomery Improvement Association offered the class-conscious industrial gentry inspiring proof that wealth and welfare were obtainable without running off to some new frontier, they also posed some crucial questions. Even if the gentry could regenerate such a Christian vision of a corporate commonwealth, would corporation capitalism be able to function if operated according to its precepts? Perhaps it would not. Perhaps the corporation economy could not function without the indirect but vital help of the citizen in the form of taxes paid to the government and then handed on to the corporation in the form of subsidies. If that were the case, then how and by what secular ideal and hierarchy of values—by what Utopia—would the class-conscious industrial gentry transform such double jeopardy into a system of true equity in which every citizen, along with the corporations, received a fair share of wealth and welfare? It might be rather difficult to convince the citizen that his sacrifices were worthwhile on the grounds that the gentry would then take an honest interest in him. For even under the best of circumstances, is having an interest taken in one a sufficient substitute for active participation in the present and future affairs of one's own society?

Those are fundamental and very difficult questions. Even to ask them is to understand why the frontier as a Utopia of escape has been so attractive in the past, and why it still exerts such influence in the middle of the 20th century. But to ask these questions is also to raise the issue as to whether Americans have any other traditions that are appropriate to the present. Is it really a choice between, on the one hand, a continuance of government by a syndicalist oligarchy relying on expansion or, on the other, a government by a class-conscious industrial gentry? To be sure, the choice does offer some measure of meaningful difference; for a class-conscious industrial gentry with the nerve to abandon the Utopia of frontier expansion would clearly provide at least the chance of a more equitable, humane, creative, and peaceful future. But if that is all Americans can offer themselves, then they are apt to become unique in the sense of becoming isolated from the mainstream of 20th-century development.

For the rest of the world, be it presently industrial or merely beginning to industrialize, is very clearly moving toward some version of a society modeled on the ideal and the Utopia of a true human community based far more on social property than upon private property. That is what the editors of *The Wall Street Journal* meant in 1958 when they candidly admitted that the United States was on "the wrong side of a social revolution." That socialist reassertion of the essence of the ancient ideal of a Christian commonwealth is a viable Utopia. It was so when the Levellers asserted it in the middle of the 17th century, and it remains so in the middle of the 20th century. It holds very simply and clearly that the only meaningful frontier lies within individual men and in their relationships with each other. It agrees with Frederick Jackson Turner that the American frontier has been "a gate of escape" from those central responsibilities and opportunities. The socialist merely says that it is time to stop running away from life.

And in Eugene Debs, America produced a man who understood that expansion was a running away, the kind of escape that was destructive of the dignity of men. He also believed and committed his life to the proposition that Americans would one day prove mature and courageous enough to give it up as a child's game; that they would one day "put away childish things" and undertake the creation of a socialist commonwealth. Americans therefore do have a third choice to consider alongside that of an oligarchy and that of a class-conscious industrial gentry. They have the chance to create the first truly democratic socialism in the world.

That opportunity is the only real frontier available to Amerians in the second half of the 20th century. If they revealed and acted upon the kind of intelligence and morality and courage that it would take to explore and develop that frontier, then they would have finally broken the chains of their own past. Otherwise, they would ultimately fall victims of a nostalgia for their childhood.

Acknowledgments

For better or worse, but unquestionably for a great deal of enjoyment on my own part, this volume is the product of the somewhat archaic notion that a man writes his own books. In Somerset Maugham's wry phrase, it is done "by applying the seat of the pants to the seat of the chair." It is of course true that no man gets into that position without assistance, and most assuredly does not stay there without encouragement, from other human beings. The main point is merely that this was not an organized project involving a vast farming out of various research assignments to students or colleagues.

For that root of all research and composition—money with which to make ends meet on the edge of the bankruptcy and income tax laws—I am grateful to three sources: The Fund for Social Analysis, the Louis B. Rabinowitz Foundation, and The World Publishing Company. I appreciate their consideration and have infinite respect for their routine, unmentioned discipline in keeping their noses—and ideologies—out of what I was doing with their money.

I owe both intellectual and emotional debts to a good many colleagues and students. The persistent and perceptive criticisms and suggestions of David Keightley of The World Publishing Company were often very helpful. Two other editors have my warm appreciation. Carey McWilliams of the *Nation* encouraged me to experiment with ideas in his journal; and in publishing a preliminary statement of the first section of this essay, William Towner of the *William and Mary Quarterly* gave me a lift at a propitious moment.

I have benefited a very great deal from a personal and intellectual friendship with my colleague George Mosse, whose deep knowledge of Europe has given him many insights into the United States. In particular, our discussions of the role of Christianity in mercantilist thought were of great value to me. I am similarly indebted to Warren Susman (Rutgers University) and Lloyd Gardner (Lake Forrest College), who exercised their fine minds on a portion of the manuscript, and on other of the ideas presented. While neither of them probably feel that it helped quite enough, I am sure that their willingness to offer serious criticism as part of their great capacity for friendship forced me at least to say what I wanted to with greater clarity and exactness.

My debts to Edward Hallett Carr, Harvey Goldberg, Fred H. Harrington, William Best Hesseltine, Merrill Jensen, Orde S. Pinckney, and Charles Vevier are perpetual. Whether offered in conversation or through their own writings, they have given me ideas and suggestions that no doubt emerge in modified form and with different emphasis, but which none the less began as their contributions. I am also deeply obligated to Professor Hans Gerth of the Department of Sociology at the University of Wisconsin. In this book, in particular, I have drawn many times on the ideas and insights gained from his lecture courses and his seminar, and from his own writings.

It also seems appropriate, in view of all the bigoted and career-building attacks, acts of purification in the form of misrepresentation, and even smart-alec criticism by supposed aristocrats, to acknowledge formally my respect for and indebtedness to Charles Austin Beard. That the Pulitzer Prize Committee has yet to find either the intelligence or the courage to honor him even posthumously is one of the most illuminating aspects of our time. He was a man of rare intellectual capacity, courage, and humaneness. As should by now be apparent, my own analyses and interpretations differ from his at many points, both in detail and in general, but that is irrelevant to the central issue. He was a great historian.

The same kind of point should be made with reference to Karl Marx. Indeed, he had even more to offer anyone seriously concerned with the problems of historical analysis and interpretation. Perhaps a corresponding friendship with him would have been the most rewarding relationship, for many of his key insights are contained in letters. It is probably one of them, the concept of "feudal socialism," which excited the curiosity and prompted the questions and research that produced this interpretation of American history. For many people, this is no doubt sufficient evidence unto the judgment. But that only makes the central point: most people damn Marx for things he neither said nor did.

Nor should Marx be acknowledged without an explicit reference to his friend and collaborator, Friedrich Engels. In many cases, it is almost impossible to separate the work of the two men. And some of Engels' letters and studies provide suggestions and analyses that can stand with the best of Marx.

Since none of them were assigned either major parts or tidbits of this project, the naming of students (some of them now graduated) is irrevocably impressionistic and indicative rather than formal and meticulous. I owe a special and collective debt to undergraduates for an almost legendary patience with my efforts to work out in lectures some of the ideas in this book, and for their sharp eyes for error and oversight. In response to their seminar papers and theses, but more especially in the course of conversations with them, I have often been stimulated by Walter LeFeber (Cornell University), Thomas McCormick (Ohio University), Carl Parinni (Lake Forrest College), Robert Smith (Texas Lutheran College), James Cooper, John Rollins, David Meissner, Lewis Kreinberg, David Eakins, Stephen Scheinberg, Frank Chalk, Michael Boylen, and Martin Sklar. I have learned from all of them.

Both footnotes and a full bibliography for a book of this nature would be poor jokes upon everyone concerned. Beginning as a student under Fred Harrington, whose command of the sources and secondary materials was at once exhilarating and infuriating, I have been at work on this essay since 1948. The source of a single quotation means almost nothing unless the entire context of associated documents and the process of reflection is also reproduced. Hence if the reader trusts or accepts the author on the basis of citing the source of a quotation, he has in reality no grounds for distrusting him because that one document is not named. History is simply not the arithmetic total of footnotes. Perhaps historians should provide their own versions of Thomas Wolfe's *Story of a Novel*, or plagiarize James Joyce under the title of *A Portrait of the Historian as a Young Monomaniac*.

I have accumulated information from many interviews and

documents. And while the private literary remains of numerous men and the archival manuscripts of the government supplied much vital data, I concluded my research very greatly impressed by the value of sitting down and at least scanning every page of the proceedings of the national legislature since the First Continental Congress; and from following a similar procedure with selected colonial and state records and the various hearings of the Congress.

I have also benefited extensively from insights and information first presented by other men and women. In addition to the materials already cited or referred to in "The Age of Mercantilism: An Interpretation of the American Political Economy, 1763–1828," *William and Mary Quarterly* (1958), and in *The Tragedy of American Diplomacy* (1959), the following items deserve particular mention. It may be worth noting, before proceeding with such enumeration, that those who care to see how a typical part of this essay was worked out in detail may consult "Samuel Adams: Calvinist, Mercantilist, Revolutionary," in *Studies on the Left* (1960).

I. GENERAL

A special comment may be helpful in connection with four very fine books. Two of them, H. N. Smith, *Virgin Land. The American West as Symbol and Myth* (1950), and W. P. Webb, *The Great Frontier* (1952), concern the role of expansion in American thought and action. I did not draw upon either of them until my own formulation of that relationship had been developed in all its essential aspects. At that point, however, I used both studies very extensively, and happily acknowledge my debt to both scholars. A third volume, R. Williams, *Culture and Society* (1958), is an exceedingly brilliant and perceptive analysis and review of the radical and conservative traditions of community in English history. No such study exists of American society, and this essay should not be misunderstood as an attempt to fill that gigantic gap; but the work by Williams did provide me with many suggestions and offered a great deal of encouragement for what I have tried to do. F. M. Bator's study, *The Question of Government Spending* (1960), appeared too late for me to use directly, but my own analysis of 20th-century American history was based on a very similar approach to that topic.

Other general studies which were particularly helpful include:

M. Buber, *Paths in Utopia* (1949); C. M. Cochrane, *Thucydides and the Science of History* (1929); M. Horkheimer, *Eclipse of Reason* (1947); B. F. Hoselitz, *Sociological Aspects of Economic Growth* (a collection of previously published essays, 1960); H. S. Hughes, *Consciousness and Society* (1958); E. Kahler, *The Tower and the Abyss* (1957); R. Kroner, *Kant's Weltanschauung* (1956); S. M. Lipset and R. Bendix, *Social Mobility in Industrial Society* (1959); R. K. Merton, *Social Theory and Social Structure* (revised ed., 1957); B. Moore, Jr., *Political Power and Social Theory* (1958); G. Myrdal, *Value in Social Theory* (1958); F. Neumann, *The Democratic and the Authoritarian State* (1957); J. Ortega y Gassett, *Man and Crisis* (1958); F. Pappenheim, *The Alienation of Modern Man* (1959); J. A. Schumpeter, *History of Economic Analysis* (1954); W. Sombart, *Weltanschauung, Science, and Economy* (1939); and F. Tönnies, *Community and Society* (an English translation appeared in 1957).

II. THE AGE OF MERCANTILISM

M. Beer, *An Inquiry into Physiocracy* (1939) and *Early British Economics* (1938); André Biéler, *La Pensée Économique et Sociale de Calvin* (1959); L. F. Brown, *The First Earl of Shaftesbury* (1933); G. L. Cherry, "The Development of the English Free-Trade Movement in Parliament, 1689–1702," *Journal of Modern History* (1953); W. D. Christie, *A Life of Anthony Ashley Cooper, First Earl of Shaftesbury* (1871); A. W. Coats, "Changing Attitudes to Labour in the Mid-Eighteenth Century," *The Economic History Review* (1958); M. W. Cranston, *John Locke* (1957); R. Davis, "English Foreign Trade, 1660–1700," *Economic History Review* (1955); L. Díon, "Natural Law and Manifest Destiny in the Era of the American Revolution," *The Canadian Journal of Economics and Political Science* (1957); C. H. George, "A Social Interpretation of English Puritanism," *Journal of Modern History* (1953); J. W. Gough, *John Locke's Political Philosophy* (1950); T. E. Gregory, "The Economics of Employment in England, 1660–1713," *Economica* (1921); C. R. Haywood, "Mercantilism and Colonial Slave Labor, 1700–1763," *The Journal of Southern History* (1957); R. W. K. Hinton, "The Mercantile System in the Time of Thomas Mun," *Economic History Review* (1955); A. J. John, "War and the English Economy," *Economic History Review* (1955); W. Kendall, *John*

Locke (*Illinois Studies in the Social Sciences*, 1941); S. G. Kurtz, *The Presidency of John Adams* (1957); W. Von Leyden (ed.), John Locke, *Essays on the Law of Nature* (1954); J. M. Low, "An Eighteenth Century Controversy in the Theory of Economic Progress," *The Manchester School of Economic and Social Studies* (1952); A. C. McLaughlin, "The Background of American Federalism," *American Political Science Review* (1918); B. Manning, "The Nobles, the People, and the Constitution," *Past and Present* (1956); R. S. Michaelsen, "Changes in the Puritan Concept of Calling or Vocation," *New England Quarterly* (1953); J. C. Miller, *Alexander Hamilton: Portrait in Paradox* (1959); C. Nettles, "The Place of Markets in the Old Colonial System," *New England Quarterly* (1933); E. E. Rich, "The First Earl of Shaftesbury's Colonial Policy," *Transactions of the Royal Historical Society* (1957); K. Samuelsson, *Ekonomi och religion* (précis and translation of excerpts, 1957); A. M. Schlesinger, *Prelude to Independence: The Newspaper War on Britain: 1764–1776* (1958); S. R. Sen, *The Economics of Sir James Steuart* (1957); R. H. Tawney, *Business and Politics under James I. Lionel Cranfield as Merchant and Minister* (1958); E. M. W. Tillyard, *The Elizabethan World Picture* (1943); R. S. Westfall, *Science and Religion in Seventeenth-Century England* (1958); C. H. Wilson, *Profit and Power* (1957); I. G. Wyllie, "The Search for an American Law of Charity," *Mississippi Valley Historical Review* (1959).

III. THE AGE OF LAISSEZ NOUS FAIRE

R. V. Bruce, *1877: Year of Violence* (1959); R. Chase, *The American Novel and Its Tradition* (1957); T. C. Cochran, *Railroad Leaders: 1845–1890* (1953); M. Curti, "The Great Mr. Locke: America's Philosopher, 1783–1861," *The Huntington Library Bulletin* (1937); D. Donald, "The Scalawag in Mississippi Reconstruction," *The Journal of Southern History* (1944); J. Dorfman, *The Economic Mind in American Civilization. Vols. I* and *II: 1606–1865* (1946); C. Goodrich, *Government Promotion of American Canals and Railroads, 1800–1890* (1960); B. Hammond, *Banks and Politics in America. From the Revolution to the Civil War* (1957); W. B. Hesseltine, "Abraham Lincoln and the Politicians," *Civil War History* (1960); D. H. Lawrence, *Studies in Classic American Literature* (1922); L. Marx, "Two Kingdoms of Force," *The Massachusetts Review*

(1959); F. O. Matthiessen, *American Renaissance* (1941); H. S. Merrill, *Bourbon Democracy of the Middle West, 1865–1896* (1953); D. C. North, "A Note on Professor Rostow's 'Take Off' into Self-Sustained Economic Growth," *The Manchester School of Economic and Social Studies* (1958); G. G. Sellers, Jr., *Jacksonian Democracy* (1958); R. Sharkey, *Money, Class, and Party* (1959); C. S. Sydor, *The Development of Southern Sectionalism, 1819–1848* (1948); G. R. Taylor, *The Transportation Revolution, 1815–1860* (1957); F. J. Turner, "The South, 1820–1830," *American Historical Review* (1907); R. W. Van Alstyne, *The American Empire* (1960); C. Vann Woodward, *Reunion and Reaction. The Compromise of 1877 and the End of Reconstruction* (1951), and "The Irony of Southern History," *Journal of Southern History* (1953); J. W. Ward, *Andrew Jackson: Symbol for an Age* (1955); B. A. Weisberger, "The Dark and Bloody Ground of Reconstruction Historiography," *Journal of Southern History* (1959); T. H. Williams, "An Analysis of Some Reconstruction Attitudes," *Journal of Southern History* (1946); E. Wilson, "Abraham Lincoln: The Union as Religious Mysticism," in *Eight Essays* (1954); G. R. Woolfolk, *The Cotton Regency* (1958); and R. H. Zoellner, "Negro Colonization: The Climate of Opinion Surrounding Lincoln, 1860–1865," *Mid-America* (1960).

IV. THE AGE OF CORPORATION CAPITALISM

E. D. Baltzell, *Philadelphia Gentlemen* (1958); A. A. Berle, Jr. and E. S. Mason (eds.), *The Corporation in Modern Society* (1959); J. Burkhead, "Changes in the Functional Distribution of Income," *Journal of the American Statistical Association* (1953); N. Chamberlain, "The Organized Business in America," *Journal of Political Economy* (1944); A. D. Chandler, Jr., "The Origins of Progressive Leadership," Appendix III in Vol. VIII of *The Letters of Theodore Roosevelt* (1954); B. Cochrane (ed.), *American Labor in Midpassage* (1959); E. S. Corwin, *Constitutional Revolution, Ltd.* (1941); E. F. Frazier, *Black Bourgeoisie* (1957); G. C. Fite, *George N. Peek and the Fight for Farm Parity* (1954); R. N. Gardner, *Sterling-Dollar Diplomacy* (1956); J. A. Garraty, "The United States Steel Corporation Versus Labor: The Early Years," *Labor History* (1960); A. H. Hansen, "Some Notes on Terborgh's 'The Bogey of Economic Maturity,' " *The Review of Economic Statistics* (1946); A. H. Hansen, "Growth or Stagnation in the American Economy,"

Review of Economic Statistics (1954); M. Horkheimer, *Eclipse of Reason* (1947); F. Hunter, *Top Leadership, U.S.A.* (1959); Iowa State University Center for Agricultural Adjustment, *Problems and Policies of American Agriculture* (1959); D. G. Johnson, "The Functional Distribution of Income in the United States, 1850–1952," *Review of Economic Statistics* (1954); M. Josephson, *Edison. A Biography* (1959); J. A. Kahl, *The American Class Structure* (1957); D. L. Kemmerer, "Economic Trends and Elections," *Current Economic Comment* (1955); G. Kolko, "The American 'Income Revolution,' " *Dissent* (1957); S. Lens, *The Crisis of American Labor* (1959); W. A. Lewis and P. J. O'Leary, "Secular Swings in Production and Trade, 1870–1913," *The Manchester School of Economic and Social Studies* (1955); D. Loth, *Swope of G. E.* (1958); B. Mandel, "Notes on the Pullman Boycott," *Explorations in Entrepreneurial History* (1954); H. P. Miller, *Income of the American People* (1955); B. Mitchell, *Depression Decade* (1947); W. Morris, *The Territory Ahead* (1958); F. Pappenheim, *The Alienation of Modern Man* (1959); R. G. Tugwell, *The Democratic Roosevelt* (1957); J. Weinstein, "Anti-War Sentiment and the Socialist Party, 1917–1918," *Political Science Quarterly* (1959); and J. Weinstein, "The Socialist Party: Its Roots and Strength, 1912–1919," *Studies on the Left* (1960).

Index

Abolitionism, 254–55, 278, 299
Acheson, Dean, 426, 485; quoted, 17–18, 371–72, 474
Adams, Brooks, 364, 368, 369, 391, 392, 485
Adams, Henry, quoted, 345
Adams, John, 98, 99, 109, 114, 115, 116, 131, 150, 167, 187; balanced government favored by 156–57; Bank of the United States opposed by, 165; break with Hamilton (1798), 175; on free trade, 122–23; and Jefferson, 174, 175, 176, 177; and Madison, 174, 175, 176; as mercantilist, 132, 139, 163; neutral policy of, as President, 174, 175; as President of United States, 174–77; navy advocated by, 139, 175; quoted, 118, 148; on Shays' Rebellion, 148; Taylor's attack on, 151; on West Indies trade, 142
Adams, John Quincy, 140, 177, 189, 192, 198, 214, 220, 229, 231, 253, 292; Jackson's victory over (1828), 205; on mercantilist philosophy and program, 210–11; and Missouri Crisis, 207; and Monroe Doctrine, 215, 216, 217; as President of United States, 210, 211, 218; quoted, 197, 204, 210, 219; *Report Upon Weights and Measures* by, 214–15
Adams, Samuel, 77, 78, 98, 99, 101, 102, 107, 140, 281; at Continental Congress, 114, 115; expansionism of, 182; on free trade, 122; as leader of colonial resistance, 107–10, 111–16 *pass.*; on Madison's feudal system, 162; and Society of the Cincinnati, 144; on West Indies trade, 142
Africa, American penetration of, 199, 339, 418, 434; revolt against white rule in, 386
Agee, James, 444

Agrarianism, of colonial planters, 82; in 1880's, 334–36; Taylor's statement of, 151, 154
Agricultural Adjustment Act, 442
Agricultural Marketing Act (1929), 436
Alabama, 205, 447–48
Alaska, strategic role of, 319
Albany Regency, 236, 237, 249
Aldrich, Nelson W., 395, 410
Alien Act, Hamilton's, 175
Allgeyer v. *Louisiana,* 329
Almanac, Franklin's, 106
Amalgamated Copper Co., 354
America's Economic Supremacy, 368, 369
America Must Choose, 454
American Agriculturist, quoted, 284
American Asiatic Association, 363
American Bankers Association, 353
American Bar Association, 304
American Board of Commissioners for Foreign Missions, 185
American Colonization Society, 199
American Economic Association, 401
American Federation of Labor, 334, 401, 431, 445
American & Foreign Power Co., 457
American Fur Trade Co., 186, 234
American Geography, 179
American Insurance Co. v. *Canter* (1828), 214
American International Corp., 420
American Magazine, 103
American National Steel Manufacturers, 304
American Philosophical Society, 91
American Protective Association, 323
American Revolution, and British mercantilism, 115
American Scene, The, 331